LANGUAGE

LANGUAGE

Leonard Bloomfield

**MOTILAL BANARSIDASS
INTERNATIONAL
DELHI**

Reprint Edition: Delhi, 2023
First Indian Edition: Delhi, 1963
First Edition: London, 1935

© MOTILAL BANARSIDASS INTERNATIONAL
All Rights Reserved

ISBN: 978-93-95458-08-5

Also available at

MOTILAL BANARSIDASS INTERNATIONAL
H. O. : 41 U.A. Bungalow Road, (Back Lane)Jawahar Nagar, Delhi - 110 007
4261 (basement) Lane #3, Ansari Road, Darya Ganj, New Delhi - 110 002
203 Royapettah High Road, Mylapore, Chennai - 600 004
12/1A, 2nd Floor, Bankim Chatterjee Street, Kolkata - 700 073
Stockist : Motilal Books, Ashok Rajpath, Near Kali Mandir, Patna - 800 004

No part of this book may be reproduced in any form or by any electronic or mechanical means including information storage and retrieval systems without permission in writing from the publishers, excepts by a reviewer who may quote brief passages in a review.

Printed & Bound by
MOTILAL BANARSIDASS INTERNATIONAL

TO

A. S. B.

PREFACE

This book is a revised version of the author's *Introduction to the Study of Language,* which appeared in 1914 (New York, Henry Holt and Company). The new version is much larger than the old, because the science of language has in the interval made progress, and because both men of science and the educated public now attribute greater value to an understanding of human speech.

Like its predecessor, this book is intended for the general reader and for the student who is entering upon linguistic work. Without such an introduction, specialized treatises are unintelligible. For the general reader an orderly survey is probably more interesting than a discussion of selected topics, for these, after all, cannot be understood without their background. No one will ask for an anecdotal treatment who has once opened his eyes to the strangeness, beauty, and import of human speech.

The deep-rooted things about language, which mean most to all of us, are usually ignored in all but very advanced studies; this book tries to tell about them in simple terms and to show their bearing on human affairs. In 1914 I based this phase of the exposition on the psychologic system of Wilhelm Wundt, which was then widely accepted. Since that time there has been much upheaval in psychology; we have learned, at any rate, what one of our masters suspected thirty years ago, namely, that we can pursue the study of language without reference to any one psychological doctrine, and that to do so safeguards our results and makes them more significant to workers in related fields. In the present book I have tried to avoid such dependence; only by way of elucidation I have told, at a few points, how the two main present-day trends of psychology differ in their interpretation. The mentalists would supplement the facts of language by a version in terms of mind, — a version which will differ in the various schools of mentalistic psychology. The mechanists demand that the facts be presented without any assumption of such auxiliary factors. I have tried to meet this demand not merely because I believe that mechanism is the necessary form of scientific discourse, but also because an exposition which stands on its own fect is more solid and more easily surveyed than one which is propped at various points by another and changeable doctrine.

I have tried everywhere to present the accepted views, not even avoiding well-used standard examples; on disputed matters I have tried to state the point at issue; and in both cases I have given references, in the Notes and Bibliography, which will enable the reader to look into things, and, if he chooses, to arrive at an opinion of his own.

Thanks are due to many scholars who contributed help and information, and to the publisher, the printer, and the very able typesetter, all of whom devoted great care to the making of this book.

L. B.

Chicago, January 1933.

PREFACE TO THE BRITISH EDITION

This edition differs from the American form of this book (New York, 1933) in two respects: the phonetic symbols conform to the usage of the International Phonetic Association, and the transcriptions of English forms represent a polite type of British ('Received' or 'Public School') pronunciation. Moreover, a few corrections have been embodied in the text. All these changes were subject to a limitation imposed by the method of manufacturing the book: the paging and alignment of the American edition had to be kept. Accordingly, the reader will find some American features (such as the spelling *-or* for *-our*) and some passages where the point of view (e.g., as to topography) is American. However, in all cases where corrections or additions seemed to have material bearing, these have been either incorporated into the text, or, where this could not be done, added in a list at the end of the book. For most of these improvements I am indebted to Professors R. G. Kent and D. Jones; the criticism and the published works of Professor Jones have aided me especially as to British pronunciation.

L. B.

Chicago, August, 1934.

CONTENTS

CHAPTER	PAGE
1. The Study of Language	3
2. The Use of Language	21
3. Speech-Communities	42
4. The Languages of the World	57
5. The Phoneme	74
6. Types of Phonemes	93
7. Modifications	109
8. Phonetic Structure	127
9. Meaning	139
10. Grammatical Forms	158
11. Sentence-Types	170
12. Syntax	184
13. Morphology	207
14. Morphologic Types	227
15. Substitution	247
16. Form-Classes and Lexicon	264
17. Written Records	281
18. The Comparative Method	297
19. Dialect Geography	321
20. Phonetic Change	346
21. Types of Phonetic Change	369
22. Fluctuation in the Frequency of Forms	392
23. Analogic Change	404
24. Semantic Change	425
25. Cultural Borrowing	444
26. Intimate Borrowing	461
27. Dialect Borrowing	476
28. Applications and Outlook	496
Notes	511
Bibliography	525
Table of Phonetic Symbols	547
Additions and Corrections	551
Index	553

LANGUAGE

CHAPTER 1

THE STUDY OF LANGUAGE

1. 1. Language plays a great part in our life. Perhaps because of its familiarity, we rarely observe it, taking it rather for granted, as we do breathing or walking. The effects of language are remarkable, and include much of what distinguishes man from the animals, but language has no place in our educational program or in the speculations of our philosophers.

There are some circumstances, however, in which the conventionally educated person discusses linguistic matters. Occasionally he debates questions of "correctness" — whether it is "better," for instance, to say *it's I* or *it's me*. His discussion of such things follows a fairly rigid pattern. If possible, he looks to the conventions of writing for an answer — as, say, for the question whether a *t* is to be pronounced in words like *often* or *soften*. Otherwise he appeals to authority: one way of speaking, he believes, is inherently right, the other inherently wrong, and certain learned men, especially the authors of grammars and dictionaries, can tell us which is which. Mostly, however, he neglects to consult these authorities, and tries, instead, to settle the matter by a kind of philosophical reasoning, which operates with terms such as "subject," "object," "predicate," and so on. This is the common-sense way of dealing with linguistic matters. Like much else that masquerades as common sense, it is in fact highly sophisticated, and derives, at no great distance, from the speculations of ancient and medieval philosophers.

It is only within the last century or so that language has been studied in a scientific way, by careful and comprehensive observation; the few exceptions will occupy us in a moment. *Linguistics*, the study of language, is only in its beginnings. The knowledge it has gained has not yet become part of our traditional education; the "grammar" and other linguistic instruction in our schools confines itself to handing on the traditional notions. Many people have difficulty at the beginning of language study, not in grasping the methods or results (which are simple enough), but in stripping off the preconceptions which are forced on us by our popular-scholastic doctrine.

1. 2. The ancient Greeks had the gift of wondering at things that other people take for granted. They speculated boldly and persistently about the origin, history, and structure of language. Our traditional lore about language is due largely to them.

Herodotus, writing in the fifth century B.C., tells us that King Psammetichus of Egypt, in order to find out which was the oldest nation of mankind (whatever this may mean), isolated two newborn infants in a park; when they began to speak, they uttered the word *bekos*, which turned out to be Phrygian for 'bread.'

In his dialogue *Cratylus*, Plato (427-347 B.C.) discusses the origin of words, and particularly the question whether the relation between things and the words which name them is a natural and necessary relation or merely the result of a human convention. This dialogue gives us a first glimpse into a century-long controversy between the *Analogists*, who believed that language was natural and therefore at bottom regular and logical, and the *Anomalists*, who denied these things and pointed out the irregularities of linguistic structure.

The Analogists believed that the origin and the true meaning of words could be traced in their shape; the investigation of this they called *etymology*. We may illustrate their theory by English examples. The word *blackbird* obviously consists of *black* and *bird:* the species was named for its color, and, indeed, blackbirds are birds and are black In the same way, the Greeks would have concluded that there was some deep-seated connection between a *gooseberry* and a *goose:* it was the etymologist's task to find this connection. The word *mushroom* would have presented a more difficult problem. The components are often altered; thus, *breakfast*, in spite of the difference in sound, is evidently the meal by which we *break* our *fast*, and *manly* a shorter form of *man-like*.

In Greek, as in English, however, most words resist this kind of analysis. Thus, *early* ends like *manly*, but the rest of the word is obscure; *woman* resembles *man*, but what is the first syllable? Then there is a residue of short, simple words that do not resemble others — words such as *man, boy, good, bad, eat, run*. In such cases the Greeks and their pupils, the Romans, resorted to guesswork. For instance, they explained the Greek word *lithos* 'stone' as derived from the phrase *lian theein* 'to run too much,' because this is what a stone does *not* do. A Latin example of this sort has become proverbial: *lucus a non lucendo* 'a grove (*lucus*) is so named on account of its not being light (*lucendo*).'

These etymologies show us, at any rate, that the Greeks realized that speech-forms change in the course of time. In the systematic study of this change modern students have found the key to most linguistic problems. The ancients never settled down to any careful study of linguistic change.

The ancient Greeks studied no language but their own; they took it for granted that the structure of their language embodied the universal forms of human thought or, perhaps, of the cosmic order. Accordingly, they made grammatical observations, but confined these to one language and stated them in philosophical form. They discovered the parts of speech of their language, its syntactic constructions, such as, especially, that of subject and predicate, and its chief inflectional categories: genders, numbers, cases, persons, tenses, and modes. They defined these not in terms of recognizable linguistic forms, but in abstract terms which were to tell the meaning of the linguistic class. These teachings appear most fully in the grammars of Dionysius Thrax (second century B.C.) and of Apollonius Dyscolus (second century A.D.).

The Greeks made also some observations of detail, but this phase of their work, unfortunately, had less effect upon posterity. Their great epic poems, the *Iliad* and the *Odyssey*, which they viewed somewhat as sacred scriptures, were composed in an ancient and otherwise unknown kind of Greek. In order to understand these texts and to make correct copies, one had to study their language. Most famous in this work was Aristarchus (about 216-144 B.C.). Other works of Greek literature were composed in conventionalized forms of various regional dialects: the Greeks had the opportunity of comparing several divergent forms of their language. When the language of the great Athenian writers of the fourth century had become antiquated, it was made a special subject of study, since it represented the ideal form of written discourse. All this work demanded careful observation of details. Some of the later grammarians, notably Herodian, the son of Apollonius Dyscolus, assembled valuable information on such topics as the inflection and accent of ancient Greek.

1. 3. The Greek generalizations about language were not improved upon until the eighteenth century, when scholars ceased to view language as a direct gift of God, and put forth various theories as to its origin. Language was an invention of ancient heroes, or else the product of a mystical Spirit of the Folk. It began in man's attempts to imitate noises (the "bow-wow" theory), or in his natural sound-producing responses (the "ding-dong" theory), or in violent outcries and exclamations (the "pooh-pooh" theory).

In the etymological explanation of speech-forms there was no improvement. Voltaire is reported to have said that etymology is a science in which the vowels count for nothing and the consonants for very little.

The Romans constructed Latin grammars on the Greek model; the most famous of these, the work of Donatus (fourth century A.D.) and of Priscian (sixth century A.D.), remained in use as text-books through the Middle Ages. In the Middle Ages, when Latin was changing from its ancient shape into the forms which we know today as the Romance languages (French, Italian, Spanish, and so on), the convention remained of writing, as well as one could, in the ancient classical form of Latin. The medieval scholar, accordingly, in both the Latin countries and others, studied only classical Latin. The scholastic philosophers discovered some features of Latin grammar, such as the distinction between nouns and adjectives and the differences between concord, government, and apposition. They contributed much less than the ancients, who had, at any rate, a first-hand knowledge of the languages they studied. The medieval scholar saw in classical Latin the logically normal form of human speech. In more modern times this doctrine led to the writing of *general grammars*, which were to demonstrate that the structure of various languages, and especially of Latin, embodies universally valid canons of logic. The most famous of these treatises is the *Grammaire générale et raisonnée* of the Convent of Port-Royal, which appeared in 1660. This doctrine persisted into the nineteenth century; it appears, for instance, in the classical scholar, Gottfried Hermann's work *De emendanda ratione Graecae grammaticae* (1801). It is still embodied in our school tradition, which seeks to apply logical standards to language. Philosophers, to this day, sometimes look for truths about the universe in what are really nothing but formal features of one or another language.

An unfortunate outgrowth of the general-grammar idea was

the belief that the grammarian or lexicographer, fortified by his powers of reasoning, can ascertain the logical basis of language and prescribe how people ought to speak. In the eighteenth century, the spread of education led many dialect-speakers to learn the upper-class forms of speech. This gave the authoritarians their chance: they wrote *normative grammars*, in which they often ignored actual usage in favor of speculative notions. Both the belief in "authority" and some of the fanciful rules (as, for instance, about the use of *shall* and *will*) still prevail in our schools.

For the medieval scholar, language meant classical Latin, as it appears in books; we find few traces of interest in any other form of speech. The horizon widened at the time of the Renaissance. At the end of the Middle Ages, the study of Greek came back into fashion; soon afterward, Hebrew and Arabic were added. What was more important, some scholars in various countries began to take an interest in the language of their own time.

The era of exploration brought a superficial knowledge of many languages. Travelers brought back vocabularies, and missionaries translated religious books into the tongues of newly-discovered countries. Some even compiled grammars and dictionaries of exotic languages. Spanish priests began this work as early as in the sixteenth century; to them we owe a number of treatises on American and Philippine languages. These works can be used only with caution, for the authors, untrained in the recognition of foreign speech-sounds, could make no accurate record, and, knowing only the terminology of Latin grammar, distorted their exposition by fitting it into this frame. Down to our own time, persons without linguistic training have produced work of this sort; aside from the waste of labor, much information has in this way been lost.

The increase of commerce and travel led also to the compilation of grammars and dictionaries for languages closer at hand. The linguistic horizon at the end of the eighteenth century can be surveyed in the glossary of 285 words in two hundred languages of Europe and Asia which P. S. Pallas (1741–1811) edited at the behest of Empress Catharine of Russia in 1786. A second edition of this, in 1791, added eighty more languages, including some African and American. In the years 1806 to 1817 there appeared a four-volume treatise under the title *Mithridates*, by J. C. Adelung and J. S. Vater, which contained the Lord's Prayer in nearly five hundred languages.

The Renaissance turned the interest of a few scholars to the older records of their own languages. Franciscus Junius (1589-1677) accomplished an enormous amount of work in the study of the ancient documents of English and of the closely related languages, Frisian, Dutch, German, Scandinavian, and Gothic. This last — a language no longer spoken today — Junius knew from the famous Silver Codex, then recently discovered, a manuscript of the sixth century A.D. containing fragments of a Gospel translation; Junius published its text, together with that of the Anglo-Saxon Gospels. George Hickes (1642-1715) continued this work, publishing a Gothic and Anglo-Saxon grammar and a *Thesaurus* of miscellaneous information about the older stages of English and the sister tongues.

1. 4. The development so far outlined shows us what eighteenth-century scholars knew about language. They stated the grammatical features of language in philosophical terms and took no account of the structural difference between languages, but obscured it by forcing their descriptions into the scheme of Latin grammar. They had not observed the sounds of speech, and confused them with the written symbols of the alphabet. This failure to distinguish between actual speech and the use of writing distorted also their notions about the history of language. They saw that in medieval and modern times highly cultivated persons wrote (and even spoke) good Latin, while less educated or careless scribes made many mistakes: failing to see that this Latin-writing was an artificial and academic exercise, they concluded that languages are preserved by the usage of educated and careful people and changed by the corruptions of the vulgar. In the case of modern languages like English, they believed, accordingly, that the speech-forms of books and of upper-class conversation represented an older and purer level, from which the "vulgarisms" of the common people had branched off as "corruptions" by a process of "linguistic decay." The grammarians felt free, therefore, to prescribe fanciful rules which they derived from considerations of logic.

These misconceptions prevented scholars from making use of the data that were at hand: the modern languages and dialects, the records of ancient languages, the reports about exotic languages, and, above all, the documents which show us successive stages of one and the same language, as for instance of Anglo-Saxon (Old English) and modern English, or of Latin and the modern Romance languages. One knew that some languages resembled each other, but the doctrine of linguistic decay discouraged systematic study of this relation, since the changes which led, say, from Latin to modern French, were viewed as haphazard corruptions.

The illusion that Latin had lived on, unchanged, beside the Romance languages, led scholars to derive contemporary languages one from the other. Mostly they took Hebrew to be the language from which all others had sprung, but some thought otherwise, as, for example, Goropius Becanus of Antwerp, who patriotically derived all languages from Dutch.

It was plain that the more familiar languages of Europe fell into three groups by virtue of close resemblances within each group, resemblances such as appear in the following words:

GERMANIC GROUP	ROMANCE GROUP	SLAVIC GROUP
'hand'		
English *hand*	French *main*	Russian *ruka*
Dutch *hand*	Italian *mano*	Polish *ręka*
German *Hand*	Spanish *mano*	Bohemian *ruka*
Danish *haand*		Serbian *ruka*
Swedish *hand*		
'foot'		
English *foot*	French *pied*	Russian *noga*
Dutch *voet*	Italian *piede*	Polish *noga*
German *Fusz*	Spanish *pie*	Bohemian *noha*
Danish *fod*		Serbian *noga*
Swedish *fot*		
'winter'		
English *winter*	French *hiver*	Russian *zima*
Dutch *winter*	Italian *inverno*	Polish *zima*
German *Winter*	Spanish *invierno*	Bohemian *zima*
Danish *vinter*		Serbian *zima*
Swedish *vinter*		

GERMANIC GROUP	ROMANCE GROUP	SLAVIC GROUP
'drink'		
English *drink*	French *boire*	Russian *pit'*
Dutch *drinken*	Italian *bere*	Polish *pic'*
German *trinken*	Spanish *beber*	Bohemian *piti*
Danish *drikke*		Serbian *piti*
Swedish *dricka*		

There was apparent also a less striking resemblance between these groups; this wider resemblance extended to some other languages, such as, notably, Greek:

'mother': Greek *mētēr*, Latin *māter* (with its modern forms in the Romance languages), Russian *mat'* (genitive case *materi* — with similar forms in the other Slavic languages), English *mother* (with similar forms in the other Germanic languages);

'two': Greek *duo*, Latin *duo*, Russian *dva*, English *two;*
'three': Greek *treis*, Latin *trēs*, Russian *tri*, English *three;*
'is': Greek *esti*, Latin *est*, Russian *jest'*, English *is* (German *ist*).

1. 5. Outside the tradition of Europe, several nations had developed linguistic doctrines, chiefly on an antiquarian basis. The Arabs had worked out a grammar of the classical form of their language, as it appears in the Koran; on the model of this, the Jews in Mohammedan countries constructed a Hebrew grammar. At the Renaissance, European scholars became acquainted with this tradition; the term *root*, for instance, as a designation for the central part of a word, comes from Hebrew grammar. In the Far East, the Chinese had gained a great deal of antiquarian linguistic knowledge, especially in the way of lexicography. A Japanese grammar seems to have grown up independently.

It was in India, however, that there arose a body of knowledge which was destined to revolutionize European ideas about language. The Brahmin religion guarded, as sacred texts, some very ancient collections of hymns; the oldest of these collections, the Rig-Veda, dates in part, at a conservative estimate, from about 1200 B.C. As the language of these texts grew antiquated, the proper way of pronouncing them, and their correct interpretation, became the task of a special class of learned men. The antiquarian interest in language which arose in this way, was carried over into a more practical sphere. Among the Hindus, as among us, different classes of society differed in speech. Apparently there

THE STUDY OF LANGUAGE 11

were forces at work which led upper-class speakers to adopt lower-class forms of speech. We find the Hindu grammarians extending their interest from the Scriptures to the upper-caste language, and making rules and lists of forms descriptive of the correct type of speech, which they called *Sanskrit*. In time they worked out a systematic arrangement of grammar and lexicon. Generations of such labor must have preceded the writing of the oldest treatise that has come down to us, the grammar of Pāṇini. This grammar, which dates from somewhere round 350 to 250 B.C., is one of the greatest monuments of human intelligence. It describes, with the minutest detail, every inflection, derivation, and composition, and every syntactic usage of its author's speech. No other language, to this day, has been so perfectly described. It may have been due, in part, to this excellent codification that Sanskrit became, in time, the official and literary language of all of Brahmin India. Long after it had ceased to be spoken as anyone's native language, it remained (as classical Latin remained in Europe) the artificial medium for all writing on learned or religious topics.

Some knowledge of Sanskrit and of the Hindu grammar had reached Europe, through missionaries, in the sixteenth and seventeenth centuries. In the eighteenth century, Englishmen in India transmitted more exact reports; round the beginning of the nineteenth century, the knowledge of Sanskrit became part of the equipment of European scholars.

1. 6. The Indian grammar presented to European eyes, for the first time, a complete and accurate description of a language, based not upon theory but upon observation. Moreover, the discovery of Sanskrit disclosed the possibility of a comparative study of languages.

To begin with, the concept of related languages was strikingly confirmed by the existence, in far-off India, of a sister of the familiar languages of Europe; witness, for example, the Sanskrit equivalents of the words above cited:

mātā 'mother,' accusative case *mātaram;*
dvāu 'two';
trayaḥ 'three';
asti 'he is.'

Even more important was the insight into linguistic structure which one got from the accurate and systematic Hindu grammar. Until now, one had been able to see only vague and fluid similarities, for the current grammars, built on the Greek model, did not clearly set off the features of each language. The Hindu grammar taught Europeans to analyze speech-forms; when one compared the constituent parts, the resemblances, which hitherto had been vaguely recognized, could be set forth with certainty and precision.

The old confused notions of linguistic relationship lived on for a brief time in the opinion that the European languages were derived from Sanskrit, but this opinion soon gave way to the obviously correct explanation, namely, that Sanskrit, Latin, Greek, and so on, were divergent later forms of some one prehistoric language. This explanation seems to have been first stated by Sir William Jones (1746–1794), the first great European Sanskrit scholar, in an address delivered in 1786: Sanskrit bears a resemblance to Greek and Latin which is too close to be due to chance, but shows, rather, that all three "have sprung from some common source which, perhaps, no longer exists," and Gothic (that is, Germanic) and Celtic probably had the same origin.

In order to work out the comparison of these languages, one needed, of course, descriptive data for each one of them. The prospect of comparison, however, with all that it revealed about ancient speech-forms and tribal migrations and the origin of peoples and customs, proved so alluring that no one undertook the humdrum task of analyzing the other languages on the model of Sanskrit. European scholars had a sound knowledge of Latin and Greek; most of them spoke some Germanic language as their mother-tongue. Confronting a precise statement of Sanskrit grammar or a carefully analyzed lexical form, they could usually recall a similar feature from some of the more familiar languages. In reality, of course, this was a makeshift; often enough the comparer had to make a preliminary investigation to establish the facts, and sometimes he went astray for lack of methodically arranged data. If European scholars had possessed descriptions of the sister languages comparable to the Hindus' description of Sanskrit, the comparative study of the *Indo-European* languages (as they are now called) would have progressed far more speedily and accurately. Yet, in spite of poor equipment, and thanks to the energy of its workers, the historical and comparative study of the Indo-European languages became one of the principal enterprises, and one of the most successful, of European science in the nineteenth century.

THE STUDY OF LANGUAGE

The languages of Persia (the so-called Iranian languages) so closely resembled Sanskrit that their kinship was certain from the start. A similar relation, though less close, was found to exist between the Baltic languages (Lithuanian, Lettish, and Old Prussian) and the Slavic. Jones' surmise that the Germanic languages were related to Latin, Greek, and Sanskrit, at once proved true, as did later his surmise about Celtic (Irish, Welsh, Cornish, Breton, and the ancient language of Gaul). Later, Armenian and Albanese, and a few ancient languages known to us only from scant written records, proved also to belong to the Indo-European family.

Although there was some dispute as to details, the general presuppositions of historical and comparative language-study soon became clear. Languages change in the course of time. Apparent exceptions, such as the medieval and modern use of Latin (or, in India, of Sanskrit), amount only to this, that by long schooling people can be trained to imitate the language of ancient writings. This antiquarian feat is utterly different from the normal transmission of speech from parents to children. All writing, in fact, is a relatively recent invention, and has remained, almost to our day, the property of only a chosen few: the effect of writing upon the forms and the development of actual speech is very slight.

If a language is spoken over a large area, or thanks to migration, in several separate areas, then it will change differently in different places, and the result will be a set of related languages, like Italian, French, Spanish, Portuguese, Roumanian, and the other Romance dialects. We infer that other groups of related languages, such as the Germanic (or the Slavic or the Celtic), which show a similar resemblance, have arisen in the same way; it is only an accident of history that for these groups we have no written records of the earlier state of the language, as it was spoken before the differentiation set in. To these unrecorded parent languages we give names like *Primitive Germanic* (*Primitive Slavic, Primitive Celtic,* and so on).[1] In the same way, finding that all these languages and groups (Sanskrit, Iranian, Armenian, Greek, Albanese, Latin, Celtic, Germanic, Baltic, Slavic) resemble each other beyond the possibility of mere chance, we call them the *Indo-European family*

---

[1] The word *primitive* is here poorly chosen, since it is intended to mean only that we happen to have no written records of the language. German scholars have a better device in their prefix *ur-* 'primeval,' with which they form, for this purpose, names like *urgermanisch, urslavisch, urkeltisch.*

of languages, and conclude, with Jones, that they are divergent forms of a single prehistoric language, to which we give the name *Primitive Indo-European*.

The method of comparison, too, was clear from the start. In general, any feature that is common to all or to several of the related languages, must have been present in their common antecedent stage, in the "parent language." Thus, from the above cited forms of the word for 'mother,' it is clear that in Primitive Indo-European this word must have begun with the sound which we indicate in writing by means of the letter *m*. Where the related languages do not agree, some or all of them must have made some change. Thus, it is clear that the second consonant in the word for 'mother' was in Primitive Indo-European a *t*-sound, and that the *th*-sound in English (as well as the earlier *d*-sound in the Old English form, *mōdor*) must be due to change.

1. 7. The beginning of a systematic comparison of the Indo-European languages was a treatise on the inflectional endings of verbs in Sanskrit, Greek, Latin, Persian, and Germanic, published in 1816 by Franz Bopp (1791-1867). In 1818 Rasmus Kristian Rask (1787-1832) showed that the words of the Germanic languages bear a regular formal relation in matters of sound, to the words of the other Indo-European languages. For instance, where the others have *p*, the Germanic languages have *f*, as in *father:* Latin *pater*, *foot:* Latin *pēs*, *five:* Greek *pente*, *few:* Latin *paucī*. In 1819 Jakob Grimm (1787-1863) published the first volume of his *Deutsche Grammatik*, which was not, as the title nowadays would indicate, a German grammar, but a comparative grammar of the Germanic languages (Gothic, Scandinavian, English, Frisian, Dutch, and German). In the second edition, in 1822, of this volume, Grimm presented a systematic exposition of the correspondences of consonants between Germanic and the other Indo-European languages; since then, these correspondences have been known to English-speaking scholars as *Grimm's Law*. These correspondences are a matter of historical detail, but their significance was overwhelming, since they showed that human action, in the mass, is not altogether haphazard, but may proceed with regularity even in so unimportant a matter as the manner of pronouncing the individual sounds within the flow of speech. Grimm's comparison of the Germanic languages remains to this day unrivaled; three more volumes appeared in 1826,

1831, and 1837; a fifth volume, which was to complete the syntax, never appeared.

In 1833 Bopp began the publication of a comprehensive treatise, a comparative grammar of the Indo-European languages. In the years 1833 to 1836 there appeared the first edition of the *Etymological Investigations* of August Friedrich Pott (1802-1887). The term *etymology*, here as in all modern discussions, has taken on a precise meaning: the etymology of a speech-form is simply its history, and is obtained by finding the older forms in the same language and the forms in related languages which are divergent variants of the same parent form. Thus, to state the etymology of the English word *mother* is to say that this form is the modern version of the ninth-century Old English *mōdor;* that this is related to Old Norse *mōðer*, Old Frisian *mōder*, Old Saxon *mōdar*, Old High German *muoter* (these are the forms in our oldest records of the respective languages), in the sense that all these are divergent variants of a single Primitive Germanic word, which we symbolize as **mōder;* and that these Germanic forms are in turn related to ("cognate with") Sanskrit *mātā*, Avestan (Old Iranian) *mātā*, Old Armenian *mair*, ancient Greek *mētēr*, Albanese *motre* (which, however, means 'sister'), Latin *māter*, Old Irish *māthir*, Lithuanian *motė* (which means 'wife'), Old Bulgarian (Slavic) *mati*, and with the other corresponding forms in each of the groups of languages here illustrated, in the sense that all these are divergent later forms of a single Primitive Indo-European word, which we symbolize as *mātēr. As this example shows, etymologies, in the modern sense, do not necessarily show us an older, more transparent meaning of words. Our modern etymologies in the Indo-European languages are due largely to the researches of Pott.

During the following decades progress was so rapid that both smaller treatises and the great handbooks rapidly became antiquated. Of the latter, Bopp's, in spite of new editions, was superseded in 1861 by the *Compendium of the Comparative Grammar of the Indo-European Languages* of August Schleicher (1823-1868). In 1886 Karl Brugmann (1849-1919) and Berthold Delbrück (1842-1922) began the publication of their *Outline of the Comparative Grammar of the Indo-European Languages;* the standard work of reference today is the second edition of this, which appeared from 1897 to 1916.

As the work went on, other, more detailed treatises were devoted to the separate branches of the Indo-European family, in the manner of Grimm's great treatise on Germanic. Friedrich Diez (1794–1876) began the serious study of the Romance languages in his *Grammar of the Romance Languages* (1836–1844); Johann Kaspar Zeuss (1806–1856) opened the field of the Celtic languages in his *Grammatica Celtica* (1853); Franz von Miklosich (1813–1891) wrote a *Comparative Grammar of the Slavic Languages* (1852–1875).

1. 8. These studies could not fail to throw light upon many an aspect of history and archaeology, but their immediate interest lay in what they told about human speech. Although the various Indo-European languages had a common origin, their later careers were independent: the student had now a vast collection of details concerning the changes in human speech, which enabled him to generalize on the manner of this change.

To draw the conclusions as to the way in which languages change, was to replace the speculation of earlier times by the results of scientific induction. William Dwight Whitney (1827–1894), an American scholar, wrote *Language and the Study of Language* (1867) and *The Life and Growth of Language* (1874). These books were translated into several European languages; today they seem incomplete, but scarcely antiquated, and still serve as an excellent introduction to language study. In 1880 there appeared the *Principles of Linguistic History* by Hermann Paul (1846–1921), which, in its successive editions (the fifth appeared in 1920), became the standard work on the methods of historical linguistics.

Paul's book of *Principles* illustrates, with a wealth of examples, the process of linguistic change which had been revealed by Indo-European studies. Not so well written as Whitney's, but more detailed and methodical, this book exercised a great influence on linguistic studies; students of a more recent generation are neglecting it, to their disadvantage. Aside from its very dry style, Paul's *Principles* suffers from faults that seem obvious today, because they are significant of the limitations of nineteenth-century linguistics.

One of these faults is Paul's neglect of descriptive language study. He admitted that descriptions of languages were necessary, but confined his actual discussion to matters of linguistic change. This shortcoming he shares with his epoch. We can study linguistic change only by comparing related languages or different historical stages of the same language. For instance, by noting the similarities and differences of English, Frisian, Dutch, German, Scandinavian, and Gothic, we can get a notion of the older language ("Primitive Germanic") from which they have differentiated in the course of time, and we can then study the changes which have occurred in each of these later languages. Or else, by comparing our records of Old English (say, in the writings of King Alfred) with modern English, we can see how English has changed in the last thousand years. Evidently our power of making this comparison depends upon our knowledge of the things to be compared. For example, our knowledge about the compounding of words (as in *blackbird* or *footsore*) in the several Germanic languages is decidedly incomplete; therefore we cannot go very far with a comparative study of this matter, which would tell us how words were compounded in Primitive Germanic, and how these habits have changed in the subsequent history of each Germanic language. The historical language students of the nineteenth century suffered under these limitations, but they seem not to have grasped the nature of the difficulty.

The other great weakness of Paul's *Principles* is his insistence upon "psychological" interpretation. He accompanies his statements about language with a paraphrase in terms of mental processes which the speakers are supposed to have undergone. The only evidence for these mental processes is the linguistic process; they add nothing to the discussion, but only obscure it. In Paul's book and largely to the present day, linguistics betrays its descent from the philosophical speculations of the ancient Greeks. Paul and most of his contemporaries dealt only with Indo-European languages and, what with their neglect of descriptive problems, refused to work with languages whose history was unknown. This limitation cut them off from a knowledge of foreign types of grammatical structure, which would have opened their eyes to the fact that even the fundamental features of Indo-European grammar, such as, especially, the part-of-speech system, are by no means universal in human speech. Believing these features to be universal, they resorted, whenever they dealt with fundamentals, to philosophical and psychological pseudo-explanations.

1. 9. Alongside the great stream of historical research, there ran, however, a small but accelerating current of general linguistic study. The Hindu grammar of Sanskrit was never quite forgotten; while many pupils used its results without knowing of its existence, the masters, who knew the antecedents of their science, appreciated its value. For the less-known Indo-European languages descriptive studies could not be avoided. It is surely no accident that the best of these, in the field of the Slavic and Baltic languages, were furnished by August Leskien (1840–1916), a scholar who took a leading part in laying the foundations of historical methods of research.

For the most part, however, descriptive studies did not merge with the main stream of historical work. Some students were attracted by the structural peculiarities of languages outside the Indo-European group, even though the history of these languages was unknown. Other students examined a variety of languages in order to get a philosophical survey of human speech; in fact, much of the older descriptive work is almost unintelligible today because it is pervaded by philosophical notions that are no longer familiar to us.

The first great book on general linguistics was a treatise on the varieties of human speech by Wilhelm von Humboldt (1767–1835), which appeared in 1836 H. Steinthal (1823–1899), beside more general writings on the fundamentals of language, published in 1861 a treatise on the principal types of language structure. G. von der Gabelentz' (1840–1893) work on the science of language (1891) is much less philosophical. This direction of study culminated in a great work on language by the philosopher and psychologist, Wilhelm Wundt (1832–1920), which appeared in 1900 as the first part of a treatise on social psychology. Wundt based his psychology of speech upon any and all accessible descriptions of languages. It is interesting today to read the Indo-Europeanist Delbrück's critique and Wundt's rejoinder, both of which appeared in the following year. Delbrück objects to Wundt's use of languages whose history is unknown; for him the only aspect of language worth studying is its change in the course of time. Wundt, on the other hand, insists upon the importance of psychological interpretation in terms of his system, while Delbruck says that it does not matter what particular system of psychology a linguist may choose.

Meanwhile some students saw more and more clearly the natural relation between descriptive and historical studies. Otto Bohtlingk

(1815–1904), who made the modern European edition of Paṇini, applied the descriptive technique to a language of totally different structure, the Yakut of Asiatic Russia (1851). Friedrich Muller (1834–1898) published an outline of linguistic science (1876–1888) which contained brief sketches of the languages of the world, regardless of whether a historical treatment was possible. Franz Nikolaus Finck (1867–1910), both in a theoretical essay (1905) and in a little volume (1910) in which he analyzed descriptively eight unrelated languages, insisted upon descriptive study as a basis for both historical research and philosophical generalization. Ferdinand de Saussure (1857–1913) had for years expounded this matter in his university lectures; after his death, they were published in book form (1915).

Most convincing in this respect was the historical treatment of language families other than the Indo-European. On the one hand, the need of descriptive data as a prerequisite for comparative work was here self-evident; on the other hand, the results showed that the processes of linguistic change were the same in all languages, regardless of their grammatical structure. The comparative study of the Finno-Ugrian languages (Finnish, Lappish, Hungarian, and their kin) began as early as 1799, and has been greatly elaborated. The second volume of Humboldt's great treatise founded the comparative grammar of the Malayo-Polynesian language family. Today we have comparative studies of other families, such as the Semitic family and the Bantu family in Africa. Students of American languages could indulge in no self-deception as to the need of descriptive data: north of Mexico alone there are dozens of totally unrelated groups of languages, presenting the most varied types of structure. In the stress of recording utterly strange forms of speech one soon learned that philosophical prepossessions were only a hindrance.

The merging of these two streams of study, the historical-comparative and the philosophical-descriptive, has made clear some principles that were not apparent to the great Indo-Europeanists of the nineteenth century, as represented, say, by Hermann Paul. All historical study of language is based upon the comparison of two or more sets of descriptive data. It can be only as accurate and only as complete as these data permit it to be. In order to describe a language one needs no historical knowledge whatever; in fact, the observer who allows such knowledge to affect his description, is bound to distort his data. Our descriptions must be unprejudiced, if they are to give a sound basis for comparative work.

The only useful generalizations about language are inductive generalizations. Features which we think ought to be universal may be absent from the very next language that becomes accessible. Some features, such as, for instance, the distinction of verb-like and noun-like words as separate parts of speech, are common to many languages, but lacking in others. The fact that some features are, at any rate, widespread, is worthy of notice and calls for an explanation; when we have adequate data about many languages, we shall have to return to the problem of general grammar and to explain these similarities and divergences, but this study, when it comes, will be not speculative but inductive.

As to change in language, we have enough data to show that the general processes of change are the same in all languages and tend in the same direction. Even very specific types of change occur in much the same way, but independently, in the most diverse languages. These things, too, will some day, when our knowledge is wider, lend themselves to a systematic survey and to fruitful generalization.

CHAPTER 2

THE USE OF LANGUAGE

2. 1. The most difficult step in the study of language is the first step. Again and again, scholarship has approached the study of language without actually entering upon it. Linguistic science arose from relatively practical preoccupations, such as the use of writing, the study of literature and especially of older records, and the prescription of elegant speech, but people can spend any amount of time on these things without actually entering upon linguistic study. As the individual student is likely to repeat the delays of history, we may do well to speak of these matters, so as to distinguish them from the subject of our study.

Writing is not language, but merely a way of recording language by means of visible marks. In some countries, such as China, Egypt, and Mesopotamia, writing was practised thousands of years ago, but to most of the languages that are spoken today it has been applied either in relatively recent times or not at all. Moreover, until the days of printing, literacy was confined to a very few people. All languages were spoken through nearly all of their history by people who did not read or write; the languages of such peoples are just as stable, regular, and rich as the languages of literate nations. A language is the same no matter what system of writing may be used to record it, just as a person is the same no matter how you take his picture. The Japanese have three systems of writing and are developing a fourth. When the Turks, in 1928, adopted the Latin alphabet in place of the Arabic, they went on talking in just the same way as before. In order to study writing, we must know something about language, but the reverse is not true. To be sure, we get our information about the speech of past times largely from written records — and for this reason we shall, in another connection, study the history of writing — but we find this to be a handicap. We have to use great care in interpreting the written symbols into terms of actual speech; often we fail in this, and always we should prefer to have the audible word.

Literature, whether presented in spoken form or, as is now our custom, in writing, consists of beautiful or otherwise notable utterances. The student of literature observes the utterances of certain persons (say, of a Shakspere) and concerns himself with the content and with the unusual features of form. The interest of the philologist is even broader, for he is concerned with the cultural significance and background of what he reads. The linguist, on the other hand, studies the language of all persons alike; the individual features in which the language of a great writer differs from the ordinary speech of his time and place, interest the linguist no more than do the individual features of any other person's speech, and much less than do the features that are common to all speakers.

The discrimination of elegant or "correct" speech is a by-product of certain social conditions. The linguist has to observe it as he observes other linguistic phenomena. The fact that speakers label a speech-form as "good" or "correct," or else as "bad" or "incorrect," is merely a part of the linguist's data concerning this speech-form. Needless to say, it does not permit him to ignore part of his material or to falsify his records: he observes all speech-forms impartially. It is part of his task to find out under what circumstances the speakers label a form in one way or the other, and, in the case of each particular form, why they label it as they do: why, for example, many people say that *ain't* is "bad" and *am not* is "good." This is only one of the problems of linguistics, and since it is not a fundamental one, it can be attacked only after many other things are known. Strangely enough, people without linguistic training devote a great deal of effort to futile discussions of this topic without progressing to the study of language, which alone could give them the key.

A student of writing, of literature or philology, or of correct speech, if he were persistent and methodical enough, might realize, after some waste of effort, that he had better first study language and then return to these problems. We can save ourselves this detour by turning at once to the observation of normal speech. We begin by observing an act of speech-utterance under very simple circumstances.

2. 2. Suppose that Jack and Jill are walking down a lane. Jill is hungry. She sees an apple in a tree. She makes a noise with her larynx, tongue, and lips. Jack vaults the fence, climbs the tree, takes the apple, brings it to Jill, and places it in her hand. Jill eats the apple.

THE USE OF LANGUAGE

This succession of events could be studied in many ways, but we, who are studying language, will naturally distinguish between the *act of speech* and the other occurrences, which we shall call *practical events*. Viewed in this way, the incident consists of three parts, in order of time:

A. Practical events preceding the act of speech.
B. Speech.
C. Practical events following the act of speech.

We shall examine first the practical events, A and C. The events in A concern mainly the speaker, Jill. She was hungry; that is, some of her muscles were contracting, and some fluids were being secreted, especially in her stomach. Perhaps she was also thirsty: her tongue and throat were dry. The light-waves reflected from the red apple struck her eyes. She saw Jack by her side. Her past dealings with Jack should now enter into the picture; let us suppose that they consisted in some ordinary relation, like that of brother and sister or that of husband and wife. All these events, which precede Jill's speech and concern her, we call the *speaker's stimulus*.

We turn now to C, the practical events which came after Jill's speech. These concern mainly the hearer, Jack, and consist of his fetching the apple and giving it to Jill. The practical events which follow the speech and concern the hearer, we call the *hearer's response*. The events which follow the speech concern also Jill, and this in a very important way: *she gets the apple into her grasp and eats it.*

It is evident at once that our whole story depends upon some of the more remote conditions connected with A and C. Not every Jack and Jill would behave like these. If Jill were bashful or if she had had bad experiences of Jack, she might be hungry and see the apple and still say nothing; if Jack were ill disposed toward her, he might not fetch her the apple, even though she asked for it. The occurrence of a speech (and, as we shall see, the wording of it) and the whole course of practical events before and after it, depend upon the entire life-history of the speaker and of the hearer. We shall assume in the present case, that all these *predisposing factors* were such as to produce the story as we have told it. Supposing this, we want to know what part the speech-utterance (B) played in this story.

If Jill had been alone, she might have been just as hungry and thirsty and might have seen the same apple. If she had sufficient strength and skill to get over the fence and climb the tree, she could get hold of the apple and eat it; if not, she would have to stay hungry. The lone Jill is in much the same position as the speechless animal. If the animal is hungry and sees or smells food, it moves toward the food; whether the animal succeeds in getting the food, depends upon its strength and skill. The state of hunger and the sight or smell of the food are the *stimulus* (which we symbolize by S) and the movements toward the food are the *reaction* (which we symbolize by R). The lone Jill and the speechless animal act in only one way, namely

$$S \longrightarrow R.$$

If this works, they get the food; if it does not work — if they are not strong or skilful enough to get the food by the actions R — they must stay hungry.

Of course, it is important for Jill's welfare that she get the apple. In most instances it is not a matter of life and death, though sometimes it is; in the long run, however, the Jill (or the animal) that gets the food has far better chances of surviving and populating the earth. Therefore, any arrangement which adds to Jill's chances of getting the apple, is enormously valuable for her. The speaking Jill in our story availed herself of just such an arrangement. She had, to begin with, the same chance of getting the apple as had the lone Jill or the speechless animal. In addition to this, however, the speaking Jill had a further chance which the others did not share. Instead of struggling with the fence and the tree, she made a few small movements in her throat and mouth, which produced a little noise. At once, Jack began to make the reactions for her; he performed actions that were beyond Jill's strength, and in the end Jill got the apple. *Language enables one person to make a reaction (R) when another person has the stimulus (S).*

In the ideal case, within a group of people who speak to each other, each person has at his disposal the strength and skill of every person in the group. The more these persons differ as to special skills, the wider a range of power does each one person control. Only one person needs to be a good climber, since he can get fruit for all the rest; only one needs to be a good fisherman, since he can supply the others with fish. *The division of labor, and, with it, the whole working of human society, is due to language.*

2. 3. We have yet to examine B, the speech-event in our story.

THE USE OF LANGUAGE

This, of course, is the part of the story with which we, as students of language, are chiefly concerned. In all of our work we are observing B; A and C concern us only because of their connection with B. Thanks to the sciences of physiology and physics, we know enough about the speech-event to see that it consists of three parts:

(B1) The speaker, Jill, moved her vocal chords (two little muscles inside the adam's-apple), her lower jaw, her tongue, and so on, in a way which forced the air into the form of sound-waves. These movements of the speaker are a reaction to the stimulus S. Instead of performing the *practical* (or *handling*) reaction R — namely, starting realistically off to get hold of the apple — she performed these vocal movements, a *speech* (or *substitute*) reaction, which we shall symbolize by a small letter r. In sum, then, Jill, as a speaking person, has not one but two ways of reacting to a stimulus:

S⟶⟶⟶⟶⟶→R (practical reaction)
S⟶⟶⟶⟶⟶→r (linguistic substitute reaction).

In the present case she performed the latter.

(B2) The sound-waves in the air in Jill's mouth set the surrounding air into a similar wave-motion.

(B3) These sound-waves in the air struck Jack's ear-drums and set them vibrating, with an effect on Jack's nerves: Jack *heard* the speech. This hearing acted as a stimulus on Jack: we saw him running and fetching the apple and placing it in Jill's grasp, much as if Jill's hunger-and-apple stimulus had been acting on him. An observer from another planet, who did not know that there was such a thing as human speech, would have to conclude that somewhere in Jack's body there was a sense-organ which told him, "Jill is hungry and sees an apple up there." In short, Jack, as a speaking person, reacts to two kinds of stimuli: *practical* stimuli of the type S (such as hunger and the sight of food) and *speech* (or *substitute*) stimuli, certain vibrations in his ear-drums, which we shall symbolize by a small letter s. When we seek Jack doing anything (fetching an apple, say), his action may be due not only, as are an animal's actions, to a practical stimulus (such as hunger in his stomach, or the sight of an apple), but, just as often, to a speech-stimulus. His actions, R, may be prompted not by one, but by two kinds of proddings:

(practical stimulus) S⟶⟶⟶→R
(linguistic substitute stimulus) s⟶⟶⟶→R.

It is evident that the connection between Jill's vocal movements (B1) and Jack's hearing (B3) is subject to very little uncertainty or variation, since it is merely a matter of sound-waves passing through the air (B2). If we represent this connection by a dotted line, then we can symbolize the two human ways of responding to a stimulus by these two diagrams:

speechless reaction: S➤————————➤R
reaction mediated by speech: S➤————➤r........s➤————➤R.

The difference between the two types is evident. The speechless reaction occurs always in the same person as does the stimulus; the person who gets the stimulus is the only one who can make the response. The response, accordingly, is limited to whatever actions the receiver of the stimulus can make. In contrast with this, the reaction mediated by speech may occur in a person who did not get the practical stimulus; the person who gets a stimulus can prompt another person to make a response, and this other person may be able to do things which the speaker cannot. The arrows in our diagrams represent the sequence of events within one person's body — a sequence of events which we think is due to some property of the nervous system. Therefore the speechless reaction can take place only in the body which received the stimulus. In the reaction mediated by speech, on the other hand, there is the link, represented by a dotted line, which consists of sound-waves in the air: the reaction mediated by speech can take place in the body of any person who hears the speech; the possibilities of reaction are enormously increased, since different hearers may be capable of a tremendous variety of acts. *The gap between the bodies of the speaker and the hearer — the discontinuity of the two nervous systems — is bridged by the sound-waves.*

The important things, biologically, are the same in both the speechless and the speaking occurrence, namely S (the hunger and sight of the food) and R (movements which get the food or fail to get it). These are the *practical* phase of the affair. The speech-occurrence, s........r, is merely a means by which S and R may occur in different individuals. The normal human being is interested only in S and R; though he uses speech, and thrives by it, he pays no attention to it. Saying the word *apple* or hearing it said, appeases no one's hunger. It, along with the rest of speech, is only a way of getting one's fellow-men to help. As students of language, however, we are concerned precisely with the speech event (s........r), worthless in itself, but a means to great ends. We distinguish between language, the subject of our study, and *real* or *practical* events, stimuli and reactions. When anything apparently unimportant turns out to be closely connected with more important things, we say that it has, after all, a "meaning"; namely, it "means" these more important things. Accordingly, we say that speech-utterance, trivial and unimportant in itself, is important because it has a *meaning:* the meaning consists of the important things with which the speech-utterance (B) is connected, namely the practical events (A and C).

2. 4. Up to a certain point, some animals respond to each others' stimuli. Evidently the marvelous co-ordination in a group of ants or bees must be due to some form of interaction. Sounds as a means for this are common enough: crickets, for instance, call other crickets by *stridulation*, noisily rubbing the leg against the body. Some animals, like man, use *vocal* noises. Birds produce sound-waves by means of the *syrinx*, a pair of reed-like organs at the head of the lungs. The higher mammals have a *larynx*, a box of cartilage (in man called the adam's-apple) at the top of the wind-pipe. Inside the larynx, at the right and left, two shelf-like muscles run along the walls; when these muscles, the *vocal chords*, are stretched taut, the outgoing breath sets them into a regular vibration which produces sound. This sound we call the *voice*.

Human speech differs from the signal-like actions of animals, even of those which use the voice, by its great differentiation. Dogs, for instance, make only two or three kinds of noise — say, barking, growling, and whining: a dog can set another dog acting by means of only these few different signals. Parrots can make a great many kinds of noise, but apparently do not make different responses to different sounds. Man utters many kinds of vocal noise and makes use of the variety: under certain types of stimuli he produces certain vocal sounds, and his fellows, hearing these same sounds, make the appropriate response. To put it briefly, in human speech, different sounds have different meanings. To study this co-ordination of certain sounds with certain meanings is to study language.

This co-ordination makes it possible for man to interact with great precision. When we tell someone, for instance, the address of a house he has never seen, we are doing something which no animal can do. Not only has each person at his service the abilities of many other persons, but this co-operation is very precise. The extent and accuracy of this working-together is the measure of success of our social organization. The term *society* or *social organism* is not a metaphor. A human social group is really a unit of a higher order than a single animal, just as a many-celled animal is a unit of a higher order than a single cell. The single cells in the many-celled animal co-operate by means of such arrangements as the nervous system; the individuals in a human society co-operate by means of sound-waves.

The different ways in which we profit by language are so obvious that we need mention only a few. We can *relay* communication. When some farmers or traders say *We want a bridge over this stream*, this news may pass through a town meeting, a state legislature, a bureau of roads, an engineering staff, and a contractor's office, running through many speakers and many relays of speech, until at last, in response to the farmers' original stimulus, a corps of workmen make the actual (practical) response movements of putting up a bridge. Closely connected with the relay character of speech is its *abstraction*. The relays of speech, between the practical stimulus and the practical response, have no immediate practical effect. Therefore they can be put into all kinds of forms, provided only one changes them back correctly before proceeding to the final, practical response. The engineer who plans the bridge does not have to handle the actual beams and girders; he works merely with speech-forms (such as numbers in calculation); if he makes a mistake, he does not destroy any materials; he need only replace the ill-chosen speech-form (say, a wrong figure) by a suitable one before he begins the actual building. In this lies the value of *talking to oneself* or *thinking*. As children, we talk to ourselves aloud, but, under the correction of our elders, we soon learn to suppress the sound-producing movements and replace them by very slight inaudible ones: we "think in words." The usefulness of thinking can be illustrated by the process of counting. Our ability to estimate numbers without using speech, is extremely limited, as anyone may see by glancing, say, at a row of books on a shelf. To say that two sets of objects "have the same number" means that if we take one object from the first set and place it next to one object of the second set, and keep on doing this without using any object more than once, we shall have no unpaired objects left over. Now, we cannot always do this. The objects may be too heavy to move, or they may be in different parts of the world, or they may exist at different times (as, say, a flock of sheep before and after a storm). Here language steps in. The numerals *one, two, three, four*, and so on, are simply a series of words which we have learned to say in a fixed order, as substitutes for the above-described process. Using them, we can "count" any set of objects by placing them into one-to-one correspondence (as mathematicians call it) with the number-words, saying *one* for one of the objects, *two* for another, *three* for the next, and so on, taking care to use each object only once, until the objects of the set are exhausted. Suppose that when we had said *nineteen*, there were no more objects left. Thereafter, at any time or place, we can decide whether any set of objects has the same number as this first set, by merely repeating the counting process with the new set. Mathematics, the ideal use of language, consists merely of elaborations of this process. The use of numbers is the simplest and clearest case of the usefulness of talking to oneself, but there are many others. We think before we act.

2. 5. The particular speech-sounds which people utter under particular stimuli, differ among different groups of men; mankind speaks many languages. A group of people who use the same system of speech-signals is a *speech-community*. Obviously, the value of language depends upon people's using it in the same way. Every member of the social group must upon suitable occasion utter the proper speech-sounds and, when he hears another utter these speech-sounds, must make the proper response. He must speak intelligibly and must understand what others say. This holds good for even the least civilized communities; wherever we find man, he speaks.

Every child that is born into a group acquires these habits of speech and response in the first years of his life. This is doubtless the greatest intellectual feat any one of us is ever required to perform. Exactly how children learn to speak is not known; the process seems to be something like this:

(1) Under various stimuli the child utters and repeats vocal sounds. This seems to be an inherited trait. Suppose he makes a noise which we may represent as *da*, although, of course, the actual movements and the resultant sounds differ from any that are used in conventional English speech. The sound-vibrations strike the child's ear-drums while he keeps repeating the move-

ments. This results in a habit: whenever a similar sound strikes his ear, he is likely to make these same mouth-movements, repeating the sound *da*. This babbling trains him to reproduce vocal sounds which strike his ear.

(2) Some person, say the mother, utters in the child's presence a sound which resembles one of the child's babbling syllables. For instance, she says *doll*. When these sounds strike the child's ear, his habit (1) comes into play and he utters his nearest babbling syllable, *da*. We say that he is beginning to "imitate." Grown-ups seem to have observed this everywhere, for every language seems to contain certain nursery-words which resemble a child's babbling — words like *mama, dada:* doubtless these got their vogue because children easily learn to repeat them.

(3) The mother, of course, uses her words when the appropriate stimulus is present. She says *doll* when she is actually showing or giving the infant his doll. The sight and handling of the doll and the hearing and saying of the word *doll* (that is, *da*) occur repeatedly together, until the child forms a new habit: the sight and feel of the doll suffice to make him say *da*. He has now the use of a word. To the adults it may not sound like any of their words, but this is due merely to its imperfection. It is not likely that children ever invent a word.

(4) The habit of saying *da* at sight of the doll gives rise to further habits. Suppose, for instance, that day after day the child is given his doll (and says *da, da, da*) immediately after his bath. He has now a habit of saying *da, da* after his bath; that is, if one day the mother forgets to give him the doll, he may nevertheless cry *da, da* after his bath. "He is asking for his doll," says the mother, and she is right, since doubtless an adult's "asking for" or "wanting" things is only a more complicated type of the same situation. The child has now embarked upon *abstract* or *displaced* speech: he names a thing even when that thing is not present.

(5) The child's speech is perfected by its results. If he says *da, da* well enough, his elders understand him; that is, they give him his doll. When this happens, the sight and feel of the doll act as an additional stimulus, and the child repeats and practises his successful version of the word. On the other hand, if he says his *da, da* imperfectly, — that is, at great variance from the adults' conventional form *doll*, — then his elders are not stimulated to give him the doll. Instead of getting the added stimulus of seeing

and handling the doll, the child is now subject to other distracting stimuli, or perhaps, in the unaccustomed situation of having no doll after his bath, he goes into a tantrum which disorders his recent impressions. In short, his more perfect attempts at speech are likely to be fortified by repetition, and his failures to be wiped out in confusion. This process never stops. At a much later stage, if he says *Daddy bringed it*, he merely gets a disappointing answer such as *No! You must say "Daddy brought it"*; but if he says *Daddy brought it*, he is likely to hear the form over again: *Yes, Daddy brought it*, and to get a favorable practical response.

At the same time and by the same process, the child learns also to act the part of a hearer. While he is handling the doll he hears himself say *da, da* and his mother say *doll*. After a time, hearing the sound may suffice to make him handle the doll. The mother will say *Wave your hand to Daddy*, when the child is doing this of his own accord or while she is holding up the child's arm and waving it for him. The child forms habits of acting in conventional ways when he hears speech.

This twofold character of the speech-habits becomes more and more unified, since the two phases always occur together. In each case where the child learns the connection S➡————➡r (for instance, to say *doll* when he sees his doll), he learns also the connection s➡————➡R (for instance, to reach for his doll or handle it when he hears the word *doll*). After he has learned a number of such twofold sets, he develops a habit by which one type always involves the other: as soon as he learns to speak a new word, he is also able to respond to it when he hears others speak it, and, vice versa, as soon as he learns how to respond to some new word, he is usually able, also, to speak it on proper occasion. The latter transference seems to be the more difficult of the two; in later life, we find that a speaker understands many speech-forms which he seldom or never employs in his own speech.

2. 6. The happenings which in our diagram are represented by a dotted line, are fairly well understood. The speaker's vocal chords, tongue, lips, and so on, interfere with the stream of his outgoing breath, in such a way as to produce sound-waves; these waves are propagated through the air and strike the hearer's ear-drums, which then vibrate in unison. The happenings, however, which we have represented by arrows, are very obscure. We do not understand the mechanism which makes people say certain things in certain situations, or the mechanism which makes them respond appropriately when these speech-sounds strike their ear-drums. Evidently these mechanisms are a phase of our general equipment for responding to stimuli, be they speech-sounds or others. These mechanisms are studied in physiology and, especially, in psychology. To study them in their special bearing on language, is to study the psychology of speech, *linguistic psychology*. In the division of scientific labor, the linguist deals only with the speech-signal (r........s); he is not competent to deal with problems of physiology or psychology. The findings of the linguist, who studies the speech-signal, will be all the more valuable for the psychologist if they are not distorted by any prepossessions about psychology. We have seen that many of the older linguists ignored this; they vitiated or skimped their reports by trying to state everything in terms of some psychological theory. We shall all the more surely avoid this fault, however, if we survey a few of the more obvious phases of the psychology of language.

The mechanism which governs speech must be very complex and delicate. Even if we know a great deal about a speaker and about the immediate stimuli which are acting upon him, we usually cannot predict whether he will speak or what he will say. We took our story of Jack and Jill as something known to us, after the fact. Had we been present, we could not have foretold whether Jill would say anything when she saw the apple, or, in case she did speak, what words she would utter. Even supposing she asked for the apple, we could not foretell whether she would preface her request by saying *I'm hungry* or whether she would say *please* or whether she would say *I want that apple* or *Get me that apple* or *I was just wishing I had an apple*, and so on: the possibilities are almost infinite. This enormous variability has led to two theories about human conduct, including speech.

The *mentalistic* theory, which is by far the older, and still prevails both in the popular view and among men of science, supposes that the variability of human conduct is due to the interference of some non-physical factor, a *spirit* or *will* or *mind* (Greek *psyche*, hence the term *psychology*) that is present in every human being. This spirit, according to the mentalistic view, is entirely different from material things and accordingly follows some other kind of causation or perhaps none at all. Whether Jill will speak or what words she will use, depends, then, upon some act of her mind or will, and, as this mind or will does not follow the patterns of succession (cause-and-effect sequences) of the material world, we cannot foretell her actions.

The *materialistic* (or, better, *mechanistic*) theory supposes that the variability of human conduct, including speech, is due only to the fact that the human body is a very complex system. Human actions, according to the materialistic view, are part of cause-and-effect sequences exactly like those which we observe, say in the study of physics or chemistry. However, the human body is so complex a structure that even a relatively simple change, such as, say, the impingement on the retina of light-waves from a red apple, may set off some very complicated chain of consequences, and a very slight difference in the state of the body may result in a great difference in its response to the light-waves. We could foretell a person's actions (for instance, whether a certain stimulus will lead him to speak, and, if so, the exact words he will utter), only if we knew the exact structure of his body at the moment, or, what comes to the same thing, if we knew the exact make-up of his organism at some early stage — say at birth or before — and then had a record of every change in that organism, including every stimulus that had ever affected the organism.

The part of the human body responsible for this delicate and variable adjustment, is the nervous system. The nervous system is a very complex conducting mechanism, which makes it possible for a change in one part of the body, (a stimulus, say, in the eye) to result in a change in some other part (a response, say, of reaching with the arm, or of moving the vocal chords and tongue). Further, it is clear that the nervous system is changed, for a time or even permanently, by this very process of conduction: our responses depend very largely upon our earlier dealings with the same or similar stimuli. Whether Jill will speak depends largely on her liking for apples and on her past experience of Jack. We remember and acquire habits and learn. The nervous system is evidently a trigger-mechanism: a very slight change may set the match to a large store of explosive material. To take the case that interests us, only so can we explain the fact that large-scale movements like Jack's fetching the apple, are set off by very slight changes, such as the minute thrumming of air-waves on his eardrum.

The working of the nervous system is not accessible to observation from without, and the person himself has no sense-organs (such as he has, for instance, for the working of the muscles in his hand) with which he himself could observe what goes on in his nerves. Therefore the psychologist must resort to indirect methods of approach.

2. 7. One such method is experiment. The psychologist submits numbers of people to carefully prearranged stimuli under the simplest conditions, and records their responses. Usually he also asks these persons to "introspect," — that is, to describe as much as possible of what goes on inside them when they get the stimulus. At this point psychologists often go astray for want of linguistic knowledge. It is a mistake, for instance, to suppose that language enables a person to observe things for which he has no sense-organs, such as the workings of his own nervous system. An observer's only advantage in reporting what goes on inside him is that he can report stimulations which an outsider cannot detect — say, a pain in his eye or a tickling in his throat. Even here, we must not forget that language is a matter of training and habit; a person may be unable to report some stimulations, simply because his stock of speech-habits provides no formula; this is the case with many of our less useful adventures, such as smaller goings-on in our internal organs. Often the very structure of our body leads to a false report; we show the physician exactly the spot where we feel a pain, and he finds the injury some distance away, at a point which his experience may teach him to locate at once from our false description. In this respect many psychologists go astray by actually training their observers to use a set of technical terms for obscure stimuli and then attaching significance to the observer's use of these terms.

Abnormal conditions in which speech is disturbed, seem to reflect general maladjustments or lesions and to throw no light on the particular mechanism of language. *Stuttering* is probably due to imperfect specialization of the two cerebral hemispheres: in the normal speaker the left hemisphere (or, if he is left-handed, the right hemisphere) dominates more delicate actions, such as those of speech; in the stutterer this one-sided specialization is incomplete. Imperfect production of specific sounds (*stammering*), where it is not due to anatomical defects in the organs of speech, seems to result from similar maladjustments. Head-wounds and diseases

THE USE OF LANGUAGE

which injure the brain often result in *aphasia*, disturbances in the manner of making speech-responses and in responding to speech. Dr. Henry Head, who had unusually good opportunities for the study of aphasia in wounded soldiers, recognizes four types.

Type 1 reacts well to other people's speech, and in milder cases, uses words for the proper objects, but mispronounces or confuses his words; in extreme cases, the sufferer can say little more than *yes* and *no*. A patient reports, with some difficulty: "I know it's not........the correct........pronunciation........I don't always........*corret* it........because I shouldn't get it right ....in five or six times........unless someone says it for me." In a more serious case, the patient, when asked his name, answers *Honus* instead of 'Thomas,' and says *erst* for 'first' and *hend* for 'second.'

Type 2 reacts fairly well to simple speech, and pronounces appropriate words and short phrases, but not in the conventional constructions; he may talk an unintelligible jargon, although each word is correct enough. To the question "Have you played any games?" a patient answers: "Played games, yes, played one, daytime, garden." He says, "Get out, lay down, go to sleep, sometimes goes away. If sit in kitchen, moving about working, makes me getting worse on it." He comments, "Funny thing, this worse, that sort of thing," and by way of explanation, writes down the words *as* and *at*. We shall see later that the structure of normal language forces us to distinguish between lexical and grammatical habits of speech; the latter are disturbed in these patients.

Type 3 reacts with difficulty to the names of objects, and has trouble in finding the right words, especially names of things. His pronunciation and arrangement are good, but he has to use ingenious circumlocutions for the words he cannot find. For 'scissors' a patient says "what you cut with"; for 'black' he says: "people who are dead, — the other people who are not dead, have this color." He may use the wrong word, as *button* for 'scissors.' The words lost are chiefly the names of concrete objects. This state seems like an exaggeration of many normal persons' difficulty in recalling people's names and the designations of objects, especially under preoccupation, excitement, or fatigue.

Type 4 often does not respond correctly to the speech of others; he has no trouble in uttering single words, but he cannot finish a connected speech. It is significant that these patients suffer from apraxia; they cannot find their way about and are confused by being set, say, on the opposite side of the street. One patient reports: "I don't seem to understand all you say, and then I forget what I've got to do." Another patient says: "When at table, I am very slow in picking out the object, say the milk-jug, which I want. I don't spot it at once . . . I see them all, but I don't spot them. When I want the salt or the pepper or a spoon, I suddenly tumble to its presence." The disturbance of speech appears in this answer of a patient: "Oh, yes! I know the difference between the Nurse and the Sister by the dress: Sister blue; Nurse — oh! I get muddled, just ordinary nurse's clothes, white, blue . . ."

Ever since 1861, when Broca showed that damage to the third frontal convolution in the left hemisphere of the brain was accompanied by aphasia, there has been dispute as to whether "Broca's center" and other regions of the cortex act as specific centers for the activity of speech. Head finds some correlation between different points of lesion and each of his four types of aphasia. The demonstrable functional identifications of cortical areas always concern some specific organ: an injury in one area of the brain is accompanied by paralysis of the right foot, an injury in another area by failure to respond to stimulation in the left-hand side of the retina, and so on. Now, speech is a very complex activity, in which stimulation of every kind leads to highly specific movements of the throat and mouth; these last, moreover, are not, in a physiologic sense, "organs of speech," for they serve biologically earlier uses in man and in speechless animals. Many injuries to the nervous system, accordingly, will interfere with speech, and different injuries will result in different kinds of difficulty, but the points of the cortex are surely not correlated with specific socially significant features of speech, such as words or syntax; this appears plainly from the fluctuating and contradictory results of the search for various kinds of "speech centers." We may expect the physiologist to get better results when he looks for correlations between points of the cortex and specific physiologic activities concerned in speech, such as the movement of special muscles or the transmission of kinesthetic stimuli from the larynx and tongue. The error of seeking correlations between anatomically defined parts of the nervous system and socially defined activities appears clearly when we see some physiologists looking for a "visual word-center" which is to control reading and writing: one might as well look for a specific brain-center for telegraphy or automobile-driving or the use of any modern invention. Physiologically, language is not a unit of function, but consists of a great many activities, whose union into a single far-reaching complex of habits results from repeated stimulations during the individual's early life.

2. 8. Another way of studying human responses is to observe them in the mass. Some actions are highly variable in each person, but fairly constant in large groups of persons. We cannot predict whether any particular unmarried adult will marry during the next twelve months, or which particular persons will commit suicide, or which ones will get into prison, but, given a large enough community, and the figures for past years (and perhaps certain other data, such as those which concern economic conditions), statisticians can foretell the number of marriages, suicides, convictions for crime, and so on, which will take place. If we found it possible and worth while to register every speech-utterance in a large community, we should doubtless be able to foretell how many times any given utterance such as *Good-morning* or *I love you* or *How much are oranges today?* would be spoken within a fixed number of days. A detailed study of this kind would tell us a great deal, especially about the changes that are constantly going on in every language.

However, there is another and simpler way of studying human action in the mass: the study of conventional actions. When we go to a strange country, we soon learn many established modes of action, such as the system of currency and of weights and measures, the rules of the road (does one keep to the right, as in America and Germany, or to the left, as in England and Sweden?), good manners, hours for meals, and so on. The traveler does not gather statistics: a very few observations put him on the track, and these are confirmed or corrected by further experience. Here the linguist is in a fortunate position: in no other respect are the activities of a group as rigidly standardized as in the forms of language. Large groups of people make up all their utterances out of the same stock of lexical forms and grammatical constructions. A linguistic observer therefore can describe the speech-habits of a community without resorting to statistics. Needless to say, he must work conscientiously and, in particular, he must record every form he can find and not try to excuse himself from this task by appealing to the reader's common sense or to the structure of some other language or to some psychological theory, and, above all, he must not select or distort the facts according to his views of what the speakers ought to be saying. Aside from its intrinsic value for the study of language, a relevant and unprejudiced description of this kind, serves as a document of major importance for psychology. The danger here lies in mentalistic views of psychology, which may tempt the observer to appeal to purely spiritual standards instead of reporting the facts. To say, for instance, that combinations of words which are "felt to be" compounds have only a single high stress (e.g. *blackbird* as opposed to *black bird*), is to tell exactly nothing, since we have no way of determining what the speakers may "feel": the observer's task was to tell us, by some tangible criterion, or, if he found none, by a list, which combinations of words are pronounced with a single high stress. A worker who accepts the materialistic hypothesis in psychology is under no such temptation; it may be stated as a principle that in all sciences like linguistics, which observe some specific type of human activity, the worker must proceed exactly as if he held the materialistic view. This practical effectiveness is one of the strongest considerations in favor of scientific materialism.

The observer who, by this mass-observation, gives us a statement of the speech-habits of a community, can tell us nothing about the changes which are going on in the language of this as of every community. These changes could be observed only by means of genuinely statistical observation through a considerable length of time; for want of this, we are ignorant of many matters concerning linguistic change. In this respect, too, the science of language is fortunate, however, because comparative and geographical methods of study, again through mass-observation, supply a good deal of what we should hope to get from statistics. The fortunate position of our science in these matters is due to the fact that language is the simplest and most fundamental of our social (that is, peculiarly human) activities. In another direction, however, the study of linguistic change profits by a mere accident, namely by the existence of written records of speech of the past.

2. 9. The stimulus which calls forth speech, leads also to some other reactions. Some of these are not visible from the outside; these are muscular and glandular actions which are of no immediate importance to the speaker's fellow-men. Others are impor-

THE USE OF LANGUAGE

tant handling responses, such as locomotion or the displacement of objects. Still other responses are visible, but not directly important; they do not change the lay-out of things, but they do, along with speech, serve as stimuli to the hearer. These actions are facial expression, mimicry, tone of voice (in so-far as it is not prescribed by the conventions of the language), insignificant handling of objects (such as fiddling with a rubber band), and, above all, *gesture*.

Gesture accompanies all speech; in kind and in amount, it differs with the individual speaker, but to a large extent it is governed by social convention. Italians use more gesture than English-speaking people; in our civilization people of the privileged class gesticulate least. To some extent, individual gestures are conventional and differ for different communities. In saying good-by we wave the hand with palm outward; Neapolitans wave it with the back outward.

Most gestures scarcely go beyond an obvious pointing and picturing. American Indians of plains or woodland tribes will accompany a story by unobtrusive gestures, foreign to us, but quite intelligible: the hand, palm in, thumb up, is held just under the eyes to represent spying; a fist is slapped into a palm for a shot; two fingers imitate a man walking, and four the running of a horse. Even where gestures are symbolic, they go little beyond the obvious, as when one points back over one's shoulder to indicate past time.

Some communities have a *gesture language* which upon occasion they use instead of speech. Such gesture languages have been observed among the lower-class Neapolitans, among Trappist monks (who have made a vow of silence), among the Indians of our western plains (where tribes of different language met in commerce and war), and among groups of deaf-mutes.

It seems certain that these gesture languages are merely developments of ordinary gestures and that any and all complicated or not immediately intelligible gestures are based on the conventions of ordinary speech. Even such an obvious transference as pointing backward to indicate past time, is probably due to a linguistic habit of using the same word for 'in the rear' and 'in the past.' Whatever may be the origins of the two, gesture has so long played a secondary rôle under the dominance of language that it has lost all traces of independent character. Tales about peoples whose language is so defective that it has to be eked out by gesture, are pure myths. Doubtless the production of vocal sound by animals, out of which language has grown, originated as a response-movement (say, contraction of the diaphragm and constriction of the throat) which happened to produce noise. It seems certain, however, that in the further development, language always ran ahead of gesture.

If one gestures by moving some object so as to leave a trace on another object, one has entered upon *marking* and *drawing*. This kind of reaction has the value of leaving a permanent mark, which may serve as a stimulus repeatedly and even after intervals of time and can be transported to stimulate persons far away. For this reason, doubtless, many peoples attribute magic power to drawings, apart from their esthetic value, which is still with us.

In some parts of the world drawing has developed into writing. The details of this process will concern us later; the point of interest here is that the action of tracing an outline becomes subordinate to language: drawing a particular set of lines becomes attached, as an accompaniment or substitute, to the utterance of a particular linguistic form.

The art of symbolizing particular forms of speech by means of particular visible marks adds a great deal to the effective uses of language. A speaker can be heard only a short ways and only for an instant or two. A written record can be carried to any place and preserved for any length of time. We can see more things at one time than we can hear, and we can deal better with visible things: charts, diagrams, written calculations, and similar devices, enable us to deal with very complex matters. The speech-stimuli of distant people, and especially of persons in the past, are available to us through writing. This makes possible an accumulation of knowledge. The man of science (but not always the amateur) surveys the results of earlier students and applies his energies at the point where they left off. Instead of always starting over again from the beginning, science progresses cumulatively and with acceleration. It has been said that, as we preserve more and more records of more and more speech-reactions of highly gifted and highly specialized individuals, we approach, as an ideal limit, a condition where all the events in the universe, past, present, and future, are reduced (in a symbolic form to which any reader may react) to the dimensions of a large library. It is no wonder that

THE USE OF LANGUAGE

the discovery of printing, which manifolds a written record to any desired number of copies, brought about, in all our manner of living, a revolution which has been under way for some centuries and is still in full swing.

There is no need of dilating upon the significance of other means for recording, transmitting, and multiplying speech, such as the telegraph, telephone, phonograph, and radio. Their importance for the simpler uses of language is obvious, as in the use of wireless telegraphy in cases of shipwreck.

In the long run, anything which adds to the viability of language has also an indirect but more pervasive effect. Even acts of speech that do not prompt any particular immediate response, may change the predisposition of the hearer for further responses: a beautiful poem, for instance, may make the hearer more sensitive to later stimuli. This general refinement and intensification of human response requires a great deal of linguistic interaction. Education or culture, or whatever name we choose to give it, depends upon the repetition and publication of a vast amount of speech.

CHAPTER 3

SPEECH-COMMUNITIES

3. 1. A speech-community is a group of people who interact by means of speech (§ 2. 5). All the so-called higher activities of man — our specifically human activities — spring from the close adjustment among individuals which we call society, and this adjustment, in turn, is based upon language; the speech-community, therefore, is the most important kind of social group. Other phases of social cohesion, such as economic, political, or cultural groupings, bear some relation to the grouping by speech-communities, but do not usually coincide with it; cultural features, especially, are almost always more widespread than any one language. Before the coming of the white man, an independent Indian tribe which spoke a language of its own, formed both a speech-community and a political and economic unit; as to religion and general culture, however, it resembled neighboring tribes. Under more complex conditions there is less correlation between language and the other groupings. The speech-community which consists of all English-speaking people is divided into two political communities: the United States and the British Empire, and each of these is in turn subdivided; economically, the United States and Canada are more closely united than politically; culturally, we are part of a great area which radiates from western Europe. On the other hand, even the narrowest of these groups, the political United States, includes persons who do not speak English: American Indians, Spanish-speakers in the Southwest, and linguistically unassimilated immigrants. Colonial occupation, as in the Philippines or India, puts a speech-community into political and economic dependence upon a foreign speech-community. In some countries the population is divided into several speech-communities that exist together without local division: a town in Poland consists of Polish-speaking and German-speaking people; by religion, the former are Catholics, the latter Jews, and, until quite recently, very few persons in either group troubled themselves to understand the other group's language.

I have said nothing about biological grouping, because this does not, like the other groupings, depend upon language for its existence. Most matings, of course, take place between persons of like speech, so that a speech-community is always something of an inbred group; the exceptions, however, are very many, both in the mating of persons of different speech, one of whom usually acquires the other's language, and, what is more important, in the assimilation into a speech-community of whole groups of foreigners, such as immigrants, conquered people, or captives. These deviations are so many that, if we had records, we should doubtless find very few persons whose ancestors of a few generations ago all spoke the same language. What concerns us most, however, is the fact that the features of a language are not inherited in the biologic sense. A child cries out at birth and would doubtless in any case after a time take to gurgling and babbling, but the particular language he learns is entirely a matter of environment. An infant that gets into a group as a foundling or by adoption, learns the language of the group exactly as does a child of native parentage; as he learns to speak, his language shows no trace of whatever language his parents may have spoken. Whatever hereditary differences there may be in the structure of the larynx, mouth, lips, and so on, of normal human beings, it is certain that these differences are not such as to affect the actions which make up language. The child learns to speak like the persons round him. The first language a human being learns to speak is his *native language;* he is a *native speaker* of this language.

3. 2. Speech-communities differ greatly in size. More than one American Indian tribe of only a few hundred persons spoke a language of its own. On the other hand, even before the coming of modern communication and travel, some speech-communities were very large: in the first centuries of the Christian Era, Latin and Greek were each spoken by millions of people over large areas round the Mediterranean. Under modern conditions, some speech-communities have grown to enormous size. Jespersen estimates the number of speakers of the principal European languages, in millions, for the years 1600 and 1912 as follows:

	English	German	Russian	French	Spanish	Italian
1600	6	10	3	14	$8\frac{1}{2}$	$9\frac{1}{2}$
1912	150	90	106	47	52	37

Figures such as these have only a very indefinite value, because one cannot always tell which local groups form a single speech-community. Tesnière, estimating the numbers round the year 1920, names Chinese as the largest speech-community, with 400 million speakers, but the term *Chinese* denotes a family of mutually unintelligible languages. Doubtless one of these, North Chinese, has today more native speakers than any other language, but I know no estimate of their number. Another language of this group, Cantonese, probably ranks among the largest speech-communities. In any case, English (to continue with Tesnière's figures) ranks second, with 170 million native speakers. Russian comes third; Tesnière divides the figures between Great Russian (80 millions), Little Russian (Ukrainian, 34 millions), and White Russian ($6\frac{1}{2}$ millions), but these are mutually intelligible varieties, about as different as British and American English. Similarly, Tesniere splits the fourth-greatest language, German, into German (80 millions) and Judeo-German ($7\frac{1}{2}$ millions), although the rest of his figures do not consider dialectal differences; Jespersen's figure of 90 millions is probably nearer right. Tesnière's remaining figures omit Javanese, which has at least 20 millions of native speakers. With these modifications his figures are: Spanish 65, Japanese 55, Bengali [1] 50, French 45, Italian 41, Turco-Tartar 39, Western Hindi [1] 38, Arabic 37, Bihari [1] 36, Portuguese 36, Eastern Hindi [1] 25, Telugu [2] 24, Polish 23, Javanese 20, Marathi [1] 19, Tamil [2] 19, Korean 17, Panjabi [1] 16, Annamite 14, Roumanian 14, Rajasthani [1] 13, Dutch 13, Bohemian-Slovak 12, Canarese [2] 10, Oriya [1] 10, Hungarian 10.

Another element of uncertainty in figures like these arises from the differences within speech-communities. Dutch and German actually form only one speech-community, in the sense that there is no break between local speech-forms, but the extreme types are mutually unintelligible, and the political groups (on the one side Flemish Belgium and the Netherlands, and on the other side, Germany, Austria, and German Switzerland) have adopted two mutually unintelligible speech-forms, Standard Dutch-Flemish and Standard German, as their official languages. On the other hand, Turco-Tartar and some of the languages of India in our list prob-

---

[1] Indo-European languages spoken in India; we should perhaps add Gujerati, with some 10 million speakers.
[2] Dravidian languages spoken in India.

ably include equally great differences, although the extremes may be connected by local gradations. A final and insurmountable difficulty lies in people's acquisition of foreign languages. If we could determine a degree of proficiency which makes a student a member of a foreign speech-community, English, studied all over the world, would receive a much larger figure. Tesnière estimates that Malay is native to some three million people, but is spoken as a foreign language, especially in commerce, by some thirty millions.

3. 3. The difficulty or impossibility of determining in each case exactly what people belong to the same speech-community, is not accidental, but arises from the very nature of speech-communities. If we observed closely enough, we should find that no two persons — or rather, perhaps, no one person at different times — spoke exactly alike. To be sure, within a relatively homogeneous set of speakers — say, the native speakers of English in the Middle Western part of the United States — the habits of speech are far more uniform than the needs of communication would demand. We see the proof of this when an outsider — say, a Southerner or an Englishman or a foreigner who has mastered English — comes into our midst: his speech may be so much like ours as to cause not the slightest difficulty in communication, and yet strikingly noticeable on account of inessential differences, such as "accent" and "idiom." Nevertheless there are great differences even among the native members of such a relatively uniform group as Middle Western American, and, as we have just seen, even greater differences within a speech-community (e.g. English) as a whole. These differences play a very important part in the history of languages; the linguist is forced to consider them very carefully, even though in some of his work he is forced provisionally to ignore them. When he does this, he is merely employing the method of abstraction, a method essential to scientific investigation, but the results so obtained have to be corrected before they can be used in most kinds of further work.

The difference between speakers is partly a matter of bodily make-up and perhaps of purely personal habit; we recognize our friends by their voices from the next room and over the telephone. Some people are more talented for speech than others: they remember more words and turns of phrase, apply them better to the situation, and combine them in more pleasing style; the extreme case is the literary genius. Sometimes convention assigns certain speech-forms to certain speakers, as when the soldier, the well-trained servant, and the child in certain schools, learn to say *sir* or *ma'm* to certain persons, who do not reciprocate. Some exclamations, such as *Goodness gracious!* or *Dear me!* are largely reserved for the use of women. In some communities very different speech-forms are conventional for the sexes. The classical instance is that of the Carib Indians; a recently authenticated one is the language of the Yana Indians in northern California. Examples of Yana words are:

	MEN'S LANGUAGE	WOMEN'S LANGUAGE
'fire'	'auna	'auh
'my fire'	'aunija	'au'nich'
'deer'	bana	ba'
'grizzly-bear'	t'en'na	t'et'

The differences between the two sets of Yana forms can be stated by means of a fairly complex set of rules.

3. 4. The most important differences of speech within a community are due to differences in *density of communication*. The infant learns to speak like the people round him, but we must not picture this learning as coming to any particular end: there is no hour or day when we can say that a person has finished learning to speak, but, rather, to the end of his life, the speaker keeps on doing the very things which make up infantile language-learning. Our description of the latter (§ 2. 5) might be taken, in many respects, as a slow-motion picture of the ordinary processes of speech. Every speaker's language, except for personal factors which we must here ignore, is a composite result of what he has heard other people say.

Imagine a huge chart with a dot for every speaker in the community, and imagine that every time any speaker uttered a sentence, an arrow were drawn into the chart pointing from his dot to the dot representing each one of his hearers. At the end of a given period of time, say seventy years, this chart would show us the density of communication within the community. Some speakers would turn out to have been in close communication: there would be many arrows from one to the other, and there would be many series of arrows connecting them by way of one, two, or three intermediate speakers. At the other extreme there would be widely separated speakers who had never heard each other speak and were connected only by long chains of arrows through many intermediate speakers. If we wanted to explain the likeness and unlikeness between various speakers in the community, or, what comes to the same thing, to predict the degree of likeness for any two given speakers, our first step would be to count and evaluate the arrows and series of arrows connecting their dots. We shall see in a moment that this would be only the first step; the reader of this book, for instance, is more likely to repeat a speech-form which he has heard, say, from a lecturer of great fame, than one which he has heard from a street-sweeper.

The chart we have imagined is impossible of construction. An insurmountable difficulty, and the most important one, would be the factor of time: starting with persons now alive, we should be compelled to put in a dot for every speaker whose voice had ever reached anyone now living, and then a dot for every speaker whom these speakers had ever heard, and so on, back beyond the days of King Alfred the Great, and beyond earliest history, back indefinitely into the primeval dawn of mankind: our speech depends entirely upon the speech of the past.

Since we cannot construct our chart, we depend instead upon the study of indirect results and are forced to resort to hypothesis. We believe that the differences in density of communication within a speech-community are not only personal and individual, but that the community is divided into various systems of sub-groups such that the persons within a sub-group speak much more to each other than to persons outside their sub-group. Viewing the system of arrows as a network, we may say that these sub-groups are separated by *lines of weakness* in this net of oral communication. The lines of weakness and, accordingly, the differences of speech within a speech-community are *local* — due to mere geographic separation — and *non-local*, or as we usually say, *social*. In countries over which a speech-community has recently spread and settled, the local differences are relatively small, as, say, in the United States (especially the western part) or Russia; in countries that have been long settled by the same speech-community the local differences are much greater, as, say, in England, where English has been spoken for some 1500 years, or in France where Latin (now called French) has been spoken for two-thousand years.

3. 5. We shall examine first the simpler case, as it appears in the United States. The most striking line of cleavage in our speech is one of social class. Children who are born into homes of privilege, in the way of wealth, tradition, or education, become native speakers of what is popularly known as "good" English; the linguist prefers to give it the non-committal name of *standard English*. Less fortunate children become native speakers of "bad" or "vulgar" or, as the linguist prefers to call it, *non-standard English*. For instance, *I have none, I haven't any, I haven't got any* are standard ("good") English, but *I ain't got none* is non-standard ("bad") English.

These two main types of American English are by no means treated alike. The standard forms are used in school, in church, and in all discourse that officially concerns the whole community, as in law-courts and legislative assemblies. All our writing (except by way of jest) is based on the standard forms, and these forms are registered in grammars and dictionaries and presented in text-books to foreigners who want to learn our language. Both groups of speakers, standard and non-standard, agree in calling the standard forms "good" or "correct" and non-standard forms "bad," "incorrect," "vulgar," or even, "not English." The speaker of standard English does not trouble himself to learn the non-standard forms, but very many speakers of non-standard English try to use the standard forms. A native of the less favored group who acquires prestige, say, in the way of wealth or political eminence, is almost sure to learn, as well as may be, the standard forms of speech; in fact, noticeable lapses in this respect — even a single *I seen it* or *I done it* — may endanger his newly acquired position.

Within the standard language there are minor differences. In this case again, the divergent forms are estimated as higher and lower. A Chicagoan, for instance, who uses the *ah*-vowel of *father* instead of the more common *a*-vowel of *man* in words like *laugh, half, bath, dance, can't*, is said to be speaking a "higher-class" kind of English. In cases like these, however, people's attitudes differ: many Chicagoans find these *ah*-forms silly and affected. Speakers of standard English often dispute as to which of two forms is "better": *it's I* or *it's me, forehead* or "*forrid*." Since the disputants do not trouble themselves to agree on a definition of "better," these disputes never reach any conclusion. This is a matter which will occupy us again.

Within the standard language, further, there are differences that obviously depend upon density of communication: different economic classes, — say, the very rich and the so-called "middle class" in its various gradations, — differ in speech. Then there are differences of education, in the way both of family tradition and of schooling. These differences are crossed by less important divisions of technical occupation: different kinds of craftsmen, merchants, engineers, lawyers, physicians, scientists, artists, and so on, differ somewhat in speech. Sports and hobbies have at least their own vocabulary. The factor of age-groups will concern us later; it is a tremendous force, but works almost unseen, and scarcely appears on the level that now concerns us, except perhaps in young people's fondness for slang.

The most stable and striking differences, even in the United States and even in our standard language, are geographic. In the United States we have three great geographic types of standard English: New England, Central-Western and Southern. Within these types there are smaller local differences: speakers of standard English from older-settled parts of the country can often tell a fellow-speaker's home within fairly narrow limits. In matters of pronunciation, especially, the range of standard English in America is wide: greatly different pronunciations, such as those, say, of North Carolina and Chicago, are accepted equally as standard. Only from the stage do we demand a uniform pronunciation, and here our actors use a British type rather than an American. In England there are similar regional types, but they are not granted equal value. The highest social recognition is given to the "public school" English of the south. The innumerable gradations from this toward the decidedly provincial types of standard, enjoy less prestige as they depart from the most favored type. The social recognition of a speaker of standard English from Scotland or Yorkshire or Lancashire, depends in part upon how closely his pronunciation approaches the upper-class southern type. In England, but scarcely in the United States, provincial colorings of standard English are tied up with differences of social level.

3. 6. Non-standard speech shows greater variety than standard. The higher the social position of the non-standard speaker, the more nearly does he approach the standard language. At the top are the transitional speakers who use an almost standard form of speech, with only a sprinkling of non-standard forms, and perhaps a pronunciation with too provincial a twang. At the bottom are the unmistakably rustic or proletarian speakers who make no pretense at using standard forms.

Apart from this continuous gradation, various groups of non-standard speakers have their own speech-forms. Occupational groups, such as fishermen, dairy workers, bakers, brewers, and so on, have, at any rate, their own technical language. Especially, minor groups who are in any way cut off from the great mass, use clearly-marked varieties of speech. Thus, sea-faring men used to speak their own type of non-standard English. Tramps and some kinds of law-breakers have many speech-forms of their own; so do circus people and other wandering entertainers. Among non-standard speakers of German, Christians and Jews, and in some places Catholics and Protestants, differ in many of their linguistic forms. If the special group is at odds with the rest of the community, it may use its peculiarities of speech as a *secret* dialect, as do the English-speaking Gipsies. Criminals in various countries have developed such secret dialects.

The greatest diversity in non-standard speech, however, is geographic. The geographic differences, which we hear even in the standard English of the United States, are more audible when we listen to non-standard speakers. In remote districts within the older-settled parts of the country these local characteristics are very pronounced, to the point where we may describe them as *local dialects*.

In older-settled speech-communities, the type exemplified by France, or by the British part of the English-speaking group, local dialects play a much greater part. In such communities the non-standard language can be divided, roughly, to be sure, and without a sharp demarcation, into *sub-standard* speech, intelligible at least, though not uniform, throughout the country, and *local dialect*, which differs from place to place to such an extent that speakers living some distance apart may fail to understand each other. Sub-standard speech, in such countries, belongs to the "lower middle class," — to the more ambitious small tradesfolk, mechanics, or city workmen, — and the local dialects are spoken by the peasants and the poorest people of the towns.

The local dialects are of paramount importance to the linguist, not merely because their great variety gives him work to do, but because the origin and history of the standard and sub-standard types of speech can be understood only in the light of the local dialects. Especially during the last decades, linguists have come to see that *dialect geography* furnishes the key to many problems.

In a country like France, Italy, or Germany — better studied in this respect than England — every village or, at most, every group of two or three villages, has its own local dialect. The differences between neighboring local dialects are usually small, but recognizable. The villagers are ready to tell in what way their neighbors' speech differs from theirs, and often tease their neighbors about these peculiarities. The difference from place to place is small, but, as one travels in any one direction, the differences accumulate, until speakers, say from opposite ends of the country, cannot understand each other, although there is no sharp line of linguistic demarcation between the places where they live. Any such geographic area of gradual transitions is called a *dialect area*.

Within a dialect area, we can draw lines between places which differ as to any feature of language. Such lines are called *isoglosses*. If a village has some unique peculiarity of speech, the isogloss based on this peculiarity will be simply a line round this village. On the other hand, if some peculiarity extends over a large part of the dialect area, the isogloss of this feature will appear as a long line, dividing the dialect area into two sections. In Germany, for instance, the northern dialects pronounce the word *bite* with a *t*-sound, as we do in English, but the southern dialects pronounce it with an *s*-sound (as in standard German *beiszen*); the isogloss which separates these two forms is a long and very irregular line, running east and west across the whole German speech area. In the north and northeast of England one can mark off an area where the past tense of *bring* has the form *brang*. *Dialect atlases*, collections of maps of a speech area with isoglosses drawn in, are an important tool for the linguist.

The speakers' attitude toward local dialects differs somewhat in different countries. In England the local dialects have little prestige; the upper-class speaker does not bother with them and the native speaker of a local dialect who rises socially will try to cast it off, even if only in exchange for some form of sub-standard speech. The Germans, on the other hand, have developed, within the last century, a kind of romantic fondness for local dialects. While the middle-class speaker, who is not quite sure of his social position, will shy away from them, some upper-class Germans make it a point to speak the local dialect of their home. In German Switzerland this goes farthest: even the upper-class Swiss, who is familiar with standard German, uses local dialect as the normal medium of communication in his family and with his neighbors.

3. 7. The main types of speech in a complex speech-community can be roughly classed as follows:

(1) *literary standard*, used in the most formal discourse and in writing (example: *I have none*);

(2) *colloquial standard*, the speech of the privileged class (example: *I haven't any* or *I haven't got any* — in England only if spoken with the southern "public school" sounds and intonation);

(3) *provincial standard*, in the United States probably not to be differentiated from (2), spoken by the "middle" class, very close to (2), but differing slightly from province to province (example: *I haven't any* or *I haven't got any*, spoken, in England, with sounds or intonations that deviate from the "public school" standard);

(4) *sub-standard*, clearly different from (1), (2), and (3), spoken in European countries by the "lower middle" class, in the United States by almost all but the speakers of type (2–3), and differing topographically, without intense local difference (example: *I ain't got none*);

(5) *local dialect*, spoken by the least privileged class; only slightly developed in the United States; in Switzerland used also, as a domestic language, by the other classes; differs almost from village to village; the varieties so great as often to be incomprehensible to each other and to speakers of (2–3–4) (Example: *a hae nane*).

3. 8. Our survey of differences within a speech-community has shown us that the members of a speech-community may speak so much alike that anyone can understand anyone else, or may differ so much that persons who live some distance apart may fail to understand each other. The former case is illustrated by an Indian tribe of a few hundred persons, the latter by a far-flung speech community like English, where an American and a dialect-speaking Yorkshireman, for instance, do not understand each other's speech. Actually, however, we can draw no line between the two cases, because there are all kinds of gradations between understanding and failing to understand. Whether the American and the Yorkshireman understand each other, may depend on the intelligence of the two individuals concerned, upon their general experience with foreign dialects or languages, upon their disposition at the moment, upon the extent to which the situation clarifies the value of the speech-utterance, and so on. Again, there are endless gradations between local and standard speech; either or both persons may make concessions which aid understanding, and these concessions will usually run in the direction of the standard language.

All this prevents our drawing a plain line round the borders of many a speech community. The clear cases are those where two mutually unintelligible languages abut on each other, as do, say, English and Spanish in our Southwest. Here each person's native language — if, for simplicity sake, we ignore the languages of Indians and recent immigrants — is either English or Spanish, and we can draw an imaginary line, a *language boundary*, which will separate the English-speakers from the Spanish-speakers. This language boundary will of course not appear as a simple and fixed line between two topographically solid communities. There will be English-speaking settlements thrown out, in the shape of *speech-islands*, into totally Spanish surroundings, and, vice versa, Spanish speech-islands surrounded by English-speaking communities. Families and individuals of either group will be found living among the other and will have to be enclosed in a separate little circle of our language boundary. Our language boundary, then, consists not only of a great irregular line, but also of many little closed curves around speech-islands, some of which contain only a single family or a single person. In spite of its geometrical complexity and of its instability from day to day, this language boundary at any rate represents a plain distinction. It is true that linguistic scholars have found enough resemblance between English and Spanish to prove beyond a doubt that these languages are related, but the resemblance and relationship are too distant to affect the question with which we are here concerned.

The same might be said, for instance, of German and Danish: across the Jutland peninsula, just north of the city of Flensburg, we could draw a boundary between the two languages, and this boundary would show, on a smaller scale, the same features as the English-Spanish boundary in our Southwest. In this case, however, the resemblance between the two languages is sufficiently close to warn us of further possibilities. The two languages are mutually unintelligible, but resemble each other so closely that it takes no linguistic research to see the relationship. If one can compare such things at all, the difference is no greater than the difference between, say, a German local dialect spoken in Sleswick and one spoken in Switzerland. German and Danish, where they abut on each other, show a difference no greater than the differences which may exist within a single locally differentiated speech-community — only that in the latter case the intermediate gradations intervene, while between German and Danish we find no intermediate dialects.

The purely relative nature of this distinction appears more plainly in other cases. We speak of French and Italian, of Swedish and Norwegian, of Polish and Bohemian as separate languages, because these communities are politically separate and use different standard languages, but the differences of local speech-forms at the border are in all these cases relatively slight and no greater than the differences which we find within each of these speech-communities. The question comes down to this: what degree of difference between adjoining speech-forms justifies the name of a language border? Evidently, we cannot weigh differences as accurately as all this. In some cases, certainly, our habits of nomenclature will not apply to linguistic conditions. The local dialects justify no line between what we call German and what we call Dutch-Flemish: the Dutch-German speech area is linguistically a unit, and the cleavage is primarily political; it is linguistic only in the sense that the political units use different standard languages. In sum, the term *speech-community* has only a relative value. The possibility of communication between groups, or even between individuals, ranges all the way from zero up to the most delicate adjustment. It is evident that the intermediate degrees contribute very much to human welfare and progress.

3. 9. The possibilities of communication are enhanced and the boundaries of the speech-community are further obscured by another very important factor, namely, people's use of foreign languages. This is by no means a modern accomplishment; among peoples of simpler civilization, such as some tribes of American Indians, well-bred persons often speak more than one of the languages of neighboring tribes. The factor of foreign-language speaking does not lend itself to measurement, since proficiency ranges all the way down to a smattering so slight as to be of almost no actual use. To the extent that the learner can communicate, he may be ranked as a *foreign speaker* of a language. We have

already seen that the usefulness of some languages, such as English or Malay, is partly due to the adherence of foreign speakers. Often enough, as among the educated classes in India, English serves as the means of communication between foreign speakers who do not understand each other's native languages.

Some people entirely give up the use of their native language in favor of a foreign one. This happens frequently among immigrants in the United States. If the immigrant does not stay in a settlement of others from his own country, and especially if he marries outside his original nationality, he may have no occasion at all to use his native language. Especially, it would seem, in the case of less educated persons, this may result, after a time, in wholesale forgetting: people of this kind understand their native language when they chance to hear it spoken, but can no longer speak it freely or even intelligibly. They have made a *shift of language;* their only medium of communication is now English, and it is for them not a native but an *adopted* language. Sometimes these persons have nevertheless acquired English very imperfectly and therefore are in the position of speaking no language well.

Another, more common case of shift of language occurs in the children of immigrants. Very often the parents speak their native language at home, and make it the native language of their children, but the children, as soon as they begin to play out of doors or to attend school, refuse to speak the home language, and in time succeed in forgetting all but a smattering of it, and speak only English. For them, English has become what we may call their *adult* language. In general, they speak it perfectly — that is, in a manner indistinguishable from that of the surrounding native speakers — but in some cases they carry over foreign peculiarities from their native language. This latter they speak very imperfectly or not at all, but their passive understanding, when they hear it, is somewhat better. A study of similar cases in Wales, where the children of Welsh-speaking parents shift to English, seems to show that this process retards the child's development.

3. 10. In the extreme case of foreign-language learning the speaker becomes so proficient as to be indistinguishable from the native speakers round him. This happens occasionally in adult shifts of language and frequently in the childhood shift just described. In the cases where this perfect foreign-language learning is not accompanied by loss of the native language, it results in *bilingualism*, native-like control of two languages. After early childhood few people have enough muscular and nervous freedom or enough opportunity and leisure to reach perfection in a foreign language; yet bilingualism of this kind is commoner than one might suppose, both in cases like those of our immigrants and as a result of travel, foreign study, or similar association. Of course, one cannot define a degree of perfection at which a good foreign speaker becomes a bilingual: the distinction is relative.

More commonly the bilingual acquires his second language in early childhood. This happens frequently in communities near a language border, or where a family lives as a speech-island, or where the parents are of different speech. Many well-to-do European families make their children bilingual by employing foreign nurses or governesses. The educated Swiss-German is bilingual in the sense that he speaks both the local dialect and the highly divergent standard German. In the United States, better-educated immigrants often succeed in making their children bilingual; this development contrasts with the shifting of language among less privileged groups. In all these cases, apparently, the two languages play somewhat different parts in the life of the bilingual. Ordinarily one language is the *home language*, while the other serves a wider range, but other dispositions also occur. The apparent frequency with which one meets bilinguals among artists and men of science may indicate a favorable effect of bilingualism on the general development of the child; on the other hand, it may mean merely that bilingualism results from generally favorable childhood surroundings.

CHAPTER 4

THE LANGUAGES OF THE WORLD

4. 1. Among the languages that are spoken today, only few are even tolerably well known to science. Of many we have inadequate information, of others none at all. The older stages of some present-day languages, and some languages no longer spoken are known to us from written records; these records, however, acquaint us with only an infinitesimal part of the speech-forms of the past. Some extinct languages are known from the scantiest of records, such as a few proper names, many more only by the name of the people who spoke them, and doubtless a vastly greater number has disappeared without a trace. More than one language now spoken, especially in Africa and in South America, will pass out of existence without being recorded.

The inadequacy of our knowledge makes it impossible to determine the relationships that may exist between many languages. In general, students who deal with slightly-known languages, have a weakness for setting up relationships on insufficient evidence. By relationship of languages we mean, of course, resemblances that can be explained only on the assumption that the languages are divergent forms of a single older language. Such resemblances show themselves in phonetic correspondences like those cited in Chapter 1, correspondences which can be determined only on the basis of extensive and accurate data. The less known the languages and the less expert the student, the greater is the danger of his making false assumptions of kinship. Even the most positive announcements often turn out, upon examination, to be based upon insufficient evidence.

4. 2. *English* is spoken by more native speakers than any other language except, presumably, North Chinese; if we count the important factor of foreign speakers, English is the most widespread of languages. The number of native speakers of English was estimated for 1920 at about 170 millions (§ 3.2). Almost all of these speakers use standard or sub-standard English; local dialects are of small extent and for the most part mutually intelligible.

English is unmistakably related to the other Germanic languages, but at the same time differs plainly from all of them. History tells us that it came to Britain as the language of invaders, the Angles, Saxons, and Jutes, who conquered the island in the fifth century of our era. The marked difference of English from the Germanic speech along the continental shore of the North Sea is explained by the millennium and a half of separation. The oldest written records of English, dating from the eighth and ninth centuries, confirm this, for their language closely resembles that of the oldest records of continental Germanic speech, which date from about the same time. The splitting off of English is a classical example of the way in which a dialect area is divided by migration.

The resemblance is closest between English and the dialects of the *Frisian* area, spoken by some 350,000 persons on the coast and coastal islands along the North Sea. This resemblance appears strikingly in the oldest Frisian texts, which date from the second half of the thirteenth century. We conclude that English is an offshoot of an *Anglo-Frisian* (or *Ingweonic*) dialect area, which must have been fairly extensive before the migration to Britain.

Outside of Frisian, the Germanic-speaking area of the European mainland (excluding Scandinavia) shows no sharp cleavages. The nearest thing to a break is a heavy bundle of isoglosses running east and west across Germany: north of the bundle one speaks *p, t, k* in words like *hope, bite, make;* south of it, sounds like *f, s, kh,* as in standard German *hoffen, beiszen, machen.* The speech of the northern type is known as Low German, that of the southern as High German; since the various isoglosses do not coincide, the distinction can be sharply drawn only if one resorts to an arbitrary definition. This difference appears already in our oldest records, which date from about the same time as those of English. Various kinds of evidence show us that the divergence of the southern type is due to changes which took place in the south during the fifth and sixth centuries of our era. The *Continental West Germanic* dialects, as they are called in contrast with Anglo-Frisian, made a vigorous eastward expansion during the Middle Ages; to the east and southeast of the main area there are many speech-islands, especially of the High German type, such as Yiddish in Poland and Russia. Continental West Germanic is spoken today by over 100 millions of persons. It has developed two great standard languages, *Dutch-Flemish*, which is used in Belgium and the Netherlands and is based on western coastal dialects of the Low-German type, and *New High German*, based on eastern central dialects of the district that was gained by medieval expansion.

Anglo-Frisian and Continental West Germanic resemble each other closely enough to be viewed as a *West Germanic* unit, in contrast with the smaller *Scandinavian* (or *North Germanic*) group. Within this group, *Icelandic* differs markedly from the rest, what with the thousand years of separation since Iceland was colonized from western Norway. Icelandic is spoken today by some 100,000 speakers. The language of the *Faroese Islands*, with about 23,000 speakers, is close to Icelandic. The rest of the area, comprising Denmark, Norway, Sweden, Gotland, and part of the Finnish coast, shows no marked cleavages; the speakers number some 15 millions. Our oldest records of North Germanic speech are inscriptions, some of which may date as early as the fourth century A.D.; the oldest manuscripts date from the twelfth century, but the wording of the texts, especially in the case of some Icelandic literature, may be several centuries older. The present-day standard languages are Icelandic, Danish, Dano-Norwegian, Norwegian Landsmaal, and Swedish.

We have some information about Germanic languages that are no longer spoken, such as the languages of the Goths, Vandals, Burgundians, and Lombards. Parts of a Bible translation in the *Gothic* language of the Visigoths, made by Bishop Ulfila in the fourth century, are preserved to us in sixth-century manuscripts, notably the Silver Codex. While the language of the Lombards seems to have been of the West Germanic type, the others, including Gothic, were closer to Scandinavian and are usually set apart as an *East Germanic* group. East Germanic settlers seem to have kept their language in the Crimea and elsewhere on the black Sea until the eighteenth century.

All the languages so far named resemble each other closely in contrast with all others, and accordingly constitute the *Germanic* family of languages; they are divergent modern forms of a single prehistoric language to which we give the name Primitive Germanic (§ 1.6).

4. 3. The kinship of the Germanic family, as a whole, with certain other languages and language families of Europe and Asia, is not superficially apparent, but has been fully established by the researches of the last century; together, all these languages make up the *Indo-European* family (§ 1.6).

To the west of the Germanic languages we find today the remnants of the *Celtic* family. *Irish* is known to us from a manuscript literature since the eighth century of our era; a few inscriptions on stone are perhaps much earlier. Irish is spoken by some 400,000 people, and its offshoot, *Scotch Gaelic*, by some 150,000; *Manx*, as a home language, alongside English, by a few hundred. Another branch of the Celtic family consists of *Welsh* and *Breton*, each with about a million speakers and known through written records since the eighth century. The latter, spoken on the northwestern coast of France, was brought there from Britain, perhaps as early as the fourth century. Another language of this branch, *Cornish*, whose earliest records date from the ninth century, died out round the year 1800. History and the evidence of place-names show that Celtic was in earlier times spoken over a large part of Europe, including what is now Bohemia, Austria, southern Germany, northern Italy, and France. It was superseded in these regions by Latin, as a result of Roman conquests, and by Germanic languages, as a result of the great migrations in the early centuries of our era. We have a few scant inscriptions, dating from round 100 B.C. in the ancient Celtic language of Gaul.

Northeast of the Germanic languages lies the *Baltic* family. The two surviving languages of this family, *Lithuanian*, spoken by some $2\frac{1}{2}$ million people, and *Lettish*, spoken by some $1\frac{1}{2}$ millions, have written records dating from the sixteenth century; thanks to the political independence of Lithuania and Latvia, both of these dialect-groups are now developing vigorous standard languages. A third language of this group, *Old Prussian*, is known to us from a few written documents of the fifteenth and sixteenth centuries; it ceased to be spoken in the seventeenth century.

South of the Baltic languages, and east and southeast of the Germanic, we find the great *Slavic* family. The eastward expansion of German in the Middle Ages overlaid various languages of the *West Slavic* branch. One of these, *Lusatian* (*Wendish, Sorbian*), survives as a speech-island of some 30,000 persons in Upper Saxony; another, *Polabian*, survived into the eighteenth century and has left a few written texts; the rest have died out, leaving a trace only in Germanized place-names. As a result of the struggle, the two great surviving West Slavic dialect areas show a peculiar

THE LANGUAGES OF THE WORLD 61

geographic configuration: a narrow streak of speech-islands trails off northward from the main *Polish* area along the Vistula toward Danzig, and *Bohemian* juts out westward as a kind of peninsula into the domain of German. Polish, recorded since the fourteenth century, is spoken by more than 20 million people. The Bohemian area, divided on the basis of standard languages, into Czech and Slovak, comprises perhaps 12 millions of speakers; the oldest records date from the thirteenth century. *East Slavic* consists of but one enormous dialect area, *Russian*, with at least 110 million speakers, and written records dating back to the twelfth century. The *South Slavic* branch is separated from the others by the intervention of Hungarian, an unrelated intruder. It consists of *Bulgarian*, with some 5 million speakers, *Serbo-Croatian*, with some 10 millions, and *Slovene*, with about $1\frac{1}{2}$ millions. Our oldest written records of Slavic speech are Old Bulgarian records from the ninth century, preserved in manuscripts written at least a century later, and a scant tenth-century text in Old Slovene. Some students find a relatively close resemblance between the Baltic and Slavic groups, and include them together as a Balto-Slavic sub-group within the Indo-European family.

To the south of the Germanic languages, *Romance* languages are spoken: the *Portuguese-Spanish-Catalan* area (with three standard languages indicated by these names) comprising in all over 100 million speakers, the *French* area with 45 millions, the *Italian* with over 40 millions, and *Ladin* (*Rhaeto-Romanic*) in Switzerland, spoken by some 16,000 persons. A further group, the *Dalmatian*, is extinct: one of the dialects, Ragusan, died out in the fifteenth century; another, Veliote, survived into the nineteenth. To the east, on the Black Sea, cut off from the western areas by the intrusion of South Slavic, lies the *Roumanian* area, estimated as having 14 millions of speakers. All the Romance languages, of course, are modern forms of *Latin*, the ancient dialect of the city of Rome. Our oldest records of Latin date from somewhere round 300 B.C. In medieval and modern time, Latin has been used as an artificial medium for writing and learned discourse. Ancient inscriptions show us, in Italy, some sister languages of Latin, notably *Oscan* and *Umbrian;* these and others, which in the course of Roman expansion were superseded by Latin, belong, together with Latin, into the *Italic* family. Some scholars believe that Italic and Celtic are connected by special resemblances, so as to form an Italo-Celtic sub-group within the Indo-European family.

East of the Adriatic, south of Serbo-Croatian, is the *Albanese* area. Albanese, known from records only since the seventeenth century, is spoken by a population of $1\frac{1}{2}$ millions. Although Albanese is full of loan-words from the surrounding languages, the native nucleus of its forms shows it to be a separate branch of the Indo-European stock.

Greek is spoken today by some 7 millions of speakers, in many local dialects and in a widespread standard language. The modern dialects are almost entirely descended from the standard language (the so-called *Koiné*) which prevailed in the first centuries of the Christian Era, having superseded the local and provincial dialects of ancient times. These Ancient Greek dialects are known to us from many inscriptions, beginning in the seventh century B.C., from fragments of writing on papyrus, beginning in the fourth century B.C., and from a copious literature (transmitted, to be sure, in much later manuscripts), whose oldest compositions, the Homeric poems, are at least as old as 800 B.C.

In Asia Minor we find one branch of the Indo-European stock, *Armenian*, spoken today by 3 or 4 million people; our oldest written records of Armenian date from the fifth century A.D.

The great Asiatic offshoot of the Indo-European family is the *Indo-Iranian* group. This consists of two sub-groups, *Iranian* and *Indic* (or *Indo-Aryan*), very different today, but in the forms of our earliest records so similar that we can with certainty view them as descendants of a Primitive Indo-Iranian parent language.

The principal dialect areas of modern Iranian are *Persian* (with a standard language of high prestige, spoken by perhaps 7 or 8 millions of people), the *Caspian* group, and *Kurdish;* then, eastward, the *Pamir* dialects, *Afghan* (*Pushto*), with some 4 million speakers, and *Baluchi;* an isolated offshoot, far to the west is *Ossete*, in the Caucasus, spoken by some 225,000 persons. Our oldest records of Iranian are the rock inscriptions, in *Old Persian*, of King Darius the Great and his successors (from the sixth to the fourth centuries B.C.), and the sacred texts, in *Avestan*, of the Zoroastrian (Parsi) religion, whose oldest portions may have been composed as early as 600 B.C., though our manuscripts are quite modern and contain a text which has undergone serious orthographic revision. Intermediate stages, except for Persian (*Pehlevi*),

THE LANGUAGES OF THE WORLD 63

are less well known, but early in the present century discoveries of manuscript fragments in Chinese Turkestan gave us knowledge of other medieval Iranian languages, which have been identified as *Parthian, Sogdian,* and *Sakian.*

The other sub-branch of Indo-Iranian, Indic, comprises a total of more than 230 millions of speakers, distributed among a number of dialect areas which cover the larger part of India and include such great languages as *Marathi* (19 millions), *Gujerati* (10 millions), *Panjabi* (16 millions), *Rajasthani* (13 millions), *Western Hindi* (38 millions), *Eastern Hindi* (25 millions), *Oriya* (10 millions), *Bihari* (36 millions), *Bengali* (50 millions). The language of the *Gipsies* (*Romani*) is an emigrant offshoot of the *Paiçachi* area in northwestern India. Our oldest written records of Indic speech, the inscriptions of King Açoka, dating from the third century B.C., show us a number of Indic dialects in what is called the *Prakrit* (or *Middle Indic*) stage; Indic languages in the Prakrit stage are known to us also from later inscriptions and from manuscript texts; among these last is *Pali,* the language of the Buddhist scriptures. An even older stage of Indic speech, the *Sanskritic* (or *Old Indic*) stage, is known to us, strangely enough, from somewhat later documents. Our oldest texts in this stage are the *Vedic* collections of hymns; the original composition of the oldest parts of the oldest collection, the Rig-Veda, is placed conservatively at 1200 B.C. These hymns form the basic part of the scriptures of the Brahmin religion. A second, slightly divergent type of Old Indic speech is known to us from the Brahmana's, the prose texts of the Brahmin religion, and from the grammar of Pāṇini (§ 1.5) and its ancillary works. This language, known as *Sanskrit,* was spoken round the fourth century B.C. by the upper class somewhere in northwestern India. As a standard dialect and later as a literary and scholastic language, it gradually came into official use all over Brahmin India; in the inscriptions it appears first round 150 B.C. and a few centuries later entirely supersedes the dialects of the Prakrit type; from that time to the present, written according to the rules of Pāṇini's grammar, it has served as the medium of an enormous body of artistic and scholarly literature.

Beside the branches so far named, all of which are represented by languages spoken today, there must have existed at different times many other offshoots of Primitive Indo-European, some closely related to surviving branches, others intermediate between them, and perhaps still others quite apart. Of some such languages we have a slight knowledge. Round the Adriatic, the *Illyrian* languages were spoken in ancient times: *Illyrian*, in which we have only a few proper names, *Venetic*, known from inscriptions that date from the fourth to the second centuries B.C., and *Messapian* in southern Italy, with inscriptions dating from 450 to 150 B.C. Of *Thracian*, in the western part of the Balkan peninsula, we have only a few names and words and a single inscription (round 400 B.C.); it seems to have been closely related to *Phrygian*, in Asia Minor, which is known to us from a set of inscriptions dating as early as the eighth century B.C. and another set from the first centuries of our era. *Macedonian* seems to have been closely related to Greek. *Ligurian* (round the present Riviera) and *Sicilian* in Sicily, may have been close to Italic. *Tocharian*, in Central Asia, is known to us from manuscript fragments of the sixth century A.D., found in Chinese Turkestan.

Primitive Indo-European, in its turn, must have been related to other languages; with one exception, however, these have either died out or else changed so much as to obscure the kinship. The one exception is *Hittite*, an ancient language of Asia Minor, known to us from cuneiform inscriptions that begin round 1400 B.C. This relationship, though distant, enables us to reconstruct some of the pre-history of Primitive Indo-European and some features of a presumable Primitive Indo-Hittite parent language.

4. 4. As the various languages of the Indo-European stock spread over their present vast territory, they must have obliterated many unrelated forms of speech. A remnant of such a language is *Basque*, spoken today by some half-million people in the western Pyrenees. Our oldest texts in Basque date from the sixteenth century. It is the only surviving form of ancient *Iberian*, once spoken over southern France and Spain, and known to us from inscriptions and place-names.

Of other such languages, now extinct, we have only scant information. In Italy, *Etruscan*, a totally unrelated neighbor that exerted a powerful influence on the Latin people, has left us copious inscriptions, which begin as early as the sixth century B.C. They are in the Greek alphabet and can be read, but not understood. The inscriptions in ancient *Rhaetian* show this language to have been an offshoot of Etruscan. An inscription of about 600 B.C. on the island of Lemnos and a series of inscriptions of the

THE LANGUAGES OF THE WORLD 65

fourth and third centuries B.C., mostly from Sardis in Asia Minor, show that Etruscan was related to *Lemnian* and *Lydian;* the texts of only the last-named have been interpreted.

From ancient *Crete* we have several inscriptions in the Greek alphabet but in an unknown language, two from the fourth century B.C. and one (from the town of Praisos) somewhat older. From a much earlier period, round 1500 B.C. we have Cretan inscriptions partly in picture-writing and partly in a simplified system derived from this.

From Asia Minor we have copious inscriptions in *Lycian*, from the fifth and fourth centuries B.C., and less extensive ones in *Carian*, from the seventh century B.C. The former are in a Greek alphabet and have been partly interpreted; the writing of the latter may be of the same provenience, but is undeciphered. In Syria and the adjacent part of Asia Minor copious inscriptions in picture-writing from about 1000 B.C. to about 550 B.C. have been attributed to the *Hittites*, but there is no reason for believing that these undeciphered inscriptions were made by the same people as our Hittite cuneiform records (§ 4.3).

Cuneiform inscriptions on rock and clay from the Near East acquaint us with extinct languages of an older time: *Sumerian* in Mesopotamia, from 4000 B.C., *Elamitic*, in Persia, from 2000 B.C.; scant records of *Cossean*, east of Mesopotamia, from 1600 B.C., *Mitanni*, east of Mesopotamia, from round 1400 B.C.; the language of *Van* (near Lake Van) from the ninth and eighth centuries B.C.; and several uninterpreted languages within the Hittite empire in Asia Minor. Of the other languages represented in records of this type, we have already mentioned Old Persian and Hittite (§ 4.3), and shall immediately speak of Babylonian-Assyrian, a Semitic language.

4. 5. Of the present-day families which border upon Indo-European, one or more may be distantly akin; the Semitic-Hamitic and the Finno-Ugrian families seem to show some resemblance to Indo-European, but, in spite of much effort, no conclusive evidence has been found.

The *Semitic-Hamitic* family consists of four branches which resemble each other but distantly: Semitic, Egyptian, Berber, and Cushite.

The *Semitic* branch appears in two offshoots. The eastern, now extinct, consists of *Babylonian-Assyrian*, known to us from inscriptions on stone and clay in cuneiform writing, from about 2500 B.C. onward; this language was superseded by Aramaic before the beginning of the Christian Era. The western branch of Semitic is divided, again, into two main offshoots, a northern and a southern. The former appears in the *Canaanite* glosses in cuneiform tablets found at Tel-el-Amarna, dating round 1400 B.C., and in the *Moabite* of the famous inscription of King Mesha, ninth century B.C. *Phoenician*, known first from inscriptions of the ninth century B.C., was spoken not only in Phoenicia, where it died out before the Christian Era, but also in the Phoenician colony of Carthage, where it lived some centuries longer. *Hebrew* is known from inscriptions of equal age and from the manuscript tradition of the Old Testament, whose earliest portion may have been composed by 1000 B.C. It was superseded by Aramaic in the second century B.C., but remained in written use through the Middle Ages; of late, there have been attempts to restore it, artificially, to the status of a spoken language. *Aramaic*, finally, consists of a group of dialects, first known from inscriptions of the eighth century B.C. In a tremendous wave of expansion, Aramaic, in the centuries just before the Christian Era, spread over Syria and large tracts of Asia, vying with Greek, and replacing many languages, among them Hebrew and Assyrian. For a millennium (from round 300 B.C. to round 650 A.D.) it served as the leading official and written language of the Near East; in the latter capacity it exercised a great effect upon Asiatic systems of writing. It was superseded, in its turn, by the spread of Arabic, and is spoken today in isolated patches by some 200,000 people. The southern branch of West Semitic is represented by several still flourishing languages. *South Arabic*, known from inscriptions ranging from about 800 B.C. to the sixth century A.D., is still spoken, in several dialects, along the southern coast of Arabia and on the island of Sokotra. *Arabic*, whose earliest record is an inscription from 328 A.D., owes its expansion, since the seventh century of our era, to the conquests of the Mohammedan Arabs. It is spoken today by some 37 millions of people and, beyond this, has served for centuries as the sacred, literary, and official language of Islam. *Ethiopian*, on the east coast of Africa (Abyssinia), is first known to us from inscriptions beginning with the fourth century A.D.; the present-day languages of this group are *Tigre*, *Tigriña*, and *Amharic*.

THE LANGUAGES OF THE WORLD 67

The Egyptian, Berber, and Cushite branches of Semitic-Hamitic are usually included under the name of *Hamitic* languages.

Egyptian is recorded for us in hieroglyphic inscriptions from 4000 B.C.; the later form of the language, known as *Coptic*, appears in a manuscript literature of Christian times. Egyptian died out, superseded by Arabic, in the seventeenth century.

The *Berber* branch of Semitic-Hamitic, is known from ancient times through inscriptions in the *Libyan* language, from the fourth century B.C.; it is represented today by various languages, such as *Tuareg* and *Kabyle*, which have maintained themselves against Arabic in northern Africa and are said to total some 6 or 7 million speakers.

The fourth branch of Semitic-Hamitic is *Cushite*, south of Egypt; it includes a number of languages, among them *Somali* and *Galla*, the latter with some 8 million speakers.

4. 6. South of the Arab and Berber areas of northern Africa, a broad belt of many languages stretches across the continent from the Ethiopian and Cushite areas in the east to the Gulf of Guinea in the west. The languages of this vast belt, spoken by a population of presumably some 50 millions, are little known. Some scholars, upon very scant evidence, believe them all to be related; others connect some of these languages with Hamitic, or some with Bantu. Among the languages of this region that are more often named, we may mention *Wolof* and *Ful* in Senegal; *Grebo*, *Ewe*, and *Yoruba* along the Guinea coast; *Haussa* in the central region; and in the east, *Nuba* in a large territory round Khartoum, south of this, *Dinka*, and still further south, *Masai*.

South of this Guinean and Soudanese belt we come upon the vast *Bantu* family of languages, which before the European invasion covered all the rest of Africa except only a southwestern district. The languages of the Bantu family, totaling some 50 millions of speakers, are very numerous; among the better known are *Luganda*, *Swaheli*, *Kaffir*, *Zulu*, *Tebele*, *Subiya*, *Herero*.

The portion of southwestern Africa that was not Bantu-speaking, belonged, before the coming of the European, to two unrelated linguistic areas: the *Bushman*, with some 50,000 speakers, and the *Hottentot*, with some 250,000.

4. 7. Returning to the continent of Eurasia, we find, to the east of the Indo-European languages and in topographic alternation with them, the great *Finno-Ugrian* family. This family consists of six major branches. The first is the *Finnish-Lapponic*. In the northerly parts of Norway, Sweden, and Finland, some 30,000 people speak *Lappish*. The other languages of the Finnish-Lapponic branch form a closer group, the Finnish (or Baltic-Finnish). The largest language of this type is *Finnish*, recorded in a fragmentary way as early as the thirteenth century and in printed books since 1544; Finnish is native to some 3 million speakers. *Esthonian*, with earliest records of about the same dates, is spoken by about a million people. Both Finnish and Esthonian have standard languages which are official in the republics of Finland and Esthonia. The other languages of the Baltic branch, *Carelian, Olonetsian, Ludian, Vepsian, Livonian, Ingrian,* and *Votian*, are far smaller, and some of them are near extinction. Four further branches of the Finno-Ugrian stock lie in patches across the extent of European and Asiatic Russia; they are *Mordvine* (a million speakers); *Cheremiss* (375,000); *Permian*, consisting of *Votyak* (420,000) and *Zyrian* (258,000), the latter with written records from the fourteenth century; *Ob-Ugrian*, consisting of *Ostyak* (18,000) and *Vogule* (5000). The sixth branch of Finno-Ugrian is *Hungarian*, brought by invaders at the end of the ninth century into central Europe. Aside from scattered words in Latin documents, the oldest written record of Hungarian dates from the thirteenth century. In a flourishing standard language and in a number of local dialects Hungarian is spoken by some 10 million persons.

To the east of the Ostyak area, along the Yenisei River, some 18,000 persons speak languages of the *Samoyede* family. These languages are dispersed over a wide area and show great local diversity. Some investigators believe that Samoyede and Finno-Ugrian are related.

4. 8. The *Turkish* (*Turco-Tartar* or *Altaic*) family of languages covers a vast main area, from Asia Minor, conquered, at the end of the Middle Ages, by the Ottoman Turks, all the way to the upper reaches of the Yenisei. These languages, with little differentiation, are spoken by some 39 millions of people; *Turkish, Tartar, Kirgiz, Uzbeg, Azerbaijani* are the more familiar language-names. Our oldest texts are some Siberian inscriptions, dating from the eighth century A.D., a Turkish-Arabic vocabulary from the eleventh century, and a Latin-Persian-Turkish vocabulary from the fourteenth. Separated from the other languages of the

THE LANGUAGES OF THE WORLD 69

group, but not very different from them, is *Yakut*, spoken by over 200,000 people in northernmost Siberia. Some students believe that Turco-Tartar is related to the Mongol and Manchu families; others, on even slighter grounds, claim a relationship of all these with Finno-Ugrian and Samoyede (in what they call a Ural-Altaic family).

The *Mongol* languages lie for the most part east of the Turco-Tartar, in Mongolia, but, in consequence of the former wandering and predatory habits of these tribes, scattered communities are found in various parts of Asia, and even in European Russia. The total number of speakers is estimated at 3 millions. The oldest known written record is an inscription from the time of Gengis Khan, in the thirteenth century.

The *Tunguse-Manchu* family lies to the north of the Mongol, dividing Yakut from the rest of the Turco-Tartar area. *Tunguse* is spoken by some 70,000 persons dwelling over a relatively large tract in Siberia. The number of actual speakers of *Manchu* is uncertain, since most of the so-called Manchus in China speak only Chinese; Deny estimates it at well under a million. As a literary and official language, Manchu has been printed since 1647; the manuscript tradition goes back to an even earlier date.

The great *Indo-Chinese* (or *Sino-Tibetan*) family consists of three branches. One of these is *Chinese*, spoken by some 400 millions of people; it forms really a vast dialect area containing many, in part mutually unintelligible, dialects or languages. These have been classified into four main groups: the *Mandarin* group (*North Chinese,* including the language of Peking; *Middle Chinese*, including Nanking; *West Chinese*, in Szechuen), the *Central Coastal* group (*Shanghai, Ningpo, Hangkow*), the *Kiangsi* group, and the *South Chinese* group (*Foochow; Amoy-Swatow; Cantonese-Hakka*). Our oldest texts are inscriptions, some of which may date as far back as 2000 B.C., but since Chinese writing uses a separate symbol for each word, with little indication of sounds, even an intelligible document may tell us little or nothing of the language: our knowledge of Chinese speech, therefore, does not set in before about 600 A.D. The second branch of Indo-Chinese is the *Tai* family, which includes *Siamese*, spoken by some 7 millions of people; the oldest record is an inscription from 1293 A.D. The third branch is *Tibeto-Burman*, consisting of four groups: in the *Tibetan* group, the language of the same name, with records reaching back to the ninth century A.D., is the most important; in the *Burmese* group, *Burmese*, with some 8 million speakers, holds a similar position; the other two groups, *Bodo-Naga-Kachin* and *Lo-lo*, consist of lesser dialects.

The *Hyperborean* family, in the extreme northeastern corner of Asia, consists of *Chukchee*, spoken by some 10,000 persons, *Koryak*, with almost as many speakers, and *Kamchadal*, with 1000.

Along the Yenisei River, *Yenisei-Ostyak*, with some 1000 speakers, and *Cottian*, probably by this time extinct, form an independent family.

No relationship has been found for several other languages of eastern Asia. *Gilyak* is spoken in the northern part of Sakhalin Island and round the mouth of the Amur River. *Ainu* is spoken by some 20,000 persons in Japan. *Japanese* has 56 million speakers; the written records begin in the eighth century. *Korean* has 17 millions of speakers.

4. 9. Turning southeastward from Europe, we find in the Caucasus region a great variety of languages. Apart from Ossete, an Iranian language (§ 4.3), these are generally classed into two families, *North Caucasian* and *South Caucasian*, with between 1 and 2 million speakers in each. The best known of these languages, *Georgian*, belongs to the latter group; the written records begin as early as the tenth century A.D.

In India, south of the Indo-Aryan languages, lies the great *Dravidian* family, including, beside many lesser languages, the great speech-areas (and standard literary languages) of *Tamil* (18 millions), *Malayalam* (6 millions), *Canarese* (10 millions; oldest inscriptions from the fifth century A.D.), *Telugu* (24 millions). A single Dravidian language, *Brahui* (with 174,000 speakers) is spoken, far off from the rest, in the mountains of Baluchistan; it seems to be a relic of a time when Dravidian occupied a much wider territory, before the invasion of Indo-Aryan and Iranian speech.

The languages of the *Munda* family are spoken by 3 millions of persons in two separate parts of India, namely, on the southern slope of the Himalayas and round the plateau of Chota Nagpur in central India.

The *Mon-Khmer* family lies in patches over southeastern Asia, including the Nicobar Islands and some districts in the Malay

Peninsula. Our oldest records are inscriptions in *Cambogian*, dating from the seventh century A.D. This family includes at present one great cultural language, *Annamite*, spoken by 14 millions of people. Some scholars believe both the Munda and the Mon-Khmer families to be related to the Malayo-Polynesian family (forming the so-called Austric family of languages).

The *Malayo-Polynesian* (or *Austronesian*) family extends from the Malay Peninsula across the Pacific to Easter Island. It consists of four branches. The *Malayan* (or *Indonesian*) branch includes *Malay*, with some 3 million native speakers and wide use as a language of commerce and civilization; further, it embraces the languages of the great islands of the East, such as *Formosan*, *Javanese* (20 millions), *Sundanese* ($6\frac{1}{2}$ millions), *Maduran* (3 millions), *Balinese* (1 million), and the many *Philippine* languages, among them *Bisaya* ($2\frac{3}{4}$ millions) and *Tagalog* ($1\frac{1}{2}$ millions); a distant offshoot is *Malagasy*, the language of Madagascar, spoken by some 3 million people. The second, *Melanesian*, branch of Malayo-Polynesian includes many languages of smaller island groups, such as the languages of the *Solomon Islands* and *Fijian*. The *Micronesian* branch contains the languages of a smaller tract, the *Gilbert*, *Marshall*, *Caroline*, and *Marianne* archipelagos and the Island of *Yap*. The fourth, *Polynesian* branch includes *Maori*, the native language of New Zealand, and the languages of the more easterly Pacific islands, such as *Samoan*, *Tahitian*, *Hawaiian*, and the language of *Easter Island*.

The other families of this part of the earth have been little studied; the *Papuan* family, on New Guinea and adjacent islands, and the *Australian* languages.

4. 10. There remains the American continent.

It is estimated that the territory north of Mexico was inhabited, before the coming of the white man, by nearly 1,500,000 Indians; in this same territory the number of speakers of American languages today cannot be much over a quarter of a million, with English making ever more rapid encroachment. As the languages have been insufficiently studied, they can be but tentatively grouped into families: estimates vary between twenty-five and fifty entirely unrelated families of languages for the region north of Mexico. Most of this region is covered by great linguistic stocks, but some areas, notably the region round Puget Sound and the coastal district of California, were closely packed with small unrelated speech-communities. At least half a dozen linguistic stocks are known to have died out. Of those that still exist, we may name a few of the largest. In the far north, the *Eskimo* family, ranging from Greenland over Baffinland and Alaska to the Aleutian Islands, forms a fairly close-knit dialect-group. The *Algonquian* family covers the northeastern part of the continent and includes the languages of eastern and central Canada (*Micmac, Montagnais, Cree*), of New England (*Penobscot, Massachusetts, Natick, Narraganset, Mohican,* and so on, with *Delaware* to the south), and of the Great Lakes region (*Ojibwa, Potawatomi, Menomini, Sauk, Fox, Kickapoo, Peoria, Illinois, Miami,* and so on), as well as a few detached languages in the west: *Blackfoot, Cheyenne,* and *Arapaho.* The *Athabascan* family covers all but the coastal fringe of northwestern Canada (*Chipewyan, Beaver, Dogrib, Sarsi,* etc.), a number of isolated groups in California (such as *Hupa* and *Matole*), and a third, large area in the south, the *Apache* and *Navajo* languages. The *Iroquoian* family was spoken in a district surrounded by Algonquian; it includes, among others, the *Huron* (or *Wyandot*) language, and the languages of the *Iroquois* type (*Mohawk, Oneida, Onondaga, Cayuga, Seneca, Tuscarora*); in a detached region to the south *Cherokee* was spoken. The *Muskogean* family includes, among other languages, *Choctaw, Chickasaw, Creek,* and *Seminole.* The *Siouan* family includes many languages, such as *Dakota, Teton, Oglala, Assiniboine, Kansa, Omaha, Osage, Iowa, Missouri, Winnebago, Mandan, Crow.* A *Uto-Aztecan* family has been proposed, on the basis of a probable relationship, to include, as three branches, the *Piman* family (east of the Gulf of California), the *Shoshonean* family (in southern California and eastward, including *Ute, Paiute, Shoshone, Comanche,* and *Hopi*), and the great *Nahuatlan* family in Mexico, including *Aztec,* the language of an ancient civilization.

The number of speakers of American languages in the rest of America is uncertain: a recent estimate places the figure for Mexico alone at $4\frac{1}{2}$ millions and for Peru and Brazil at over 3 millions each, with a total of over 6 millions for Mexico and Central America and of over $8\frac{1}{2}$ millions for South America. The number of languages and their relationships are quite unknown; some twenty or so independent families have been set up for Mexico and Central America, and round eighty for South America. In the former region, beside Nahuatlan, we may mention the *Mayan*

THE LANGUAGES OF THE WORLD

family in Yucatan as the bearer of an ancient civilization. In South America, we note, in the northwest, the *Arawak* and *Carib* families, which once prevailed in the West Indies; the *Tupi-Guarani*, stretched along the coast of Brazil, the *Araucanian* in Chile, and *Kechuan*, the language of the Inca civilization. Both the Aztec and the Maya had developed systems of writing; as both the systems were largely hieroglyphic and have been only in part deciphered, these records do not give us information about the older forms of speech.

CHAPTER 5

THE PHONEME

5. 1. In Chapter 2 we distinguished three successive events in an act of speech: A, the speaker's situation; B, his utterance of speech-sound and its impingement on the hearer's ear-drums; and C, the hearer's response. Of these three types of events, A and C include all the situations that may prompt a person to speak and all the actions which a hearer may perform in response; in sum, A and C make up the world in which we live. On the other hand, B, the speech-sound, is merely a means which enables us to respond to situations that would otherwise leave us unaffected, or to respond more accurately to situations that otherwise might prompt less useful responses. In principle, the student of language is concerned only with the actual speech (B); the study of speakers' situations and hearers' responses (A and C) is equivalent to the sum total of human knowledge. If we had an accurate knowledge of every speaker's situation and of every hearer's response — and this would make us little short of omniscient — we could simply register these two facts as the *meaning* (A–C) of any given speech-utterance (B), and neatly separate our study from all other domains of knowledge. The fact that speech-utterances themselves often play a part in the situation of a speaker and in the response of a hearer, might complicate things, but this difficulty would not be serious. Linguistics, on this ideal plane, would consist of two main investigations: *phonetics*, in which we studied the speech-event without reference to its meaning, investigating only the sound-producing movements of the speaker, the sound-waves, and the action of the hearer's ear-drum, and *semantics*, in which we studied the relation of these features to the features of meaning, showing that a certain type of speech-sound was uttered in certain types of situations and led the hearer to perform certain types of response.

Actually, however, our knowledge of the world in which we live is so imperfect that we can rarely make accurate statements about the meaning of a speech-form. The situations (A) which lead to an utterance, and the hearer's responses (C), include many things that have not been mastered by science. Even if we knew much more than we do about the external world, we should still have to reckon with the predispositions of the speaker and the hearer. We cannot foretell whether, in a given situation, a person will speak, or if so, what words he will use, and we cannot foretell how he will respond to a given speech.

It is true that we are concerned not so much with each individual as with the whole community. We do not inquire into the minute nervous processes of a person who utters, say, the word *apple*, but content ourselves rather with determining that, by and large, for all the members of the community, the word *apple* means a certain kind of fruit. However, as soon as we try to deal accurately with this matter, we find that the agreement of the community is far from perfect, and that every person uses speech-forms in a unique way.

5. 2. The study of language can be conducted without special assumptions only so long as we pay no attention to the meaning of what is spoken. This phase of language study is known as *phonetics* (*experimental phonetics, laboratory phonetics*). The phonetician can study either the sound-producing movements of the speaker (*physiological phonetics*) or the resulting sound-waves (*physical* or *acoustic phonetics*); we have as yet no means for studying the action of the hearer's ear-drum.

Physiological phonetics begins with inspection. The *laryngoscope*, for instance, is a mirror-device which enables an observer to see another person's (or his own) vocal chords. Like other devices of the sort, it interferes with normal speech and can serve only for very limited phases of observation. The x-ray does good service where its limitations can be overcome; tongue-positions can be photographed, for instance, if one lays a thin metal strip or chain along the upper surface of the tongue. Other devices give a transferred record. For instance, a false palate covered with coloring-matter is put into the mouth; after the speaker utters a sound, the places where the tongue has touched the palate are recognizable by the removal of the coloring-matter. In most devices of this sort a bulb is attached to some part of the speaker's vocal organs, say to the adam's-apple; the mechanism transforms the movement into up-and-down movements of a pen-point which touches a strip of paper. The strip of paper is kept moving at an even rate of speed, so that the up-and-down movement of the pen-point appears on the paper as a wavy line. This recording device is called a *kymograph*. In acoustic phonetics one secures imprints of the sound-waves. Records of this kind are familiar to us in the form of phonograph-disks; phoneticians have not yet succeeded in analyzing most features of such records.

A considerable part of our information about speech-sounds is due to the methods we have just outlined. However, laboratory phonetics does not enable us to connect speech-sounds with meanings; it studies speech-sounds only as muscular movements or as disturbances in the air, without regard to their use in communication. On this plane we find that speech-sounds are infinitely complex and infinitely varied.

Even a short speech is continuous: it consists of an unbroken succession of movements and sound-waves. No matter into how many successive parts we break up our record for purposes of minute study, an even finer analysis is always conceivable. A speech-utterance is what mathematicians call a *continuum;* it can be viewed as consisting of any desired number of successive parts.

Speech-utterances are infinitely varied. Everyday experience tells us that different persons speak differently, for we can recognize people by their voices. The phonetician finds that no two utterances are exactly alike.

Evidently the working of language is due to a resemblance between successive utterances. Utterances which in ordinary life we describe as consisting of "the same" speech-forms — say, successive utterances of the sentence *I'm hungry* — evidently contain some constant features of sound-wave, common to all utterances of this "same" speech-form. Only on this assumption can we account for our ordinary use of language. The phonetician, however, cannot make sure of these constant features, as long as he ignores the meaning of what is said. Suppose, for instance, that he had records of an utterance which we could identify as representing the syllable *man*, spoken on two different pitch-schemes. If the language of these utterances were English, we should say that both contained the same speech-form, namely, the word *man*, but if the language were Chinese, the two records might represent two different speech-forms, since in Chinese differences of pitch-scheme are connected with different meanings:

THE PHONEME 77

the word *man* with a high rising pitch, for instance means 'deceive,' and the word *man* with a falling pitch means 'slow.' As long as we pay no attention to meanings, we cannot decide whether two uttered forms are "the same" or "different." The phonetician cannot tell us which features are significant for communication and which features are immaterial. A feature which is significant in some languages or dialects, may be indifferent in others.

5. 3. The fact that two utterances of the syllable *man* with different pitch-schemes are "the same" speech-form in English, but "different" speech-forms in Chinese, shows us that the working of language depends upon our habitually and conventionally discriminating some features of sound and ignoring all others. The features of sound in any utterance, as they might be recorded in the laboratory, are the *gross acoustic features* of this utterance. Part of the gross acoustic features are indifferent (*non-distinctive*), and only a part are connected with meanings and essential to communication (*distinctive*). The difference between distinctive and non-distinctive features of sound lies entirely in the habit of the speakers. A feature that is distinctive in one language, may be non-distinctive in another language.

Since we can recognize the distinctive features of an utterance only when we know the meaning, we cannot identify them on the plane of pure phonetics. We know that the difference between the English forms *man* and *men* is distinctive, because we know from ordinary life that these two forms are used under different circumstances. It is possible that some science other than linguistics may define this difference in accurate terms, providing even for the case where we use *man* for more than one individual (*man wants but little here below*). In any case, however, this difference cannot be recognized by purely phonetic observation: the difference between the vowel sounds of *man* and *men* is in some languages non-distinctive.

To recognize the distinctive features of a language, we must leave the ground of pure phonetics and act as though science had progressed far enough to identify all the situations and responses that make up the meaning of speech-forms. In the case of our own language, we trust to our everyday knowledge to tell us whether speech-forms are "the same" or "different." Thus, we find that the word *man* spoken on various pitch-schemes is in English still "the same" word, with one and the same meaning, but that *man* and *men* (or *pan* and *pen*) are "different" words, with different meanings. In the case of a strange language we have to learn such things by trial and error, or to obtain the meanings from someone that knows the language.

The study of *significant* speech-sounds is *phonology* or *practical phonetics*. Phonology involves the consideration of meanings. The meanings of speech-forms could be scientifically defined only if all branches of science, including, especially, psychology and physiology, were close to perfection. Until that time, phonology and, with it, all the semantic phase of language study, rests upon an assumption, the fundamental assumption of linguistics: we must assume that *in every speech-community some utterances are alike in form and meaning*.

5. 4. A moderate amount of experimenting will show that the significant features of a speech-form are limited in number. In this respect, the significant features contrast with the gross acoustic features, which, as we have seen, form a continuous whole and can be subdivided into any desired number of parts. In order to recognize the distinctive features of forms in our own language, we need only determine which features of sound are "different" for purposes of communication. Suppose, for instance, that we start with the word *pin:* a few experiments in saying words out loud soon reveal the following resemblances and differences:

(1) *pin* ends with the same sound as *fin, sin, tin,* but begins differently; this kind of resemblance is familiar to us because of our tradition of using end-rime in verse;

(2) *pin* contains the sound of *in,* but adds something at the beginning;

(3) *pin* ends with the same sound as *man, sun, hen,* but the resemblance is smaller than in (1) and (2);

(4) *pin* begins with the same sound as *pig, pill, pit,* but ends differently;

(5) *pin* begins with the same sound as *pat, push, peg,* but the resemblance is smaller than in (4);

(6) *pin* begins and ends like *pen, pan, pun,* but the middle part is different;

(7) *pin* begins and ends differently from *dig, fish, mill,* but the middle part is the same.

In this way, we can find forms which partially resemble *pin*, by altering any one of *three* parts of the word. We can alter first one and then a second of the three parts and still have a partial resemblance: if we alter the first part and then the second, we get a series like *pin-tin-tan;* if we alter the first part and then the third, we get a series like *pin-tin-tick;* if we alter the second part and then the third, we get a series like *pin-pan-pack:* and if we alter all three parts, no resemblance is left, as in *pin-tin-tan-tack*.

Further experiment fails to reveal any more replaceable parts in the word *pin:* we conclude that the distinctive features of this word are three indivisible units. Each of these units occurs also in other combinations, but cannot be further analyzed by partial resemblances: each of the three is *a minimum unit of distinctive sound-feature, a phoneme.* Thus we say that the word *pin* consists of three phonemes: the first of these occurs also in *pet, pack, push,* and many other words; the second also in *fig, hit, miss,* and many other words; the third also in *tan, run, hen,* and many other words. In the case of *pin* our alphabetic writing represents the three phonemes by three letters, *p, i,* and *n,* but our conventions of writing are a poor guide; in the word *thick,* for instance, our writing represents the first phoneme by the two-letter group *th* and the third by the two-letter group *ck*.

A little practice will enable the observer to recognize a phoneme even when it appears in different parts of words, as *pin, apple, mop*. Sometimes our stock of words does not readily bring out the resemblances and differences. For instance, the word *then* evidently consists of three phonemes, but (especially under the influence of our way of writing) we might question whether the initial phoneme was or was not the same as in *thick;* once we hit upon the pair *thigh* and *thy,* or upon *mouth* and *mouthe,* we see that they are different.

5. 5. Among the gross acoustic features of any utterance, then, certain ones are distinctive, recurring in recognizable and relatively constant shape in successive utterances. These distinctive features occur in lumps or bundles, each one of which we call a phoneme. The speaker has been trained to make sound-producing movements in such a way that the phoneme-features will be present in the sound-waves, and he has been trained to respond only to these features and to ignore the rest of the gross acoustic mass that reaches his ears.

It would be useless to try to produce the distinctive features in a pure state, free from non-distinctive accompaniments. For example, an English word, as such, has no distinctive pitch-scheme — the features of pitch which appear in any utterance of it are non-distinctive — but of course we cannot speak a word like *man* without any features of pitch: in any one utterance of it there will be some pitch-scheme — even, rising, falling, high, middle, low, and so on. The phonemes of a language are not sounds, but merely features of sound which the speakers have been trained to produce and recognize in the current of actual speech-sound — just as motorists are trained to stop before a red signal, be it an electric signal-light, a lamp, a flag, or what not, although there is no disembodied redness apart from these actual signals.

In fact, when we observe closely, especially in a language foreign to us, we often notice the wide range of non-distinctive features and the relatively slight consistency of the distinctive features. The Menomini Indian, in a word like that for 'water,' which I shall here render as *nipēw*, seems to us to be speaking the middle consonant sometimes as a *p* and sometimes as a *b*. For his language, the phonemic (that is, essential) feature is merely a closure of the lips without escape of breath through the nose. Everything else, including the features by which English distinguishes between *p* and *b*, is non-distinctive. On the other hand, a slight puff of breath before the consonant, or else a slight catch in the throat — either of which will probably escape the ear of an English hearer — would produce in the Menomini language two entirely different phonemes, each of which contrasts with the plain *p-b* phoneme.

In the same way, a Chinese observer who had not been forewarned, would probably have some trouble before he realized that English words have the same meaning (are "the same") regardless of their pitch-scheme.

In part, the non-distinctive features receive a fairly conventional treatment. When a foreign speaker reproduces the phonemic values of our language so as to make himself understood, but does not distribute the non-distinctive features in accordance with our habit, we say that he speaks our language well enough, but with a foreign "accent." In English, for instance, we produce the initial phonemes of words like *pin*, *tin*, *kick* with a slight puff of breath (aspiration) after the opening of the closure, but when an *s* precedes, as in *spin*, *stick*, *skin*, we usually leave off this puff of breath. As this difference is not distinctive, a foreign speaker who fails to reproduce it, is still intelligible, but his speech will seem queer to us. Frenchmen are likely to fail in this matter, because in French the phonemes which resemble our *p*, *t*, *k* are spoken always without aspiration. On the other hand, an Englishman or American who speaks French well enough to be understood, is likely still to displease his hearers by using the aspiration after *p*, *t*, *k*.

Non-distinctive features occur in all manner of distributions. In most types of American English, the *t*-phoneme in words like *water* or *butter* is often reduced to an instantaneous touch of the tongue-tip against the ridge behind the upper gums: in our habit, the sound so produced suffices to represent the phoneme. In England this variant is unknown, and is likely to be interpreted as a variant of the phoneme *d*, — so that the American may find that he is not understood when he asks for *water*.

In the ordinary case, there is a limit to the variability of the non-distinctive features: the phoneme is kept distinct from all other phonemes of its language. Thus, we speak the vowel of a word like *pen* in a great many ways, but not in any way that belongs to the vowel of *pin*, and not in any way that belongs to the vowel of *pan*: the three types are kept rigidly apart.

5. 6. The fact that distinctions which are phonemic in one language or dialect are indifferent in others, and the fact that the borders between different phonemes differ in different languages and dialects, appears most clearly when we hear or try to speak a foreign language or dialect. We have just seen an instance of how American English may be misunderstood in England. The vowel of words like *job, bomb, hot* is in American English much closer than in British English to the vowel of words like *far, balm, pa;* in some kinds of American English the two sets of words have in fact the same vowel. The Englishman of the south, moreover, has lost the *r*-sound in words like *far*. A London cabman did not understand me when I asked to be driven to the *Comedy Theatre*: I had forgotten myself and spoken the American form of the first vowel in *comedy*, and this the Englishman could take only as a representative of the vowel phoneme in a word like *car* — so that I was really asking for a *Carmody Theatre*, which does not exist.

When we try to speak a foreign language or dialect, we are likely to replace its phonemes by the most similar phonemes of our own language or dialect. Sometimes our native phoneme and the foreign one overlap, so that part of the time our reproduction is correct, but part of the time it falls outside the range of the foreign sound.

Thus, an American who pronounces the French word *même* ('same') with the vowel of the English word *ma'm*, will only part of the time produce a sound which meets the conventional requirements of the French phoneme; most of the time he will be producing a sound which differs decidedly from the vowel which the Frenchman is accustomed to hear.

What saves the situation in such cases is the native's complementary inaccuracy. When we hear foreign speech-sounds we respond to them as if they contained the characteristics of some acoustically similar phoneme of our native language. The discrepancy disturbs us, and we say that the foreigner speaks indistinctly or with a strange "accent," but we do not know where the difference lies. In our example, accordingly, the Frenchman will mostly understand the American's pronunciation of *même*, even when it contains a vowel sound that would never occur in the Frenchman's own pronunciation. However, if our rendition deviates too far from the foreign phoneme, and especially if it comes close to some other phoneme of the foreign language, we shall be misunderstood; thus, some varieties of the American's *ma'm* which he uses for French *même*, will be unintelligible because the Frenchman accepts them as renditions of a different phoneme which occurs, for instance, in words like *lame* ('blade').

The confusion is more serious when two or three of the foreign phonemes resemble some one native phoneme of ours. Our infantile language-learning trains us to ignore differences that are not phonemic in our language. The English-speaker will not hear any difference between the Menomini forms *a' käh* 'yes, indeed,' and *ahkäh* 'kettle,' and the first part of the word *akähsemen* 'plum.' In the first of these forms, the phoneme which resembles our *k* is preceded by a slight catch in the throat (a glottal stop) which I have designated here by an apostrophe; in the second, the *k* is preceded by a puff of breath (aspiration), which I have designated by *h;* in the third form these features are absent. The English-speaker was trained in childhood not to respond to a catch in the throat or a slight huskiness before a consonant sound: if a fellow-speaker occasionally produces such a noise, we pay no attention to it.

The Menomini, for his part, cannot distinguish differences like that of our *t* and *d*. Words like *bad* and *bat* sound alike to him. This appears, for instance, in the fact that the Menomini have translated the word *Swede* into their language as if it were *sweet*, by the term *sayēwenet* 'one who is sweet.' There is a Menomini phoneme which resembles both our *t* and *d*, and doubtless the Menomini speaker often utters variants of this phoneme which fall within the range of our *t*-phoneme, and occasionally variants which fall within the range of our *d*-phoneme, but his infantile training taught him to ignore these differences of sound.

When we try to speak a foreign language, we reproduce, in such cases, several foreign phonemes by one single phoneme of our own. The native speaker, in turn, responds to our phoneme as if it were one of his. Thus, the German hears no difference between the initial phoneme of *tin* and that of *thin*, since both of them resemble one of his native phonemes. When he speaks English, he uses this German phoneme. Hearing him, we respond to it as though it were our *t*-phoneme; we are right, at any rate, in concluding that he does not distinguish between *tin* and *thin*. In quite the same way, when the English-speaker hears German, he will respond to two different phonemes of that language as though they were identical with the English phoneme that is initial in words like *cat*, and he will fail, in consequence, to distinguish between some words that are quite different in the habits of the German.

In other cases, the one phoneme which we substitute for several phonemes of the foreign language, is acoustically intermediate, and to the native speaker we seem to be interchanging the sounds. For instance, many Germans (such as Alsatians) have only one phoneme, of intermediate acoustic quality, in the sphere of our *p* and *b*, and in speaking our language they use this for both of our phonemes. When they do this in a word like *pie*, we are struck by the deviation in the direction of *b* and respond as though to the word *buy;* on the other hand, when they use their intermediate phoneme in a word like *buy*, we are struck by the deviation in the direction of *p*, and respond as though we had heard *pie*. Hence it seems to us (or to a Frenchman) that the German can pronounce both *p* and *b*, but perversely keeps interchanging the two.

The greatest difficulty arises where a language makes significant use of features that play no such part in our language. An English-speaker who hears Chinese (or any of quite a few other languages), will fail to understand or to speak intelligibly, until he discovers and trains himself to hear and to reproduce the distinctions of relative pitch which are significant in every syllable. He does not respond to them at first, because as an infant he was trained not to notice the different pitch-schemes which occur in successive utterances of a word like *man;* the Chinese infant, on the other hand, was trained to respond to several types of such pitch-schemes.

When the foreign language has only one phoneme in a general acoustic type where our language has more than one, it often seems to us as if the foreigner were using very different sounds without a reasonable distinction. Thus, the Menomini's or the Alsatian's one *p-b* phoneme will strike our ears now as *p* and now as *b*.

Some persons have an aptitude for hearing and reproducing foreign speech-sounds; we say that such persons are good imitators or have a "good ear." Most other people, if they hear enough of a foreign language, or if they are carefully instructed, will in time learn to understand and make themselves understood. Practical phoneticians sometimes acquire great virtuosity in discriminating and reproducing all manner of strange sounds. In this, to be sure, there lies some danger for linguistic work. Having learned to discriminate many kinds of sounds, the phonetician may turn to some language, new or familiar, and insist upon recording all the distinctions he has learned to discriminate, even when in this language they are non-distinctive and have no bearing whatever. Thus, having learned, say in the study of Chinese, to hear the difference between an aspirated *p, t, k,* (as we usually have it in words like *pin, tin, kick*) and a similar sound without aspiration (as a Frenchman forms it, and as we usually have it in words like *spin, stick, skin*), the phonetician may clutter up his record of English by marking the aspiration wherever he hears it, while in reality its presence or absence has nothing to do with the meaning of what is said. The chief objection to this procedure is its inconsistency. The phonetician's equipment is personal and accidental; he hears those acoustic features which are discriminated in the languages he has observed. Even his most "exact" record is bound to ignore innumerable non-distinctive features of sound; the ones that appear in it are selected by accidental and personal factors. There is no objection to a linguist's describing all the acoustic features that he can hear, provided he does not confuse these with the phonemic features. He should remember that his

THE PHONEME 85

hearing of non-distinctive features depends upon the accident of his personal equipment, and that his most elaborate account cannot remotely approach the value of a mechanical record.

Only two kinds of linguistic records are scientifically relevant. One is a mechanical record of the gross acoustic features, such as is produced in the phonetics laboratory. The other is a record in terms of phonemes, ignoring all features that are not distinctive in the language. Until our knowledge of acoustics has progressed far beyond its present state, only the latter kind of record can be used for any study that takes into consideration the meaning of what is spoken.

In fact, the laboratory phonetician usually knows, from other sources, the phonemic character of the speech-sounds he is studying; he usually formulates his problems not in purely acoustic terms, but rather in terms which he has borrowed from practical phonetics.

5. 7. In order to make a record of our observations, we need a system of written symbols which provides one sign for each phoneme of the language we are recording. Such a set of symbols is a *phonetic alphabet*, and a record of speech in the shape of these symbols is a *phonetic transcription* (or, simply, a *transcription*).

The principle of a symbol for each phoneme is approached by our traditional alphabetic writing, but our traditional writing does not carry it out sufficiently for the purposes of linguistic study. We write *sun* and *son* differently, although the phonemes are the same, but *lead* (noun) and *lead* (verb) alike, though the phonemes are different. The words *oh, owe, so, sew, sow, hoe, beau, though* all end with the same phoneme, variously represented in writing; the words *though, bough, through, cough, tough, hiccough* end with different phonemes but are all written with the letters -*ough*. Our letter *x* is superfluous because it represents the same phonemes as *ks* (as in *tax*) or *gz* (as in *examine*); our letter *c* is superfluous because it represents the same phoneme as *k* (in *cat*) or as *s* (in *cent*). Although we have the letter *j* for the initial phoneme in *jam*, we also use the letter *g* (as in *gem*) for this same phoneme. Standard English, as spoken in Chicago, has thirty-two simple primary phonemes: the twenty-six letters of our alphabet are too few for a phonetic record. For some phonemes we use combinations of two letters (*digraphs*), as *th* for the initial phoneme in *thin*, *ch* for that in *chin*, *sh* for that in *shin*, and *ng* for the final phoneme in *sing*. This leads to further inconsistencies: in *then* we use *th* for a different phoneme, and in *hothouse* for the two phonemes which are normally represented by the separate letters *t* and *h;* in *Thomas* the *th* has the value of the phoneme ordinarily represented by *t*. In *singer* we use *ng* for a single phoneme, as in *sing*, but in *finger* the letters *ng* represent this phoneme plus the phoneme ordinarily represented by the letter *g*, as in *go*. Traditional alphabetic writing is accurate only in the case of a few languages, such as Spanish, Bohemian, Polish, and Finnish, where it has been shaped or revised by persons who had worked out the phonemic system of their language.

5. 8. On account of the imperfections of traditional writing and the lack of a sufficient number of characters in our (so-called "Latin") alphabet, scholars have devised many phonetic alphabets.

Some of these schemes depart entirely from our traditional habits of writing. Bell's "Visible Speech" is the best-known of these, chiefly because Henry Sweet (1845–1912) used it. The symbols of this alphabet are simplified and conventionalized diagrams of the vocal organs in position for the utterance of the various phonemes. Visible Speech is hard to write and very costly to print.

Another system which departs from the historical tradition is Jespersen's "Analphabetic Notation." Here every phoneme is represented by a whole set of symbols which consist of Greek letters and Arabic numerals, with Latin letters as exponents. Each Greek letter indicates an organ and each numeral a degree of opening; thus, α indicates the lips and 0 indicates closure, so that $\alpha 0$ will appear in the formula for any phoneme during whose utterance the lips are closed, such as our *p*, *b*, and *m* phonemes. The formula for the English *m* phoneme, as in *man*, is $\alpha 0\ \delta 2\ \epsilon 1$, where $\delta 2$ means that the back of the palate is lowered, and $\epsilon 1$ means that the vocal chords are in vibration. The advantages of this notation are evident, but of course it is not intended for the recording of whole utterances.

Most phonetic alphabets are modifications of the traditional alphabet. They supplement the ordinary letters by such devices as small capitals, letters of the Greek alphabet, distorted forms of conventional letters, and letters with little marks, *diacritical signs*, attached to them (e.g. $\bar{a}$ and $\ddot{a}$). There are many alphabets of this type, such as that of Lepsius, used for African languages; of Lundell, used for Swedish dialects; of Bremer, used for German dialects; of the American Anthropological Association, used for American Indian languages. In this book we shall use the alphabet of the International Phonetic Association; this alphabet was developed by Ellis, Sweet, Passy, and Daniel Jones. A crude form of phonetic alphabet appears in the "keys to pronunciation" of most dictionaries. Similar devices have grown up in the traditional writing of some languages, devices such as the two dots over vowel letters in German writing (ä, ö, ü) or the diacritical marks in Bohemian writing (č for our *ch*, š for our *sh*); the Russian and Serbian alphabets supplement the Greek alphabet with a number of extra letters.

In principle, one phonetic alphabet is about as good as another, since all we need is a few dozen symbols, enough to supply one for each phoneme of whatever language we are recording. In their application, however, all phonetic alphabets suffer from serious drawbacks. When they were invented, the principle of the phoneme had not been clearly recognized. The inventors meant their alphabets to be rich and flexible enough to offer a symbol for every acoustic variety that could be heard in any language. It is evident, today, that a record of this kind would amount to nothing less than a mechanical recording of the sound-waves, which would be the same for no two utterances. In practice, the phonemic principle somehow slipped in: usually one wrote a symbol for each phoneme, but these symbols were highly differentiated and cluttered up with diacritical marks, for the purpose of indicating "exact" acoustic values. The varieties that were in this way distinguished, were merely those which phoneticians happened to have noticed. Henry Sweet devised a relatively simple system, based on the Latin alphabet, which he called *Romic*, for use alongside of Visible Speech. When the phonemic principle became clear to him, he realized that his Romic notation would still be sufficient if one greatly simplified it. Accordingly he used a simplified form, with a symbol for each phoneme, and called it *Broad Romic;* he still believed, however, that the more complex form, *Narrow Romic*, was somehow "more accurate" and better suited to scientific purposes.

Out of Sweet's Romic there has grown the alphabet of the International Phonetic Association, which consists, accordingly, of the Latin symbols, supplemented by a number of artificial letters, and a few diacritical marks. In a modified form, we shall use it in this book, placing between square brackets, as is customary, everything that is printed in phonetic symbols.

5. 9. The principle on which the International Alphabet is based, is to employ ordinary letters in values approximating the values they have in some of the chief European languages, and to supplement these letters by artificial signs or by the use of diacritical marks whenever the number of phonemes of a type exceeds the number of ordinary letters. Thus, if a language has one phoneme of the general type of our *t*-sound, we symbolize this phoneme by the ordinary letter [t], regardless of whether this phoneme is acoustically quite like the English or the French *t*-sound, but if the language has two phonemes of this general type, we can symbolize only one of them by [t], and for the second one we must resort to the use of a capital [T], or an italic [*t*], or some other similar device. If a language has two phonemes of the general type of our *e*-sound as in *pen*, we use the letter [e] for one of them, and the supplementary symbol [ɛ] for the other, as in *pan* [pɛn].

These principles, which the International Phonetic Association formulated as early as 1912, have been neglected even by its members; most students have failed to break away from the tradition of the time when the phonemic principle had not yet been recognized. Thus, we find most writers using queer symbols for English phonemes because it has been recognized that English phonemes differ from the most similar types of French phonemes. For instance, having pre-empted the symbol [o] for the phoneme of French *eau* [o] ('water'), these authors do not use this letter for recording the English vowel in *son*, because this English phoneme is unlike the French phoneme. In the present edition of this book, where the examples are given in British pronunciation, I follow the customary transcription, e.g. top [tɔp].

Where several languages or dialects are under discussion, each one must be recorded in terms of its own phonemes; the differences, so far as we are able to state them, may deserve a verbal description, but must not be allowed to interfere with our symbols. Thus, even a phonetician who thinks he can describe in accurate terms the differences between the phonemes of standard English as spoken in Chicago and as spoken in London, will add nothing to the value of his statements by using queer symbols for one or the

THE PHONEME

other of these two sets of phonemes, and he will only make things still harder if he uses outlandish symbols for both of them, because he happens to know that the ordinary letters have been used for recording the somewhat different phonemes of some other language.

The principle of a single symbol for a single phoneme may be modified without harm only where no ambiguity can result. It may be advisable, where no ambiguity can result, to depart from the strict principle when this saves the use of extra symbols that might be disturbing to the reader or costly to print. In some languages, sounds like our [p, t, k] with a slight puff of breath after them, are distinct from sounds like the French [p, t, k] without this aspiration; if the language has no phoneme designated by [h], or if it has such a phoneme but this phoneme never occurs after [p, t, k], then it is safe and economical to use the compound symbols [ph, th, kh] for the former type.

5. 10. The matter of recording languages is complicated not only by the existence of several phonetic alphabets and by inconsistencies in their application, but also by the frequent use of two other devices alongside phonetic transcription.

One of these devices is the *citation* of forms in their traditional orthography. This is often done where the language in question uses the Latin alphabet. The author either supposes that his reader knows the pronunciation, or else, in the case of ancient languages, he may not care to guess at the pronunciation. Citation is often helpful to readers who are familiar with the ordinary orthography; it is only fair, however, to add a transcription, e.g. French *eau* [o] 'water.' Even in the case of ancient languages it is often useful to add a guess at the pronunciation, e.g. Old English *geoc* [jok] 'yoke.' Only in the case of languages like Bohemian or Finnish, whose traditional orthography is entirely phonetic, can one dispense with a transcription. In the case of Latin, a citation with a macron over long vowels is sufficient (e.g. *amāre* 'to love'), since, so far as we know, Latin orthography was phonetic except that it failed to indicate the distinction between long and short vowels.

For languages which use alphabets other than the Latin, citation is less often employed. It is customary in the case of Greek, less often of Russian, but is in every way to be deplored. Some luxurious publications indulge even in Hebrew, Arabic, and Sanskrit type for citing these languages. The only reasonable exceptions here are forms of writing like the Chinese and the ancient Egyptian, whose symbols, as we shall see, have meaning-values that cannot be represented in phonetic terms.

For languages which use writing of some form other than the Latin alphabet, *transliteration* is often employed instead of transcription. Transliteration consists in assigning some letter of the Latin alphabet (or some group of letters or some artificial symbol) to each character of the original alphabet, and thus reproducing the traditional orthography in terms of Latin letters. Unfortunately, different traditions have grown up for transliterating different languages. Thus, in transliterating Sanskrit, the Latin letter *c* is used to represent a Sanskrit letter which seems to have designated a phoneme much like our initial phoneme in words like *chin*, but in transliterating the Slavic alphabet, the letter *c* is used to represent a letter which designates a phoneme resembling our *ts* combination in *hats*. For most linguistic purposes it would be better to use a phonetic transcription.

5. 11. It is not difficult (even aside from the help that is afforded by our alphabetic writing) to make up a list of the phonemes of one's language. One need only proceed with a moderate number of words as we did above with the word *pin*, to find that one has identified every phoneme. The number of *simple primary phonemes* in different languages runs from about fifteen to about fifty. Standard English, as spoken in Chicago, has thirty-two. *Compound phonemes* are combinations of simple phonemes which act as units so far as meaning and word-structure are concerned. Thus, the diphthong in a word like *buy* can be viewed as a combination of the vowel in *far* with the phoneme that is initial in *yes*. Standard English has twelve such combinations.

It is somewhat harder to identify the *secondary phonemes*. These are not part of any simple meaningful speech-form taken by itself, but appear only when two or more are combined into a larger form, or else when speech-forms are used in certain ways — especially as sentences. Thus, in English, when we combine several simple elements of speech into a word of two or more syllables, we always use a secondary phoneme of *stress* which consists in speaking one of these syllables louder than the other or others: in the word *foretell* we speak the *tell* louder than the *fore*, but in *foresight* the *fore* is louder than the *sight*. The noun *contest* has the stress on the first syllable, the verb *contest* on the second. Features of *pitch* appear in English as secondary phonemes chiefly at the end of sentences, as in the contrast between a question (*at four o'clock?*) and an answer (*at four o'clock*). It is worth noticing that Chinese, as well as many other languages, uses features of pitch as primary phonemes. The secondary phonemes are harder to observe than the primary phonemes, because they occur only in combinations or in particular uses of simple forms (e.g. *John?* in contrast with *John*).

The principles we have outlined would probably enable anyone familiar with the use of writing to work out a system of transcribing his language. In this book the English examples will be transcribed, unless otherwise indicated, according to the pronunciation of educated speakers in the south of England. This requires thirty-two symbols for primary phonemes and eight for secondary phonemes; however, following the customary scheme of transcription, we shall use several additional symbols.

PRIMARY PHONEMES

[ɑ:]	*half*	[hɑ:f]	[g]	*give*	[giv]	[p]	*pick*	[pik]
[ʌ]	*up*	[ʌp]	[h]	*hut*	[hʌt]	[r]	*red*	[red]
[b]	*big*	[big]	[i]	*inn*	[in]	[s]	*set*	[set]
[d]	*dig*	[dig]	[j]	*yes*	[jes]	[ʃ]	*shop*	[ʃɔp]
[dʒ]	*jam*	[dʒem]	[k]	*cut*	[kʌt]	[t]	*tip*	[tip]
[ð]	*then*	[ðen]	[l]	*lamb*	[lɛm]	[tʃ]	*chin*	[t in]
[e]	*egg*	[eg]	[m]	*met*	[met]	[θ]	*thin*	[θin]
[ɛ]	*add*	[ɛd]	[n]	*net*	[net]	[u]	*put*	[put]
[ə]	*better*	[ˈbetə]	[ŋ]	*sing*	[siŋ]	[v]	*van*	[vɛn]
[ə.]	*bird*	[bə:d]	[ɔ]	*odd*	[ɔd]	[w]	*wet*	[wet]
[f]	*fat*	[fɛt]	[ɔ:]	*ought*	[ɔ:t]	[z]	*zip*	[zip]
			[ʒ]	*rouge*	[ruwʒ]			

COMPOUND PRIMARY PHONEMES

[aj]	*buy*	[baj]	[aw]	*cow*	[kaw]	[ɛə]	*care*	[kɛə]
[ej]	*bay*	[bej]	[ow]	*low*	[low]	[iə]	*fear*	[fiə]
[ij]	*bee*	[bij]	[uw]	*do*	[duw]	[ɔə]	*door*	[dɔə]
[ɔj]	*boy*	[bɔj]	[juw]	*few*	[fjuw]	[uə]	*sure*	[ʃuə]

SECONDARY PHONEMES

[ˈˈ], placed before primary symbols, loudest stress: *That's mine!* [ðɛt s ˈˈmajn!].

[ˈ], placed before primary symbols, ordinary stress : *examine* [igˈzɛmin], *I've seen it* [aj v ˈsijn it].
[ˌ], placed before primary symbols, less loud stress : *milkman* [ˈmilkˌmɛn], *Keep it up* [ˌkijp it ˈʌp].
[ˌ], placed under one of the primary symbols [l, n], a slight stress which makes this primary phoneme louder than what precedes and what follows : *brittler* [ˈbritlə̩], *buttoning* [ˈbʌtn̩iŋ].
[.], placed after primary symbols, the falling pitch at the end of a statement : *I've seen it* [aj v ˈsijn it].
[?], placed after primary symbols, the rising pitch at the end of a yes-or-no question : *Have you seen it?* [həv ju ˈsijn it?].
[!], placed after primary symbols, the distortion of the pitch-scheme in exclamations : *It's on fire!* [it s ɔn ˈfajə], *Seven o'clock?!* [ˈsevn əˈklɔk?!].
[,], placed between primary symbols, the pause, often preceded by rising pitch, that promises continuation of the sentence : *John, the older boy, is away at school* [ˈʤɔn, ðij ˈowldə ˈbɔj, iz əˈwej ət ˈskuwl].

CHAPTER 6

TYPES OF PHONEMES

6. 1. While the general principles which we surveyed in the last chapter will enable an observer to analyze the phonetic structure of his own speech, they yield very little help, at the start, for the understanding of a strange language. The observer who hears a strange language, notices those of the gross acoustic features which represent phonemes in his own language or in other languages he has studied, but he has no way of knowing whether these features are significant in the language he is observing. Moreover, he fails to notice acoustic features which are not significant in his own language and in the other languages he has studied, but are significant in the new language. His first attempts at recording contain irrelevant distinctions, but fail to show essential ones. Even a mechanical record will not help at this stage, since it would register the gross acoustic features, but would not tell which ones were significant. Only by finding out which utterances are alike in meaning, and which ones are different, can the observer learn to recognize the phonemic distinctions. So long as the analysis of meaning remains outside the powers of science, the analysis and recording of languages will remain an art or a practical skill.

Experience shows that one acquires this skill more easily if one is forewarned as to the kinds of speech-sounds that are distinctive in various languages — although it is true that any new language may show some entirely unforeseen distinction. This information is most easily acquired if it is put into the form of a rough description of the actions of the vocal organs. This rough description is what we mean by the term *practical phonetics*. After the observer has found out which of the gross acoustic features are significant in a language, his description of the significant features can be illustrated by a mechanical record.

6. 2. We have no special organs for speech; speech-sounds are produced by the organs that are used in breathing and eating. Most speech-sounds are produced by interference with the outgoing breath. Exceptions to this are *suction-sounds* or *clicks*. As a non-linguistic sign of surprised commiseration (and also as a signal to urge horses), we sometimes make a click — the novelist represents it by *tut, tut!* — with the tongue against the ridge just back of the upper teeth. As speech-sounds, various clicks, formed in different parts of the mouth, are used in some African languages.

6. 3. The first interference which the outgoing breath may meet, is in the *larynx*. The larynx is a box of cartilage at the head of the wind-pipe, visible from the outside as the adam's-apple. Within the larynx, at the right and left, are two shelf-like muscular protuberances, the *vocal chords*. The opening between them, through which the breath passes, is called the *glottis*. In ordinary breathing the vocal chords are relaxed and the breath passes freely through the glottis. At the rear of the larynx, the vocal chords are attached to two movable cartilaginous hinges, the *arytenoids*. Thanks to delicate muscular adjustments, both the vocal chords and the arytenoids can be set into a number of positions. The extreme positions are the wide-open position of ordinary breathing and the firmly closed position which occurs when one holds one's breath with the mouth wide open. Various languages make use of various intermediate positions of the glottis.

One of these positions is the position for *voicing*. In voicing, the vocal chords are drawn rather tightly together, so that the breath can get through only from instant to instant. In getting through, the breath-stream sets the vocal chords into vibration; the frequency ranges from around eighty to around one-thousand vibrations per second. These vibrations, communicated to the outer air, strike our ears as a *musical sound*, which we call the *voice*. The voice does not play a part in all speech-sounds: we distinguish between *voiced* and *unvoiced* (or *breathed*) speech-sounds. If one places a finger on the adam's-apple, or, better, if one presses one's palms tightly over one's ears, and then utters a voiced sound, such as [v] or [z], the voice will be felt as a trembling or vibration, while unvoiced sounds, such as [f] or [s] will lack this buzzing accompaniment. It seems that in every language at least a few phonemes have lack of voicing among their fixed characteristics. During the production of most unvoiced sounds the glottis is wide open, as in ordinary breathing.

Various adjustments enable us to alter the loudness and the pitch of the voice-sound as well as its quality of resonance. These last variations, such as the "head register," "chest register,"

TYPES OF PHONEMES

"muffled sound," "metallic sound," and the like, have not been physiologically analyzed.

Among the positions intermediate between breathing and voicing, several deserve mention. If the vocal chords are so far separated that the voice no longer sounds pure, but is accompanied by the friction-sound of the breath passing through the glottis, we get a *murmur*. In English, the unstressed vowels are often spoken with murmur instead of voice. As a phoneme, the murmur occurs in Bohemian, where it may be transcribed by the symbol [h], which is used in the conventional orthography of this language. If the glottis is still farther opened, the voice ceases and only a *friction-sound* remains; this friction-sound characterizes our phoneme [h], as in *hand* [hend]. Another intermediate position is the *whisper*, in which only the cartilage-glottis — that is, the space between the arytenoids — is open, but the vocal chords are in contact. In what we ordinarily call "whispering," the whisper is substituted for the voice and the unvoiced sounds are produced as in ordinary speech.

The sound-waves produced by the vibration of the vocal chords in voicing, are modified by the shape and by the elasticity of the channel through which they pass before they reach the outer air. If we compare the vocal chords to the reeds of a wind-instrument, we may view the mouth, or rather, the whole cavity from the vocal chords to the lips, including, in some cases the nasal cavity, as a *resonance-chamber*. By setting the mouth into various positions, by cutting off the exit either through the mouth or through the nose, and by tightening or loosening the muscles of this region, we vary the configuration of the outgoing sound-waves.

In contrast with musical sound, *noises*, which consist of irregular combinations of sound-waves, can be produced by means of the glottis, the tongue, and the lips. Some voiced sounds, such as [a, m, l], are *purely musical*, that is, relatively free from noise, while others, such as [v, z], consist of a noise plus the musical sound of voicing. Unvoiced sounds consist merely of noises; examples are [p, f, s].

6. 4. When the breath leaves the larynx, it passes, in normal breathing, through the nose. During most speech, however, we cut off this exit by raising the *velum*. The velum is the soft, movable back part of the palate; at the rear it ends in the *uvula*, the little lobe that can be seen hanging down in the center of the mouth.

TYPES OF PHONEMES

If one stands before a mirror, breathing quietly through nose and mouth, and then speaks a clear [a], one can see the raising of the velum, especially if one watches the uvula. When the velum is raised, its edge lies against the rear wall of the breath-passage, cutting off the exit of the breath through the nose. Most sounds of speech are purely *oral;* the velum is completely raised and no breath escapes through the nose. If the velum is not completely raised, some of the breath escapes through the nose and the speech-sounds have a peculiar resonance; such sounds are called *nasalized* sounds. In English the difference between purely oral and nasalized sounds is not distinctive; we often nasalize our vowels before and after the phonemes [m, n, n], and we nasalize more than usual when we are tired or relaxed. In some languages, however, nasalized sounds, most commonly vowels, are separate phonemes, distinct from similar sounds without nasalization. The usual symbols for nasalization are a small hook under a letter (this is used in the traditional orthography of Polish), or a tilde over a letter (Portuguese orthography and International Phonetic Association). French has four nasalized vowels as phonemes, distinct from the corresponding purely oral vowels: *bas* [ba] 'stocking,' but *banc* [bɑ̃] 'bench'; *mot* [mo] 'word,' but *mont* [mõ] 'mountain.'

If the velum is not raised and the exit of the breath through the mouth is in any way cut off, then, as in ordinary breathing, all the breath escapes through the nose. Phonemes where this is the case are *nasal.* In English we have three nasals: [m], in which the lips are closed; [n], in which the tongue is pressed against the gums; and [ŋ], as in *sing* [siŋ], in which the back of the tongue is pressed against the palate. These are purely musical sounds, characterized by the resonances which the different shapes of the oral-nasal cavity give to the musical sound of the voice. Some languages, however, have unvoiced nasals as phonemes; these are audible not so much by the very slight friction-noise of the breath-stream, as by the contrast with preceding or following sounds and by the intervening non-distinctive glide-sounds that are produced while the vocal organs change their position.

A good test of nasalization is to hold a card horizontally with one edge pressed against the upper lip and the opposite edge against a cold pane of glass· if one now produces a purely oral sound, such as [ɑː] the pane will be misty only under the card; if one produces

TYPES OF PHONEMES

a nasalized sound, such as [ã], the moisture will appear both above and below the card; and if one produces a purely nasal sound, such as [m], the moisture on the pane appears only above the card.

6. 5. We change the shape of the *oral cavity* by placing the lower jaw, the tongue, and the lips into various positions, and we affect the resonance also by tightening or loosening the muscles of the throat and mouth. By these means every language produces, as phonemes, a number of *musical sounds*, such as our [ɑː] in *palm* [pɑ m], our [i] in *pin* [pin], our [u] in *put* [put], our [r] in *rubber* ['rʌbə], and so on. In some of these the tongue actually touches the roof of the mouth, but leaves enough room at one or both sides for the breath to escape without serious friction-noise; such sounds are *laterals*, of the type of our [l], as in *little* ['litl]. In unvoiced laterals, which occur in Welsh and in many American languages, the friction-noise of the breath-stream is more audible than in unvoiced nasals.

We make noises in the mouth by movements of the tongue and lips. If we place these organs (or the glottis) so as to leave a very narrow passage, the outgoing breath produces a friction-noise: phonemes characterized by this noise are *spirants* (*fricatives*). They may be unvoiced, as are our [f] and [s], or voiced, like our [v] and [z]. Since the amount of friction can be varied to any degree, there is no real boundary between spirants and musical sounds such as [i] or [l]; especially the voiced varieties occur in different languages with many degrees of closure.

If we place the tongue or the lips (or the glottis) so as to leave no exit, and allow the breath to accumulate behind the closure, and then suddenly open the closure, the breath will come out with a slight pop or explosion; sounds formed in this way are *stops* (*plosives, explosives*), like our unvoiced [p, t, k] and our voiced [b, d, g]. The characteristic feature of a stop is usually the explosion, but the making of the closure (the *implosion*) or even the brief period of time during closure, may suffice to characterize the phoneme; thus, in English we sometimes leave off the explosion of a final [p, t, k]. These varieties are audible by contrast with what precedes or follows (as a sudden stoppage of sound or as a moment of silence), or else through the transitional sounds during the movement of tongue or lips; also, during the closure of a voiced stop one can hear the muffled sound of the voice.

Since lips, tongue, and uvula are elastic, they can be placed so that the breath sets them into vibration, with alternate moments of contact and opening. Such *trills* occur in many languages; an example is the British English "rolled *r*," as in *red* or *horrid*.

We shall take up the chief types of phonemes in the following order:

noise-sounds:
stops,
trills,
spirants;
musical sounds:
nasals,
laterals,
vowels.

6. 6. *Stops* occur as phonemes in perhaps every language. English distinguishes three types as to position: *labial* (more exactly, *bilabial*), in which the two lips form the closure [p, b]; *dental* (more exactly, *alveolar*, or better *gingival*), in which the tip of the tongue makes closure against the ridge just back of the upper gums [t, d]; and *velar* (in older writings mis-called *guttural*), in which the back of the tongue is pressed against the velum [k, g].

These last two types occur in many varieties, thanks to the mobility of the tongue. Contact can be made by the *tip* of the tongue (*apical* articulation) or by a larger area, the *blade*, round the tip (*coronal* articulation); it can be made against the edges of the upper teeth (*interdental* position), against the backs of the upper teeth (*postdental* position), against the ridge back of the upper teeth (*gingival* position), or against points still higher up on the palate (*cerebral* or *cacuminal* or, better, *inverted* or *domal* position). Thus, apical articulation in the domal position (the tip of the tongue touching almost the highest point in the roof of the mouth) occurs as a non-distinctive variant alongside the gingival [t, d] in American English. In French the nearest sounds to our [t, d] are pronounced not gingivally but as postdentals (the tip or blade touching the back of the teeth). In Sanskrit and in many modern languages of India, postdentals [t, d] and domals (usually transcribed by a letter with a dot under it, or by italics, or, as in this book, by small capitals [T, D]) are distinct phonemes.

Similarly, different parts of the back of the tongue (*dorsal* articulation) may be raised so as to touch different parts of the palate; one distinguishes, usually, between *anterior* or *palatal* position and *posterior* or *velar* position, and, still farther back, *uvular* position. In English the velars [k, g] are closed farther forward before some sounds, as in *kin, give*, and farther backward before others, as in *cook, good* — both types in contrast with, say, *calm, guard* — but these variants are not distinctive. In some languages, such as Hungarian, there are separate phonemes of the palatal and velar types, which we distinguish in transcription by such devices as [c] for the palatal and [k] for the velar unvoiced stop. In Arabic a velar unvoiced stop [k] and a uvular unvoiced stop [q] are distinct phonemes.

A *glottal* or *laryngal* stop is produced by bringing the vocal chords tightly together and then letting them spring apart under the pressure of the breath. We sometimes produce this sound before an initial stressed vowel when speaking under a strain, and in German this is the normal usage; as a phoneme, the glottal stop occurs in many languages, as, for instance, in Danish, where there is a distinctive difference, for example, between *hun* [hun] 'she' and *hund* [hunʔ] 'dog.'

As to the manner of forming the closure, aside from the difference of *unvoiced* and *voiced*, the amount of breath-pressure and the vigor of action in the lips or tongue may be variously graded: pressure and action are gentle in *lenes*, vigorous in *fortes;* in *solutio:-lenes* the opening-up is relatively slow, so as to weaken the explosion. The unvoiced stops may be followed by a puff of unvoiced breath (*aspiration*) or preceded by one (*pre-aspiration*); the voiced stops, similarly, may be preceded or followed by unvoiced breath or by a murmur. The closure may be made simultaneously in two positions, as in the [gb] stops of some African languages; many languages have *glottalized* oral stops, with a glottal stop occurring simultaneously, or just before, or just after the opening of the [p, t, k]. In English the unvoiced stops are aspirated fortes, but other types occur as non-distinctive variants, notably the unaspirated lenis type after [s], as in *spin, stone, skin*. Our voiced stops are lenes; at the beginning or at the end of a word they are not voiced through their whole duration. In French the unvoiced stops [p, t, k] are fortes and, as a non-distinctive variant, may be accompanied by a simultaneous glottal stop, but are never aspirated; the voiced [b, d, g] are lenes, more fully voiced than in

English. In North Chinese, aspirated and unaspirated unvoiced stops are different phonemes, e.g. [pha] versus [pa], and voiced stops occur only as non-distinctive variants of the latter. Many South-German dialects distinguish unvoiced unaspirated fortes and lenes, which we may transcribe by [p, t, k] and [b, d, g]; voiced variants are not distinctive. Sanskrit had four such types of stops: unvoiced unaspirated [p], aspirated [ph], and voiced unaspirated [b], aspirated [bh].

6. 7. The commonest *trill* is the *apical* or *tongue-tip trill*, in which the tongue-tip vibrates in a few rapid strokes against the gums; this is the "rolled" r of British English, Italian, Russian, and many other languages. Bohemian distinguishes two phonemes of this type, the one accompanied by a strong friction sound. The *uvular trill*, in which the uvula vibrates against the uplifted back of the tongue, occurs in Danish, in the commoner pronunciation of French, German, and Dutch, and in varieties of English (the "Northumbrian burr"); in these languages, as well as in Norwegian and Swedish, the uvular and the tongue-tip trill are geographic variants of the same phoneme. The phonetic symbol for a trill is [r]; if a language has more than one trill phoneme, [R] is a handy character.

If the tongue-tip is allowed to make only a single swing, with one rapid contact against the gums or palate, we have a *tongue-flip*. In the Central-Western type of American English, a voiced gingival tongue-flip occurs as a non-distinctive variant of [t] in forms like *water, butter, at all;* different types of tongue-flip occur in Norwegian and Swedish dialects.

6. 8. The positions in which *spirants* are formed in English differ from those of the stops. In one pair, the *labiodentals* [f, v], the breath-stream is forced to pass between the upper teeth and the lower lip. In the *dentals* [θ, ð], as in *thin* [θin], *then* [ðen], the blade of the tongue touches the upper teeth. Our *gingival* spirants [s, z] are *hisses* or *sibilants:* that is, the tongue is constricted, so as to bulge up at the sides and leave only a narrow channel along the center, through which the breath is forced sharply against the gums and teeth, giving a sonorous hiss or buzz. If we draw the tongue a little ways out of this position — in English we draw it back — the breath is directed less sharply against the gums and teeth, and seems to eddy round before finding an exit: in English these *hushes* or *abnormal sibilants* are separate phonemes

TYPES OF PHONEMES

[ʃ, 3], as in *shin* [ʃin], *vision* ['viӡn]. In each of these positions we have a pair, voiced and unvoiced. Many other varieties occur, such as *bilabial* spirants, in which the narrowing is made between the two lips (an unvoiced variety in Japanese, a voiced in Spanish). In French the hisses are formed postdentally; to our ears the Frenchman seems to have a slight lisp. German, which has no [ӡ], protrudes the lips for [ʃ], so as to accentuate the eddying sound. Swedish has a [ʃ] with very wide opening, which sounds queer to English ears.

English has no *dorsal* spirants, but they occur in many languages, in a great variety of positions, including lateral types. German has an unvoiced *palatal* spirant, in which the middle of the tongue is raised against the highest part of the palate; as a non-distinctive variant of this, it uses a *velar* type, an unvoiced spirant in the position of our [k, g, ŋ]. The customary transcription of German uses two symbols, [ç] for the palatal variety, as in *ich* [iç] 'I', and [x] for the velar variety, as in *ach* [ax] 'oh,' but only one symbol is needed, since the varieties depend upon the preceding phoneme. Voiced spirants [ɣ] of the same position occur in some types of German pronunciation as variants of the stop [g]; in Dutch and in modern Greek they occur as separate phonemes. *Uvular* spirants occur in Danish as variants of the uvular trill, in other languages as distinct phonemes.

In English we have an unvoiced *glottal* spirant, [h] as in *hit* [hit], *when* [hwen], *hew* [hjuw], in which friction is produced by the passage of the breath through the slightly opened glottis; Bohemian has a similar sound in which the friction is accompanied by voice vibrations (murmur). A further pair of glottal spirants, unvoiced ("hoarse *h*") and voiced ("ayin"), occurs in Arabic; their characteristic feature is said to be a tightening of the throat-muscles.

As to manner, spirants show perhaps less variety than stops. Among languages which distinguish two varieties of manner, French voices its [v, z, ӡ] more completely than does English. Some languages have glottalized spirants (preceded, accompanied, or followed by a glottal stop).

6. 9. The positions of *nasals* are much like those of stops; in English [m, n, ŋ] are spoken in the same three positions as the stops: [m] is bilabial, like [p, b], the [n] is gingival, like [t, d], and [ŋ], as in *sing* [siŋ], *sink* [siŋk], *singer* ['siŋə], *finger* ['fiŋgə], is formed in the same way as are [k, g], the velar stops. On the same principle, French speaks its [n] in postdental position, like its [t, d]. On the other hand, French has no velar nasal, but has a palatal nasal, in which the closure is made by raising the middle of the tongue against the highest part of the palate, as in *signe* [siɲ] 'sign.' As in the stops, Sanskrit and modern Indian languages distinguish between a dental [n] and a domal [ɴ].

6. 10. In English the lateral [l] is apical, in gingival position; at the end of words we use a non-distinctive variety in which the middle of the tongue is excessively lowered; contrast *less* with *well*. In German and French the [l] is spoken with the surface of the tongue more raised; the acoustic impression is quite different; in French, moreover, the contact is postdental. Italian has a palatal lateral, distinct from the dental, with the back of the tongue touching the highest point of the palate but leaving free passage for the breath at one or both sides: *figlio* ['fiʎo] 'son.' Some American languages have a whole series of laterals, with differences of position, glottalization, or nasalization. Unvoiced laterals, especially if the contact is extensive, take on a spirant character; voiced laterals, especially if the point of contact is minute, merge with vowels; thus, one of the two lateral phonemes of Polish strikes our ear almost as a [w]. On the other hand, the Central-Western American English vowel [r], as in *red* [red], *fur* [fr̩], *far* [far], is closely akin to a lateral: the tip of the tongue is raised to domal (inverted) position, but does not quite make a contact. In transcription we use the same symbol [r] as for the trill of other languages; this is convenient, because our sound and the British English trill in *red* are geographic variants of the same phoneme.

6. 11. *Vowels* are modifications of the voice-sound that involve no closure, friction, or contact of the tongue or lips. They are ordinarily voiced; some languages, however, distinguish different voice-qualities, such as *muffled* vowels, *murmured* vowels, with slow vibration of the vocal chords, or *whispered* vowels, in which friction between the arytenoids replaces vibration of the vocal chords.[1]

---

[1] In contrast with vowels, the other sounds (stops, trills, spirants, nasals, laterals) are sometimes called *consonants*. Our school grammar uses the terms "vowel" and "consonant" in an inconsistent way, referring to letters rather than sounds. In the description of individual languages, it is often convenient to use these terms in other ways and to supplement them by such as *sonant* or *semivowel*, whose application we shall see in the next chapter.

TYPES OF PHONEMES

Every language distinguishes at least several different vowel phonemes. The differences between these phonemes seem to be largely differences of tongue-position, and to consist, acoustically, of differences in the distribution of overtones. Even these principles are disputed; in what follows I shall state the tongue-positions according to the generally accepted scheme, which has this merit, that it agrees with the relations of the vowels that are exhibited in the phonetic and grammatical systems of many languages. Other factors that enter into the distinction of vowel phonemes, are the tenseness and looseness of the tongue and other muscles, and different positions of the lips, such as protrusion and retraction.

The Central-Western type of American English distinguishes nine vowel phonemes. One of these, [r], which we have already discussed, is peculiar in its inverted tongue-position. The other eight form what we may call a *two-four system*. As to position, they occur in pairs; each pair consists of a *front* vowel, formed by raising the middle of the tongue toward the highest part of the palate, and a *back* vowel, formed by raising the back of the tongue toward the velum. The four pairs differ as to nearness of the tongue to the palate; thus we have four degrees of raising: *high*, *higher mid*, *lower mid*, and *low*. Instead of the terms *high* and *low*, some writers use *close* and *open*. This gives us the following scheme:

	Front	Back
high	i	u
higher mid	e	o
lower mid	ɛ	ɔ
low	a	ɑ

Examples: *in, inn* [in], *egg* [eg], *add* [ɛd], *alms* [amz], *put* [put], *up* [op], *ought* [ɔt], *odd* [ɑd]. These phonemes are subject to a good deal of non-distinctive variation, some of which depends upon the surrounding phonemes and will interest us later.

Southern British English has much the same system, but the distribution of the back-vowel phonemes is different, in that the degrees of closure of the vowels in words like *up* and *odd* are the reverse of ours: higher mid in *odd* [ɔd], low in *up* [ʌp]. However, there has arisen a convention of transcribing British English, not by the symbols here indicated in accord with the principles of the IPA alphabet, but by means of queer symbols which are intended to remind the reader, irrelevantly enough, of the difference between English and French vowel phonemes:

	Chicago pronunciation according to IPA principles	British pronunciation according to IPA principles	British pronunciation, actual practice
inn	in	in	in
egg	eg	eg	eg
add	ɛd	ɛd	ɛd
alms	amz	amz	ɑːmz
put	put	put	put
odd	ɑd	od	ɔd
ought	ɔt	ɔt	ɔːt
up	ɔp	ɐp	ʌp

The ninth vowel phoneme, which we transcribe for Central-Western American English by [r], as in *bird* [br̩d], has no uniform correspondent in Southern British English or in New-England or Southern American English. Before vowels, British English has a tongue-tip trill, which we transcribe by [r], as in *red* [red]; where Central-Western American has [r] after vowels, British has merely a modification (in some cases, a lengthening) of the vowel, which is indicated by a colon [ː], as in *part* [pɑːt], *form* [fɔːm]; where in Central-Western American the [r] is neither preceded nor followed by a vowel, British English uses a *mixed vowel*, intermediate between front and back positions, which is transcribed by [əː] or [ə], as in *bird* [bəːd] or *bitter* ['bitə].

6. 12. Some Central-Western types of American English lack the distinction of [a] and [ɑ]. The low vowel of such speakers strikes my ear as an [a], both in *alms* and in *odd;* in their phonemic system, however, its position is neither "front," nor "back," but indifferent, since this pronunciation has only one low-vowel phoneme. A similar system, without the eccentric [r] vowel, occurs also in Italian. We may call this a *seven-vowel* system:

	Front	Indifferent	Back
high	i		u
higher mid	e		o
lower mid	ɛ		ɔ
low		a	

Italian examples are: *si* [si] 'yes.' *pesca* ['peska] 'fishing,' *pesca* ['pɛska] 'peach,' *tu* [tu] 'thou,' *pollo* ['pollo] 'chicken,' *olla* ['ɔlla] 'pot,' *ama* ['ama] 'loves.'

TYPES OF PHONEMES

Some languages have simpler systems, such as the *five-vowel* system of Spanish or Russian:

	FRONT	INDIFFERENT	BACK
high	i		u
mid	e		o
low		a	

Spanish examples: *si* [si] 'yes,' *pesca* ['peska] 'fishing,' *tu* [tu] 'thou,' *pomo* ['pomo] 'apple,' *ama* ['ama] 'loves.'

Even simpler is the *three-vowel* system which appears in some languages, such as Tagalog:

	FRONT	INDIFFERENT	BACK
high	i		u
low		a	

The fewer the phonemes in a vowel-system, the more room is there for non-distinctive variation of each phoneme. In Spanish the mid vowels, for instance, vary, to our ear, between higher and lower positions, with much the same acoustic qualities as in Italian, where these differences represent different phonemes. The Russian vowels are subject to wide variation, which depends chiefly on the preceding and following phonemes; especially one variant of the high front vowel, as in [sin] 'son,' strikes our ear very strangely, because in this variant the tongue is drawn back much farther than in any variant of the English high front vowel. The three-vowel system of Tagalog, finally, allows each phoneme a range that seems enormous to our hearing; the variants of the Tagalog phonemes symbolized above by the characters [i] and [u], range all the way from positions like those of our high vowels to positions like those of our lower mid vowels.

6. 13. Different positions of the lips play no part in American English vowels, except for one minor fact which we shall take up later. In many languages, however, lip-positions accentuate the quality of different vowels: the front vowels are supported by *retraction* of the lips (drawing back the corners of the mouth), and the back vowels by *protrusion* or *rounding* of the lips. In general, the higher the vowel, the more pronounced is the action of the lips. These features appear in most European languages and contribute to the difference between their and our vowels. Even here we find decided differences; the Scandinavian languages, especially Swedish, round their back vowels more than do the other European languages: a Swedish [o], as in *bo* [boː] 'to dwell,' has about the tongue-position of a German or French [o], as in German *so* [zoː] 'thus' or French *beau* [bo] 'beautiful,' but it has the extreme lip-rounding of a German or French high vowel [u], as in German *du* [duː] 'thou' or French *bout* [bu] 'end'; it strikes us as a kind of intermediate sound between an [o] and an [u].

The languages just named make use of lip-positions also for the distinction of phonemes. The commonest distinction of this kind is that between the ordinary front vowels (with retracted lip-position) and *rounded front vowels*, with the lip-position of the corresponding back vowels. Thus, French, beside eight vowel phonemes in a distribution like that of American English, has three rounded front vowels:

	Front		Back
	Unrounded	Rounded	(Rounded)
high	i	y	u
higher mid	e	ø	o
lower mid	ɛ	œ	ɔ
low	a		ɑ

Examples:

fini [fini] 'done,' *été* [ete] 'summer,' *lait* [lɛ] 'milk,' *bat* [ba] 'beats,'

rue [ry] 'street,' *feu* [fø] 'fire,' *peuple* [pœpl] 'people,'

roue [ru] 'wheel,' *eau* [o] 'water,' *homme* [ɔm] 'man,' *bas* [bɑ] 'low.'

To these are added four nasalized vowels (see above, § 6.4), as distinct phonemes: *pain* [pɛ̃] 'bread,' *bon* [bõ] 'good,' *un* [œ̃] 'one,' *banc* [bɑ̃] 'bench.' Furthermore, French has a shorter variety of [œ], which is transcribed as [ə], as in *cheval* [ʃəval] 'horse.'

The symbols [y, ø] are taken from the traditional orthography of Danish; that of German (and of Finnish) uses the symbols *ü* and *ö*.

One can learn to produce rounded front vowels by practising lip-positions before a mirror: after learning to produce front vowels of the types [i, e, ɛ] with the corners of the mouth drawn back, and back vowels of the types [u, o, ɔ] with the lips protruded and rounded, one speaks an [i] and then tries to keep the tongue-position unchanged while rounding the lips as for an [u]; the result is an

[y]. In the same way one passes from [e] to [ø] and from [ɛ] to [œ].

A further distinction is created by the use of *unrounded back vowels*, in contrast with rounded. This additional factor produces in Turkish a *three-dimensional* vowel system: each vowel phoneme is either front or back, high or low, rounded or unrounded:

	FRONT		BACK	
	UNROUNDED	ROUNDED	UNROUNDED	ROUNDED
high	i	y	ï	u
low	e	ø	a	o

6. 14. Another factor in vowel-production is the *tense* or *loose* position of the muscles: to our ears, vowels of the former type sound clearer and perhaps excessively precise, since the English vowels are all loose. Some authors use the terms *narrow* and *wide* instead of *tense* and *loose*. The most striking characteristic, to our ear, of the French vowels is their tense character. It is relative tenseness, too, which in addition to lip-action, makes the Italian vowels very different from those of English, although the two languages make the same number of distinctions.

Tenseness and looseness are utilized for distinctions of phonemes in German and Dutch. In German, and, to a lesser extent, in Dutch, the tense vowels are also of longer duration (a factor which will concern us later) than the loose. If we indicate tenseness, combined with greater length, by a colon after the symbol, we obtain for these languages the following system, with a pair of phonemes in each position [1]:

	FRONT		INDIFFERENT	BACK
	UNROUNDED	ROUNDED		(ROUNDED)
high	i: i	y: y		u: u
mid	e: e	ø: ø		o: o
low			a: a	

German examples:
ihn [i:n] 'him,' *in* [in] 'in,' *Beet* [be:t] 'flower-bed,' *Bett* [bet] 'bed,' *Tür* [ty:r] 'door,' *hübsch* [hypʃ] 'pretty,' *König* ['kø:nik] 'king,' *zwölf* [tsvølf] 'twelve,'

Fusz [fu:s] 'foot,' *Flusz* [flus] 'river,' *hoch* [ho:x] 'high,' *Loch* [lox] 'hole,' *kam* [ka:m] 'came,' *Kamm* [kam] 'comb.'

The differences between the vowel phonemes of different lan-

---
[1] Dutch lacks the short [ø].

guages are not sufficiently understood. It is likely, moreover, that one and the same phoneme may often be produced, in the same language, by very different actions of the vocal organs, but with similar, and for the native hearer identical, acoustic effects: it is supposed that in such cases the deviation of one organ (say, a different tongue-position) is compensated by different action of some other organ (such as a different action of the larynx).

CHAPTER 7

MODIFICATIONS

7. 1. The typical actions of the vocal organs described in the last chapter may be viewed as a kind of basis, which may be modified in various ways. Such modifications are: the length of time through which a sound is continued; the loudness with which it is produced; the musical pitch of the voice during its production; the position of organs not immediately concerned in the characteristic action; the manner of moving the vocal organs from one characteristic position to another. This distinction between basic speech-sounds and modifications is convenient for our exposition, but it is not always recognized in the phonetic system of languages; many languages place some of the latter features quite on a par with phonemes of the former sort. We have seen, for instance, that features of pitch are utilized as primary phonemes in Chinese, and features of duration distinguish primary phonemes in German. On the other hand, most languages do recognize the distinction to this extent, that they use some of the modifying features as secondary phonemes — phonemes which are not part of the simplest linguistic forms, but merely mark combinations or particular uses of such forms.

7. 2. *Duration* (or *quantity*) is the relative length of time through which the vocal organs are kept in a position. Some languages distinguish between two or more durations of speech-sounds. Thus, we have seen (§ 6.14) that in German the tense vowels are longer than the loose; this difference of length is more striking than that of tenseness. The sign for a long phoneme is a colon after the symbol for the sound, as German *Beet* [be:t] 'flower-bed,' in contrast with *Bett* [bet] 'bed.' If more degrees of length are to be indicated, a single dot or other signs can be used. Another method of indicating long quantity is to write the symbol twice; this is done in Finnish orthography, e.g. *kaappi* 'cupboard' with long [a] and long [p].

In American English, vowel-quantity is not distinctive. The low and lower mid vowels, as in *pan, palm, pod, pawn,* are longer than the other vowels, as in *pin, pen, pun, pull*. All our vowels, moreover, are longer before voiced sounds than before unvoiced; thus, the [ɛ] in *pan, pad* is longer than in *pat, pack* and the [i] in *pin, bid* longer than in *pit, bit*. These differences are, of course, not distinctive, since they depend upon the height of the vowel and upon the following phonemes.

In dealing with matters of quantity, it is often convenient to set up an arbitrary unit of relative duration, the *mora*. Thus, if we say that a short vowel lasts one mora, we may describe the long vowels of the same language as lasting, say, one and one-half morae or two morae.

In French, the distinction between long and short vowels works in a peculiar way. Long vowels occur only before the last consonant or consonant-group of a word: the mere presence of a long vowel in French thus indicates that the next consonant or consonant-group ends a word. In this position, moreover, the length of a vowel is for the most part determined entirely by the nature of the phonemes themselves. The nasalized vowels [ã, ɛ̃, õ, œ̃] and the vowels [o, ø] are in this position always long: *tante* [tãt] 'aunt,' *faute* [foːt] 'fault.' The remaining vowels are always long if the final consonant is [j, r, v, vr, z, ʒ], as in *cave* [kaːv] 'cellar,' *vert* [vɛːr] 'green.' Only in the cases not covered by these two rules, is the vowel-quantity ever distinctive, as in *bête* [bɛːt] 'beast' versus *bette* [bɛt] 'beet.'

Long consonants occur in English in phrases and compound words, such as *pen-knife* ['pen ˌnajf] or *eat two* ['ijt 'tuw]; within a single word [nn] occurs in a variant pronunciation of forms like *meanness* ['mijnnis] beside ['mijnis]. A distinction of two consonant-quantities within simple words is normal in Italian, as in *fatto* ['fatto] 'done,' but *fato* ['fato] 'fate,' in Finnish, and in many other languages. In Swedish and Norwegian a consonant is long always and only after a stressed short vowel; the difference of consonant-quantities, accordingly, is not distinctive. In Dutch there are no long consonants; even when like consonants meet in a phrase, only one consonant mora is spoken, so that the phrase consisting of *dat* [dat] 'that' and *tal* [tal] 'number' is pronounced ['da 'tal].

7. 3. *Stress* — that is, intensity or loudness — consists in greater amplitude of sound-waves, and is produced by means of more energetic movements, such as pumping more breath, bringing the

MODIFICATIONS

vocal chords closer together for voicing, and using the muscles more vigorously for oral articulations. In English we have three secondary phonemes which consist of increased stress, in contrast with what we may call unstressed passages of phonemes. Our *highest stress* ["] marks emphatic forms, usually in contrast or contradiction; our *high stress* or *ordinary stress* ['] appears normally on one syllable of each word; our *low stress* or *secondary stress* [ˌ] appears on one or more syllables of compound words and long words. In phrases, the high stress of certain words is replaced by a low stress or entirely omitted. Examples:

This is *my* birthday present [ˈðis iz ˈˈmaj ˈbəːθdej ˌpreznt].
It *isn't my* fault, and it *is your* fault [it ˈˈiz nt ˈˈmaj ˈfɔːlt, ən it ˈˈiz ˈˈjɔː ˈfɔːlt].
I'm going out [aj m ˌgowiŋ ˈawt.]
Let's go back [ˈlet s ˌgow ˈbɛk.]
business man [ˈbiznis ˌmɛn]
gentleman [ˈdʒentlmən]
dominating [ˈdɔmiˌnejtiŋ]
domination [ˌdɔmiˈnejʃn]

This system is paralleled in all the Germanic languages, and in many others, such as Italian, Spanish, the Slavic languages, Chinese. In stress-using languages like these, the stress characterizes combinations of linguistic forms; the typical case is the use of one high stress on each word in the phrase, with certain unstressed or low-stressed words as exceptions. However, some languages of this type contain simple linguistic forms (such as unanalyzable words) of more than one syllable, which may be differentiated, accordingly, by the place of the stress; thus Russian ['gorot] 'city' and [mo'ros] 'frost' are both simple words, containing no prefix or suffix; here, accordingly, the *place of stress* has the value of a primary phoneme.

Other languages use degrees of loudness as non-distinctive features. In the Menomini language a sentence sounds, as to ups and downs of stress, quite like an English sentence, but these ups and downs are determined entirely by the primary phonemes and bear no relation to the meaning. In French the distribution of stress serves only as a kind of gesture: ordinarily the end of a phrase is louder than the rest; sometimes, in emphatic speech, some other syllable is especially loud; often enough one hears a long succession of syllables with very little fluctuation of stress.

7. 4. Among stress-using languages there are some differences in the manner of applying stress. In English there is a non-distinctive variation by which the vowels of unstressed words and syllables appear in a "weakened" form: they are shorter and formed with looser muscles, the voice is sometimes reduced to a murmur, and the tongue-positions tend toward a uniform placing, somewhere near higher mid position. The degree of weakening varies from utterance to utterance, and differs a great deal in different geographic and social types of English. The vowels of the least-stressed syllables are decidedly short and loose; these vowels are a very lax [i], as in *landed* ['lɛndid], *glasses* ['glaɪsiz], *heavy* ['hevi]; a very lax mid vowel, resembling [ə:] but decidedly shorter, which we transcribe as [ə], as in *bitter* ['bitə], *bottom* ['bɔtəm], *parrot* ['pɛrət]; and, finally, syllabic [l] and [n], as in *bottle* ['bɔtl], *button* ['bʌtn]. Where we have the same form stressed in some combinations and unstressed in others, we may get a plain contrast. Thus:

con- ['kɔn-]: *convict*, noun ['kɔnvikt]:
    [kən-]: *convict*, verb [kən'vikt].
re- ['rij-]: *reflex* ['rijfleks], ['re-]: *refuse*, noun ['refjuws]:
    [ri-]: *reflect* [ri'flekt], *refuse*, verb [ri'fjuwz].
pro- ['prow-]: *protest*, noun ['prowtest], ['prɔ-]: *progress*, noun
    ['prɔgres] beside ['prowgres].
    [prə-]: *protest*, verb [prə'test], *progress*, verb [prə'gres].
vac- ['vejk-]: *vacant* ['vejkənt]:
    [vək-]: *vacation* [və'kejʃn].
-bel [-'bel]: *rebel*, verb [ri'bel]:
    [-bl]: *rebel*, noun ['rebl].
-tom [-'tɔm]: *atomic* [ə'tɔmik]:
    [-tɛm]: *atom* ['ɛtəm].
-tain [-'tejn]: *maintain* [mən'tejn, mejn'tejn]:
    [-tin]: *maintenance* ['mejntinəns].

In cases like these, various grades of weakening exist side by side and are used according to the speed and the mood (formal, familiar, and so on) of utterance. There are also local and social differences. American English says *dictionary* ['dikʃn̩ˌejrij], *secretary* ['sekreˌtejrij] (compare *secretarial* [ˌsekre'tejrij]); British English uses weaker forms, saying ['dikʃn̩ri, 'sekr̩tri]. On the other hand, in forms like *Latin* ['lɛtn̩], *Martin* ['martn̩] this degree of weakening is decidedly sub-standard in England, where the standard forms are ['letin, 'mɑːtin].

MODIFICATIONS

Not all languages that use stress as a distinctive feature weaken their unstressed vowels. The Germanic languages other than English produce the vowels of unstressed syllables quite like those of stressed syllables. The unstressed vowels in German *Monat* ['mo:nat] 'month,' *Kleinod* ['klajno:t] 'gem,' *Armut* ['armu:t] 'poverty,' are quite like the stressed vowels in *hat* [hat] 'has,' *Not* [no:t] 'distress,' *Mut* [mu:t] 'courage.' In these languages only one vowel, the short [e], appears in a weakened variant when it is unstressed. Thus, in German *hatte* ['hate] 'had' or *gebadet* [ge'ba:det] 'bathed,' the [e]-vowel is spoken shorter and with the tongue less raised and fronted than in a form like *Bett* [bet] 'bed,' and in a form like *baden* ['ba:den] 'to bathe,' the second syllable is acoustically quite like the second syllable of an English form like *sodden* ['sɔdn], and very different from a German *denn* [den] 'then.' Phoneticians often indicate this weakening by using the character [ə] for the unstressed form of [e], transcribing *hatte* ['hatə], *baden* ['ba:dən] or ['ba:dn̩], but this is unnecessary, since the accent-mark suffices to indicate the weakening.

Other stress-using languages, such as Italian, Spanish, Bohemian, Polish, do not use special variants for any of the unstressed vowels; compare, for instance, our *restitution* [ˌresti'tuwšn̩] with an Italian *restituzione* [restitutsi'one]. In a Bohemian word like *kozel* ['koẑel] 'goat,' the [e] is just as fully formed as in *zelenec* ['zelenets] 'evergreen.'

7. 5. Another difference between stress-using languages concerns the point at which the increase of loudness sets in. In English, if the first syllable of a word has a stress, the increase of loudness begins exactly at the beginning of the word. Accordingly, there is a difference between pairs like the following:

a name [ə 'nejm]   *an aim* [ən 'ejm]
that sod ['ðɛt 'sɔd]   *that's odd* ['ðɛt s 'ɔd]
that stuff ['ðɛt 'stʌf]   *that's tough* ['ðɛt s 'tʌf]

The same habit prevails in German and Scandinavian; German, in fact, marks the onset of stress so vigorously that it often takes the shape of a (non-distinctive) glottal stop before the initial vowel of a stressed word or element, as in *ein Arm* [ajn 'arm] 'an arm,' or in *Verein* [fer-'ajn] 'association,' where the *ver-* is an unstressed prefix.

In many stress-using languages, on the other hand, the point of onset of a stress is regulated entirely by the character of the primary phonemes. In Dutch, for instance, when there is a single consonant before the vowel of a stressed syllable, this consonant always shares in the loudness, regardless of word-division or other factors of meaning: *een aam* 'an aam' (measure of forty gallons) and *een naam* 'a name' are both [eˈnaːm], and a phrase like *het ander oog* 'the other eye' is [eˈtandeˈroːx]. The same habit prevails in Italian, Spanish, and the Slavic languages.

7. 6. Differences of *pitch*, that is, frequency of vibration in the musical sound of the voice, are used in English, and perhaps in most languages, as secondary phonemes. The actual acoustic forms are highly variable; there is also some geographic variation. The Englishman's rising pitch in *Thank you!* is striking to American ears, and his rising pitch in some statements often makes them sound to us like a yes-or-no question. Moreover, we use features of pitch very largely in the manner of gestures, as when we talk harshly, sneeringly, petulantly, caressingly, cheerfully, and so on. In English, and in the languages of Europe generally, pitch is the acoustic feature where gesture-like variations, non-distinctive but socially effective, border most closely upon genuine linguistic distinctions. The investigation of socially effective but non-distinctive patterns in speech, an investigation scarcely begun, concerns itself, accordingly, to a large extent with pitch. For the same reason, it is not easy to define the cases where features of pitch have in our language a genuine status as secondary phonemes.

It is clear that the end of a sentence (a term we shall have to define later) is always marked by some special distribution of pitch. We can speak the words *It's ten o'clock, I have to go home*, as a single sentence, with a *final-pitch* only at the end, or as two sentences, with a final-pitch on *clock* and another at the end: *It's ten o'clock. I have to go home.* After a final-pitch we may pause for any length of time, or stop talking.

Within the domain of final-pitch we can distinguish several phonemic differences. *It's ten o'clock*, as a statement, differs from *It's ten o'clock?* as a question; the latter ends with a rise, instead of a fall. Among questions, there is a difference of pitch-scheme between a yes-or-no question, such as *It's ten o'clock?* or *Did you see the show?* and a supplement-question, which is to be answered by some special word or phrase, as *What time is it?* or *Who saw the show?* with a lesser rise at the end. In transcription we may indicate the latter type by placing the question-mark upside down

[¿]. The distinction appears plainly in the contrast between a supplement-question and a yes-or-no question which asks whether this supplement-question is to be answered: *Who saw the show?* ['huw 'sɔː ðə 'ʃow¿] asks for the person, but ['huw 'sɔː ðə 'ʃow?] means 'Is this what you were asking about?'

These three types of final-pitch appear side by side in the following example. If someone said *I'm the man who — who —*, his interlocutor might help him out by saying, with the final-pitch of a statement, *Who took the money* [huw 'tuk ðə 'mʌni.]. This contrasts with the supplement-question *Who took the money?* ['huw 'tuk ðə 'mʌni¿], to which an interlocutor who wanted to make sure that this was the question, or to use it as a formal starting-point, might answer by a yes-or-no question, *Who took the money?* ['huw 'tuk ðə 'mʌni?] (*I'll tell you who took it. . .*).

It appears, further, that sentences of all three of these types may be distorted as to pitch, and also as to stress, when the speaker is responding to a strong stimulus. We are doubtless justified in setting up a single secondary phoneme of *exclamatory pitch*, symbol [!], for this type, and in supposing that the varieties within this type, such as the intonations of anger, surprise, call, sneer, and the like, are non-distinctive, gesture-like variations. The exclamatory phoneme appears in conjunction with all three of the final-pitch phonemes. Contrast *John* [ʤɔn.] as an answer to a question, with *John!* ['ʤɔn!] as a call for the hearer's (John's) presence or attention; similarly *John?* ['ʤɔn?] as a simple question ('Is that John?') contrasts with the same question accompanied by exclamatory pitch: *John?!* ['ʤɔn?!] ('It isn't John, I hope!'); finally, *Who was watching the door* [¿] contrasts with the exclamatory *Who was watching the door* [¿!] in an emergency or a calamity.

As a fifth secondary phoneme of pitch in English we must recognize *pause-pitch* or *suspension-pitch* [,], which consists of a rise of pitch before a pause within a sentence. It is used, in contrast with the final-pitches, to show that the sentence is not ending at a point where otherwise the phrasal form would make the end of a sentence possible: *I was waiting there* [,] *when in came the man. John* [,] *the idiot* [,] *missed us.* (Contrast: *John the Baptist was preaching.*) *The man* [,] *who was carrying a bag* [,] *came up to our door.* Only one man is in the story; contrast: *The man who was carrying a bag came up to our door*, which implies that several men are in the story.

7. 7. In English both stress and pitch, then, are used only as secondary phonemes, but there are some differences between the functions of the two. The stress phonemes step in only when two or more elements of speech are joined into one form: a simple word, like *John*, contains no distinctive feature of stress; to hear a distinctive feature of stress we must take a phrase or a compound word or, at least, a word containing two or more parts, such as *contest*. The pitch phonemes, on the other hand, occur in every utterance, appearing even when a single word is uttered, as in *John! John? John*. On the other hand, the pitch phonemes in English are not in principle attached to any particular words or phrases, but vary, with differences of meaning, in otherwise identical forms.

Many languages differ from English in using secondary phonemes of pitch as we use those of stress, in words and phrases that consist of more than one element. In Swedish and Norwegian, a word of two syllables, for instance, has an ordinary high stress on one of them, quite as it would in English, but, in addition to this, the stressed syllables are distinguished by two different schemes of pitch. The stress may be accompanied by a rising pitch, giving much the same acoustic impression as an English high stress, as in Norwegian ['bøner] 'peasants' or ['aksel] 'shoulder,' or, with a distinctive difference, it may be accompanied by a falling pitch, as in [˝bøner] 'beans' or [˝aksel] 'axle.' This distinctive word-pitch is all the more remarkable because in all other respects Swedish and Norwegian closely resemble English in their use of secondary phonemes of pitch and stress.

The Japanese language is said to distinguish two relative pitches, normal and higher; thus, [hana] 'nose' has normal pitch on both syllables, ['hana] 'beginning' has higher pitch on the first syllable, and [ha'na] 'flower' on the second; there seem to be no secondary phonemes of word-stress.

In still other languages features of pitch are used as primary phonemes. North Chinese distinguishes four of these, which we may symbolize by numbers:

[^{1}] high level: [ma^1] 'mother'
[^{2}] high rising: [m̩a^2] 'hemp'
[^{3}] low rising: [ma^3] 'horse'
[^{4}] low falling: [ma^4] 'scold.'

Cantonese is said to have six such tones. Primary phonemes of pitch, in fact, appear in very many languages, either in a few simple

MODIFICATIONS

types, as in Lithuanian, Serbian, and ancient Greek, or in what seems to us a bewildering variety, as in some African languages.

It is worth noticing that we have in American English a non-distinctive variation of pitch on our stressed vowels: before an unvoiced sound, as in *map* or *mat*, the pitch-scheme is simple, but before a voiced sound, as in *mad* or *man*, we have ordinarily, and under loud stress quite clearly, a rising-falling pitch.

7. 8. Once we have obtained some notion of how a phoneme is formed, we may observe various *modifications* in the way it is produced. The English phonemes [k, g], for instance, are made by closure of the back of the tongue against the velum: if we observe carefully, we find that the closure is made farther forward when the next phoneme is a front vowel, as in *kin* [kin], *keen* [kijn], *give* [giv], *gear* [giə], and farther backward before a back vowel, as in *cook* [kuk], *coop* [kuwp], *good* [gud], *goose* [guws], in contrast with what we may call the normal position, as in *car* [kɑ:], *cry* [kraj], *guard* [gɑ:d], *gray* [grej]. The English phoneme [h] is formed with the oral position of the following vowel. These variants are not distinctive, since they depend entirely upon the following phoneme. In languages where differences of this sort are distinctive, we have really no right to call them "modifications," for in these languages they are essential features of the phoneme. We might just as well use the term "modification" of the action or inaction of the voice during the production of a noise-sound, or of the presence or absence of nasalization, or of the rounding or retraction of the lips during the production of a vowel. Nevertheless, it is convenient to view in this way some less familiar features which are phonemic in certain languages.

The most important of these is *palatalization:* during the production of a consonant the tongue and lips take up, so far as is compatible with the main features of the phoneme, the position of a front vowel, such as [i] or [e]. Thus, we may say that in English [k] and [g] are subject to a non-distinctive palatalization before a front vowel. Palatalization occurs as a distinctive feature notably in some of the Slavic languages. In Russian, for instance, most consonant phonemes occur in pairs, with the distinctive difference of *plain* versus *palatalized*. For the transcription of the latter, various devices have been used, such as a dot, curve, or caret-sign over the symbol, or an exponent *i* or an accent-mark after it, or the use of italic letters. We shall adopt the last-named device, as the most convenient for printing. In a Russian word like [pat͡] 'five' the corners of the mouth are retracted and the tongue is raised into front-vowel position during the formation of both consonants. In the case of the [t] this means, of course, that while the tip and edge of the tongue are making closure against the backs of the upper teeth, the blade of the tongue is raised toward the palate; similarly in words like ['dadа] 'uncle' or ['nana] 'nurse.' The distinctive character of the difference appears in cases like [bit] 'way of being,' [bit] 'to be,' [bit] 'to beat.'

Some languages distinguish *velarized* consonants, in which the tongue is retracted as for a back vowel. If the lips are rounded during the production of a consonant, it is said to be *labialized*. These two modifications appear together in *labiovelarized* consonants.

7. 9. The manner in which the vocal organs pass from inactivity to the formation of a phoneme, or from the formation of one phoneme to that of the next, or from the formation of a phoneme to inactivity, will often show varieties which we label as *transitions*. This term is fair enough when the differences are not distinctive, but when they are distinctive, we have really no right to describe some of the essential features of the phonemes as basic and others as transitional.

In passing from silence to a voiced stop, as in *bay, day, gay,* we begin the voicing gradually, and in passing from these sounds to silence, as in *ebb, add, egg,* we gradually lessen the voicing. This contrasts with the French manner, where the stops in these positions are fully voiced, from the very beginning to the very end. In passing from silence to a stressed vowel, we usually make a gradual onset of the voice, while the North German first closes the glottis and then suddenly begins full voicing, so as to produce a (non-distinctive) glottal stop. Occasionally, as a non-distinctive variant, we start in the German style and the German in ours. In French and in sub-standard southern English a third variety of onset is non-distinctive, in which the glottis passes through the [h]-position. In standard English and in German this variety is distinctive, as in English *heart* [hɑ:t] versus *art* [ɑ:t]. In passing from a vowel to silence, the languages so far named use a gentle off-glide, but others pass through the [h]-position or end sharply with a glottal stop, and in still others these differences are phonemic. In passing from an unvoiced stop to a voiced sound,

MODIFICATIONS

especially a vowel, one may begin the voicing at the very moment of explosion, or the voicing may lag for an instant; in either case it may begin gently or with a glottal stop; these differences are phonemic in some languages, and were discussed in § 6.6. Before or after palatalized consonants there may be a *glide* resembling a front vowel; velarized consonants, similarly, may be accompanied by a back-vowel glide.

In successions of consonants the chief transitional feature seems to be the difference between *close* and *open* transition. In English we use close transition. When we pass from one stop to another, we form the second closure before opening the first: in a word like *actor* ['ɛktə], for instance, the tip of the tongue touches the gums for the [t] before the back of the tongue is removed from the velum to release the [k]. French uses open transition: in a word like *acteur* [aktœːr] 'actor,' the [k] is opened before the tongue-tip touches the teeth for the [t]. Similarly, combinations of stop plus spirant in English have close transition, as in *Betsy, cupful, it shall*: before the stop is opened, the organs are already placed, as far as possible, into the position of the following spirant, so that the explosion of the stop is incomplete. This contrasts with the open transition of French, where the stop is fully exploded before the spirant begins, as in *cette scène* [sɛt sɛːn] 'this scene,' *étappe facile* [etap fasil] 'easy stage,' *cette chaise* [sɛt ʃɛːz] 'this chair.' The same difference appears in so-called *double* consonants, combinations in which the same consonant phoneme appears twice in succession. In English, forms like *grab-bag* ['grɛb ˌbɛg], *hot time* ['hɔt 'tajm], *pen-knife* ['pen ˌnajf] show only one closure for the groups [bb, tt, nn]; this closure merely lasts longer than the closure of a single consonant. The double consonant is marked also by the difference of stress between the implosion (in our examples, weak) and the explosion (in our examples, strong). In French, similar groups, as in *cette table* [sɛt tabl] 'this table,' normally show two openings, with an implosion and an explosion for each of the two consonant units.

If both types of transition occur in a language, the difference may be utilized as a phonemic distinction. Thus, Polish has mostly open transition, like that of French, as in *trzy* [tʃi] 'three,' but the combination of [t] and [ʃ] occurs also with close transition, as a separate phoneme, which we may designate by [tʃ], as in *czy* [tʃi] 'whether.' There is also, again as a separate phoneme, a palatalized variety of this, [tʃ], as in *ci* [tʃi] 'to thee.'

E.

This last example shows us *compound phonemes* — that is, sounds resembling a succession of two or more phonemes of the same language, but in some way distinguished from such a succession, and utilized as separate phonemes. Many compound phonemes consist, like those in our example, of a stop plus a spirant or other open consonant; phonemes of this sort are called *affricates*. In English, where all consonant groups have close transition, this could not be used as a phonemic feature. Nevertheless, English has two affricate phonemes, [tʃ] as in *church* [tʃəːtʃ], and [dʒ] as in *judge* [dʒʌdʒ]. These affricates are always palatalized, and it is this feature which distinguishes them from combinations of [t] plus [ʃ], as in *beet-sugar* [ˈbijt ˌʃugə], *it shall* [it ˈʃɛl] and of [d] plus [ʒ], as in *did Jeanne* [did ˈʒɑːn].

7. 10. The treatment of successions of vowels and predominantly musical sounds shows great variety, and many types of transition are distinctive in one or another language.

In any succession of sounds, some strike the ear more forcibly than others: differences of *sonority* play a great part in the transition effects of vowels and vowel-like sounds. Thus, other things (especially, the stress) being equal, a low vowel, such as [a], is more sonorous than a high vowel, such as [i]; any vowel is more sonorous than a consonant; a nasal, trill, or lateral more than a stop or spirant; a sibilant [s, z], with its concentration of the breath-stream into a narrow channel, more than another spirant; a spirant more than a stop; a voiced sound more than an unvoiced. In any succession of phonemes there will thus be an up-and-down of sonority. In a series like [tatatata], the [a]'s will be more sonorous than the [t]'s. In the following example four degrees of sonority are distinguished by means of numbers:

Jack caught a red bird
[dʒɛk kɔːt ə red bəɪd]
314   414   1 213 313.

Evidently some of the phonemes are more sonorous than the phonemes (or the silence) which immediately precede or follow. This is true of the phonemes marked 1 in our example, and is true, for instance, of the [e] in *egg* [eg] and of the [ɔː] in *saw* [sɔː]. Any phoneme which is louder than the phoneme (or the silence) which precedes, and at the same time louder than the phoneme (or the silence) which follows, is a *crest of sonority* or a *syllabic*; the other phonemes are *non-syllabic*. Thus the [e] in *red* and the [əː] in

MODIFICATIONS

bird are syllabics, but the [r] in *red* and the [d] in *red* and *bird* are non-syllabics. An utterance is said to have as many *syllables* (or *natural syllables*) as it has syllabics. The ups and downs of *syllabication* play an important part in the phonetic structure of all languages.

In every language, only certain ones of the phonemes ever occur as syllabics, but in principle any sound may be more sonorous than its surroundings. The interjections *pst!* [pst!] and *sh!* [ʃ!] with which we demand silence, differ from ordinary English words in using [s] and [ʃ] as syllabics. Actually, most of the phonemes in any language are used only as non-syllabics, as, in English, [p, t, k]; we call these *consonants*. Other phonemes, fewer in number, occur only as syllabics, as, in English, [e, ʌ, a]; we call these *vowels*. In most languages there is a third, intermediate group of *sonants*, phonemes which occur in both syllabic and non-syllabic positions; thus, in American English, of the Central-Western type, [r] is syllabic in *bird* [brd], but non-syllabic in *red* [red].

Whether a sonant in any word is syllabic or non-syllabic, is determined in different ways in different languages. If the syllabic or non-syllabic character of a sonant depends entirely upon the surrounding phonemes (as in *bird* versus *red*), then the difference is not distinctive, and, so far as transcription is concerned, we do not need more than one symbol. In many cases, however, the syllabic or non-syllabic character of the sonant is determined arbitrarily, and constitutes a phonemic difference. Thus, in *stirring* ['stɹ̩iŋ] the [r] is syllabic, but in *string* [striŋ] it is non-syllabic; in the second syllable of *pattern* ['pɛtr̩n] the [r] is syllabic and the [n] is non-syllabic, but in the second syllable of *patron* ['pejtrn̩] the [r] is non-syllabic and the [n] is syllabic. In such cases we need separate symbols for the two phonemes. Unfortunately, our habits of transcription in this regard are neither uniform nor consistent. In a few cases we use different symbols: [i, u, y] are generally used for syllabic values, and [j, w, ɥ], respectively, for the corresponding non-syllabics; many transcribers, however, use the former symbols also for certain non-syllabic occurrences. Another device is to place a little curve above or below symbols like [i, u, y, e, o, a] to indicate non-syllabic function. On the other hand, the symbols [r, l, m, n] usually have a dot, circle, or vertical line placed under them to denote syllabic function.

When the syllabic or non-syllabic function of a sonant is determined by the surrounding phonemes (or silence), the distribution is *natural*. Thus, in standard German, the phonemes [i, u] are non-syllabic when they precede or follow a vowel, and in all other positions they are syllabic. Non-syllabic [u] occurs only after [a], as in *Haus* [haws] 'house'; non-syllabic [i] occurs after [a], as in *Ei* [aj] 'egg,' after [o] (or [ø]), as in *neu* [noj, nøj] 'new,' and before vowels and [u], as in *ja* [jaː] 'yes,' *jung* [juŋ] 'young.' The variants after a vowel are decidedly lowered, and the non-syllabic [i] before syllabics is spoken with close contact, so as to give a decided friction-sound, but these differences are not distinctive; traditionally, transcribers use the symbols [i, u] for the former type, but [j] for the latter.

In many instances the syllabic or non-syllabic value of a sonant is determined in other ways than by natural distribution. Some languages use a slight increase of stress to make a sonant syllabic in cases where natural sonority does not suffice. Thus, in some English pronunciations, forms like *bottling, brittler, buttoning* are spoken with three syllables: a slight increase of stress on the [l] or [n] produces a moment of greater prominence. We transcribe this as *bottling* [ˈbɔtl̩iŋ], *brittler* [ˈbritlə], *buttoning* [ˈbʌtn̩iŋ]. Here the *syllabic-stress* acts as a secondary phoneme; it is symbolized by the mark [ˌ]. In Central-Western American English this syllabic-stress plays an important part; it produces contrasts such as *stirring* [ˈstr̩iŋ] versus *string* [striŋ], *mackerel* [ˈmɛkr̩l] versus *minstrel* [ˈminstr̩l], *battery* [ˈbɛtrij] versus *pantry* [ˈpɛntrij], *apron* [ˈejpr̩n] versus *pattern* [ˈpɛtr̩n]; and it makes possible such forms as *bearer* [ˈbejr̩r̩], *error* [ˈɛr̩r̩], *stirrer* [ˈstr̩r̩]. In these forms of English, then, the syllabic-stress is a distinctive feature, a secondary phoneme.

In British and some varieties of American English we have, further, combinations of vowels with [ə], in which the prior member is syllabic, thanks to greater stress: [iə] in *fear* [fiə], [uə] in *sure* [ʃuə], [ɛə] in *fair, fare* [fɛə], [ɔə] in *coarse, course* [kɔəs]. There is no need of a special sign for this non-syllabic use of the [r-əː] phoneme, since the preceding vowel sign indicates its character. The prior members differ markedly from the independent forms of the vowels [i, u, ɛ, ɔ]; for the same reason there is no need of separate symbols. The same holds true of the greatly modified forms of vowels and diphthongs before [r] in some varieties of American pronunciation: *fear* [fijr], *fair, fare* [fejr], *fire* [fajr], *sure*

MODIFICATIONS

[ʃuwr], *coarse, course* [kowrs], *Mary* [ˈmejrij], *merry* [ˈmerij], *marry* [ˈmɛrij], *hoarse* [howrs], *horse* [hors], *war* [wɔr], *sorry* [ˈsɑrij]. In these combinations, various types of American English show various modifications of the normal vowels and diphthongs.

By the use of syllabic-stress some languages reverse the relations of natural sonority; thus, South German dialects have the [i, u, y] syllabic and the [a] non-syllabic in forms like [liab] 'dear,' [guat] 'good,' [gryan] 'green.'

Another type of distribution is the use of *articulatory differences* to set off the syllabic and non-syllabic functions of the sonants. Usually this consists in forming the non-syllabic variety with more closure than the syllabic variety. In English, the sonants [i] and [u] occur as non-syllabics before and after vowels; symbolizing these non-syllabic occurrences by [j] and [w], we have [j] in *yes* [jes], *say* [sej], *buy* [baj], *boy* [bɔj] and [w] in *well* [wel], *go* [gow], *now* [naw]. In these examples the non-syllabic function of [j, w] is sufficiently determined by natural sonority, since a more open vowel precedes or follows. Therefore the actual variations in the manner of forming the sounds are here non-distinctive: the [j, w] after vowels, especially in the types [aj, ɔj, aw] are very open, and the [a] also is quite different from an ordinary [a]; before a vowel, as in *yes, well*, the [j] has a higher and more fronted tongue-position than a syllabic [i], and the [w] has a higher tongue-position than a syllabic [u] and is formed with a slight contraction of the lips. Now, these latter differences are utilized, in English, as phonemic differences: even where the function is not determined by natural sonority, we distinguish the closer non-syllabic [j, w] as separate phonemes, from the more open syllabic [i, u]. Thus, we distinguish between [uw] in *ooze* [uwz] and [wu] in *wood* [wud], and between [ij] in *ease* [ijz] and a rare [ji], as in slang *yip* [jip] 'to squeal,' and we have even groups like [jij, wuw], as in *yeast* [jijst], *woo* [wuw]. When two different members of the set, [i, u, r] come together in a stressed syllable, the first is non-syllabic: *you* [juw], *yearn* [jəːn], *win* [win], *work* [wəːk], *rid* [rid], *room* [rum]. This is made possible by our producing [j] and [w] with more tense articulation before a syllabic sonant or vowel than before a non-syllabic sound (*bit*) or in final position (*say*). A non-syllabic sonant which, thanks to some modification, is phonemically distinct from the corresponding syllabic sonant is called a *semi-vowel*.

In the same way, French produces its high vowels [i, u, y] with greater closure and tensity when they are non-syllabic, as in *hier* [jɛːr] 'yesterday,' *oie* [wa] 'goose,' *ail* [aːj] 'garlic,' *huile* [ɥil] 'oil,' and treats these types as separate semivowel phonemes, distinguishing, for instance, between *oui* [wi] 'yes' and *houille* [uːj] 'anthracite,' and employing the sequence [ij], as in *fille* [fiːj] 'daughter.'

7. 11. Vowels and sonants combine into compound phonemes, which are known as *diphthongs*, or, if there are three components, as *triphthongs*. Whether a succession of phonemes is to be viewed as a compound phoneme, depends entirely upon the phonetic structure of the language. In English, successions like [je] in *yes* or [we] in *well* are treated as two phonemes, like any sequence of consonant plus vowel, but combinations of vowel plus semivowel are treated as compound phonemes. We have seven such combinations, as well as one triphthong of semivowel-vowel-semivowel:

see	[sij]	*seeing*	['sijiŋ]
say	[sej]	*saying*	['sejiŋ]
buy	[baj]	*buying*	['bajiŋ]
boy	[bɔj]	*boyish*	['bɔjiʃ]
do	[duw]	*doing*	['duwiŋ]
go	[gow]	*going*	['gowiŋ]
bow	[baw]	*bowing*	['bawiŋ]
hew	[hjuw]	*hewing*	['hjuwiŋ]

We shall see in the next chapter that in the phonetic structure of our speech-forms, these groups play the same part as simple vowel phonemes. The peculiar non-distinctive modifications of the components, especially of [a, j, w], which we noticed above, often appear in diphthongs, but this is of secondary importance; the essential feature is the peculiar structural treatment. Another peculiarity is the tense character of [ij] and [uw]: the muscles of the tongue and lips are more strongly contracted than in the simple vowels [i, u]. Many phoneticians class these types as tense long vowels, transcribing them as [iː] and [uː].

A further set of four diphthongs is furnished by the groups of vowel plus non-syllabic [ə]:

fear	[fiə]	*sure*	[ʃuə]
fair	[fɛə]	*shore*	[ʃɔə]

MODIFICATIONS

In some pronunciations these modified varieties differ from any simple vowel, witness Central-Western American

Mary ['mejrij]   *wore* [wowr], *hoarse* [howrs]
merry ['merij]   *horse* [hors]
marry ['mɛrij]   *war* [wɔr].

Many types of pronunciation, however, lack some or all of these differences; in these types either some of the diphthongs or some of the simple vowels do not occur before [r].

Diphthongs occur also in languages that do not treat syllabic and non-syllabic vowels as separate phonemes. In German the combinations [aj] as in *Eis* [ajs] 'ice,' [oj] as in *neu* [noj] 'new,' and [aw], as in *Haus* [haws] 'house,' are treated, structurally, as unit phonemes. As in English, the constituents differ greatly from their ordinary form: the non-syllabics have mid-vowel quality rather than high, and the [oj], especially, exists in several varieties, resembling, in some pronunciations, rather a combination of rounded front vowels, say [øɥ].

Diphthongs like the English and German, where the syllabic part precedes, are called *falling* diphthongs, in contrast with *rising* diphthongs, in which the non-syllabic part precedes. Thus, in French, combinations like [jɛ], as in *fier* [fjɛːr] 'proud,' and [wa], as in *moi* [mwa] 'I,' are treated structurally as unit phonemes; in Italian, the combinations [jɛ, wɔ] are treated as diphthongs; the same is true of [je, we] in Spanish.

Some languages have compound phonemes of syllabic vowels and non-syllabic consonants. In Lithuanian the phonemes [l, r, m, n] are never syllabic, but combinations like [al, ar, am, an] are treated structurally and accentually as diphthongs, quite on a par with [aj] or [aw].

7. 12. Since syllabication is a matter of the relative loudness of phonemes, it can be re-enforced or opposed by adjustments of stress. The re-enforcing habit prevails probably in most languages. In French, where stress is not distinctive, every syllable is re-enforced by a slight increase of stress on its syllabic; if there is only one non-syllabic before the syllabic, the rise begins on this non-syllabic; if there are two, different groups are treated differently: *pertinacité* [pɛr-ti-na-si-te] 'pertinacity,' *patronnesse* [pa-trɔ-nɛs] 'patroness.' This distribution of minute rises and falls of stress is non-distinctive, since it is determined entirely by the character of the primary phonemes. It gives the language, to our ears, a rapid, pattering or drumming sound. The same habit prevails also in many stress-using languages, such as Italian, Spanish, Polish, Bohemian, and even in Russian, which not only has distinctive stress, but also weakens the unstressed vowels. Thus, in Italian *pertinacia* [per-ti-ˈna-tʃa] 'stubbornness' or *patronessa* [pa-tro-ˈnes-sa] 'patroness,' the syllables are divided by ups and downs of stress, which are well-marked in the accented syllables, and slight in the others.

English and the other Germanic languages do not mark off the unstressed syllables by ups and downs of stress. In a word like *dimity* [ˈdimiti] or *patroness* [ˈpejtrənis], the stress merely drops off after its high point on the first syllable. Evidently there are three syllables, because there are three crests of natural sonority, but it would be impossible to say where one syllable ends and the next begins. In forms like *pertinacity* [ˌpɔːtiˈnɛsiti] or *procrastination* [prəˌkrɛstiˈnejʃn], the beginnings of the stressed syllables are plainly marked by the onset of stress, but no other syllable-boundaries are in any way marked off.

The distribution of stress may create crests of sonority which are independent of the natural sonority of the phonemes. We have seen that in English the phonemes [l, n] may be louder than the surrounding phonemes, and therefore syllabic, thanks to a slight increase of stress.

The distribution of stress may even overcome relations of natural sonority. In a combination like [dzd], the [z] is more sonorous than the [d]'s, and in [kst] the [s] is more sonorous than the stops, but in English our single high stress on forms like *adzed* [ɛdzd], *text* [tekst], *step* [step] is so loud that it drowns out these small differences of sonority. Some stress-using languages in this way drown out even the sonority of predominantly musical sounds: thus, Russian speaks the following, thanks to stress, as one-syllable words: [lba] 'of the forehead,' [rta] 'of the mouth'; Polish, similarly *trwa* [trva] 'it lasts,' *msza* [mʃa] 'mass.'

CHAPTER 8

PHONETIC STRUCTURE

8. 1. Descriptions of speech-sounds like those in the last two chapters, are due merely to chance observation. These descriptions are made in terms of a speaker's movements: more refined physiological observation may show that some of them are wrong. What is more serious, the differences and varieties that are observed, such as, say, the difference between French and English unvoiced stops [p, t, k], are not selected by any fixed principles (such as acoustic phonetics may some day give us), but owe their currency to the chance that some observer with a good ear had heard both of the languages concerned. Just as observation of South German dialects or of certain American Indian languages adds to the varieties of unvoiced stops that could be gathered from standard English and standard French, so the study of almost any new dialect will increase the repertoire of differences which a phonetician can hear. The extent of observation is haphazard, it's accuracy doubtful, and the terms in which it is reported are vague. Practical phonetics is a skill, for the student of languages often a very useful skill, but it has little scientific value.

For this reason it is beyond our power to analyze the general acoustic effect of a language. We can explain certain superficial effects: the "pattering" run of Italian (to English ears) is due to the syllable-division; the "guttural" sound of Dutch (to our sense), to the use of a uvular trill (§ 6.7) and of velar spirants (§ 6.8). In general, however, such observations of the "basis of articulation" are bound to be vague. English (in contrast, say, with French or German) retracts the jaw; the Central and Western type of American English adds a tendency to raise the tip of the tongue. German and French (in contrast with English) advance the jaw and use the muscles more vigorously — German in large, sweeping movements, French in smaller and more precise ones, especially in the front of the mouth. Danish draws the muscles in toward the median line. Such observations are often helpful toward understanding or imitating a pronunciation, but they are hazy and inaccurate. We must wait for laboratory phonetics to give us precise and trustworthy statements.

The important thing about language, however, is not the way it sounds. The speaker's movement, the disturbance in the air, and the hearer's ear-drum vibrations (the B of § 2.2) are, in themselves, of very little moment. The important thing about language is its service in connecting the speaker's stimulus (A in § 2.2) with the hearer's response (C in § 2.2). This connection depends, as we have seen (§ 5.4), upon only a relatively few features of the acoustic form, upon the features which we call phonemes. For the working of language, all that is necessary is that each phoneme be unmistakably different from all the others. Except for this differentiation, its range of variety and its acoustic character are irrelevant. Any language can be replaced, for all its essential values, by any system of sharply distinct signals, provided that one signal is made to replace each phoneme of the language. Such a replacement is made in a correct phonetic transcription — one which satisfies the demands of accuracy and relevancy by using one and only one symbol for each phoneme. Imperfectly and yet sufficiently well for practical purposes, such a replacement is made in traditional alphabetic writing. The importance of a phoneme, then, lies not in the actual configuration of its sound-waves, but merely in the difference between this configuration and the configurations of all the other phonemes of the same language.

For this reason even a perfected knowledge of acoustics will not, by itself, give us the phonetic structure of a language. We shall always have to know which of the gross acoustic features are, by virtue of meanings, "the same," and which "different" for the speakers. The only guide to this is the speaker's situation and the hearer's response. Any description which fails to discriminate the distinctive features from the non-distinctive, can tell us little or nothing about the structure of a language. In this respect, a mechanical record has at least the virtue of not distorting the acoustic facts. The "exact" freehand records of zealous phonetic experts are likely to insist upon irrelevant acoustic differences that owe their notation merely to the circumstance that the observer has learned to respond to them. On this basis, it is possible to find the same set of "sounds" in languages of entirely different phonemic structure. For instance, both languages might show seven similar vowel "sounds," but in Language B these might be seven

PHONETIC STRUCTURE 129

different phonemes, while in Language A [ɛ] and [ɔ] might be non-distinctive variants of [a], and [e, o] respectively of [i, u]. Both languages might seem to show two durations of vowels, but these might be phonemic in Language A (as in German), while in Language B they might be non-distinctive variants. Both might show plain and aspirated unvoiced stops, as different phonemes in Language A and as mere non-distinctive variants in Language B. Both might have a series of voiced spirants, but these might be distinctive in Language B, while in Language A they existed merely as variants of stops between vowels.

Only the phonemes of a language are relevant to its structure — that is, to the work it does. A description of the non-distinctive features might be of great interest, but for this it would have to be more complete and more copious than any that have so far been made.

8. 2. A list or table of the phonemes of a language should therefore ignore all non-distinctive features. Such lists or tables are usually made on the basis of practical-phonetic classifications, thus:

STANDARD ENGLISH

stops, unvoiced	p		t			k		
voiced	b		d			g		
affricate, unvoiced				tʃ				
voiced				dʒ				
spirants, unvoiced		f θ	s	ʃ			h	
voiced		v ð	z	ʒ				
nasals	m		n			ŋ		
lateral			l					
trill			r					
semivowels			j	w				
vowels, high			i	u				
higher mid			e ə:	ɔː				
lower mid			ɛ	o				
low			ʌ	ɑː				

secondary phonemes:
    stress   " ' ˌ
    syllabic-stress
    pitch   ¿ ? ! ,

Tables like these, even when they exclude non-distinctive features, are nevertheless irrelevant to the structure of the language, because they group the phonemes according to the linguist's notion of their physiologic character, and not according to the parts which the several phonemes play in the working of the language. Our table does not show, for instance, that [l, n] sometimes serve as syllabics in unstressed syllables (§ 7.10). It does not show which vowels are the syllabic correspondents of the semivowels [j] and [w], or the peculiarity of articulation, thanks to which these semivowels figure as separate phonemes, in contrast with the simpler distribution of [ə:] versus [r]. It does not show which vowels and semivowels combine into compound phonemes. To show these structural facts, we should need a supplementary table something like this:

I. *Primary phonemes:*
  A. *Consonants*, always or sometimes non-syllabic:
    1. *Mutes*, always non-syllabic: [p t k b d g tʃ dʒ f θ s ʃ h v ð z ʒ m ŋ]
    2. *Sonants*, sometimes syllabic:
      a. *Consonantoids*, syllabicity determined partly by syllabic-stress; not diphthong-forming: [n l]
      b. *Vocaloids*, diphthong-forming:
        (1) *Semi-consonant*, syllabicity determined entirely by surroundings: [r–ə:]
        (2) *Semivowels*, syllabicity determined also by manner of articulation:
          (a) *Non-syllabic:* [j w]
          (b) *Syllabic:* [i u]
  B. *Vowels*, always syllabic:
    1. *Diphthongs and triphthong*, compound phonemes: [ij uw ej ow aj aw ɔj juw iə uə ɛə ɔə eɔə]
    2. *Simple vowels:* [e ɛ ʌ ɔ ɔ: ɑ:]
II. *Secondary phonemes:*
  A. *Syllabic-stress*, applied to semi-consonants: [ˌ]
  B. *Form-stress*, applied to meaningful forms: [" ' ˌ]
  C. *Pitch*, relating to end of utterance:
    1. *Medial:* [,]
    2. *Final:* [. ¿ ? !]

8. 3. The parts which our phonemes play in the structure of our language are in reality much more diverse than this; in fact, we can easily show that no two of them play exactly the same part.

PHONETIC STRUCTURE

Since every utterance contains, by definition, at least one syllabic phoneme, the simplest way to describe the phonetic structure of a language is to state which non-syllabic phonemes or groups of non-syllabic phonemes (*clusters*) appear in the three possible positions: *initial*, before the first syllabic of an utterance; *final*, after the last syllabic of an utterance; and *medial*, between syllabics.

In this respect the diphthongs and triphthong play in English the same part as do the simple vowels; it is precisely this fact that compels us to class them as compound phonemes and not as mere successions of phonemes.

For convenience, I shall place a number before each phoneme or group of phonemes that shows any peculiarity in its structural behavior.

Taking first the initial non-syllabics, we find at the outset that two phonemes never begin an utterance; they are (1) [ŋ, ʒ]. We ignore foreign forms, such as the French name *Jeanne* [ʒan].

Further, six of the non-syllabics that occur in initial position never appear as members of an initial cluster: (2) [v, ð, z, tʃ, dʒ, j].

The initial clusters all begin with one of the following non-syllabics: (3) [p, t, k, b, d, g, f, θ, s, ʃ, h]. Here we find an accord between the structural grouping and our physiologic description, since our structural group (3) embraces exactly the physiologic groups of stops and unvoiced spirants.

If the first consonant of the cluster is (4) [s], it may be followed by one of the set (5) [p, t, k, f, m, n], as in *spin, stay, sky, sphere, small, snail*.

All the initials of group (3) and the combinations of (4) [s] with (6) [p, t, k] may be followed by one of the set (7) [w, r, l], with the following restrictions:

(8) [w] never comes after (9) [p, b, f, ʃ], and never after the combination of (4) [s] with (10) [t]. The actual clusters, then, are illustrated by the words *twin, quick, dwell, Gwynne, thwart, swim, when* [hwen], *squall*.

(11) [r] never comes after (12) [s, h]. The clusters, therefore, are those which begin the words *pray, tray, crow, bray, dray, gray, fray, three, shrink, spray, stray, scratch*.

(13) [l] never comes after (14) [t, d, θ, ʃ, h], and never after the combination of (4) [s] with (15) [k]. The clusters, accordingly, are those which appear in *play, clay, blue, glue, flew, slew, split*.

8. 4. We come now to the final clusters. These are subject to the general rule that the same phoneme never occurs in two adjoining positions: there are no such final groups as [ss] or [tt]. This rule holds good also for initial clusters and is implied by our description of them, but it does not hold good, as we shall see, for medial clusters.

We have undertaken to view combinations of vowel plus [j] or [w] as compound phonemes (diphthongs) and accordingly cannot count the semivowels in these combinations as final non-syllabics or parts of clusters. If, accordingly, we eliminate these cases (e.g. *say* [sej], *go* [gow]), we find that (16) [h, j, w] do not occur as final non-syllabics or members of final clusters. All the remaining non-syllabics occur in both of these functions.

English final clusters consist of two, three, or four non-syllabics. One can describe the combinations most simply by saying that each cluster consists of a *main final* consonant, which may be preceded by a *pre-final*, which in turn may be preceded by a *second pre-final;* further, the main final may be followed by a *post-final*. This gives us six possibilities:

	WITHOUT POST-FINAL	WITH POST-FINAL
main final alone:	*bet* [-t]	*bets* [-ts]
pre-final plus main final:	*test* [-st]	*tests* [-sts]
second pre-final plus pre-final plus main final:	*text* [-kst]	*texts* [-ksts].

The consonants which occur as post-finals are (17) [t, d, s, z]. In a form like *test* or *text* we call the [-t] a main final, because there exist forms like *tests*, *texts*, in which a further consonant (a post-final) is added, but in a form like *wished* [wiʃt] we call the [-t] a post-final because the cluster [-ʃt] is not paralleled by any cluster with the addition of a further consonant: we have no such final cluster as, say, [-ʃts].

The occurrence of the post-finals is limited by three important restrictions. The post-finals (18) [t, s] are the only ones that occur after the main finals (19) [p, t, k, tʃ, f, θ, s, ʃ]; these same post-finals never occur after any other sounds; and the post-finals (20) [t, d] are the only ones that occur after the main finals (21) [tʃ, dʒ, s, z, ʃ, ʒ]. It is worth noticing that set (19) agrees, except for the absence of [h], with the physiological class of unvoiced sounds,

PHONETIC STRUCTURE

and that set (21) embraces the physiological classes of affricates and sibilants. These restrictions group the main finals into six classes:

Those in (19) but not in (21) may be followed by [t, s], as [p] in *help, helped, helps;*

those in neither (19) nor (21) may be followed by [d, z], as [b] in *grab, grabbed, grabs;*

those in (19) and (21) may be followed only by [t], as [tʃ] in *reach, reached;*

those in (21) but not in (19) may be followed only by [d], as [dʒ] in *urge, urged;*

[t] in (19) but not in (21), owing to the rule of no doubling, may be followed only by [s], as in *wait, waits;*

[d] in neither (19) nor (21), owing to the same rule, may be followed only by [z], as in *fold, folds.*

We turn now to the pre-finals. The main consonants (22) [g, ð, ʒ, ŋ, r] are never accompanied by a pre-final, and the consonants (23) [b, g, tʃ, dʒ, v, ʃ, r] never occur as pre-finals. The combinations that remain are subject to the following further restrictions:

The pre-finals (24) [l, r] do not occur before the main final (25) [z]. Their combinations, accordingly, are those which appear in the following examples: *harp, barb, heart, hard, hark, march, barge, scarf, carve, hearth, farce, harsh, arm, barn, help, bulb, belt, held, milk, filch, bilge, pelf, delve, wealth, else, Welsh, elm, kiln.*

The pre-final (25) [n] occurs only before the main finals (27) [t, d, tʃ, dʒ, θ, s, z], as in *ant, sand, pinch, range, month, once, bronze.*

The pre-final (28) [m] occurs only before the main finals (29) [p, t, f, θ], as in *camp, dreamt, nymph;* the combination with (30) [θ] occurs with the second pre-final (11) [r]: *warmth.*

The pre-final (31) [ŋ] occurs only before (32) [k; θ], as in *link, length.*

The pre-final (4) [s] occurs only before (6) [p, t, k], as in *wasp, test, ask.* Before (10) [t] it may be preceded by the second pre-final (15) [k], as in *text.*

The pre-finals (33) [ð, z] occur only before the main final (28) [m], as in *rhythm, chasm.*

The pre-final (10) [t] occurs only before the main finals (34) [θ, s], as in *eighth* [ejtθ], *Ritz* (compare, with post-final [t] added, the slang *ritzed* [ritst] 'snubbed'). The combination with the main final (4) [s] occurs also with second pre-final (11) [r] in *quartz.*

The pre-final (35) [d] occurs only before (36) [θ, z], as in *width, adze*.

The pre-finals (37) [p, k] occur only before the main finals (18) [t, s], as in *crypt, lapse, act, tax*. Of these two, the pre-final (15) [k] before the main final (4) [s] occurs also with the second pre-final (31) [ŋ], as in *minx* (compare, with a post-final [t] added, the slang *jinxed* [dʒiŋkst] 'gave bad luck'); the other, [p], occurs with the second pre-final (28) [m]: *glimpse, tempt*.

The pre-final (38) [f] occurs only before (10) [t], as in *lift*.

The medial non-syllabics of English consist of all the combinations of final plus initial, ranging from *hiatus*, complete lack of a non-syllabic, as in *saw it* ['sɔːit], to such clusters as in *glimpsed strips* [-mpst str-], including repetitions of the same phoneme, as in *that time* [-t t-] or *ten nights* [-n n-].

8. 5. A survey of the 38 functional sets of non-syllabics will show that this classification suffices to define every non-syllabic phoneme in our language. In the same way, most or possibly all of our syllabic phonemes could be defined by the parts they play in the structure of our language. Since different types of standard English differ in the distributions of the syllabic phonemes, I shall mention only a few of the pattern features.

The syllabic semivowel [u] does not occur initially or finally; it occurs medially only before [t, k, d, s, ʃ, m, l], as in *put, took, wood, puss, push, room, pull*. Of the vowels, only [ɑː] and [ɔː] and the unstressed [ə] and [i] occur at the end of a word. In Southern British and some forms of American English the vowels and diphthongs merge with a following [r] in final position and before consonants into special types of articulation (§ 6.11): [ij-r] appears as [iə]: *fear, feared*, [uw-r] as [uə]: *cure, cured*, [ej-r] as [ɛə]: *care, cared*, [ow-r] as [ɔə] or [ɔː]: *bore, bored*, [ɑː-r] as [ɑː]: *spar, sparred*. Structurally, we may either set up these equivalences (as was done in § 8.4, where [r] was listed as a pre-final and second pre-final), or we may simply say that the syllabics [ɑː, iə, uə, ɛə, ɔə, əː] are peculiar in adding an [r] before a syllabic [*stirring, fearing, curing, caring, sparring, boring*]. In either case we observe that [iəd, ɛəd] with other than a post-final [d] are rare: *weird, laird* are structurally peculiar words; so is *cairn*, with [ɛən]. Although [i, e, ɛ, ɔ, ʌ] occur before [r], as in *spirit, merit, carry, sorry, curry*, they do not appear before the equivalent of a final or anteconsonantal [r].

PHONETIC STRUCTURE 135

The vowel [ɔː] does not occur before [g] and the vowel [ɑː] does not occur after the initial non-syllabic sonant [w]. Before pre-final [l] the only permitted diphthongs are [ij, aj, ow], and the first two occur only when [d] follows, as in *field, mild, old, colt*. Before pre-final [n] only [aj, aw] occur with any freedom, as in *pint, mount, bind, bound;* [ɔj, ej] occur when [t] follows, as in *paint, point*. The diphthongs do not occur before [ŋ].

The triphthong [juw] differs from ordinary combinations of [j] plus vowel or diphthong (*yank, year, Yale*) in that it occurs after initial consonants, as in *pew, cue, beauty, gules, few, hew, view, muse*, and after the clusters [sp, st, sk], as in *spew, stew, skew*. After dentals, especially [θ, s, z, l], some speakers use [juw] and others [uw]: *thews, sue, presume, lute;* similarly, but with a wider prevalence of the [juw] variant, after [t, d, n], as in *tune, dew, new*. The triphthong does not occur after initial [tʃ, dʒ, ʃ, ð, r] and consonant plus [l].

We shall find that the grammatical structure of a language implies groupings of the phonemes which supplement the groups definable on the basis of succession (§ 13.6).

8. 6. The structural pattern differs greatly in different languages, and leads us to recognize different types of compound phonemes. German, for instance, has, on the whole, a structural scheme much like that of English, but with some striking differences. The voiced stops and spirants [b, d, g, v, z] never occur in final position. The initial groups can be simply described only if one takes the affricate combinations [pf, ts] as compound phonemes, as in *Pfund* [pfunt] 'pound,' *zehn* [tseːn] 'ten,' *zwei* [tsvaj] 'two.' The only diphthongs are [aj, aw, oj]; the simplicity of structure in this respect, leads phoneticians to transcribe them rather by [ai, au, oi], since no ambiguity can arise. The French system differs not only as to the particular clusters, but also in more general respects. The diphthongs are rising, such as [jɛ, wa]. The greatest difference is in the use of the vowel phoneme [ə], whose occurrence is governed largely by the phonetic pattern, so that it may be said to play the part of a secondary rather than of a primary phoneme. The phoneme [ə] occurs wherever without it there would arise an unpermitted cluster of consonants. Thus, it occurs in *le chat* [lə ʃa] 'the cat,' because [lʃ] is not permitted as an initial cluster, but not in *l'homme* [l ɔm] 'the man,' where no cluster arises. It appears in *cheval* [ʃəval] 'horse,' since the cluster [ʃv] is not permitted initially, but since this cluster is permitted in medial position, one says *un cheval* [œ̃ ʃval] 'a horse.' The medial clusters are limited, for the most part to two consonants; thus, [rt] is permitted as a final cluster, as in *porte* [pɔrt] 'carries,' but if an initial consonant follows, [ə] is inserted, as in *porte bien* [pɔrtə bjɛ̃] 'carries well.' An entirely different system appears in a language like Plains Cree. The structure groups the phonemes into five sets: (1) the vowels [a, a:, e:, i, i:, u, o:]; these are the only syllabic phonemes; (2) consonants of four types: stops [p, t, k], including the affricate tʃ]; spirants [s, h]; nasals [m, n]; semivowels [j, w]. The initial possibilities are: no consonant; any one consonant; stop, spirant, or nasal plus semivowel. The medial possibilities are: any one consonant; stop, spirant, or nasal plus semivowel; spirant plus stop; spirant plus stop plus semivowel. The only final possibility is one consonant. The Fox language, with a somewhat similar patterning, permits of no final consonant: every utterance ends in a short vowel.

While English is especially rich in consonant clusters, it is easy to find others, such as initial [pf-, pfl-, pfr-, ts-, tsv-, ʃv-, kn-, gn-] in German, e.g. *Pflaume* [ˈpflawme] 'plum,' *schwer* [ʃveːr] 'heavy,' *Knie* [kniː] 'knee,' or the clusters in Russian [tku] 'I weave,' [mnu] 'I squeeze,' [ʃtʃi] 'cabbage-soup,' [lʃtʃu] 'I flatter.' Final clusters foreign to English appear, for example, in German *Herbst* [herpst] 'autumn' and Russian [borʃtʃ] 'beet-soup.'

8. 7. Once we have defined the phonemes as the smallest units which make a difference in meaning, we can usually define each individual phoneme according to the part it plays in the structural pattern of the speech-forms. We observe, especially, that the structural pattern leads us to recognize also compound phonemes, which resemble successions of other phonemes, but play the part of a simple phoneme, and that very slight acoustic differences, such as, in English, the syllabic-stress on [l, n], or the greater tensity of [j, w] compared to syllabic [i, u], may give rise to separate phonemes.

The phonemes so defined are the units of signaling; the meaningful forms of a language can be described as arrangements of primary and secondary phonemes. If we take a large body of speech, we can count it the relative frequencies of phonemes and of combinations of phonemes. This task has been neglected by linguists and very imperfectly performed by amateurs, who confuse phonemes with printed letters. Taking the total number of phonemes in the text used as 100 per cent, a recent count for English shows the following percentage frequencies for consonant phonemes:

n	7.24	ð	3.43	p	2.04	g	.74
t	7.13	z	2.97	f	1.84	j	.60
r	6.88	m	2.78	b	1.81	tʃ	.52
s	4.55	k	2.71	h	1.81	dʒ	.44
d	4.31	v	2.28	ŋ	.96	θ	.37
l	3.74	w	2.08	ʃ	.82	ʒ	.05

The figures for [r, l, m, n] include the occurrences in syllabic function; those for [j] and [w] do not include the occurrences of these phonemes as parts of diphthongs or triphthong. The count of vowel phonemes is too confused to allow of plain reading. Apparently, [e] is the most-used, with a frequency of over 8 per cent; next comes [ij], with over 6 per cent; then [ɛ], with 3.5 per cent. The figures for groups of phonemes are unusable. From this and similar counts it is evident that the phonemes of a language perform very different rôles as to frequency. Moreover, there seems to be some resemblance between languages; thus, in languages which use two types of stops, such as our [p, t, k] versus [b, d, g], the stop of the unvoiced type in each pair is more frequent than its voiced mate, — for instance, [t] more frequent than [d]. A serious study of this matter is much to be desired.

8. 8. We have seen three ways of studying the sounds of speech. Phonetics in the strict sense — that is, laboratory phonetics — gives us a purely acoustic or physiological description. It reveals only the gross acoustic features. In practice, the laboratory phonetician usually singles out for study some feature which his lay knowledge recognizes as characteristic of a phoneme. Practical phonetics is an art or skill, not a science; the practical phonetician frankly accepts his everyday recognition of phonemic units and tries to tell how the speaker produces them. The term phonology is sometimes placed in contrast with the two forms of phonetics: phonology pays no heed to the acoustic nature of the phonemes, but merely accepts them as distinct units. It defines each phoneme by its rôle in the structure of speech-forms. It is important to remember that practical phonetics and phonology presuppose a knowledge of meanings: without this knowledge we could not ascertain the phonemic features.

The description of a language, then, begins with phonology, which defines each phoneme and states what combinations occur. Any combination of phonemes that occurs in a language, is *pronounceable* in this language, and is a *phonetic form*. The combination [mnu], for instance is unpronounceable in English, but the combination [men] is pronounceable and is a phonetic form.

When the phonology of a language has been established, there remains the task of telling what meanings are attached to the several phonetic forms. This phase of the description is *semantics*. It is ordinarily divided into two parts, *grammar* and *lexicon*.

A phonetic form which has a meaning, is a *linguistic form*. Thus, any English sentence, phrase, or word is a linguistic form, and so is a meaningful syllable, such as, say, [mɛl] in *maltreat*, or [mʌn] in *Monday;* a meaningful form may even consist of a single phoneme, such as the [s] which means 'more than one' in plural-forms like *hats, caps, books*. In the following chapters we shall see how meanings are connected with linguistic forms.

CHAPTER 9

MEANING

9. 1. The study of speech-sounds without regard to meanings is an abstraction: in actual use, speech-sounds are uttered as signals. We have defined the *meaning* of a linguistic form as the situation in which the speaker utters it and the response which it calls forth in the hearer. The speaker's situation and the hearer's response are closely co-ordinated, thanks to the circumstance that every one of us learns to act indifferently as a speaker or as a hearer. In the causal sequence

speaker's situation ⇒⟶ speech ⇒⟶ hearer's response,

the speaker's situation, as the earlier term, will usually present a simpler aspect than the hearer's response; therefore we usually discuss and define meanings in terms of a speaker's stimulus.

The situations which prompt people to utter speech, include every object and happening in their universe. In order to give a scientifically accurate definition of meaning for every form of a language, we should have to have a scientifically accurate knowledge of everything in the speakers' world. The actual extent of human knowledge is very small, compared to this. We can define the meaning of a speech-form accurately when this meaning has to do with some matter of which we possess scientific knowledge. We can define the names of minerals, for example, in terms of chemistry and mineralogy, as when we say that the ordinary meaning of the English word *salt* is 'sodium chloride (NaCl),' and we can define the names of plants or animals by means of the technical terms of botany or zoölogy, but we have no precise way of defining words like *love* or *hate*, which concern situations that have not been accurately classified — and these latter are in the great majority.

Moreover, even where we have some scientific (that is, universally recognized and accurate) classification, we often find that the meanings of a language do not agree with this classification. The whale is in German called a 'fish': *Walfisch* ['val-ˌfiʃ] and the bat a 'mouse': *Fledermaus* ['fie:der-ˌmaws]. Physicists view the color-spectrum as a continuous scale of light-waves of different lengths, ranging from 40 to 72 hundred-thousandths of a millimetre, but languages mark off different parts of this scale quite arbitrarily and without precise limits, in the meanings of such color-names as *violet, blue, green, yellow, orange, red*, and the color-names of different languages do not embrace the same gradations. The kinship of persons seems a simple matter, but the terminologies of kinship that are used in various languages are extremely hard to analyze.

The statement of meanings is therefore the weak point in language-study, and will remain so until human knowledge advances very far beyond its present state. In practice, we define the meaning of a linguistic form, wherever we can, in terms of some other science. Where this is impossible, we resort to makeshift devices. One is *demonstration*. If someone did not know the meaning of the word *apple*, we could instruct him by handing him an apple or pointing at an apple, and continuing, as long as he made mistakes, to handle apples and point at them, until he used the word in the conventional way. This is essentially the process by which children learn the use of speech-forms. If a questioner understood enough of our language, we could define the word *apple* for him by *circumlocution* — that is, in the manner of our dictionaries, by a roundabout speech which fitted the same situations as does the word *apple*, saying, for instance: "The well-known, firm-fleshed, smooth-skinned, round or oblong pome fruit of the trees of the genus Malus, varying greatly in size, shape, color, and degree of acidity." Or else, if we knew enough of the questioner's language, we could answer him by *translation* — that is, by uttering a roughly equivalent form of his language; if he were a Frenchman, for instance, we could give *pomme* [pɔm] as the meaning of *apple*. This method of definition appears in our bilingual dictionaries.

9. 2. The situations which prompt us to utter any one linguistic form, are quite varied; philosophers tell us, in fact, that no two situations are ever alike. Each one of us uses the word *apple*, in the course of a few months, of many individual pieces of fruit which differ in size, shape, color, odor, taste, and so on. In a favorable case, such as that of the word *apple*, all the members of the speech-community have been trained, from childhood, to use

MEANING

the speech-form whenever the situation (in this case, the object) presents certain relatively definable characteristics. Even in cases like this, our usage is never quite uniform and most speech-forms have less clear-cut meanings. Nevertheless, it is clear that we must discriminate between *non-distinctive* features of the situation, such as the size, shape, color, and so on of any one particular apple, and the *distinctive*, or *linguistic meaning* (the *semantic* features) which are common to all the situations that call forth the utterance of the linguistic form, such as the features which are common to all the objects of which English-speaking people use the word *apple*.

Since our study ordinarily concerns only the distinctive features of form and meaning, I shall henceforth usually omit the qualification *linguistic* or *distinctive*, and speak simply of *forms* and *meanings*, ignoring the existence of non-distinctive features. A form is often said to *express* its meaning.

9. 3. Even if we had an accurate definition of the meaning that is attached to every one of the forms of a language, we should still face a difficulty of another sort. A very important part of every situation is the state of the speaker's body. This includes, of course, the predisposition of his nervous system, which results from all of his experiences, linguistic and other, up to this very moment — not to speak of hereditary and pre-natal factors. If we could keep an external situation ideally uniform, and put different speakers into it, we should still be unable to measure the equipment each speaker brought with him, and unable, therefore, to predict what speech-forms he would utter, or, for that matter, whether he would utter any speech at all.

If we had perfect definitions, we should still discover that during many utterances the speaker was not at all in the situation which we had defined. People very often utter a word like *apple* when no apple at all is present. We may call this *displaced speech*. The frequency and importance of displaced speech is obvious. We recall the infant "asking for" his doll (§ 2.5). Relayed speech embodies a very important use of language: speaker A sees some apples and mentions them to speaker B, who has not seen them; speaker B relays this news to C, C to D, D to E, and so on, and it may be that none of these persons has seen them, when finally speaker X goes and eats some. In other ways, too, we utter linguistic forms when the typical stimulus is absent. A starving beggar at the door says *I'm hungry*, and the housewife gives him food: this incident, we say, embodies the *primary* or *dictionary meaning* of the speech-form *I'm hungry*. A petulant child, at bed-time, says *I'm hungry*, and his mother, who is up to his tricks, answers by packing him off to bed. This is an example of displaced speech. It is a remarkable fact that if a foreign observer asked for the meaning of the form *I'm hungry*, both mother and child would still, in most instances, define it for him in terms of the dictionary meaning. Lying, irony, jesting, poetry, narrative fiction, and the like, are probably as old and certainly as widespread as language. As soon as we know the dictionary meaning of a form, we are fully able to use it in displaced speech; our dictionaries and handbooks of foreign languages need tell us only the dictionary meaning. The displaced uses of speech are derived in fairly uniform ways from its primary value, and require no special discussion; nevertheless, they add to our uncertainty as to the forms that a given speaker will utter (if he speaks at all) in a given situation.

9. 4. Adherents of mentalistic psychology believe that they can avoid the difficulty of defining meanings, because they believe that, prior to the utterance of a linguistic form, there occurs within the speaker a non-physical process, a *thought, concept, image, feeling, act of will,* or the like, and that the hearer, likewise, upon receiving the sound-waves, goes through an equivalent or correlated mental process. The mentalist, therefore, can define the meaning of a linguistic form as the characteristic mental event which occurs in every speaker and hearer in connection with the utterance or hearing of the linguistic form. The speaker who utters the word *apple* has had a mental image of an apple, and this word evokes a similar image in a hearer's mind. For the mentalist, language is *the expression of ideas, feelings, or volitions.*

The mechanist does not accept this solution. He believes that *mental images, feelings,* and the like are merely popular terms for various bodily movements, which, so far as they concern language, can be roughly divided into three types:

(1) large-scale processes which are much the same in different people, and, having some social importance, are represented by conventional speech-forms, such as *I'm hungry* (*angry, frightened, sorry, glad; my head aches,* and so on);

(2) obscure and highly variable small-scale muscular contractions and glandular secretions, which differ from person to person,

MEANING

and, having no immediate social importance, are not represented by conventional speech-forms;

(3) soundless movements of the vocal organs, taking the place of speech-movements, but not perceptible to other people ("thinking in words," § 2.4).

The mechanist views the processes in (1) simply as events which the speaker can observe better than anyone else; the various problems of meaning, such as that of displaced speech (the naughty child saying *I'm hungry*), exist here no less than elsewhere. The mechanist believes that the processes in (2) are private habits left over, as traces, from the vicissitudes of education and other experience; the speaker reports them as *images, feelings,* and so on, and they differ not only for every speaker, but for every occasion of speech. The speaker who says, "I had the mental image of an apple," is really saying, "I was responding to some obscure internal stimuli of a type which was associated at some time in my past with the stimuli of an apple." The sub-vocal speech in (3) seems to the mechanist merely a derivative of the habit of actual speech-utterance; when we are assured that a speaker has inaudibly performed the speech-movements of a certain utterance ("thought it in words"), we face exactly the same problem as when he has audibly uttered the same speech-form. In sum, then, the "mental processes" seem to the mechanist to be merely traditional names for bodily processes which either (1) come within the definition of meaning as speaker's situation, or (2) are so distantly correlated with speech-utterance as to be negligible factors in the speaker's situation, or (3) are mere reproductions of the speech-utterance.

Although this difference of opinion plays a decisive part in our views about the fundamentals of language, as of other human activities, and although mentalists lean heavily upon their terminology in all discussion of meaning, the dispute has really very little to do with problems of linguistic meaning. The events which the mentalist designates as mental processes and the mechanist classifies otherwise, affect in every case only one person: every one of us responds to them when they occur within him, but has no way of responding to them when they occur in anyone else. The mental processes or internal bodily processes of other people are known to each one of us only from speech-utterances and other observable actions. Since these are all we have to work with, the mentalist in practice defines meanings exactly as does the mechanist, in terms of actual situations; he defines *apple* not as "the image of the well-known, firm-fleshed, etc. . . . fruit," but, like the mechanist, omits the first three of these words, and, in fact, for all speakers except himself, merely infers that the image was present, either from the fact that the speaker used the word *apple*, or from some more definite utterance of the speaker's ("I had a mental image of an apple"). In practice, then, all linguists, both mentalists and mechanists, define meanings in terms of the speaker's situation and, whenever this seems to add anything, of the hearer's response.

9. 5. Linguistic meanings are more specific than the meanings of non-linguistic acts. A great deal of human co-operation is effected without language, by such means as gestures (for instance, pointing at something), the handling of objects (placing an object into someone's hand, dashing an object to the ground), contact (nudging, caressing), non-linguistic sounds, both non-vocal (snapping the fingers, applause) and vocal (laughing, crying), and so on. We must mention especially, in this last connection, the non-linguistic (non-distinctive) features of speech-sound, such as plaintive, angry, commanding, drawling "tones of voice"; the manner of speech, in fact, is, next to speech itself, our most effective method of signaling. Linguistic forms, however, result, for the most part, in far more accurate, specific, and delicate co-ordination than could be reached by non-linguistic means; to see this, one need only listen to a few chance speeches: *Four feet three and a half inches. — If you don't hear from me by eight o'clock, go without me. — Where's the small bottle of ammonia?* Apparent exceptions, such as elaborate systems of gesture, deaf-and-dumb language, signaling-codes, the use of writing, telegraphy, and so on, turn out, upon inspection, to be merely derivatives of language.

Since we have no way of defining most meanings and of demonstrating their constancy, we have to take the specific and stable character of language as a presupposition of linguistic study, just as we presuppose it in our everyday dealings with people. We may state this presupposition as the *fundamental assumption of linguistics* (§ 5.3), namely:

In certain communities (speech-communities) some speech-utterances are alike as to form and meaning.

This virtue of speech-forms is bought at the cost of rationality. The non-linguistic modes of communication are based directly upon our bodily make-up, or else arise directly from simple social situations, but the connection of linguistic forms with their meanings is wholly arbitrary. What we call *horse*, the German calls *Pferd* [pfe:rt], the Frenchman *cheval* [ʃəval], the Cree Indian [misatim], and so on; one set of sounds is as unreasonable as any other.

Our fundamental assumption implies that each linguistic form has a constant and specific meaning. If the forms are phonemically different, we suppose that their meanings also are different — for instance, that each one of a set of forms like *quick, fast, swift, rapid, speedy*, differs from all the others in some constant and conventional feature of meaning. We suppose, in short, that there are no actual *synonyms*. On the other hand, our assumption implies also that if the forms are semantically different (that is, different as to linguistic meaning), they are not "the same," even though they may be alike as to phonetic form. Thus, in English, the phonetic form [bɛə] occurs with three different meanings: *bear* 'to carry; to give birth to,' *bear* 'ursus,' and *bare* 'uncovered.' Similarly, [pɛə] represents two nouns (*pear* and *pair*) and a verb (*pare*), and many other examples will occur to the reader. Different linguistic forms which have the same phonetic form (and differ, therefore, only as to meaning) are known as *homonyms*. Since we cannot with certainty define meanings, we cannot always decide whether a given phonetic form in its various uses has always the same meaning or represents a set of homonyms. For instance, the English verb *bear* in *bear a burden, bear troubles, bear fruit, bear offspring*, can be viewed as a single form or as a set of two or perhaps even more homonyms. Similarly, *charge*, in *charge the cannon with grapeshot, charge the man with larceny, charge the gloves to me, charge him a stiff price*, can be viewed in several ways; *the infantry will charge the fort* seems to be different. The quality *sloth* and the animal *sloth* probably represent a pair of homonyms to some speakers and a single meaning to others. All this shows, of course, that our basic assumption is true only within limits, even though its general truth is presupposed not only in linguistic study, but by all our actual use of language.

9. 6. Although the linguist cannot define meanings, but must appeal for this to students of other sciences or to common knowledge, yet, in many cases, having obtained definitions for some forms, he can define the meanings of other forms in terms of these first ones. The mathematician, for instance, who is here acting as a linguist, cannot define such terms as *one* and *add*, but if we give him a definition of these, he can define *two* ('one added to one'), *three* ('one added to two'), and so on, without end. What we see plainly in mathematical language, where the denotations are very precise, appears also in many ordinary speech-forms. If the meanings of the English past tense and of the word *go* are defined, the linguist can define *went* as 'the past of *go*.' If the difference *male : female* is defined for the linguist, he can assure us that this is the difference between *he : she, lion : lioness, gander : goose, ram : ewe*. The linguist has this assurance in very many cases, where a language, by some recognizable phonetic or grammatical feature, groups a number of its forms into *form-classes:* in any one form-class, every form contains an element, the *class-meaning*, which is the same for all forms of this form-class. Thus, all English substantives belong to a form-class, and each English substantive, accordingly, has a meaning, which, once it is defined for us (say, as 'object'), we can attribute to every substantive form in the language. English substantives, further, are subdivided into the two classes of singular and plural; granted a definition of the meanings of these two classes, we attribute one of these meanings to every substantive.

In every language we find certain forms, *substitutes*, whose meaning consists largely or entirely of class-meanings. In English, the pronouns are the largest group of substitutes. The pronouns show us a very interesting combination of meanings. The principal features are class-meanings; thus, *somebody, someone* have the class-meanings of substantives, singulars, personals; *he* has the class-meanings of substantives, singulars, personals, males; *it* has the class-meanings of substantives, singulars, non-personals; *they* has the class-meanings of substantives and plurals. In the second place, a pronoun may contain an element of meaning which makes the pronoun represent some particular substantive form of the language. Thus, the pronouns *some* and *none* tell us that the particular substantive is one which has been recently mentioned (*Here are apples : take some*); in contrast with this, *something, somebody, someone, nothing, nobody, no one* tell nothing about the species. Thirdly, some pronouns contain an element of meaning which tells us which particular objects in a species are concerned. Thus, *he, she, it, they* imply that not only the species (say, *policeman*) has been mentioned, but also that the particular object of this species (say, *Officer Smith*, or *the one at this corner*) has been identified. This feature of meaning, once defined, will be found in various other forms of our language; it occurs, apparently without admixture, as the meaning of the article *the*, for this little word tells us only that the following substantive denotes an identified individual of a species.

In sum, then, we may say that certain meanings, once they are defined, can be recognized as recurring in whole series of forms. In particular, the last-named type, which has to do with the identification of individual objects of a species, in the way of selection, inclusion, exclusion, or numbering, elicits very uniform responses from different persons, and recurs with relative uniformity in different languages; these types of meaning, accordingly, give rise to the specially accurate form of speech which we call mathematics.

9. 7. Vocal gestures, serving an inferior type of communication, occur not only outside of speech, as in an inarticulate outcry, but also in combination with speech-forms, in the disposition of non-distinctive features of speech-sound, such as the "tone of voice." Some conventional speech-forms, in fact, seem to lie on the border-line; thus, we have seen that, in English, the exclamations *pst* [pst] and *sh* [ʃ], with which we demand silence, violate the phonetic pattern by the use as syllabics of the relatively un-sonorous phonemes [s, ʃ]. Less striking deviations from the phonetic pattern sometimes occur in words whose meaning resembles that of a pointing gesture. In English the initial phoneme [ð] occurs only in words of demonstrative and related meanings, such as *this, that, the, then, there, though;* in Russian, the phoneme [e] occurs initially in none but demonstrative words, such as ['eto] 'this.'

Non-phonemic, gesture-like features may become fairly fixed. In Plains Cree the word [eː] 'yes' is ordinarily spoken with a diphthongal glide in the vowel and a final glottal stop, somewhat as [eeːʔ], although neither of these features is phonemic in the language. In our slang fashions, peculiar pitch-schemes occasionally become fixed for certain values; in the last years, *Yeah?* and *Is that so?* with a peculiar modification of the question-pitch, have been used as facetious vulgarisms, expressing disbelief.

The latter expression has also a form *Is zat so?* which illustrates another phase of unusual linguistic features, *facetious mispronun-*

ciation. To say *Please, oxcuse me*, for instance, is a form of tired wit. These distortions get their value from a resemblance to other linguistic forms (as in our example, the word *ox*) or to the speech-forms of foreigners, sub-standard speakers, and children, as in the facetious use of [ɔj] for [r] in words like *bird* (imitating the sub-standard speech of New York City), or in the use of baby-talk (*Atta boy! Atta dirl!*).

Certain expressions have slurred and shortened by-forms in which the phonetic pattern is lost; these are common formulas of social intercourse, such as greetings and terms of address. Thus, *How do you do?* is shortened in all manner of ways into forms which cannot be recorded in terms of English phonemes, but only suggested by such sketches as [ʤˈduw] or [dˈduw]; *How are you?* is something like [hwaj, haj]; *madam* appears as [m̩] in *Yes'm*. These by-forms occur only in the formula; in asking *How do you do it?* [ˈhaw ʤu ˈduw it.] for example, we do not use the over-slurred form. These shortened forms occur in various languages; their relation to normal speech is obscure, but evidently they represent a kind of *sub-linguistic* communication, in which the ordinary meaning of the forms plays no part.

We can mention any sound by means of a rough imitation in terms of vocal sound, as when we tell the calls of animals, or when we report the noise of an engine. In this way we can also mention speech-sounds; talking about a person who lisps, for instance, someone may say, "I am tired of his eternal *yeth, yeth* " The commonest case is *hypostasis*, the mention of a phonetically normal speech-form, as when we say, "That is only an *if*," or "There is always a *but*," or when we talk about "the word *normalcy*" or "the name *Smith*." One may even speak of parts of words, as I shall speak in this book of "the suffix -*ish* in *boyish*." Hypostasis is closely related to *quotation*, the repetition of a speech.

9. 8. The peculiarities of the forms discussed in the last paragraph consist in deviations from the ordinary tie-up of phonetic form with dictionary meaning. When there is no such deviation, and only a normal phonetic form with a dictionary meaning is to be considered, the latter will still exhibit great complexity. We have already seen that present-day knowledge does not suffice to unravel all the entanglements of meaning, but there are two main features of the dictionary meaning of speech-forms which demand such comment as we are able to make.

MEANING

Very many linguistic forms are used for more than one typical situation. In English, we speak of the *head* of an army, of a procession, of a household, or of a river, and of a *head* of cabbage; of the *mouth* of a bottle, cannon, or river; of the *eye* of a needle, and of hooks and *eyes* on a dress; of the *teeth* of a saw; of the *tongue* of a shoe or of a wagon; of the *neck* of a bottle and of a *neck* of the woods; of the *arms, legs,* and *back* of a chair; of the *foot* of a mountain; of *hearts* of celery. A man may be a *fox*, an *ass*, or a *dirty dog;* a woman, a *peach, lemon, cat,* or *goose;* people are *sharp* and *keen* or *dull,* or else *bright* or *foggy,* as to their wits; *warm* or *cold* in temperament; *crooked* or *straight* in conduct; a person may be *up in the air, at sea, off the handle, off his base,* or even *beside himself,* without actually moving from the spot. The reader will be able to add examples practically without limit; there is no greater bore than the enumeration and classification of these "metaphors."

The remarkable thing about these variant meanings is our assurance and our agreement in viewing one of the meanings as *normal* (or *central*) and the others as *marginal* (*metaphoric* or *transferred*). The central meaning is favored in the sense that we understand a form (that is, respond to it) in the central meaning unless some feature of the practical situation forces us to look to a transferred meaning. If we hear someone say *There goes a fox!* we look for a real fox, and if this is out of the question, we are likely to take the utterance as displaced speech (say, as make-believe or as part of a fairy-tale). Only if some situational feature forces us — say, if the speaker is pointing at a man — do we take the form in the transferred sense. Even if we heard someone say, *The fox promised to help her,* we should think of a fairy-tale rather than of *fox* 'unscrupulous and clever person.' Sometimes the practical feature that forces us to take a form in transferred meaning, has been given by speech: *Old Mr. Smith is a fox* is bound to be taken in transferred meaning, because we do not call real foxes "Mr." or give them family-names. *He married a lemon* forces us to the transferred meaning only because we know that men do not go through a marriage ceremony with a piece of fruit. On the other hand, special practical situations may change all this. People who lived close to the Fox Indians might, without special constraint, take *fox* in our examples in the transferred sense 'member of the Fox nation.'

In some cases a transferred meaning is linguistically determined by an accompanying form. The word *cat* always has a transferred meaning when it is accompanied by the suffix *-kin* (*catkin*), and the word *pussy* when it is compounded with *willow* (*pussy-willow*); similarly, the word *eye* when it has the suffix *-let* (*eyelet*). The words *dog, monkey, beard* when they appear with the marks of verb derivation (say, with a preceding *to*), always have transferred meaning (*to dog someone's footsteps; don't monkey with that; to beard a lion in his den*). These linguistic features may be purely negative: *give out*, used without an object (*his money gave out; our horses gave out*), always has a transferred meaning ('become exhausted') In these cases the structure of the language recognizes the transferred meaning. Even a linguist who made no attempt to define meanings would have to specify that *give out*, intransitive, meant something different (was a different form) from *give out*, transitive (*he gave out tickets*).

In many cases we hesitate whether to view the form as a single form with several meanings or as a set of homonyms. Examples of this are *air* 'atmosphere; tune, melody; manner' (this last including *airs* 'haughty manners'), *key* 'instrument for locking and unlocking; set of tones in music,' *charge* 'attack; load; accuse; debit,' *sloth* 'name of an animal; laziness.'

We are likely to make the mistake of thinking that the transferred meanings of our language are natural and even inevitable in human speech — the more so, as they appear also in other European languages. This last, however, is merely a result of our common cultural traditions; while transferred meanings occur in all languages, the particular ones in any given language are by no means to be taken for granted. Neither in French nor in German can one speak of the *eye* of a needle or of an *ear* of grain. To speak of the *foot* of a mountain seems natural to any European, but it would be nonsense in Menomini and doubtless in many other languages. On the other hand, in Menomini [unaːʔnɛw] 'he places him in position' has also the transferred meaning 'he picks lice from him.' In Russian, [noˈga] 'leg' is not used of the leg of a chair or table; this transferred meaning appears only in the diminutive [ˈnoʃka] 'little leg; leg of a chair or table.' Accordingly, when the linguist tries to state meanings, he safely ignores the uses of displaced speech, but does his best to register all cases of transferred meaning.

All this applies also to another type of deviant meaning, the *narrowed* meaning, with this difference, that we are far more ready to accept a form in a narrowed meaning. The practical situation guides us at once to take *car* in different narrowed senses in *The diner is the second car forward* ('railroad-carriage'); *Does the car stop at this corner?* ('street-car'); *Bring the car close to the curb* ('motor-car'). When we hear the command to *call a doctor*, we take it at once to mean a *doctor of medicine*. A *burner* is primarily a person or instrument that burns things, but usually, in a narrowed sense, a gas-tap arranged to give a certain kind of flame. A *bulb* among gardeners is one thing and among electricians another. A *glass* is usually a drinking-glass or a looking-glass; *glasses* are usually eye-glasses. Narrowed meanings are hard to define, because, after all, every occurrence of a form is prompted by some one practical situation which need not contain all the possibilities of meaning: *apple* is used now of a green one, now of a red one, and so on.

The language itself, by formal characteristics, recognizes narrowed meanings in certain combinations. For instance, *blackbird* is not merely any 'black bird': in this combination the meaning of *black* is greatly narrowed; similarly *blueberry*, *whitefish*, and the like.

Widened meanings are less common. In general, *cat* is the domestic animal, but now and then we use the word to include lions, tigers, and so on; the word *dog*, however, is not similarly used to include wolves and foxes. On the other hand, *hound* is used poetically and facetiously of any kind of dog. Often, the widened meaning is recognized in the structure of the language, and appears only when certain accompanying forms are present. Thus *meat* is edible flesh, but in *meat and drink* and in *sweetmeats* it is food in general; *fowl* is an edible bird, but in *fish, flesh, or fowl* or *the fowl of the air* it is any bird.

Often enough the speakers of a language do not distinguish a central and a marginal meaning in cases where an outsider might see two situationally different values; thus, *day* in English means a period of twenty-four hours (Swedish *dygn* [dyŋn]) or the light part of this period (in contrast with *night;* Swedish *dag* [da:g]).

9. 9. The second important way in which meanings show instability, is the presence of supplementary values which we call *connotations*. The meaning of a form for any one speaker is nothing

F

more than a result of the situations in which he has heard this form. If he has not heard it very many times, or if he has heard it under very unusual circumstances, his use of the form may deviate from the conventional. We combat such personal deviations by giving explicit definitions of meaning; this is a chief use of our dictionaries. In the case of scientific terms, we manage to keep the meaning nearly free from connotative factors, though even here we may be unsuccessful; the number *thirteen*, for instance, has for many people a strong connotation.

The most important connotations arise from the social standing of the speakers who use a form. A form which is used by a less privileged class of speakers often strikes us as coarse, ugly, and vulgar. *I ain't got none, I seen it, I done it* sound nasty to the speaker of standard English. This may be offset by some special factor: the speech-forms of tramps or criminals may bear a connotation of devil-may-care wit, and those of a rustic type may strike us as homely but poetic. A form used by a more privileged class of speakers may strike us as over-formal or prettified and affected. Most speakers of Central-Western American English find this connotation in the use of [ɑ] instead of [ɛ] in forms like *laugh, bath, can't* and of [juw] instead of [uw] in forms like *tune, sue, stupid.*

Connotations of local provenience are closely akin to these; a Scotch or an Irish locution has its own tang; so have, in America, certain real or supposed Anglicisms, such as *luggage* (for *baggage*) or *old chap, old dear* as terms of address.

Even in communities that have no writing, some forms are recognized (rightly or wrongly) as *archaisms;* in communities that have written records, these serve as additional sources of archaic forms. Examples are, in English, the old second-person singular forms (*thou hast*), the third-person forms in *-th* (*he hath*), the old present subjunctive (*if this be treason*), the pronoun *ye*, and many forms like *eve, e'en, e'er, morn, anent,* and so on. Sometimes fully current locutions may preserve some special *aphoristic form;* thus, an old sentence-construction survives in a few proverbs, such as *First come, first served* or *Old saint, young sinner.*

The connotation of *technical* forms gets its flavor from the standing of the trade or craft from which they are taken. Sea-terms sound ready, honest, and devil-may-care: *abaft, aloft, the cut of his jib, stand by;* legal terms precise and a bit tricky: *without let or hindrance, in the premises, heirs and assigns;* criminals' terms crass but to the point: *a stickup, a shot (of whiskey), get pinched.*

The connotation of *learned* forms is vaguer but more frequent: almost any colloquial form has a parallel form with learned connotation.

NORMAL	LEARNED
He came too soon.	He arrived prematurely.
It's too bad.	It is regrettable.
Where're you going?	What is your destination?
now	at present
if he comes	in case (in case that, in the event that, in the contingency that) he comes; should he come, . . .
so (that) you don't lose it.	in order that you may not lose it, lest you lose it.

As these examples show, the learned, elegant, and archaic types of connotation merge in many a form. In formal speech and in writing, we customarily prefer learned forms, up to a certain degree: he who uses too many learned forms is a stilted speaker or a tiresome writer.

Foreign speech-forms bear connotations of their own, which reflect our attitude toward foreign peoples. The foreign features of form may consist in peculiarities of sound or of phonetic pattern: *garage, mirage, rouge, a je ne sais quoi; olla podrida, chile con carne; dolce far niente, fortissimo; Zeitgeist, Wanderlust; intelligentsia.* In other instances, the foreign feature lies in the construction, as in the French types *marriage of convenience* and *that goes without saying.* This flavor is turned to facetious use in *mock-foreign* forms, such as *nix come erouse* (mock-German), *ish gabibble* ('it's none of my concern,' supposedly Judeo-German). Schoolboys use mock-Latinisms, such as the nonsense-form *quid sidi quidit,* or *macaronic* verse: *Boyibus kissibus priti girlorum, girlibus likibus, wanti somorum.*

Some languages, and most notably, perhaps, English, contain a great mass of *semi-foreign* or *foreign-learned* forms — a class of forms with a separate style of pattern and derivation. Our text-books of rhetoric distinguish these forms, as the "Latin-French" part of our vocabulary, from the "native" or "Anglo-Saxon" forms. The connotation, however, does not depend directly upon the actual provenience of the forms. The word *chair,* for instance, is Latin-French in origin, but does not belong to the foreign-learned part of our vocabulary. The chief formal characteristic of our foreign-learned forms is perhaps the use of certain accented suffixes and combinations of suffixes, such as [-iti] *ability;* [-'ejʃn] *education.* Another feature is the use of certain phonetic alternations, such as [sijv] in *receive,* but [sep] in *reception* and [sij] in *receipt,* or [vajd] in *provide,* but [vid] in *provident,* [viz] in *visible,* and [viʒ] in *provision.* These peculiarities suffice to mark certain words and constituents of words as foreign-learned, especially certain prefixes (*ab-, ad-, con-, de-, dis-, ex-, in-, per-, pre-, pro-, re-, trans-*); these prefixes themselves in part show peculiar phonetic alternations, as in *con-tain* but *collect, correct,* and *ab-jure* but *abs-tain.* Semantically, our foreign-learned forms are peculiar in the capricious and highly specialized meanings of the combinations; it seems impossible, for instance, to set up any consistent meaning for elements like [sijv] in *conceive, deceive, perceive, receive* or [tend] in *attend, contend, distend, pretend,* or [d(j)uws] in *adduce, conduce, deduce, induce, produce, reduce.* The connotative flavor of these forms lies in the learned direction: a speaker's ability to use these forms measures his education. Errors in their use (*malapropisms*) mark the semi-educated speaker. The less educated speaker fails to understand many of these forms, and is to this extent shut out from some types of communication; he may take vengeance by using *mock-learned* forms, such as *absquatulate, discombobulate, rambunctious, scrumptious.* Many languages contain a foreign-learned layer of this kind: the Romance languages have a Latin type, largely identical with ours; Russian, beside a fair sprinkling of this type, has learned forms from Old Bulgarian; Turkish has a stratum of Persian and Arabic words, and Persian of Arabic; the languages of India similarly use Sanskrit forms.

Opposed to the foreign-learned connotation, the *slangy* connotation is facetious and unrestrained: the users of slang forms are young persons, sportsmen, gamblers, vagrants, criminals, and, for that matter, most other speakers in their relaxed and unpretentious moods. Examples are familiar, such as *guy, gink, gazebo, gazook, bloke, bird* for 'man,' *rod* or *gat* for 'pistol,' and so on; the slang form may at the same time be foreign, as *loco* 'crazy,' *sabby* 'understand,' *vamoose* 'go away,' from Spanish. The value is largely facetious; when the slang form has been in use too long, it is likely to be replaced by some new witticism.

MEANING

9. 10. The varieties of connotation are countless and indefinable and, as a whole, cannot be clearly distinguished from denotative meaning. In the last analysis, every speech-form has its own connotative flavor for the entire speech-community and this, in turn, is modified or even offset, in the case of each speaker, by the connotation which the form has acquired for him through his special experience. It may be well, however, to speak briefly of two more types of connotation which stand out with at least relative clearness.

In many speech-communities certain *improper* speech-forms are uttered only under restricted circumstances; a speaker who utters them outside the restriction is shamed or punished. The strictness of the prohibition ranges from a mild rule of *propriety* to a severe *tabu*. The improper forms belong for the most part to certain spheres of meaning, but often enough there exist by their side forms with the same denotation but without the improper connotation, as *prostitute* by the side of the improper form *whore*.

Some improper forms denote objects or persons that are not to be named in a casual way, or perhaps not to be named at all. In English, various terms of religion, such as *God, devil, heaven, hell, Christ, Jesus, damn* are proper only in serious speech. Violation of the rule exposes the speaker to reproof or avoidance; on the other hand, in certain groups or under certain conditions, the violation connotes vigor and freedom. In many communities the names of persons are tabu under some circumstances or to some people. The male Cree Indian, for example, does not speak the names of his sisters and of some other female relatives; he explains the avoidance by saying, "I respect her too much."

Another direction of impropriety is the tabu on so-called *obscene* forms. In English there is a severe tabu on some speech-forms whose meaning is connected with excretory functions, and on some that deal with reproduction.

A third type of improper connotation is less universal among us; the avoidance of *ominous* speech-forms, which name something painful or dangerous. One avoids the words *die* and *death* (*if anything should happen to me*) and the names of some diseases. Other peoples avoid mention of the left hand, or of thunderstorms.

In some communities one avoids the names of game animals, either during the hunt or more generally. Under special conditions (as, on the war-path), many speech-forms may be avoided, or *inverted* speech, saying the opposite of what one means, may be in order.

9. 11. The second more specialized type of connotation that here deserves to be pointed out, is *intensity*. The most characteristic intense forms are *exclamations*. For these we have in English not only a special secondary phoneme [!], but also certain special speech-forms, *interjections*, such as *oh! ah! ouch!* These forms all reflect a violent stimulus, but differ in connotation from an ordinary statement in which the speaker merely says that he is undergoing a strong stimulus.

Certain speech-forms have an *animated* flavor, akin to the exclamatory, as, for instance, the placing first of certain adverbs: *Away ran John; Away he ran.* In connected narrative a similar flavor appears in less violent transpositions: *Yesterday he came (and said . . .)* is more lively than *He came yesterday . . .* In English the *historical present*, in narrating past events, is either elegant, as in the summary of a play or story, or, in ordinary speech, slightly vulgar: *Then he comes back and says to me . . .*

English is especially rich in another type of intense forms, the *symbolic* forms. Symbolic forms have a connotation of somehow illustrating the meaning more immediately than do ordinary speech-forms. The explanation is a matter of grammatical structure and will concern us later; to the speaker it seems as if the sounds were especially suited to the meaning. Examples are *flip, flap, flop, flitter, flimmer, flicker, flutter, flash, flush, flare, glare, glitter, glow, gloat, glimmer, bang, bump, lump, thump, thwack, whack, sniff, sniffle, snuff, sizzle, wheeze.* Languages that have symbolic forms show some agreement, but probably more disagreement as to the types of sounds and meanings which are associated. A special type of symbolic form, which is quite widely distributed, is the repetition of the form with some phonetic variation, as in *snip-snap, zig-zag, riff-raff, jim-jams, fiddle-faddle, teeny-tiny, ship-shape, hodge-podge, hugger-mugger, honky-tonk.*

Closely akin to these are *imitative* or *onomatopoetic* intense forms, which denote a sound or an object which gives out a sound: the imitative speech-form resembles this sound: *cock-a-doodle-doo, meeow, moo, baa.* Many bird names are of this sort: *cuckoo, bob-white, whip-poor-will.* Doubled forms are common: *bow-wow, ding-dong, pee-wee, choo-choo, chug-chug.* These forms differ from

MEANING

language to language: the French dog says *gnaf-gnaf* [ɲaf ɲaf]; the German bell says *bim-bam*.

Among the forms just cited, some have an *infantile* connotation; they are *nursery-forms*. The most familiar are *papa* and *mama*. In English almost any doubled syllable may be used, in almost any meaning, as a nursery-word; each family develops its private supply of the type [ˈdijdi, ˈdajdaj, ˈdajdi, ˈmijmi, ˈwɑːwɑː]. This custom provides speech-forms which the infant can reproduce with relative ease, and it helps adults to turn the infant's utterances into conventional signals.

The *pet-name* or *hypochoristic* connotation largely merges with that of the nursery. In English, relatively few pet-names like *Lulu*, have the doubled nursery form; in French this type is common: *Mimi, Nana*, and so on. English pet-names are less uniform: *Tom, Will, Ed, Pat, Dan, Mike* can be described structurally as shortenings of the full name; this is not the case in *Bob* for *Robert*, *Ned* for *Edward*, *Bill* for *William*, *Dick* for *Richard*, *Jack* for *John*. Some have the diminutive suffix [-i], as *Peggy, Maggie* for *Margaret, Fanny* for *Frances, Johnny, Willie, Billy*.

There is some intensity also in the connotation of *nonsense-forms*. Some of these, though conventional, have no denotation at all, as *tra-la-la, hey-diddle-diddle, tarara-boom-de-ay*; others have an explicitly vague denotation, as *fol-de-rol, gadget, conniption fits*. Any speaker is free to invent nonsense-forms; in fact, any form he invents is a nonsense-form, unless he succeeds in the almost hopeless task of getting his fellow-speakers to accept it as a signal for some meaning.

CHAPTER 10

GRAMMATICAL FORMS

10. 1. Our discussion so far has shown us that every language consists of a number of signals, *linguistic forms*. Each linguistic form is a fixed combination of signaling-units, the *phonemes*. In every language the number of phonemes and the number of actually occurring combinations of phonemes, is strictly limited. By uttering a linguistic form, a speaker prompts his hearers to respond to a situation; this situation and the responses to it, are the *linguistic meaning* of the form. We assume that each linguistic form has a constant and definite meaning, different from the meaning of any other linguistic form in the same language. Thus, hearing several utterances of some one linguistic form, such as *I'm hungry*, we assume (1) that the differences in sound are irrelevant (unphonetic), (2) that the situations of the several speakers contain some common features and that the differences between these situations are irrelevant (unsemantic), and (3) that this linguistic meaning is different from that of any other form in the language. We have seen that this assumption cannot be verified, since the speaker's situations and the hearer's responses may involve almost anything in the whole world, and, in particular, depend largely upon the momentary state of their nervous systems. Moreover, when we deal with the historical change of language, we shall be concerned with facts for which our assumption does not hold good. In the rough, however, our assumption is justified by the mere fact that speakers co-operate in a very refined way by means of language-signals. In describing a language, we are concerned primarily with the working of this cooperation at any one time in any one community, and not with its occasional failures or with its changes in the course of history. Accordingly, the descriptive phase of linguistics consists in a somewhat rigid analysis of speech-forms, on the assumption that these speech-forms have constant and definable meanings (§ 9.5).

Our basic assumption does have to be modified, however, right at the outset, in a different way. When we have recorded a fair

GRAMMATICAL FORMS

number of forms in a language, we always discover a feature which we have so far ignored in our discussion: the *partial* resemblance of linguistic forms. Suppose we hear a speaker say

John ran,

and a little later hear him or some other speaker say

John fell.

We recognize at once that these two forms, *John ran* and *John fell,* are in part phonetically alike, since both of them contain an element *John* [ʤɔn], and our practical knowledge tells us that the meanings show a corresponding resemblance: whenever a form contains the phonetic element [ʤɔn], the meaning involves a certain man or boy in the community. In fact, if we are lucky, we may hear someone utter the form

John!

all by itself, without any accompaniment.

After observing a number of such cases, we shall be constrained to modify the basic assumption of linguistics to read: In a speech-community some utterances are alike *or partly alike* in sound and meaning.

The common part of partly like utterances (in our example, *John*) consists of a phonetic form with a constant meaning: it answers, therefore, to the definition of a linguistic form. The parts which are not common to the partly-like utterances (in our example, *ran* in the one utterance, and *fell* in the other) may, in the same way, turn out to be linguistic forms. Having heard the form *John ran,* we may later hear the form *Bill ran,* and perhaps even (say, in answer to a question) an isolated *Ran.* The same will happen with the component *fell* in *John fell:* we may hear a form like *Dan fell* or even an isolated *Fell.*

In other cases, we may wait in vain for the isolated form: Knowing the forms *John, Bill,* and *Dan,* we may hear the forms, *Johnny, Billy,* and *Danny* and hope to hear now an isolated *-y* [-i] with some such meaning as 'little,' but in this instance we shall be disappointed. In the same way, familiar with the forms *play* and *dance,* we may hear the forms *playing* and *dancing,* and then hope, in vain, to hear an isolated *-ing* [-iŋ], which might reassure us as to the somewhat vague meaning of this syllable. In spite of the fact that some components do not occur alone, but only as parts of larger forms, we nevertheless call these components linguistic forms, since they are phonetic forms, such as [i] or [iŋ], with constant meanings. A linguistic form which is never spoken alone is a *bound* form; all others (as, for instance, *John ran* or *John* or *run* or *running*) are *free* forms.

In other cases we wait in vain for the occurrence of a form even as part of some other form. For instance, having heard the form *cranberry*, we soon recognize the component *berry* in other forms, such as *blackberry*, and may even hear it spoken alone, but with the other component of *cranberry* we shall have no such luck. Not only do we wait in vain to hear an isolated **cran*, but, listen as we may, we never hear this element outside the one combination *cranberry*, and we cannot elicit from the speakers any other form which will contain this element *cran-*. As a practical matter, observing languages in the field, we soon learn that it is unwise to try to elicit such forms; our questions confuse the speakers, and they may get rid of us by some false admission, such as, "Oh, yes, I guess *cran* means red." If we avoid this pitfall, we shall come to the conclusion that the element *cran-* occurs only in the combination *cranberry*. However, since it has a constant phonetic form, and since its meaning is constant, in so far as a *cranberry* is a definite kind of *berry*, different from all other kinds, we say that *cran-*, too, is a linguistic form. Experience shows that we do well to generalize this instance: *unique elements*, which occur only in a single combination, are linguistic forms.

Sometimes we may be unable to decide whether phonetically like forms are identical in meaning. The *straw-* in *strawberry* is phonetically the same as the *straw-* in *strawflower* and as the isolated *straw*, but whether the meanings are "the same," we cannot say. If we ask the speakers, they will answer sometimes one way, sometimes another; they are no more able to tell than we. This difficulty is part of the universal difficulty of semantics: the practical world is not a world of clear-cut distinctions.

10. 2. We see, then, that some linguistic forms bear partial phonetic-semantic resemblances to other forms; examples are, *John ran, John fell, Bill ran, Bill fell; Johnny, Billy; playing, dancing; blackberry, cranberry; strawberry, strawflower*. A linguistic form which bears a partial phonetic-semantic resemblance to some other linguistic form, is a *complex form*.

The common part of any (two or more) complex forms is a linguistic form; it is a *constituent* (or *component*) of these complex forms. The constituent is said to be *contained in* (or to be *included in* or to *enter into*) the complex forms. If a complex form, beside the common part, contains a remainder, such as the *cran-* in *cranberry*, which does not occur in any other complex form, this remainder also is a linguistic form; it is a *unique constituent* of the complex form. The constituent forms in our examples above are: *John, ran, Bill, fell, play, dance, black, berry, straw, flower, cran-* (unique constituent in *cranberry*), *-y* (bound-form constituent in *Johnny, Billy*), *-ing* (bound-form constituent in *playing, dancing*). In any complex form, each constituent is said to *accompany* the other constituents.

A linguistic form which bears no partial phonetic-semantic resemblance to any other form, is a *simple* form or *morpheme*. Thus, *bird, play, dance, cran-, -y, -ing* are morphemes. Morphemes may show partial phonetic resemblances, as do, for instance, *bird* and *burr*, or even homonymy, as do *pear, pair, pare*, but this resemblance is purely phonetic and is not paralleled by the meanings.

From all this it appears that every complex form is entirely made up, so far as its phonetically definable constituents are concerned, of morphemes. The number of these *ultimate constituents* may run very high. The form *Poor John ran away* contains five morphemes: *poor, John, ran, a-* (a bound form recurring, for instance, in *aground, ashore, aloft, around*), and *way*. However, the structure of complex forms is by no means as simple as this; we could not understand the forms of a language if we merely reduced all the complex forms to their ultimate constituents. Any English-speaking person who concerns himself with this matter, is sure to tell us that the *immediate constituents* of *Poor John ran away* are the two forms *poor John* and *ran away;* that each of these is, in turn, a complex form; that the immediate constituents of *ran away* are *ran*, a morpheme, and *away*, a complex form, whose constituents are the morphemes *a-* and *way;* and that the constituents of *poor John* are the morphemes *poor* and *John*. Only in this way will a proper analysis (that is, one which takes account of the meanings) lead to the ultimately constituent morphemes. The reasons for this will occupy us later.

10. 3. A morpheme can be described phonetically, since it consists of one or more phonemes, but its meaning cannot be analyzed within the scope of our science. For instance, we have seen that the morpheme *pin* bears a phonetic resemblance to other morphemes, such as *pig, pen, tin, ten,* and, on the basis of these resemblances, can be analyzed and described in terms of three phonemes (§ 5.4), but, since these resemblances are not connected with resemblances of meaning, we cannot attribute any meaning to the phonemes and cannot, within the scope of our science, analyze the meaning of the morpheme. The meaning of a morpheme is a *sememe*. The linguist assumes that each sememe is a constant and definite unit of meaning, different from all other meanings, including all other sememes, in the language, but he cannot go beyond this. There is nothing in the structure of morphemes like *wolf, fox,* and *dog* to tell us the relation between their meanings; this is a problem for the zoölogist. The zoölogist's definition of these meanings is welcome to us as a practical help, but it cannot be confirmed or rejected on the basis of our science.

A workable system of signals, such as a language, can contain only a small number of signaling-units, but the things signaled about — in our case, the entire content of the practical world — may be infinitely varied. Accordingly, the signals (linguistic forms, with morphemes as the smallest signals) consist of different combinations of the signaling-units (phonemes), and each such combination is arbitrarily assigned to some feature of the practical world (sememe). The signals can be analyzed, but not the things signaled about.

This re-enforces the principle that linguistic study must always start from the phonetic form and not from the meaning. Phonetic forms — let us say, for instance, the entire stock of morphemes in a language — can be described in terms of phonemes and their succession, and, on this basis, can be classified or listed in some convenient order, as, for example, alphabetically; the meanings — in our example, the sememes of a language — could be analyzed or systematically listed only by a well-nigh omniscient observer.

10. 4. Since every complex form is made up entirely of morphemes, a complete list of morphemes would account for all the phonetic forms of a language. The total stock of morphemes in a language is its *lexicon*. However, if we knew the lexicon of a language, and had a reasonably accurate knowledge of each sememe, we might still fail to understand the forms of this language. Every utterance contains some significant features that are not accounted for by the lexicon. We saw, for instance, that the five morphemes, *John, poor, ran, way, a-* which make up the form *Poor John ran away,* do not fully account for the meaning of this utterance. Part of this meaning depends upon the arrangement — for example, upon the order of succession — in which these morphemes appear in the complex form. Every language shows part of its meanings by the *arrangement* of its forms. Thus, in English, *John hit Bill* and *Bill hit John* differ in meaning by virtue of the two different orders in which the morphemes are uttered.

The meaningful arrangements of forms in a language constitute its *grammar*. In general, there seem to be four ways of arranging linguistic forms.

(1) *Order* is the succession in which the constituents of a complex form are spoken. The significance of order appears strikingly in contrasts such as *John hit Bill* versus *Bill hit John*. On the other hand, **Bill John hit* is not an English form, because our language does not arrange these constituents in this order; similarly, *play-ing* is a form, but **ing-play* is not. Sometimes differences of order have connotative values; thus, *Away ran John* is livelier than *John ran away*.

(2) *Modulation* is the use of secondary phonemes. Secondary phonemes, we recall (§ 5.11), are phonemes which do not appear in any morpheme, but only in grammatical arrangements of morphemes. A morpheme like *John* [dʒɔn] or *run* [rʌn] is really an abstraction, because in any actual utterance the morpheme is accompanied by some secondary phoneme which conveys a grammatical meaning. In English, if the morpheme is spoken alone, it is accompanied by some secondary phoneme of pitch (§ 7.6): it is either *John!* or *John?* or *John* [.] — this last with falling final-pitch, as, in answer to a question — and there is no indifferent or abstract form in which the morpheme is not accompanied by any final-pitch. In English complex forms, some of the constituents are always accompanied by secondary phonemes of stress (§ 7.3); thus, the difference in the place of stress distinguishes the noun *convict* from the verb *convict*.

(3) *Phonetic modification* is a change in the primary phonemes of a form. For instance, when the forms *do* [duw] and *not* [nɔt] are combined into a complex form, the [uw] of *do* is ordinarily replaced by [ow], and, whenever this happens, the *not* loses its vowel, so that the combined form is *don't* [dow nt]. In this example the modification is optional, and we have also the unmodified

forms in *do not*, with a difference of connotation. In other cases we have no choice. Thus, the suffix *-ess* with the meaning 'female,' as in *count-ess*, is added also to *duke* [d(j)uwk], but in this combination the form *duke* is modified to *duch-* [dʌtʃ-], for the word is *duchess* ['dʌtʃis].

Strictly speaking, we should say that the morpheme in such cases has two (or, sometimes, more) different phonetic forms, such as *not* [nɔt] and [nt], *do* [duw] and [dow], *duke* and *duch-*, and that each of these *alternants* appears under certain conditions. In our examples, however, one of the alternants has a much wider range than the other and, accordingly, is a *basic alternant*. In other cases, the alternants are more on a par. In *run* and *ran*, for instance, neither alternant is tied to the presence of any accompanying form, and we might hesitate as to the choice of a basic alternant. We find, however, that in cases like *keep : kep-t* the past-tense form contains an alternant (*kep-*) which occurs only with a certain accompanying form (*-t*); accordingly, to obtain as uniform as possible a statement, we take the infinitive form (*keep, run*) as basic, and describe the alternant which appears in the past tense (*kev-, ran*) as a phonetically modified form. We shall see other instances where the choice is more difficult; we try, of course, to make the selection of a basic alternant so as to get, in the long run the simplest description of the facts.

(4) *Selection* of forms contributes a factor of meaning because different forms in what is otherwise the same grammatical arrangement, will result in different meanings. For instance, some morphemes spoken with exclamatory final-pitch, are calls for a person's presence or attention (*John! Boy!*), while others, spoken in the same way, are commands (*Run! Jump!*), and this difference extends also to certain complex forms (*Mr. Smith! Teacher!* versus *Run away! Backwater!*). The forms which, when spoken with exclamatory final-pitch, have the meaning of a call, may be said, by virtue of this fact, to make up a *form-class* of the English language; we may call it the form-class of "personal substantive expressions." Similarly, the forms which, when spoken with exclamatory final-pitch, have the meaning of a command, make up, by virtue of this fact, the English form-class of "infinitive expressions." Whether an exclamation is a call or a command, depends upon the selection of the form from the one or the other of these two classes.

GRAMMATICAL FORMS

The meaning of a complex form depends in part upon the selection of the constituent forms. Thus, *drink milk* and *watch John* name actions, and, as we have just seen, are infinitive expressions, but *fresh milk* and *poor John* name objects and are substantive expressions. The second constituents, *milk*, and *John*, are the same; the difference depends upon the selection of the first constituent. By virtue of this difference, the forms *drink* and *watch* belong to one English form-class (that of "transitive verbs"), and the forms *fresh* and *poor* to another (that of "adjectives").

The features of selection are usually quite complicated, with form-classes divided into sub-classes. In English, if we combine a form like *John* or *the boys* (form-class of "nominative substantive expressions") with a form like *ran* or *went home* (form-class of "finite verb expressions"), the resultant complex form means that this object 'performs' this action (*John ran, the boys ran, John went home, the boys went home*). These features of selection, however, are supplemented by a further habit: we say *John runs fast* but *the boys run fast*, and we never make the reverse combinations of *John* with *run fast*, or of *the boys* with *runs fast*. The form-class of nominative expressions is divided into two sub-classes ("singular" and "plural") and the form-class of finite verb expressions likewise, into two sub-classes ("singular" and "plural"), such that in the complex forms which mean that an object performs an action, the two constituents agree as to the "singular" or "plural" sub-class. In Latin, the form *pater filium amat* (or *filium pater amat*) means 'the father loves the son,' and the form *patrem filius amat* (or *filius patrem amat*) means 'the son loves the father'; the forms *pater* 'father' and *filius* 'son' belong to a form-class ("nominative case") whose forms, in combination with a verb like *amat* 'he loves,' denote the 'performer' of the action; the forms *patrem* 'father' and *filium* 'son' belong to a different form-class ("accusative case"), whose forms, in combination with a verb like *amat*, denote the 'undergoer' ('object' or 'goal') of the action.

The features of selection are often highly arbitrary and whimsical. We combine *prince, author, sculptor* with the suffix *-ess* in *princess, authoress, sculptress* (in this last case with phonetic modification of [r] to [r]), but not *king, singer, painter*. By virtue of this habit, the former words belong to a form-class from which the latter words are excluded.

10. 5. The features of grammatical arrangement appear in various combinations, but can usually be singled out and separately described. A simple feature of grammatical arrangement is a *grammatical feature* or *taxeme*. A taxeme is in grammar what a phoneme is in the lexicon — namely, the smallest unit of form. Like a phoneme, a taxeme, taken by itself, in the abstract, is meaningless. Just as combinations of phonemes, or, less commonly, single phonemes, occur as actual lexical signals (phonetic forms), so combinations of taxemes, or, quite frequently, single taxemes, occur as conventional grammatical arrangements, *tactic forms*. A phonetic form with its meaning is a linguistic form; a tactic form with its meaning is a *grammatical form*. When we have occasion to contrast the purely lexical character of a linguistic form with the habits of arrangement to which it is subject, we shall speak of it as a *lexical form*. In the case of lexical forms, we have defined the smallest meaningful units as morphemes, and their meanings as sememes; in the same way, the smallest meaningful units of grammatical form may be spoken of as *tagmemes*, and their meanings as *episememes*.

The utterance *Run!*, for example, contains two grammatical features (taxemes), namely, the modulation of exclamatory final-pitch, and the selective feature which consists in the use of an infinitive verb (as opposed, for instance, to the use of a noun, as in *John!*). Each of these two taxemes happens to be, in English, a tactic form, since each is currently used as a unit of signaling. Taking each of them with its meaning, we describe them as units of grammatical form (tagmemes). The tagmeme of exclamatory final-pitch occurs with any lexical form and gives it a grammatical meaning (an episememe) which we may roughly describe perhaps, as 'strong stimulus.' The tagmeme of selection by which infinitive forms are marked off as a form-class, has a grammatical meaning (an episememe) which we may call a *class-meaning* and roughly define as 'action.'

A tagmeme may consist of more than one taxeme. For instance, in forms like *John ran; poor John ran away; the boys are here; I know,* we find several taxemes. One constituent belongs to the form-class of nominative expressions (*John, poor John, the boys, I*) The other constituent belongs to the form-class of finite verb expressions (*ran, ran away, are here, know*). A further taxeme of selection assigns certain finite verb expressions to certain nominative expressions; thus, the constituents are not interchangeable in the three examples *I am, John is, you are*. A taxeme of order places the nominative expression before the finite verb expression: we do not say *ran John. Further taxemes of order, in part reversing the basic one, appear in special cases like *did John run? away ran John; will John?* A taxeme of modulation appears only in special cases, when the nominative expression is unstressed, as in *I know* [aj 'now]. Taxemes of phonetic modification appear also in certain special cases, such as *John's here*, with [z] for *is*, or *I'd go*, with [d] for *would*. Now, none of these taxemes, taken by itself, has any meaning, but, taken all together, they make up a grammatical form, a tagmeme, whose meaning is this, that the one constituent (the nominative expression) 'performs' the other constituent (the finite verb expression).

If we say *John ran!* with exclamatory pitch, we have a complex grammatical form, with three tagmemes. One of these is 'strong stimulus,' the second is '(object) performs (action),' and the third has the episememe of 'complete and novel' utterance, and consists, formally, in the selective feature of using an actor-action phrase as a sentence.

10. 6. Any utterance can be fully described in terms of lexical and grammatical forms; we must remember only that the meanings cannot be defined in terms of our science.

Any morpheme can be fully described (apart from its meaning) as a set of one or more phonemes in a certain arrangement. Thus, the morpheme *duke* consists of the phonemes, simple and compound, [d], [juw], [k], in this order; and the morpheme *-ess* consists of the phonemes [i], [s], in this order. Any complex form can be fully described (apart from its meaning) in terms of the immediate constituent forms and the grammatical features (taxemes) by which these constituent forms are arranged. Thus, the complex form *duchess* ['dʌtʃis] consists of the immediate constituents *duke* [djuwk] and *-ess* [is], arranged in the following way:

Selection. The constituent *duke* belongs to a special class of English forms which combine with the form *-ess*. This form-class includes, for instance, the forms *count, prince, lion, tiger, author, waiter*, but not the forms *man, boy, dog, singer*; it is a sub-class of a larger form-class of male personal nouns. The form *-ess* constitutes a little form-class of its own, by virtue of the fact that it (and it alone) combines with precisely the forms in the class just described. All these facts, taken together, may be viewed as a single taxeme of selection.

Order. The form *-ess* is spoken after the accompanying form.

Modulation. The form *-ess* is spoken unstressed; the accompanying form has a high stress.

Phonetic modification. The [juw] of *duke* is replaced by [ʌ], and the [k] by [tʃ].

Given the forms *duke* and *-ess*, the statement of these four grammatical features fully describes the complex form *duchess*.

Any actual utterance can be fully described in terms of the lexical form and the accompanying grammatical features. Thus, the utterance *Duchess!* consists of the lexical form *duchess* and the two taxemes of exclamatory final-pitch and selection of a substantive expression.

If some science furnished us with definitions of the meanings of the units here concerned, defining for us the meanings (sememes) of the two morphemes (*duke* and *-ess*) and the meanings (episememes) of the three tagmemes (arrangement of *duke* and *-ess;* use of exclamatory final-pitch; selection of a substantive expression), then the meaning of the utterance *Duchess!* would be fully analyzed and defined.

10. 7. The grammatical forms are no exception to the necessary principle — strictly speaking, we should call it an assumption — that a language can convey only such meanings as are attached to some formal feature: the speakers can signal only by means of signals. Many students of language have been misled in this matter by the fact that the formal features of grammar are not phonemes or combinations of phonemes which we can pronounce or transcribe, but merely *arrangements* of phonetic forms. For this our scholastic tradition may be largely to blame; if it were not for this tradition, there would perhaps be nothing difficult about the fact, for instance, that in English, *John hit Bill* and *Bill hit John* signal two different situations, or that *convict* stressed on the first syllable differs in meaning from *convict* stressed on the second syllable, or that there is a difference of meaning between *John!* and *John?* and *John.*

A form like *John* or *run*, mentioned in the abstract, without, for instance, any specification as to final-pitch, is, properly speaking, not a real linguistic form, but only a lexical form; a linguistic form, as actually uttered, always contains a grammatical form.

No matter how simple a form we take and how we utter it, we have already made some selection by virtue of which the utterance conveys a grammatical meaning in addition to its lexical content, and we have used some pitch-scheme which, in English at any rate, lends it a grammatical meaning such as 'statement' 'yes-or-no question,' 'supplement-question,' or 'exclamation.'

The grammatical forms of a language can be grouped into three great classes:

(1) When a form is spoken alone (that is, not as a constituent of a larger form), it appears in some *sentence-type*. Thus, in English, the use of the secondary phoneme [!] gives us the sentence-type of exclamation, and the use of a substantive expression gives us the type of a call (*John!*).

(2) Whenever two (or, rarely, more) forms are spoken together, as constituents of a complex form, the grammatical features by which they are combined, make up a *construction*. Thus, the grammatical features by which *duke* and *-ess* combine in the form *duchess*, or the grammatical features by which *poor John* and *ran away* combine in the form *poor John ran away*, make up a construction.

(3) A third great class of grammatical forms must probably be set up for the cases where a form is spoken as the conventional substitute for any one of a whole class of other forms. Thus, the selective feature by which the form *he* in English is a conventional substitute for a whole class of other forms, such as *John, poor John, a policeman, the man I saw yesterday, whoever did this*, and so on (which forms, by virtue of this habit, constitute form-class of "singular male substantive expressions"), must doubtless be viewed as an example of a third class of grammatical forms, to which we may give the name of *substitutions*.

CHAPTER 11

SENTENCE-TYPES

11. 1. In any utterance, a linguistic form appears either as a constituent of some larger form, as does *John* in the utterance *John ran away,* or else as an independent form, not included in any larger (complex) linguistic form, as, for instance, *John* in the exclamation *John!* When a linguistic form occurs as part of a larger form, it is said to be in *included position;* otherwise it is said to be in *absolute position* and to constitute a *sentence.*

A form which in one utterance figures as a sentence, may in another utterance appear in included position. In the exclamation just cited, *John* is a sentence, but in the exclamation *Poor John!* the form *John* is in included position. In this latter exclamation, *poor John* is a sentence, but in the utterance *Poor John ran away,* it is in included position. Or again, in the utterance just cited, *poor John ran away* is a sentence, but in the utterance *When the dog barked, poor John ran away,* it is in included position.

An utterance may consist of more than one sentence. This is the case when the utterance contains several linguistic forms which are not by any meaningful, conventional grammatical arrangement (that is, by any construction) united into a larger form, e.g.: *How are you? It's a fine day. Are you going to play tennis this afternoon?* Whatever practical connection there may be between these three forms, there is no grammatical arrangement uniting them into one larger form: the utterance consists of three sentences.

It is evident that the sentences in any utterance are marked off by the mere fact that each sentence is an independent linguistic form, not included by virtue of any grammatical construction in any larger linguistic form. In most, or possibly all languages, however, various taxemes mark off the sentence, and, further, distinguish different types of sentence.

In English and many other languages, sentences are marked off by modulation, the use of secondary phonemes. In English, secondary phonemes of pitch mark the end of sentences, and distinguish three main sentence-types: *John ran away* [.] *John*

SENTENCE-TYPES

ran away [?] *Who ran away* [¿]. To each of these, further, we may add the distortion of exclamatory sentence-pitch, so that we get in all, six types, as described in § 7.6.

This use of secondary phonemes to mark the end of sentences makes possible a construction known as *parataxis*, in which two forms united by no other construction are united by the use of only one sentence-pitch. Thus, if we say *It's ten o'clock* [.] *I have to go home* [.] with the final falling pitch of a statement on *o'clock*, we have spoken two sentences, but if we omit this final-pitch (substituting for it a pause-pitch), the two forms are united, by the construction of parataxis, into a single sentence: *It's ten o'clock* [,] *I have to go home* [.]

Another feature of sentence-modulation in English and many other languages, is the use of a secondary phoneme to mark emphatic parts of a sentence. In English we use highest stress for this ("Now it's *my* turn," § 7.3). The emphatic element in English may be marked also by the use of special constructions (It was *John* who did that) and by word-order (*Away* he ran); in languages where stress is not significant, such methods prevail, as in French *C'est Jean qui l'a fait* [s ɛ ʒã ki l a fɛ] 'It is *John* who did it.' Some languages use special words before or after an emphatic element, as Tagalog [ikaw 'ŋaʔ aŋ nag'saːbi nijan] 'you (emphatic particle) the one-who-said that,' i.e. 'You yourself said so'; Menomini ['joːhpeh 'niw, kan 'wenah 'waːpah] 'Today (emphatic particle), not (emphatic particle) tomorrow.' Our high stress can even strike forms that are normally unstressed: *of, for,* and *by* the people; *im*migration and *e*migration.

11. 2. Beside features of modulation, features of selection may serve to mark off different sentence-types. This is the case in some of the examples just given, where a special construction, or the use of a special particle, marks an emphatic element. In English, supplement-questions are distinguished not only by their special pitch-phoneme [¿], but also by a selective taxeme: the form used as a supplement-question either consists of a special type of word or phrase, which we may call an *interrogative substitute,* or else contains such a word or phrase; *Who? With whom? Who ran away? With whom was he talking?*

Perhaps all languages distinguish two great sentence-types which we may call *full sentences* and *minor sentences.* The difference consists in a taxeme of selection: certain forms are *favorite sentence-forms;* when a favorite sentence-form is used as a sentence, this is a full sentence, and when any other form is used as a sentence, this is a minor sentence. In English we have two favorite sentence-forms. One consists of *actor-action* phrases — phrases whose structure is that of the actor-action construction: *John ran away. Who ran away? Did John run away?* The other consists of a *command* — an infinitive verb with or without modifiers: *Come! Be good!* This second type is always spoken with exclamatory sentence-pitch; the infinitive may be accompanied by the word *you* as an actor: *You be good!* As these examples show, the meaning of the full sentence-type is something like 'complete and novel utterance' — that is, the speaker implies that what he says is a full-sized occurrence or instruction, and that it somehow alters the hearer's situation. The more deliberate the speech, the more likely are the sentences to be of the full type. The nature of the episememe of full sentences has given rise to much philosophic dispute; to define this (or any other) meaning exactly, lies beyond the domain of linguistics. It is a serious mistake to try to use this meaning (or any meanings), rather than formal features, as a starting-point for linguistic discussion.

Quite a few of the present-day Indo-European languages agree with English in using an actor-action form as a favorite sentence-type. Some, such as the other Germanic languages and French, agree also in that the actor-action form is always a phrase, with the actor and the action as separate words or phrases. In some of these languages, however — for instance, in Italian and Spanish and in the Slavic languages — the actor and the action are bound forms which make up a single word: Italian *canto* ['kant-o] 'I sing,' *canti* ['kant-i] 'thou singest,' *cant-a* ['kant-a] 'he (she, it) sings,' and so on. A word which contains a favorite sentence-form of its language is a *sentence-word*.

Some languages have different favorite sentence-types. Russian has an actor-action type of sentence-word finite verbs, like those of Italian: [po'ju] 'I sing,' [po'joʃ] 'thou singest,' [po'jot] 'he (she, it) sings,' and so on. In addition to this, it has another type of full sentence: [i'van du'rak] 'John (is) a fool,' [sol'dat 'xrabr] 'the soldier (is) brave,' [o'tets 'doma] 'Father (is) at home.' In this second type, one component, which is spoken first, is a substantive; the other form is a substantive to which the first s equated, or an adjective (adjectives have a special form for this use), or an adverbial form.

When a language has more than one type of full sentence, these types may agree in showing constructions of two parts. The common name for such bipartite favorite sentence-forms is *predications*. In a predication, the more object-like component is called the *subject*, the other part the *predicate*. Of the two Russian types, the former is called a *narrative* predication, the latter an *equational* predication. For a language like English or Italian, which has only one type of bipartite sentence, these terms are superfluous, but often employed: *John ran* is said to be a predication, in which the actor (*John*) is the subject and the action (*ran*) the predicate.

Latin had the same types of full sentence as Russian, but the narrative type existed in two varieties: one with an actor-action construction: *cantat* 'he (she, it) sings,' *amat* 'he (she, it) loves,' and one with a goal-action construction: *cantātur* 'it is being sung,' *amātur* 'he (she, it) is loved.' The equational type was less common than in Russian: *beātus ille* 'happy (is) he.'

Tagalog has five types of predication, with this common feature: either the subject precedes and a particle [aj] (after vowels, [j]) intervenes, or the reverse order is used without the particle.

There is, first, an equational type: [aŋ 'ba:ta j maba'it] 'the child is good,' or, with inverse order, [maba'it aŋ 'ba:taʔ] 'good (is) the child.' Then there are four narrative types, in which the predicates are *transient* words, which denote things in four different relations to an action. The four types of transient words are:

actor: [pu'mu:tul] 'one who cut'
goal: [pi'nu:tul] 'something cut'
instrument: [ipi'nu:tul] 'something cut with'
place: [pinu'tu:lan] 'something cut on or from.'

These transient words are by no means confined, like our verbs, to predicative position; they can figure equally well, for instance, in equational sentences, as: [aŋ pu'mu:tul aj si 'hwan] 'the one who did the cutting was John,' but in the predicate position they produce four types of narrative predication:

actor-action: [sja j pu'mu:tul naŋ 'ka:huj] 'he cut some wood'
goal-action: [pi'nu:tul nja aŋ 'ka:huj] 'was-cut by-him the wood,' i.e. 'he cut the wood'

instrument-action: [ipi'nuːtul nja aŋ 'guːluk] 'was-cut-with by-him the bolo-knife,' i.e. 'he cut with the bolo'

place-action: [pinu'tuːlan nja aŋ 'kaːhuj] 'was-cut-from by-him the wood,' i.e. 'he cut (a piece) off the wood.'

Georgian distinguishes between an action-type, as ['v-tsʔer] 'I-write' and a sensation-type, as ['m-e-smi-s] 'me-sound-is,' i.e. 'I hear.' Such distinctions are never carried out with scientific consistency; Georgian classifies sight in the action-type: ['v-naxav] 'I-see.'

Not all favorite sentence-forms have bipartite structure: the command in English consists of merely an infinitive form (*come; be good*) and only occasionally contains an actor (*you be good*). In German, beside a favorite sentence-type of actor-action which closely resembles ours, there is an *impersonal* variety, which differs by not containing any actor: *mir ist kalt* [miːr ist 'kalt] 'to-me is cold,' that is, 'I feel cold;' *hier wird getanzt* ['hiːr virt ge'tantst] 'here gets danced,' that is, 'there is dancing here.' In Russian, there is an impersonal type which differs from the equational predication by the absence of a subject: ['nuʒno] 'it is necessary.'

11. 3. English has a sub-type of full sentences which we may call the *explicit-action* type; in this type the action centers round the verb *do, does, did*. This taxeme of selection appears in the contrast between, say, *I heard him* and *I did hear him*. The explicit-action type has several uses. When the verb is an emphatic element (spoken with highest stress), the normal type emphasizes the lexical content (the sememe) of the verb, as in "I *heard* him" (but did not see him), or in "*Run* home!" (don't walk); the explicit-action type emphasizes the occurrence (as opposed to non-occurrence) or the time (present or past) of the action, as in "I *did* hear him," or "*Do* run home!" Secondly, we use the explicit-action type wherever the verb is modified by *not*, as in *I didn't hear him* or *Don't run away;* thus, English, by a taxeme of selection, distinguishes a *negative* type of full sentence.

Further, within our explicit-action type, we distinguish a sub-type in which the verb *do, does, did* precedes the actor. This *inverted* type occurs in *formal* yes-or-no questions, along with question-pitch; *Did John run away? Didn't John run away?* in contrast with the uninverted (*informal*) type: *John ran away? John didn't run away?*

SENTENCE-TYPES

The features just discussed are not so widely paralleled among languages as the more general characteristics of English full sentences. In German, for instance, the negative adverb is not tied up with a special-sentence-type: *Er kommt nicht* [eːr 'komt 'nixt] 'he comes not' is like *Er kommt bald* [eːr 'komt 'balt] 'he comes soon.' Other languages, however, resemble English in using special sentence-types with negative value. In Finnish, negative sentences have a special construction: the verb (which, as in Italian, includes actor and action in one sentence-word) is a special negative verb, which may be modified by an infinitive-like form of another verb:

luen	'I read'	*en lue*	'I-don't read'
luet	'thou readest'	*et lue*	'thou-dost-not read'
lukee	'he reads'	*ei lue*	'he-doesn't read.'

In Menomini there are three main types of full sentence, equational, narrative, and negative:

narrative: [piːw] 'he-comes'
equational: [enuʔ pajiat] 'he — the one who comes,' that is, 'It's he that's coming'
negative: [kan upianan] 'not he-comes (negative),' that is, 'He does not come.'

In the negative type the two parts are, on the one side, the negative word [kan] in its various inflections and, on the other, the rest of the sentence, marked by the use of special verb-forms.

Special types of full sentences for formal questions are more widespread. German uses actor-action forms in which the verb precedes the actor: *Kommt er?* ['komt eːr?] 'comes he?' in contrast with *Er kommt* [eːr 'komt] 'he comes.' French also uses special interrogative constructions: 'Is John coming?' is either *Jean vient-il?* [ʒã vjɛ̃t i?] 'John comes he?' or *Est-ce que Jean vient?* [ɛ s kə ʒã vjɛ̃?] 'Is it that John comes?' In Menomini the three main types of full sentence have each an interrogative sub-type:

narrative: [piːʔ?] 'Is he coming?'
equation: [enut pajiat?] 'he (interrogative) the one who comes?' that is, 'Is it he that is coming?'
negative: [kanɛːʔ upianan?] 'not (interrogative) he-comes (negative)?' that is, 'Isn't he coming?'

Other languages lack a special sentence-type for formal yes-or-no questions, but some of them use special interrogative words, as Latin *venitne?* [we'nit ne?] 'Is he coming?' and *num venit?* 'You don't mean to say he is coming?' (expectation of negative reply), in contrast with *venit?* 'He is coming?' This use of special little words (particles) to mark a formal yes-or-no question, appears in many languages, such as Russian, Chinese, Tagalog, Cree.

Most languages agree with English in marking supplement-questions by the presence of special words, but the details differ: in Tagalog and in Menomini, for instance, the supplement-question is always an equational sentence, e.g., Menomini [awɛːʔ pajiat¿] 'who the-one-who-comes?' that is, 'Who is coming?'

The English command is an example of a special sentence-type used in exclamations. Other languages also have special types of full sentence for some kinds of exclamations. In Menomini there are two such, one of *surprise*, where the occurrence is new or unforeseen, and one of *disappointment* at the non-occurrence of something expected:

SURPRISE

narrative: [piasah!] 'and so he's coming!'
equational: [enusaʔ pajiat!] 'and so it's he that's coming!'
negative: [kasaʔ upianan!] 'and so he isn't coming!'

DISAPPOINTMENT

narrative: [piapah!] 'but he was coming!'
equational: [enupaʔ pajiat!] 'but he was the one who was coming!'
negative: [kapaʔ upianan!] 'but he wasn't coming!'

11. 4. A sentence which does not consist of a favorite sentence-form is a *minor sentence*. Some forms occur predominantly as minor sentences, entering into few or no constructions other than parataxis; such forms are *interjections*. Interjections are either special words, such as *ouch, oh, sh, gosh, hello, sir, ma'm, yes,* or else phrases (*secondary interjections*), often of peculiar construction, such as *dear me, goodness me, goodness gracious, goodness sakes alive, oh dear, by golly, you angel, please, thank you, good-bye.*

In general, minor sentences seem to be either *completive* or *exclamatory*. The *completive* type consists of a form which merely supplements a situation — that is, an earlier speech, a gesture, or the mere presence of an object: *This one. Tomorrow morning. Gladly, if I can. Whenever you're ready. Here. When? With whom? Mr. Brown: Mr. Smith* (in introducing people). *Drugs. State Street.* They occur especially as answers to questions; for this use we have the special completive interjections, *yes* and *no*. Even in this regard languages differ: French says *si* 'yes' in answer to negative questions, such as 'Isn't he coming?' but *oui* [wi] 'yes' in answer to others, such as 'Is he coming?' Some languages have no such interjections. Polish answers with ordinary adverbs, affirmatively with *tak* 'thus, so' and negatively with *nie* [ne] 'not.' Finnish answers affirmatively by an ordinary form, e.g. *Tulette-ko kaupungista?* — *Tulemme*. 'Are you coming from town?' — 'We are coming,' and negatively by its negative verb: *Tunnette-ko herra Lehdon? — En* (or *En tunne*) 'Do you know Mr. Lehto?' — 'I don't' (or 'I don't know').

Exclamatory minor sentences occur under a violent stimulus. They consist of interjections or of normal forms that do not belong to favorite sentence-types, and often show parataxis: *Ouch, damn it! This way, please!* A substantive form naming a hearer is used in English as a demand for his presence or attention: *John! Little boy! You with the glasses!* With parataxis: *Hello, John! Come here, little boy!* The interjections *sir* and *ma'am* are especially devoted to this use; in the same way Russian uses an interjection [s], as [da-s] 'yes, sir; yes, ma'am,' without distinction of sex. Many languages have special *vocative* forms for this use, as Latin *Balbus* (man's name), vocative *Balbe*, or Fox [iʃkwɛːwa] 'woman,' vocative [iʃkwe], and [iʃkwɛːwak] 'women,' vocative [iʃkwɛːtike]. In Menomini the terms of relationship have special, highly irregular vocative forms: [nɛʔnɛh] 'my older brother,' vocative [nanɛːʔ] or [nekiːjah] 'my mother,' vocative [neʔɛːh]. Other words are spoken as vocatives with short vowels instead of long: [mɛtɛːmuh] 'woman,' vocative [mɛtɛmuh]. In Sanskrit, vocative forms were unstressed.

Occasionally we find minor sentences of aphoristic type (§ 9.9) used with much the same value as full sentences; English examples are *The more you have, the more you want. The more, the merrier. First come, first served. Old saint, young sinner.*

11. 5. In most languages the sentence is characterized also by a selective feature more general than all those we have been discussing: some linguistic forms, which we call *bound forms* (§ 10.1), are never used as sentences. English examples are the *-ess* [is] in *countess, lioness, duchess*, etc., or the *-ish* [iʃ] in *boyish, childish, greenish*, etc., or the *-s* [s] in *hats, books, cups*, etc. These are genuine linguistic forms and convey a meaning, but they occur only in construction, as part of a larger form. Forms which occur as sentences are *free forms*. Not every language uses bound forms: modern Chinese, for instance, seems to have none.

A free form which consists entirely of two or more lesser free forms, as, for instance, *poor John* or *John ran away* or *yes, sir*, is a *phrase*. A free form which is not a phrase, is a *word*. A word, then, is a free form which does not consist entirely of (two or more) lesser free forms; in brief, a word is a *minimum free form*.

Since only free forms can be isolated in actual speech, the word, as the minimum of free form, plays a very important part in our attitude toward language. For the purposes of ordinary life, the word is the smallest unit of speech. Our dictionaries list the words of a language; for all purposes except the systematic study of language, this procedure is doubtless more useful than would be a list of morphemes. The analysis of linguistic forms into words is familiar to us because we have the custom of leaving spaces between words in our writing and printing. People who have not learned to read and write, have some difficulty when, by any chance, they are called upon to make word-divisions. This difficulty is less in English than in some other languages, such as French. The fact that the spacing of words has become part of our tradition of writing, goes to show, however, that recognition of the word as a unit of speech is not unnatural to speakers; indeed, except for certain doubtful cases, people easily learn to make this analysis.

In our school tradition we sometimes speak of forms like *book, books*, or *do, does, did, done* as "different forms of the same word." Of course, this is inaccurate, since there are differences of form and meaning between the members of these sets: the forms just cited are different linguistic forms and, accordingly, different words.

In other cases, inconsistencies in our habits of writing may make us uncertain. We write *John's* in *John's ready*, where it is two words (*John* and [z], an alternant of *is*) and in *John's hat*, where it is one word (consisting of *John* and the bound form [-z], possessive). We write *the boy's* as though it were two or three words, but, strictly speaking, it is only one word, since the immediate constituents are *the boy* and [-z] possessive, and the latter is a bound form; this appears clearly in cases like *the king of England's* or *the man I saw yesterday's*, where the meaning shows that the [-z] is in construction with the entire preceding phrase, so that the two are united into a single long word.

11. 6. In the case of many languages, however, it is impossible to distinguish consistently, on the one hand, between phrases and words and, on the other hand, between words and bound forms. The linguist cannot wait indefinitely for the chance of hearing a given form used as a sentence — that is, spoken alone. Some forms are rarely so used. Inquiry or experiment may call forth very different responses from hearers. Are English forms like *the*, *a*, *is*, and ever spoken alone? One can imagine a dialogue: *Is? — No; was.* The word *because* is said to be a woman's answer. An impatient listener says *And?* We can imagine a hesitant speaker who says *The . . .* and is understood by his hearers. Aside from such far-fetched situations, the general structure of a language may make one classification more convenient than another for our purpose. The form *the*, though rarely spoken alone, plays much the same part in our language as the forms *this* and *that*, which freely occur as sentences; this parallelism leads us to class *the* as a word:

this thing : *that thing* : *the thing*
this   : *that*   : (*the*).

In other cases, the difficulty is due to features of phonetic modification. The forms [z] in *John's ready*, [m] in *I'm hungry*, or [nt] in *Don't!* are unpronounceable in English, but we have to class them as words, for they are merely alternants of the pronounceable forms *is*, *am*, *not*. In French we have even the case of a single phoneme representing two words: *au* [o] in a phrase like *au roi* [o rwa] 'to the king,' arises by phonetic modification of the two words *à* [a] 'to' and *le* [lə] 'the'; this [o] is homonymous with the words *eau* 'water' and *haut* 'high.'

In other cases the doubtful forms are units of grammatical selection rather than of modification, and yet, in view of the total structure of their language, may be best classified as words. French, again, has several forms of this sort. Absolute forms like *moi* [mwa] 'I, me' and *lui* [lɥi] 'he, him' are replaced in certain constructions by shorter forms that do not ordinarily appear in absolute use, such as *je* [ʒə] 'I,' *me* [mə] 'me,' *il* [il] 'he,' *le* [lə] 'him'; for instance: *je le connais* [ʒə l kɔnɛ] 'I know him,' *il me connaît* [i m kɔnɛ] 'he knows me.' The replacement of the absolute forms by these *conjunct* forms is to be described as a feature of selection rather than of modification; nevertheless, the conjunct forms, largely because of their parallelism with the absolute forms, have the status of words.

A less important border-line case is the use of bound forms in hypostasis (§ 9.7), as when we speak of a girl in her *teens*, taking up all kinds of *isms* and *ologies*.

At the other extreme we find forms which lie on the border between words and phrases. A form like *blackbird* resembles a two-word phrase (*black bird*), but we shall find that a consistent description of English is bound to class this form as a single (compound) word. In this case there is a clear-cut difference, since in *blackbird* the second word (*bird*), has a weaker stress instead of a normal high stress, a difference which in English is phonemic, and this formal difference correlates with the semantic difference between *blackbird* and *black bird*. The distinction is not always so clear: *ice-cream* ['ajs ˌkrijm], spoken with only one high stress, will be classed as a (compound) word, but the variant pronunciation *ice cream* ['ajs 'krijm], with two high stresses, will be classed as a two-word phrase. Similar variants exist in types like *messenger boy, lady friend*.

This criterion of stress fails us in forms like *devil-may-care* (as in *a devil-may-care manner*) or *jack-in-the-pulpit* (as the name of a plant). If the former were *devil-may-care-ish*, we should not hesitate to class it as a word, since here one of the immediate constituents is the bound form *-ish*. The forms of the type *devil-may-care* are classed as words (phrase-words) because of certain other features which, within the system of the English language, place them on a level with other words. One of these is their peculiar function; as a phrase *devil-may-care* would be an actor-action form, but as a phrase-word it fills the position of an adjective. Another is their indivisibility: the plant-name *jack-in-the-pulpit* cannot be modified by putting the word *little* in front of *pulpit*, but the corresponding phrase permits of this and other expansions.

This latter principle, namely that a word cannot be interrupted by other forms, holds good almost universally. Thus, one can say *black — I should say, bluish-black — birds*, but one cannot similarly interrupt the compound word *blackbirds*. The exceptions to this principle are so rare as to seem almost pathological. Gothic had a bound form [ga-] which was prefixed especially to verbs: ['se:hwi] 'he should see,' [ga'se:hwi] 'he should be able to see.'

SENTENCE-TYPES

Yet occasionally we find words included between this [ga-] and the main body of the verb, as in the translation of *Mark* 8, 23: ['frah ina ga- u hwa 'se:hwi] 'he asked him whether [u] he saw anything [hwa].'

None of these criteria can be strictly applied: many forms lie on the border-line between bound forms and words, or between words and phrases; it is impossible to make a rigid distinction between forms that may and forms that may not be spoken in absolute position.

11. 7. The word is not primarily a phonetic unit: we do not, by pauses or other phonetic features, mark off those segments of our speech which could be spoken alone. In various ways, however, different languages give phonetic recognition to the word-unit: some, like French, very little, and others, like English, very much.

As a free form, the word is capable of being spoken in absolute position; accordingly, it is subject to the phonetic patterning of its language. It is sure to contain at least one of the phonemes which normally serve as syllabics; interjections, such as our *sh* [ʃ] and *pst* [pst], occasionally violate this principle. The initial and final consonants and clusters in the word are necessarily such, as can occur at the beginning and at the end of speech; thus, no English word begins with [ŋ] or [mb] and none ends with [h] or [mb].

Beyond this, many languages place further restrictions on the phonetic structure of the word. We may find that some of the permitted medial clusters do not occur within the body of a single word; in English, permitted clusters like [ʃtʃ, vt, tsv, ststr], as in *rash child, give ten, it's very cold, least strong*, and double consonants, like [nn, tt, bb], as in *ten nights, that time, nab Bill*, do not occur within simple words. On the other hand, French, with its insertion of [ə], and languages like Fox or Samoan, which use no final consonants, tolerate no more clusters within a phrase than within a word.

Some languages have the peculiar restriction, known as *vowel-harmony*, of tolerating only certain combinations of vowels in the successive syllables of a word. Thus, in Turkish, the vowels of a word are either all front vowels [i, y, e, ö], as in [sevildirememek] 'not to be able to cause to be loved,' or all back vowels [ï, u, a, o], as in [ˌazïldïramamak] 'not to be able to cause to be written'.

In Chinese we have the extreme of structural word-marking; each word consists of one syllable and of two or three primary phonemes: a non-syllabic simple or compound phoneme as initial, a syllabic simple or compound phoneme as final; and one of the pitch-schemes (§ 7.7); the initial non-syllabic may be lacking; the language has no bound forms.

In English and many other languages, each word is marked by containing one and only one high stress (*forgiving; convict*, verb; *convict*, noun). In some of these languages the word-unit is even more plainly marked, in that the position of a word-stress bears a definite relation to the beginning or to the end of the word: in Bohemian and in Icelandic the first syllable is stressed, in Cree the third-last (the *antepenult*), in Polish the next-to-last (the *penult*). In Latin the penult was stressed, as in *amamus* [a'ma:mus] 'we love,' unless this syllable had a short vowel followed by no more than one consonant, in which case the antepenult was stressed, as in *capimus* ['kapimus] 'we take.' In languages like these, the stress is a *word-marker*, which indicates the beginnings or ends of words, but, since its position is fixed, it cannot distinguish between different words. In Italian, Spanish, and modern Greek, the stress comes always on one of the last three syllables of a word. In ancient Greek a word had either a simple accent on one of the last three syllables or a compound accent on one of the last two, with some further restrictions based on the nature of the primary phonemes in these syllables.

Among stress-using languages, some, like English, start the stress at the beginning of a word whose stress comes on the first syllable; witness contrasts like *a name* versus *an aim* or *that scold* versus *that's cold* (§ 7.5); others, such as Dutch, Italian, Spanish, and the Slavic languages, regulate the onset of stress by purely phonetic habits, starting the stress on a consonant which precedes a stressed vowel, even though this consonant belongs to another word, as in Italian *un altro* [u'n altro] 'another.' A language like French, which uses no stress-phonemes, cannot in this way mark its word-units.

Phonetic recognition of the word-unit, in cases like the above, is disturbed chiefly by two factors. Words which contain, among their ultimate constituents, two or more free forms, generally have the phonetic character of phrases. In English, compound words have the same medial clusters as phrases: *stove-top* [vt], *chest-strap* [ststr], *pen-knife* [nn], *grab-bag* [bb]; phrase-derivatives may even have more than one high stress: *old-maidish* [ˈowld ˈmejdiʃ], *jack-in-the-pulpit* [ˈdʒɛk in ðə ˈpulpit].

On the other hand, words in included position are subject to modulations and phonetic modifications which may remove the phonetic characteristics of word-marking. Thus *not* in the phrase *don't* [ˈdow nt] loses both its high stress and its syllabic; compare, similarly, *lock it*, with *locket*, *feed her* [ˈfijd ə] with *feeder*, and so on. English unstressed words are phonetically like affixal syllables. In the normal pronunciation *at all* [eˈt ɔːl] the stress begins on the [t] of *at*. These included variants, in which a word loses the phonetic features that characterize words in absolute position, will concern us in the next chapter. In the present connection it is worth noticing, however, that in a small way these modified phrases may nevertheless involve phonetic recognition of the word-unit, because they contain phonetic sequences that do not occur in single words. Thus, the final sequence [ownt] is permitted in English, but occurs only in the phrases *don't* and *won't*, and not in any one word. In South German dialects some initial clusters, such as [tn, tʃt] occur in phrases, thanks to phonetic modification of the first word, as in [t naxt] 'the night,' [t ʃtaːʃt] 'thou standest,' but not in any one word. In North Chinese a phrase may end in syllabic plus [r], as in [cjaw³ ˈma r³] 'little horse,' but only as a result of phonetic modification of two words, — in our example, [ma³] 'horse' and [r²] 'son, child, small.'

In the few languages which use no bound forms, the word has a double importance, since it is the smallest unit not only of free form but also of linguistic form in general. In languages which use bound forms, the word has great structural importance because the constructions in which free forms appear in phrases differ very decidedly from the constructions in which free or bound forms appear in words. Accordingly, the grammar of these languages consists of two parts, called *syntax*, and *morphology*. However, the constructions of compound words and, to some extent, of phrase-derivatives, occupy an intermediate position.

CHAPTER 12

SYNTAX

12. 1. Traditionally, the grammar of most languages is discussed under two heads, *syntax* and *morphology*. The sentence-types, which we surveyed in the last chapter, are placed under the former heading, and so are the types of substitution (which we shall consider in Chapter 15), but grammatical *constructions*, which we shall now examine, are dealt with partly under the heading of morphology. There has been considerable debate as to the usefulness of this division, and as to the scope of the two headings. In languages that have bound forms, the constructions in which bound forms play a part differ radically from the constructions in which all the immediate constituents are free forms. Accordingly, we place the former under the separate heading of morphology. The difficulty is this, that certain formal relations, such as the relation between *he* and *him*, consist in the use of bound forms, while the semantic difference between these forms can be defined in terms of syntactic construction; *he* serves, for instance, as an actor (*he ran*) and *him* as an undergoer (*hit him*). Nevertheless, the traditional division is justified: it merely happens that in these cases the meanings involved in the morphologic construction are definable in terms of syntax instead of being definable merely in terms of practical life. *Syntactic* constructions, then, are constructions in which none of the immediate constituents is a bound form. Border-line cases between morphology and syntax occur chiefly in the sphere of compound words and phrase-words.

12. 2. The free forms (words and phrases) of a language appear in larger free forms (phrases), arranged by taxemes of modulation, phonetic modification, selection, and order. Any meaningful, recurrent set of such taxemes is a *syntactic construction*. For instance, the English actor-action construction appears in phrases like these:

John ran   *Bill fell*
John fell *Our horses ran away.*
Bill ran

In these examples we see taxemes of selection. The one constituent (*John, Bill, our horses*) is a form of a large class, which we call *nominative expressions;* a form like *ran* or *very good* could not be used in this way. The other constituent (*ran, fell, ran away*) is a form of another large class, which we call *finite verb expressions;* a form like *John* or *very good* could not be used in this way. Secondly, we see a taxeme of order: the nominative expression *precedes* the finite verb expression. We need not stop here to examine the various other types and sub-types of this construction, which show different or additional taxemes. The meaning of the construction is roughly this, that whatever is named by the substantive expression is an actor that *performs* the action named by the finite verb expression. The two immediate constituents of the English actor-action construction are not interchangeable: we say that the construction has two *positions*, which we may call the positions of *actor* and of *action*. Certain English words and phrases can appear in the actor position, certain others in the action position. The positions in which a form can appear are its *functions* or, collectively, its *function*. All the forms which can fill a given position thereby constitute a *form-class*. Thus, all the English words and phrases which can fill the actor position in the actor-action construction, constitute a great form-class, and we call them nominative expressions; similarly, all the English words and phrases which can fill the action position on the actor-action construction, constitute a second great form-class, and we call them finite verb expressions.

12. 3. Since the constituents of phrases are free forms, the speaker may separate them by means of *pauses*. Pauses are mostly non-distinctive; they occur chiefly when the constituents are long phrases; in English they are usually preceded by a pause-pitch.

We have seen (§ 11.1) that free forms which are united by no other construction may be united by *parataxis*, the mere absence of a phonetic sentence-final, as in *It's ten o'clock* [,] *I have to go home* [.] In ordinary English parataxis a pause-pitch appears between the constituents, but we have also a variety of *close parataxis* without a pause-pitch, as in *please come* or *yes sir*.

A special variety of parataxis is the use of *semi-absolute* forms, which grammatically and in meaning duplicate some part of the form with which they are joined in parataxis, as in *John, he ran away*. In French this type is regularly used in some kinds of questions, as *Jean quand est-il venu?* [žɑ̃ kɑ̃t ɛt i vny?] 'John, when did he come?'

Parenthesis is a variety of parataxis in which one form interrupts the other; in English the parenthetic form is ordinarily preceded and followed by a pause-pitch: *I saw the boy* [,] *I mean Smith's boy* [,] *running across the street* [.] In a form like *Won't you please come?* the *please* is a *close* parenthesis, without pause-pitch.

The term *apposition* is used when paratactically joined forms are grammatically, but not in meaning, equivalent, e.g. *John* [,] *the poor boy*. When the appositional group appears in included position, one of its members is equivalent to a parenthesis: *John* [,] *the poor boy* [,] *ran away* [.] In English we have also *close* apposition, without a pause-pitch, as in *King John, John Brown, John the Baptist, Mr. Brown, Mount Everest*.

Often enough non-linguistic factors interfere with construction; what the speaker has said is nevertheless meaningful, provided he has already uttered a free form. In *aposiopesis* the speaker breaks off or is interrupted: *I thought he* — . In *anacolouthon* he starts over again: *It's high time we* — *oh, well, I guess it won't matter.* When a speaker hesitates, English and some other languages offer special parenthetic *hesitation-forms*, as [ə] or [ɛ] in *Mr.* — *ah* — *Sniffen* or *Mr.* — *what you may call him* — *Sniffen* or *that* — *thingamajig* — *transmitter.*

12. 4. Features of modulation and of phonetic modification play a great part in many syntactic constructions; they are known as *sandhi*.[1] The form of a word or phrase as it is spoken alone is its *absolute* form; the forms which appear in included positions are its *sandhi-forms*. Thus, in English, the absolute form of the indefinite article is *a* ['ej]. This form appears in included position only when the article is an emphatic element and the next word begins with a consonant, as in "not *a* house, but *the* house." If the next word begins with a vowel, we have instead a sandhi-form, *an* ['ɛn], as in "not *an* uncle, but *her* uncle."

A feature of modulation appears in the fact that when *a, an* is not an emphatic element, it is spoken as an unstressed syllable, as in *a house* [ə 'haws], *an arm* [ən 'ɑːm]. In English, a word in absolute form has one high stress; hence we may say that in a sandhi-form without high stress a word is spoken as if it were part

---

[1] This term, like many technical terms of linguistics, comes from the ancient Hindu grammarians. Literally, it means 'putting together.'

SYNTAX

of another word. Various languages use sandhi-forms of this sort; they are known as *atonic* forms. This term is not altogether appropriate, since the peculiarity is not always a lack of stress. In the French phrase *l'homme* [l ɔm] 'the man,' the article *le* [lə] is atonic, because its sandhi-form [l] could not be spoken alone on account of the phonetic pattern (lack of a vowel). In the Polish phrase [do nuk] 'to the feet,' the preposition *do* 'to' is atonic precisely because it has the stress, for the stress in this language is placed on the next-to-last syllable of each word, and falls on *do* only because this word is treated as part of the following word.

An atonic form which is treated as part of the following word — this is the case in our examples so far — is a *proclitic*. An atonic form which is treated as if it were part of the preceding word is an *enclitic;* thus, in *I saw him* [aj 'sɔː.im], the [aj] is proclitic, but the [im] enclitic.

The sandhi which substitutes *an* for *a*, and the sandhi by which *this* and other words are unstressed in phrasal combinations, are examples of *compulsory sandhi*. Other English sandhi habits are *optional*, because paralleled by unaltered variants, which have usually a formal or elevated connotation; for instance, the dropping of [h] in *him* does not take place in the more elevated variant *I saw him* [aj ˈsɔː him]. Beside the sandhi-forms in *did you?* [ˈdidʒuw?], *won't you* [ˈwowntʃuw?], *at all* [əˈtɔːl] (in American English with the voiced tongue-flip variant of [t]), we have the more elegant variants [ˈdid juw? ˈwownt juw? ət ˈɔːl].

Sandhi-forms may be unpronounceable when taken by themselves; this is the case in a number of English examples:

ABSOLUTE FORM	SANDHI-FORM
is [ˈiz]	[z] *John's ready.*
	[s] *Dick's ready.*
has [ˈhɛz]	[z] *John's got it.*
am [ˈɛm]	[m] *I'm ready.*
are [ˈɑː]	[ə] *We're waiting.*
have [ˈhɛv]	[v] *I've got it.*
had [ˈhɛd]	[d] *He'd seen it.*
would [ˈwud]	[d] *He'd see it.*
will [ˈwil]	[l] *I'll go.*
	[l] *That'll do.*
them [ˈðem]	[əm] *Watch 'em.*

ABSOLUTE FORM	SANDHI-FORM
not ['nɔt]	[n̥t] *It isn't.*
	[nt] *I won't.*
	[t] *I can't.*
and ['ɛnd]	[n̥] *bread and butter.*

The French language has a great deal of sandhi. Thus, the article *la* [la] 'the' (feminine) loses the [a] before a vowel or diphthong: *la femme* [la fam] 'the woman,' but *l'encre* [l ãkr] 'the ink,' *l'oie* [l wa] 'the goose.' The adjective *ce* [sə] 'this' (masculine) adds [t] before the same sounds: *ce couteau* [sə kuto] 'this knife,' but *cet homme* [sɔt ɔm] 'this man.' A plural pronoun adds [z] before the initial vowel of a verb: *vous faites* [vu fɛt] 'you make,' but *vous êtes* [vuz ɛːt] 'you are.' A plural noun-modifier behaves similarly: *les femmes* [le fam] 'the women,' but *les hommes* [lez ɔm] 'the men.' A first-person or second-person verb adds [z], a third-person verb [t], before certain initial vowels: *va* [va] 'go thou,' but *vas-y* [vaz i] 'go thou there'; *elle est* [ɛl ɛ] 'she is,' but *est-elle?* [ɛt ɛl?] 'is she?' A few masculine adjectives add sandhi-consonants before a vowel: *un grand garçon* [œ̃ grã garsõ] 'a big boy,' but *un grand homme* [œ̃ grãt ɔm] 'a great man.'

In languages with distinctions of pitch in the word, modifications of pitch may play a part in sandhi. Thus, in Chinese, beside the absolute form ['i¹] 'one,' there are the sandhi-forms in [ᵢi⁴ phi² 'ma³] 'one horse' and [i² ko 'ʒən²] 'one man.'

Sandhi-modification of initial phonemes is less common than that of the end of a word; it occurs in the Celtic languages, as, in modern Irish:

ABSOLUTE FORM	SANDHI-FORM
['boː] 'cow'	[an 'voː] 'the cow'
	[ar 'moː] 'our cow'
['uv] 'egg'	[an 'tuv] 'the egg'
	[na 'nuv] 'of the eggs'
	[a 'huv] 'her egg'
['baːn] 'white'	['boː 'vaːn] 'white cow'
['bog] 'soft'	['roː 'vog] 'very soft'
['briʃ] 'break'	[do 'vriʃ] 'did break.'

12. 5. Our examples so far illustrate *special* or *irregular* cases of sandhi, peculiar to certain forms and constructions. *General* or *regular* sandhi applies to any and all words in a short (*close-knit*) phrase. In some forms of English, such as New England and southern British, words which in absolute position have a final vowel, add [r] before an initial vowel: *water* ['wɔːtə] but *the water is* [ðə 'wɔːtər iz]; *idea* [aj'diə] but *the idea is* [ðij aj'diər iz]. When three consonants come together in French, the word-final adds [ə]; thus, *porte* [pɔrt] 'carries' and *bien* [bjɛ̃] 'well' appear in the phrase as *porte bien* [pɔrtə bjɛ̃] 'carries well.' A word whose first syllable in absolute form contains [ə], either because the word has no other syllabic or because otherwise it would begin with an unpermitted cluster (§ 8.6), loses this [ə] in the phrase whenever no unpermitted group would result: *le* [lə] 'the' but *l'homme* [l ɔm] 'the man'; *cheval* [ʃəval] 'horse,' but *un cheval* [œ̃ ʃval] 'a horse'; *je* [ʒə] 'I,' *ne* [nə] 'not,' *le* [lə] 'it,' *demande* [dəmãd] 'ask,' but *je ne le demande pas* [ʒə n lə dmãd pa] 'I don't ask it' and *si je ne le demande pas* [si ʒ nə l dəmãd pa] 'if I don't ask it.'

In Sanskrit there is a great deal of general sandhi; for instance, final [ah] of the absolute form appears in the following sandhi-variants: absolute [deːˈvah] 'a god,' sandhi-forms: [deːˈvas ˈtatra] 'the god there,' [deːˈvaç carati] 'the god wanders,' [deːˈva eːti] 'the god goes,' [deːˈvoː dadaːti] 'the god gives,' and, with change also of a following initial, before [ˈatra] 'here,' [deːˈvoː tra] 'the god here.' Certain words, however, behave differently; thus, [ˈpunah] 'again' gives [ˈpunar dadaːti] 'again he gives,' [ˈpunar ˈatra] 'again here.' The divergent words may be marked off by some structural feature. Thus, in some Dutch pronunciations the absolute forms *heb* [ˈhep] 'have' and *stop* [stɔp] 'stop' behave differently in sandhi: *heb ik?* [ˈheb ek?] 'have I?' but *stop ik?* [ˈstɔp ek?] 'do I stop?' The forms which have the voiced consonant in sandhi have it also whenever it is not at the end of the word, as *hebben* [ˈhebe] 'to have,' in contrast with *stoppen* [ˈstɔpe] 'to stop.' Sandhi-distinctions based on morphologic features like this, may be called *reminiscent sandhi*.

Sandhi may go so far as to restrict the word-final in a phrase beyond the ordinary medial restrictions of a language. Thus, the sequence [ta] is permitted medially in Sanskrit, as in [ˈpatati] 'he falls,' but [t] at the end of the word is in close-knit phrases replaced by [d] before a vowel: absolute [ˈtat] 'that,' but [ˈtad asti] 'that is.'

12. 6. Taxemes of selection play a large part in the syntax of most languages; syntax consists largely in defining them — in stating, for instance, under what circumstances (with what accompanying forms or, if the accompanying forms are the same, with what difference of meaning) various form-classes (as, say, indicative and subjunctive verbs, or dative and accusative nouns, and so on) appear in syntactic constructions. We have seen that the selective taxemes delimit form-classes. These classes are most numerous in the languages that use most taxemes of selection. The syntactic constructions of a language mark off large classes of free forms, such as, in English, the nominative expression or the finite verb expression. Since different languages have different constructions, their form-classes also are different. We shall see that the great form-classes of a language are most easily described in terms of *word-classes* (such as the traditional "parts of speech"), because the form-class of a phrase is usually determined by one or more of the words which appear in it.

In languages which make a wide use of selective taxemes, the large form-classes are subdivided into smaller ones. For instance, the English actor-action construction, in addition to the general selective taxemes, shows some more specialized taxemes of the same sort. With the nominative expressions *John* or *that horse* we can join the finite verb expression *runs fast*, but not the finite verb expression *run fast;* with the nominative expressions *John and Bill* or *horses* the reverse selection is made. Accordingly, we recognize in each of these two form-classes a division into two sub-classes, which we call *singular* and *plural*, such that a singular nominative expression is joined only with a singular finite verb expression, and a plural nominative expression only with a plural finite verb expression. It would not do to define these sub-classes by meaning — witness cases like *wheat grows* but *oats grow*. Further examination shows us several varieties of selection: (1) many finite verb expressions, such as *can, had, went*, appear with any actor; (2) many, such as *run : runs*, show the twofold selection just described; (3) one, *was : were*, shows a twofold selection that does not agree with the preceding; (4) one, finally, *am : is : are*, shows a threefold selection, with a special form that accompanies the actor *I*, precisely the actor form as to which (2) and (3) disagree:

	(1)	(2)	(3)	(4)
A	*I can*	*I run*	*I was*	*I am*
B	*the boy can*	*the boy runs*	*the boy was*	*the boy is*
C	*the boys can*	*the boys run*	*the boys were*	*the boys are*
	A = B = C	A = C	A = B	

Thus we find among nominative expressions and among finite verb expressions a threefold subdivision, due to taxemes of selection; among nominative expressions sub-class A contains only the form *I;* sub-class B contains those which are joined with finite verb expressions such as *runs, was, is,* and sub-class C contains those which are joined with finite verb expressions such as *run, were, are.* In fact, we can base our definition of the three sub-classes on the selection of the three finite verb forms *am : is : are.* Conversely, we define the sub-classes of finite verb expressions by telling with which nominative expressions (say, *I : the boy : the boys*) they occur.

The narrower type of selection in cases like this one is in principle no different from the more inclusive type by which our language distinguishes great form-classes like nominative expressions and finite verb expressions, but there are some differences of detail. The narrower type of selection, by which great form-classes are subdivided into selective types, is called *agreement.* In a rough way, without real boundaries, we can distinguish three general types of agreement.

12. 7. In our example, the agreement is of the simplest kind, which is usually called *concord* or *congruence:* if the actor is a form of sub-class A, the action must be a form of sub-class A, and so on. Sometimes one of the subdivisions is otherwise also recognized in the structure of the language; thus, in our example, classes B and C of nominative expressions are otherwise also definable in our language; namely, by the use of the modifiers *this, that* with class B, but *these, those* with class C: we say *this boy, this wheat,* but *these boys, these oats.* Accordingly, we view the subdivision of nominative expressions into singulars and plurals as more fundamental than that of finite verb expressions, and say that the latter *agree with* or *stand in congruence* with the former. For the same reason, we say that the forms *this, that, these, those* stand in congruence with the accompanying substantive form. Congruence plays a great part in many languages; witness for example the inflection of the adjectives in most Indo-European languages in congruence with various sub-classes (number, gender, case) of the noun: German *der Knabe* [der 'kna:be] 'the boy,' *ich sehe den Knaben* [ix 'ze:e den 'kna:ben] 'I see the boy,' *die Knaben* [di: 'kna:ben] 'the boys,' where the selection of *der, den, die* agrees with the sub-classes of the noun (singular and plural, nominative and accusative); in *das Haus* [das 'haws] 'the house,' the form *das*, as opposed to *der*, is selected in agreement with the so-called *gender-classes* into which German nouns are divided. These genders are arbitrary classes, each of which demands different congruence-forms in certain kinds of accompanying words. German has three gender-classes; for each of these I give phrases showing the congruence of the definite article and of the adjective *kalt* 'cold':

"masculine gender": *der Hut* [der 'hu:t] 'the hat,' *kalter Wein* [ˌkalter 'vajn] 'cold wine'

"feminine gender": *die Uhr* [di: 'u:r] 'the clock' *kalte Milch* [ˌkalte 'milx] 'cold milk'

"neuter gender": *das Haus* [das 'haws] 'the nouse,' *kaltes Wasser* [ˌkaltes 'vaser] 'cold water.'

French has two genders, "masculine," *le couteau* [lə kuto] 'the knife,' and "feminine," *la fourchette* [la furʃɛt] 'the fork.' Some languages of the Bantu family distinguish as many as twenty gender-classes of nouns.

12. 8. In other cases the subsidiary taxeme of selection has to do with the syntactic position of the form. For instance, we say *I know* but *watch me, beside me*. The choice between the forms *I* (*he, she, they, we*) and *me* (*him, her, them, us*) depends upon the position of the form: the *I*-class appears in the position of actor, the *me*-class in the position of goal in the action-goal construction (*watch me*) and in the position of axis in the relation-axis construction (*beside me*). This type of selection is called *government;* the accompanying form (*know, watch, beside*) is said to *govern* (or to *demand* or to *take*) the selected form (*I* or *me*). Government, like congruence, plays a great part in many languages, including many of the Indo-European family. Thus, in Latin, different verbs govern different case-forms in the substantive goal: *videt bovem* 'he sees the ox,' *nocet bovī* 'he harms the ox,' *ūtitur bove* 'he uses the ox,' *meminit bovis* 'he remembers the ox.' Similarly, different main clauses may govern different forms of subordinate verbs, as in French *je pense qu'il vient* [ʒə pɑ̃s k i vjɛ̃] 'I think he is coming,' but *je ne pense pas qu-il vienne* [ʒə n pɑ̃s pɑ k i vjɛn] 'I don't think he is coming.'

Identity and non-identity of objects are in many languages distinguished by selective features akin to government. In English we say *he washed him* when actor and goal are not identical, but *he washed himself* (a *reflexive* form) when they are the same person. Swedish thus distinguishes between identical and non-identical actor and possessor: *han tog sin hatt* [han 'to:g si:n 'hat] 'he took his (own) hat' and *han tog hans hatt* [hans 'hat] 'his (someone else's) hat.' The Algonquian languages use different forms for non-identical animate third persons in a context. In Cree, if we speak of a man and then, secondarily, of another man, we mention the first one as ['na:pe:w] 'man,' and the second one, in the so-called *obviative* form, as ['na:pe:wa]. Thus, the language distinguishes between the following cases, where we designate the principal person as A and the other (the obviative) as B:

['utinam u'tastutin] 'he (A) took his (A's) hat'
['utinam utastu'tinijiw] 'he (A) took his (B's) hat'
[utina'mijiwa u'tastutin] 'he (B) took his (A's) hat'
[utina'mijiwa utastu'tinijiw] 'he (B) took his (B's) hat.'

12. 9. In the third type of agreement, *cross-reference*, the subclasses contain an actual mention of the forms with which they are joined. This mention is in the shape of a substitute-form, resembling our pronouns. In non-standard English this occurs in such forms as *John his knife* or *John he ran away;* here the form *his knife* actually mentions a male possessor, who is more explicitly mentioned in the accompanying semi-absolute form *John;* similarly, the *he* in *he ran away* mentions the actor *John* — contrast *Mary her knife* and *Mary she ran away*. In French, cross-reference occurs in the standard language especially in certain types of questions, such as *Jean où est-il?* [ʒɑ̃ u ɛt i?] 'John where is he?' that is, 'Where is John?' (§ 12.3). A Latin finite verb, such as *cantat* 'he (she, it) sings,' includes substitutive mention of an actor. It is joined in cross-reference with a substantive expression that makes specific mention of the actor, as in *puella cantat* '(the) girl she-sings.' In many languages verb-forms include substitutive (pronominal) mention of both an actor and an undergoer, as, in Cree [wa:pame:w] 'he saw him or her'; accordingly, more specific mention of both actor and undergoer is in cross-reference ['wa:-pame:w 'atimwa a'wa na:pe:w] 'he-saw-him (obviative) a-dog (obviative) that man'; that is, 'the man saw a dog.' Similarly, in many languages, a possessed noun includes pronominal mention of a possessor, as, in Cree, ['astutin] 'hat,' but [ni'tastutin] 'my hat,' [ki'tastutin] 'thy hat,' [u'tastutin] 'his, her, its hat'; hence, when the possessor is mentioned in another word or phrase, we have cross-reference, as in ['tʃa:n u'tastutin] 'John his-hat,' i.e. 'John's hat.'

12. 10. Every syntactic construction shows us two (or sometimes more) free forms combined in a phrase, which we may call the *resultant* phrase. The resultant phrase may belong to a form-class other than that of any constituent. For instance, *John ran* is neither a nominative expression (like *John*) nor a finite verb expression (like *ran*). Therefore we say that the English actor-action construction is *exocentric:* the resultant phrase belongs to the form-class of no immediate constituent. On the other hand, the resultant phrase may belong to the same form-class as one (or more) of the constituents. For instance, *poor John* is a proper-noun expression, and so is the constituent *John;* the forms *John* and *poor John* have, on the whole, the same functions. Accordingly, we say that the English character-substance construction (as in *poor John, fresh milk,* and the like) is an *endocentric* construction.

The exocentric constructions in any language are few. In English we have, beside the actor-action construction, also that of relation-axis, as *beside John, with me, in the house, by running away;* the constituents are a prepositional expression and an accusative expression, but the resultant phrase has a function different from either of these, appearing in entirely different syntactic positions (e.g. as a modifier of verbs: *sit beside John,* or of nouns: *the boy beside John*). Another exocentric construction of English is that of *subordination.* The constituents in one type (*clause-subordination*) are a subordinating expression and an actor-action phrase, as in *if John ran away;* the resultant phrase has the function of neither constituent, but serves as a modifier (subordinate clause). In the other type (*phrase-subordination*) the constituents are a subordinating expression and any other form, especially a substantive: *as I, than John,* and the resultant phrase has the function of a modifier (*as big as I, bigger than John*). Although the resultant phrase in an exocentric construction has a function different from the function of any constituent, yet one of these constituents is usually peculiar to the construction and serves to characterize the resultant phrase; thus, in English, finite verbs, prepositions, and subordinating conjunctions regularly appear in the exocentric constructions just illustrated, and suffice to characterize them.

Endocentric constructions are of two kinds, *co-ordinative* (or *serial*) and *subordinative* (or *attributive*). In the former type the resultant phrase belongs to the same form-class as two or more of the constituents. Thus, the phrase *boys and girls* belongs to the same form-class as the constituents, *boys, girls;* these constituents are the *members* of the co-ordination, and the other constituent is the *co-ordinator*. Sometimes there is no co-ordinator: *books, papers, pens, pencils, blotters (were all lying . . .)*; sometimes there is one for each member, as in *both Bill and John, either Bill or John*. There may be minor differences of form-class between the resultant phrase and the members; thus *Bill and John* is plural, while the members are each singular.

In subordinative endocentric constructions, the resultant phrase belongs to the same form-class as one of the constituents, which we call the *head:* thus, *poor John* belongs to the same form-class as *John*, which we accordingly call the head; the other member, in our example *poor*, is the *attribute*. The attribute may in turn be a subordinative phrase: in *very fresh milk* the immediate constituents are the head *milk*, and the attribute *very fresh*, and this phrase, in turn, consists of the head *fresh* and the attribute *very*. In this way there can be several *ranks* of subordinative position; in *very fresh milk* there are three: (1) *milk*, (2) *fresh*, (3) *very*. In the same way, the head also may show an attributive construction: the phrase *this fresh milk* consists of the attribute *this* and the head *fresh milk*, and this, in turn, of the attribute *fresh* and the head *milk*.

12. 11. If all the syntactic constructions which go to make up a phrase are endocentric, then the phrase will contain among its ultimate constituents some word (or several words, members of a co-ordination) whose form-class is the same as that of the phrase. This word is the *center* of the phrase. In the phrase *all this fresh milk*, the word *milk* is the center, and in the phrase *all this fresh bread and sweet butter*, the words *bread* and *butter* are the centers. Since most of the constructions in any language are endocentric, most phrases have a center: the form-class of a phrase is usually the same as that of some word that is contained in the phrase.

The exceptions are phrases of exocentric construction, and these, too, we have seen, are definable in terms of word-classes. The syntactic form-classes of phrases, therefore, can be derived from the syntactic form-classes of words: the form-classes of syntax are most easily described in terms of *word-classes*. Thus, in English, a substantive expression is either a word (such as *John*) which belongs to this form-class (a *substantive*), or else a phrase (such as *poor John*) whose center is a substantive; and an English finite verb expression is either a word (such as *ran*) which belongs to this form-class (a *finite verb*), or else a phrase (such as *ran away*) whose center is a finite verb. An English actor-action phrase (such as *John ran* or *poor John ran away*) does not share the form-class of any word, since its construction is exocentric, but the form-class of actor-action phrases is defined by their construction: they consist of a nominative expression and a finite verb expression (arranged in a certain way), and this, in the end, again reduces the matter to terms of word-classes.

The term *parts of speech* is traditionally applied to the most inclusive and fundamental word-classes of a language, and then, in accordance with the principle just stated, the syntactic form-classes are described in terms of the parts of speech that appear in them. However, it is impossible to set up a fully consistent scheme of parts of speech, because the word-classes overlap and cross each other.

In speaking of form-classes we use the term *expression* to include both words and phrases: thus *John* is a *substantive*, *poor John* a *substantive phrase*, and both forms are *substantive expressions*.

Within the great form-classes which contain both words and (thanks to endocentric constructions) a vast number of phrasal combinations, there may be sub-classes due to small differences of phrasal construction. For instance, when an attribute like *fresh, good*, or *sweet* is joined to the head *milk*, as in *fresh milk*, this resultant phrase is still capable of joining with other attributes, as in *good, sweet, fresh milk:* the phrase has entirely the same functions as its center (and head), namely the word *milk*. If, however, we join a form like *milk* or *fresh milk* with the attribute *this*, the resultant phrase, *this milk* or *this fresh milk* has not quite the same function as the head or center, since the resultant phrase cannot be joined with attributes like *good, sweet:* the construction in *this milk, this fresh milk* is *partially closed*. The possibilities in this direction, in fact, are limited to adding the attribute *all*, as in *all this milk* or *all this fresh milk*. When the attribute *all* has been added, the construction is *closed:* no more attributes of this type (adjectives) can be added.

12. 12. An example of a taxeme of *order* is the arrangement by which the actor form precedes the action form in the normal type of the English actor-action construction: *John ran*. In languages which use highly complex taxemes of selection, order is largely non-distinctive and connotative; in a Latin phrase such as *pater amat fīlium* 'the father loves the son,' the syntactic relations are all selective (cross-reference and government) and the words appear in all possible orders (*pater fīlium amat, fīlium pater amat*, and so on), with differences only of emphasis and liveliness. In English, taxemes of order appear in the difference between actor-action and action-goal, as in *John ran* and *catch John;* the difference between *John hit Bill* and *Bill hit John* rests entirely upon order. In general, however, taxemes of order in English occur along with taxemes of selection. Languages which in this respect and in the general configuration of their syntax resemble English, may still show great differences as to taxemes of order. Thus, standard German differs from English in allowing only one attribute (word or phrase) of the verb to precede a finite verb: *heute spielen wir Ball* ['hojte 'ʃpi:len vi:r 'bal] 'today play we ball.' Further, it places several elements last in the sentence: certain adverbs, as *ich stehe um sieben Uhr auf* [ix 'ʃte:e um 'zi:ben 'u:r 'awf] 'I get at seven o'clock up'; participles, as *ich habe ihn heute gesehen* [ix ˌha:be i:n 'hojte geˈze:n] 'I have him today seen'; infinitives, as *ich werde ihn heute sehen* [ix ˌverde i:n 'hojte 'ze:n] 'I shall him today see'; the verb of a dependent clause: *wenn ich ihn heute sehe* [ven ix i:n 'hojte 'ze:e] 'if I him today see.'

French has a complicated and rigid system of ordering certain substitute ("conjunct") accompaniments of its verbs. In the ordinary (non-interrogative) sentence-type, it distinguishes seven positions of these elements, which precede the finite verb:

(1) actors, such as *je* [ʒə] 'I,' *il* [il] 'he, it,' *ils* [il] 'they,' *on* [õ] 'one,' *ce* [sə] 'it, that'

(2) the negative adverb *ne* [nə] 'not'

(3) farther goals of first and second persons, such as *me* [mə] 'to me,' *vous* [vu] 'to you,' and of the reflexive *se* [sə] 'to himself, herself, themselves'

(4) nearer goals, such as *me* [mə] 'me,' *vous* [vu] 'you,' *se* [sə] 'himself, herself, themselves,' *le* [lə] 'him, it,' *les* [le] 'them'

(5) farther goals of the third person: *lui* [lɥi] 'to him, to her,' *leur* [lœ:r] 'to them'

(6) the adverb *y* [i] 'there, thither, to it, to them'

(7) the adverb *en* [ã] 'from there, of it, of them.'

For example: (1-2-3-4) *il ne me le donne pas* [i n mə l dɔn pɑ] 'he does not give it to me'

(1-3-6-7) *il m'y en donne* [i m j ã dɔn] 'he gives me some of it there'

(1-4-5) *on le lui donne* [õ lə lɥi dɔn] 'one gives it to him'

(1-2-6-7) *il n'y en a pas* [i n j ãn a pɑ] 'there aren't any,' literally 'it has not of them there.'

Occasionally order serves finer distinctions. In French most adjectives follow their nouns: *une maison blanche* (yn mezõ blɑ̃ʃ] 'a white house'; a certain few precede: *une belle maison* [yn bɛl mezõ] 'a pretty house'; others precede only with transferred meanings or with emphatic or intense connotations: *une barbe noire* [yn barbə nwa:r] 'a black beard': *une noire trahison* [yn nwa:r traizõ] 'a black betrayal'; *un livre excellent* [œ̃ li:vr ɛksɛlã] 'an excellent book': *un excellent livre* 'a splendid book!' A few show greater differences of meaning: *un livre cher* [œ̃ li:vrə ʃɛ:r] 'a costly book': *un cher ami* [œ̃ ʃɛ:r ami] 'a dear friend,' *sa propre main* [sa prɔprə mɛ̃] 'his own hand': *une main propre* [yn mɛ̃ prɔpr] 'a clean hand.'

Viewed from the standpoint of economy, taxemes of order are a gain, since the forms are bound to be spoken in some succession; nevertheless, few languages allow features of order to work alone: almost always they merely supplement taxemes of selection.

12. 13. The languages of the Indo-European family are peculiar in having many parts of speech; no matter upon what constructions we base our scheme, a language like English will show at least half a dozen parts of speech, such as substantive, verb, adjective, adverb, preposition, co-ordinating conjunction, and subordinating conjunction, in addition to interjections. Most languages show a smaller number. A distribution into three types is quite frequent (Semitic, Algonquian); usually one resembles our substantives and one our verbs. It is a mistake to suppose that our part-of-speech system represents universal features of human expression. If such classes as objects, actions, and qualities exist apart from our language, as realities either of physics or of human psychology, then, of course, they exist all over the world, but it would still be true that many languages lack corresponding parts of speech.

In languages with few parts of speech, the syntactic form-classes appear rather in phrases. Often the class of a phrase is indicated by some special word, a *marker;* strictly speaking, the marker and the form which it accompanies are joined in an exocentric construction which determines the class of the phrase. Aside from this selective feature, the constructions are likely to be distinguished by word-order.

The classical instance is Chinese. The parts of speech are *full words* and *particles* (that is, markers). The principal constructions are three.

(1) The favorite sentence-construction is one of *subject* and *predicate*, much like the English actor-action construction; the subject precedes the predicate: [tha^1 'xaw^3] 'he is good,' [tha^1 'laj^2] 'he came.' In certain cases, depending on differences of form-class, the predicate is marked by the particle [ʃɔ^4] at its beginning: [tha^1 ʃə^4 'xaw^3 ˌʒən^2] 'he (p.) good man,' that is, 'he is a good man.'

(2) There is an endocentric construction in which the *attribute* precedes the *head;* in meaning this resembles the similar English constructions: ['xaw^3 ˌʒən^2] 'good man,' ['man^4 ˌtʃhy^4] 'slowly go,' that is, 'go slowly.' The attribute is in certain cases marked by the particle [ti^1] at its end: ['tiŋ^3 ˌxaw^3 ti^2 'ʒən^2] 'very good man'; [ˌwo^3 ti^2 'fu^4 tʃhin^1] 'I (p.) father,' that is, 'my father'; ['tso^4 tʃo^2 ti^1 ˌʒən^2] 'sit (p.) person,' that is, 'a sitting person'; ['wo^3 'çje^3 ˌtsə^4 ti 'pi^3] 'I write (p.) brush,' that is, 'the brush I write with' —in this example the attribute is a phrase of subject-predicate construction; ['maj^3 ti 'ʃu^1] 'buy (p.) book,' that is 'the purchased book.'

(3) A second endocentric construction, in which the attribute follows the head, resembles rather the English action-goal and relation-axis constructions: [ˌkwan^1 'man^2] 'shut the door,' [ˌtsaj^4 'tʃuŋ^1 kwo] 'in China.' We may call this, somewhat inexactly, the *action-goal* construction, to distinguish it from (2).

Taxemes of selection consist largely in the marking off of a form-class which serves as subject in (1), as head in (2), and as goal in (3), resembling the English substantive expression. To this form-class (we may call it the *object expression*) only a few words may be said to belong in their own right; these are substitute-words of the type [tha¹] 'he, she' or [wo³] 'I.' The other object expressions are phrases with various markers. The commonest of these markers are certain particles which precede as attributes of type (2), such as [tʃə⁴] 'this,' [na⁴] 'that,' [na³] 'which?' Thus, [ˈtʃə⁴ ko⁴] 'this piece,' that is, 'this (thing).' In most instances these markers do not immediately join with a full word; but only with certain ones, like the [ko⁴] 'piece' in the last example, which hereby constitute a form-class of *numeratives;* the phrase of marker plus numerative joins the ordinary full word in construction (2), as: [tʃə ko ˈʒən²] 'this (individual) man'; [ˌwu³ ˌljaŋ⁴ ˈtʃhə¹] 'five (individual) cart,' that is 'five carts.' Another kind of object expression is characterized by the particle [ti¹] at its end: [ˌmaj⁴ ˈʃu¹ ti] 'sell book (p.),' that is 'bookseller.'

In this way complex phrases are built up: [tha¹ ˈtaw⁴ ˈthjen² li³ ˈtʃhy⁴] 'he enter field interior go,' that is, 'he goes into the field'; here the first word is the subject, the rest of the phrase the predicate; in this predicate the last word is the head and the other three are an attribute; this attribute consists of the action [taw⁴] 'enter' and the goal [ˈthjen² li³] 'field interior,' in which the first word is an attribute of the second. In the sentence [ni³ ˈmej² pa³ ˈmaj³ ˈmej² ti ˌtʃhjen³ ˈkej³ wo³] 'you not take buy coal (p.) money give I,' the first word is the subject, the rest the predicate; this predicate consists of an attribute, [mej²] 'not' and a head; within this head, the first five words are again an attribute and the last two [ˈkej³ wo³] 'give I' a head, whose construction is action and goal. In the five-word attribute [pa³ ˌmaj³ ˈmej² ti ˌtʃhjen³] 'take buy coal (p.) money,' the first word is an action and the rest a goal; this goal consists of the head [tʃhjen³] 'money' and the attribute [ˌmaj³ ˈmej² ti] which is marked as such by the particle [ti¹] appended to the phrase [ˌmaj³ ˈmej²] 'buy coal,' whose construction is action-goal. Thus the sentence means 'you not taking buy-coal-money give me,' that is 'you haven't given me money to buy coal.'

In Tagalog, the parts of speech are, again, full word and particle, but here the full words are subdivided into two classes which we may call *static* and *transient.* The latter resemble our verbs in forming a special kind of predicate (the narrative type, with four sub-types, § 11.2) and in showing morphologic distinctions of tense and mode, but they differ from our verbs because, on the one hand, they are not restricted to the function of predicate and, on the other hand, there exist non-narrative predicates. The chief constructions are subject and predicate, marked optionally by order (predicate precedes subject) or by the particle [aj] and order (subject precedes predicate marked by initial [aj]), as illustrated in § 11.2. The subject and the equational predicate are selectively marked: the class of forms which fill these positions resembles the English substantive expression and, even more, the Chinese object expression. A few substitute-words, such as [a'ku] 'I' and [si'ja] 'he, she,' belong to this class by their own right; all other object expressions are phrases, characterized by the presence of certain attributes, as [isa ŋ 'baːtaʔ] 'one child,' or by certain particles, chiefly [si] before names, as [si 'hwan] 'John,' and [aŋ] before other forms, as [aŋ 'baːtaɪ] 'the child, a child,' [aŋ pu'la] 'the red,' that is, 'the redness,' [aŋ 'puːtul] 'the cut,' or, to illustrate transient forms, [aŋ pu'muːtul] 'the one who cut,' [aŋ pi'nuːtul] 'that which was cut,' [aŋ ipi'nuːtul] 'that which was cut with,' [aŋ pinu'tuːlan] 'that which was cut from.' There are four attributive constructions. In one, a particle [na], after vowels [ŋ], intervenes between head and attribute, in either order, as [aŋ 'baːta ŋ sumu:'suːlat] or [aŋ sumu:'suːlat na 'baːtaʔ] 'the writing child'; [aŋ pu'la ŋ pan'ju] 'the red handkerchief,' [aŋ pan'ju ŋ i'tu] 'this handkerchief.' Another, more restricted attributive construction lacks the particle, as [hin'diː a'ku] 'not I,' [hin'diː maba'it] 'not good.' In the third attributive construction the attribute is an object expression in a special form: thus, [a'ku] 'I' is replaced by [ku], and [si'ja] 'he, she' by [ni'ja], and the particle [si] by [ni], the particle [aŋ] by [naŋ]: [aŋ pu'la naŋ pan'ju aj matiŋ'kad] 'the red of the handkerchief is bright'; [aŋ 'baːta j ku'maːin naŋ 'kaːnin] 'the child ate (some) rice,' (actor-action); [ki'naːin naŋ 'baːtaʔ aŋ 'kaːnin] 'the rice was eaten by the child' (goal-action); see also the examples in § 11.2. In the fourth attributive construction, too, the attribute is an object expression: [si] is replaced by [kaj] and [aŋ] by [sa]; the attribute tells of a place: [aŋ baːta j na'naːug sa 'baːhaj] 'the child came out of the house, out of a house.'

12. 14. The details of syntax are often complicated and hard to describe. On this point, any fairly complete grammar of a language like English, German, Latin, or French, will prove more enlightening than would an abstract discussion. Syntax is obscured, however, in most treatises, by the use of philosophical instead of formal definitions of constructions and form-classes. As a single illustration of the more complex syntactic habits, we shall survey the main features of one construction in present-day (colloquial standard) English — the construction which we may call *character-substance*, as in *fresh milk*.

This construction is attributive, and the head is always a *noun-expression* — that is, a noun or an endocentric phrase with a noun as center. The noun is a word-class; like all form-classes, it is to be defined in terms of grammatical features, some of which, in fact, appear in what follows. When it has been defined, it shows a class-meaning which can be roughly stated as 'object of such and such a *species*'; examples are *boy, stone, water, kindness*. The attribute in our construction is always an *adjective expression* — that is, an adjective or an endocentric phrase with an adjective as center. The *adjective* is in English a word-class (part of speech), definable precisely by its function in the character-substance construction which we are now to discuss; its class-meaning will emerge from our discussion as something like '*character* of specimens of a species of objects'; examples are *big, red, this, some*. Beside these features of selection, the character-substance construction contains a feature of order: the adjective expression precedes the noun expression: *poor John, fresh milk*.

The adjectives are divided into two classes, *descriptive* and *limiting*, by the circumstance that when adjectives of both these classes occur in a phrase, the limiting adjective precedes and modifies the group of descriptive adjective plus noun. Thus, in a form like *this fresh milk*, the immediate constituents are the limiting adjective *this*, and the noun phrase *fresh milk*, which consists, in turn, of the descriptive adjective *fresh* and the noun *milk*. This difference subdivides our character-substance construction into two sub-types, the *quality-substance* construction, where the attribute is a descriptive adjective expression, and the *limitation-substance* construction, where the attribute is a limiting adjective.

The quality-substance construction and the form-class of descriptive adjectives are both divided into several types by features of order. For instance, we say *big black sheep* and never **black big sheep, kind old man* and never **old kind man*, and so on. We shall not stop to examine these sub-types. The meaning of the form-class of descriptive adjectives is roughly '*qualitative* character of specimens.'

The form-class of limiting adjectives is much smaller than that of descriptive adjectives, and constitutes, in fact, what we shall later define as an *irregular* form-class — that is, a form-class which has to be described in the shape of a list of the forms; however, the boundary between limiting and descriptive adjectives is not completely definable. The class-meaning of limiting adjectives will appear from the following discussion as something like '*variable* character of specimens.'

Our limiting adjectives fall into two sub-classes of *determiners* and *numeratives*. These two classes have several subdivisions and are crossed, moreover, by several other lines of classification.

The determiners are defined by the fact that certain types of noun expressions (such as *house* or *big house*) are always accompanied by a determiner (as, *this house, a big house*). The class-meaning is, roughly, '*identificational* character of specimens.' This habit of using certain noun expressions always with a determiner, is peculiar to some languages, such as the modern Germanic and Romance. Many languages have not this habit; in Latin, for instance, *domus* 'house' requires no attribute and is used indifferently where we say *the house* or *a house*.

A number of features subdivides the determiners into two classes, *definite* and *indefinite*. Of these features, we shall mention only one: a definite determiner can be preceded by the numerative *all* (as in *all the water*) but an indefinite determiner (as, *some* in *some water*) cannot.

The definite determiners are: any possessive adjective (*John's book, my house*) and the words *this* (*these*), *that* (*those*), *the*. The class of possessive adjectives is definable in terms of morphology. It is worth observing that Italian, which has a character-substance construction much like ours, does not use possessive adjectives as determiners: *il mio amico* [il mio a'miko] 'the my friend' (that is, 'my friend') contrasts with *un* [un] *mio amico* 'a my friend' (that is, 'a friend of mine'). The class-meaning of definite determiners is '*identified* specimens.' A precise statement of how the specimens are identified, is a practical matter outside the linguist's control; the identification consists in possession by some person (*John's book*), spatial relation to the speaker (*this house*), description by some accompanying linguistic form (*the house I saw*), or purely situational features (*the sky, the chairman*), among which earlier mention by speech is to be reckoned ("I saw a man, but *the man* did not see me"). Among the definite determiners, *this* : *these* and *that* : *those* are peculiar in showing congruence with the number-class of the noun (*this house* : *these houses*).

The indefinite determiners are *a* (*an*), *any*, *each*, *either*, *every*, *neither*, *no*, *one*, *some*, *what*, *whatever*, *which*, *whichever*, and the phrasal combinations *many a*, *such a*, *what a*. The class-meaning is '*unidentified* specimens.'

The word *a* is peculiar in its sandhi-form *an*, used before vowels. The word *one* occurs not only as an indefinite determiner (*one man*), but also in some entirely different functions (as in *a big one*, *if one only knew*); this phenomenon may be designated as *class-cleavage*. The meanings of the various indefinite determiners are in part linguistically definable in terms of grammatical features of wider bearing than our present subject. For instance, *what* and *which* are interrogative, introducing supplement-questions, which prompt the hearer to supply a speech-form (*what man? which man?*) *Whatever* and *whichever* are relative, marking their noun as part of a subordinate clause (*whatever book you take*, . . .). *No* and *neither* are negative, ruling out all specimens. *Each*, *which*, and *whichever* imply a limited field of selection: that is, the specimens concerned belong to an identified part (or to the identified whole) of the species (*which book? which parent?*); *either* and *neither* go farther in limiting the field to two specimens.

Some of the determiners are atonic (barring, of course, the case where they are emphatic elements): *my*, *our*, *your*, *his*, *her*, *its*, *their*, *the*, *a;* others are sometimes atonic or spoken with secondary stress.

The types of noun expressions which always have a determiner, are preceded, when no more specific determiner is present, by the articles, definite *the* and indefinite *a*, whose meaning is merely the class-meaning of their respective form-classes. A grammatical classification, such as definite and indefinite, which always accompanies some grammatical feature (here the types of noun expression which demand a determiner), is said to be *categoric*. The definite and indefinite categories may be said, in fact, to embrace the entire class of English noun expressions, because even those types of noun expression which do not always take a determiner, can be classed as definite or indefinite: *John*, for instance, as definite, *kindness* as indefinite.

According to the use and non-use of determiners, English noun expressions fall into a number of interesting sub-classes:

I. *Names* (*proper nouns*) occur only in the singular number, take no determiner, and are always definite: *John, Chicago.* The class meaning is 'species of object *containing only one specimen.*' Here and in what follows, space forbids our entering into details, such as the class-cleavage by which a name occurs also as a common noun, in cases like homonymy (*two Johns, this John*); nor can we take up sub-classes, such as that of river-names, which are always preceded by *the* (*the Mississippi*).

II. *Common nouns* occur in both categories, definite and indefinite. The class-meaning is 'species of object *occurring in more than one specimen.*' In the plural number they require a determiner for the definite category (*the houses*), but not for the indefinite (*houses,* corresponding to the singular form *a house*).

A. *Bounded nouns* in the singular number require a determiner (*the house, a house*). The class meaning is 'species of object occurring in more than one specimen, *such that the specimens cannot be subdivided or merged.*'

B. *Unbounded nouns* require a determiner for the definite category only (*the milk : milk*). The class-meaning is 'species of object occurring in more than one specimen, *such that the specimens can be subdivided or merged.*'

1. *Mass nouns* never take *a* and have no plural (*the milk : milk*). The class-meaning is that of B with the added proviso that the specimens '*exist independently.*'

2. *Abstract nouns* in the indefinite singular without a determiner include all the specimens (*life is short*); with a determiner and in the plural, the specimens are separate (*a useful life; nine lives*). The class-meaning is that of B with the proviso that the specimens '*exist only as the demeanor (quality, action, relation) of other objects.*'

Among the subdivisions of II, class-cleavage is frequent and interesting, as, *an egg, eggs* (A), but "he got *egg* on his necktie" (B1); *coffee* (B1), but *an expensive coffee* (A).

The limiting adjectives of the other class, numeratives, fall into various sub-classes, of which we shall merely mention a few. Two of them, *all* and *both* precede a determiner (*all the apples*); the rest follow (*the other apples*). Two, however, precede *a* in phrases which are determiners: *many a, such a.* The numeratives *few, hundred, thousand,* and those formed with the suffix *-ion* (*million* and so on), are preceded by *a* in phrases which serve as numeratives with plural nouns (*a hundred years*). The numeratives *same, very, one* — this last differs by class-cleavage from the determiner *one* — are used only with definite nouns (*this same book, the very day, my one hope*); the numeratives *much, more, less* are used only with indefinite nouns (*much water*); the numerative *all* is used with both kinds of nouns but only with definite determiners (*all the milk; all milk*). Some, such as *both, few, many*, and the higher numbers, are used only with plural nouns; others, such as *one, much, little*, only with singular nouns. Some numeratives are used also in other syntactic positions, as, *many* and *few* as predicate adjectives (*they were many*), and *all, both* as semi-predicative attributes (*the boys were both there*). Some other interesting lines of classification among the English numeratives will appear when we take up the substitutive replacement of noun expressions in Chapter 15.

CHAPTER 13

MORPHOLOGY

13. 1. By the *morphology* of a language we mean the constructions in which bound forms appear among the constituents. By definition, the resultant forms are either bound forms or words, but never phrases. Accordingly, we may say that morphology includes the constructions of words and parts of words, while syntax includes the constructions of phrases. As a border region we have phrase-words (*jack-in-the-pulpit*) and some compound words (*blackbird*), which contain no bound forms among their immediate constituents, and yet in some ways exhibit morphologic rather than syntactic types of construction.

In general, morphologic constructions are more elaborate than those of syntax. The features of modification and modulation are more numerous and often irregular — that is, confined to particular constituents or combinations. The order of the constituents is almost always rigidly fixed, permitting of no such connotative variants as *John ran away : Away ran John*. Features of selection minutely and often whimsically limit the constituents that may be united into a complex form.

Accordingly, languages differ more in morphology than in syntax. The variety is so great that no simple scheme will classify languages as to their morphology. One such scheme distinguishes *analytic* languages, which use few bound forms, from *synthetic*, which use many. At one extreme is a completely analytic language, like modern Chinese, where each word is a one-syllable morpheme or a compound word or phrase-word; at the other, a highly synthetic language like Eskimo, which unites long strings of bound forms into single words, such as [aːwlisa-ut-issʔar-si-niarpu-ŋa] 'I am looking for something suitable for a fish-line.' This distinction, however, except for cases at the former extreme, is relative; any one language may be in some respects more analytic, but in other respects more synthetic, than some other language. Another scheme of this sort divided languages into four morphologic types, *isolating*, *agglutinative*, *polysynthetic*, and *in-*

flecting. Isolating languages were those which, like Chinese, used no bound forms; in agglutinative languages the bound forms were supposed merely to follow one another, Turkish being the stock example; polysynthetic languages expressed semantically important elements, such as verbal goals, by means of bound forms, as does Eskimo; inflectional languages showed a merging of semantically distinct features either in a single bound form or in closely united bound forms, as when the suffix *-ō* in a Latin form like *amō* 'I love' expresses the meanings 'speaker as actor,' 'only one actor,' 'action in present time,' 'real (not merely possible or hypothetical) action.' These distinctions are not co-ordinate, and the last three classes were never clearly defined.

13. 2. Since the speaker cannot isolate bound forms by speaking them alone, he is usually unable to describe the structure of words. The statement of morphology requires systematic study. The ancient Greeks made some progress in this direction, but, in the main, our technique was developed by the Hindu grammarians. No matter how refined our method, the elusive nature of meanings will always cause difficulty, especially when doubtful relations of meaning are accompanied by formal irregularities. In the series *goose, gosling, gooseberry, gander*, we shall probably agree that the first two forms are morphologically related, in the sense that [gɔz-] in *gosling* is a phonetic modification of *goose*, but the [guz-] in *gooseberry* does not fit the meaning, and, on the other hand, the formal resemblance [g-] of *goose* and *gander* is so slight that one may question whether it really puts the practical relation of meaning into linguistic form. This last difficulty appears also in the pair *duck : drake*, with their common [d... k]. One soon learns that one cannot look to the speakers for an answer, since they do not practise morphologic analysis; if one bothers them with such questions, they give inconsistent or silly answers. If the history of a language is known, one often finds that the ambiguity was absent in some older state of the language — it appears, for instance, that some centuries ago 'gooseberry' was **grose-berry* and had nothing to do with a *goose* — but facts of this sort evidently do not tell us how things work in the present state of the language.

In describing the modulations and modifications which occur in syntax, we naturally take the absolute form of a word or phrase as our starting-point, but a bound form which occurs in several shapes will lead to several entirely different forms of description, according to our choice of a *basic alternant*. For instance, the plural-suffix of English nouns appears ordinarily in three shapes: [-iz] *glasses*, [-z] *cards*, [-s] *books;* by taking each of these three, in turn, as one's starting-point, one can arrive at three entirely different statements of the facts.

Very often there are further difficulties. Sometimes a grammatical feature, such as a phonetic modification, appears to express a meaning which is usually expressed by a linguistic form, as in *man : men*, where modification of the vowel takes the place of the plural-suffix. In other cases there is not even a grammatical feature: a single phonetic form, in the manner of homonymy, represents two meanings which are usually distinguished by means of a linguistic form, as, singular and plural noun in *the sheep (grazes) : the sheep (graze)*. Here the Hindus hit upon the apparently artificial but in practice eminently serviceable device of speaking of a *zero element:* in *sheep : sheep* the plural-suffix is replaced by zero — that is, by nothing at all.

13. 3. What with these and other difficulties, any inconsistency of procedure is likely to create confusion in a descriptive statement of morphology. One must observe, above all, the principle of immediate constituents (§ 10.2). This principle leads us, at the outset, to distinguish certain classes of words, according to the *immediate constituents:*

A. *Secondary words*, containing free forms:
   1. *Compound words*, containing more than one free form: *door-knob, wild-animal-tamer*. The included free forms are the *members* of the compound word: in our examples, the members are the words *door, knob, tamer*, and the phrase *wild animal*.
   2. *Derived secondary words*, containing one free form: *boyish, old-maidish*. The included free form is called the *underlying form;* in our examples the underlying forms are the word *boy* and the phrase *old maid*.

B. *Primary words*, not containing a free form:
   1. *Derived primary words*, containing more than one bound form: *re-ceive, de-ceive, con-ceive, re-tain, de-tain, con-tain*.
   2. *Morpheme-words*, consisting of a single (free) morpheme: *man, boy, cut, run, red, big*.

The principle of immediate constituents will lead us, for example, to class a form like *gentlemanly* not as a compound word, but as a derived secondary word, since the immediate constituents are the bound form *-ly* and the underlying word *gentleman;* the word *gentlemanly* is a secondary derivative (a so-called *de-compound*) whose underlying form happens to be a compound word. Similarly, *door-knobs* is not a compound word, but a de-compound, consisting of the bound form [-z] and the underlying word *door-knob*.

The principle of immediate constituents leads us to observe the *structural order* of the constituents, which may differ from their actual sequence; thus, *ungentlemanly* consists of *un-* and *gentlemanly*, with the bound form added at the beginning, but *gentlemanly* consists of *gentleman* and *-ly* with the bound form added at the end.

13. 4. As examples of relatively simple morphologic arrangements we may take the constructions of secondary derivation that appear in English plural nouns (*glass-es*) and past-tense verbs (*land-ed*).

As to selection, the bound forms are in both cases unique, but the underlying forms belong to two great form-classes: the plural nouns are derived from *singular nouns* (as, *glasses* from *glass*) and the past-tense verbs from *infinitive verbs* (as, *landed* from *land*). Other, subsidiary taxemes of selection will concern us later.

As to order, the bound form, in both cases, is spoken after the underlying form.

By a feature of modulation common to nearly all constructions of English morphology, the underlying form keeps its stress, and the bound form is unstressed.

The taxemes of phonetic modification are more elaborate, and will show us some peculiarities that appear in the morphology of many languages.

To begin with, the bound form appears in several *alternants*, different shapes which imply, in this case, features of phonetic modification:

glass : *glasses* [-iz]
pen : *pens* [-z]
book : *books* [-s].

If we collect examples, we soon find that the shape of the bound form is determined by the last phoneme of the accompanying form:

[-iz] appears after sibilants and affricates (*glasses, roses, dishes, garages, churches, bridges*); [-z] appears after all other voiced phonemes (*saws, boys, ribs, sleeves, pens, hills, cars*); and [-s] after all other unvoiced phonemes (*books, cliffs*). Since the differences between the three alternants [-iz, -z, -s] can be described in terms of phonetic modification, we say that they are *phonetic alternants*. Since the distribution of the three alternants is regulated according to a linguistically recognizable characteristic of the accompanying forms, we say that the alternation is *regular*. Finally, since the deciding characteristic of the accompanying forms is phonemic (namely, the identity of the last phoneme), we say that the alternation is *automatic*.

Regular alternations play a great part in the morphology of most languages. Not all regular alternations are phonetic or automatic. In German, for instance, the singular nouns are divided, by certain syntactic features, into three form-classes which are known as genders (§ 12.7); now, German plural nouns are derived from singulars by the addition of bound forms which differ according to the gender of the underlying singular:

masculine nouns add [-e], with certain vowel-changes: *der Hut* [huːt] 'hat': *Hute* ['hyːte] 'hats'; *der Sohn* [zoːn] 'son': *Söhne* ['zøːne] 'sons'; *der Baum* [bawm] 'tree': *Bäume* ['bojme] 'trees'

neuter nouns add [-e] without vowel-change: *das Jahr* [jaːr] 'year': *Jahre* ['jaːre] 'years'; *das Boot* [boːt] 'boat': *Boote* ['boːte] 'boats'; *das Tier* [tiːr] 'animal': *Tiere* ['tiːre] 'animals'

feminine nouns add [-en]: *die Uhr* [uːr] 'clock, watch': *Uhren* ['uːren] 'clocks, watches'; *die Last* [last] 'burden': *Lasten* ['lasten] 'burdens'; *die Frau* [fraw] 'woman': *Frauen* ['frawen] 'women.'

This alternation (aside from special features which we need not consider) is regular, but it is not phonetic, since, of the three alternants, [-e] with vowel change, [-e], and [-en], the last is not, in the system of the language, phonetically akin to the first two; and the alternation is not automatic, but *grammatical*, since it depends not upon phonetic, but upon grammatical (in this instance, syntactic) peculiarities of the underlying forms.

13. 5. We have not yet described in terms of phonetic modification, the kinship of the three alternants [-iz, -z, -s] of the bound form that appears in English plural nouns. It is evident that three entirely different statements are possible, according to our choice of one or another of the three forms as our starting-point. Our aim is to get, in the long run, the simplest possible set of statements that will describe the facts of the English language. To try out the different possible formulae with this aim in view, often involves great labor. In the present instance our trouble is small, because our alternation has an exact parallel in English syntax: the enclitic word whose absolute form is *is* ['iz], alternates quite like our plural suffix:

> *Bess's ready* [iz, əz] [1]
> *John's ready* [z]
> *Dick's ready* [s].

Since in this case the absolute form *is* necessarily serves as the starting-point of description, we reach the simplest formula if we take [-iz] as the *basic alternant* also of the bound form. We can say, then, that in English any morpheme of the form [iz, ez], unstressed, loses its vowel after all phonemes except sibilants and affricates, and then replaces [z] by [s] after unvoiced sounds. This covers also the alternation of the third-person present-tense verb suffix in *misses : runs : breaks* and of the possessive-adjective suffix in *Bess's, John's, Dick's*. Moreover, it leads us to use a parallel formula in the case of the past-tense suffix of verbs. This suffix appears in three similar alternants:

> *land   : landed* [-id]
> *live   : lived* [-d]
> *dance : danced* [-t],

and we need not hesitate, now, to take [-id] as the basic form for our description and to say that this form loses its vowel after all phonemes except dental stops, and then replaces [d] by [t] after all unvoiced sounds.

13. 6. A survey of English plural nouns will soon show that the statement we have made holds good for an indefinitely large number of forms, but not for a certain limited number of exceptions.

In some instances the constituent form in the plural differs phonetically from the underlying singular noun:

> *knife* [najf]   : *knives* [najv-z]
> *mouth* [mawθ] : *mouths* [mawð-z]
> *house* [haws] : *houses* ['hawz-iz].

---

[1] The types of English pronunciation which distinguish between [ə] and [i] in unstressed position, use [i] in both the bound form (*glasses*) and the word (*Bess's*).

We can describe the peculiarity of these plurals by saying that the final [f, θ, s] of the underlying singular is replaced by [v, ð, z] before the bound form is added. The word "before" in this statement means that the alternant of the bound form is the one appropriate to the substituted sound; thus, the plural of *knife* adds not [-s], but [-z]: "first" the [-f] is replaced by [-v], and "then" the appropriate alternant [-z] is added. The terms "before, after, first, then," and so on, in such statements, tell the *descriptive order*. The actual sequence of constituents, and their structural order (§ 13.3) are a part of the language, but the descriptive order of grammatical features is a fiction and results simply from our method of describing the forms; it goes without saying, for instance, that the speaker who says *knives*, does not "first" replace [f] by [v] and "then" add [-z], but merely utters a form (*knives*) which in certain features resembles and in certain features differs from a certain other form (namely, *knife*).

If the English plural nouns which exhibit this voicing of a final spirant in the underlying form, showed any common phonetic or grammatical feature that distinguished them from other nouns, we could describe this peculiarity as a regular alternant. This, however, seems not to be the case; we have also plurals like *cliffs, myths, creases*, where [f, θ, s] of the underlying form appears unchanged. We can make our general statement cover one group, but will then have to furnish a *list* of the cases that do not fall under the general statement. A set of forms that is not covered by a general statement, but has to be presented in the shape of a list, is said to be *irregular*. We try, of course, to arrange our description so that as many forms as possible will be included in general statements. The choice is often decided for us by the circumstance that one group of forms is of indefinite extent and therefore amenable to a general statement, but not to a list. In the case of English nouns in [-s], we obviously face this condition, for *house : houses* is the only instance where [-s] is replaced by [z] in the plural, while an indefinite number of plural nouns retains the [-s] of the underlying form (*glasses, creases, curses, dances*, and so on). Our list, in this case, includes only one form, *houses*, a *unique* irregularity. The list of plurals which substitute [ð] for the [-θ] of the underlying form is not large, embracing only the forms *baths, paths, cloths, mouths* (and for some speakers also *laths, oaths, truths, youths*); on the other side we find a number of current forms, such as *months, widths, drouths, myths, hearths,* and, what is more decisive, the habit of keeping [-θ] in the formation of plurals that are not traditional and may be formed by a speaker who has not heard them: *the McGraths, napropaths, monoliths.* In the case of [-f] the list is larger: *knives, wives, lives, calves, halves, thieves, leaves, sheaves, beeves, loaves, elves, shelves* (and for some speakers also *hooves, rooves, scarves, dwarves, wharves*); we decide to call these irregular on the strength not only of counter-instances, such as *cliffs, toughs, reefs, oafs,* but also of less common or occasional forms, such as (*some good*) *laughs,* (*general*) *staffs, monographs.*

Where the two treatments occur side by side, as in *laths* [lɑːθs] or [lɑːðz], *roofs* or *rooves,* there is usually some slight difference of connotation between the variants. The noun *beef,* as a mass-noun (§ 12.14), has no ordinary plural by its side; the plural *beeves* is a *specialized* derivative, since it deviates in its meaning of 'oxen, cattle,' with archaic-poetic connotation.

We may note in passing that the grammatical features we have discussed, determine features of the phonetic pattern (§ 8.5), by defining groups like *sibilant-affricate, dental stop, voiced, unvoiced,* and establishing the relation [f, θ, s] versus [v, ð, z], and [t] versus [d].

We may describe "voicing of final spirant plus suffix [-iz, -z, (-s)]" as an *irregular alternant* of the regular plural-suffix [-iz, -z, -s]; the irregularity consists in a phonetic modification of the underlying form. The same modification is accompanied by modification of the syllabic in the uniquely irregular *staff : staves.* In *cloth* [klɔːθ] : *clothes* [klowz] we have a uniquely irregular plural with specialized meaning ('garments, clothing'), beside the irregular plural *cloths* [klɔːðz] with normal meaning.

The homonymous third-person present-tense suffix of verbs is accompanied by phonetic modification of the underlying form in *do* [duw] : *does* [dʌz], *say* [sej] : *says* [sez], *have* [hɛv] : *has* [hɛz].

The past-tense suffix [-id, -d, -t] is accompanied by phonetic modification in the irregular forms *say : said, flee : fled, hear* [hiə] *: heard* [hɔːd], *keep : kept* (and, similarly, *crept, slept, swept, wept; leaped* and *leapt* are variants), *do : did, sell : sold* (and, similarly, *told*), *make : made, have : had.*

13. 7. In some cases the bound form appears in an unusual shape. In *die : dice* the alternant [-s] appears against the general habit; in *penny · pence* the same feature is accompanied by modification (loss of [-i]) in the underlying form, together with specialization of meaning, in contrast with the normal variant *pennies*. In the past tense, we find [-t] instead of [-d] in the archaic-flavored variants *burnt, learnt*. If we say that in English the unpermitted final cluster [-dt] is replaced by [-t], we can class here, with [-t] instead of [-id], the forms *bent, lent, sent, spent, built*.

Both constituents show irregular phonetic modification in *feel : felt* and similarly in *dealt, knelt, dreamt, meant*. If we say that the unpermitted final clusters [-vt, -zt] are replaced by [-ft,-st], we can class here also *leave : left* and *lose : lost*. The bound form appears in the alternant [-t] instead of [-d], and the underlying form replaces the syllabic and all that follows by [ɔː] in *seek* [sijk]*: sought* [sɔːt] and, similarly, in *bought, brought, caught, taught, thought*.

In the extreme case, an alternant bears no resemblance to the other alternants. In *ox : oxen* the bound form added in the plural is [-n] instead of [-iz, -z, -s]. If the language does not show parallel cases which warrant our describing the deviant form in terms of phonetic modification, an alternant of this sort is said to be *suppletive;* thus, [-n] in *oxen* is a suppletive alternant of [-iz, -z, -s], because English grammar shows no phonetic modification of [-iz] to [-n]. In other instances it is the underlying form which suffers suppletion. Beside the ordinary derivation of *kind : kinder, warm : warmer*, and so on, we have *good : better*, where the underlying word *good* is replaced by an entirely different form *bet-*, which we describe, accordingly, as a suppletive alternant of *good*. In the same way, the infinitive *be* suffers suppletion, by [i-], in the third-person present-tense form *is* [iz]. In *child : children*, a suppletive alternant [-rən] of the bound form is accompanied by phonetic modification of the underlying word.

Another extreme case is that of *zero-alternants* (§ 13.2), in which a constituent is entirely lacking, as in the plurals *sheep, deer, moose, fish*, and so on. These plurals are irregular, for although some of them (for instance, species of fish, like *perch, bass, pickerel*, large enough to be eaten in separate specimens, and not named after other objects) can be classified by purely practical features of meaning, they have no formal characteristic by which we could define them. The past-tense suffix of verbs shows a zero-alternant in *bet, let, set, wet, hit, slit, split, cut, shut, put, beat, cast, cost, burst, shed, spread, wed*. The third-person present-tense suffix has a zero-alternant in *can, shall, will, must, may,* and, in certain constructions (for instance, with the modifier *not*), in *need, dare;* this is a regular grammatical alternation, since these verbs are definable by their syntactic function of taking an infinitive modifier without the preposition *to*. Our possessive-adjective suffix [-iz, -z, -s] has a zero-alternant in one instance, namely, after an underlying form which ends in the plural-suffix [-iz, -z, -s,] as *the-boys'*.

A zero-alternant may go with modification of the accompanying form. Thus, the plural nouns *geese, teeth, feet, mice, lice, men, women* ['wimən] add no bound form to the singular, but contain a different syllabic. In these plurals a grammatical feature, phonetic modification, expresses a meaning (namely, the sememe *'more than one object'*) which is normally expressed by a linguistic form (namely, the morpheme [-iz, -z, -s]). We may say that "substitution of [ij]" (for the stressed syllabic of the underlying form) in *geese, teeth, feet,* "substitution of [aj]" in *mice, lice,* "substitution of [e]" in *men,* and "substitution of [i]" in *women,* are alternants of the normal plural-suffix — *substitution-alternants* or *substitution-forms*. In our past-tense verbs we find substitution of various syllabics taking the place of [-id, -d, -t], as:

[ɔ] *got, shot, trod*

[ɛ] *drank, sank, shrank, rang, sang, sprang, began, ran, swam, sat, spat*

[e] *bled, fed, led, read, met, held, fell*

[i] *bit, lit, hid, slid*

[ɔ] *saw, fought*

[ʌ] *clung, flung, hung, slung, swung, spun, won, dug, stuck, struck*

[u] *shook, took*

[ej] *ate, gave, came, lay*

[aw] *bound, found, ground, wound*

[ow] *clove, drove, wove, bore, swore, tore, wore, broke, spoke, woke, chose, froze, rose, smote, wrote, rode, stole, shone;* with *dove* as a variant beside regular *dived*

[(j)uw] *knew, blew, flew, slew, drew, grew, threw.*

In *stand : stood* we have a more complex case with an alternant describable as "substitution of [u] and loss of [n]."

A zero-alternant replaces the bound form, and a suppletive alternant the underlying form, in cases like *be : was, go : went, I : my, we : our, she : her, bad : worse.*

In cases like *have* [hɛv] : *had* [hɛ-d] or *make* [mejk] : *made* [mej-d], one of the constituents is modified by the loss of a phoneme. This loss may be described as a *minus-feature;* like zero-features or substitution-features, minus-features may occur independently. For instance, in a French adjective, the regular type has only one form, regardless of whether the adjective accompanies a masculine or a feminine noun, e.g. *rouge* [ru:ʒ] 'red': *un livre rouge* [œ̃ li:vrə ru:ʒ] 'a red book,' masculine, and *une plume rouge* [yn plym ru:ʒ] 'a red feather or pen,' feminine. In a fairly large irregular type, however, the masculine and feminine forms differ: *un livre vert* [vɛ:r] 'a green book,' but *une plume verte* [vɛrt] 'a green feather or pen.' Thus:

Masculine	Feminine
plat [pla] 'flat'	*platte* [plat]
laid [lɛ] 'ugly'	*laide* [lɛd]
distinct [distɛ̃] 'distinct'	*distincte* [distɛ̃kt]
long [lõ] 'long'	*longue* [lõg]
bas [bɑ] 'low'	*basse* [bɑ:s]
gris [gri] 'gray'	*grise* [gri:z]
frais [frɛ] 'fresh'	*fraîche* [frɛ:ʃ]
gentil [ʒɑ̃ti] 'gentle'	*gentille* [ʒɑ̃ti:j]
léger [leʒe] 'light'	*légère* [leʒɛ:r]
soul [su] 'drunk'	*soule* [sul]
plein [plɛ̃] 'full'	*pleine* [plɛ:n]

It is evident that two forms of description are here possible. We could take the masculine forms as a basis and tell what consonant is added in each case in the feminine form, and this would, of course, result in a fairly complicated statement. On the other hand, if we take the feminine form as our basis, we can describe this irregular type by the simple statement that the masculine form is derived from the feminine by means of a minus-feature, namely, loss of the final consonant and of the cluster [-kt]. If we take the latter course, we find, moreover, that all the other differences between the two forms, as to vowel quantity and as to nasalization (as in our last example), re-appear in other phases of French morphology and can in large part be attributed to the phonetic pattern.

The last part of our discussion has shown us that a word may have the character of a secondary derivative and yet consist of only one morpheme, accompanied by a zero-feature (*sheep*, as a plural; *cut* as a past), by a substitution-feature (*men, sang*), by suppletion (*went, worse*), or by a minus-feature (French *vert*, masculine). We class these words as secondary derivatives and recognize their peculiarity by calling them *secondary morpheme-words*.

13. 8. The bound forms which in secondary derivation are added to the underlying form, are called *affixes*. Affixes which precede the underlying form are *prefixes*, as *be-* in *be-head;* those which follow the underlying form are called *suffixes*, as [-iz] in *glasses* or *-ish* in *boyish*. Affixes added within the underlying form are called *infixes;* thus, Tagalog uses several infixes which are added before the first vowel of the underlying form: from ['suːlat] 'a writing' are derived [suˈmuːlat] 'one who wrote,' with the infix [-um-], and [siˈnuːlat] 'that which was written,' with infix [-in-]. *Reduplication* is an affix that consists of repeating part of the underlying form, as Tagalog [suː-ˈsuːlat] 'one who will write,' [ˈgaːmit] 'thing of use': [gaː-ˈgaːmit] 'one who will use.' Reduplication may be of various extent: Fox [waːpamɛːwa] 'he looks at him': [waː-waːpamɛːwa] 'he examines him,' [waːpa-waːpamɛːwa] 'he keeps looking at him.' It may differ phonetically in some conventional way from the underlying word: ancient Greek [ˈphajnej] 'it shines, it appears': [pam-ˈphajnej] 'it shines brightly'; Sanskrit [ˈbharti] 'he bears': [ˈbi-bharti] 'he bears up,' [ˈbhari-bharti] 'he bears off violently.'

13. 9. We have seen that when forms are partially similar, there may be a question as to which one we had better take as the underlying form, and that the structure of the language may decide this question for us, since, taking it one way, we get an unduly complicated description, and, taking it the other way, a relatively simple one. This same consideration often leads us to *set up* an artificial underlying form. For instance, in German the voiced mutes [b, d, g, v, z] are not permitted finals, and are in final position replaced by the corresponding unvoiced phonemes. Accordingly we get sets like the following:

Underlying word	Derived word
Gras [graːs] 'grass'	*grasen* [ˈgraːz-en] 'to graze'
Haus [haws] 'house'	*hausen* [ˈhawz-en] 'to keep house, to carry on'
Spasz [ʃpaːs] 'jest'	*spaszen* [ˈʃpaːs-en] 'to jest'
aus [aws] 'out'	*auszen* [ˈaws-en] 'on the outside.'

It is evident that if we took the underlying words in their actual shape as our basic forms, we should have to give a long list to tell which ones appeared in derivatives with [z] instead of [s]. On the other hand, if we start from an artificial underlying form with [-z], as [graːz-, hawz-], in contrast with [spaːs, aws], we need give no list and can account for the uniform final [-s] which actually appears in the independent forms, by the rule of permitted finals. Similarly for the other voiced mutes, as in

 rund [runt] 'round' *runde* ['rund-e] 'round ones'
 bunt [bunt] 'motley' *bunte* ['bunt-e] 'motley ones,'

where we set up a theoretical basic form [rund-] in contrast with [bunt]. We have seen that in some languages these theoretical forms appear also in the phrase, by reminiscent sandhi (§ 12.5).

Similarly, some languages permit no final clusters and yet show included free forms with clusters. Compare the following noun-forms in Menomini:

Singular (suffix zero)	Plural (suffix [-an])
[nenɛːh] 'my hand'	[nenɛːhkan] 'my hands'
[metɛːh] 'a heart'	[metɛːhjan] 'hearts'
[wiːkiːh] 'birch-bark'	[wiːkiːhsan] 'pieces of birch-bark'
[nekɛːʔtʃenɛh] 'my thumb'	[nekɛːʔtʃenɛːhtʃjan] 'my thumbs'
[peːhtʃekunaːh] 'medicine-bundle'	[peːhtʃekunaːhtjan] 'medicine-bundles.'

It is evident that a description which took the singular forms as a basis would have to show by elaborate lists what consonants, as, [k, j, s, tʃj, tj], are added before a suffix; the simple and natural description is to take as a starting-point the free forms not in their absolute shape, but in the form which appears before suffixes, as [wiːkiːhs-] and the like.

Another example is furnished by Samoan, which permits no final consonants at all, and therefore has sets like the following:

Without suffix	With suffix [-ia]
[tani] 'weep'	[tanisia] 'wept'
[inu] 'drink'	[inumia] 'drunk'
[ulu] 'enter'	[ulufia] 'entered.'

It is clear that a useful description will here set up the basic forms in theoretical shape, as [tanis-, inum-, uluf-].

13. 10. Modulation of secondary phonemes often plays a part in morphologic constructions. In English, affixes are normally unstressed, as in *be-wail-ing, friend-li-ness* and the like. In our foreign-learned vocabulary, shift of stress to an affix is a taxeme in many secondary derivatives. Thus, some suffixes have *pre-suffixal stress:* the accent is on the syllable before the suffix, regardless of the nature of this syllable; thus, *-ity* in *able : ability, formal : formality, major : majority;* [-jn̩] in *music : musician, audit: audition, educate : education;* [-ik] in *demon : demonic, anarchist : anarchistic, angel : angelic.* In the derivation of some of our foreign-learned nouns and adjectives from verbs, the stress is put on the prefix: from the verb *insert* [in'sə:t] we derive the noun *insert* ['insə:t]; similarly *contract, convict, convert, converse, discourse, protest, project, rebel, transfer.* In other cases this modulation appears along with a suffix: *conceive : concept, perceive : percept, portend : portent;* in some, the underlying verb has to be theoretically set up, as in *precept.*

In some languages modulation has greater scope. In Sanskrit, with some suffixes the derivative form keeps the accent of the underlying form:

['ke:ça-] 'hair' : ['ke:ça-vant-] 'having long hair'
[pu'tra-] 'son' : [pu'tra-vant-] 'having a son.'

Others are accompanied by shift of accent to the first syllable:

['puruʃa-] 'man' : ['pa:wruʃ-e:ja-] 'coming from man'
[va'sti-] 'bladder' : ['va:st-e:ja-] 'of the bladder.'

Others have presuffixal accent:

['puruʃa-] 'man' : [puru'ʃa-ta:-] 'human nature'
[de:'va-] 'god' : [de:'va-ta:-] 'divinity.'

Other affixes are themselves accented:

['r ʃi-] 'sage' : [a:rʃ-e:'ja-] 'descendant of a sage'
[sa'rama:-] (proper noun) : [sa:ram-e:'ja-] 'descended from Sarama.'

Others require an accentuation opposite to that of the underlying word:

['atithi-] 'guest' : [a:ti'th-ja-] 'hospitality'
[pali'ta-] 'gray' : ['pa:lit-ja-] 'grayness.'

Tagalog uses both stress and vowel-lengthening as auxiliary phonemes; three suffixes of the form [-an] differ in the treatment of these modulations.

Suffix [-an]¹ is characterized by presuffixal stress and by long vowel in the first syllable of the underlying form:

['iːbig] 'love' : [iː'biːgan] 'love-affair'
[i'num] 'drink' : [iː'nuːman] 'drinking-party.'

The meaning is 'action (often reciprocal or collective) by more than one actor.'

Suffix [-an]² is stressed when the underlying word has stress on the first syllable; otherwise it is treated like [-an]¹:

['tuːlug] 'sleep' : [tulu'gan] 'sleeping-place'
[ku'luŋ] 'enclose' : [kuː'luːŋan] 'place of imprisonment.'

The meaning is 'place of action, usually by more than one actor, or repeated.'

Suffix [-an]³ has presuffixal stress when the underlying word is stressed on the first syllable; it is stressed when the underlying word is stressed on the last syllable; there is no vowel-lengthening beyond what is demanded by the phonetic pattern:

(a) ['saːgiŋ] 'banana' : [sa'giːŋan] 'banana-grove'
   [ku'luŋ] 'enclose' : [kulu'ŋan] 'cage, crate'
(b) ['puːtul] 'cut' : [pu'tuːlan] 'that which may be cut from'
   [la'kas] 'strength' : [laka'san] 'that upon which strength may be expended.'

The meaning is (a) 'an object which serves as locality of the underlying object, action, etc.,' and (b) 'that which may be acted upon.'

In languages with auxiliary phonemes of pitch, these may play a part in morphology. Thus, in Swedish, the suffix *-er* of agent-nouns shows the normal compound word-pitch of polysyllables (§ 7.7) in the resultant form: the verb-stem [leːs-] 'read' forms *läser* ['leːser] 'reader'; but the *-er* of the present tense demands simple word-pitch in the resultant form: (*han*) *läser* ['leːser] '(he) reads.'

13. 11. In all observation of word-structure it is very important to observe the principle of immediate constituents. In Tagalog, the underlying form ['taːwa] 'a laugh' appears reduplicated in the derivative [taː'taːwa] 'one who will laugh'; this form, in turn, underlies a derivative with the infix [-um-], namely [tuma:'ta:wa] 'one who is laughing.' On the other hand, the form ['pi:lit] 'effort' *first* takes the infix [-um-], giving [pu'mi:lit] 'one who compelled,' and is *then* reduplicated, giving [-pu:pu'mi:lit], which underlies [nag-pu:pu'mi:lit] 'one who makes an extreme effort.' Close observation of this principle is all the more necessary because now and then we meet forms which compromise as to immediate constituents. Tagalog has a prefix [paŋ-], as in [a'tip] 'roofing' : [paŋ-a'tip] 'that used for roofing; shingle.' The [ŋ] of this prefix and certain initial consonants of an accompanying form are subject to a phonetic modification — we may call it *morphologic sandhi* — by which, for instance, our prefix joins with ['pu:tul] 'a cut' in the derivative [pa-'mu:tul] 'that used for cutting,' with substitution of [m] for the combination of [-ŋ] plus [p-]. In some forms, however, we find an inconsistency as to the structural order; thus, the form [pa-mu-'mu:tul] 'a cutting in quantity' implies, by the actual sequence of the parts, that the reduplication is made "before" the prefix is added, but at the same time implies, by the presence of [m-] for [p-] in both reduplication and main form, that the prefix is added "before" the reduplication is made. A carelessly ordered description would fail to bring out the peculiarity of a form like this.

13. 12. In languages of complex morphology we can thus observe a *ranking* of constructions: a complex word can be described only as though the various compoundings, affixations, modifications, and so on, were added *in a certain order* to the basic form. Thus, in English, the word *actresses* consists, in the first place, of *actress* and [-iz], just as *lasses* consists of *lass* and [-iz]; *actress*, in turn consists of *actor* and *-ess*, just as *countess* consists of *count* and *-ess; actor*, finally, consists of *act* and [-ə]. There would be no parallel for a division of *actresses*, say into *actor* and *-esses.* In languages of this type, then, we can distinguish several *ranks* of morphologic structure.

In many languages these ranks fall into classes: the structure of a complex word reveals first, as to the more immediate constituents, an outer layer of *inflectional* constructions, and then an inner layer of constructions of *word-formation*. In our last example, the outer, inflectional layer is represented by the construction of *actress* with [-iz], and the inner, word-formational layer by the remaining constructions, of *actor* with *-ess* and of *act* with [-ə].

MORPHOLOGY 223

This distinction cannot always be carried out. It is based on several features. The constructions of inflection usually cause closure or partial closure (§ 12.11), so that a word which contains an inflectional construction (an *inflected* word) can figure as a constituent in no morphologic constructions or else only in certain inflectional constructions. The English form *actresses*, for instance, can enter into only one morphologic construction, namely the derivation of the possessive adjective *actresses'* (with the zero-alternant of [-iz, -z, -s], § 13.7). This latter form, in turn, cannot enter into any morphologic construction; it has complete closure.

Another peculiarity of inflection, in contrast with word-formation, is the rigid parallelism of underlying and resultant forms. Thus, nearly all English singular nouns underlie a derived plural noun, and, vice versa, nearly all English plural nouns are derived from a singular noun. Accordingly, English nouns occur, for the most part in parallel sets of two: a singular noun (*hat*) and a plural noun derived from the former (*hats*). Given one of these, the speaker is usually capable of producing the other. Each such set of forms is called a *paradigmatic set* or *paradigm*, and each form in the set is called an *inflected form* or *inflection*. Some languages have large paradigms, which contain many inflections. In Latin, for instance, the verb appears in some 125 inflectional forms, such as *amāre* 'to love,' *amō* 'I love,' *amās* 'thou lovest,' *amat* 'he loves,' *amāmus* 'we love,' *amem* 'I may love,' *amor* 'I am loved,' and so on; the occurrence of one form usually guarantees the occurrence of all the others. It is this parallelism of the inflections which forces us to treat a single phonetic form, like *sheep* as a set of homonyms, a singular noun *sheep* (corresponding to *lamb*) and a plural noun *sheep* (corresponding to *lambs*). It is this parallelism also, which leads us to view entirely different phonetic forms, like *go : went*, as morphologically related (by suppletion): *go* as an infinitive (parallel, say, with *show*) and *went* as a past-tense form (parallel, then, with *showed*).

The parallelism, to be sure, is sometimes imperfect. *Defective* paradigms lack some of the inflections; thus, *can, may, shall, will, must* have no infinitive, *must* has no past tense, *scissors* no singular. If, as in these cases, the lacking form happens to underlie the actually existing ones, we do best to set up a theoretical underlying form, such as a non-existent infinitive *can or singular *scissor-. On the other hand, some irregular paradigms are *over-differenti-*

ated. Thus, corresponding to a single form of an ordinary paradigm like *play* (*to play, I play, we play*), the paradigm of *be* has three forms (*to be, I am, we are*), and, corresponding to the single form *played*, it has the forms (*I*) *was*, (*we*) *were, been*. The existence of even a single over-differentiated paradigm implies homonymy in the regular paradigms.

The parallelism of inflected forms goes hand in hand with a further characteristic: the different inflections differ in syntactic function. If we say *the boys chauffe*, our syntactic habit of congruence (§ 12.7) requires us, when *the boy* is the actor, to supply also the form *chauffes*. In the case of the present and past inflections of the English verb this is not true: the parallelism of *plays : played* is not required by any habits of our syntax, but is carried out none the less rigidly.

If there are several ranks of inflection, we get compound paradigms; the inflections of the English noun, for instance, consist of an outer construction, the derivation of the possessive adjective, and an inner one, the derivation of the plural:

	SINGULAR	PLURAL
nominative-accusative	*man*	*men*
possessive adjective	*man's*	*men's*

In the Latin verb we find a very complicated compound paradigm: an outer layer for different actors or undergoers, distinguished as to person (speaker, hearer, third person), number (singular, plural), and voice (actor, undergoer), an inner layer for differences of tense (present, past, future) and mode (real, hypothetical, unreal), and an innermost layer for a difference as to completion of the act (imperfectic, perfectic).

13. 13. We come, finally, to an important characteristic of inflection, akin to those we have mentioned, the *derivational unity* of paradigms. The inflectional forms of a paradigm do not each enter into composition and derivation, but the paradigm as a whole is represented by some one form. In English, the forms of a noun-paradigm are represented by the singular, as in *manslaughter, mannish*, and those of the verb-paradigm by the infinitive, as in *playground, player*. An English paradigm consists of an underlying word (itself a member of the paradigm) and some secondary derivatives containing this underlying word; as a constituent in further derivation and composition, the paradigm, as a whole, is represented by the underlying form; the English language, accordingly, may be said to have *word-inflection*, *word-derivation*, and *word-composition*.

In many languages, especially in those which have a more complex morphology, none of the forms in a paradigm can conveniently be viewed as underlying the others. Thus, the regular paradigms of the German verb contain a common element which is not equal to any of the inflectional forms. For instance, the paradigm represented by the forms *lachen* ['lax-en] '(to) laugh,' (*ich*) *lache* ['lax-e] '(I) laugh,' (*er*) *lacht* [lax-t] '(he) laughs,' (*er*) *lachte* ['lax-te] '(he) laughed,' *gelacht* [ge-'lax-t] 'laughed' (participle), and so on, shows a common element *lach-* [lax-] in all the inflectional forms, but none of these inflectional forms consists simply of the element *lach-* without an affix. In secondary derivation and composition the paradigm is represented by this same form, as in *Lacher* ['lax-er] 'laugher' and *Lachkrampf* ['lax-ˌkrampf] 'laughing-spasm.' This *lach-*, strictly speaking, is a bound form; it is called the *kernel* or *stem* of the paradigm. The German verb is an example of *stem-inflection*, *stem-derivation*, and *stem-composition*. In our description, we usually treat the stem as if it were a free form.

In some languages of this type, the common element of the paradigm differs from the stem which represents the paradigm in derivatives and compounds. Thus, an ancient Greek noun-paradigm has stem-inflection. It contains a common element, a kernel, much like the German verb-stem, e.g. [hipp-] 'horse':

	Singular	Plural
nominative	['hipp-os]	['hipp-oj]
vocative	['hipp-e]	['hipp-oj]
accusative	['hipp-on]	['hipp-ows]
dative	['hipp-o:j]	['hipp-ojs]
genitive	['hipp-ow]	['hipp-o:n]

In secondary derivation, however, this paradigm is represented not by the common element [hipp-], but by a special *deriving-form* [hipp-o-] as in [hip'po-te:s] 'horseman,' or with loss of the [o] by phonetic modification, in [hipp-i'kos] 'pertaining to horses.' Similarly, as a compound-member, the paradigm is represented by a special *compounding-form*, homonymous with the preceding: [hippo-'kantharos] 'horse-beetle.' Thus, we distinguish between the *kernel* [hipp-], which actually (subject, however, in principle, to phonetic modification) appears in all the forms, and the *stem* [hipp-o-], which underlies the further derivatives.

Some exceptions to the principle of paradigmatic unity are only apparent. The possessive-adjective form in the English compounds like *bull's-eye* or the plural form in *longlegs* are due, as we shall see, to the phrasal structure of these compounds. Real exceptions do, however, occur. German has a suffix *-chen* [-xen] 'small,' which forms secondary derivatives from nouns, as: *Tisch* [tiʃ] 'table' : *Tischchen* ['tiʃ-xen] 'little table.' In the system of German morphology, this is a construction of word-formation, but in a certain few instances the suffix [-xen] is added to nouns which already have plural inflection: beside *Kind* [kint] 'child': *Kindchen* ['kint-xen] 'little child,' the plural inflection *Kinder* ['kinder] 'children' underlies the derivative *Kinderchen* ['kinder-xen] 'little children.' If a language contained too many cases of this sort, we should simply say that it did not distinguish such morphologic layers as are denoted by the terms inflection and word-formation.

CHAPTER 14

MORPHOLOGIC TYPES

14. 1. Of the three types of morphologic constructions which can be distinguished according to the nature of the constituents — namely, composition, secondary derivation, and primary derivation (§ 13.3) — the constructions of compound words are most similar to the constructions of syntax.

Compound words have two (or more) free forms among their immediate constituents (*door-knob*). Under the principle of immediate constituents, languages usually distinguish compound words from phrase-derivatives (as, *old-maidish*, a secondary derivative with the underlying phrase *old maid*), and from de-compounds (as, *gentlemanly*, a secondary derivative with the underlying compound word *gentleman*). Within the sphere of compound words, the same principle usually involves a definite structural order; thus, the compound *wild-animal-house* does not consist, say, of three members *wild*, *animal*, and *house*, and not of the members *wild* and *animal-house*, but of the members *wild animal* (a phrase) and *house*; and, similarly, the compound *doorknob-wiper* consists, unmistakably, of the members *door-knob* and *wiper*, and not, for instance, of *door* and *knob-wiper*.

The grammatical features which lead us to recognize compound words, differ in different languages, and some languages, doubtless, have no such class of forms. The gradations between a word and a phrase may be many; often enough no rigid distinction can be made. The forms which we class as compound words exhibit some feature which, in their language, characterizes single words in contradistinction to phrases.

In meaning, compound words are usually more specialized than phrases; for instance, *blackbird*, denoting a bird of a particular species, is more specialized than the phrase *black bird*, which denotes any bird of this color. It is a very common mistake to try to use this difference as a criterion. We cannot gauge meanings accurately enough; moreover, many a phrase is as specialized in meaning as any compound: in the phrases *a queer bird* and *meat and drink,* the words *bird, meat* are fully as specialized as they are in the compounds *jailbird* and *sweetmeats.*

14. 2. In languages which use a single high stress on each word, this feature distinguishes compound words from phrases. In English the high stress is usually on the first member; on the other member there is a lesser stress, as in *door-knob* ['dɔə-ˌnɔb], *upkeep* ['ʌp-ˌkijp]. Certain compounds have the irregularity of leaving the second member unstressed, as in *gentleman* ['d͡ʒentlmən], *Frenchman* ['frent͡ʃmən]; contrast *milkman* ['milk-ˌmɛn]. Certain types of compounds, chiefly some whose members are adverbs and prepositions, stress the second member: *without, upon.* Accordingly, wherever we hear lesser or least stress upon a word which would always show high stress in a phrase, we describe it as a compound-member: *ice-cream* ['ajs-ˌkrijm] is a compound, but *ice cream* ['ajs 'krijm] is a phrase, although there is no denotative difference of meaning. However, a phrase as prior member in a compound keeps all its high stresses: in *wild-animal-house* ['wajld-'ɛniml-ˌhaws] the stress assures us only that *house* is a compound-member; the rest of the structure is shown by other criteria.

As to the phonetic pattern, compound words are generally treated like phrases: in English, clusters like [vt] in *shrovetide* or [nn] in *pen-knife* do not occur within simple words. Sandhi-like phonetic modifications mark a compound as a single word only when they differ from the sandhi of syntax in the same language. Thus *gooseberry* ['guzbri] is marked as a compound because the substitution of [z] for [s] is not made in English syntax, but only in morphology, as in *gosling* ['gɔzliŋ]. Similarly, in French, *pied-à-terre* [pjet-a-tɛːr] 'temporary lodging' (literally 'foot-on-ground') beside *pied* [pje] 'foot,' or *pot-au-feu* [pɔt-o-fo] 'broth' (literally 'pot-on-the-fire') beside *pot* [po] 'pot,' or *vinaigre* [vin-ɛgr] 'vinegar' (literally 'sour-wine') beside *vin* [vɛ̃] 'wine,' are marked as compounds, because French nouns do not exhibit these types of sandhi in the phrase, but only in word-constructions, such as *pieter* [pjete] 'toe the mark,' *potage* [pɔtaːʒ] 'thick soup,' *vinaire* [vinɛːr] 'pertaining to wine'; contrast, for instance, the phrase *vin aigre* [vɛ̃ ɛgr] 'sour wine.'

More striking phonetic modifications may mark a compound; thus, in the following examples the prior member suffers greater modification than it does in any phrase of its language: *holy* ['howli] : *holiday* ['hɔlidej], *moon* : *Monday, two* [tuw] : *twopence* ['tʌpns]; Old English ['fe:ower] 'four': ['fiðer-ˌfe:te] 'four-footed'; the second member, in Sanskrit [na:wh] 'ship': [ati-'nuh] 'gone from the ship'; ancient Greek [pa'te:r] 'father': [ew-'pato:r] 'well-fathered'; Gothic *dags* 'day' : *fidur-dōgs* 'four days old'; both members, in English *breakfast* ['brekfəst], *blackguard* ['blɛgə:d], *boatswain* ['bowsn], *forecastle* ['fowksl]; in some cases there is also a variant form without modification, as in *forehead* ['fɔrid], *waistcoat* ['weskət]. In extreme cases, of course, the form may be so unlike the independent word that we may hesitate between calling it a compound-member or an affix: a form like *fortnight* ['fɔ:t-ˌnajt], lies on the border between compound and simple word.

The order of the members in a compound word may be fixed, while that of the phrase is free, as in *bread-and-butter* ['bred-n-ˌbʌtə] 'slices of bread spread with butter,' contrasting with the phrase, as in *she bought bread and butter, she bought butter and bread*. This criterion is likely to break down, however, because the order in a phrase, too, may be fixed: we have also a specialized phrase ['bred n 'bʌtə] with the same order and the same meaning as the compound. Contrasting order is a surer mark : French *blanc-bec* [blã-bɛk] 'callow young person' (literally 'white-beak') is characterized as a compound, because adjectives like *blanc* in the phrase always follow their noun: *bec blanc* 'white beak.' English examples are *to housekeep, to backslide, to undergo*, since in a phrase a noun goal like *house* and adverbs of the type *back, under* would follow the verb (*keep house, slide back*).

14. 3. The commonest, but also the most varied and most difficult to observe, of the features which lead us to distinguish compound words from phrases, are grammatical features of selection.

The plainest contrast appears in languages with *stem-composition* (§ 13.13). A stem like German *lach-*, which represents a whole verb paradigm in a German compound like *Lachkrampf* ['lax-ˌkrampf] 'laughing-spasm,' but does not actually occur as an independent word, makes the compound unmistakably different from any phrase. Even more plainly, a compounding-stem, such as ancient Greek [hippo-] 'horse,' may differ formally from all the inflections of its paradigm, and, in any case, characterizes a compound by its invariability; thus, [hippo-] joins some other stem, such as ['kantharo-] 'beetle,' to form a compound stem, [hippo-'kantharo-] 'horse-beetle,' but remains unchanged in all the inflectional forms of this compound: nominative [hippo'kantharo-s], accusative [hippo'kantharo-n], and so on.

Even when the compound-member is formally equal to some word, it may characterize the compound. In ancient Greek a noun-stem is inflected by means of suffixes. Accordingly, the first member of a compound noun-stem will remain the same in all forms of the paradigm. Thus, the phrase 'new city' will show various inflectional forms of two paradigms:

> nominative [ne'a: 'polis]
> accusative [ne'a:n 'polin]
> genitive [ne'a:s 'poleo:s],

and so on, but the compound stem [ne'a:-poli-] 'Naples,' whose first member is in nominative singular form, will show this first member unchanged in all the inflections:

> nominative [ne'a:polis]
> accusative [ne'a:polin]
> genitive [nea:'poleo:s].

In German, the adjective has word-inflection; the underlying form is used as a complement of verbs: *Das ist rot* [das ist 'ro:t] 'that is red,' and the derived inflections appear as modifiers of nouns: *roter Wein* ['ro:ter 'vajn] 'red wine.' The absence of inflectional suffixes therefore characterizes the compound-member in a form like *Rotwein* ['ro:t-₁vajn] 'red-wine.'

The use of prefixes and suffixes may decide for us what is the beginning and what the end of a word or stem. In German, the past participle of verbs is formed by the addition to the stem of a prefix [ge-] and a suffix [-t], as in *gelacht* [ge-'lax-t] 'laughed.' The position of these affixes, accordingly, shows us that a form like *geliebkost* [ge-'li:p₁ko:s-t] 'caressed' is one word, derived from a compound stem, but that a form like *liebgehabt* ['li:p ge-₁hap-t] 'liked' is a two-word phrase. This gives us a standard for the classification of other inflectional forms, such as the infinitives *liebkosen* ['li:p-₁ko:zen] 'to caress' and *liebhaben* .['li:p ₁ha:ben] 'to like.'

Sometimes the compound-member resembles an inflectional form, but one which would be impossible in the phrase. The [-z, -s] on the prior members of *bondsman, kinsman, landsman, marksman* resembles the possessive-adjective suffix, but possessive adjectives like *bond's, land's* and so on, would not be so used in the phrase. In French, the adjective *grande* [grãd] great, as in *une grande maison* [yn grãd mezõ] 'a big house,' drops the final consonant (§ 13.7) to make the inflectional form used with masculine nouns: *un grand garçon* [œ̃ grã garsõ] 'a big boy'; but, as a compound-member, the latter form appears also with certain feminine nouns: *grand'mère* [grã-mɛːr] 'grandmother,' *grand'porte* [grã-pɔrt] 'main entry.' Compound-members of this type are especially common in German: *Sonnenschein* [ˈzonen-ˌʃajn] 'sunshine' has the prior member *Sonne* in a form which, as a separate word in a phrase, could only be plural; in *Geburtstag* [geˈburts-ˌtaːk] 'birthday,' the [-s] is a genitive-case ending, but would not be added, in an independent word, to a feminine noun like *die Geburt* 'birth.'

A compound-member may be characterized by some feature of word-formation which differs from what would appear in an independent word. In ancient Greek there was a highly irregular verb-paradigm, containing such forms as [daˈmaoː] 'I tame,' [eˈdmeːtheː] 'he was tamed,' and so on, which grammarians conveniently describe on the basis of a stem-form [dameː-]. From this paradigm there is derived, on the one hand, the independent agent-noun [dmeːˈteːr] 'tamer,' and, on the other hand, with a different suffix, an agent-noun [-damo-], which is used only as a second member of compound words, as in [hipˈpo-damo-s] 'horse-tamer.' Compounds with special features of word-formation are known as *synthetic compounds*. Synthetic compounds occurred especially in the older stages of the Indo-European languages, but the habit is by no means extinct. In English, the verb *to black* underlies the independent agent-noun *blacker* (as in *a blacker of boots*), but forms also, with a zero-element, the agent-noun *-black* which appears in the compound *boot-black;* similarly, *to sweep* forms *sweeper* and the second member of *chimney-sweep.* Even forms like *long-tailed* or *red-bearded* are not aptly described as containing the words *tailed, bearded* (as in *tailed monkeys, bearded lady*); the natural starting-point is rather a phrase like *long tail* or *red beard*, from which they differ by the presence of the suffix *-ed*. This is the same thing as saying that we use compounds of the type *long-tailed, red-bearded* regardless of the existence of words like *tailed, bearded:* witness forms like *blue-eyed, four-footed, snub-nosed*. Another modern English synthetic type is that of *three-master, thousand-legger*.

In English, we freely form compounds like *meat-eater* and *meat-*

eating, but not verb-compounds like **to meat-eat*; these exist only in a few irregular cases, such as *to housekeep, to bootlick*. Now, to be sure, words like *eater* and *eating* exist alongside the compounds; the synthetic feature consists merely in the restriction that a phrase like *eat meat* is paralleled by compounds only when *-er* or *-ing* is at the same time added. We may designate the types *meat-eating* and *meat-eater* as *semi-synthetic* compounds.

14. 4. Among the word-like features of the forms which we class as compound words, indivisibility (§ 11.6) is fairly frequent: we can say *black — I should say, bluish-black — birds*, but we do not use the compound word *blackbird* with a similar interruption. In some instances, however, other features may lead us to class a form as a compound word, even though it is subject to interruption. In Fox, a form like [ne-pjɛːtʃi-wa:pam-a:-pena] 'we have come to see him (her, them)' has to be classed as a compound word, because the inflectional prefix [ne-] 'I (but not thou)' and the inflectional suffixes [-a:-] 'him, her, them' and [-pena] 'plural of first person' unmistakably mark the beginning and end of a word (§ 14.3). The members of the compound are the particle [pjɛːtʃi] 'hither' and the verb-stem [wa:pam-] 'see (an animate object).' Nevertheless, the Fox language sometimes inserts words and even short phrases between the members of such compounds, as in [ne-pjɛːtʃi-ketaːnesa-wa:pam-a:-pena] 'we have come to see her, thy daughter.' In German, compound-members can be combined serially; *Singvögel* ['ziŋ-ˌføːgel] 'songbirds,' *Raubvögel* ['rawp-ˌføːgel] 'birds of prey,' *Sing- oder Raubvögel* ['ziŋ-oːder-'rawp-ˌføːgel] 'songbirds or birds of prey.'

Generally, a compound-member cannot, like a word in a phrase, serve as a constituent in a syntactic construction. The word *black* in the phrase *black birds* can be modified by *very* (*very black birds*), but not so the compound-member *black* in *blackbirds*. This feature serves to class certain French forms as compound words: thus, *sage-femme* [saːʒ-fam] 'midwife' is to be classed as a compound, in contrast with a homonymous phrase meaning 'wise woman,' because only in the latter can the constituent *sage* 'wise' be accompanied by a modifier: *très sage femme* [trɛ saːʒ fam] 'very wise woman.' This restriction, like the preceding, is occasionally absent in forms which by other features are marked as compound words. In Sanskrit, where stem-composition plainly marks the prior member of compound words, this member is

MORPHOLOGIC TYPES

nevertheless occasionally accompanied by a modifying word, as in [citta-prama'thini: de:'va:na:m 'api] 'mind-disturbing of-gods even,' that is 'disturbing to the minds even of gods,' where the genitive plural noun ('of gods') is a syntactic modifier of the compound-member [cit'ta-] 'mind.'

14. 5. The description and classification of the forms which the structure of a language leads us to describe as compound words, will depend upon the characteristic features of this language. Linguists often make the mistake of taking for granted the universal existence of whatever types of compound words are current in their own language. It is true that the main types of compound words in various languages are somewhat similar, but this similarity is worthy of notice; moreover, the details, and especially the restrictions, vary in different languages. The differences are great enough to prevent our setting up any scheme of classification that would fit all languages, but two lines of classification are often useful.

One of these two lines of classification concerns the *relation of the members*. On the one hand, we have *syntactic* compounds, whose members stand to each other in the same grammatical relation as words in a phrase; thus, in English, the members of the compounds *blackbird* and *whitecap* (the difference between these two examples will concern us later) show the same construction of adjective plus noun as do the words in the phrases *black bird* and *white cap*. On the other hand, we have *asyntactic* compounds like *door-knob*, whose members stand to each other in a construction that is not paralleled in the syntax of their language — for English has no such phrasal type as **door knob*.

The syntactic compound differs from a phrase only in the essential features which (in its language) distinguish compound words from phrases — in English, then, chiefly by the use of only one high stress. It may differ lexically from the corresponding phrase, as does *dreadnaught;* the corresponding phrase, *dread naught*, has an archaic connotation, and the normal phrase would be *fear nothing*. We can set up sub-classes of syntactic compounds according to the syntactic constructions which are paralleled by the members, as, in English, adjective with noun (*blackbird, whitecap, bull's-eye*), verb with goal noun (*lickspittle, dreadnaught*). verb with adverb (*gadabout*), past participle with adverb (*castaway*), and so on.

Many compounds are intermediate between the syntactic and asyntactic extremes: the relation of the members parallels some syntactic construction, but the compound shows more than the minimum deviation from the phrase. For instance, the compound verb *to housekeep* differs from the phrase *keep house* by the simple feature of word-order. In such cases we may speak of various kinds of *semi-syntactic* compounds. The difference of order appears also in *upkeep* versus *keep up*, and in the French *blanc-bec* versus *bec blanc* (§ 14.2). In *turnkey* versus *turn the key* or *turn keys*, the difference lies in the use of the article or of the number-category. Even types like *blue-eyed, three-master, meat-eater*, viewed as synthetic compounds, can be said to correspond to *blue eyes, three masts, eat meat*, and to differ from these phrases by simple formal characteristics, including the addition of the bound forms *-ed, -er* to the second member. In French, *boîte-à-lettres* [bwaːt-a-letr], literally 'box-for-letters,' and *boîte-aux-lettres* [bwaːt-o-letr], literally 'box-for-the-letters,' both meaning 'mail-box, post-box,' differ in the choice of preposition and in the use of the article from the normal phrasal type, which would give *boîte pour des lettres* [bwaːt puːr de letr] 'box for letters'; the use of *a* and certain other prepositions in place of more specific ones, and differences of article (especially of zero in place of the phrasal article represented by the form *des*), are in French well-marked features which enable us to set up a class of semi-syntactic compounds.

Where semi-syntactic compounds are definable, they can be further classified in the same manner as syntactic compounds: thus, in the semi-syntactic *blue-eyed* the members have the same construction as in the syntactic *blackbird*, in *three-master* the same as in *three-day*, in *housekeep, turnkey* the same as in *lickspittle*, in *upkeep* the same as in *gadabout*.

Asyntactic compounds have members which do not combine in syntactic constructions of their language. Thus, in *door-knob, horsefly, bedroom, salt-cellar, tomcat* we see two nouns in a construction that does not occur in English syntax. Other asyntactic types of English compounds are illustrated by *fly-blown, frost-bitten — crestfallen, footsore, fireproof, foolhardy — by-law, by-path, everglade — dining-room, swimming-hole — bindweed, cry-baby, driveway, playground, blowpipe — broadcast, dry-clean, foretell — somewhere, everywhere, nowhere.* Compounds with obscure members, such as *smokestack, mushroom*, or with unique members, such as *cranberry, huckleberry, zigzag, choo-choo,* are, of course, to be classed as asyntactic.

Although the relation between the members of asyntactic compounds is necessarily vague, yet we can sometimes extend the main divisions of syntactic and semi-syntactic compounds to cover also the asyntactic class. In English, for instance, the coordinative or copulative relation which we see in a semi-syntactic compound like *bittersweet* (compare the phrase *bitter and sweet*), can be discerned also in asyntactic compounds like *zigzag, fuzzy-wuzzy, choo-choo*. Most asyntactic compounds seem to have a kind of attribute-and-head construction: *door-knob, bulldog, cranberry*. To the extent that one can carry out this comparison, one can therefore distinguish between *copulative* compounds (Sanskrit *dvandva*) and *determinative* (*attributive* or *subordinative*) compounds (Sanskrit *tatpurusha*); these divisions will cross those of syntactic, semi-syntactic, and asyntactic compounds. One may even be able to mark off smaller divisions. The Hindu grammarians distinguished among copulative compounds a special sub-group of *repetitive* (*amredita*) compounds, with identical members, as in *choo-choo, bye-bye, goody-goody*. In English, we can mark off also a class in which the members show only some elementary phonetic difference, as *zigzag, flimflam, pell-mell, fuzzy-wuzzy*. The Hindus found it convenient to set off, among the determinatives, a special class of syntactic attribute-and-head compounds (*karmadharaya*), such as *blackbird*.

14. 6. The other frequently usable line of classification concerns the relation of the compound as a whole to its members. One can often apply to compounds the distinction between *endocentric* and *exocentric* constructions which we met in syntax (§ 12.10). Since a *blackbird* is a kind of a *bird*, and a *door-knob* a kind of a *knob*, we may say that these compounds have the same function as their head members; they are endocentric. On the other hand, in *gadabout* and *turnkey* the head member is an infinitive verb, but the compound is a noun; these compounds are exocentric (Sanskrit *bahuvrihi*). To take a copulative type as an example, the adjective *bittersweet* ('bitter and sweet at the same time') is endocentric, since the compound, like its co-ordinated members, *bitter* and *sweet*, has the function of an adjective, but the plant-name *bittersweet* is exocentric, since, as a noun, it differs in grammatical function from the two adjective members.

Another type of English exocentric compounds consists of adjectives with noun head: *two-pound, five-cent, half-mile, (in) apple-pie (order)*.

The difference of form-class may be less radical, but still recognizable in the system of the language. In English, the nouns *longlegs, bright-eyes, butterfingers* are exocentric, because they occur both as singulars, and, with a zero-affix, as plurals (*that longlegs, those longlegs*). In French, the noun *rouge-gorge* [ruːʒ-gɔrʒ] 'robin' (literally 'red-throat') is exocentric, because it belongs to the masculine gender-class (*le rouge-gorge* 'the robin'), while the head member belongs to the feminine gender (*la gorge* 'the throat'). In the English type *sure-footed, blue-eyed, straight-backed* the synthetic suffix [-id, -d, -t] goes hand in hand with the exocentric value (adjective with noun head); however, one might perhaps hesitate as to the classification, since *-footed, -eyed, -backed* might be viewed as adjectives (compare *horned, bearded*). Types like *clambake, upkeep* are better described as endocentric, in English grammar, because the head members *-bake* and *-keep* can be viewed as nouns of action derived, with a zero-feature, from the verbs; if English did not use many zero-features in derivation and did not form many types of action nouns, we should have to class these compounds as exocentric. Similarly, our description will probably work out best if we class *bootblack, chimney-sweep* as endocentric, with *-black* and *-sweep* as agent-nouns.

On the other hand, the large class of English compounds that is exemplified by *whitecap, longnose, swallow-tail, blue-coat, blue-stocking, red-head, short-horn* has noun function and a noun as head member, and yet is to be classed as exocentric, because the construction implies precisely that the object does not belong to the same species as the head member: these compounds mean 'object possessing such-and-such an object (second member) of such-and-such quality (first member).' This appears in the fact that the number-categories (*longlegs*) and the personal-impersonal categories (*nose . . . it; longnose . . . he, she*) do not always agree. In *three-master, thousand-legger* the synthetic suffix goes hand in hand with this exocentric relation. Nevertheless, there are borderline cases which may prevent a clear-cut distinction. The compound *blue-bottle* is endocentric if we view the insect as 'like a bottle,' but exocentric if we insist that the 'bottle' is only part of the insect.

The Hindus distinguished two special sub-classes among exocentric compounds, namely *numeratives* (*dvigu*), nouns with a number as prior member, such as, in English, *sixpence, twelvemonth, fortnight*, and *adverbials* (*avyayībhava*), adverbs with noun head, such as *bareback, barefoot, hotfoot*, or with noun subordinate, such as *uphill, downstream, indoors, overseas*.

14. 7. In *secondary derivative words* we find one free form, a phrase (as in *old-maidish*) or a word (as in *mannish*), as an immediate constituent; in the latter case, the underlying word may be a compound word (as in *gentlemanly*) or, in its own turn, a derived word (as in *actresses*, where the underlying word *actress* is itself a secondary derivative from the underlying word *actor*). We have seen, however, that for the description of some languages, we do well to set up *theoretical underlying forms*, namely *stems*, which enable us to class certain forms as secondary derivatives although, strictly speaking, they do not contain a free form (§ 13.13). A similar device is called for in the description of forms like English *scissors, oats*, where we set up a theoretical *scissor-, oat-* as underlying forms, just as we class *cranberry, oatmeal, scissor-bill* as compound words.

The underlying free form, actual or theoretical, is accompanied either by an affix, or, as we saw, in Chapter 13, by a grammatical feature.

In many languages, secondary derivatives are divided, first of all, into inflectional forms and word-formational forms (§ 13.12), but we may do well to recall that languages of this sort nevertheless often contain border-line forms, such as, in English, *beeves* or *clothes*, which predominantly resemble inflectional types, but show a formal-semantic deviation. In the same way, *learned* ['lə:nid], *drunken, laden, sodden, molten*, and the slang *broke* 'out of funds' deviate from the strictly inflectional past participles *learned* [lə:nd], *drunk, loaded, seethed, melted, broken*.

The inflectional forms are relatively easy to describe, since they occur in parallel paradigmatic sets; the traditional grammar of familiar languages gives us a picture of their inflectional systems. It may be worth noticing, however, that our traditional grammars fall short of scientific compactness by dealing with an identical feature over and over again as it occurs in different paradigmatic types. Thus, in a Latin grammar, we find the nominative-singular sign *-s* noted separately for each of the types *amīcus* 'friend,' *lapis* 'stone,' *dux* 'leader,' *tussis* 'cough,' *manus* 'hand,' *faciēs* 'face,' when, of course, it should be noted only once, with a full statement as to where it is and where it is not used.

Word-formation offers far more difficulty, and is largely neglected in our traditional grammars. The chief difficulty lies in determining which combinations exist. In very many cases we have to resign ourselves to calling a construction irregular and making a list of the forms. Only a list, for instance, can tell us from which English male nouns we derive a female noun by means of the suffix *-ess*, as in *countess, lioness*, and it will probably require a subsidiary list to tell in which of these derivatives a final [ə] is replaced by non-syllabic [r], as in *waiter : waitress, tiger : tigress* — for the type without this change, as in *author : authoress* is probably regular. Special cases, such as *duke : duchess, master : mistress, thief : thievess* demand separate mention.

Once we have established a construction of this kind, we may be able to set up a typical meaning and then, as in the case of inflection, to look for parallels. Our suffix *-ess*, for instance, has a definable linguistic meaning, not only because of the parallel character of all the sets like *count : countess, lion : lioness*, but also because English grammar, by the distinction of *he : she*, recognizes the meaning of the *-ess* derivatives. Accordingly, we are able to decide, much as we are in the case of inflection, whether a given pair of forms, such as *man : woman*, does or does not show the same relation. This enables us to draw up supplementary statements, resembling our descriptions of paradigms, which show the various formal aspects of some grammatically determined semantic unit. Thus, we find the sememe 'female of such-and-such male' expressed not only by the suffix *-ess*, but also by composition, as in *elephant-cow, she-elephant, nanny-goat*, and by suppletion, as in *ram : ewe, boar : sow;* some such pairs show inverse derivation, the male derived from the female, as *goose : gander, duck : drake*.

Similarly, we should probably need a complete list to tell which English adjectives underlie comparative forms in *-er* of the type *kinder, shorter, longer*, and, having this list, we could recognize semantically equivalent pairs, such as *good : better, much : more, little : less, bad : worse*.

In other groups the semantic relations are not grammatically definable. Thus, we derive a great many verbs from nouns by means of various changes, including a zero-element, but the meanings of these derived verbs in relation to the underlying noun are manifold: *to man, to dog, to beard, to nose, to milk, to tree, to table, to skin, to bottle, to father, to fish, to clown,* and so on. Or, again, we derive verbs from adjectives in several varieties of the meanings 'to become so-and-so' and 'to make (a goal) so-and-so,' with various formal devices:

zero: *to smoothe*
zero, from comparative: *to lower*
zero, from quality-noun: *old : to age*
modification of vowel: *full : to fill*
suppletion (?) : *dead : to kill.*
prefixes: *enable, embitter, refresh, assure, insure, belittle*
suffix *-en: brighten*
suffix *-en,* from quality-noun: *long : lengthen.*

To this list we must add a large number of foreign-learned types, such as *equal : equalize, archaic : archaize, English : anglicize, simple : simplify, vile : vilify, liquid : liquefy, valid : validate, long : elongate, different : differentiate, debile : debilitate, public : publish.*

When derivation is made by means of grammatical features, such as phonetic modification (*man : men ; mouth : to mouthe*) or modulation (*convict* verb : *convict* noun) or suppletion (*go : went*) or zero-elements (*cut* infinitive : *cut* past tense; *sheep* singular : *sheep* plural; *man* noun : *to man* verb), we may have a hard time deciding which form of a set we had better describe as the underlying form. In English, we get a simpler description if we take irregular paradigms (such as *man : men* or *run : ran*) as underlying, and regular paradigms (such as *to man* or *a run*) as derived. In most cases this criterion is lacking; thus, we shall find it hard to decide, in cases like *play, push, jump, dance,* whether to take the noun or the verb as the underlying form. Whatever our decision, the derivative word (e.g. *to man* derived from the noun *man,* or *a run* derived from the verb *to run*) will often contain no affixes, and will be described (for reasons that will shortly appear) as a *secondary root-word.*

In the same way, phrase-derivatives, such as *old-maidish,* derived from the phrase *old maid,* offer no special difficulty so long as they contain a derivational affix, such as *-ish,* but when the phrase is accompanied only by a zero-feature, as in *jack-in-the-pulpit* or *devil-may-care,* we have the difficult type of *phrase-words.* These differ from phrases in their uninterrupted and syntactically inexpansible character, and often in their exocentric value.

14. 8. *Primary words* contain no free forms among their immediate constituents. They may be *complex*, consisting of two or more bound forms, as *per-ceive, per-tain, de-ceive, de-tain*, or they may be *simple*, as *boy, run, red, and, in, ouch*.

The bound forms which make up complex primary words, are determined, of course, by features of partial resemblance, as in the examples just cited. In many languages the primary words show a structural resemblance to secondary words. Thus, in English, the primary words *hammer, rudder, spider* resemble secondary words like *dance-r, lead-er, ride-r*. The part of the primary word which resembles the derivational affix of the secondary word (in our examples, *-er*) can be described as a *primary affix*. Thus, the primary words *hammer, rudder, spider* are said to contain a primary suffix *-er*. The remaining part of the primary word — in our examples, the syllable [hɛm-] in *hammer*, [rʌd-] in *rudder*, [spajd-] in *spider* — is called the *root*. The root plays the same part in primary words as the underlying form (e.g. *dance, lead, ride*) in secondary words (*dancer, leader, rider*).

This distinction between primary affixes and roots is justified by the fact that the primary affixes are relatively few and vague in meaning, while the roots are very numerous and therefore relatively clear-cut as to denotation.[1]

In accordance with this terminology, primary words that do not contain any affix-like constituents (e.g. *boy, run, red*) are classed as *primary root-words*. The roots which occur in primary root-words are free roots, in contrast with bound roots which occur only with a primary affix, such as the root [spajd-] in *spider*.

Primary affixes may be extremely vague in meaning and act merely as an obligatory accompaniment (a *determinative*) of the root. In English, the commonest primary suffixes do not even tell the part of speech; thus, we have, with *-er*, *spider, bitter, linger, ever, under;* with *-le, bottle, little, hustle;* with *-ow, furrow,*

---

[1] Early students of language, who confused description with the entirely different (and much harder) problem of ascertaining historical origins, somehow got the notion that roots possessed mysterious qualities, especially in the way of age. Now and then one still hears the claim that the roots which we set up must once upon a time have been spoken as independent words. The reader need scarcely be told that this is utterly unjustified; the roots, like all bound forms, are merely units of partial resemblance between words. Our analysis guarantees nothing about earlier stages of the language which we are analyzing.

yellow, borrow. In other cases the meaning is more palpable; thus, *-ock*, in *hummock, mattock, hassock,* and so on, forms nouns denoting a lumpy object of moderate size, and this is confirmed by its use as a secondary suffix (class-cleavage) in words like *hillock, bullock.* Our foreign-learned prefixes get a vague but recognizable meaning from contrasts like *con-tain, de-tain, per-tain, re-tain.* In some languages, however, primary affixes bear relatively concrete meanings. The Algonquian languages use primary suffixes that denote states of matter (wood-like solid, stone-like solid, liquid, string-like thing, round thing), tools, parts of the body, animals, woman, child (but not, apparently, adult males). Thus, in Menomini, the verb-form [kepa:hkwaham] 'he puts a cover on it,' has a stem [kepa:hkwah-], which consists of the root [kep-] 'obstruction of opening,' and the primary suffixes [-a:hkw-] 'wood or other solid of similar consistency,' and [-ah-] 'act on inanimate object by tool.' Similarly, in Menomini, [akuapi:nam] 'he takes it from the water,' the verb-stem consists of the root [akua-] 'removal from a medium,' and the suffixes [-epi:-] 'liquid' and [-en-] 'act on object by hand'; [ni:sunak] 'two canoes' is a particle consisting of the root [ni:sw-] 'two' and the primary suffix [-unak] 'canoe.' These affixes are used also in secondary derivation. Some of them are derived from independent words or stems; thus, in Fox, [pjɛ:tehkwɛ:wɛ:wa] 'he brings a woman or women' is an intransitive verb (that is, cannot be used with a goal-object, — much as if we could say *he woman-brings) containing the primary suffix [-ehkwɛ:wɛ:-] 'woman,' which is derived from the noun [ihkwɛ:wa] 'woman.' In Menomini, the cognate [-ehkiwɛ:-], as in [pi:tehkiwɛ:w] (same meaning), does not stand in this relation to any noun, because the old noun for 'woman' is here obsolete, and the actual word is [metɛ:muh] 'woman.' In some languages the use of primary affixes derived from nouns covers much the same semantic ground as our syntactic construction of verb with goal-object. This habit is known as *incorporation;* the classical instance is Nahuatl, the language of the Aztecs, where a noun like [naka-tl] 'meat' is represented by a prefix in a verb-form like [ni-naka-kwa] 'I-meat-eat,' that is, 'I eat meat.'

A root may appear in only one primary word, as is the case with most ordinary English roots, such as *man, boy, cut, red, nast-* (in *nasty*), *ham-* (in *hammer*), or it may appear in a whole series of primary words, as is the case with many of our foreign-learned roots, like [-sijv] in *deceive, conceive, perceive, receive.* In either case, the primary word may underlie a whole series of secondary derivatives; thus, *man* underlies *men, man's, men's, mannish, manly, (to) man (mans, manned, manning); deceive* underlies *deceiver, deceit, deception, deceptive; conceive* underlies *conceivable, conceit, concept, conception, conceptual; perceive* underlies *perceiver, percept, perceptive, perception, perceptible, perceptual;* and *receive* underlies *receiver, receipt, reception, receptive, receptacle.* Moreover, secondary derivatives like these may exist where the primary word is lacking; thus, we have no such primary word as **preceive,* but we have the words *precept, preceptor,* which are best described as secondary derivatives of a theoretical underlying form **pre-ceive.*

The roots of a language make up its most numerous class of morphological forms and accordingly bear its most varied and specific meanings. This is clearest in languages which have roots as free forms, as, in English, *boy, man, cut, run, red, blue, green, brown, white, black.* The clear-cut meaning will be found also in bound roots, such as *yell-* in *yellow, purp-* in *purple, nast-* in *nasty,* and so on. In most languages, however, there are also roots of very vague meaning, such as, in English, the foreign-learned roots of the type *-ceive, -tain, -fer (conceive, contain, confer,* and so on). This is particularly the case in languages whose primary affixes are relatively varied and specific in meaning.

Once we have set up a root, we face the possibility of its modification. This possibility is obvious when the root occurs as an ultimate constituent in a secondary derivative: thus, in the secondary derivative *duchess* the modification of the underlying word *duke* is at the same time a modification of the root *duke,* and in the secondary derivatives *sang, sung, song,* the modifications of the underlying *sing,* are necessarily modifications of the root *sing.* The alternant shapes of roots are in some languages so varied that the describer may well hesitate as to the choice of a basic form. In ancient Greek we find the alternants [dame:-, dme:-, dmo:-, dama-, dam-] in the forms [e-'dame:] 'he tamed,' [e-'dme:-the:] 'he was tamed,' ['dmo:-s] 'slave,' [da'ma-o:] 'I tame,' [hip'po-dam-o-s] 'horse-tamer.' Our whole description of Greek morphology, including even the distribution of derivatives into primary and secondary types, will depend upon our initial choice of a basic form for roots of this sort. In the Germanic languages, modification of the root, with or without affix-like determinatives, occurs in words of symbolic connotation, as *flap, flip, flop*. If we take *flap* as the basic form of this root, we shall describe *flip, flop* as derivatives, formed by substitution of [i] 'smaller, neater' and by substitution of [ɔ] 'larger, duller.' Similar cases are, with substitution of [i]: *snap : snip, snatch : snitch, snuff : sniff, bang : bing, yap : yip;* of [ij]: *squall : squeal, squawk : squeak, crack : creak, gloom : gleam, tiny : teeny,* of [ʌ]: *mash : mush, flash : flush, crash : crush.* At first glance, we should describe these forms as secondary derivatives, since the word *flap* can be said to underlie the words *flip, flop,* but it is possible that a detailed description of English morphology would work out better if we viewed words like *flip, flop* as primary modifications of "the root *flap-*," instead of deriving them from the actual word *flap*.

The roots of a language are usually quite uniform in structure. In English they are one-syllable elements, such as *man, cut, red;* many of them are free forms, occurring as root-words, but many, such as [spajd-] in *spider*, [hɛm-] in *hammer*, and, especially, foreign-learned roots like [-sijv] in *conceive, perceive*, are bound forms. Some of these bound roots end in clusters that do not occur in word-final, as [lʌmb-] in *lumber* or [liŋg-] in *linger*. In Russian, the roots are monosyllabic, with the exception of some that have [l] or [r] between vowels of the set [e, o], as in ['golod-] 'hunger,' ['gorod-] 'city.' We have seen an example of the variability of a root in ancient Greek; for this language, as well as, apparently, for Primitive Indo-European, we probably have to set up roots of several different shapes, monosyllabic, such as [do:-] 'give,' and disyllabic, such as [dame:-] 'tame.' In North Chinese, all the roots are monosyllabic free forms consisting, phonetically, of an initial consonant or cluster (which may be lacking), a final syllabic (including diphthongal types with non-syllabic [j, w, n, ŋ]), and a pitch-scheme. The Malayan languages have two-syllable roots, with stress on one or the other syllable, as in the Tagalog root-words ['ba:haj] 'house' and [ka'maj] 'hand.' In the Semitic languages the roots consist of an unpronounceable skeleton of three consonants; accordingly, every primary word adds to the root a morphologic element which consists of a vowel-scheme. Thus, in modern Egyptian Arabic, a root like [k-t-b] 'write' appears in words like [katab] 'he wrote,' [ka:tib] 'writing (person),' [kita:b] 'book,' and, with prefixes, [ma-ka:tib] 'places for writing, studies,' [ma-ktab] 'place for writing, study,' [je-ktub] 'he is writing;' similarly, the root [g-l-s] 'sit' appears in [galas] 'he sat,' [ga:lis] 'sitting person,' [ma-ga:lis] 'councils,' [ma-glas] 'council.'

In a few languages, such as Chinese, the structure of the roots is absolutely uniform; in others, we find some roots that are shorter than the normal type. It is a remarkable fact that these shorter roots belong almost always to a grammatical or a semantic sphere which can be described, in terms of English grammar, as the sphere of pronoun, conjunction, and preposition. In German, which has much the same root structure as English, the definite article contains a root [d-], for in the forms *der, dem, den,* and so on, the rest of the word (*-er, -em, -en,* and so on) is in each case a normal inflectional ending, appearing also in the inflectional forms of an adjective like 'red': *rot-er, rot-em, rot-en.* The same applies to the interrogative pronoun 'who?' with forms like *wer, wem, wen.* In Malayan and in Semitic, many words in this semantic sphere have only one syllable, as, in Tagalog, [at] 'and,' or the syntactic particles [aŋ] 'sign of object-expression,' [aj] 'sign of predication,' [na] 'sign of attribution.' This semantic sphere is roughly the same as that in which English uses atonic words.

14. 9. Perhaps in most languages, most of the roots are morphemes. Even in cases like English *sing : sang : sung : song* or *flap : flip : flop,* a relevant description will view one of the forms as basic and the others as secondary derivatives or as primary derivatives with phonetic modification of the root. In other cases, however, we find clearly-marked phonetic-semantic resemblances between elements which we view as different roots. The pronominal words of English are probably best described as containing monosyllabic roots that resemble each other, especially as to the initial consonants:

[ð-]: *the, this, that, then, there, thith-er, thus.*

[hw-]: *what, when, where, whith-er, which, why;* modified to [h] in *who, how.*

[s-]: *so, such.*

[n-]: *no, not, none, nor, nev-er, neith-er.*

Complex morphologic structure of the root is much plainer in the case of English symbolic words; in these we can distinguish, with varying degrees of clearness, and with doubtful cases on the border-line, a system of initial and final *root-forming morphemes*, of vague signification. It is plain that the intense, symbolic connotation is associated with this structure. Thus, we find recurrent initials:

[fl-] 'moving light': *flash, flare, flame, flick-er, flimm-er.*
[fl-] 'movement in air': *fly, flap, flit (flutt-er).*
[gl-] 'unmoving light': *glow, glare, gloat, gloom (gleam, gloam-ing, glimm-er), glint.*
[sl-] 'smoothly wet': *slime, slush, slop, slobb-er, slip, slide.*
[kr-] 'noisy impact': *crash, crack (creak), crunch.*
[skr-] 'grating impact or sound': *scratch, scrape, scream.*
[sn-] 'breath-noise': *sniff (snuff), snore, snort, snot.*
[sn-] 'quick separation or movement': *snap (snip), snatch (snitch).*
[sn-] 'creep': *snake, snail, sneak, snoop.*
[dʒ-] 'up-and-down movement': *jump, jounce, jig (jog, jugg-le), jangle (jingle).*
[b-] 'dull impact': *bang, bash, bounce, biff, bump, bat.*

In the same vague way, we can distinguish finals:

[-ɛʃ] 'violent movement': *bash, clash, crash, dash, flash, gash, mash, gnash, slash, splash.*
[-ɛə] 'big light or noise': *blare, flare, glare, stare.*
[-awns] 'quick movement': *bounce, jounce, pounce, trounce.*
[-im], mostly with determinative [-ə], 'small light or noise': *dim, flimmer, glimmer, simmer, shimmer.*
[-ʌmp] 'clumsy': *bump, clump, chump, dump, frump, hump, lump, rump, stump, slump, thump.*
[-ɛt], with determinative [-ə], 'particled movement': *batter, clatter, chatter, spatter, shatter, scatter, rattle, prattle.*

In this last instance we see a formal peculiarity which confirms our classification. In English morphology there is no general restriction to the occurrence of [-ə] or [-l̩] as suffixes, and, in particular, they are not ruled out by the presence of [r, l] in the body of the word: forms like *brother, rather, river, reader, reaper* or *little, ladle, label* are common enough. The symbolic roots, however, that contain an [r], are never followed by the determinative suffix [-ə], but take an [-l̩] instead, and, conversely, a symbolic root containing [l] is never followed by [-l̩], but only by [-ə]: *brabble* and *blabber* are possible as English symbolic types, but not *brabber* or *blabble.*

The analysis of minute features, such as the root-forming morphemes, is bound to be uncertain and incomplete, because a phonetic similarity, such as, say, the [b-] in *box, beat, bang*, represents a linguistic form only when it is accompanied by a semantic similarity, and for this last, which belongs to the practical world, we have no standard of measurement.

CHAPTER 15

SUBSTITUTION

15. 1. Having surveyed sentence-types (Chapter 11) and constructions (Chapters 12, 13, 14), we turn now to the third type of meaningful grammatical arrangement, *substitution* (§ 10.7).

A *substitute* is a linguistic form or grammatical feature which, under certain conventional circumstances, replaces any one of a class of linguistic forms. Thus, in English, the substitute *I* replaces any singular-number substantive expression, provided that this substantive expression denotes the speaker of the utterance in which the substitute is used.

The grammatical peculiarity of substitution consists in selective features: the substitute replaces only forms of a certain class, which we may call the *domain* of the substitute; thus, the domain of the substitute *I* is the English form-class of substantive expressions. The substitute differs from an ordinary linguistic form, such as *thing, person, object*, by the fact that its domain is grammatically definable. Whether an ordinary form, even of the most inclusive meaning, such as *thing*, can be used of this or that practical situation, is a practical question of meaning; the equivalence of a substitute, on the other hand, is grammatically determined. For instance, no matter whom or what we address, we may mention this real or pretended hearer in the form of a substantive expression by means of the substitute *you* — and for this we need no practical knowledge of the person, animal, thing, or abstraction that we are treating as a hearer.

In very many cases, substitutes are marked also by other peculiarities: they are often short words and in many languages atonic; they often have irregular inflection and derivation (*I : me : my*) and special syntactic constructions. In many languages they appear as bound forms and may then be characterized by morphologic features, such as their position in structural order.

15. 2. One element in the meaning of every substitute is the *class-meaning* of the form-class which serves as the domain of the substitute. The class-meaning of the substitute *you*, for example, is the class-meaning of English substantive expressions; the class-meaning of *I* is that of singular substantive expressions, and the class-meaning of the substitutes *they* and *we* is that of plural substantive expressions.

Some substitutes add a more specific meaning which does not appear in the form-class, but even in these cases a set of several substitutes systematically represents the whole domain. Thus, *who* and *what* together cover the class-meaning of English substantive expressions. In the same way, *he*, *she*, and *it* together cover the class-meaning of singular substantive expressions; within the set, *he* and *she* cover the same sub-domain as *who*, and *it* the same sub-domain as *what*, but the distinction between *he* and *she* implies a further and independent subdivision. Our selection of substitutes, then, divides English substantive expressions into the sub-classes of *personal* (replaced by *who* and *he-she*) and *non-personal* (replaced by *what* and *it*), and it subdivides the personal singulars into the sub-classes of *male* (replaced by *he*) and *female* (replaced by *she*).

In addition to the class-meaning, every substitute has another element of meaning, the *substitution-type*, which consists of the conventional circumstances under which the substitution is made. Thus, *I* replaces any singular substantive expression (this domain gives us the class-meaning of *I*), provided that this substantive expression denotes the speaker of the very utterance in which the *I* is produced: this is the substitution-type of *I*. The circumstances under which a substitution is made are practical circumstances, which the linguist, for his part, cannot accurately define. In detail, they differ greatly in different languages; in speaking a foreign language, we have great difficulty in using the proper substitute-forms.

15. 3. Nevertheless, it will be worth our while to leave, for a moment, the ground of linguistics, and to examine the problems which here confront the student of sociology or psychology. We find, at once, that the various types of substitution represent elementary circumstances of the act of speech-utterance. The substitution-types in *I*, *we*, and *you* are based upon the speaker-hearer relation. The types of *this*, *here*, *now* and *that*, *there*, *then* represent relations of distance from the speaker or from the speaker and the hearer. The interrogative type of *who*, *what*, *where*, *when* stimulates the hearer to supply a speech-form. The negative type of *nobody, nothing, nowhere, never* excludes the possibility of a speech-form. These types are remarkably widespread and uniform (except for details) in the languages of the world; among them we find the practical relations to which human beings respond more uniformly than to any others — numerative and identificational relations, such as positive-negative, *all, some, any, same, other*, and, above all, the numbers, *one, two, three*, and so on. These are the relations upon which the language of science is based; the speech-forms which express them make up the vocabulary of mathematics. Many of these substitution-types have to do with species and individuals: they select or identify individuals (*all, some, any, each, every, none*, and so on) out of a species. Perhaps every language has a form-class of object-expressions, with a class-meaning of the type 'species occurring in individual specimens.' Accordingly, the substitutes for object-expressions, *pronominals*, will usually show the most varied substitution-types. In English, where object-expressions are a special part of speech, the *noun*, the substitutes for the noun make up a part of speech, the *pronoun;* together, these two constitute a greater part of speech, the *substantive*. The pronouns differ from nouns, for one thing, in not being accompanied by adjective modifiers (§ 12.14).

To a large extent, some substitution-types are characterized, further, by the circumstance that the form for which substitution is made, has occurred in recent speech. Thus, when we say *Ask that policeman, and he will tell you*, the substitute *he* means, among other things, that the singular male substantive expression which is replaced by *he*, has been recently uttered. A substitute which implies this, is an *anaphoric* or *dependent* substitute, and the recently-uttered replaced form is the *antecedent*. This distinction, however, seems nowhere to be fully carried out: we usually find some *independent* uses of substitutes that are ordinarily dependent, as, for instance, the independent use of *it* in *it's raining*. Independent substitutes have no antecedent: they tell the form-class, and they may even have an elaborate identificational or numerative substitution-type — as, for instance, *somebody, nobody* — but they do not tell which form of the class (for instance, which particular noun) has been replaced.

On the whole, then, substitution-types consist of elementary features of the situation in which speech is uttered. These features are so simple that, for the most part, they could be indicated by gestures: *I, you, this, that, none, one, two, all,* and so on. Especially the substitutes of the 'this' and 'that' types resemble interjections in their semantic closeness to non-linguistic forms of response; like interjections, they occasionally deviate from the phonetic pattern of their language (§ 9.7). Since, aside from the class-meaning, the substitution-type represents the whole meaning of a substitute, we can safely say that the meanings of substitutes are, on the one hand, more inclusive and abstract, and, on the other hand, simpler and more constant, than the meanings of ordinary linguistic forms. In their class-meaning, substitutes are one step farther removed than ordinary forms from practical reality, since they designate not real objects but grammatical form-classes; substitutes are, so to speak, linguistic forms of the second degree. In their substitution-type, on the other hand, substitutes are more primitive than ordinary linguistic forms, for they designate simple features of the immediate situation in which the speech is being uttered.

The practical usefulness of substitution is easy to see. The substitute is used more often than any one of the forms in its domain; consequently, it is easier to speak and to recognize. Moreover, substitutes are often short forms and often, as in English, atonic, or, as in French, otherwise adapted to quick and easy utterance. In spite of this economy, substitutes often work more safely and accurately than specific forms. In answer to the question *Would you like some fine, fresh cantaloupes?* The answer *How much are cantaloupes?* is perhaps more likely to be followed by a delay or aberration of response ("misunderstanding') than the answer *How much are they?* This is especially true of certain substitutes, such as *I,* whose meaning is unmistakable, while the actual mention of the speaker's name would mean nothing to many a hearer.

15. 4. Returning to the ground of linguistics, we may be somewhat bolder, in view of what we have seen in our practical excursion, about stating the meanings of substitutes. We observe, also, that in many languages, the meanings of substitutes recur in other forms, such as the English limiting adjectives (§ 12.14).

The meaning of the substitute *you* may be stated thus:

A. *Class-meaning:* the same as that of the form-class of substantive expressions, say 'object or objects';
B. *Substitution-type:* 'the hearer.'

SUBSTITUTION

The meaning of the substitute *he* may be stated thus:
A. *Class-meanings:*
  1. *Definable in terms of form-classes:*
     (a) the same as that of the form-class of singular substantive expressions, say 'one object';
     (b) the same as that of the form-class defined by the substitutes *who, someone*, say 'personal';
  2. *Creating an otherwise unestablished form-class: he* is used only of certain singular personal objects (the rest are replaced, instead, by *she*), which, accordingly, constitute a sub-class with a class-meaning, say 'male';
B. *Substitution-types:*
  1. *Anaphora: he* implies, in nearly all its uses, that a substantive designating a species of male personal objects has recently been uttered and that *he* means one individual of this species; say 'recently mentioned';
  2. *Limitation: he* implies that the individual is identifiable from among all the individuals of the species mentioned; this element of meaning is the same as that of the syntactic category of definite nouns (§ 12.14) and can be stated, say, as 'identified.'

15. 5. Substitutes whose substitution-type consists of nothing but anaphora, are (*simple*) *anaphoric* substitutes: apart from their class-meanings (which differ, of course, according to the grammatical form-classes of different languages), they say only that the particular form which is being replaced (the antecedent) has just been mentioned. In English, finite verb expressions are anaphorically replaced by forms of *do, does, did,* as in *Bill will misbehave just as John did.* The antecedent here is *misbehave;* accordingly, the replaced form is *misbehaved.* A few English verb-paradigms, such as *be, have, will, shall, can, may, must,* lie outside the domain of this substitution: *Bill will be bad just as John was* (not *did*). Nouns, in English are anaphorically replaced by *one,* plural *ones,* provided they are accompanied by an adjective attribute: *I prefer a hard pencil to a soft one, hard pencils to soft ones.* This use of *one* as an anaphoric pronoun differs by class-cleavage from the several attributive uses of the word *one* (§ 12.14), especially in forming a plural, *ones.* The details of this anaphoric substitution will concern us later (§ 15.8-10).

In subordinate clauses introduced by *as* or *than*, we have in English a second kind of anaphora for a finite verb expression: we say not only *Mary dances better than Jane does*, but also *Mary dances better than Jane*. We can describe this latter type by saying that (after *as* and *than*) an actor (*Jane*) serves as an anaphoric substitute for an actor-action expression (*Jane dances*), or we can say that (after *as* and *than*) a *zero-feature* serves as an anaphoric substitute for a finite verb expression accompanying an actor expression. Another case of an anaphoric zero-feature in English is the replacement of infinitive expressions after the preposition *to* (as in *I haven't seen it, but hope to*) and after the finite verbs which take an infinitive attribute without *to* (as in *I'll come if I can*). Similarly, we have zero-anaphora for participles after forms of *be* and *have*, as in *You were running faster than I was; I haven't seen it, but Bill has*. Zero-anaphora for nouns with an accompanying adjective occurs freely in English only for mass nouns, as in *I like sour milk better than fresh*. For other nouns we use the anaphoric *one, ones*, except after certain limiting adjectives.

While some forms of simple anaphoric substitution seem to occur in every language, there are great differences of detail. The use of *one, ones*, is peculiar to English; related languages of similar structure use zero-anaphora quite freely for nouns after adjectives, as, German *grosze Hunde und kleine* ['gro:se 'hunde unt 'klajne] 'big dogs and little ones'; French *des grandes pommes et des petites* [de gr ã d pɔm e de ptit] 'big apples and small ones.' In some languages the subject in the full sentence-types can be replaced by zero-anaphora; thus, in Chinese, to a statement like [wo³ 'juŋ⁴ i² khwaj 'pu⁴] 'I need one piece (of) cloth,' the response may be ['juŋ⁴ i⁴ 'phi¹ mo?] 'Need one roll (interrogative particle)?' In Tagalog this happens in subordinate clauses, as in the sentence [aŋ 'puːnuʔ aj tuˈmuːbuʔ haŋˈgaŋ sa mag buːŋa] 'the tree (predicative particle) grew until (attributive particle) bore-fruit.'

15. 6. Perhaps all languages use pronominal substitutes which combine anaphora with definite identification: the replaced form is an identified specimen of the species named by the antecedent. This, we have seen, is the value of the English pronoun *he*, as in *Ask a policeman, and he will tell you*. Substitutes of this kind are often, but misleadingly, called "anaphoric"; a better name would be *definite*. In most languages, including English, the definite substitutes are not used when the antecedent is the speaker or the hearer or includes these persons; for this reason, the definite substitutes are often spoken of as *third-person* substitutes. They usually share various peculiarities with the substitutes that refer to the hearer and to the speaker.

The English definite or third-person pronouns, *he, she, it, they,* differ for singular and plural replaced forms, and, in the singular, for *personal* and *non-personal* antecedents: personal *he, she,* versus non-personal *it*. We have seen that the difference of singular and plural is otherwise also recognized by the language (as, for instance, in the inflection of nouns: *boy, boys*), and we shall see that the same is true of the difference of personal and non-personal. Within the personal class, however, the distinction between *he* used with a male antecedent, and *she,* with a female antecedent, is otherwise imperfectly recognized in our language (as, in the use of the suffix *-ess,* § 14.7). The distinction, then, between the pronoun-forms *he* and *she,* creates a classification of our personal nouns into *male* (defined as those for which the definite substitute is *he*) and *female* (similarly defined by the use of the substitute *she*). Semantically, this classification agrees fairly well with the zoölogical division into sexes.

In languages with noun-genders (§ 12.7), the third-person pronouns usually differ according to the gender of the antecedent. Thus, in German, *masculine* nouns, such as *der Mann* [der 'man] 'the man,' *der Hut* [hu:t] 'the hat,' have the third-person substitute *er* [e:r], as when *er ist grosz* [e:r ist 'gro:s] 'he, it is big,' is said of either a man or a hat, or of any other antecedent that belongs to the "masculine" congruence-class;

feminine nouns, such as *die Frau* [di: 'fraw] 'the woman,' *die Uhr* [u:r] 'the clock,' have the third-person substitute *sie* [zi:], as in *sie ist grosz,* 'she, it is big';

neuter nouns, such as *das Haus* [das 'haws] 'the house,' or *das Weib* [vajp] 'the woman,' have the third-person substitute *es* [es], as in *es ist grosz*.

This distinction, unlike that of *he* and *she* in English, accords with a distinction in the form of noun-modifiers (such as *der : die : das* 'the').

The meaning of definite identification — that is, the way in which the individual specimen is identified from among the species named by the antecedent — varies for different languages and would probably be very hard to define. It is important to notice, however, that in languages which have a category of "definite" noun-modifiers (such as, in English *the, this, that, my, John's,* etc., § 12.14), the definite pronoun identifies the individual in the same fashion as a definite modifier identifies its head noun; thus, a *he* after the antecedent *policeman* is equivalent in denotation, except for the peculiar value that lies in the use of a substitute, to the phrase *the policeman*. We need mention only a few widespread peculiarities, such as the case, not very common in English, that the definite pronoun is spoken before its antecedent: *He is foolish who says so*. If the antecedent is a predicate complement after a form of the verb *to be*, the definite pronoun is normally *it*, regardless of number, personality, or sex: *it was a two-storey house; it's he; it's me (I), it's the boys*. Instead of an infinitive phrase as an actor (*to scold the boys was foolish*), we more commonly use *it*, with the infinitive phrase following in close parataxis (§ 12.2): *it was foolish to scold the boys*. An actor-action phrase, such as *you can't come*, does not serve as an actor; but does appear in close parataxis with *it* as an actor: *it's too bad you can't come*. This *anticipatory* use of the definite pronoun extends, in German, to almost any actor, with the restriction that the pronoun comes first; thus, beside *ein Mann kam in den Garten* [ajn 'man 'kaːm in den 'garten] 'a man came into the garden,' there is the form *es kam ein Mann in den Garten*, where the use of *es* resembles the English use of the adverb *there*. If the noun in parataxis is plural, this German *es* accompanies a plural verb: beside *zwei Männer kamen in den Garten* [tsvaj 'mener 'kaːmen] 'two men came into the garden,' there is the form *es kamen zwei Männer in den Garten*.

In French, the definite pronoun replaces an adjective: *êtes-vous heureux? — je le suis* [ɛːt vu œrø? — ʒə l sɥi.] 'Are you happy? — I am.' A step beyond this, we find definite pronouns in marginal uses without any antecedent, as in English slang *beat it* 'run away,' *cheese it* 'look out,' *he hot-footed it home* 'he ran home,' *let 'er go*. We use *they* as an actor for people in general: *they say Smith is doing very well*. The commonest use of this sort is the *pseudo-impersonal* use of a definite pronoun as a merely formal actor, in languages that have a favorite actor-action construction: *it's raining; it's a shame*. This may occur alongside a genuine impersonal construction (§ 11.2). Thus, in German, beside the genuine impersonal *mir war kalt* [miːr vaːr 'kalt] 'to-me was cold; I felt cold,' *hier wird getanzt* ['hiːr virt ge'tantst] 'here gets danced; there is dancing here,' the definite pronoun *es* may appear as an actor, provided it comes first in the phrase: *es war mir kalt; es wird hier getanzt.* In Finnish, the impersonal and the pseudo-impersonal are used for different meanings: *puhutaan* 'there is talking' is a genuine impersonal, but *sadaa* 'it's raining' contains a definite substitute actor 'he, she, it,' just as does *puhuu* 'he, she, it is talking.'

15. 7. The definite substitutes in most languages are not used when the replaced form designates the speaker or the hearer or groups that include these persons; in this case a different type, the *personal* substitute is used. The *first-person* substitute *I* replaces mention of the speaker, and the *second-person* substitute *thou*, of the hearer. These are independent substitutes, requiring no antecedent utterance of the replaced form.

In addition to the *I* and *thou* substitutes, most languages use also forms for groups of people that include the speaker or the hearer or both. Thus, in English, for a group of people which includes the speaker, the substitute is *we;* if the speaker is not included, but the hearer is, the substitute is *ye.* Many languages distinguish all three of these possibilities, as, Tagalog, which, beside [a'ku] 'I' and [i'kaw] 'thou,' has the plural-like forms:

speaker only included (*exclusive* first person plural): [ka'mi] 'we'

speaker and hearer included (*inclusive* first person plural): ['taːju] 'we'

hearer only included (second person plural): [ka'ju] 'ye.'

Similarly, languages which distinguish a dual number, allow of five combinations, as in Samoan: 'I-and-he,' 'I-and-thou,' 'ye-two,' 'I-and-they,' 'I-and-thou-and-he (-or-they),' 'thou-and-they.' A few languages distinguish also a *trial* number ('three persons') in their personal pronouns.

The English forms *thou, ye* are, of course, archaic; modern English is peculiar in using the same form, *you*, both for the hearer and for a group of persons that includes the hearer.

Many languages use different second-person substitutes according to different social relations between speaker and hearer. Thus, French uses *vous* [vu] 'you' much like English, for both singular and plural, but if the hearer is a near relative, an intimate friend, a young child, or a non-human being (such as a god), there is a special *intimate* singular-form *toi* [twa]. German uses the third-person plural pronoun 'they' for both singular and plural second person: *Sie spaszen* [ziː ˈʃpaːsen] is both 'they are jesting' and 'you (singular or plural) are jesting,' but the intimate forms, used much like those of French, distinguish singular and plural: *du spaszest* [du: ʃpaːsest] 'thou art jesting,' *ihr spaszt* [iːr ʃpaːst] 'ye are jesting.'

The meaning of second-person substitutes is limited in some languages by the circumstance that they are not used in deferential speech; instead, the hearer is designated by some honorific term (*your Honor, your Excellency, your Majesty*). In Swedish or in Polish, one says, for instance, 'How is *Mother* feeling?' or 'Will *the gentleman* come to-morrow?' where the terms here italicized denote the hearer. Some languages, such as Japanese and Malay, distinguish several substitutes for both first and second persons, according to deferential relations between speaker and hearer.

The personal substitutes and the definite ("third-person") substitutes in many languages group themselves, by virtue of common features, into a kind of closed system of *personal-definite* substitutes. In English, both sets *he, she, it, they* and *I, we, you* (*thou, ye*), are atonic in the phrase; most of them have a special accusative case-form (*me, us, him, her, them, thee*); most of them derive their possessive adjectives irregularly (*my, our, your, his, her, their, thy*), and some of these adjectives have a special form for zero anaphora (*mine*, etc., § 15.5). In French, the personal-definite pronouns have special (*conjunct*) forms when they serve as actors or goals of verbs (§ 12.12); these have case-inflection for different positions, which is otherwise foreign to French substantives; moreover, they underlie possessive adjectives, as *moi* [mwa] 'I,' *mon chapeau* [mõ ʃapo] 'my hat,' while other substantives do not: *le chapeau de Jean* [lə ʃapo d ʒã] 'the hat of John; John's hat.' Very commonly the personal-definite substitutes have special syntactic constructions. Thus, in English, German, and French, the finite verb has special congruence-forms for different persons as actors: I *am : thou art : he is;* French *nous savons* [nu savõ] 'we know,' *vous savez* [vu save] 'you know,' *elles savent* [ɛl saːv] 'they (feminine) know,' *ils savent* [i saːv] 'they know.'

The personal-definite pronouns may even have a fairly systematic structure. Thus, in the Algonquian languages, an initial element [ke-] appears in the forms that include the hearer; if the hearer is not included, [ne-] denotes the speaker; if neither is included, the initial is [we-], as, in Menomini:

[kenah] 'thou'   [kenaʔ] 'we' (inclusive)   [kenuaʔ] 'ye'
[nenah] 'I'   [nenaʔ] 'we' (exclusive)
[wenah] 'he'   [wenuaʔ] 'they.'

Samoan, with a distinction of dual and plural numbers, has:
[aʔu] 'I'   [ima:ua] 'we two' (excl.)   [ima:tou] 'we' (excl.)
            [ita:ua] 'we two' (incl.)   [ita:tou] 'we' (incl.)
[ʔoe] 'thou' [ʔoulua] 'ye two'   [ʔoutou] 'ye'
[ia] 'he'   [ila:ua] 'they two'   [ila:tou] 'they.'

The dual-trial-plural distinction appears in the language of Annatom Island (Melanesian):
[ainjak] 'I,' [aijumrau] 'we two' (excl.), [aijumtai] 'we three' (excl.), [aijama] 'we' (excl.),
[akaijau] 'we two' (incl.), [akataij] 'we three' (incl.), [akaija] 'we' (incl.),
[aiek] 'thou,' [aijaurau] 'ye two,' [aijautaij] 'ye three,' [aijaua] 'ye,'
[aien] 'he,' [arau] 'they two,' [ahtaij] 'they three,' [ara] 'they.'

In many languages, personal-definite substitutes appear as bound forms. Thus, Latin had definite-personal actors or goals in the finite verb-forms:

amō 'I love,' *amās* 'thou lovest,' *amat* 'he (she, it) loves,' *amāmus* 'we love,' *amātis* 'ye love,' *amant* 'they love,'

amor 'I am loved,' *amāris* 'thou art loved,' *amātur* 'he (she, it) is loved,' *amāmur* 'we are loved,' *amāminī* 'ye are loved,' *amantur* 'they are loved.'

Some languages, in the same way, include both actor and goal, as Cree: [nisa:kiha:w] 'I love him,' [nisa:kiha:wak] 'I love them,' [kisa:kiha:w] 'thou lovest him,' [nisa:kihik] 'he loves me,' [nisa:kihikuna:n] 'he loves us (excl.),' [kisa:kihitina:n] 'we love thee,' [kisa:kihitin] 'I love thee,' and so on, through a large paradigm.

Likewise, in Cree, the possessor of an object appears in a bound form: [nitastutin] 'my hat,' [kitastutin] 'thy hat,' [utastutin] 'his hat,' and so on. In all these cases, the third-person bound form may stand in cross-reference with a noun antecedent: Latin *pater amat* 'father he-loves; the father loves' (§ 12.9).

The personal-definite system may be elaborated by distinctions of identity and non-identity, such as the difference of *me* and *myself*, where the latter form implies identity with the actor (*I washed myself*, § 12.8), or the Scandinavian *hans* 'his' and *sin* 'his (own).' These differences appear also in bound forms, as in the obviative forms of Algonquian (§ 12.8); similarly, ancient Greek, beside an ordinary bound actor, as in ['elowse] 'he washed,' had a *middle-voice* form, where the actor is at the same time affected by the action: [e'lowsato] 'he washed himself' or 'he washed for himself.'

Other specializations are less common; thus, Cree, beside a verb with actor and goal, such as [ninituma:w] 'I ask for him, call him,' [ninitute:n] 'I ask for it,' and a form with actor and two goals, [ninitutamawa:w] 'I ask him for it,' has also a form with actor, goal, and interested person [ninitutamwa:n] 'I ask for it with reference to him,' that is, 'for his use' or 'at his behest.'

15. 8. *Demonstrative* or *deictic* substitution-types are based on relative nearness to the speaker or hearer. In English we have two such types, for nearer and for farther away; they coincide with the values of the limiting adjectives *this* and *that* (§ 12.14). Demonstrative substitutes may be dependent (that is, they may refer anaphorically to an antecedent speech-form that names the species), or independent. In either case, however, they identify the individual object within the (named or unnamed) species. Demonstrative pronoun substitution, in English, is made by the pronouns *this* (*these*), *that* (*those*), which differ, by class-cleavage, from the limiting adjectives, or by phrases consisting of these limiting adjectives plus the anaphoric *one* (§ 15.5). These forms are not ordinarily used to replace personal nouns — for the anticipatory use in *This is my brother; these are my brothers* cannot be viewed as personal. The dependent substitutes in the singular are *this one, that one*, and the independent *this, that;* hence we have the distinction between, say, *of these books, I like this one better than that one*, but, of unnamed objects, *I like this better than that*. In the plural, however, *these* and *those* are in either case used without the anaphoric *ones*.

In French we can see a more differentiated system. There are three types of demonstrative limitation and substitution: a general type from which two special types are differentiated by the addition of the adverbs *ci* [si] for nearer position and *là* [la] for farther away. The forms of the limiting adjective, the dependent pronoun, and the independent pronoun, are distinct:

	ADJECTIVE	DEPENDENT PRONOUN	INDEPENDENT PRONOUN
singular			*ce* [sə]
masculine	*ce* [sə]	*celui* [səlɥi]	
feminine	*cette* [sɛt]	*celle* [sɛl]	

SUBSTITUTION

	ADJECTIVE	DEPENDENT PRONOUN	INDEPENDENT PRONOUN
plural			
masculine	*ces* [se]	*ceux* [sø]	
feminine	*ces* [se]	*celles* [sɛl]	

Thus: *cette plume-ci* [sɛt plym si] 'this pen,' *de ces deux plumes, je préfère celle-ci à celle-là* [də se dø plym, ʒə prefeːr sɛl si a sɛl la] 'of these two pens, I prefer this one to that one'; but, of unnamed things, *je préfère ceci à cela* [sə si a sə la] 'I prefer this to that.' The pronouns without *ci* and *là* are confined to certain constructions: *de ces deux plumes, je préfere celle que vous avez* [sɛl kə vuz ave] 'of these two pens, I prefer the one you have'; independent: *c'est assez* [s ɛt ase] 'that's enough.'

Demonstrative substitution-types are not always fully distinct from definite, and, similarly, demonstrative limiting modifiers may merge with mere definite markers of the type 'the.' In German, more than one dialect has only a single paradigm whose forms are used proclitically as a definite article, *der Mann* [der 'man] 'the man,' and with accent as a demonstrative limiting adjective, *der Mann* ['deːr 'man] 'that man,' and as a pronoun, *der* ['deːr] 'that one.' This last use, in German, is but slightly distinguished from that of the definite pronoun *er* [eːr] 'he'; the chief difference, perhaps, is the use of *der* (not *er*) in the second of two paratactic full sentences: *es war einmal ein Mann, der hatte drei Söhne* [es 'vaːr ajn₁maːl ajn 'man, deːr ₁hate ₁draj 'zøːne] 'there was once a man, he (literally, 'that-one') had three sons.'

Many languages distinguish more types of demonstrative substitution; thus, some English dialects add *yon*, for things farthest away, to the distinction of *this* and *that*. Latin had *hic* for things nearest the speaker, *iste* for those nearest the hearer; and *ille* for those farthest away. The Kwakiutl language makes the same distinctions, but doubles the number by distinguishing also between 'in sight' and 'out of sight.' Cree has [awa] 'this,' [ana] 'that,' and [oːja] 'that recently present but now out of sight.' Eskimo has a whole series: [manna] 'this one,' [anna] 'that one in the north,' [qanna] 'that one in the south,' [panna] 'that one in the east,' [kanna] 'that one down there,' [sanna] 'that one down in the sea,' [iŋŋa] 'that one,' and so on.

Outside of pronouns, we have the adverbial forms *here : there, hither : thither, hence : thence, now : then;* the *th*-forms, however, merge with simple anaphoric use, as in *Going to the circus? I'm going there too.* Similarly, *so* (and archaically also *thus*) is both demonstrative and, more usually, anaphoric (*I hope to do so*). Forms like (*do it*) *this way, this sort* (*of thing*), *this kind* (*of thing*) are on the border between substitutes and ordinary linguistic forms.

15. 9. *Interrogative* substitutes prompt the hearer to supply either the species or the identification of the individual; in English, accordingly, interrogative substitutes occur only in supplement-questions. Of pronouns, we have the independent *who?* (accusative *whom?*) for personals and *what?* for non-personals; these ask for both species and individual. For non-personals only we have also the independent *which?* asking for identification of the individual object from a limited field, but not for the species. The dependent substitutes, asking for the identification of the individual from a limited field, are *which one? which ones?*

Outside the pronouns, we have the interrogative substitutes *where? whither? whence? when? how? why?* Interrogative verb-substitutes occur in some languages, as in Menomini [weʔse:kew$_ʔ$] 'what sort is he?'

The limitation of interrogative forms to certain syntactic positions is quite common. Frequently we find them restricted to positions in the predicate of a binary sentence-type. The word-order and the plural verb-form in *who are they? what are those things?* are features of this kind. In present-day French, the non-personal *quoi?* [kwa$_ʔ$] 'what?' is scarcely ever used as actor or goal, but instead, figures as a predicate complement, appearing in the conjunct form *que* [kə], as in *qu'est-ce que c'est?* [k ɛ s kə s ɛ$_ʔ$] 'what is it that this is? what's this?' and *qu'est-ce qu'il a vu?* [k ɛ s k il a vy$_ʔ$] 'what is it that he has seen? what did he see?' In some languages the interrogative substitutes are always predicates of equational sentences, as, in Tagalog, [ˈsi:nu aŋ nagbiˈgaj sa iˈju$_ʔ$] 'who the one-who-gave to you? who gave it to you?' or, in Menomini [awɛ:ʔ pɛ:muhnɛt$_ʔ$] 'who the-one-walking-by? who is walking there?'

15. 10. The various possibilities of selecting individual objects from a species are represented by all manner of substitute-forms, especially of pronouns. In English, nearly all forms of this sort consist of limiting adjectives with the anaphoric *one, ones* (§ 15.5) or of substantive uses, by class-cleavage, of the same words. There

SUBSTITUTION

are many distinctions, not always rigidly carried out, between dependent and independent substitution, and in the latter, between personal and non-personal classes. The various limiting adjectives differ in treatment; these differences add another line of classification among them (§ 12.14).

(1) Some limiting adjectives are, like ordinary adjectives, followed by *one, ones* to form anaphoric substitutes. We have seen that this is the case of the singular *this, that* and, under certain conditions, of *which? what?* It is true also of *each, every, whatever, whichever,* and of the phrasal expressions *many a, such a, what a.* Thus, we say *he was pleased with the children and gave each one a penny.* As independent substitutes we use *this, that, which, what, whichever, whatever* of non-personals only; corresponding to *every,* we have personal *everybody, everyone* and non-personal *everything; each* has no independent form.

(2) We have both simple pronoun use or combination with the anaphoric *ones, one,* in the case of *either, former, latter, last, neither, other, such,* and the ordinals, *first, second,* etc. The variants differ chiefly in connotation. Thus, we say *Here are the books; take either (one).* The word *other* forms a special sub-class, in that it has a plural form, *others: You keep this book and I'll take the others (the other ones).* In independent use these words serve chiefly as non-personals.

(3) The remaining limiting adjectives are peculiar in not taking the anaphoric *one, ones.* Thus, we say: *Here are the books; take one (two, three, any, both, all, a few, some,* and so on). The independent substitutes show great variety. Thus, *all* is used as a non-personal: *All is not lost; That's all.* On the other hand, *one,* as an atonic, is personal: *One hardly knows what to say.* Several form compounds for independent use, such as the personal *somebody, someone, anybody, anyone* and the non-personal *something, anything.*

(4) Several limiting adjectives show an eccentric treatment. The article *the* with the anaphoric *one, ones* forms a dependent substitute, provided some other modifier follows: *the one(s) on the table;* otherwise it does not appear in pronominal use, and the definite pronoun serves instead. The article *a* in combination with another adjective does not influence the treatment of the latter: *many a one; another (one).* Otherwise, the article *a* is accompanied by the anaphoric *one* only in the emphatic form *not a one.* All other pronominal uses show us *one* replacing *a:* to

take an apple there corresponds the pronominal *take one*. The determiner *no* is paralleled by the dependent substitute *none*, but ordinarily we use instead the combination of *not* with *any* (*I didn't see any*); the independent substitutes are the compounds *nobody, no one, nothing* (archaic *naught*).

Among these substitution-types, the negative is, of course, represented in all languages, and often shows special peculiarities; to it belong also the non-pronominal *nowhere, never,* and sub-standard *nohow*. In many languages, as in most forms of sub-standard English, these substitutes are accompanied by the general negative adverb: *I can't see nothing*. The numerative types (*all, one, two, three,* and so on) seem also to be universal. As to the selective types, however, there is great room for variety; other languages have substitution-types that are not exactly matched in English. Thus, Russian ['ne-xto] 'someone' implies that the speaker can (but does not) identify the individual ('someone told me the other day that . . . '), while [xto-ni-'but] does not imply this ability ('there's someone at the door'). Still another type, ['koj-xto] implies that a different individual is selected on different occasions ('now and then someone tries').

15. 11. Substitutes frequently are tied up with special syntactic functions; thus, we have seen that interrogative substitutes in English and many other languages are confined to certain positions in the sentence. Some languages have special pronouns for predicative use. Thus, in Menomini, beside such forms as [nenah] 'I,' [enuh] 'that one' (animate), [eneh] 'that' (inanimate), there are parallel forms which occur only as predicates; the normal substitute appears in [kɛhke:nam eneh] 'he-knows-it that (thing); he knows that,' but the predicative form in [eneʔ kɛ:hkenah] 'that (thing) that-which-he-knows; that is what he knows,' or in [enuʔ kɛ:hkenah] 'that (person) the-one-who-knows-it; that one is the one who knows it.' These predicative forms vary inflectionally for the same categories as a verb, such as interrogative [enet kɛ:hkenah?] 'is it that which he knows? is that the thing he knows?' or surprised present [enesaʔ kɛ:hkenah!] 'and so that is what he knows!' and so on.

Our *relative* substitutes belong to a fairly widespread, but by no means universal type: the substitute indicates that the phrase in which it figures, is an included (or completive) form. In English, the phrase has the favorite full-sentence structure (actor-action construction), and is marked by the relative substitute as not constituting a full sentence. Our relatives *who (whom), which, where, when, that* differ from other substitutes by class-cleavage. They, or their immediate phrase, come first in the clause. We have, firstly, the anaphoric type, *that*, and personal *who*, non-personal *which: the boy who (that) ran away, the book which (that) he read; the house in which we lived.* If the relative substitute fills in its clause the position of verbal goal, prepositional axis, or predicate complement, we have here also a zero-substitute: *the man I saw, the house we lived in, the hero he was.* In ordinary speech, English relative clauses identify the individual antecedent; in more formal style we have also non-identifying relative clauses with paratactic sentence-modulation: *the man, who was carrying a big bag, came up to the gate.*

In languages with case-forms, the inflection of the relative pronoun is normally determined by the forms in its clause: *I saw the boy who ran away; the boy whom I saw ran away.* In Latin, a normal form would be *in hāc vītā quam nunc ego dēgō* 'in this life which I now lead,' where the antecedent, *vītā* happens to be in the ablative case (as axis of the preposition *in*), and the relative pronoun, *quam* 'which,' in the accusative case, as goal of the verb *dēgō*. However, languages with complicated inflection now and then show *attraction* of the relative pronoun into an inflectional form that belongs properly to the antecedent: the Latin form *vītā in hāc quā nunc ego dēgō*, with the same denotation as the above normal form, has the relative pronoun *quā* in the ablative case, concording with the antecedent, instead of the accusative case demanded by its position in the clause.

Independent relative substitutes, having no antecedent, allow the clause to replace an indication of species: *take what(ever) you want; ask whom(ever) you like; whoever says so is mistaken.* In English such clauses are used also as paratactic modifiers of a full sentence: *whatever he says, I don't believe him.* The same difference between dependent and independent use appears in our adverbial substitutes: dependent *the time (when) he did it; the house where we lived;* independent *we'll see him when he gets here; we visit them whenever we can; we take them where(ver) we find them.*

CHAPTER 16

FORM–CLASSES AND LEXICON

16. 1. The meaningful features of linguistic signaling are of two kinds: lexical forms, which consist of phonemes, and grammatical forms, which consist of taxemes (features of arrangement, § 10.5). If we extend the term *lexical* to cover all forms that can be stated in terms of phonemes, including even such forms as already contain some grammatical features (e.g. *poor John* or *duchess* or *ran*), then the parallelism of lexical and grammatical features can be exhibited in a set of terms like the following:
  (1) Smallest and meaningless unit of linguistic signaling: *phememe;*
    (a) lexical: *phoneme;*
    (b) grammatical: *taxeme;*
  (2) Smallest meaningful unit of linguistic signaling: *glosseme;* the meaning of a glosseme is a *noeme;*
    (a) lexical: *morpheme;* the meaning of a morpheme is a *sememe;*
    (b) grammatical: *tagmeme;* the meaning of a tagmeme is an *episememe;*
  (3) Meaningful unit of linguistic signaling, smallest or complex: *linguistic form;* the meaning of a linguistic form is a *linguistic meaning;*
    (a) lexical: *lexical form;* the meaning of a lexical form is a *lexical meaning;*
    (b) grammatical: *grammatical form;* the meaning of a grammatical form is a *grammatical meaning.*

Every lexical form is connected in two directions with grammatical forms. On the one side, the lexical form, even when taken by itself, in the abstract, exhibits a meaningful grammatical *structure*. If it is a complex form, it shows some morphologic or syntactic construction (*duchess, poor John*), and if it is a morpheme, it may still exhibit morphologic features (a modified morpheme, e.g. *men* or *ran*, § 13.7); in an unmodified morpheme (*man, run*) we may view the absence of grammatical construction as a positive

FORM-CLASSES AND LEXICON

characteristic. On the other side, the lexical form in any actual utterance, as a concrete linguistic form, is always accompanied by some grammatical form: it appears in some function, and these privileges of occurrence make up, collectively, the grammatical *function* of the lexical form. The lexical form appears in certain sentence-types or, if it is a bound form, in none at all; it appears in certain positions of certain constructions or, if it is an interjection, in few or none; it appears as replaced form in certain substitutions, or, if it be a substitute, as substitute in certain substitutions. The functions of lexical forms are created by the taxemes of selection which help to make up grammatical forms. Lexical forms which have any function in common, belong to a common *form-class*.

The functions of lexical forms appear as a very complex system. Some functions are common to a great number of forms and define a large form-class; for instance, the functions which define the English form-class of substantive expressions (serving in the sentence-type of call, filling the positions of actor with a verb, of goal with a verb, of axis with a preposition; underlying a possessive adjective, and so on), are common to an almost unlimited number of words and phrases. Different functions may create overlapping form-classes; thus, the function of filling the actor position is common to substantive expressions and to marked infinitive phrases (*to scold the boys would be foolish*). Other functions may be limited to a very few lexical forms or to only a single one; thus, phrases with the noun *way* as center seem to be the only substantive expressions which function as adverbs of manner, with the interrogative substitute *how?* (*this way, the way I do,* and so on).

Particular lexical forms may, by *class-cleavage* (§ 12.14) exhibit unusual combinations of function. Thus, *egg* is in English a bounded noun, (*the egg, an egg*) but occurs also as a mass noun (*he spilled egg on his necktie*). *Salt* is a mass noun and accordingly underlies a plural only in the specialized meaning 'kinds of,' but, by class-cleavage, there is also a plural *salts* (as in *Epsom salts*) with the meaning 'consisting of particles,' in a class with *oats, grits,* and the like. *Man* is a (bounded, personal) male noun (*a man, the man, . . . he*), but by class-cleavage is treated also as a proper noun, parallel in this with *God,* as in *man wants but little, man is a mammal.* The word *one* by a complicated class-cleavage belongs to five form-classes: as a determiner (§ 12.14) it fulfils the requirement that bounded singular nouns be preceded by a modifier of this class (*one house, one mile*); as an ordinary numerative it occurs with the definite determiners (*the one man, this one book, my one friend*); it replaces *a* with anaphora of the noun (§ 15.10) when no other modifier is present (*Here are some apples; take one*); it occurs as an independent pronoun for 'any person in general' and in this use is always atonic and underlies the derivatives *one's* and *oneself* (*one can't help oneself*); finally, it is the anaphoric substitute for nouns after an adjective, and in this use forms a plural, *ones* (*the big box and the small one, these boxes and the ones in the kitchen*, § 15.5).

16. 2. The grammar of a language includes, then, a very complex set of habits (taxemes of selection) by which every lexical form is used only in certain conventional functions; every lexical form is assigned always to the customary form-classes. To describe the grammar of a language, we have to state the form-classes of each lexical form, and to determine what characteristics make the speakers assign it to these form-classes.

The traditional answer to this question appears in our school grammars, which try to define the form-classes by the *class-meaning* — by the feature of meaning that is common to all the lexical forms in the form-class. The school grammar tells us, for instance, that a noun is "the name of a person, place, or thing." This definition presupposes more philosophical and scientific knowledge than the human race can command, and implies, further, that the form-classes of a language agree with the classifications that would be made by a philosopher or scientist. Is *fire*, for instance, a thing? For over a century physicists have believed it to be an action or process rather than a thing: under this view, the verb *burn* is more appropriate than the noun *fire*. Our language supplies the adjective *hot*, the noun *heat*, and the verb *to heat*, for what physicists believe to be a movement of particles (molecules) in a body. Similarly, school grammar defines the class of plural nouns by its meaning "more than one" (person, place, or thing), but who could gather from this that *oats* is a plural while *wheat* is a singular? Class-meanings, like all other meanings, elude the linguist's power of definition, and in general do not coincide with the meanings of strictly-defined technical terms. To accept definitions of meaning, which at best are makeshifts, in place of an identification in formal terms, is to abandon scientific discourse.

Class-meanings are merely composites, or, one might say, greatest common factors, of the grammatical meanings which accompany the forms. To state a class-meaning is to find some formula that includes the grammatical meanings in which the forms occur. An English finite verb expression (*runs, ran away, is very kind, scolded the boys,* and so on) occurs only in one position of one construction, namely as action in the actor-action construction (*John ran away*). Even when it is used alone, it appears only as a completive sentence which, accordingly, presupposes an actor. Now, we can state the meaning of the actor-action construction very roughly as 'A performs B,' where A is the nominative expression (*John*) and B the finite verb expression (*ran away*). This statement defines for us the meanings of the two positions; the meaning of the actor-position is 'performer of B,' and that of the action-position is 'performed by A.' Therefore, since English finite verb expressions occur only and always in this latter position, their class-meaning is the same as that of their one position, namely, 'performed by an object.' If we define the class-meaning of the larger form-class of verbs as 'action,' then the class-meaning of English finite verb expressions is '(action) performed by an actor.'

When a form-class has more than one function, its class-meaning is harder to state, but is still merely a derivative of the grammatical meanings in which the forms occur. English substantive expressions occur, for instance, in the position of actor in the actor-action construction (*John ran*), with the positional meaning 'performer of an action.' They occur in the position of goal in the action-goal construction (*hit John*), with a positional meaning something like 'undergoer of an action.' They occur in the position of axis in the relation-axis construction (*beside John*), with a positional meaning of, say, 'center from which a relation holds good.' They occur in morphologic construction with the possessive suffix (*John's*), with the positional meaning of 'possessor.' Without listing all the other functions of English substantive expressions, we can say that the class-meaning common to all the lexical forms in this form-class is 'that which can be the performer of an action, the undergoer of an action, the center from which a relation holds good, the possessor of objects,' and so on. Whether we can sum this up in a shorter formula, depends upon our resources of terminology; for instance, we can sum up the class-meaning just given, under the term 'object.'

These instances suffice to show that class-meanings are not

clearly-definable units which could serve as a basis for our work, but only vague situational features, undefinable in terms of our science. The people who speak English and keep their substantive expressions within the accepted functions, do not guide themselves by deciding whether each lexical form denotes an object. Form-classes, like other linguistic phenomena, can be defined, not in terms of meaning, but only in terms of linguistic (that is, lexical or grammatical) features.

16. 3. The form-class of a lexical form is determined for the speakers (and consequently for the relevant description of a language) by the structure and constituents of the form, by the inclusion of a special constituent (a *marker*), or by the identity of the form itself.

(1) A complex form is usually assigned to a form-class by its structure and constituents. An endocentric phrase, for instance, such as *fresh milk*, belongs to the same form-class as its head or center (§ 12.10). An exocentric phrase, such as *in the house*, contains some characteristic constituent (as, in our example, the preposition *in*) which determines its form-class. Thus, the form-class of a phrase is usually determined, at bottom, by the form-class of one or more of the included words. For this reason the speaker (and the grammarian) need not deal separately with each phrase; the form-class of almost any phrase is known if we know the syntactic constructions and the form-classes of words. The form-classes of words are therefore fundamental for syntax. Our school grammar recognizes this: it tries, by a mistaken method, to be sure, to determine the form-classes of words, particularly the most inclusive of these form-classes (*parts of speech*), and then shows how phrases are constructed.

(2) Sometimes the function of a phrase is determined by some special constituent, a *marker*. For instance, in English, a phrase consisting of the preposition *to* and an infinitive expression, belongs to the special form-class of *marked infinitive phrases*, whose function differs from that of unmarked infinitive expressions, since they serve as actors (*to scold the boys was foolish*) and as attributes of nouns, verbs, and adjectives (*a chance to go; he hopes to go; glad to go*). The determining adjectives form noun phrases which are distinguished by closure: *this fresh milk* cannot take adjective modifiers as can *fresh milk* or *milk* (§ 12.10). Whenever a form-class of small extent determines a peculiar function in phrases, we may

regard its forms as markers. Thus, our determining adjectives, our prepositions, our co-ordinating conjunctions, and our subordinating conjunctions, may be viewed as markers; they are small form-classes, and the presence of any of their forms in a phrase determines something about the form-class of this phrase. Other examples of markers are the particles of Chinese or Tagalog (§ 12.13).

(3) Finally, lexical forms may belong *arbitrarily* or *irregularly* to a form-class that is indicated neither by their structure nor by a marker. For instance, the phrase *in case* has the structure of preposition plus substantive and yet serves as a subordinating conjunction: *In case he isn't there, don't wait for him.* The phrases *this way, that way, the other way, the same way* have substantive structure, but are used as verb-modifiers of the special sub-class (manner) that has the interrogative substitute *how?* Similarly, quite a few English nouns and noun phrases serve as verb-modifiers in the *when?* class, either alone or in phrases: *Sunday, last winter, tomorrow morning.* The form-classes of English words are largely arbitrary: there is nothing to tell us that *man, boy, lad, son, father* are male nouns, that *run, bother* are verbs, that *sad, red, green* are adjectives, and so on. In particular, of course, the form-class of every morpheme is arbitrarily determined. A complete description of a language will list every form whose function is not determined either by structure or by a marker; it will include, accordingly, a *lexicon*, or list of morphemes, which indicates the form-class of each morpheme, as well as lists of all complex forms whose function is in any way irregular.

16. 4. Form-classes are not mutually exclusive, but cross each other and overlap and are included one within the other, and so on. Thus, in English, the nominative expressions (which serve as actors) include both substantives and marked infinitives (*to scold the boys would be foolish*). On the other hand, among the substantives are some pronoun-forms which, by over-differentiation, do not serve as actors: *me, us, him, her, them, whom.* One group of substantives, the gerunds (*scolding*), belongs to a form-class with infinitives and with other verb-forms, in serving as head for certain types of modifiers, such as a goal (*scolding the boys*). For this reason a system of parts of speech in a language like English cannot be set up in any fully satisfactory way: our list of parts of speech will depend upon which functions we take to be the most important.

One can often distinguish, however, between great form-classes like the above, and petty form-clases like that of *foot, goose, tooth* or of *ox* (with irregular plural-forms). Large form-classes which completely subdivide either the whole lexicon or some important form-class into form-classes of approximately equal size, are called *categories*. Thus, the English parts of speech (substantive, verb, adjective, and so on) are categories of our language. So are singular and plural substantives, since these two form-classes, of approximately equal size, completely subdivide the form-class of substantives. In general, inflectional forms, what with the parallel occurrence in every paradigm, represent categories — for instance, the various forms of the verb-paradigm, including the congruence-forms of finite verbs (*am : is : are* or *was : were*) and, crossing these, the tenses and modes of finite verbs (*he is : he was : he were*).

Not all categories, however, are inflectional. The selection of the pronouns *he* versus *she* divides our personal nouns into the categories of male and female; yet there is no inflection or regular derivation to distinguish these, but only a sporadic use of markers (*count : countess, Paul : Pauline, Albert : Alberta*) or of entirely irregular derivation (*duck : drake, goose : gander*) or of composition (*he-goat, billy-goat, bull-buffalo*) or suppletion (*son : daughter, ram : ewe*) or merely class-cleavage (*a teacher . . . he; a teacher . . . she; Francis : Frances*).

Again, some categories are syntactic, and appear not in inflection, but in phrases. Such are the categories of indefinite and definite substantives (*a book : the book*), or, in our verbs, the aspects (*wrote : was writing*), completion (*wrote : had written*), or voice (*wrote : was written*).

The categories of a language, especially those which affect morphology (*book : books, he : she*), are so pervasive that anyone who reflects upon his language at all, is sure to notice them. In the ordinary case, this person, knowing only his native language, or perhaps some others closely akin to it, may mistake his categories for universal forms of speech, or of "human thought," or of the universe itself. This is why a good deal of what passes for "logic" or "metaphysics" is merely an incompetent restating of the chief categories of the philosopher's language. A task for linguists of the future will be to compare the categories of different languages and see what features are universal or at least widespread. Thus, a form-class comparable to our substantive expressions, with a class-meaning something like 'object,' seems to exist everywhere, though in many languages it is not an arbitrary class, like our substantive part of speech, but depends largely upon the presence of markers, as in Malayan or Chinese (§ 12.13).

16. 5. Our knowledge of the practical world may show that some linguistic categories agree with classes of real things. It may be, for instance, that our non-linguistic world consists of objects, actions, qualities, manners, and relations, comparable with the substantives, verbs, adjectives, adverbs, and prepositions of our language. In this case it would still be true, however, that many other languages do not recognize these classes in their part-of-speech system. Moreover, we should still have to determine the English parts of speech not by their correspondence with different aspects of the practical world, but merely by their functions in English syntax.

This appears plainly in the circumstance that languages with an elaborate part-of-speech system always contain *abstract forms;* they have parallel forms with the same lexical meaning for use in different syntactic positions. Thus, a verb like *run* or an adjective like *smooth* cannot serve as an actor, but we have for this function the abstract noun forms *run* (as in *the run will warm you up*) and *smoothness*. It is an error to suppose that abstract forms like these occur only in the languages of literate peoples; they occur in all languages that limit different form-classes to different syntactic positions.

Linguistic categories, then, cannot be defined in philosophical terms; having defined them in formal terms, we may have great difficulty in describing their meaning. To show this, we need only glance at some of the more familiar categories.

Number, as it appears in our singulars and plurals, seems to be close to some universal trait of human response; yet, cases like *oats* versus *wheat*, or *Epsom salts* versus *table salt*, seem to have little non-linguistic justification.

The categories of *gender* in English are close to our non-linguistic recognition of personality and sex, but even here some animals (*the bull* . . . *he* or *it*) and other things (*the good ship* . . . *she* or *it*) are variously treated. The gender-categories of most Indo-European languages, such as the two of French or the three of German (§ 12.7), do not agree with anything in the practical world, and this is true of most such classes. In the Algonquian languages, all persons and animals belong to one category, an 'animate' gender, but so do some other objects, such as 'raspberry,' 'kettle,' and 'knee'; all other objects (including, for instance, 'strawberry,' 'bowl,' 'elbow') belong to the other, 'inanimate' gender. Some of the Bantu languages run up to as high as twenty such classes; distinctions of number, however, are merged with the gender-classification.

Case-categories, ranging from two, as in English (*he : him*), up to twenty or so, as in Finnish, resemble various situations of the practical world, but never with any consistency. Thus, in German, the goal of a verb is in the accusative case, as in *er bat mich* [e:r 'ba:t mix] 'he asked me (for something),' but certain verbs have it in the dative case, as *er dankte mir* [e:r 'daŋkte mi:r] 'he thanked me'; compare the Latin examples in § 12.8.

The categories of *tense* have a surface rationality, especially in a language like Latin, which distinguishes present (*cantat* 'he sings'), past (*cantāvit* 'he sang'), and future (*cantābit* 'he will sing'), but even here one soon finds that these categories disagree with our non-linguistic analysis: the "historical present" is used in Latin, as in English, of past events, and the meanings of the Latin tense-forms are mixed up with considerations other than relative time.

The English categories of *aspect* distinguish between 'punctual' action (some grammarians call it 'perfective'), envisaged as a unit (*he wrote the letter*), and 'durative' action (some call it 'imperfective'), which extends over a segment of time during which other things can happen (*he was writing the letter*). This distinction is at best hard to define for the practical world, and in English suffers marked dislocations; some verbs, for instance, appear persistently in punctual form (*I think he is there; he is funny*) and are durative only in special constructions or meanings (*I am thinking of him; he is being funny*). In Russian, which has much the same aspects as English, certain verbs, such as 'eat' and 'drink,' appear persistently in durative form.

A common verb-category that is lacking in English, is *iteration*, which distinguishes between an action occurring once and a repeated action, as, in Russian [on be'ʒal do'moj] 'he was running home' (on one particular occasion) and [on 'begal do'moj] 'he ran home; he was running home' (repeatedly, e.g. every day).[1]

---

[1] In English, iteration plays no part in the verb-form: *he played tennis every day* (punctual) and *he was playing tennis every day* (durative) are like *he played a set of*

Perfection contrasts contemporary, 'imperfectic' action with 'perfectic' action, whose effect is contemporary: *he writes* versus *he has written; he is writing* versus *he has been writing; he wrote* versus *he had written; he was writing* versus *he had been writing.* The difference is scarcely definable in terms of practical situation, and different languages show different distributions.

English has many *modes*, distinguishing various approaches of an action to its actual occurrence. Morphologically, English distinguishes between 'real' (*he is here*) and 'unreal' (*if he were here*); syntactically, English recognizes a whole series by the peculiarity of certain irregular ('auxiliary') verbs which are followed by an infinitive without *to: he will write, shall write, can write, must write, may write.* We may observe that in these combinations the infinitive is rather persistently punctual, and only now and then durative (*I shall be writing*); in Russian, the future tense, which corresponds fairly well to our *shall* and *will* phrases, distinguishes aspect just as exactly as do the present and past tenses. The uses of different modes are tied up in many languages with differences of syntactic position and congruence. In English, for instance, the unreal appears only in clauses introduced by *if* or *though*, or in combination with the phrasal mode-forms (*he would help us*, unreal of *he will help us*). Similar complications appear in the uses of the various modes of other languages, as, in French, *je pense qu'il vient* [ʒə pãs k i vjɛ̃] 'I think he is coming,' with the verb of the clause in the 'indicative' (actual) mode, but *je ne pense pas qu'il vienne* [ʒə n pãs pa k i vjɛn] 'I don't think he is coming,' with the verb of the clause in the 'subjunctive' (possible) mode.

16. 6. We saw in § 16.3 that the function of some forms is determined by their constituents or their construction. Any function that is so determined is said to be *regular*, and a function which is not so determined is said to be *irregular*. Thus, if we know that the words *fox* and *ox* are singular common nouns, wavering between non-personal and male personal gender, then we can say that *fox* has the regular function of combining with the plural-suffix [-iz] in the form *foxes* (since this function is shared by an unlimited number of singular nouns), but that *ox* has the irregular

tennis (punctual) and *he was playing a set of tennis* (durative). In Latin, French, and modern Greek, repeated action and durative action are merged in one class: French *il écrivait* [il ekrivɛ] is both 'he was writing' and 'he wrote (repeatedly); he used to write.' In Russian, repeated actions are classed as durative, but, within the durative class, are distinct, at least for certain verbs, from single actions.

function of combining with the plural-suffix [-ŋ]. Linguists usually apply the terms *regular* and *irregular* to the form itself, saying, for instance, that the noun *fox* is regular and the noun *ox* irregular; we must specify, of course, the function with respect to which these terms hold good, since in their other functions the nouns *fox* and *ox* are quite alike. By another extension of these terms, linguists apply them also to the resultant forms in which the functions appear, saying, for instance, that the plural noun *foxes* is regular and the plural noun *oxen* irregular.

The speaker can use a form in a regular function even when he has never heard the resultant form: he may utter a form like *foxes*, for instance, even when he has never heard this particular plural. He can use a form in an irregular function only if he has heard it used in this function: the form *oxen* is uttered only by speakers who have heard it from other speakers. In the description of a language, accordingly, regular functions are stated for whole form-classes, in the mass: we can state the regular plural-formation of English nouns without attempting to list all the nouns in the language. Irregular functions, on the other hand, force us to list all the forms of the class: we have to mention the noun *ox* as taking *-en* in the plural, and the nouns *foot, tooth, goose* as taking substitution of [ij] in the plural, and so on.

If we insist on this distinction, we may say that any form which a speaker can utter without having heard it, is regular in its immediate constitution and embodies regular functions of its constituents, and any form which a speaker can utter only after he has heard it from other speakers, is irregular. Strictly speaking, then, every morpheme of a language is an irregularity, since the speaker can use it only after hearing it used, and the reader of a linguistic description can know of its existence only if it is listed for him. The lexicon is really an appendix of the grammar, a list of basic irregularities. This is all the more evident if meanings are taken into consideration, since the meaning of each morpheme belongs to it by an arbitrary tradition. In a language like English, where each morpheme is arbitrarily assigned to some grammatical class, this feature also is an irregularity: the speaker must learn from experience and the describer must list the fact that *pin* is a noun, *spin* a verb, *thin* an adjective, *in* a preposition, and so on. This task also is customarily assigned to the lexicon; the grammar lists only the kinds of irregularity that are not present in all

FORM-CLASSES AND LEXICON 275

the morphemes of a language, and the terms *regular* and *irregular* are used only of features that appear in the grammar.

If we make this restriction, it is obvious that most speech-forms are regular, in the sense that the speaker who knows the constituents and the grammatical pattern, can utter them without ever having heard them; moreover, the observer cannot hope to list them, since the possibilities of combination are practically infinite. For instance, the classes of nominative expressions and finite verb expressions in English are so large that many possible actor-action forms — say, *a red-headed plumber bought five oranges* — may never before have been uttered; by the same token, however, we cannot be sure that this is true of any particular combination which we may chance to hear. A grammatical pattern (sentence-type, construction, or substitution) is often called an *analogy*. A regular analogy permits a speaker to utter speech-forms which he has not heard; we say that he utters them *on the analogy* of similar forms which he has heard.

An irregular analogy, on the other hand, may cover a number of forms, but a speaker will rarely utter a new form on the analogy of those which he has heard. For instance, the phrases *at least, at most, at best, at worst, at first, at last* are built up on the same pattern (*at* plus adjective in *-st*), but the analogy is limited to a very few forms. In *at all* (where the adjective does not end in *-st* and the sandhi is irregular) or in *don't* we have a unique analogy. When the automobile came into use, one speaker was as well able as another to form the compound *automobile-driver*, on the analogy of *cab-driver, truck-driver*, and so on; a compound like *cranberry*, on the other hand, with its unique first member, is uttered only by speakers who have heard it. If we take meanings into consideration, we can say the same of a speaker who uses the term *blackbird* of the species of bird to which it customarily applies, for the compound bears this meaning by an arbitrary tradition. A form like *charlestoner* 'one who performs the dance called *charleston*' is formed on the regular analogy of *dancer, waltzer, two-stepper*, and so on; a form like *duchess* (§ 10.6) is unique. On the border-line we have cases like the feminines in *-ess*, which on the whole are limited to traditional forms: we say *poetess, sculptress*, but not **paintress;* occasionally, however, a speaker will extend this analogy, uttering such forms as, say, *profiteeress, swindleress*. Even our root-forming morphemes (§ 14.9) have some flexibility; hearing a form like *squunch* in a meaning 'step with suction-noise on wet ground,' we cannot tell whether the speaker has heard it or is using the analogy of [skw-], as in *squirt, squash,* and [-ʌntʃ], as in *crunch.*

The regular analogies of a language are habits of substitution. Suppose, for instance, that a speaker had never heard the form *give Annie the orange,* but that he had heard or spoken a set of forms like the following:

Baby is hungry.   Poor Baby!   Baby's orange.   Give Baby the orange!
Papa is hungry.   Poor Papa!   Papa's orange.   Give Papa the orange!
Bill is hungry.   Poor Bill!   Bill's orange.   Give Bill the orange!
Annie is hungry. Poor Annie!   Annie's orange. . . . .

He has the habit, now, — the analogy, — of using *Annie* in the same positions as *Baby, Papa, Bill,* and accordingly, in the proper situation, will utter the new form *Give Annie the orange!* When a speaker utters a complex form, we are in most cases unable to tell whether he has heard it before or has created it on the analogy of other forms. The utterance of a form on the analogy of other forms is like the solving of a proportional equation with an indefinitely large set of ratios on the left-hand side:

$$\left. \begin{array}{l} \textit{Baby is hungry : Annie is hungry} \\ \textit{Poor Baby : Poor Annie} \\ \textit{Baby's orange : Annie's orange} \end{array} \right\} = \textit{Give Baby the orange} : x$$

or

$$\left. \begin{array}{l} \textit{dog : dogs} \\ \textit{pickle : pickles} \\ \textit{potato : potatoes} \\ \textit{piano : pianos} \end{array} \right\} = \textit{radio} : x$$

16. 7. The power or wealth of a language consists of the morphemes and the tagmemes (sentence-types, constructions, and substitutions). The number of morphemes and tagmemes in any language runs well into the thousands. In every language, moreover, many complex forms carry specialized meanings which cannot figure in a purely linguistic description but are practically of great importance. The linguist can determine, for instance, that English compounds of the type *blackbird, bluebird, whitefish,* or phrases of the type *give out, fall out, throw up,* bear specialized meanings, but he cannot evaluate these meanings, although in practical life they are fully as useful as any sememe.

Popularly, the wealth of a language is supposed to depend upon the number of different words which it uses, but this number is indeterminate, since words are freely formed according to the analogies of morphologic construction. For instance, having counted *play*, *player*, and *dance*, shall we count *dancer* as a fourth word, even though it contains no additional glosseme? If so, then the number of words in any language is practically infinite. When we are told that Shakspere used 20,000 different words in his writings, and Milton in his poems some 8,000, we mistakenly conclude that less eloquent speakers use far fewer. It is an indication of Shakspere's genius that he used so many different words in so small a volume of speech as is contained in his works, but this volume of speech is small compared to the amount which even a taciturn person will utter in the course of a year. The myths about peasants, workingmen, or savages who use only a few hundred words have no foundation in fact; in so far as one can count words (ignoring, for instance, the inflected forms of a language like ours), every adult speaker uses at least somewhere round 20,000 to 30,000 words; if he is educated — that is, if he knows technical and learned words — he uses many more. Everyone, moreover, understands more words than he uses.

The relative frequency of the various lexical and grammatical units (morphemes and tagmemes) in a language can be studied wherever we have copious records of normal utterances. In the next chapters we shall see that our lack of such records is one of the impediments to the historical study of language — for fluctuations in the frequency of glossemes play an important part in the changes that occur in every language.

The frequency of most lexical forms is doubtless subject to a great deal of superficial fluctuation, according to the practical circumstances. A word like *thimble*, say, or *stove*, might not occur at all in long stretches of speech; yet such forms as these are used by everyone when the occasion presents itself. The most frequent forms, on the other hand, both lexical and, especially, grammatical, are constantly demanded by the structure of the language. Such counting as has been done has been confined to words. It is found that the commonest words (*the*, *to*, *is*, etc.) make up a consistently high percentage of what is spoken.

16. 8. The practical question as to what things can be said in different languages, is often confused with questions of word-meanings and of categories. One language will use a phrase where another uses a single word and still another a bound form. A meaning that is categoric in one language (as, for instance, plurality of objects in English) may appear only under particular practical stimuli in another language. As to denotation, whatever can be said in one language can doubtless be said in any other: the difference will concern only the structure of the forms, and their connotation. What one language expresses by a single morpheme will in another language require perhaps a long phrase; what one language says in a word may appear in another language as a phrase or as an affix. Elements of meaning that appear in one language because they belong to some category, even though they are irrelevant to the practical situation, will be absent in another language. In English we say *Pike's Peak is high* with a present-tense verb; in Chinese or in Russian there would be no present-tense element in a similar message.

It is a striking fact that the smallest units of signaling, the glossemes, of different languages, differ vastly in practical value. This is true even of closely related languages. Where we say *ride*, German says *reiten* ['rajten] for riding on an animal, but *fahren* ['fa:ren] for other kinds of riding, as in a vehicle. Where we say *on*, German says *auf* when the force of gravity helps the contact, as in 'on the table,' but otherwise *an*, as in 'on the wall.' Our *morning* matches the French *matin* [matɛ̃], except when the morning is viewed as a segment of time during which something else can happen, as in 'I slept all morning' or 'during the morning'; in this case French uses a derivative *matinée* [matine]. Even things which are easily defined and classified, receive the most diverse treatment in different languages. Nothing could be more definite than terms for simple biological relationship between persons. Yet, beside words corresponding to our *brother* and *sister*, German has a plural *Geschwister* [ge'ʃvister] that includes both sexes, as in *Wieviele Geschwister haben Sie?* [vi: 'fi:le ge'ʃvister 'ha:ben zi:?] 'How many brothers and (or) sisters have you?' Some languages have here one word, regardless of gender, as Tagalog [kapa'tid]; our *brother* corresponds to a Tagalog phrase [kapa'tid na la'la:ki], where the last word means 'male,' and our *sister* to [kapa'tid na ba'ba:ji], with the attribute 'female.' On the other hand, some languages insist upon relative age: Chinese ['ko^1 ko^1] 'elder brother,' ['tʃjuŋ^1 ti^4] 'younger brother,' ['tʃje^3 tʃje^3] 'elder sister,' ['mej⁴ mej⁴] 'younger sister.' An even more complicated terminology appears in Menomini, which we can best elucidate if we use the term *sibling* to mean 'brother or sister.' In Menomini the terms are [nɛʔnɛh] 'my elder brother,' [neme:h] 'my elder sister,' [nɛhse:h] 'my younger sibling,' [neko:ʔsemaw] 'my sibling of opposite sex' (i.e. 'my brother' when a woman says it, 'my sister' when a man says it), [ne:hkah] 'my brother (man speaking),' [ne:tɛkɛh] 'my sister (woman speaking).' The general term [ni:tɛsjanak] 'my siblings' is used in the plural when the siblings are of both sexes and not all younger than the possessor.

Terms of relationship not only vary as in the above examples, but also are used in situations that one cannot define. The Menomini terms for 'brother' and 'sister' are used also for cousins, provided the related parents are of the same sex: a man says [ne:hkah] of his father's brother's son, and so on. Moreover, these and some other terms are inherited: my father's brother's son's son is also [ne:hkah]. Consequently, the meaning really hinges on the consistency with which these relationships are remembered and recognized.

In the same way, plant-names, for example, are perhaps nowhere used in a way that would be consistent with a botanist's classification — even aside from such vague terms as *tree, shrub, bush, herb, reed, grass*.

Even in such a sphere as that of the numbers, languages show many deviations. Our system of decimal numbers (*twenty-two, thirty-five*, etc.) shows traces of a duodecimal or twelves system (*eleven, twelve* instead of *one-teen, *two-teen). Other irregularities are formal, as *two : twenty : second : half*, or *three : thirteen, thirty, third*. Furthermore, the connotation of certain numbers like *three, seven, thirteen*, and of additional terms like *dozen, score, gross*, cannot be stated mathematically. In Danish there is an admixture of a vigesimal or twenties system. In French one counts from 'sixty' to 'seventy-nine' without a special word for the intervening multiple of ten: 'seventy' is *soixante-dix* [swasɑ̃t-dis] 'sixty-ten'; 'seventy-one' is *soixante et onze* [swasɑ̃t e õz] 'sixty and eleven,' and so on; ' eighty ' is *quatre-vingt* [katrə vẽ] 'four-twenties,' and then one counts up twenty more to reach one-hundred; thus, 'ninety-two' is *quatre-vingt douze* [katrə vẽ du:z] 'four-twenties-twelve.' Peoples who have little use for higher numbers may use very few: the Kham Bushmen are said to count by simple numbers only to 'three,' and to use 'two and two' for 'four,' and so on.

In other spheres which are subject to scientific analysis, this may still provide no gauge for the linguistic classification. Color, for instance, is a matter of frequency of refracted or reflected light-waves. The visible spectrum is an unbroken scale of frequencies. Different languages use different color-names (such as our *red, orange, yellow, green, blue, violet*, § 9.1) for different parts of this scale. We should have a hard time deciding at what points on the actual scale the domain of each English color-name begins and ends. If we showed people colors in minute grades of variety, we should find that between the frequencies which were named consistently, say, as *yellow* and as *green*, there would be a border-zone, where the naming wavered. If we went outside the European culture-sphere, we should find entirely different distributions.

For most of our meanings we have not even this approach to an external standard. Terms which relate to social behavior, such as *love, friend, kind, hate* could be defined in terms of ethnology, folk-lore, and sociology, provided these studies had reached a perfection and accuracy undreamed of today. Terms which relate to states of the speaker's body that are perceptible only to him, such as *queasy, qualmish, sad, gay, glad, happy*, could be defined only if we had a minute knowledge of what goes on inside a living person's body. Even all this would not suffice for linguistic meanings that have less practical bearing, such as categories of noun-gender or verbal aspect. There seems to be no practical criterion by which the gender of a noun in German, French, or Latin could be determined: to define the meaning of the episememe 'masculine' in such a language would be simply to list the markers of masculine nouns and the nouns that belong arbitrarily to the class, and to say that whatever is common, in the practical world, to all these objects, is the "meaning" of the masculine gender-category. The same is true of the verbal aspects of English: the difference between *wrote* and *was writing* is so elusive and differs so much for different verbs and in different phrases, that the definer, after stating the main principles, cannot do better than to resort to a demonstration by means of examples.

CHAPTER 17

WRITTEN RECORDS

17. 1. The language of any speech-community appears to an observer as a complicated signaling-system, of the kind that has occupied us in the preceding chapters of this book. A language presents itself to us, at any one moment, as a stable structure of lexical and grammatical habits.

This, however, is an illusion. Every language is undergoing, at all times, a slow but unceasing process of *linguistic change*. We have direct evidence of this change in the case of communities which possess written records of their earlier speech. The English of the King James Bible or of Shakspere is unlike the English of today. The fourteenth-century English of Chaucer is intelligible to us only if we use a glossary. The ninth-century English of King Alfred the Great, of which we have contemporary manuscript records, seems to us like a foreign language; if we could meet English-speakers of that time, we should not understand their speech, or they ours.

The speed of linguistic change cannot be stated in absolute terms. A speaker has no difficulty, in youth, in conversing with his grandparents, or, in age, in conversing with his grandchildren, yet a thousand years — say, thirty to forty generations — have sufficed to change the English language to the extent we have just indicated. During these generations, it must have seemed to each London-English mother that her children were learning to speak the same kind of English as she had learned in her infancy. Linguistic change is far more rapid than biological change, but probably slower than the changes in other human institutions.

Linguistic change interests us especially because it offers the only possibility of explaining the phenomena of language. Speakers acquire their habits from earlier speakers; the only explanation of their habits lies in the habits of these earlier speakers. If we ask, for instance, why present-day speakers use the form *dog* for the animal 'canis domesticus,' or, let us say, why they add the suffix [-iz, -z, -s] to derive plural from singular nouns, the obvious answer is that they acquired these habits, in infancy, from the older people round them; if we then ask the same questions about the habits of these older people, we are referred to the habits of still older people, and so on, back into time, without limit. If we could realize our diagram of density of communication (§ 3.4), in which every speaker was represented by a dot and every utterance by an arrow from the dot that represented the speaker to the dot or dots that represented the hearer or hearers, we should find that the network reached indefinitely back into time.

In the normal case, then, the explanation for a speech-habit is simply the existence of the same habit at an earlier time. Where linguistic change has been at work, however, the explanation will be the existence of some other habit at an earlier time, plus the occurrence of the change. Our lexical habit, for instance, of using the word *meat* 'edible flesh,' is not very old; a few centuries ago, the word *flesh* was used in this meaning, and the word *meat* meant 'food.' The explanation of our present-day habit, in this case, consists in (1) the earlier habit, and (2) the intervening change. Since linguistic change never stops, it sooner or later affects every habit in a language; if we know enough of the speech of the past, the second type of explanation will apply to every present-day speech-form.

Since written records give us direct information about the speech-habits of the past, the first step in the study of linguistic change, wherever we have written records, is the study of these records.

We today are so used to reading and writing that we often confuse these activities with language itself (§ 2.1). Writing is a relatively recent invention. It has been in use for any considerable length of time in only a few speech-communities, and even in these its use has been confined, until quite recently, to a very few persons. A speech-utterance is the same, whether it receives a written record or not, and, in principle, a language is the same, regardless of the extent to which speech-utterances of this language are recorded in writing. For the linguist, writing is, except for certain matters of detail, merely an external device, like the use of the phonograph, which happens to preserve for our observation some features of the speech of past times.

17. 2. Writing is an outgrowth of drawing. Probably all peoples make pictures by painting, drawing, scratching, or carving. These pictures, aside from other uses (§ 2.9), sometimes serve as messages or reminders — that is, they modify the conduct of the beholder — and they may be persistently used in this way. The Indians of North America are skilful draftsmen, and in older times made extensive practical use of pictures. Thus, we are told of an Ojibwa Indian who owned a long strip of birch-bark with a series of pictures, which he used to remind himself of the succession of verses in a sacred song. The third picture, for instance, represents a fox, because the third verse of the song says something about a fox, and the sixth picture represents an owl, because the sixth verse says, "It is an ill omen." A Mandan Indian sent the following picture to a fur-trader: in the center are two crossed lines; at one side of these lines are outline drawings of a gun and of a beaver, with twenty-nine parallel strokes above the picture of the beaver; at the other side of the crossed lines are drawings of a fisher, an otter, and a buffalo. This means: "I am ready to trade a fisher-skin, an otter-skin, and a buffalo-hide for a gun and thirty beaver-pelts."

Records and messages of this sort are usually spoken of as "picture-writing," but this term is misleading. The records and messages, like writing, have the advantage of being permanent and transportable, but they fall short of writing in accuracy, since they bear no fixed relation to linguistic forms and accordingly do not share in the delicate adjustment of the latter.

We have no record of any people's progress from this use of pictures to the use of real writing, and can only guess at the steps. In the use of pictures we can often see the beginnings of the transition, and traces of it remain in the actual systems of writing.

Real writing uses a limited number of conventional symbols. We must suppose, therefore, that in the transition the pictures became conventionalized. The way of outlining each animal, for instance, becomes so fixed that even a very imperfect sketch leaves no doubt as to the species of animal. To some degree this is true of the pictures of American Indians. In actual systems of writing we often find symbols which still betray this origin. In the so-called *hieroglyphic* writing of ancient Egypt, most of the symbols are conventional but realistic pictures, and many of them actually denote the name of the object which they represent; thus, the picture of a goose (drawn always in the same way) denotes the word [sɨ?] [1] which means 'goose.' In Chinese writing, some of the symbols, such as, for instance, the symbol for the word [ma³] 'horse,' still resemble a picture of the meaning of the word, and this is sometimes true of the older shapes of characters whose modern form shows no such resemblance.

When the picture has become rigidly conventionalized, we may call it a *character*. A character is a uniform mark or set of marks which people produce under certain conditions and to which, accordingly, they respond in a certain way. Once this habit is established, the resemblance of the character to any particular object is of secondary importance, and may be obliterated by changes in the convention of forming the character. These changes are often due to the nature of the writing-materials. Some of the characters of the *cuneiform* writing of the ancient Mesopotamian peoples still betray their origin in pictures, but for the most part this is not the case: the characters consist of longer and shorter wedge-shaped strokes in various arrangements, and evidently got this shape because they were scratched into tough clay. In the hieroglyphic writing of ancient Egypt the characters were carefully painted, but for rapid writing with a reed brush on papyrus the Egyptians developed a simplified and rounded version (known as *hieratic* writing) whose characters have lost all resemblance to pictures. Our own writing is ultimately derived from the ancient Egyptian, but no one could recognize pictures in our letters; as a matter of fact, our letter F still has the two horns of the snail which was pictured in the hieroglyphic ancestor of this letter.

The other, more important phase of the transition from the use of pictures to real writing, is the association of the characters with linguistic forms. Most situations contain features that do not lend themselves to picturing; the picture-user resorts to all sorts of devices that will elicit the proper response. Thus, we saw the Indian drawing twenty-nine strokes above his beaver to represent the number of beaver-pelts. Instead of depicting the process of exchange by a series of pictures, he represented it by two crossed lines with the sets of traded objects at either side. The Ojibwa represented "ill omen" by an owl, in accordance, no doubt, with some tribal belief.

When the picture-user was confronted by a problem of this kind, we may suppose that he actually spoke to himself, and tried out

[1] We do not know the vowel sounds of ancient Egyptian.

various wordings of the troublesome message. Language, after all, is our one way of communicating the kind of things that do not lend themselves to drawing. If we make this supposition, we can understand that the picture-users might, in time, arrange the characters in the order of the spoken words of their language, and that they might develop a convention of representing every part — say, every word — of the spoken utterance by some character. We can only guess at the steps of this transition: real *writing* presupposes it.

In real writing, some characters have a twofold value, for they represent both a picturable object and a phonetic or linguistic form; other characters, having lost their pictorial value, represent only a phonetic or linguistic form; purely pictorial characters that are not associated with speech-forms sink into subsidiary use. The linguistic value predominates more and more, especially as the characters become conventionalized in shape, losing their resemblance to pictured objects. The characters become *symbols* — that is marks or groups of marks that conventionally represent some linguistic form. A symbol "represents" a linguistic form in the sense that people write the symbol in situations where they utter the linguistic form, and respond to the symbol as they respond to the hearing of the linguistic form. Actually, the writer utters the speech-form before or during the act of writing and the hearer utters it in the act of reading; only after considerable practice do we succeed in making these speech-movements inaudible and inconspicuous.

17. 3. Apparently, *words* are the linguistic units that are first symbolized in writing. Systems of writing which use a symbol for each word of the spoken utterance, are known by the misleading name of *ideographic* writing. The important thing about writing is precisely this, that the characters represent not features of the practical world ("ideas"), but features of the writers' language; a better name, accordingly, would be *word-writing* or *logographic writing*.

The main difficulty about logographic writing is the providing of symbols for words whose meaning does not lend itself to pictorial representation. Thus, the Egyptians used a character that represented a tadpole, to symbolize a word that meant 'one-hundred thousand,' presumably because tadpoles were very numerous in the swamps. The Chinese symbol for the word 'good' is a combination of the symbols for 'woman' and for 'child.'

The most important device of this sort is to use the symbol of some phonetically similar word whose meaning is picturable. Thus, the ancient Egyptians used the character that depicted a goose, not only for the word [sỉ] 'goose,' but also for the word [sỉ] 'son,' and they used the character that depicted a conventionalized checkerboard, not only for [mn] 'checkers,' but also for [mn] 'remain.' Chinese writing used the conventionalized character depicting a wheat-plant not only for a word that meant 'wheat,' but also for the homonymous word that meant 'come' — in present-day North Chinese, [laj²]. The ambiguity that arises in this way, leads to a further development: one adds some character that shows which of the similar words is to be read; these additional characters are called *classifiers* or *determinants*. In Chinese writing, which carries the logographic system to perfection, the *phonetic* (as the basic symbol is called) and the classifier are united into a single compound character. Thus, the symbol for [ma³] 'horse' and the symbol for [ny³] 'woman' are united into a compound character, which serves as the symbol for the word [ma¹] 'mother.' The symbol for [faŋ¹] 'square' combines with the symbol for [thu²] 'earth' into a compound symbol for [faŋ¹] 'district'; with the symbol for [sr¹] 'silk,' it forms a compound symbol representing the word [faŋ³] 'spin.' The phonetic part of the compound symbol, as these examples show, does not always accurately represent the sound of the word; we have to suppose, however, that at the time and in the dialect where this development took place, the compound symbols (that is, such as were there and then created) were phonetically accurate.

The logographic system, as we see it in Chinese writing, has the disadvantage that one has to learn a symbol for every word of the language. The compound symbols of Chinese writing can all be analyzed into 214 constituents ("radicals"), but, even so, the labor of learning to read and write is enormous. On the other hand, this system has a great advantage in that the symbols are non-committal as to the phonetic shape of the words. The Chinese speak a number of mutually unintelligible dialects, but in writing and printing they adhere to certain conventions of lexicon and word-order and are thus able to read each others' writings and, with some training, also the writings of their ancient literature.

WRITTEN RECORDS 287

Our numerals (derived from ancient India) are examples of logographic writing. A symbol like 4 is intelligible to many nations, although we read it as [fɔə], the Germans as [fiːr], the French as [katr], and so on. Moreover, since we arrange the numerals according to a fixed convention, we can read each others' numeral phrases even though our languages differ as to the structure of these phrases: 91, for instance, is everywhere intelligible, although we say not ['najn 'wʌn] but ['najnti 'wʌn], and the Germans say, in opposite order, ['ajn unt 'nojntsix] 'one and ninety,' and the French [katrə vɛ̃ ɔ̃z] 'four twenties eleven,' and the Danes ['eʔn ɔ hal 'fɛmʔs] 'one and half five-times.'

17. 4. In the device of representing unpicturable words by phonetically similar picturable words, we see the emergence of the phonetic factor in writing. Once a symbol is associated with a particular word, the phonetic features of this word may suffice to bring about the writing of the symbol. In Chinese, where the words are of uniform structure, this transference has been made only from word to word, and the compound characters, in accordance with this structure, are written as units and held down to uniform size. In the writing of other languages, where words are of various lengths, we find word-symbols used for phonetically similar parts of longer words. Thus, the Egyptians wrote the symbol for [mn] 'checkerboard' twice over to represent the word [mnmn] 'move.' By a succession of the symbols for [mc̦] 'duster' and [ᴅr] 'basket,' they wrote the word [mc̦ᴅr] 'ear.' In accordance with the structural variety, they represented words not always by one symbol, but also by various arrangements of logograms, phonetics, and classifiers. Similarly, in Aztec writing, the place-name *Teocaltitlan*, literally 'god-house-people,' was represented by the symbols for *tentli* 'lips,' *otli* 'path,' *calli* 'house,' and *tlantli* 'teeth'; this is the more intelligible as the *-tli* in these words is an inflectional suffix.

The symbols in this way may take on a more and more constant *phonographic* value: they become *phonograms* — that is, symbols not for linguistic forms, but for phonetic forms. The commonest result seems to be a set of *syllabic* symbols, each one of which denotes one syllabic sound with (or without) preceding and following non-syllabics. The cuneiform writing of the ancient Mesopotamians reached this stage; it had characters for such syllables as [ma, mi, mu, am, im, um, muk, mut, nam, tim]. Throughout

K

its use, as it passed from nation to nation, it carried along logographic features. For instance, the ancient Sumerian word for 'god' was [an]; when the Babylonians learned the use of writing, they took over the Sumerian symbol as a logogram for the Babylonian word [ilu] 'god,' and as a classifier which they placed before the names of gods. This kind of retention often occurs when a system of writing is adapted to a new language; thus, we retain Latin abbreviations, such as & (Latin *et*) for *and;* etc. (Latin *et cetera* 'and other things') for *and so forth;* i.e. (Latin *id est*) for *that is;* e.g. (Latin *exempli gratia* 'for the sake of an example') for *for instance;* lb. (Latin *libra*) for *pound,* and so on.

In Babylonian writing the syllabic principle was never fully carried out; thus, a single symbol (a vertical wedge with two small wedges aslant at the left) represented the syllables [ud, ut, uᴛ, tam, par, pir, laẋ, xiʃ] and, logographically, the words [uːmu] 'day,' [ʃamʃu] 'sun,' and [piçu] 'white.' In its Old Persian form, cuneiform writing had developed into a genuine syllabary, with a relatively small number of symbols, each representative of some one syllable. In general, syllabic systems of writing are widespread and seem to be easily devised. The ancient Greeks on the island of Cyprus used a syllabary of some sixty-five symbols. The Japanese largely use Chinese logographs, but supplement them with two syllabaries, both of which are derived from Chinese characters. The Vai, in Guinea, are said to have a system of 226 syllabic signs. When persons acquainted with modern writing devise a system for an illiterate people, they sometimes find it easiest to teach syllabic writing. Thus, Sikwaya, a Cherokee, devised a set of eighty-five syllabic symbols for his language; the Fox Indians have several syllabaries, all based on English script forms; and the Cree have a syllabary consisting of simple geometrical characters.

17. 5. It seems that only once in the history of writing there has been any advance beyond the syllabic principle. Some of the Egyptian hieroglyphic and hieratic symbols were used for syllables containing only one consonant; in the use of these, differences of the accompanying vowel were disregarded, and the resultant ambiguities were removed by the use of classifiers and logograms. In all, there were twenty-four of these symbols for one-consonant syllables. At an early date — certainly before 1500 B.C. — Semitic-speaking people became acquainted with Egyptian

WRITTEN RECORDS

writing, and hit upon the idea of setting down words of their language by means of the twenty-four simplest Egyptian symbols. This was feasible because the structure of Semitic identifies each root by its consonant-scheme (§ 14.8); the non-indication of vowels could leave a reader in doubt only as to some features of word-derivation which he might, in most instances, guess from the context.

Our oldest examples of this Semitic writing are the Sinai Inscriptions, which date from somewhere round 1800 to 1500 B.C. One later style of writing these characters is known as the South Semitic; it is represented by old inscriptions and, in modern times, by the Ethiopian alphabet. The other, North Semitic, style, was used by the Phoenicians, the Hebrews, and the Arameans. The Aramaic varieties include the style which we see in the modern "Hebrew" type, the Syrian style, and the writing of modern Arabic. It is the North Semitic character, in its Phoenician and its Aramaic varieties, that has spread, with many changes, over Asia and Europe.

The syllabaries used in India seem to be derived in part from Aramaic, and mostly from Phoenician writing. For the languages of India, indication of the vowel phonemes was necessary. The Indians used each Semitic character for the syllable of consonant plus [a] and then devised additional marks (*diacritical signs*) which they added to the symbol to designate the combination of the consonant with some other vowel. Thus, a simple sign means [ba], and the same sign with various marks means [ba:, bi, bi:, bu, bu:) and so on. Further, the Indians devised a mark which meant that the consonant was followed by no vowel at all, and a set of symbols for vowels without any consonant. At the same time, they increased the number of basic symbols until they had one for each consonant phoneme. In this way they arrived at a ystem which recorded their speech-forms with entire phonetic accuracy.

17. 6. Of all the offshoots, immediate and other, of Semitic writing, we need trace only the one which includes our own system of writing. The ancient Greeks took over the Phoenician system and made a decisive change. Some of the Phoenician symbols represented syllables containing consonants that were foreign to Greek; thus, A represented glottal stop plus vowel, O a laryngal spirant plus vowel, and I the consonant [j] plus vowel. The Greeks used these superfluous symbols to indicate vowel values, combining two symbols, such as TA or TO or TI, to represent a single syllable. In this way they arrived at the principle of *phonemic* or *alphabetic* writing — the principle of using a symbol for each phoneme. They fell short of complete accuracy only because they failed to invent enough symbols for vowels: they never distinguished between the long and short quantities, distinctive in their language, of the vowels [a, i, u]. They did later devise diacritical marks to indicate the position and the two qualities of their word-accent, and some signs of punctuation to indicate sentence-modulation.

From the Greeks the alphabet spread to other Mediterranean peoples. The Romans received it apparently through the mediation of the Etruscans. In the Middle Ages it passed from the Greeks to the Bulgarians, Serbians, and Russians, and from the Romans, directly or indirectly, to the other nations of Europe.

The transfer of writing to a new language occurs, apparently, in this way, that some bilingual person who knows writing in one language, hits upon the notion of using the alphabet also for his other language. He may retain whatever defects the alphabet had in the first language and he may retain letters that are necessary in the first language but superfluous in the new one, and he may fail to devise new letters for additional phonemes of the new language. On the other hand, he or his successors may be clever enough to mend these defects, either by inventing new characters or by putting superfluous characters to good use, or by semi-phonetic devices, such as using combinations of letters for a single phoneme.

The phonetic pattern of Latin was such that the Greek alphabet, as the Romans got it (probably from the Etruscans), was almost sufficient. One defect, the use of the symbol C for both [k] and [g], they mended by inventing the modified symbol G for [g]. A more serious matter was the lack of symbols to distinguish long and short vowels; the practice of placing a stroke over the letter or of writing the letter twice to indicate length, never gained much ground. There was no need for indicating the word-accent, since this in Latin was automatically regulated according to the primary phonemes.

The Germanic-speaking peoples took over the Graeco-Roman alphabet, we do not know when or where, in a shape somewhat different from the ordinary Greek or Latin styles. This form of the alphabet, known as the *runes*, was used for short inscriptions, chiefly of magic or religious character, such as epitaphs. The runes were not used skilfully, but they did include letters for some typically Germanic phonemes, [θ, w, j]. The customary order of the alphabet, too, was different from that of the Graeco-Roman prototype; it ran: [f u θ a r k g w h n i j p ɛ z s t b e m l ŋ o d]. For this reason the runic alphabet is sometimes called the *futhark*. The oldest runic inscriptions date from round 300 A.D. Later, as the Germanic-speaking peoples were christianized by Romance and Irish missionaries, they gave up the runes in favor of the Latin alphabet. However, the Gothic bishop Ulfila, who in the fourth century devised an alphabet for his Bible-translation, retained several runic letters, and the Old English priests, in the eighth century, when they took to writing English, retained the runic characters for [θ] and [w], since the Latin alphabet provided none. It was only after the Norman Conquest that English writers gave up these letters in favor of the combinations *th* and *vv* (whence our *w*). The five Latin vowel letters have never sufficed for English; on the other hand, we retain the superfluous letters *c*, *q*, and *x*. The writing of present-day English lacks symbols for the phonemes [ɑ:, ɛ, ɔ:, θ, ð, ʃ, ʒ, tʃ, ŋ] and for the stress-accent. This lack is only partially repaired by the use of digraphs, such as *th*, *sh*, *ch*, *ng*.

Occasionally we find our alphabet fully adapted to the phonetic system of some language. In the ninth century, the apostles Cyril and Method added enough extra letters to the Greek alphabet to make it cover the primary phonemes of the Old Bulgarian language. This Slavic alphabet, in its modern form, is well suited to the Slavic languages; for Serbian, some extra characters have been added. Several modern languages have adequate forms of the Latin alphabet; in the case of Bohemian and of Finnish, this result has been reached by the use of diacritical marks, and in the case of Polish by the use also of digraphs, such as *cz* for [tʃ] and *sz* for [ʃ].

17. 7. The principle of alphabetic writing — one symbol for each phoneme — is applicable, of course, to any language. The inadequacy of the actual systems is due largely to the conservatism of the people who write. The writer does not analyze the phonetic system of his speech, but merely writes each word as he has seen it in the writings of his predecessors. When the art of writing becomes well established in a community, not only the spellings of words, but even lexical and grammatical forms become conventional for written records. In this way, a *literary dialect* may become established and obligatory for written records, regardless of the writer's actual dialect.

This conservatism, as time goes on, works also in another way: the conventions of writing remain unaltered even though the speech-forms have undergone linguistic change. For instance, in Latin writing the letter C represented the phoneme [k]. When the Irish and the English took over the Latin alphabet, they used this letter for their [k]-phonemes; in Old English, *cu* spelled [kuː] 'cow,' *cinn* spelled [kinn] 'chin,' and *scip* spelled [skip] 'ship.' Later on, the phoneme [k] underwent certain changes in the various dialects of Latin. In Italy, [k] before front vowels became [tʃ]; Latin ['kentum] 'hundred,' for instance, became Italian ['tʃɛnto]. The Romans wrote their word as *centum;* the Italians still write *cento*. In France, the Latin [k] before front vowels has become [s], as in [sã] 'hundred,' but the French still write this word as *cent*. In English, we have taken our foreign-learned words from French, with the [s] pronunciation, but also with the traditional spelling with C, as in the word *cent* [sent]. In Latin, the letters A, E, I, O, U were used for the phonemic types [a, e, i, o, u], and they were taken into English writing in these values. Thus, in medieval English writing, a graph like *name* represented a form like ['naːme] 'name.' In the fifteenth century, English spelling became conventionally fixed in much its present shape. Since that time, however, our vowel phonemes have undergone a great deal of change. The result has been that we use the Latin vowel-letters not only in entirely new values — this, after all, would do no harm — but in inconsistent ways. We have kept on using the letter A in graphs like *name, hat, all, far,* although these words have now entirely different syllabic phonemes. Sounds which existed when our spelling became habitual, but have since been lost by linguistic change, are still represented in our writing by silent letters, as in *name, know, gnat, bought, would*.

Once a system of spelling has become antiquated in its relation to the spoken sounds, learned scribes are likely to invent pseudo-archaic spellings. The words *debt, doubt, subtle* contained no [b]-sound in Old French, whence English received them, and were written both in French and in English as *dette, doute, sutil;* the present-day spellings with *b* were invented by scribes who knew the far-off Latin antecedents of the French words, *debitum, dubito, subtilis*. The letter *s* in *isle* reflects the Old French spelling *isle* (from Latin *insula*); at the time when the word was taken into English it no longer had an [s] (compare modern French *île* [iːl]) and was appropriately spelled *ile*. The scribes not only favored the spelling with *s*, but even introduced the letter *s* into two similar words which had never contained any [s]-sound, namely the native English *island* (from Old English *iglond*) and the French loan-word *aisle* (French *aile*, from Latin *āla*). People who saw the runic letter þ in ancient English writings but did not know its value [θ], took it to be a form of the letter *y* and arrived at the notion that the article *the* was in older English *ye*.

17. 8. It is evident, from all this, that written records give us only an imperfect and often distorted picture of past speech, which has to be deciphered and interpreted, often at the cost of great labor. To begin with, the values, logographic or phonographic, of the written signs may be unknown. In this case, the problem of decipherment is sometimes desperate. The best help is a bilingual inscription, in which by the side of the undeciphered text there is a version in some known language; other aids are some knowledge of the language or of the contents of the inscription. In 1802 Georg Friedrich Grotefend succeeded in deciphering cuneiform inscriptions in Old Persian, and round the middle of the nineteenth century a succession of workers (E. Hincks, Rawlinson, Oppert) deciphered those in Babylonian-Assyrian; in both instances the decipherers made ingenious use of their knowledge of related languages. The cuneiform texts in other languages (Sumerian, the language of Van, and Hittite) were deciphered thanks to bilingual texts, such as dictionary-like tablets of word-lists in Sumerian, Assyrian, and Hittite. In 1821 Jean Francois Champollion began the decipherment of ancient Egyptian writings by using the famous Rosetta Stone (found by the French in 1799; now in the British Museum), which bears parallel inscriptions in hieroglyphics, in a later form of Egyptian writing, and in Greek. In 1893 Vilhelm Thomsen deciphered the Old Turkish Orkhon inscriptions; Thomsen saw that the writing was alphabetical and the language of the Turk family. The hieroglyph-like inscriptions of the Hittites and those of the ancient Cretans have never been deciphered; of the Maya picture-writing in Central America only some characters, denoting months, days, numbers, and colors, have been interpreted.

If the system of writing is known, but the language is not, the situation is little better. The most famous instance of this is the

Etruscan language in ancient Italy; we have extensive texts in a form of the Greek alphabet, but cannot interpret them, beyond reading personal names and a few other words. We have dice with the first six numbers written on the faces, but cannot determine the order of these numbers. The Lydian inscriptions in Asia Minor are intelligible, thanks to a bilingual text in Lydian and Aramaic; the alphabet is Greek, and the language apparently related to Etruscan.

17. 9. When both the system of writing and the language are intelligible, we aim, of course, to learn from the texts all we can get as to phonetics, grammar, and lexicon. The phonetic values of the characters in ancient writings can never be surely known; thus, the actual sounds represented even by the alphabetic symbols of languages like Ancient Greek, Latin, Gothic, or Old English, are in part uncertain. When the writing has become conventional and unphonetic, the lapses of scribes or the way they write uncommon words, may betray the real phonetic values. Our Old English manuscripts show the same inflectional system from the ninth century until well into the eleventh century, distinguishing the vowels of unstressed syllables and the presence of final m and n; but occasional lapses of the scribes betray the fact that already in the tenth century most of these vowels had changed to [e] and the final [m] and [n] had been lost; such lapses are, for instance, spellings like *worde* for usual *worda* 'of words,' *fremme* for normal *fremman* 'to make,' *gode* for *godum* 'to good ones.' When an English writer in the fifteenth century spells *behalf* without an l, we infer that he no longer pronounced the [l] in this word, although the tradition of writing insists upon the symbol to this day. So-called *inverse* spellings tell the same story. Old English had a sound [x] in words like *light, bought, eight*, which is still reflected in our spelling with *gh*. When we find the word *deleite* (a loan from Old French *deleiter*), which never contained the sound [x], spelled *delight*, then we may be sure that the [x] was no longer spoken in words like *light:* for the writers, the *gh* was now a mere silent graph, indicative only of vowel-quantity.

A serious factor in the linguistic interpretation of written documents is their transmission. Inscriptions, chiefly on stone or metal or, as in the cuneiform texts, on clay, are generally original notations; we need reckon only with one scribe's errors of spelling or dictation. Most writing, however, is made on perishable material,

WRITTEN RECORDS

and has come to our time through successive copyings. Our manuscripts of Greek and Latin writings date from the Middle Ages, often from the later Middle Ages or from the early modern period; only fragments have been preserved on papyrus in the sands of Egypt. It is rare good fortune when we have a contemporary manuscript of an ancient text, like the Hatton manuscript of Alfred the Great's translation of Pope Gregory's *Pastoral Care*. The scribes not only made mistakes in copying, especially where they did not understand the text, but they even tampered with it, by way of improving the language or falsifying the content. The study of ancient writing, *paleography*, and the technique of reconstructing ancient texts from one or more imperfect copies, *textual criticism*, have developed into separate branches of science. Unfortunately, textual critics have sometimes lacked linguistic knowledge; our printed editions of ancient texts may fail to report linguistically valuable forms that appear in the manuscripts.

Sometimes the text which appears in our written records has undergone re-spelling into a new alphabet or a new system of orthography. This is the case with our text of the ancient Greek Homeric poems, and with our texts of the Avesta. We try, in such cases, to reconstruct the original spellings and to detect misleading or erroneous features in the traditional text.

17. 10. There are a few side-issues which sometimes help us in the linguistic interpretation of written records. In the forms of composition which we group together under the name of *verse*, the author binds himself to observe certain phonetic patterns. In modern English verse, for instance, the author shapes his wording so that stress-phonemes come at certain intervals, and that words of like ending, from the stressed syllabic to the end, occur in pairs or larger sets, again at certain intervals. Thus, if we know that a poet composed under a convention of exact rimes, we can gather from his rime-words a great deal of information that may not appear in the spellings. Chaucer rimed — to quote the words in their present-day spellings — *mean* with *clean*, but not with *keen, queen, green:* he evidently spoke different vowels in these two sets of words. On the other hand, inconsistencies are equally illuminating. When the Alsatian poet Brant, at the end of the fifteenth century, rimes the word for 'not' both in the Alsatian form [nit], as, for instance, with *Bitt* [bit] 'request,' and in the present-day standard German form [nixt], as, for instance, with

Geschicht [ge'ʃixt] 'story,' we know that in his day the modern standard form, *nicht* [nixt] 'not' had already gained currency alongside the provincial form of the word. Even when rimes are used traditionally after they cease to be phonetically true, as, in modern English poetry, rimes like *move : love* or *scant : want*, a study of the tradition may be of interest.

Other types of verse lead to similar deductions. In old Germanic poetry, high-stressed words occurred in alliterative sets with the same initial consonant, as in *house and home, kith and kin*. Accordingly when in ancient Icelandic verses of the Eddic poems we find ['wega, 'vega] 'strike' alliterating with [rejŏr] 'wroth,' we conclude that the men who coined this alliteration still pronounced the latter word with an initial [wr-], although the spelling of our manuscripts, in accordance with the later language, no longer shows the [w]. In Greek and Latin verse the succession of long and short syllables was regulated; a syllable containing a long vowel or a diphthong, or any vowel followed by more than one consonant, counted as long; the position of words in verse thus often informs us as to vowel-quantities, which are only in part shown by Greek orthography and not at all by Latin.

Another occasional help toward the interpretation of written records is the transcription of speech-forms from one language into another. At the beginning of the Christian era we find the name of *Caesar* written in Greek texts as *kaisar:* since the Greek language has not undergone a change of [k] to [tʃ] or the like, and the Greek *k*, accordingly, represented always a phoneme of the [k] type, this transcription makes it likely that Latin at that time still preserved the [k-]. The old Chinese transcriptions of Indo-Aryan names in Buddhist texts give information about the sounds which were attached to Chinese logographic symbols.

Finally, written records may contain statements of a linguistic nature, as in the case of Sanskrit grammar and lexicon (§ 1.6); the Hindus, moreover, were excellent phoneticians and interpreted the written symbols in physiologic terms. Often enough, however, we have to distrust the information in our texts. The Latin grammarians give us little help as to speech-sounds; the English phoneticians of the early modern period, likewise, confused sounds with spellings and give very poor guidance as to the actual pronunciation of their time.

CHAPTER 18

THE COMPARATIVE METHOD

18. 1. We saw in Chapter 1 that some languages resemble each other to a degree that can be explained only by historical connection. Some resemblance, to be sure, may result from universal factors. Such features as phonemes, morphemes, words, sentences, constructions, and substitution-types, appear in every language; they are inherent in the nature of human speech. Other features, such as noun-like and verb-like form-classes, categories of number, person, case, and tense, or grammatical positions of actor, verbal goal, and possessor, are not universal, but still so widespread that better knowledge will doubtless some day connect them with universal characteristics of mankind. Many features that are not widespread — among them some very specific and even minute ones — are found in distant and wholly unrelated languages; these features, too, may be expected some day to throw light on human psychology.

Other resemblances between languages bear no significance whatever. Modern Greek ['mati] means 'eye,' and so does the Malay word [mata]. If we knew nothing of the history of these languages, we should have to work through their lexicons and grammars in search of other resemblances, and then weigh the probabilities of historical connection, taking into account both the number of resemblances and their structural position. Actually, our knowledge of the past forms both of Greek and of Malay shows us that the resemblance of the two words for 'eye' is accidental. Modern Greek ['mati] is a relatively recent development from an ancient Greek [om'mation] 'little eye,' and this word was in ancient Greek connected, as a secondary derivative, with an underlying word ['omma] 'eye.' The Malay word [mata], on the other hand, had in ancient times much the same phonetic shape as today. Even if, against all present seeming, it should turn out, some day, that these two languages are related, the relationship would lie far back of Primitive Indo-European and Primitive Malayo-Polynesian time, and the resemblance of the modern words for 'eye' would have nothing to do with this relationship.

Still other resemblances are due to the borrowing of speech-forms. In modern Finnish there are many words like *abstraktinen* 'abstract,' *almanakka* 'almanac,' *arkkitehti* 'architect,' *ballaadi* 'ballad,' and so on through the dictionary — cultural words of general European distribution, which have been borrowed, in the last centuries, from one European language into the other, and evidence nothing about kinship. To be sure, we cannot always distinguish between this sort of transmission and the normal handing on of linguistic habits within a speech-community, but for the most part the two processes are very different. If the Finno-Ugrian languages should be related to the Indo-European, then the kinship dates from a time when the words *abstract, almanac*, etc., were not yet in use.

18. 2. When we say, in contrast with these cases, that a resemblance between languages is due to *relationship*, we mean that these languages are later forms of a single earlier language. In the case of the Romance languages, we have written records of this parent language, namely, Latin. After the Latin language had spread over a large area, it underwent different linguistic changes in different parts of this area, so that today these different parts differ greatly in speech, and we call the divergent speech-forms "Italian," "French," "Spanish," and so on. If we could follow the speech, say of Italy, through the last two-thousand years, we could not pick out any hour or year or century when "Latin" gave way to "Italian"; these names are entirely arbitrary. By and large, any feature that is common to all the modern territorial forms of Latin, was present in the Latin of two-thousand years ago; on the other hand, when the modern forms of Latin disagree as to any feature, then some or all of them have, in this feature, undergone some change during the last two-thousand years. The resemblances appear especially in features that are common in everyday speech — in the commonest constructions and form-classes and in the intimate basic vocabulary. The features of difference, moreover, appear in systematic groups, with each territorial form diverging in its own characteristic way.

In most cases we are less favorably situated, in that we possess no written records of the uniform parent speech. The Germanic languages, for instance, resemble each other much as do the Romance, but we have no records from a time when the differences had not yet arisen. The *comparative method*, however, makes the same inferences in both cases. In the latter case we merely lack the confirmation of the written record. We assume the existence, at some time in the past, of a *Primitive Germanic* parent language, but the speech-forms of this language are known to us only by inference. When we write them down, we indicate this by placing an asterisk before them.

18. 3. Compare, for instance, the following words in present-day standard English, Dutch, German, Danish, and Swedish:

	English	Dutch	German	Danish	Swedish
'man'	mɛn	man	man	manʔ	man
'hand'	hɛnd	hant	hant	hɔnʔ	hand
'foot'	fut	vuːt	fuːs	foːð	foːt
'finger'	'fiŋgə	'viŋer	'fiŋer	'feŋʔər	'fiŋer
'house'	haws	høys	haws	huːʔs	huːs
'winter'	'wintə	'winter	'vinter	'venʔdər	'vinter
'summer'	'sʌmə	'zoːmer	'zomer	'sɔmər	ᵛsomar
'drink'	driŋk	'driŋke	'triŋken	'dregə	ᵛdrika
'bring'	briŋ	'breŋe	'briŋen	'breŋə	ᵛbriŋa
'lived'	livd	'leːvde	'leːpte	'leːvəðə	ᵛleːvde

This list could be extended almost indefinitely; the resemblances are so many and they so thoroughly pervade the basic vocabulary and grammar, that neither accident nor borrowing will explain them. We need only turn to languages outside the Germanic group to see the contrast, as in 'hand': French [mɛ̃], Russian [ru'ka], Finnish *käsi;* or 'house': French [mezõ], Russian [dom], Finnish *talo.* Another remarkable feature is the systematic grouping of the differences within the Germanic family. Where Swedish has the compound intonation, there Danish lacks the glottal stop; where the others have initial [f], there Dutch has initial [v]; where the others have [d], there German has [t]. In fact, whole series of forms show the same divergences from one Germanic language to the other. Thus, the divergent syllabic phonemes in the word *house* are paralleled in a whole set of forms:

	English	Dutch	German	Danish	Swedish
'house'	haws	høys	haws	huːʔs	huːs
'mouse'	maws	møys	maws	muːʔs	muːs
'louse'	laws	løys	laws	luːʔs	luːs
'out'	awt	øyt	aws	uːð	uːt
'brown'	brawn	brøyn	brawn	bruːʔn	bruːn

The fact that the differences themselves follow a system, — that the divergence, say, of English and German [aw] and Dutch [øy] appears in a whole series of forms — confirms our surmise that these forms are historically connected. The divergence, we suppose, is due to characteristic changes undergone by some or all of the related languages. If we extend our observation to cover more of the dialects in each area, we find many other varieties, with a similar parallelism. In particular, we find, in our example, that forms with the vowel [u:], such as [hu:s, mu:s] etc., occur also in local dialects of the English, Dutch, and German areas — as, for instance, in Scotch English.

Further, availing ourselves of the written records of these languages, we find that the oldest records from the English and Dutch-German areas, dating round the eighth and ninth centuries of our era, write the forms in our example uniformly with the letter *u*, as *hus, mus, lus, ut* (southern German *uz*), *brun*. Since the writing of these peoples was based on Latin, where the letter *u* represented vowels of the type [u], we conclude that the divergences in the syllabic of our forms had not yet arisen in the ninth century, and that the syllabic in those days was [u] in all the Germanic languages; other evidence leads us to believe that the vowel was long [u:]. Accordingly, we conclude that the Primitive Germanic parent language spoke these forms with [u:] as the syllabic. It is important to observe, however, that this description of the phoneme is only a supplementary detail; even if we made no surmise as to the acoustic character of the Primitive Germanic phoneme, the regularity of the correspondences, in the way of agreement and in the way of parallel disagreement, could still be explained only on the supposition that some one phoneme of the parent language appeared in the syllabic position of the forms *house, mouse*, and so on.

18. 4. It is interesting to compare these inferences with the inferences that are made in the more favorable case, where the parent language is known to us from written records. The resemblance between the Romance languages is much like that between the Germanic languages.

	ITALIAN	LADIN	FRENCH	SPANISH	ROUMANIAN
'nose'	'naso	nas	ne	'naso	nas
'head'	'kapo	kaf	ʃef	'kabo	kap
'goat'	'kapra	'kavra	ʃɛ:vr	'kabra	'kaprə
'bean'	'fava	'fave	fɛ:v	'aba	'fawə[1]

[1] Macedonian

THE COMPARATIVE METHOD 301

Here we follow the same procedure as with the Germanic correspondences, observing the local types in each area, and the spellings of the older records. The difference is only this, that written notations of the form of the parent language, Latin, are in most instances available. The Romance words in our example are modern forms of the Latin words which appear in our records as *nasum, caput, capram, fabam.*

After we have learned to draw inferences from the Romance forms, we may find discrepancies between the result of our inferences and the written records of Latin. These discrepancies are especially interesting because of the light they throw on the value of our inferences in cases where no record of the parent language is available. Take, for instance, the syllabic in the following types:

	ITALIAN	LADIN	FRENCH	SPANISH	ROUMANIAN
'flower'	'fjore	flur	flœ:r		'floarə
'knot'	'nodo	nuf	nø		nod
'vow'	'voto	vud	vø	bodas[1]	
'tail'	'koda	'kua	kø	'kola [2]	'koadə

The Latin prototypes appear in the first three of these words, as well as in a number of similar cases, with a syllabic *o*, which we interpret as [o:]: *florem, nodum, uotum.* In our fourth word, accordingly, we infer that the Latin prototype contained this same vowel and had the form *['ko:dam]. An inference of this kind is a *reconstruction;* we mark the reconstructed form, *['ko:dam] or *cōdam, with an asterisk. Now, in the written records of Latin, the word for 'tail' appears in a different shape, namely as *caudam* (accusative singular; the nominative is *cauda*). This disagrees with our reconstruction, for ordinarily Latin *au* (presumably [aw]) is reflected in the Romance languages by a different type of vowel-correspondence. Thus, Latin *aurum* 'gold' and *causam* 'thing, affair' appear as:

	ITALIAN	LADIN	FRENCH	SPANISH	ROUMANIAN
'gold'	'ɔro		ɔ:r	'oro	aur
'thing'	'kɔsa	'koze	ʃo:z	'kosa	

It is true that our Latin manuscripts, written in the Middle Ages, occasionally spell the word for 'tail' as *coda*, but this may be due merely to the errors of copyists; the older manuscripts from which

[1] Plural form, meaning 'wedding.'
[2] Re-shaped from Old Spanish *coa*, presumably ['koal].

ours were copied may have had the usual Latin form *cauda*. This error would be natural for copyists whose school pronunciation of ancient Latin did not distinguish between Latin *o* and *au*, and would be almost inevitable for copyists who spoke a form of Latin in which our word already had, as in the present-day languages, the vowel of *florem, nodum, votum* and not that of *aurum, causam*. That some people were in this latter position appears from the gloss, preserved to us in ninth-century manuscripts, which explains the word *cauda* by saying that it means *coda:* apparently, the former seemed antique and difficult, while the latter was intelligible. The conclusive support for our reconstruction appears in this, that inscriptions of early date show occasional spellings of *o* in words that ordinarily have *au*, as POLA for the name *Paulla* in an inscription dating from the year 184 B.C. Further, we learn that this *o*-pronunciation for *au*-forms was a vulgarism. Suetonius (who died about 160 A.D.) tells us that the rhetorician Florus corrected the Emperor Vespasian (died 79 A.D.) for saying *plostra* instead of the more elegant *plaustra* 'wagons'; the next day, the emperor got back at him by calling him *Flaurus* instead of *Florus*. As to our word, a grammarian of the fourth century A.D. speaks of *cauda* and *coda* as variant pronunciations. Moreover, we occasionally find over-elegant forms, like Vespasian's *Flaurus* for *Florus;* an inscription dating from before the beginning of the Christian Era has the spelling AVSTIA for *ostia* [o:stia] 'doors.' In sum, we conclude that our reconstructed **coda* *[ko:da] is by no means illusory, but represents a less elegant pronunciation which really existed in ancient time.

Cases like this give us confidence in the reconstructed forms. Latin writing did not indicate vowel-quantities; a graph like *secale* 'rye' could represent several phonetic types. As this word does not occur in verse, where its position would show us the vowel-quantities (§ 17.10), we should be unable to determine its form, had we not the evidence of the comparative method: forms like Italian *segola* ['segola], French *seigle* [sɛ:gl] show us that the Latin graph represents the form ['se:kale]. Students of the Romance languages reconstruct a Primitive Romance ("Vulgar Latin") form before they turn to the written records of Latin, and they interpret these records in the light of the reconstructed form.

18. 5. A reconstructed form, then, is a formula that tells us which identities or systematic correspondences of phonemes appear in a set of related languages; moreover, since these identities and correspondences reflect features that were already present in the parent language, the reconstructed form is also a kind of phonemic diagram of the ancestral form.

In the oldest records of the Germanic languages we find the following forms of the word *father:*

Gothic, text composed in the fourth century A.D., preserved in a sixth-century manuscript: *fadar*, presumably ['fadar]; the phoneme represented by *d* may have been a spirant.

Old Norse, in thirteenth-century manuscripts of texts that were, in part, composed much earlier: *faðer*, *faðir*, presumably ['faðer].

Old English, ninth-century manuscripts: *fæder*, presumably ['feder].[1]

Old Frisian, thirteenth-century manuscripts of texts that were composed somewhat earlier: *feder*, presumably ['feder].

Old Saxon (that is, northerly parts of the Dutch-German area), ninth-century manuscripts: *fader*, presumably ['fader].

Old High German (southerly parts of the Dutch-German area), ninth-century manuscripts: *fater*, presumably ['fater].

We sum up these facts by putting down the Primitive Germanic prototype as *['fader]; moreover, we claim that this summarizing formula at the same time shows us the phonemic structure of the prehistoric form.

Our formula embodies the following observations.

(1) All the Germanic languages stress the first syllable of this word, as of most others. We indicate this in our formula by an accent-mark, or, since accent on the first syllable is normal in Germanic, by writing no accent-mark at all. This means, at the same time, that in the Primitive Germanic parent language this word shared with most other words a phonemic feature (call it x) which appears in all the actual Germanic languages as a high stress on the first syllable of the word. Of course, it is almost a certainty that this feature x in the parent speech was the same as appears in all the actual Germanic languages, namely, a high stress on the first syllable, but this additional surmise in no way affects the validity of the main conclusion.

(2) All the old Germanic languages begin the word with [f].

---

[1] The Old English syllable [-der] has in modern English changed to [-ðǝ]; hence we say *father, mother, gather,* etc., where Old English had [-der].

If we had not the older records, we should have to consider the fact that some present-day dialects of the English and of the Dutch-German areas have here a voiced spirant of the type [v], but the geographic distribution would even then show us that [f] was the older type. In any case, the structural value of the symbol [f] in our formula is merely this, that the word *father* in the Germanic languages begins, and in Primitive Germanic began, with the same phoneme as the words *foot, five, fee, free, fare,* and so on, all of which we symbolize by formulas with initial [f].

(3) The [a] in our formula says that we have here the same correspondence as in words like the following:

water: Gothic ['wato:], Old Norse [vatn], Old English ['wɛter], Old Frisian ['weter], Old Saxon ['watar], Old High German ['wassar], Primitive Germanic formulas *['water, 'wato:];

acre: Gothic ['akrs], Old Norse [akr], Old English ['ɛker], Old Frisian ['ekker], Old Saxon ['akkar], Old High German ['akxar], Primitive Germanic formula *['akraz];

day: Gothic [dags], Old Norse [dagr], Old English [dɛj], Old Frisian [dej], Old Saxon [dag], Old High German [tag], Primitive Germanic formula *['dagaz].

In this case the deviations, namely Old English [ɛ] and Old Frisian [e] beside the [a] of the other languages, do not occur in all forms; all the dialects have [a], for instance, in cases like the following:

fare: Gothic, Old English, Old Saxon, Old High German ['faran], Old Norse, Old Frisian ['fara], Primitive Germanic formula *['faranan].

In fact, the English [ɛ] and the Frisian [e] occur under fixed phonetic conditions — namely, in monosyllables, like *day,* and before an [e] of the next syllable, as in *father, water, acre.* This deviation, we infer, is due to a later change, perhaps in a common intermediate Anglo-Frisian parent language. We are safe, in any case, in setting up, for all these words, a single structural phonemic unit [a] in the Primitive Germanic parent language.

(4) The acoustic value of the Gothic letter which we have transliterated as *d* is doubtful; it may have been a stop of the type [d] or a spirant of the type [ð], or it may have fluctuated, in which case [d] and [ð] were variants of one phoneme. The old Scandinavian graph speaks for [ð] in this area. The West Germanic languages have an unmistakable [d], which, in this as in other

THE COMPARATIVE METHOD

cases, appears in South German as [t]. In our Primitive Germanic formula we indicate all this by the symbol [d] or [ð]; the former is preferable because easier to print. Our formula identifies the phoneme with that which appears in cases like the following:

mother: Old Norse ['moːðer], Old English ['moːdor], Old Frisian ['moːder], Old Saxon ['moːdar], Old High German ['muotar], Primitive Germanic formula *['moːder];

mead: Old Norse [mjɔðr], Old English ['meodo], Old Frisian ['mede], Old High German ['metu], Primitive Germanic formula *['meduz];

ride: Old Norse ['riːða], Old English ['riːdan], Old Frisian ['riːda], Old High German ['riːtan], Primitive Germanic formula *['riːdanan].

(5) The next phoneme shows us a divergence in Gothic, which is obviously due to later change: Gothic always has *ar* for the unstressed *er* of the other languages, e.g.: Gothic ['hwaθar], Old English ['hwɛðer] 'which of the two.'

(6) The dialects agree as to the last phoneme, [r].

18. 6. While we have no written records to confirm our reconstructions of Primitive Germanic, we occasionally get almost this from the very ancient Scandinavian runic inscriptions (§ 17.6). Take, for instance, the following reconstructions:

guest: Gothic [gasts], Old Norse [gestr], Old English, Old Frisian [jest], Old Saxon, Old High German [gast], Primitive Germanic formula *['gastiz];

horn: all the old dialects [horn], Primitive Germanic formula *['hornan].

Here our Primitive Germanic reconstructions are longer than the actually attested forms. Space forbids our entering into the reasons that lead us to set up the additional phonemes; suffice it to say that in most cases, as in *guest*, these additional phonemes are made entirely definite by the forms in the actual dialects, while in others, such as *horn*, the presence of additional phonemes in Primitive Germanic is certain from the comparison of the Germanic languages, although the nature of these phonemes is decided only by the considerations which we now approach. I have chosen the words *guest* and *horn* as examples because they occur in a runic inscription on a golden horn, dating probably round 400 A.D., found near Gallehus in Denmark. Transliterated, the inscription reads:

ek hlewagastiz holtiŋaz horna tawido

'I, Fame-Guest, the Holting (man of the family of Holt), made the horn.' The same words in our Primitive Germanic formulas, would appear as *['ek 'hlewa-₁gastiz 'holtingaz 'hornan tawido:n], and the inscription confirms the final syllable of our reconstruction of *guest*, and the vowel, at any rate, of the final syllable in our reconstruction of *horn*.

The Finnish, Estonian, and Lappish languages, belonging to the Finno-Ugrian family (§ 4.7) and therefore unrelated to ours, contain many words which they must have borrowed from a Germanic language at an ancient time — all evidence points to the beginning of the Christian Era. As these languages have since that time gone through entirely different changes than have the Germanic languages, these borrowed forms give us independent evidence as to the ancient form of Germanic words. Our reconstructions of Primitive Germanic forms, like *ring*, Old English [hring], Old Norse [hringr], as *['hringaz], or *king*, Old English ['kyning], as *['kuningaz], or *gold*, Old English [gold] as *['golθan], or *yoke*, Old English [jok], as *['jokan], are confirmed by such Finnish loan-words as *rengas* 'ring,' *kuningas* 'king,' *kulta* 'gold,' *jukko* 'yoke.'

18. 7. The comparative method gives us an even more powerful check upon our Primitive Germanic reconstructions. Since the Germanic languages are a branch of the Indo-European family, our Primitive Germanic forms enter as units into comparison with forms of the other Indo-European languages. The reconstructed forms of Primitive Indo-European give us a scheme of a still earlier structure, out of which the Primitive Germanic structure has grown.

Among our last examples there are two good instances. Our reconstruction of Primitive Germanic *['gastiz] 'guest' matches the Latin form *hostis* 'stranger.' From the comparison of the Slavic forms, Old Bulgarian [gostı], Russian [gost̡], and so on, we reconstruct a Primitive Slavic *[ˈgostı]; this, however, is under strong suspicion of having been borrowed from a Germanic dialect and must therefore stay out of account. The comparison of the Latin form, however, leads us to set up a Primitive Indo-European formula *[ghostis], which tells us, in shorthand fashion, that the Latin second syllable confirms the final phonemes of our Primitive Germanic formula.

Similarly, on the basis of Gothic [ga'juk] 'pair' and the other old Germanic forms of the word *yoke*, namely, Old Norse [ok], Old English [jok], Old High German [jox], we set up a Primitive Germanic formula *['jokan], confirmed by the Finnish loan-form *jukko*. The phonemes in the second syllable of this reconstructed form would be in some respects indeterminate, were it not that this formula enters in turn into comparison with other forms of the Indo-European group. Sanskrit [ju'gam] leads us to set up a Primitive Indo-Iranian *[ju'gam]. Further, we have Greek [zu'gon] and Latin ['jugum]. The Slavic forms, such as Old Bulgarian [igo], Russian ['igo], lead us to set up a Primitive Slavic formula *['igo]. Cornish *iou*, Welsh *iau*, point to a Primitive Celtic *['jugom]. Even languages which have reshaped our word, Lithuanian ['jungas] and Armenian *luc*, give some evidence as to the structure of the word in Primitive Indo-European. All of this evidence we subsume in the formula, Primitive Indo-European *[ɟu'gom].

The case of the word *father* shows us an inference of a more complex character. Sanskrit [pi'taː], Greek [pa'teːr], Latin ['pater], Old Irish ['aðir], Primitive Germanic *['fader], are the principal forms which lead us to set up the Primitive Indo-European formula as *[pə'teːr]. The initial phoneme here illustrates the simplest case, a constant and normal set of correspondences: initial [p] of the Indo-European languages in general is matched by [f] in Germanic, and by zero in Celtic; Latin ['porkus] 'pig,' Lithuanian ['ᵛparʃas], corresponds to Primitive Germanic *['farhaz], Old English [fearh] (modern *farrow*), and Old Irish [ork], and the Primitive Indo-European formula is *['por*k*os].

The second phoneme in our formula shows a more complex case. In our Primitive Indo-European formulas we distinguish three short-vowel phonemes, [a, o, ə], although no Indo-European language has this threefold distinction. We do this because the correspondences between the languages show three different combinations. We use the symbol [a] in those cases where Indo-Iranian, Greek, Latin, and Germanic agree in having [a], as in

acre: Sanskrit ['aɟrah], Greek [a'gros], Latin ['ager], Primitive Germanic *['akraz]: Primitive Indo-European formula *[agros].

We use the symbol [o] for the many cases where Indo-Iranian and Germanic have [a], but Greek, Latin, and Celtic have [o], as in

eight: Sanskrit [aʃ'ʈaːw], Greek [ok'toː], Latin ['oktoː], Primitive Germanic *['ahtaw], Gothic ['ahtaw], Old German ['ahto]: Primitive Indo-European formula *[o*k*'toːw].

We use the symbol [ə] for the cases where Indo-Iranian has [i], while the other languages have the same phoneme as in the forms of the first set:

stead: Sanskrit ['sthitih] 'a standing,' Greek ['stasis], Primitive Germanic *['stadiz], Gothic [staθs], Old High German [stat]: Primitive Indo-European formula *[sthətis].

Evidently the forms of the word *father* show this last type of correspondence; hence we use [ə] in our formula. The morphologic structure of Primitive Indo-European, as it appears in the totality of our formulas, confirms our threefold distinction [a, o, ə], in that these three units take part in three different types of morphologic alternation.

The third symbol in our formula, which is the last we shall consider, illustrates a very interesting type of inference. Ordinarily when the other Indo-European languages have a [t], the Germanic languages have a [θ]. Thus,

brother: Sanskrit ['bhra:ta:], Greek ['phra:te:r] ('member of a phratry'), Latin ['fra:ter], Old Bulgarian [bratru], Primitive Germanic *['bro:θer], Gothic ['bro:θar], Old Norse ['bro:ðer], Old English ['bro:ðor], Old High German ['bruoder]: Primitive Indo-European formula *['bhra:te:r];

three: Sanskrit ['trajah], Greek ['trejs], Latin [tre:s], Old Bulgarian [trıje], Primitive Germanic *[θri:z], Old Norse [θri:r], Old High German [dri:]: Primitive Indo-European formula *['trejes].

The word *father*, together with some others, is anomalous in Primitive Germanic in containing [d] instead of [θ]. One might, of course, assume that two distinct Primitive Indo-European phonemes were here involved, which had coincided as [t] in all the Indo-European languages except Germanic, which alone distinguished them as [θ] versus [d]. In 1876, however, Karl Verner (1846–1896), a Danish linguist, showed that in a number of the cases where Germanic has the troublesome [d], this consonant follows upon a vowel or diphthong which is unstressed in Sanskrit and Greek; this correlation occurs in enough instances, and, in the morphologic structure, systematically enough, to exclude the factor of accident. The contrast of the words *brother* and *father* illustrates this correlation. Since the place of the word-accent is determined by the primary phonemes in Italic, Celtic, and Germanic, we can easily believe that its position in each of these languages is due to later change. Sanskrit and Greek, moreover, agree so often, although the place of the accent in both is highly irregular, that we do not hesitate to attribute this feature to the parent language. We thus face a definite succession of events in the period between Primitive Indo-European and Primitive Germanic — a period to which we give the name *pre-Germanic:*

Primitive Indo-European: [t] a unit phoneme; word-accent on different syllables in different words:
*['bhra:te:r] 'brother' *[pə'te:r] 'father'
Pre-Germanic period:
first change: [t] becomes [θ]:
*['bra:θe:r] *[fa'θe:r]
second change: [θ] after unstressed syllabic becomes [d], presumably a voiced spirant:
*['bra:θe:r] *[fa'de:r]
third change: the accent is shifted to the first syllable of each word; this brings us to
Primitive Germanic *['bro:θer] *['fader].

In a similar way, the correspondences reveal the pre-history of each branch of the Indo-European family. Thus, in the case of Latin *cauda* and *cōda* 'tail,' the Lithuanian word ['kuodas] 'tuft' probably represents the same form of the parent speech; if so, then, in the light of other correspondences, in which Lithuanian [uo] and Latin [o:] appear side by side, we may take *cōda* to be the older of the two Latin forms, and *cauda* to be a hyper-urban (over-elegant) variant (§ 18.4).

Our Primitive Indo-European reconstructions are not subject to any check by means of earlier recorded or reconstructed forms. In the last decades, to be sure, it has been ascertained that the Hittite language, known to us from records in cuneiform writing from 1400 B.C. onward, is distantly related to Indo-European. Accordingly, it has been possible to uncover a few features of a Primitive Indo-Hittite parent language — that is, to trace the earlier history of a few of the features of Primitive Indo-European.

18. 8. The comparative method tells us, in principle, nothing about the acoustic shape of reconstructed forms; it identifies the phonemes in reconstructed forms merely as recurrent units. The Indonesian languages show us a striking example of this. Each language has only a few phonemes of the types [d, g, l, r], but the variety of the correspondences assures us of a larger number of phonemes in the parent language. The acoustic character of these phonemes can only be guessed at; the symbols by which we represent them are merely labels for correspondences. It is worth noticing that we have older written records for none of these languages except Javanese; this in no way affects the application of the comparative method. The eight normal types of correspondence will appear sufficiently if we consider three languages: Tagalog (on the island of Luzon in the Philippines), Javanese, and Batak (on the island of Sumatra). In the following examples the consonant under discussion appears in the middle of the word.

		Tagalog	Javanese	Batak	Primitive Indonesian
(1)		l	l	l	l
	'choose'	'pi:liʔ	pilik	pili	*pilik
(2)		l	r	r	L
	'lack'	'ku:laŋ	kuraŋ	huraŋ	*kuLaŋ
(3)		l	r	g	g
	'nose'	i'luŋ	iruŋ	iguŋ	*iguŋ
(4)		l	ᴅ	d	ᴅ
	'desire'	'hi:lam	iᴅam	idam	*hiᴅam¹
(5)		r	d	d	d
	'point out'	'tu:ruʔ	tuduk	tudu	*tuduk
(6)		r	d	d	d
	'spur'	'ta:riʔ	tadi	tadi	*tadi
(7)		g	g	g	g
	'sago'	'sa:gu	sagu	sagu	*tagu ²
(8)		g	zero	r	ɣ
	'addled'	bu'guk	vuʔ	buruk	*buɣuk

18. 9. The comparative method assumes that each branch or language bears independent witness to the forms of the parent language, and that identities or correspondences among the related languages reveal features of the parent speech. This is the same thing as assuming, firstly, that the parent community was completely uniform as to language, and, secondly, that this parent community split suddenly and sharply into two or more daughter communities, which lost all contact with each other.

¹ Javanese [ᴅ] is a domal stop, distinct from the dental [d]. The Tagalog word means 'pain, smart.' The Batak form here given is not listed for the Toba dialect, from which our other examples are taken, but it occurs in the Dairi dialect.
² The Tagalog form means 'exudation'; in poetic use, also 'sap.'

Often enough, the comparative method assumes successive splittings of this sort in the history of a language. It assumes that Germanic split off neatly from Primitive Indo-European. After this split, any change in Germanic was independent of changes in the sister languages, and any resemblance between Germanic and the sister languages betokens a common inheritance. The differences between Primitive Indo-European and Primitive Germanic are due to changes which occurred during the *pre-Germanic* period. In exactly the same way, the comparative method interprets the special similarities among the West Germanic languages (in contrast with Scandinavian and Gothic) by saying that a West Germanic community split off, neatly and suddenly, from the uniform Primitive Germanic parent community. After this splitting off comes a pre-West-Germanic period, during which there arose the differences that characterize Primitive West Germanic. Again, on the basis of peculiarities common to English and Frisian (such as, especially, the [ɛ, e] for Primitive West Germanic [a], which we noticed above), we may speak of a pre-Anglo-Frisian period, during which there occurred the changes which led to Primitive Anglo-Frisian. Upon this there followed a pre-English period, which leads to the forms that appear in our earliest records of English. Thus, the comparative method reconstructs uniform parent languages existing at points in time, and deduces the changes which took place after each such parent language split, up to the next following parent language or recorded language. The comparative method thus shows us the ancestry of languages in the form of a family-tree, with successive branchings: the points at which branches separate are designated by the word *primitive;* the branches between the points are designated by the prefix *pre-*, and represent periods of linguistic change (Figure 1).

18. 10. The earlier students of Indo-European did not realize that the family-tree diagram was merely a statement of their method; they accepted the uniform parent languages and their sudden and clear-cut splitting, as historical realities.

In actual observation, however, no speech-community is ever quite uniform (§ 3.3). When we describe a language, we may ignore the lack of uniformity by confining ourselves to some arbitrarily chosen type of speech and leaving the other varieties for later discussion, but in studying linguistic change we cannot do this, because all changes are sure to appear at first in the shape of variant features.

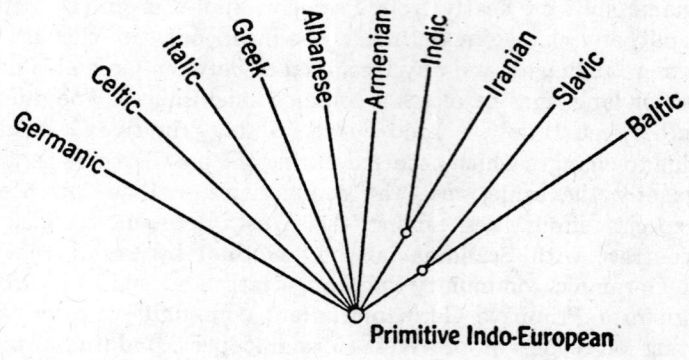

FIGURE 1. (Above) Family-tree diagram of the relationship of the Indo-European languages. (Below) Part of a family-tree diagram, showing the epochs in the history of English.

At times, to be sure, history shows us a sudden cleavage, such as is assumed by the comparative method. A cleavage of this sort occurs when part of a community emigrates. After the Angles, Saxons, and Jutes settled in Britain, they were fairly well cut off from their fellows who remained on the Continent; from that

THE COMPARATIVE METHOD

time on, the English language developed independently, and any resemblance between English and the continental dialects of West Germanic can be taken, in the ordinary case, as evidence for a feature that existed before the emigration of the English. When the Gipsies, in the Middle Ages, started from northwestern India on their endless migration, the changes in their language, from that time on, must have been independent of whatever linguistic changes occurred in their former home.

A less common case of clear-cut division of a speech-community,

FIGURE 2. Eastern Europe: the splitting of speech-areas by invasion. Latin, once a unit, was split, in the early Middle Ages, by the intrusion of Slavic. In the ninth century this area, in turn, was split by the intrusion of Hungarian.

is splitting by the intrusion of a foreign community. Under the Roman Empire, Latin was spoken over a solid area from Italy to the Black Sea. In the early Middle Ages, Slavs came in from the north and settled so as to cut this area completely in two: since that time, the development of Roumanian, in the east, has gone on independently of the development of the other Romance languages, and a feature common to both Roumanian and the western Romance languages is presumably guaranteed as Latin. In the ninth century, the great Slavic area in turn suffered a similar split, for the Magyars (Hungarians), coming from the east, settled so as to cut the Slavic area into a northern and a southern part (see Figure 2). Since that time, accordingly, the changes in South Slavic (Slovene, Serbian, Bulgarian) have been independent of those in the northern area of Slavic, and any common features of the two areas presumably date from before the split.

Such clear-cut splitting, however, is not usual. The differences among the Romance languages of the western area are evidently not due to geographic separation or to the intrusion of foreign speech-communities. Aside from English and from Icelandic, the same holds good of the Germanic languages, including the sharply defined difference between West Germanic and Scandinavian, which border on each other in the Jutland peninsula. Evidently some other historical factor or factors beside sudden separation may create several speech-communities out of one, and in this case we have no guarantee that all changes after a certain moment are independent, and therefore no guarantee that features common to the daughter languages were present in the parent language. A feature common, let us say, to French and Italian, or to Dutch-German and Danish, may be due to a common change which occurred after some of the differences were already in existence.

18. 11. Since the comparative method does not allow for varieties within the parent language or for common changes in related languages, it will carry us only a certain distance. Suppose, for instance, that within the parent language there was some dialectal difference: this dialectal difference will be reflected as an irreconcilable difference in the related languages. Thus, certain of the inflectional suffixes of nouns contain an [m] in Germanic and Balto-Slavic, but a [bh] in the other Indo-European languages, and there is no parallel for any such phonetic correspondence.

THE COMPARATIVE METHOD 315

(a) Primitive Indo-European *[-mis], instrumental plural: Gothic ['wulfam] 'to, by wolves,'

Primitive Indo-European *[-mi:s], instrumental plural: Lithuanian [nakti'mis] 'by nights,' Old Bulgarian [nɔʃtɪmi],

Primitive Indo-European *[-mos], dative-ablative plural: Lithuanian [vil'kams] 'to wolves,' Old Bulgarian [vlkomʊ],

(b) Primitive Indo-European *[-bhis], instrumental plural: Sanskrit [pad'bhih] 'by feet,' Old Irish ['ferav] 'by men,'

Primitive Indo-European *[-bhjos], dative-ablative plural: Sanskrit [pad'bhjah] 'to, from the feet,'

Primitive Indo-European *[-bhos], dative-ablative plural: Latin ['pedibus] 'to, from the feet,' Old Celtic [ma:trebo] 'to the mothers.'

In cases like these, the comparative method does not show us the form of the parent speech (which is defined as a uniform language), but shows us irreconcilably different forms, whose relation, as alternants or as dialectal variants, it does not reveal. Yet these cases are very many.

On the other hand, if, like the older scholars, we insist that the discrepancy is due to a common change in the history of Germanic and Balto-Slavic, then, under the assumptions of the comparative method, we must say that these two branches had a period of common development: we must postulate a Primitive Balto-Slavo-Germanic speech-community, which split off from Primitive Indo-European, and in turn split into Germanic and Balto-Slavic. If we do this, however, we are at once involved in contradictions, because of other, discordant but overlapping, resemblances. Thus, Balto-Slavic agrees with Indo-Iranian, Armenian, and Albanese, in showing sibilants in certain forms where the other languages have velars, as in the word for 'hundred':

Sanskrit [ça'tam], Avestan [satəm], Lithuanian ['ʃimtas], but Greek [he-ka'ton], Latin ['kentum], Old Irish [ke:ð], Primitive Indo-European *[km'tom]. We suppose that the parent language in such cases had palatalized velar stops.

Likewise, where the four branches just named have velar stops, there the others, in many forms, have combinations of velars with a labial element, or apparent modifications of these; we suppose that the parent language had labialized velar stops, as in the interrogative substitute stem:

Sanskrit [kah] 'who?' Lithuanian [kas], Old Bulgarian [kʊ-to], but Greek ['po-then] 'from where?' Latin [kwo:] 'by whom, by what?' Gothic [hwas] 'who?' Primitive Indo-European *[k^{w}os] 'who?' and derivatives.

Only in a limited number of cases do the two sets of languages agree in having plain velar stops. Accordingly, many scholars suppose that the earliest traceable division of the Primitive Indo-European unity was into a western group of so-called "*centum*-languages" and an eastern group of "*satem*-languages," although, to be sure, Tocharian, in Central Asia, belonged to the former group. This division, it will be seen, clashes with any explanation that supposes Balto-Slavic and Germanic to have had a common period of special development.

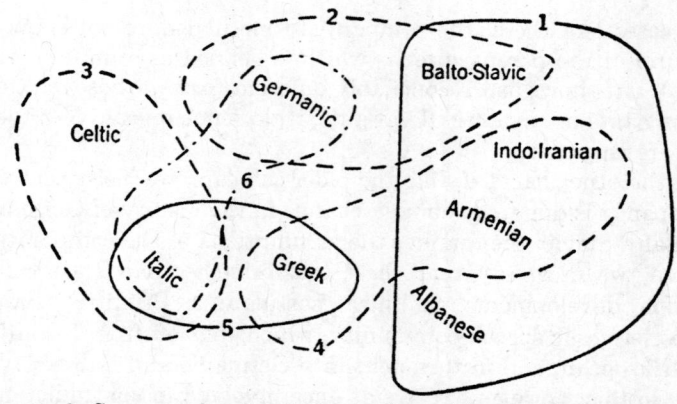

FIGURE 3. Some overlapping features of special resemblance among the Indo-European languages, conflicting with the family-tree diagram. — Adapted from Schrader.
1. Sibilants for velars in certain forms.
2. Case-endings with [m] for [bh].
3. Passive-voice endings with [r].
4. Prefix ['e-] in past tenses.
5. Feminine nouns with masculine suffixes.
6. Perfect tense used as general past tense.

Again, we find special resemblances between Germanic and Italic, as, for instance, in the formation and use of the past-tense verb, or in some features of vocabulary (*goat* : Latin *haedus;* Gothic *gamains* : Latin *communis* 'common'). These, too, conflict with the special resemblances between Germanic and Balto-Slavic. In the same way, Italic on the one side shares peculiarities with Celtic and on the other side with Greek (Figure 3).

THE COMPARATIVE METHOD

18. 12. As more and more of these resemblances were revealed, the older scholars, who insisted upon the family-tree diagram, faced an insoluble problem. Whichever special resemblances one took as evidence for closer relationships, there remained others, inconsistent with these, which could be explained only by an entirely different diagram. The decision, moreover, was too important to be evaded, since in each case it profoundly altered the value of resemblances. If Germanic and Balto-Slavic, for instance, have passed through a period of common development, then any agreement between them guarantees nothing about Primitive Indo-European, but if they have not passed through a period of common development, then such an agreement, on the family-tree principle, is practically certain evidence for a trait of Primitive Indo-European.

The reason for these contradictions was pointed out in 1872 by Johannes Schmidt (1843-1901), in a famous essay on the interrelationship of the Indo-European languages. Schmidt showed that special resemblances can be found for any two branches of Indo-European, and that these special resemblances are most numerous in the case of branches which lie geographically nearest each other. Johannes Schmidt accounted for this by the so-called *wave-hypothesis*. Different linguistic changes may spread, like waves, over a speech-area, and each change may be carried out over a part of the area that does not coincide with the part covered by an earlier change. The result of successive waves will be a network of isoglosses (§ 3.6). Adjacent districts will resemble each other most; in whatever direction one travels, differences will increase with distance, as one crosses more and more isogloss-lines. This, indeed, is the picture presented by the local dialects in the areas we can observe. Now, let us suppose that among a series of adjacent dialects, which, to consider only one dimension, we shall designate as A, B, C, D, E, F, G, . . . X, one dialect, say F, gains a political, commercial, or other predominance of some sort, so that its neighbors in either direction, first E and G, then D and H, and then even C and I, J, K, give up their peculiarities and in time come to speak only the central dialect F. When this has happened, F borders on B and L, dialects from which it differs sharply enough to produce clear-cut language boundaries; yet the resemblance between F and B will be greater than that between F and A, and, similarly, among L, M, N, . . . X, the dialects nearest to F will show a greater resemblance to F, in spite of the clearly marked boundary, than will the more distant dialects. The presentation of these factors became known as the *wave-theory*, in contradistinction to the older *family-tree theory* of linguistic relationship. Today we view the wave process and the splitting process merely as two types — perhaps the principal types — of historical processes that lead to linguistic differentiation.

18. 13. The comparative method, then, — our only method for the reconstruction of prehistoric language, — would work accurately for absolutely uniform speech-communities and sudden, sharp cleavages. Since these presuppositions are never fully realized, the comparative method cannot claim to picture the historical process. Where the reconstruction works smoothly, as in the Indo-European word for *father*, or in observations of less ambitious scope (such as, say, reconstructions of Primitive Romance or Primitive Germanic), there we are assured of the structural features of a speech-form in the parent language. Wherever the comparison is at all ambitious as to the reach of time or the breadth of the area, it will reveal incommensurable forms and partial similarities that cannot be reconciled with the family-tree diagram. The comparative method can work only on the assumption of a uniform parent language, but the incommensurable forms (such as *[-mis] and *[-bhis] as instrumental plural case endings in Primitive Indo-European) show us that this assumption is not justified. The comparative method presupposes clear-cut splitting off of successive branches, but the inconsistent partial similarities show us that later changes may spread across the isoglosses left by earlier changes; that resemblance between neighboring languages may be due to the disappearance of intermediate dialects (wave-theory); and that languages already in some respects differentiated may make like changes.

Sometimes additional facts help us to a decision. Thus, the adjective Sanskrit ['pi:va:] 'fat,' Greek ['pi:o:n] occurs only in Indo-Iranian and Greek, but its existence in Primitive Indo-European is guaranteed by the irregular formation of the feminine form, Sanskrit ['pi:vari:], Greek ['pi:ejra]; neither language formed new feminines in this way. On the other hand, the Germanic word *hemp*, Old English ['henep], Middle Dutch ['hannep], and so on, corresponds to Greek ['kannabis]; nevertheless, we learn from Herodotus (fifth century B.C.) that hemp was known to the Greeks only as a foreign plant, in Thrace and Scythia: the word came into Greek (and thence into Latin) and into Germanic (and thence, presumably, into Slavic) from some other language — very likely from a Finno-Ugrian dialect — at some time before the pre-Germanic changes of [k] to [h] and of [b] to [p]. But for this piece of chance information, the correspondence of the Greek and Germanic forms would have led us to attribute this word to Primitive Indo-European.

18. 14. The reconstruction of ancient speech-forms throws some light upon non-linguistic conditions of early times. If we consider, for instance, that the composition of our earliest Indic records can scarcely be placed later than 1200 B.C., or that of the Homeric poems later than 800 B.C., we are bound to place our reconstructed Primitive Indo-European forms at least a thousand years earlier than these dates. We can thus trace the history of language, often in minute detail, much farther back than that of any other of a people's institutions. Unfortunately, we cannot transfer our knowledge to the latter field, especially as the meanings of speech-forms are largely uncertain. We do not know where Primitive Indo-European was spoken, or by what manner of people; we cannot link the Primitive Indo-European speech-forms to any particular type of prehistoric objects.

The noun and the verb *snow* appear so generally in the Indo-European languages that we can exclude India from the range of possible dwellings of the Primitive Indo-European community. The names of plants, even where there is phonetic agreement, differ as to meaning; thus, Latin ['fa:gus], Old English [bo:k] mean 'beech-tree,' but Greek [phe:'gos] means a kind of oak. Similar divergences of meaning appear in other plant-names, such as our words *tree*, *birch*, *withe* (German *Weide* 'willow'), *oak*, *corn*, and the types of Latin *salix* 'willow,' *quercus* 'oak,' *hordeum* 'barley' (cognate with German *Gerste*), Sanskrit ['javah] 'barley.' The type of Latin *glans* 'acorn' occurs with the same meaning in Greek, Armenian, and Balto-Slavic.

Among animal-names, *cow*, Sanskrit [ga:wh], Greek ['bows], Latin [bo:s], Old Irish [bo:], is uniformly attested and guaranteed by irregularities of form. Other designations of animals appear in only part of the territory; thus, *goat*, as we have seen, is confined to Germanic and Italic; the type Latin *caper*: Old Norse *hafr* 'goat' occurs also in Celtic; the type Sanskrit [a'jah], Lithuanian [oˇʒi:s] is confined to these two languages; and the type of Greek ['ajks] appears also in Armenian and perhaps in Iranian. Other animals for which we have one or more equations covering part of the Indo-European territory, are horse, dog, sheep (the word *wool* is certainly of Primitive Indo-European age), pig, wolf, bear, stag, otter, beaver, goose, duck, thrush, crane, eagle, fly, bee (with *mead*, which originally meant 'honey'), snake, worm, fish. The types of our *milk* and of Latin *lac* 'milk' are fairly widespread, as are the word *yoke* and the types of our *wheel* and German *Rad* 'wheel,' and of *axle*. We may conclude that cattle were domesticated and the wagon in use, but the other animal-names do not guarantee domestication.

Verbs for weaving, sewing, and other processes of work are widespread, but vague or variable in meaning. The numbers apparently included 'hundred' but not 'thousand.' Among terms of relationship, those for a woman's relatives by marriage ('husband's brother,' 'husband's sister,' and so on) show widespread agreement, but not those for a man's relatives by marriage; one concludes that the wife became part of the husband's family, which lived in a large patriarchal group. The various languages furnish several equations for names of tools and for the metals gold, silver, and bronze (or copper). Several of these, however, are loan-words of the type of *hemp;* so certainly Greek ['pelekus] 'axe,' Sanskrit [para'çuh] is connected with Assyrian [pilakku], and our *axe* and *silver* are ancient loan-words. Accordingly, scholars place the Primitive Indo-European community into the Late Stone Age.

CHAPTER 19

DIALECT GEOGRAPHY

19. 1. The comparative method, with its assumption of uniform parent languages and sudden, definitive cleavage, has the virtue of showing up a residue of forms that cannot be explained on this assumption. The conflicting large-scale isoglosses in the Indo-European area, for instance, show us that the branches of the Indo-European family did not arise by the sudden breaking up of an absolutely uniform parent community (§ 18.11, Figure 3). We may say that the parent community was dialectally differentiated before the break-up, or that after the break-up various sets of the daughter communities remained in communication; both statements amount to saying that areas or parts of areas which already differ in some respects may still make changes in common. The result of successive changes, therefore, is a network of isoglosses over the total area. Accordingly, the study of local differentiations in a speech-area, *dialect geography*, supplements the use of the comparative method.

Local differences of speech within an area have never escaped notice, but their significance has only of late been appreciated. The eighteenth-century grammarians believed that the literary and upper-class standard language was older and more true to a standard of reason than the local speech-forms, which were due to the ignorance and carelessness of common people. Nevertheless, one noticed, in time, that local dialects preserved one or another ancient feature which no longer existed in the standard language. Toward the end of the eighteenth century there began to appear *dialect dictionaries*, which set forth the lexical peculiarities of non-standard speech.

The progress of historical linguistics showed that the standard language was by no means the oldest type, but had arisen, under particular historical conditions, from local dialects. Standard English, for instance, is the modern form not of literary Old English, but of the old local dialect of London which had become first a provincial and then a national standard language, absorbing, meanwhile, a good many forms from other local and provincial dialects. Opinion now turned to the other extreme. Because a local dialect preserved some forms that were extinct in the standard language, it was viewed as a survival, unchanged, of some ancient type; thus, we still hear it said that the speech of some remote locality is "pure Elizabethan English." Because the admixture of forms from other dialects had been observed only in the standard language, one jumped at the conclusion that local dialects were free from this admixture and, therefore, in a historical sense, more regular. At this stage, accordingly, we find *dialect grammars*, which show the relation of the sounds and inflections of a local dialect to those of some older stage of the language.

Investigation showed that every language had in many of its forms suffered displacements of structure, which were due to the admixture of forms from other dialects. Old English [f], for instance, normally appears as [f] in standard English, as in *father, foot, fill, five*, and so on, but in the words *vat* and *vixen*, from Old English [fɛt] and ['fyksen] 'female fox,' it appears as [v], evidently because these forms are admixtures from a dialect which had changed initial [f] to [v]; and, indeed, this initial [v] appears regularly in some southern English dialects (Wiltshire, Dorset, Somerset, Devon), in forms like ['vaðə, vut, vil, vajv]. Some students hoped, therefore, to find in local dialects the phonemic regularity (that is, adherence to older patterns) that was broken in the standard language. In 1876 a German scholar, Georg Wenker, began, with this end in view, to survey the local dialects in the Rhine country round Düsseldorf; later he extended his survey to cover a wider area, and published, in 1881, six maps as a first instalment of a *dialect atlas* of northern and central Germany. He then gave up this plan in favor of a survey which was to cover the whole German Empire. With government aid, Wenker got forty test-sentences translated, largely by schoolmasters, into more than forty-thousand German local dialects. Thus it was possible to mark the different local varieties of any one feature on a map, which would then show the geographic distribution. Since 1926 these maps, on a reduced scale, have been appearing in print, under the editorship of F. Wrede.

The result, apparent from the very start, of Wenker's study, was a surprise: the local dialects were no more consistent than the standard language in their relation to older speech-forms. *Dialect geography* only confirmed the conclusion of comparative study, namely, that different linguistic changes cover different portions of an area. The new approach yielded, however, a close-range view of the network of isoglosses.

19. 2. At present, then, we have three principal forms of dialect study. The oldest is lexical. At first, the dialect dictionaries included only the forms and meanings which differed from standard usage. This criterion, of course, is irrelevant. Today we expect a dictionary of a local dialect to give all the words that are current in non-standard speech, with phonetic accuracy and with reasonable care in the definition of meanings. A dialect dictionary for a whole province or area is a much bigger undertaking. It should give a phonemic scheme for each local type of speech, and therefore can hardly be separated from a phonologic study. We expect a statement of the geographic area in which every form is current, but this statement can be given far better in the form of a map.

Grammars of local dialects largely confine themselves to stating the correspondence of the phonemes and of the inflectional forms with those of an older stage of the language. The modern demand would be rather for a description such as one might make of any language: phonology, syntax, and morphology, together with copious texts. The history of the forms can be told only in connection with that of the area as a whole, since every feature has been changed or spared only in so far as some wave of change has reached or failed to reach the speakers of the local dialect. The grammar of a whole area represents, again, a large undertaking. The first work of this kind, the single-handed performance of a man of the people, was the Bavarian grammar, published in 1821, of Johann Andreas Schmeller (1785–1852); it is still unsurpassed. For English, we have the phonology of the English dialects in the fifth volume of Ellis's *Early English Pronunciation*, and Joseph Wright's grammar, published in connection with his *English Dialect Dictionary*. Here too, of course, we demand a statement of the topographic extent of each feature, and this, again, can be more clearly given on a map.

Except for the complete and organized description of a single local dialect, then, the map of distribution is the clearest and most compact form of statement. The dialect atlas, a set of such maps, allows us to compare the distributions of different features by comparing the different maps; as a practical help for this comparison, the German atlas provides with each map a loose transparent sheet reproducing the principal isoglosses or other marks of the map. Aside from the self-understood demands of accuracy and consistency, the value of a map depends very largely on the completeness with which the local dialects are registered: the finer the network, the more complete is the tale. In order to record and estimate a local form, however, we need to know its structural pattern in terms of the phonemic system of the local dialect. Furthermore, several variant pronunciations or grammatical or lexical types may be current, with or without a difference of denotation, in a local dialect, and these variants may be decidedly relevant to the history of the change which produced them. Finally, to reproduce the whole grammar and lexicon would require so vast a number of maps that even a very large atlas can only give samples of distribution; we ask for as many maps as possible. In view of all this, a dialect atlas is a tremendous undertaking, and in practice is likely to fall short in one or another respect. The sentences on which the German atlas is based, were written down in ordinary German orthography by schoolmasters and other linguistically untrained persons; the material does not extend to great parts of the Dutch-German area, such as the Netherlands and Belgium, Switzerland, Austria, Baltic German, Yiddish, Transylvanian, and the other speech-islands. The data are largely phonologic, since the informant, except for striking lexical or grammatical differences, would merely transcribe the forms into a spelling that represented the local pronunciation; yet the phonologic aspect is precisely what will be least clear in such a transcription. The data for the French atlas were collected by a trained phonetician, Edmond Edmont; one man, of course, could visit only a limited number of localities and stay but a short time in each. Accordingly, the maps register only something over six-hundred points in the French area (France and adjoining strips in Belgium, Switzerland, and Italy), and the forms were collected in each case from a single informant by means of a questionnaire of some two-thousand words and phrases. However fine his ear, Edmont could not know the phonologic pattern of each local dialect. The results for both phonetics and lexicon are more copious than those of the German atlas, but the looseness of the network and the lack of whole sentences are drawbacks. The atlas itself was planned and worked out by Jules Gilliéron (1854–1926), and has appeared in full (1896–1908), together with a supplement for Corsica. An Italian atlas, by K. Jaberg and J. Jud, has been appearing since 1928; it tries for great accuracy and pays close attention to meanings. Smaller atlases exist for Swabia (by H. Fischer, 28 maps, published, in connection with a careful treatise, in 1895), for Denmark (by V. Bennicke and M. Kristensen, 1898–1912), for Roumania (by G. Weigand, 1909), for Catalonia (by A. Griera, 1923 ff.), and for Brittany (by P. Le Roux, 1924 ff.). Other atlases are in preparation, including a survey of New England under the direction of H. Kurath. A single-handed observer can cover a small part of an area, as did Karl Haag in his study of a district in Southern Swabia (1898); or else, he may restrict himself to one or two features but follow them over a larger district, as did G. G. Kloeke in his study of the vowel phonemes of the words *mouse* and *house* in the Netherlands and Belgium (1927).

Needless to say, the map or atlas may be accompanied by a treatise that interprets the facts or accounts for their origin, as in the publications of Fischer, Haag, and Kloeke. The great atlases have given rise to many studies, such as, notably, Gilliéron's various books and essays, based on the French atlas, and a whole series of studies, under the editorship of F. Wrede, by workers on the German maps.

19. 3. Our knowledge is confined, so far, to the conditions that prevail in long-settled areas. In these, there is no question of uniformity over any sizable district. Every village, or, at most, every cluster of two or three villages, has its local peculiarities of speech. In general, it presents a unique combination of forms, each of which also appears, in other combinations, in some of the neighboring localities. On the map, accordingly, each settlement or small cluster of settlements will be cut off from each of its neighbors by one or more isoglosses. As an example, Figure 4, reproducing a small portion of Haag's map, shows the Swabian village of Bubsheim (about ten miles east by southeast of Rottweil). The nearest neighbors, within a distance of less than five miles, are all separated from Bubsheim by isoglosses; only two of these neighbors agree with each other as to all of the features that were studied by Haag. The appended table (Figure 5) shows under the name of each locality, the forms in which its dialect differs from the forms of Bubsheim, which are given in the first column; where no form is given, the dialect agrees with Bubsheim. The number before each form is the same as the number attached to the corresponding isogloss in Figure 4.

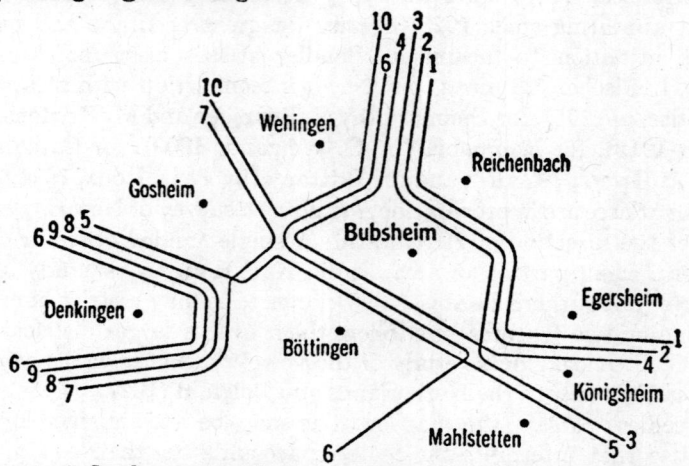

FIGURE 4. Isoglosses around the German village of Bubsheim (Swabia), after Haag. The village of Denkingen has been added, with a few of its isoglosses, in order to show the recurrence of Line 6.

If we followed the further course of these isoglosses, we should find them running in various directions and dividing the territory into portions of differing size. The isoglosses numbered 1, 2, and 3 in our Figures, cut boldly across the German area; Bubsheim agrees, as to these features, with the south and southwest. In contrast with these important lines, others, such as our number 9, surround only a small district: the form ['trũ:ke] 'drunk,' which is listed for Denkingen, is spoken only in a small patch of settlements. The isogloss we have numbered as 6 appears on our map as two lines; these are really parts of an irregularly winding line: Denkingen agrees with Bubsheim as to the vowel of the verb *mow*, although the intermediate villages speak differently. We find even isoglosses which divide a town into two parts; thus, along the lower Rhine, just southwest of Duisburg, the town of Kaldenhausen is cut through by a bundle of isoglosses: the eastern and western portions of the town speak different dialects.

The reason for this intense local differentiation is evidently to be sought in the principle of density (§ 3.4). Every speaker is constantly adapting his speech-habits to those of his interlocutors;

DIALECT GEOGRAPHY

Bubsheim	Reichenbach, Egesheim	Königsheim	Mahlstetten	Böttingen	Denkingen	Gosheim	Wehingen
1. ofə 'stove'	oːfə						
2. uffi 'up'	nuff						
3. tsiːt 'time'	tsejt	tsejt					
4. bɑ̃w 'bean'		bɔ̃ː	bɔ̃ː	bɔ̃ː	bɔ̃ː	bɔ̃ː	bɔ̃ː
5. ɛ̃ːt 'end'			ɐ̃jt	ɐ̃jt	ajt		
6. mɛːjə 'to mow'				mɐjə		mɐjə	mɐjə
7. farb 'color'					faːrb	faːrb	
8. alt 'old'					aːlt		
9. truŋkə 'drunk'					trũːkə		
10. gɑ̃w 'to go'							gɔ̃ː

FIGURE 5. Ten speech-forms in the local dialect of Bubsheim in Swabia, with the divergent forms of neighboring dialects. Where no form is given, the dialect agrees with Bubsheim. The numbers are those of the isoglosses on the map, Figure 4. — After Haag.

he gives up forms he has been using, adopts new ones, and, perhaps oftenest of all, changes the frequency of speech-forms without entirely abandoning any old ones or accepting any that are really new to him. The inhabitants of a settlement, village, or town, however, talk much more to each other than to persons who live elsewhere. When any innovation in the way of speaking spreads over a district, the limit of this spread is sure to be along some line of weakness in the network of oral communication, and these lines of weakness, in so far as they are topographical lines, are the boundaries between towns, villages, and settlements.

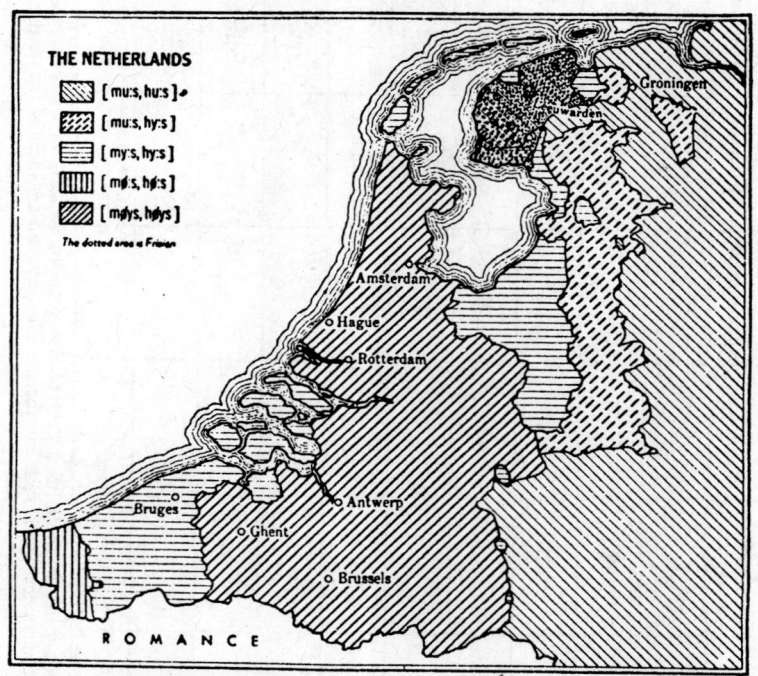

FIGURE 6. Distribution of syllabic sounds in the words *mouse* and *house* in the Netherlands. — After Kloeke.

19. 4. Isoglosses for different forms rarely coincide along their whole extent. Almost every feature of phonetics, lexicon, or grammar has its own area of prevalence — is bounded by its own isogloss. The obvious conclusion has been well stated in the form of a maxim: *Every word has its own history.*

DIALECT GEOGRAPHY

The words *mouse* and *house* had in early Germanic the same vowel phoneme, a long [u:]. Some modern dialects — for instance, some Scotch dialects of English — preserve this sound apparently unchanged. Others have changed it, but keep the ancient structure, in the sense that these two words still have the same syllabic phoneme; this is the case in standard English and in standard German, where both words have [aw], and in standard Dutch, where both have [øɥ]. In the study above referred to, Kloeke traces the syllabics of these two words through the present-day local dialects of Belgium and the Netherlands. Our Figure 6 shows Kloeke's map on a reduced scale.

An eastern area, as the map shows, has preserved the Primitive Germanic vowel [u:] in both words: [mu:s, hu:s].

Several patches, of various size, speak [y:] in both words: [my:s, hy:s].

A district in the extreme west speaks [ø:] in both words: [mø:s, hø:s].

A great central area speaks a diphthong of the type [øɥ] in both words: [møɥs, høɥs]. Since this is the standard Dutch-Flemish pronunciation, it prevails in the usage of standard speakers also in the other districts, but this fact is not indicated on the map.

In these last three districts, then, the sound is no longer that of Primitive Germanic and medieval Dutch, but the structure of our two words is unchanged, in so far as they still agree in their syllabic phoneme.

Our map shows, however, three fair-sized districts which speak [u:] in the word *mouse*, but [y:] in the word *house;* hence, inconsistently, [mu:s, hy:s]. In these districts the structural relation of the two words has undergone a change: they no longer agree as to their syllabic phoneme.

We see, then, that the isogloss which separates [mu:s] from [my:s] does not coincide with the isogloss which separates [hu:s] from [hy:s]. Of the two words, *mouse* has preserved the ancient vowel over a larger territory than *house*. Doubtless a study of other words which contained [u:] in medieval times, would show us still other distributions of [u:] and the other sounds, distributions which would agree only in part with those of *mouse* and *house*.

At some time in the Middle Ages, the habit of pronouncing [y:] instead of the hitherto prevalent [u:] must have originated in some cultural center — perhaps in Flanders — and spread from there over a large part of the area on our map, including the central district which today speaks a diphthong. On the coast at the north of the Frisian area there is a Dutch-speaking district known as *het Bilt*, which was diked in and settled under the leadership of Hollanders at the beginning of the sixteenth century, and, as the map shows, uses the [y:]-pronunciation. It is [y:], moreover, and not the old [u:], that appears in the loan-words which in the early modern period passed from Dutch into the more easterly (Low German) dialects of the Dutch-German area, and into foreign languages, such as Russian and Javanese. The Dutch that was carried to the colonies, such as the Creole Dutch of the Virgin Islands, spoke [y:]. The spellings in written documents and the evidence of poets' rimes confirm this: the [y:]-pronunciation spread abroad with the cultural prestige of the great coastal cities of Holland in the sixteenth and seventeenth centuries.

This wave of cultural expansion was checked in the eastern part of our district, where it conflicted with the expansion of another and similar cultural area, that of the North German Hanseatic cities. Our isoglosses of *mouse* and *house*, and doubtless many others, are results of the varying balance of these two cultural forces. Whoever was impressed by the Hollandish official or merchant, learned to speak [y:]; whoever saw his superiors in the Hanseatic upper class, retained the old [u:]. The part of the population which made no pretensions to elegance, must also have long retained the [u:], but in the course of time the [y:] filtered down even to this class. This process is still going on: in parts of the area where [u:] still prevails — both in the district of [mu:s, hu:s] and in the district of [mu:s, hy:s] — the peasant, when he is on his good behavior, speaks [y:] in words where his everyday speech has [u:]. This flavor of the [y:]-variants appears strikingly in the shape of hyper-urbanisms: in using the elegant [y:], the speaker sometimes substitutes it where it is entirely out of place, saying, for instance, [vy:t] for [vu:t] 'foot,' a word in which neither older nor present-day upper-class Dutch ever spoke an [y:].

The word *house* will occur much oftener than the word *mouse* in official speech and in conversation with persons who represent the cultural center; *mouse* is more confined to homely and familiar situations. Accordingly, we find that the word *house* in the upper-class and central form with [y:] spread into districts where the word *mouse* has persisted in the old-fashioned form with [u:]. This shows us also that the Holland influence, and not the Hanseatic, was the innovator and aggressor; if the reverse had been the case, we should find districts where *house* had [u:] and *mouse* had [y:].

In the sixteenth and seventeenth centuries, even while the [y:]-pronunciation was making its conquests, there arose, it would seem in Antwerp, a still newer pronunciation with [øɥ] instead of the hitherto elegant [y:]. This new style spread to the Holland cities, and with this its fortune was made. The [øɥ]-pronunciation, as in standard Dutch *huis* [høɥs], *muis* [moɥs], is today the only truly urbane form. On our map, the area of this [øɥ] looks as if it had been laid on top of a former solid area of [y:], leaving only disconnected patches uncovered along the edge. This picture of disconnected patches at the periphery is characteristic of older styles, in language or in other activities, that have been superseded by some new central fashion. It is characteristic, too, that the more remote local dialects are taking up a feature, the [y:]-pronunciation, which in more central districts and in the more privileged class of speakers, has long ago been superseded by a still newer fashion.

19. 5. The map in our last example could not show the occurrence of the present-day standard Dutch-Flemish pronunciation with [øɥ] in the districts where it has not conquered the local dialects. To show this would be to cover our whole map with a dense and minute sprinkling of [øɥ]-forms, for the educated or socially better-placed persons in the whole area speak standard Dutch-Flemish.

The persistence of old features is easier to trace than the occurrence of new. The best data of dialect geography are furnished by *relic forms*, which attest some older feature of speech. In 1876, J. Winteler published what was perhaps the first adequate study of a single local dialect, a monograph on his native Swiss-German dialect of the settlement Kerenzen in the Canton of Glarus. In this study, Winteler mentions an archaic imperative form, [lɑx] 'let,' irregularly derived from the stem [lɑs-], and says that he is not certain that anyone still used it at the time of publication; most speakers, at any rate, already used the widespread and more regular form [lɑs] 'let.' A later observer, C. Streiff, writing in 1915, has not heard the old form; it has been totally replaced by [lɑs].

In the same way, Winteler quotes a verse in which the Glarus people are mocked for their use of the present-tense plural verb-

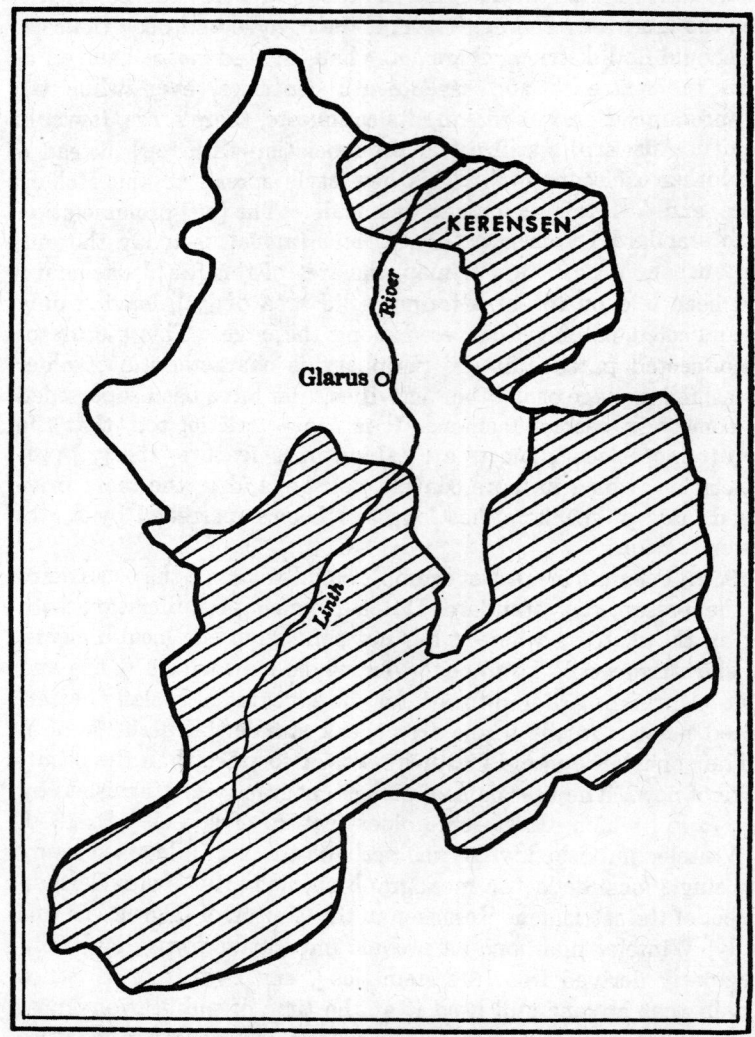

FIGURE 7. The Canton of Glarus, Switzerland. — In 1915 the shaded areas still used the provincial [hajd, wajd] as plurals of "have" and "want to"; the unshaded area used the general Swiss-German forms [hand, wand]. — After Streiff.

forms [hajd] '(we, ye, they) have' and [wajd] '(we, ye, they) want to,' forms which sounded offensively rustic to their neighbors, who used the more generally Swiss provincial forms [hand, wand]. Forty years later, Streiff reports a similar verse, in which the people of the central region of the canton (including the largest

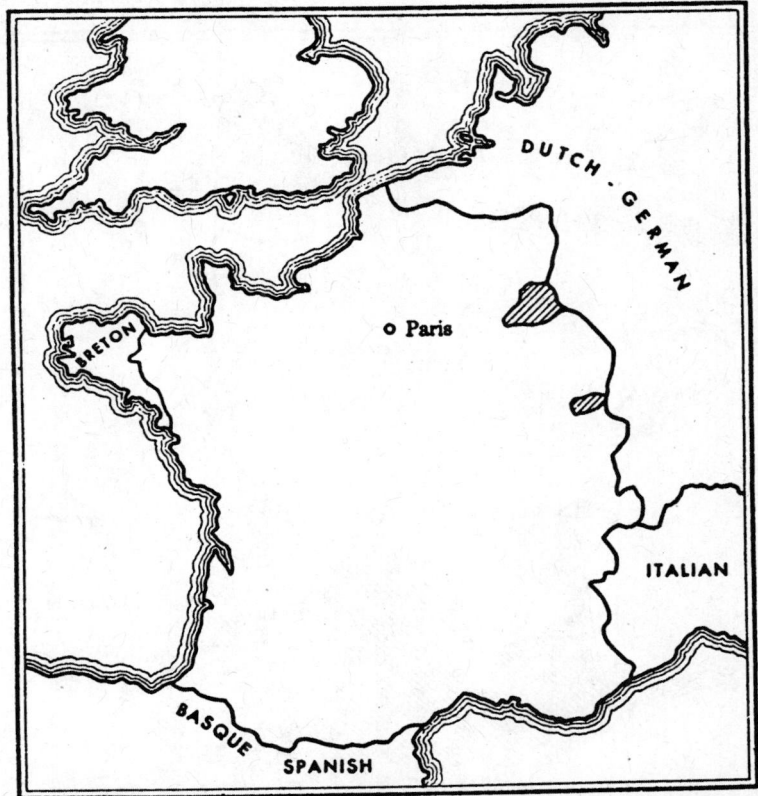

FIGURE 8. The French speech-area. — A discontinuous isogloss encloses the two marginal shaded areas in which reflexes of Latin *multum* "much, very" are still in use. — After Gamillscheg.

community and seat of government, the town of Glarus) mock the inhabitants of the outlying valleys for their use of these same forms, [hajd, wajd]. Our Figure 7, based on Streiff's statements, shows the distribution in 1915: the more urbane and widespread [hand, wand] prevail in the central district along the river Linth, which includes the capital, Glarus, and communicates freely with the city of Zurich (toward the northwest); the old rustic forms are used in the three more remote valleys, including the settlement of Kerenzen.

The relic form, as this example shows, has the best chance of survival in remote places, and therefore is likely to appear in

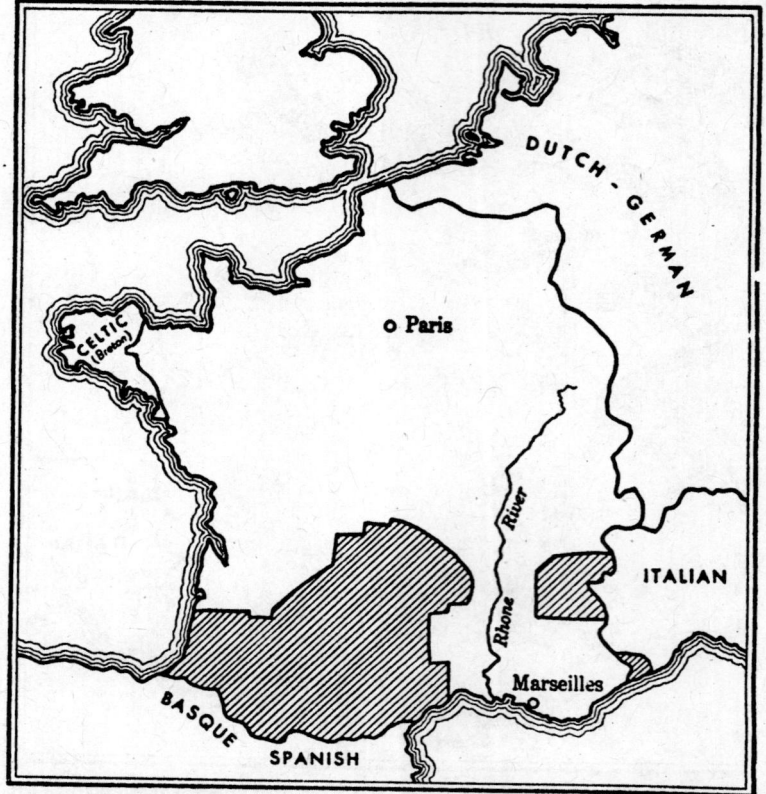

FIGURE 9. The French speech-area. — The unshaded district uses reflexes of Latin *fallit* in the meaning "it is necessary." The shaded areas use other forms. — After Jaberg.

small, detached areas. The Latin form *multum* 'much,' surviving, for instance, in Italian *molto* ['molto] and Spanish *mucho* ['mutʃo] 'much,' *muy* [muj] 'very,' has been replaced in nearly all of the French area by words like standard French *très* [tre] 'very,' a modern form of Latin *trans* 'through, beyond, exceeding,' and *beaucoup* [boku] 'very,' which represents a Latin **bonum colpum* 'a good blow or stroke.' Figure 8 shows the two detached marginal areas in which modern forms of Latin *multum* are still in use.

In Latin, the word *fallit* meant 'he, she, it deceives.' By way of a meaning 'it fails,' this word came to mean, in medieval French, 'it is lacking,' and from this there has developed the modern French use of *il faut* [i fo] 'it is necessary; one must.' This highly specialized development of meaning can hardly have occurred independently in more than one place; the prevalence of the modern locution in the greater part of the French area must be due to spread from a center, presumably Paris. Figure 9 shows us, in the unshaded district, the prevalence of phonetic equivalents of standard French *il faut* in local dialects. The shaded districts use other forms, principally reflexes of Latin *calet* 'it's hot.' It is evident that the modern form spread southward along the Rhône, which is a great highway of commerce. We see here how an isogloss running at right angles to a highway of communication, will not cross it with unchanged direction, but will swerve off, run parallel with the highway for a stretch, and then either cross it or, as in our example, reappear on the other side, and then run back before resuming its former direction. The bend or promontory of the isogloss shows us which of the two speech-forms has been spreading at the cost of the other.

19. 6. If we observe a set of relic forms that exhibit some one ancient feature, we get a striking illustration of the principle that each word has its own history. The Latin initial cluster [sk-] has taken on, in the French area, an initial [e-], a so-called *prothetic vowel*, as, for example, in the following four words with which our Figure 10 is concerned:

	LATIN		MODERN STANDARD FRENCH	
'ladder'	*scala*	['ska:la]	*échelle*	[eʃɛl]
'bowl'	*scutella*	[sku'tella]	*écuelle*	[ekɥɛl]
'write'	*scribere*	['skri:bere]	*écrire*	[ekri:r]
'school'	*schola*	['skola]	*école*	[ekɔl]

Our figure shows us six disconnected and, as to commerce, remote districts which still speak forms without the added vowel, such as [kwe:l] 'bowl,' in one or more of these four words. These districts include 55 of the 638 places that were observed by Edmont (§ 19.2). The districts are:

A. A fairly large area in Belgium, overlapping the political border of the French Republic at one point (Haybes, Department of the Ardennes), and covering 23 points of the Atlas.

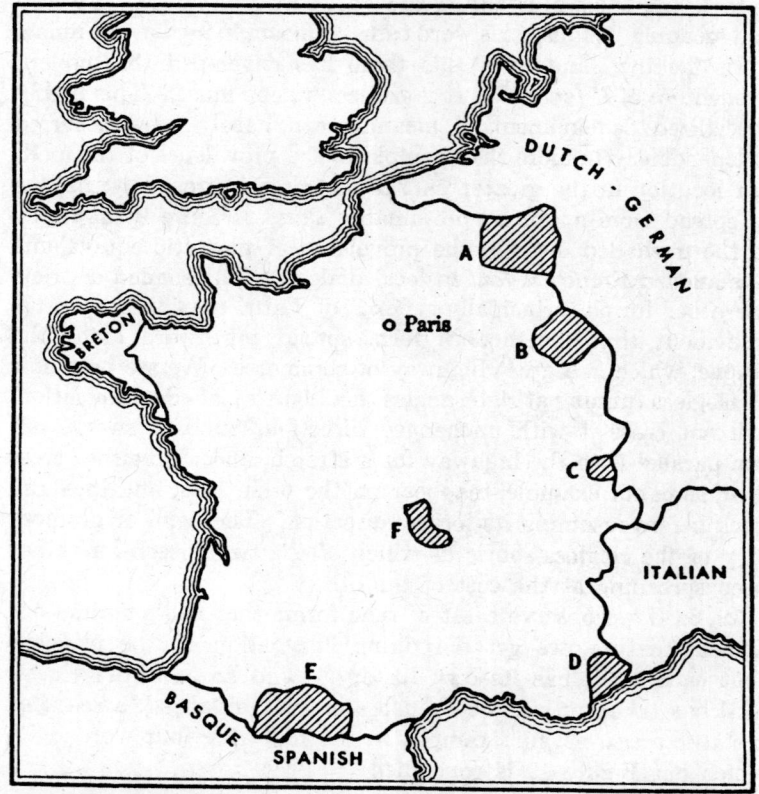

FIGURE 10. The French speech-area. — The shaded districts speak reflexes of Latin [sk-] without an added initial vowel. — After Jaberg.

B. A somewhat smaller area in the Departments of the Vosges and of Meurthe-et-Moselle, overlapping into Lorraine, 14 points.

C. The village of Bobi in Switzerland, 1 point.

D. Mentone and two other villages in the Department of Alpes-Maritimes on the Italian border, 3 points.

E. A fair-sized district along the Spanish border, in the Department of Hautes-Pyrénées, and overlapping into the neighboring Departments, 11 points.

F. A small interior district in the hill-country of the Auvergne, Departments of Haute-Loire and Puy-de-Dôme, 3 points.

Words in which forms without added vowel are still spoken	Number of places where forms without added vowel are still spoken						
	BY DISTRICTS						TOTAL
	A	B	C	D	E	F	
ladder, bowl, write, school	2						2
ladder, bowl, write	11					1	12
ladder, bowl, school				1	3		4
bowl, write, school			1				1
ladder, bowl	5	6		1			12
ladder, write	1						1
ladder, school					5		5
bowl, write	2*					1	3*
ladder	2	8			3		13
bowl				1			1
write						1	1
TOTAL	23	14	1	3	11	3	55*

* One point is doubtful as to bowl

FIGURE 11. Prothetic vowel in French. — Occurrence of the forms in the shaded areas of Figure 10, by communities.

What interests us is the fact that most of the settlements in these backward districts have adopted the prothetic vowel in one, two, or three of our words. Thus, in district B, the village of Sainte-Marguerite (Vosges) says [tʃo:l] 'ladder' and [kwe:l] 'bowl,' but, in the modern style, [ekrir] 'write' and [eko:l] 'school.' Moreover, the dialects do not agree as to the words in which the innovation is made; thus, in contrast with the preceding case, the village of Gavarnie (Hautes-Pyrénées), in our district E, says ['ska:lo] 'ladder' and ['sko:lo] 'school,' but [esku'de:lo] 'bowl' and [eskri'be] 'write.' Only two points, both in district A, have preserved the old initial type in all four of our words; the others show various combinations of old and new forms. Figure 11 gives, in the first column, the combinations of words in which the old form is still in use, then the number of points (by districts and in total) where each combination has survived. In spite of the great variety

Words in which forms without added vowel are still spoken	Number of places where forms without added vowel are still spoken						
	BY DISTRICTS						TOTAL
	A(23)	B(14)	C(1)	D(3)	E(11)	F(3)	
'ladder'	21	14		2	11	1	49
'bowl'	20*	6	1	3	3	2	35*
'write'	16	1				3	20
'school'	2		1	1	8		12

One point is doubtful

FIGURE 12. Prothetic vowel in French. — Occurrence of the forms in the shaded areas of Figure 10, by words.

that appears in this table, the survey by individual words, in Figure 12, shows that the homely terms 'ladder' and 'bowl' appear more often in the old form than do 'write' and 'school,' which are associated with official institutions and with a wider cultural outlook. To be sure, at Bobi (district C) it is precisely 'ladder' which has the new form, but wherever the field of observation is larger, as in districts A, B, and E, or in the total, the terms for 'ladder' and 'bowl' tend to lead in the number of conservative forms.

19. 7. The final result of the process of spread is the complete submergence of the old forms. Where we find a great area in which some linguistic change has been uniformly carried out, we may be sure that the greater part of the uniformity is due to geographic leveling. Sometimes place-names show us the only trace of the struggle. In the German area generally, two ancient diphthongs, which we represent as [ew] and [iw] are still distinct, as in standard New High German, with [i:] for ancient [ew], *Fliege* 'fly' (noun), *Knie* 'knee,' *Stiefvater* 'step-father,' *tief* 'deep,' but, with [oj] for ancient [iw], *scheu* 'shy,' *teuer* 'dear,' *neun* 'nine.' The dialect of Glarus has apparently lost the distinction, as have adjoining dialects, wherever a labial or velar consonant followed the diphthong:

old [ew] before labial or velar:

	Primitive Germanic Type	Glarus
fly	*['flewgo:n]	['fly:gə]
knee	*['knewan]	[xny:]
step-	*['stewpa-]	['ʃty:f-fɑtər]

old [iw]:

shy	*['skiwhjaz]	[ʃy:x]
dear	*['diwrjaz]	[ty:r]
nine	*['niwni]	[ny:n]

Apparently, then, these two old types are both represented in Glarus by modern [y:], in accordance with the general South-German development. A single form suggests that the [y:] for old [ew] is really an importation, namely, the word *deep*, Primitive Germanic type *['dewpaz], which appears in Glarus as [tœjf]. Our suspicion that the diphthong [œj] is the older representative of [ew] before labials and velars in this region, is confirmed by a place-name: ['xnœj-grɑ:t], literally 'Knee-Ridge.'

The southwestern corner of German-speaking Switzerland has changed the old Germanic [k] of words like *drink* to a spirant [x] and has lost the preceding nasal, as in ['tri:xə] 'to drink.' This is today a crass localism, for most of Switzerland, along with the rest of the Dutch-German area, speaks [k]. Thus, Glarus says ['triŋkə] 'to drink,' in accord with standard German *trinken*. Place-names, however, show us that the deviant pronunciation once extended over a much larger part of Switzerland. Glarus, well to the east, alongside the common noun ['wɪŋkəl] 'angle, corner,' has the place-name of a mountain pasture ['wɪxlə] 'Corners,' and alongside [xrɑŋk] 'sick' (formerly, 'crooked') the name of another pasture ['xrawx-tɑːl] 'Crank-Dale,' that is, 'Crooked-Valley.'

19. 8. Dialect geography thus gives evidence as to the former extension of linguistic features that now persist only as relic forms. Especially when a feature appears in detached districts that are separated by a compact area in which a competing feature is spoken, the map can usually be interpreted to mean that the detached districts were once part of a solid area. In this way, dialect geography may show us the stratification of linguistic features; thus, our Figure 6, without any direct historical supplementation, would tell us that the [uː]-forms were the oldest, that they were superseded by the [yː]-forms, and these, in turn, by the diphthongal forms.

Since an isogloss presumably marks a line of weakness in the density of communication, we may expect the dialect map to show us the communicative conditions of successive times. The inhabitants of countries like England, Germany, or France, have always applied provincial names to rough dialectal divisions, and spoken of such things as "the Yorkshire dialect," "the Swabian dialect," or "the Norman dialect." Earlier scholars accepted these classifications without attempting to define them exactly; it was hoped, later, that dialect geography would lead to exact definitions. The question gained interest from the wave-theory (§ 18.12), since the provincial types were examples of the differentiation of a speech-area without sudden cleavage. Moreover, the question took on a sentimental interest, since the provincial divisions largely represent old tribal groupings: if the extension of a dialect, such as, say, the "Swabian dialect" in Germany, could be shown to coincide with the area of habitation of an ancient tribe, then language would again be throwing light on the conditions of a bygone time.

In this respect, however, dialect geography proved to be disappointing. It showed that almost every village had its own dialectal features, so that the whole area was covered by a network of isoglosses. If one began by setting up a list of characteristic provincial peculiarities, one found them prevailing in a solid core, but shading off at the edges, in the sense that each characteristic was bordered by a whole set of isoglosses representing its presence in different words — just as the *house* and *mouse* isoglosses for [y:] and [u:] do not coincide in the eastern Netherlands (Figure 6). A local dialect from the center of Yorkshire or Swabia or Normandy could be systematically classed in terms of its province, but at the outskirts of such a division there lie whole bands of dialects which share only part of the provincial characteristics. In this situation, moreover, there is no warrant for the initial list of characteristics. If these were differently selected — say, without regard to the popularly current provincial classification — we should obtain entirely different cores and entirely different zones of transition.

Accordingly, some students now despaired of all classification and announced that within a dialect area there are no real boundaries. Even in a domain such as that of the western Romance languages (Italian, Ladin, French, Spanish, Portuguese) it was urged that there were no real boundaries, but only gradual transitions: the difference between any two neighboring points was no more and no less important than the difference between any two other neighboring points. Opposing this view, some scholars held fast to the national and provincial classifications, insisting, perhaps with some mystical fervor, on a terminology of cores and zones.

It is true that the isoglosses in a long-settled area are so many as to make possible almost any desired classification of dialects and to justify almost any claim concerning former densities of communication. It is easy to see, however, that, without prejudice of any kind, we must attribute more significance to some isoglosses than to others. An isogloss which cuts boldly across a whole area, dividing it into two nearly equal parts, or even an isogloss which neatly marks off some block of the total area, is more significant than a petty line enclosing a localism of a few villages. In our Figures 4 and 5, isoglosses 1, 2, 3, which mark off southwestern German from the rest of the German area, are evidently more significant than, say, isogloss 9, which encloses only a few villages. The great isogloss shows a feature which has spread over a large domain; this spreading is a large event, simply as a fact in the history of language, and, may reflect, moreover, some non-linguistic cultural movement of comparable strength. As a criterion of description, too, the large division is, of course, more significant than small ones; in fact, the popular classification of dialects is evidently based upon the prevalence of certain peculiarities over large parts of an area.

Furthermore, a set of isoglosses running close together in much the same direction — a so-called *bundle* of isoglosses — evidences a larger historical process and offers a more suitable basis of classification than does a single isogloss that represents, perhaps, some unimportant feature. It appears, moreover, that these two characteristics, topographic importance and bundling, often go hand in hand. Thus, France is divided by a great bundle of isoglosses running east and west across the area. This division reflects the medieval division of France into the two cultural and linguistic domains of French and Provençal.

The most famous bundle of this kind, perhaps, is the east-and-west bundle which runs across the Dutch-German area, separating Low German from High German. The difference is in the treatment of the Primitive Germanic unvoiced stops [p, t, k], which in the south have been shifted to spirants and affricates. If we take standard Dutch and standard German as representatives of the two types, our isoglosses separate forms like these:

	Northern	Southern
make	['ma:ke]	['maxen]
I	[ik]	[ix]
sleep	['sla:pe]	['ʃla:fen]
thorp 'village'	[dorp]	[dorf]
pound	[punt]	[pfunt]
bite	['bejte]	['bajsen]
that	[dat]	[das]
to	[tu:]	[tsu:]

The isoglosses of these and other forms that contain Primitive Germanic [p, t, k] run in a great bundle, sometimes coinciding, but at other times diverging, and even crossing each other. Thus, round Berlin, the isogloss of *make*, together with a good many others, makes a northward bend, so that there one says [ik] 'I' with unshifted [k], but ['maxen] 'make' with [k] shifted to [x]; on the other hand, in the west the isogloss of *I* swerves off in a northwesterly direction, so that round Düsseldorf one says [ix] 'I' with the shifted sound, but ['ma:ken] 'make' with the old [k] preserved.

DIALECT GEOGRAPHY

In this way we find that the topographic distribution of linguistic features within a dialect area is not indifferent, and exhibits decided cleavages. We must make only two obvious reservations: we cannot guarantee to preserve the popular terminology by provinces, but, if we retain provincial names, must redefine them; and we can bound our divisions either imperfectly, by zones, or arbitrarily, by selecting some one isogloss as the representative of a whole bundle.

19. 9. Having found the linguistic divisions of an area, we may compare them with other lines of cleavage. The comparison shows that the important lines of dialectal division run close to political lines. Apparently, common government and religion, and especially the custom of intermarriage within the political unit, lead to relative uniformity of speech. It is estimated that, under older conditions, a new political boundary led in less than fifty years to some linguistic difference, and that the isoglosses along a political boundary of long standing would persist, with little shifting, for some two-hundred years after the boundary had been abolished. This seems to be the primary correlation. If the important isoglosses agree with other lines of cultural division — as, in northern Germany, with a difference in the construction of farm-houses — or if they agree with geographic barriers, such as rivers or mountain-ranges, then the agreement is due merely to the fact that these features also happen to concord with political divisions.

This has been shown most plainly in the distribution of the important German isoglosses along the Rhine. Some forty kilometers east of the Rhine the isoglosses of the great bundle that separates Low German and High German begin to separate and spread out northwestward and southwestward, so as to form what has been called the "Rhenish fan" (Figure 13). The isogloss of northern [k] versus southern [x] in the word *make*, which has been taken, arbitrarily, as the critical line of division, crosses the Rhine just north of the town of Benrath and, accordingly, is called the "Benrath line." It is found, now, that this line corresponds roughly to an ancient northern boundary of the territorial domains of Berg (east of the Rhine) and Jülich (west of the Rhine). The isogloss of northern [k] versus southern [x] in the word *I* swerves off northwestward, crossing the Rhine just north of the village of Ürdingen, and is known accordingly, as the "Ürdingen

M

line;" some students take this, rather than the line of *make*, as the arbitrary boundary between Low and High German. The Ürdingen line corresponds closely to the northern boundaries of the pre-Napoleonic Duchies, abolished in 1789, of Jülich and Berg — the states whose earlier limit is reflected in the Benrath line — and of the Electorate of Cologne. Just north of Ürdingen, the town of Kaldenhausen is split by the Ürdingen line into a western section which says [ex] and an eastern which says [ek];

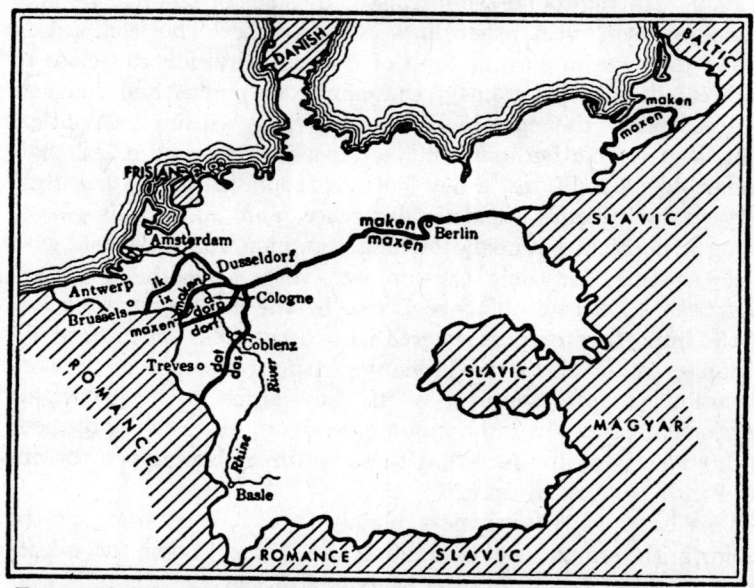

FIGURE 13. The Dutch-German speech-area, showing the isogloss of [k] versus [x] in the word *make*, and, in the western part, the divergence of three other isoglosses which in the east run fairly close to that of *make*. — After Behaghel.

we learn that up to 1789 the western part of the town belonged to the (Catholic) Electorate of Cologne, and the eastern part to the (Protestant) County of Mörs. Our map shows also two isoglosses branching southwestward. One is the line between northern [p] and southern [f] in the word [dorp – dorf] 'village'; this line agrees roughly with the southern boundaries in 1789 of Jülich, Cologne, and Berg, as against the Electorate of Treves. In a still more southerly direction there branches off the isogloss between northern [t] and southern [s] in the word [dat – das] 'that,' and this line, again, coincides approximately with the old southern boundary of the Electorate and Archbishopric of Treves.

All this shows that the spread of linguistic features depends upon social conditions. The factors in this respect are doubtless the density of communication and the relative prestige of different social groups. Important social boundaries will in time attract isogloss-lines. Yet it is evident that the peculiarities of the several linguistic forms themselves play a part, since each is likely to show an isogloss of its own. In the Netherlands we saw a new form of the word *house* spreading farther than a new form of the homely word *mouse* (§ 19.4). We can hope for no scientifically usable analysis, such as would enable us to predict the course of every isogloss: the factors of prestige in the speakers and of meaning (including connotation) in the forms cut off our hope of this. Nevertheless, dialect geography not only contributes to our understanding of the extra-linguistic factors that affect the prevalence of linguistic forms, but also, through the evidence of relic forms and stratifications, supplies a great many details concerning the history of individual forms.

CHAPTER 20

PHONETIC CHANGE

20. 1. Written records of earlier speech, resemblance between languages, and the varieties of local dialects, all show that languages change in the course of time. In our Old English records we find a word *stan* 'stone,' which we interpret phonetically as [sta:n]; if we believe that the present-day English word *stone* [stown] is the modern form, by unbroken tradition, of this Old English word, then we must suppose that Old English [a:] has here changed to modern [ow]. If we believe that the resemblances are due not to accident, but to the tradition of speech-habits, then we must infer that the differences between the resemblant forms are due to changes in these speech-habits. Earlier students recognized this; they collected sets of resemblant forms (etymologies) and inferred that the differences between the forms of a set were due to linguistic change, but, until the beginning of the nineteenth century, no one succeeded in classifying these differences. The resemblances and differences varied from set to set. An Old English *bat*, which we interpret phonetically as [ba:t], is in one meaning paralleled by modern English *boat* [bowt], but in another meaning by modern English *bait* [bejt]. The initial consonants are the same in Latin *dies* and English *day*, but different in Latin *duo* and English *two*. The results of linguistic change presented themselves as a hodge-podge of resemblances and differences. One could suspect that some of the resemblances were merely accidental ("false etymologies"), but there was no test. One could reach no clear formulation of linguistic relationship — the less so, since the persistence of Latin documents through the Middle Ages alongside of documents in the Romance languages distorted one's whole view of linguistic chronology.

It is not useless to look back at those times. Now that we have a method which brings order into the confusion of linguistic resemblances and throws some light on the nature of linguistic relationship, we are likely to forget how chaotic are the results of linguistic change when one has no key to their classification.

PHONETIC CHANGE

Since the beginning of the nineteenth century we have learned to classify the differences between related forms, attributing them to several kinds of linguistic change. The data, whose variety bewildered earlier students, lend themselves with facility to this classification. Resemblances which do not fit into our classes of change, are relatively few and can often be safely ruled out as accidental; this is the case, for instance, with Latin *dies* : English *day*, which we now know to be a false etymology.

The process of linguistic change has never been directly observed; we shall see that such observation, with our present facilities, is inconceivable. We are assuming that our method of classification, which works well (though not by any means perfectly), reflects the actual factors of change that produced our data. The assumption that the simplest classification of observed facts is the true one, is common to all science; in our case, it is well to remember that the observed facts (namely, the results of linguistic change as they show themselves in etymologies) resisted all comprehension until our method came upon the scene. The first step in the development of method in historical linguistics was the seeking out of uniform *phonetic correspondences;* we take these correspondences to be the results of a factor of change which we call *phonetic change*.

20. 2. At the beginning of the nineteenth century we find a few scholars systematically picking out certain types of resemblance, chiefly cases of *phonetic* agreement or correspondence. The first notable step was Rask's and Grimm's observation (§ 1.7) of correspondences between Germanic and other Indo-European languages. From among the chaotic mass of resemblant forms, they selected certain ones which exhibited uniform phonetic correlations. Stated in present-day terms, these correlations appear as follows:

(1) Unvoiced stops of the other languages are paralleled in Germanic by unvoiced spirants:

[p − f] Latin *pēs* : English *foot;* Latin *piscis* : English *fish;* Latin *pater* : English *father;*

[t − θ] Latin *trēs* : English *three;* Latin *tenuis* : English *thin;* Latin *tacēre* 'to be silent' : Gothic ['θahan];

[k − h] Latin *centum* : English *hundred;* Latin *caput* : English *head;* Latin *cornū* : English *horn*.

(2) Voiced stops of the other languages are paralleled in Germanic by unvoiced stops:

[b — p] Greek ['kannabis] : English *hemp;*
[d — t] Latin *duo* : English *two;* Latin *dens* : English *tooth;* Latin *edere* : English *eat;*
[g — k] Latin *grānum* : English *corn;* Latin *genus* : English *kin;* Latin *ager* : English *acre.*

(3) Certain aspirates and spirants of the other languages (which we denote today as "reflexes of Primitive Indo-European voiced aspirates") are paralleled in Germanic by voiced stops and spirants:

Sanskrit [bh], Greek [ph], Latin [f], Germanic [b, v]: Sanskrit ['bhara:mi] 'I bear,' Greek ['phero:], Latin *ferō* : English *bear;* Sanskrit ['bhra:ta:], Greek ['phra:te:r], Latin *frāter* : English *brother;* Latin *frangere* : English *break;*

Sanskrit [dh], Greek [th], Latin [f], Germanic [d, ð]: Sanskrit ['a-dha:t] 'he put,' Greek ['the:so:] 'I shall put,' Latin *fēcī* 'I made, did' : English *do;* Sanskrit ['madhu] 'honey, mead,' Greek ['methu] 'wine' : English *mead;* Sanskrit ['madhjah], Latin *medius* : English *mid;*

Sanskrit [h], Greek [kh], Latin [h], Germanic [g, ɣ]: Sanskrit [hã'sah] : English *goose;* Sanskrit ['vahati] 'he carries on a vehicle,' Latin *vehit* : Old English *wegan* 'to carry, move, transport'; Latin *hostis* 'stranger, enemy' : Old English *giest* 'guest.'

The only reason for assembling cases like these is the belief that the correlations are too frequent or in some other way too peculiar to be due to chance.

20. 3. Students of language have accepted these correlations (calling them, by a dangerous metaphor, Grimm's "law"), because the classification they introduce is confirmed by further study: new data show the same correspondences, and cases which do not show these correspondences lend themselves to other classifications.

For instance, from among the cases which do not show Grimm's correspondences, it is possible to sort out a fair-sized group in which unvoiced stops [p, t, k] of the other languages appear also in Germanic; thus, the [t] of the other languages is paralleled by Germanic [t] in cases like the following:

Sanskrit ['asti] 'he is,' Greek ['esti], Latin *est* : Gothic [ist] 'is';
Latin *captus* 'taken, caught' : Gothic [hafts] 'restrained';
Sanskrit [aʃ'та:w] 'eight,' Greek [ok'to:] Latin *octō* : Gothic ['ahtaw].

PHONETIC CHANGE

Now, in all these cases the [p, t, k] in Germanic is immediately preceded by an unvoiced spirant [s, f, h], and a survey of the cases which conform to Grimm's correspondences shows that in them the Germanic consonant is never preceded by these sounds. Grimm's correlations have thus, by leaving a residue, led us to find another correlation: after [s, f, h] Germanic [p, t, k] parallel the [p, t, k] of the other Indo-European languages.

Among the residual forms, again, we find a number in which initial voiced stops [b, d, g] of Germanic are paralleled in Sanskrit not by [bh, dh, gh], as Grimm would have it, but by [b, d, g], and in Greek not by the expected [ph, th, kh], but by [p, t, k]. An example is Sanskrit ['bo:dha:mi] 'I observe,' Greek ['pewthomaj] 'I experience' : Gothic [ana-'biwdan] 'to command,' Old English ['be:odan] 'to order, announce, offer,' English *bid*. In 1862, Hermann Grassmann (1809–1877) showed that this type of correlation appears wherever the next consonant (the consonant after the intervening vowel or diphthong) belongs to Grimm's third type of correspondences. That is, Sanskrit and Greek do not have aspirate stops at the beginning of two successive syllables, but, wherever the related languages show this pattern, have the first of the two stops unaspirated: corresponding to Germanic *[bewda-], we find in Sanskrit not *[bho:dha-] but [bo:dha-], and in Greek not *[phewtho-] but [pewtho-]. Here too, then, the residual data which are marked off by Grimm's correspondences, reveal a correlation.

In this case, moreover, we get a confirmation in the structure of the languages. In Greek, certain forms have a reduplication (§ 13.8) in which the first consonant of the underlying stem, followed by a vowel, is prefixed: ['do:so:] 'I shall give,' ['di-do:mi] 'I give.' We find, now, that for stems with an initial aspirate stop the reduplication is made with a plain stop: ['the:so:] 'I shall put,' ['ti-the:mi] 'I put.' The same habit appears elsewhere in Greek morphology; thus, there is a noun-paradigm with nominative singular ['thriks] 'hair,' but other case-forms like the accusative ['trikha]: when the consonant after the vowel is aspirated, the initial consonant is [t] instead of [th]. Similarly, in Sanskrit, the normal reduplication repeats the first consonant: ['a-da:t] 'he gave,' ['da-da:mi] 'I give,' but for an initial aspirate the reduplication has a plain stop: ['a-dha:t] 'he put,' ['da-dha:mi] 'I put,' and similar alternations appear elsewhere in Sanskrit morphology.

These alternations are obviously results of the sound-change discovered by Grassmann.

20. 4. If our correspondences are not due to chance, they must result from some historical connection, and this connection the comparative method reconstructs, as we have seen, by the assumption of common descent from a parent language. Where the related languages agree, they are preserving features of the parent language, such as, say, the [r] in the word *brother*, the [m] in the words *mead* and *mid* (§ 20.2), or the [s] in the verb-forms for 'he is' (§ 20.3). Where the correspondence connects markedly different phonemes, we suppose that one or more of the languages have changed. Thus we state Grimm's correspondences by saying:

(1) Primitive Indo-European unvoiced stops [p, t, k] changed in pre-Germanic to unvoiced spirants [f, θ, h];

(2) Primitive Indo-European voiced stops [b, d, g] changed in pre-Germanic to unvoiced stops [p, t, k];

(3) Primitive Indo-European voiced aspirate stops [bh, dh, gh] changed in pre-Germanic to voiced stops or spirants [b, d, g], in pre-Greek to unvoiced aspirate stops [ph, th, kh], in pre-Italic and pre-Latin to [f, θ, h]. In this case the acoustic shape of the Primitive Indo-European phonemes is by no means certain, and some scholars prefer to speak of unvoiced spirants [f, θ, x]; similarly, we do not know whether the Primitive Germanic reflexes were stops or spirants, but these doubts do not affect our conclusions as to the phonetic pattern

The correspondences where [p, t, k] appear also in Germanic demand a restriction for case (1): immediately after a consonant (those which actually occur are [s, p, k]), the Primitive Indo-European unvoiced stops [p, t, k] were not changed in pre-Germanic.

Grassmann's correspondences we state historically by saying that at a certain stage in the history of pre-Greek, forms which contained two successive syllables with aspirate stops, lost the aspiration of the first stop. Thus, we reconstruct:

Primitive Indo-European	>	pre-Greek	>	Greek
*['bhewdhomaj]		*['phewthomaj]		['pewthomaj]
*['dhidhe:mi]		*['thithe:mi]		['tithe:mi]
*['dhrighm̥]		*['thrikha]		['trikha].

On the other hand, in the nominative singular of the word for 'hair,' we suppose that there never was an aspirate after the vowel:

Primitive Indo-European *[dhriks] appears as Greek [thriks]. We infer a similar change for pre-Indo-Iranian: a Primitive Indo-European *[bhewdho-] appearing in Sanskrit as [bo:dha-], a Primitive Indo-European *[dhedhe:-] as [dadha:-], and so on.

A further step in the reconstruction of the historical events proceeds from the fact that the loss of aspiration results in Sanskrit in [b, d, g], but in Greek in [p, t, k]. This implies that the Primitive Indo-European [bh, dh, gh] had already become unvoiced [ph, th, kh] in pre-Greek when the loss of aspiration took place. Since this unvoicing does not occur in Indo-Iranian, we conclude that the de-aspiration in pre-Greek and the de-aspiration in pre-Indo-Iranian took place independently.

The interpretation, then, of the phonetic correspondences that appear in our resemblant forms, assumes that *the phonemes of a language are subject to historical change.* This change may be limited to certain phonetic conditions; thus, in pre-Germanic, [p, t, k] did not change to [f, θ, h] when another unvoiced consonant immediately preceded, as in *[kəptos] > Gothic [hafts]; in pre-Greek, [ph, th, kh] became [p, t, k] only when the next syllable began with an aspirate. This type of linguistic change is known as *phonetic change* (or *sound change*). In modern terminology, the assumption of sound-change can be stated in the sentence: *Phonemes change.*

20. 5. When we have gathered the resemblant forms which show the recognized correlations, the remainders will offer two self-evident possibilities. We may have stated a correlation too narrowly or too widely: a more careful survey or the arrival of new data may show the correction. A notable instance of this was Grassmann's discovery. The fact that residues have again and again revealed new correlations, is a strong confirmation of our method. Secondly, the resemblant forms may not be divergent pronunciations of the same earlier form. Grimm, for instance, mentioned Latin *dies* : English *day* as an etymology which did not fall within his correlations, and since his time no amount of research has revealed any possibility of modifying the otherwise valid correlation-classes so that they may include this set. Similarly, Latin *habēre* 'to have' : Gothic *haban*, Old High German *habēn*, in spite of the striking resemblance, conflicts with types of correlation that otherwise hold good. In such cases, we may attribute the resemblance to accident, meaning by this that it is not due to any historical connection; thus, Latin *dies* : English *day* is now regarded by everyone as a "false etymology." Or else, the resemblance may be due to grammatical resemblance of forms in the parent language; thus, Latin *habēre* 'to have' and Old High German *habēn* 'to have' may be descendants, respectively, of two stems, *[gha'bhe:-] and *[ka'bhe:-] which were morphologically parallel in Primitive Indo-European. Finally, our resemblant forms may owe their likeness to a historical connection other than descent from a common prototype. Thus, Latin *dentālis* 'pertaining to a tooth' and English *dental* resemble each other, but do not show the correlations (e.g. Latin *d* : English *t*) which appear in Latin and English reflexes of a common Primitive Indo-European prototype. The reason is that *dental* is merely the English-speaker's reproduction of the Latin word.

To sum up, then, the residual forms which do not fit into recognized types of phonetic correlation may be:

(1) descendants of a common ancestral form, deviant only because we have not correctly ascertained the phonetic correlation, e.g. Sanskrit ['bo:dha:mi] and English *bid*, before Grassmann's discovery;

(2) not descendants of a common ancestral form, in which case the resemblance may be due to

 (a) accident, e.g. Latin *dies* : English *day;*

 (b) morphologic partial resemblance in the parent language, e.g. Latin *habēre* : English *have;*

 (c) other historical relations, e.g. Latin *dentālis* : English *dental.*

If this is correct, then the study of residual resemblant forms will lead us to discover new types of phonetic correlation (1), to weed out false etymologies (2a), to uncover the morphologic structure of the parent speech (2b), or to recognize types of linguistic change other than sound-change (2c). If the study of residual forms does not lead to these results, then our scheme is incorrect.

20. 6. During the first three quarters of the nineteenth century no one, so far as we know, ventured to limit the possibilities in the sense of our scheme. If a set of resemblant forms did not fit into the recognized correlations, scholars felt free to assume that these forms were nevertheless related in exactly the same way as the normal forms — namely, by way of descent from a common ancestral form. They phrased this historically by saying that a speech-sound might change in one way in some forms, but might change in another way (or fail to change) in other forms. A Primitive Indo-European [d] might change to [t] in pre-Germanic in most forms, such as *two* (: Latin *duo*), *ten* (: Latin *decem*), *tooth* (: Latin *dens*), *eat* (: Latin *edere*), but remain unchanged in some other forms, such as *day* (: Latin *dies*).

On the whole, there was nothing to be said against this view — in fact, it embodied a commendable caution — unless and until an extended study of residual forms showed that possibilities (1) and (2a, b, c) were realized in so great a number of cases as to rule out the probability of sporadic sound-change. In the seventies of the nineteenth century, several scholars, most notably, in the year 1876, August Leskien (§ 1.9), concluded that exactly this had taken place: that the sifting of residual forms had resulted so often in the discovery of non-contradictory facts (1, 2b, 2c) or in the weeding out of false etymologies (2a), as to warrant linguists in supposing that the change of phonemes is absolutely regular. This meant, in terms of our method, that all resemblances between forms which do not fall into the recognized correspondence-classes are due to features of sound-change which we have failed to recognize (1), or else are not divergent forms of a single prototype, either because the etymology is false (2a), or because some factor other than sound-change has led to the existence of resemblant forms (2b, c). Historically interpreted, the statement means that sound-change is merely a change in the speakers' manner of producing phonemes and accordingly affects a phoneme at every occurrence, regardless of the nature of any particular linguistic form in which the phoneme happens to occur. The change may concern some habit of articulation which is common to several phonemes, as in the unvoicing of voiced stops [b, d, g] in pre-Germanic. On the other hand, the change may concern some habit of articulating successions of phonemes, and therefore take place only under particular phonetic conditions, as when [p, t, k] in pre-Germanic became [f, θ, h] when not preceded by another sound of the same group or by [s]; similarly, [ph, th, kh] in pre-Greek became [p, t, k] only when the next syllable began with an aspirate. The limitations of these *conditioned sound-changes* are, of course, purely phonetic, since the change concerns only a habit of articulatory movement; phonetic change is independent of non-phonetic factors, such as the meaning, frequency, homonymy, or what not, of any particular linguistic form. In present-day terminology the whole assumption can be briefly put into the words: *phonemes change*, since the term *phoneme* designates a meaningless minimum unit of signaling.

The new principle was adopted by a number of linguists, who received the nickname of "neo-grammarians." On the other hand, not only scholars of the older generation, such as Georg Curtius (1820–1885), but also some younger men, most notably Hugo Schuchardt (1842–1927), rejected the new hypothesis. The discussion of the pro's and con's has never ceased; linguists are as much divided on this point today as in the 1870's.

A great part of this dispute was due merely to bad terminology. In the 1870's, when technical terms were less precise than today, the assumption of uniform sound-change received the obscure and metaphorical wording, "Phonetic laws have no exceptions." It is evident that the term "law" has here no precise meaning, for a sound-change is not in any sense a law, but only a historical occurrence. The phrase "have no exceptions" is a very inexact way of saying that non-phonetic factors, such as the frequency or meaning of particular linguistic forms, do not interfere with the change of phonemes.

The real point at issue is the scope of the phonetic correspondence-classes and the significance of the residues. The neo-grammarians claimed that the results of study justified us in making the correspondence-classes non-contradictory and in seeking a complete analysis of the residues. If we say that Primitive Indo-European [d] appears in Germanic as [t], then, according to the neo-grammarians, the resemblance of Latin *dies* and English *day* or of Latin *dentālis* and English *dental*, cannot be classed simply as "an exception" -- that is, historically, as due to the pre-Germanic speakers' failure to make the usual change of habit — but presents a problem. The solution of this problem is either the abandonment of the etymology as due to accidental resemblance (Latin *dies* : English *day*), or a more exact formulation of the phonetic correspondence (Grassmann's discovery), or the recognition of some other factors that produce resemblant forms (Latin *dentālis* borrowed in English *dental*). The neo-grammarian insists, particularly, that his hypothesis is fruitful in this last direction: it sorts out the resemblances that are due to factors other than phonetic change, and accordingly leads us to an understanding of these factors.

The actual dispute, then, concerns the weeding-out of false etymologies, the revision of our statements of phonetic correspondence, and the recognition of linguistic changes other than sound-change.

20. 7. The opponents of the neo-grammarian hypothesis claim that resemblances which do not fit into recognized types of phonetic correspondence may be due merely to sporadic occurrence or deviation or non-occurrence of sound-change. Now, the very foundation of modern historical linguistics consisted in the setting up of phonetic correspondence-classes: in this way alone did Rask and Grimm bring order into the chaos of resemblances which had bewildered all earlier students. The advocates of sporadic sound-change, accordingly, agree with the neo-grammarians in discarding such etymologies as Latin *dies* : English *day*, and retain only a few, where the resemblance is striking, such as Latin *habēre* : Old High German *habēn*, or Sanskrit [ko:kilah], Greek ['kokkuks], Latin *cuculus* : English *cuckoo*. They admit that this leaves us no criterion of decision, but insist that our inability to draw a line does not prove anything: exceptional sound-changes occurred, even though we have no certain way of recognizing them.

The neo-grammarian sees in this a serious violation of scientific method. The beginning of our science was made by a procedure which implied regularity of phonetic change, and further advances, like Grassmann's discovery, were based on the same implicit assumption. It may be, of course, that some other assumption would lead to an even better correlation of facts, but the advocates of sporadic sound-change offer nothing of the kind; they accept the results of the actual method and yet claim to explain some facts by a contradictory method (or lack of method) which was tried and found wanting through all the centuries that preceded Rask and Grimm.

In the historical interpretation, the theory of sporadic sound-change faces a very serious difficulty. If we suppose that a form like *cuckoo* resisted the pre-Germanic shift of [k] to [h] and still preserves a Primitive Indo-European [k], then we must also suppose that during many generations, when the pre-Germanic people had changed their way of pronouncing Primitive Indo-

European [k] in most words, and were working on through successive acoustic types such as, say, [kh — kx — x — h], they were still in the word *cuckoo* pronouncing an unchanged Primitive Indo-European [k]. If such things happened, then every language would be spotted over with all sorts of queer, deviant sounds, in forms which had resisted sound-change or deviated from ordinary changes. Actually, however, a language moves within a limited set of phonemes. The modern English [k] in *cuckoo* is no different from the [k] in words like *cow, calf, kin*, which has developed normally from the Primitive Indo-European [g]-type. We should have to suppose, therefore, that some later change brought the preserved Primitive Indo-European [k] in *cuckoo* into complete equality with the Germanic [k] that reflects a Primitive Indo-European [g], and, since every language moves within a limited phonetic system, we should have to suppose that in every case of sporadic sound-change or resistance to sound-change, the discrepant sound has been reduced to some ordinary phonemic type in time to escape the ear of the observer. Otherwise we should find, say, in present-day standard English, a sprinkling of forms which preserved sounds from eighteenth-century English, early modern English, Middle English, Old English, Primitive Germanic, and so on — not to speak of deviant sounds resulting from sporadic changes in some positive direction.

Actually, the forms which do not exhibit ordinary phonetic correlations, conform to the phonemic system of their language and are peculiar only in their correlation with other forms. For instance, the modern standard English correspondents of Old English [o:] show some decided irregularities, but these consist simply in the presence of unexpected phonemes, and never in deviation from the phonetic system. The normal representation seems to be:

[ɔ] before [s, z] plus consonant other than [t]: *goshawk, gosling, blossom;*

[ɔː] before Old English consonant plus [t]: *soft, sought* (Old English *sōhte*), *brought, thought;*

[u] before [k] *book, brook* (noun), *cook, crook, hook, look, rook, shook, took;*

[ʌ] before [n] plus consonant other than [t] and before consonant plus [r̩]: *Monday, month; brother, mother, other, rudder;*

[ow] before [nt] and [r] and from the combination of Old English

PHONETIC CHANGE

[o:w]: *don't; floor, ore, swore, toward, whore; blow* ('bloom'), *flow, glow, grow, low* (verb), *row, stow;*

[uw] otherwise: *do, drew, shoe, slew, too, to, woo, brood, food, mood, hoof, roof, woof, cool, pool, school, stool, tool, bloom, broom, doom, gloom, loom, boon, moon, noon, soon, spoon, swoon, whoop, goose, loose, boot, moot, root, soot, booth, sooth, tooth, smooth, soothe, behoove, prove, ooze.*

If we take the correlation of Old English [o:] with these sounds as normal under the phonetic conditions of each case, then we have the following residue of contradictory forms:

[ɔ] *shod, fodder, foster.*
[aw] *bough, slough;*
[e] *Wednesday;*
[ʌ] *blood, flood, enough, tough, gum, done, must, doth, glove;*
[ow] *woke;*
[u] *good, hood, stood, bosom, foot,* and optionally *hoof, roof, broom, soot;*
[uw] *moor, roost.*

All of these seven deviant types contain some ordinary English phoneme; the [ʌ], for instance, in *blood*, etc., is the ordinary [ʌ]-phoneme, which represents Old English [u] in words like *love, tongue, son, sun, come.* In every case, the discrepant forms show not queer sounds, but merely normal phonemes in a distribution that runs counter to the expectations of the historian.

20. 8. As to the correction of our correspondence-groups by a careful survey of the residual cases, the neo-grammarians soon got a remarkable confirmation of their hypothesis in Verner's treatment of Germanic forms with discrepant [b, d, g] in place of [f, θ, h] (§ 18.7). Verner collected the cases like Latin *pater* : Gothic ['fadar], Old English ['fɛder], where Primitive Indo-European [t] appears in Germanic as [d, ð], instead of [θ]. Now, the voicing of spirants between vowels is a very common form of sound-change, and has actually occurred at various times in the history of several Germanic languages. Primitive Germanic [θ] appears as a voiced spirant, coinciding with the reflex of Primitive Germanic [d], in Old Norse, which says, for instance, ['bro:ðer], with the same consonant as ['faðer]. In Old English, too, the Primitive Germanic [θ] had doubtless become voiced between vowels, as in ['bro:ðor], although it did not coincide with [d], the reflex of Primitive Germanic [d], as in ['fɛder]. In both Old

Norse and Old English, Primitive Germanic [f] had become voiced [v] between vowels, as in Old English *ofen* ['oven] 'oven' (Old High German *ofan* ['ofan]), coinciding with the [v] that represented Primitive Germanic [b], as in Old English *yfel* ['yvel] 'evil' (Old High German *ubil* ['ybil]). Nothing could be more natural, therefore, if one admitted the possibility of irregular sound-change, than to suppose that the voicing of intervocalic spirants had begun sporadically in some words already in pre-Germanic time, and that a Primitive Germanic *['fader] alongside *['broːθer] represented merely the beginning of a process that was to find its completion in the Old Norse, Old English, and Old Saxon of our actual records. Yet in 1876 Verner's study of the deviant forms showed an unmistakable correlation: in a fair number of cases and in convincing systematic positions, the deviant [b, d, g] of Germanic appeared where Sanskrit and Greek (and therefore, presumably, Primitive Indo-European) had an unaccented vowel or diphthong before the [p, t, k], as in Sanskrit [pi'taː], Greek [pa-'teːr] : Primitive Germanic *['fader], contrasting with Sanskrit ['bhraːtaː], Greek ['phraːteːr] : Primitive Germanic *['broːθer]. Similarly, Sanskrit ['çvaçurah] 'father-in-law,' reflecting, presumably a Primitive Indo-European *['swe*k*uros], shows in Germanic the normal reflex of [h] for [*k*], as in Old High German ['swehar], but Sanskrit [çva'çruːh] 'mother-in-law,' reflecting a Primitive Indo-European *[swe'*k*ruːs] appears in Germanic with [g], as in Old High German ['swigar], representing the Primitive Indo-European [*k*] after the unstressed vowel.

A confirmation of this result was the fact that the unvoiced spirant [s] of Primitive Indo-European suffered the same change under the same conditions: it appears in Germanic as [s], except when the preceding syllabic was unaccented in Primitive Indo-European; in this case, it was voiced in pre-Germanic, and appears as Primitive Germanic [z], which later became [r] in Norse and in West Germanic. In a number of irregular verb-paradigms the Germanic languages have medial [f, θ, h, s] in the present tense and in the singular indicative-mode forms of the past tense, but [b, d, g, z] in the plural and subjunctive forms of the past tense and in the past participle, as, for instance, in Old English:

['weorθan] 'to become,' [heː 'wearθ] 'he became,' but [weː 'wurdon] 'we became';

['ke:osan] 'to choose,' [he: 'ke:as] 'he chose,' but [we: 'kuron] 'we chose';

['wesan] 'to be,' [he: 'wɛs] 'he was,' but [we: 'wɛ:ron] 'we were.'

This alternation, Verner showed, corresponds to the alternation in the position of the word-accent in similar Sanskrit paradigms, as, in the verb-forms cognate with the above:

['vartate:] 'he turns, becomes,' [va-'varta] 'he turned,' but [va-vrti'ma] 'we turned';

*['ɟo:ʃati] 'he enjoys,' [ɟu-'ɟo:ʃa] 'he enjoyed,' but [ɟu-ɟuʃi'ma] 'we enjoyed';

['vasati] 'he dwells,' [u-'va:sa] 'he dwelt,' but [u:ʃi'ma] 'we dwelt.'

This was so striking a confirmation of the hypothesis of regular sound-change, that the burden of proof now fell upon the opponents of the hypothesis: if the residual forms can show such a correlation as this, we may well ask for very good reasons before we give up our separation of forms into recognized correspondences and remainders, and our principle of scanning residual forms for new correspondences. We may doubt whether an observer who was satisfied with a verdict of "sporadic sound-change" could ever have discovered these correlations.

In a small way, the accidents of observation sometimes furnish similar confirmations of our method. In the Central Algonquian languages — for which we have no older records — we find the following normal correspondences, which we may symbolize by "Primitive Central Algonquian" reconstructed forms:

	Fox	Ojibwa	Menomini	Plains Cree	Primitive Central Algonquian
(1)	hk	ʃk	tʃk	sk	tʃk
(2)	ʃk	ʃk	sk	sk	ʃk
(3)	hk	hk	hk	sk	xk
(4)	hk	hk	hk	hk	hk
(5)	k	ng	hk	hk	nk

Examples:

(1) Fox [kehkjɛ:wa] 'he is old,' Menomini [ketʃki:w], PCA *[ketʃkjɛ:wa].

(2) Fox [aʃkutɛ:wi] 'fire,' Ojibwa [iʃkudɛ:], Menomini [esko:tɛ:w], Cree [iskute:w], PCA *[iʃkutɛ:wi].

(3) Fox [mahkese:hi] 'moccasin,' Ojibwa [mahkizin], Menomini [mahke:sen], Cree [maskisin], PCA *[maxkesini].

(4) Fox [no:hkumesa] 'my grandmother,' Ojibwa [no:hkumis], Menomini [no:hkumeh], Cree [no:hkum], PCA *[no:hkuma].

(5) Fox [takeʃkawɛ:wa] 'he kicks him,' Ojibwa [tangiʃkawa:d], Menomini [tahkɛ:skawe:w], Cree [tahkiskawe:w], PCA *[tankeʃkawɛ:wa].

Now, there is a residual morpheme in which none of these correspondences holds good, namely the element which means 'red':

(6) Fox [meʃkusiwa] 'he is red,' Ojibwa [miʃkuzi], Menomini [mehko:n], Cree [mihkusiw], PCA *[meçkusiwa].

Under an assumption of sporadic sound-change, this would have no significance. After the sixth correspondence had been set up, however, it was found that in a remote dialect of Cree, which agrees in groups (1) to (5) with the Plains Cree scheme, the morpheme for 'red' has the peculiar cluster [htk], as in [mihtkusiw] 'he is red.' In this case, then, the residual form showed a special phonetic unit of the parent speech.

The assumption of regular (that is, purely phonemic) sound-change is justified by the correlations which it uncovers; it is inconsistent to accept the results which it yields and to reject it whenever one wants a contradictory assumption ("sporadic sound-change") to "explain" difficult cases.

20. 9. The relation of our residual forms to factors of linguistic history other than sound-change, is the crucial point in the dispute about the regularity of sound-change. The neo-grammarians could not claim, of course, that linguistic resemblances ever run in regular sets. The actual data with which we work are extremely irregular, — so irregular that centuries of study before the days of Rask and Grimm had found no useful correlations. The neo-grammarians did claim, however, that factors of linguistic change other than sound-change will appear in the residual forms after we have ruled out the correlations that result from sound-change. Thus, Old English [a:] in stressed syllables appears in modern English normally as [ow], as in *boat* (from Old English [ba:t]), *sore, whole, oath, snow, stone, bone, home, dough, goat,* and many other forms. In the residue, we find forms like Old English [ba:t] : *bait,* Old English [ha:l] : *hale,* Old English [swa:n] 'herdsman' : *swain.* Having found that Old English [a:] appears in modern standard English as [ow], we assign the forms with the discrepant modern English [ej] to a residue. The forms in this residue are not the results of a deviant, sporadic sound-change of Old English [aː] to modern English [ej]; their deviation is due not to sound-change, but to another factor of linguistic change. The forms like *bait, hale, swain* are not the modern continuants of Old English forms with [aː], but borrowings from Scandinavian. Old Scandinavian had [ej] in forms where Old English had [aː]; Old Scandinavian (Old Norse) said [stejnn, bejta, hejll, swejnn] where Old English said [staːn, baːt, haːl, swaːn]. The regularity of correspondence is due, of course, to the common tradition from Primitive Germanic. After the Norse invasion of England, the English language took over these Scandinavian words, and it is the Old Norse diphthong [ej] which appears in the deviant forms with modern English [ej].

In cases like these, or in cases like Latin *dentālis* : English *dental*, the opponents of the neo-grammarian hypothesis raise no objection, and agree that *linguistic borrowing* accounts for the resemblance. In many other cases, however, they prefer to say that irregular sound-change was at work, and, strangely enough, they do this in cases where only the neo-grammarian hypothesis yields a significant result.

Students of dialect geography are especially given to this confusion. In any one dialect we usually find an ancient unit phoneme represented by several phonemes — as in the case of Old English [oː] in modern English *food, good, blood*, and so on (§ 20.7). Often one of these is like the old phoneme and the others appear to embody one or more phonetic changes. Thus, in Central-Western American English, we say *gather* with [ɛ], *rather* with [ɛ] or with [a], and *father* always with [a]. Some speakers have [juw] in words like *tune, dew, stew, new;* some have [uw] in the first three types, but keep [juw] ordinarily after [n-]; others speak [uw] in all of them. Or, again, if we examine adjacent dialects in an area, we find a gradation: some have apparently carried out a sound-change, as when, say, in Dutch, some districts in our Figure 6 have [yː] for ancient [uː] in the words *mouse* and *house;* next to these we may find dialects which have apparently carried out the change in some of the forms, but not in others, as when some districts in our Figure 6 say [hyːs] with the changed vowel, but [muːs] with the unchanged; finally, we reach a district where the changed forms are lacking, such as, in Figure 6, the area where the old forms [muːs, huːs] are still being spoken. Under a hypothesis of sporadic sound-change, no definite conclusions could be drawn, but under the assumption of regular sound-change, distributions of this sort can at once be interpreted: an irregular distribution shows that the new forms, in a part or in all of the area, are due not to sound-change, but to borrowing. The sound-change took place in some one center and, after this, forms which had undergone the change spread from this center by linguistic borrowing. In other cases, a community may have made a sound-change, but the changed forms may in part be superseded by unchanged forms which spread from a center which has not made the change. Students of dialect geography make this inference and base on it their reconstruction of linguistic and cultural movements, but many of these students at the same time profess to reject the assumption of regular phonetic change. If they stopped to examine the implications of this, they would soon see that their work is based on the supposition that sound-change is regular, for, if we admit the possibility of irregular sound-change, then the use of [hy:s] beside [mu:s] in a Dutch dialect, or of ['raðə] *rather* beside ['geðə] *gather* in standard English, would justify no deductions about linguistic borrowing.

20. 10. Another phase of the dispute about the regularity of sound-change concerns residual forms whose deviation is connected with features of meaning. Often enough, the forms that deviate from ordinary phonetic correlation belong to some clearly marked semantic group.

In ancient Greek, Primitive Indo-European [s] between vowels had been lost by sound-change. Thus, Primitive Indo-European *['gewso:] 'I taste' (Gothic ['kiwsa] 'I choose') appears in Greek as ['gewo:] 'I give a taste'; Primitive Indo-European *['genesos] 'of the kin' (Sanskrit ['janasah]) appears as Greek ['geneos], later ['genows]; Primitive Indo-European *['e:sm̥] 'I was' (Sanskrit ['a:sam]) appears in Greek as [ˇe:a], later [ˇe:].

Over against cases like these, there is a considerable residue of forms in which an old intervocalic [s] seems to be preserved in ancient Greek. The principal type of this residue consists of aorist-tense (that is, past punctual) verb-forms, in which the suffix [-s-] of this tense occurs after the final vowel of a root or verb-stem. Thus, the Greek root [plew-] 'sail' (present tense ['plewo:] 'I sail,' paralleled by Sanskrit ['plavate:] 'he sails') has the aorist form ['eplewsa] 'I sailed'; the Greek aorist ['etejsa] 'I paid a penalty' parallels

Sanskrit ['aca:jʃam] 'I collected'; the Greek root [ste:-] 'stand' (present tense ['histe:mi] 'I cause to stand') has the aorist form ['este:sa] 'I caused to stand,' parallel with Old Bulgarian [staxʊ] 'I stood up,' Primitive Indo-European type *['esta:sm̥]; a Primitive Indo-European aorist type *['ebhu:sm̥] (Old Bulgarian [byxʊ] 'I became') is apparently represented by Greek ['ephu:sa] 'I caused to grow.' Opponents of the neo-grammarian method suppose that when intervocalic [s] was weakened and finally lost during the pre-Greek period, the [s] of these forms resisted the change, because it expressed an important meaning, namely that of the aorist tense. A sound-change, they claim, can be checked in forms where it threatens to remove some semantically important feature.

The neo-grammarian hypothesis implies that sound-change is unaffected by semantic features and concerns merely the habits of articulating speech-sounds. If residual forms are characterized by some semantic feature, then their deviation must be due not to sound-change, but to some other factor of linguistic change — to some factor which is connected with meanings. In our example, the sound-change which led to the loss of intervocalic [s] destroyed every intervocalic [s]; forms like Greek ['este:sa] cannot be continuants of forms that existed before that sound-change. They were created after the sound-change was past, as new combinations of morphemes in a complex form, by a process which we call *analogic new combination* or *analogic change*. In many forms where the aorist-suffix was not between vowels, it had come unscathed through the sound-change. Thus, a Primitive Indo-European aorist *['ele:jkʷsm̥] 'I left' (Sanskrit ['ara:jkʃam]) appears in Greek, by normal phonetic development, as ['elejpsa]; Primitive Indo-European *[eje:wksm̥] 'I joined' (Sanskrit ['aja:wkʃam]) appears as Greek ['ezewksa]; the Primitive Indo-European root *[ɡews-] 'taste' (Greek present ['gewo:], cited above), combining with the aorist-suffix, would give a stem *[ɡe:ws-s-]: as double [ss] was not lost in pre-Greek, but merely at a later date simplified to [s], the Greek aorist ['egewsa] 'I gave a taste' is the normal phonetic type. Accordingly, the Greek language possessed the aorist suffix [-s-]; at all times this suffix was doubtless combined with all manner of verbal stems, and our aorists with the [-s-] between vowels are merely combinations which were made after the sound-change which affected [-s-] had ceased to work. On models like the inherited present-tense ['gewo:] with aorist ['egewsa], one formed, for the present-tense ['plewo:], a new aorist ['eplewsa]. In sum, the residual forms are not due to deflections of the process of sound-change, but reveal to us, rather, a different factor of linguistic change — namely, analogic change.

In much the same way, some students believe that sounds which bear no important meaning are subject to excess weakening and to loss by irregular sound-change. In this way they explain, for instance, the weakening of *will* to [l] in forms like *I'll go*. The neo-grammarian would attribute the weakening rather to the fact that the verb-form in phrases like these is atonic: in English, unstressed phonemes have been subjected to a series of weakenings and losses.

20. 11. The neo-grammarians define sound-change as a purely phonetic process; it affects a phoneme or a type of phonemes either universally or under certain strictly phonetic conditions, and is neither favored nor impeded by the semantic character of the forms which happen to contain the phoneme. The effect of sound-change, then, as it presents itself to the comparatist, will be a set of regular phonemic correspondences, such as Old English [sta:n, ba:n, ba:t, ga:t, ra:d, ha:l]: modern English [stown, bown, bowt, gowt, rowd, howl] *stone, bone, boat, goat, road (rode), whole*. However, these correspondences will almost always be opposed by sets or scatterings of deviant forms, such as Old English [ba:t, swa:n, ha:l] versus modern English [bejt, swejn, hejl] *bait, swain, hale*, because phonetic change is only one of several factors of linguistic change. We must suppose that, no matter how minute and accurate our observation, we should always find deviant forms, because, from the very outset of a sound-change, and during its entire course, and after it is over, the forms of the language are subject to the incessant working of other factors of change, such as, especially, borrowing and analogic combination of new complex forms. The occurrence of sound-change, as defined by the neo-grammarians, is not a fact of direct observation, but an assumption. The neo-grammarians believe that this assumption is correct, because it alone has enabled linguists to find order in the factual data, and because it alone has led to a plausible formulation of other factors of linguistic change.

Theoretically, we can understand the regular change of phonemes, if we suppose that language consists of two layers of habit. One layer is phonemic: the speakers have certain habits of voicing, tongue-movement, and so on. These habits make up the phonetic system of the language. The other layer consists of formal-semantic habits: the speakers habitually utter certain combinations of phonemes in response to certain types of stimuli, and respond appropriately when they hear these same combinations. These habits make up the grammar and lexicon of the language.

One may conceivably acquire the phonetic habits of a language without using any of its significant forms; this may be the case of a singer who has been taught to render a French song in correct pronunciation, or of a mimic who, knowing no French, can yet imitate a Frenchman's English. On the other hand, if the phonemes of a foreign language are not completely incommensurable with ours, we may utter significant forms in this language without acquiring its phonetic habits; this is the case of some speakers of French and English, who converse freely in each others' languages, but, as we say, with an abominable pronunciation.

Historically, we picture phonetic change as a gradual favoring of some non-distinctive variants and a disfavoring of others. It could be observed only by means of an enormous mass of mechanical records, reaching through several generations of speakers. The hypothesis supposes that such a collection — provided that we could rule out the effects of borrowing and analogic change — would show a progressive favoring of variants in some one direction, coupled with the obsolescence of variants at the other extreme. Thus, Old English and Middle English spoke a long mid vowel in forms like *gos* 'goose' and *ges* 'geese.' We suppose that during a long period of time, higher variants were favored and lower variants went out of use, until, in the eighteenth century, the range of surviving variants could be described as a high-vowel type [u:, i:]; since then, the more diphthongal variants have been favored, and the simple-vowel types have gone out of use.

The non-distinctive acoustic features of a language are at all times highly variable. Even the most accurate phonetic record of a language at any one time could not tell us which phonemes were changing. Moreover, it is certain that these non-distinctive, sub-phonemic variants are subject to linguistic borrowing (imitation) and to analogic change (systematization). This appears from the fact that whenever the linguist deals with a sound-change — and certainly in some cases his documents or his observations must date from a time very shortly after the occurrence of the change — he finds the results of the sound-change disturbed by these other factors. Indeed, when we observe sub-phonemic variants, we sometimes find them distributed among speakers or systematized among forms, quite in the manner of linguistic borrowing and of analogic change. In the Central-Western type of American English, vowel-quantities are not distinctive, but some speakers habitually (though perhaps not invariably) use a shorter variant of the phoneme [a] before the clusters [rk, rp], as in *dark, sharp*, and before the clusters [rd, rt] followed by a primary suffix [-r̩, n-], as in *barter, Carter, garden, marten (Martin)*. Before a secondary suffix, [-r̩, -n̩], however, the longer variant is used, as in *starter, carter* ('one who carts'), *harden;* here the existence of the simple words (*start, cart, hard*), whose [a] is not subject to shortening, has led to the favoring of the normal, longer variant. The word *larder* (not part of the colloquial vocabulary) could be read with the shorter variant, but the agent-noun *larder* ('one who lards') could be formed only with the longer type of the [a]-phoneme. This distribution of the sub-phonemic variants is quite like the results of analogic change, and, whatever its origin, the distribution of this habit among speakers is doubtless effected by a process of imitation which we could identify with linguistic borrowing. If the difference between the two variants should become distinctive, then the comparatist would say that a sound-change had occurred, but he would find the results of this sound-change overlaid, from the very start, by the effects of borrowing and of analogic change.

We can often observe that a non-distinctive variant has become entirely obsolete. In eighteenth-century English, forms like *geese, eight, goose, goat* had long vowels of the types [i:, e:, u:, o:], which since then have changed to the diphthongal types [ij, ej, uw, ow]. This displacement has had no bearing on the structure of the language; a transcription of present-day standard English which used the symbols [i:, e:, u:, o:] would be perfectly adequate. It is only the phonetician or acoustician who tells us that there has been a displacement in the absolute physiologic and accustic configuration of these phonemes. Nevertheless, we can see that the non-diphthongal variants, which at first were the predominant ones, are today obsolete. The speaker of present-day standard English who tries to speak a language like German or French which has undiphthongized long vowels, has a hard

PHONETIC CHANGE

time learning to produce these types. It is as hard for him to articulate these acoustic types (which existed in English not so many generations ago) as it is for the Frenchman or the German to produce the English diphthongal types. The speaker learns only with difficulty to produce speech-sounds that do not occur in his native language, even though the historian, irrelevantly, may assure him that an earlier stage of his language possessed these very sounds.

We can speak of sound-change only when the displacement of habit has led to some alteration in the structure of the language. Most types of American English speak a low vowel [ɑ] in forms like *got, rod, not*, where British English has kept an older mid-vowel type [ɔ]. In some types of American standard English, this [ɑ] is distinct from the [a] of forms like *calm, far, pa* — so that *bother* does not rime with *father*, and *bomb*, is not homonymous with *balm:* there has been no displacement of the phonemic system. In other types of American standard English, however, the two phonemes have coincided: *got, rod, bother, bomb, calm, far, pa, father, balm* all have one and the same low vowel [a], and we say, accordingly, that a sound-change has taken place. Some speakers of this (as well as some of the other) type pronounce *bomb* as [bom]: this form is due to some sort of linguistic borrowing and accordingly cannot exhibit the normal correlation.

The initial clusters [kn-, gn-], as in *knee, gnat*, lost their stop sound early in the eighteenth century: hereby *knot* and *not, knight* and *night, gnash* and *Nash* became homonymous. English-speakers of today learn only with difficulty to produce initial clusters like these, as, say, in German *Knie* [kni:] 'knee.'

In Dutch-German area, the Primitive Germanic phoneme [θ] changed toward [ð] and then toward [d]; by the end of the Middle Ages this [d] coincided, in the northern part of the area, with Primitive Germanic [d]. Hence modern standard Dutch has initial [d] uniformly, both in words like *dag* [dax] 'day,' *doen* [du:n] 'do,' *droom* [dro:m] 'dream,' where English has [d], and in words like *dik* [dik] 'thick,' *doorn* [do:rn] 'thorn,' *drie* [dri:] 'three,' where English has [θ]. The distinction has been entirely obliterated, and could be re-introduced only by borrowing from a language in which it has been preserved. Needless to say, the Dutchman or North German has as hard a time learning to utter an English [θ] as though this sound had never existed in his language.

The favoring of variants which leads to sound-change is a historical occurrence; once it is past, we have no guarantee of its happening again. A later process may end by favoring the very same acoustic types as were eliminated by an earlier change. The Old and Middle English long vowels [iː, uː], as in [wiːn, huːs], were eliminated, in the early modern period, by change toward the diphthongal types of the present-day *wine, house*. At about the same time, however, the Old and Middle English long mid vowels, as in [geːs, goːs], were being raised, so that eighteenth-century English again had the types [iː, uː] in words like *geese, goose*. The new [iː, uː] arrived too late to suffer the change to [aj, aw] which had overtaken the Middle English high vowels. Similarly, we must suppose that the pre-Greek speakers of the generations that were weakening the phoneme [s] between vowels, could learn only with difficulty to utter such a thing as a distinct simple [s] in intervocalic position, but, after the change was over, the simplification of long [ss] re-introduced this phonetic type, and (doubtless independently of this) new combinations of the type ['esteːsa] (§ 20.10) were again fully pronounceable. In this way, we can often determine the succession (*relative chronology*) of changes. Thus, it is clear that in pre-Germanic time, the Primitive Indo-European [b, d, g] can have reached the types of Primitive Germanic [p, t, k] only *after* Primitive Indo-European [p, t, k] had already been changed somewhat in the direction of the types of Primitive Germanic [f, θ, h] — for the actual Germanic forms show that these two series of phonemes did not coincide (§ 20.2).

CHAPTER 21

TYPES OF PHONETIC CHANGE

21. 1. Phonetic change, as defined in the last chapter, is a change in the habits of performing sound-producing movements. Strictly speaking, a change of this kind has no importance so long as it does not affect the phonemic system of the language; in fact, even with perfect records at our command, we should probably be unable to determine the exact point where a favoring of certain variants began to deserve the name of a historical change. At the time when speakers of English began to favor the variants with higher tongue-position of the vowels in words like *gōs* 'goose' and *gēs* 'geese,' the dislocation was entirely without significance. The speakers had no way of comparing the acoustic qualities of their vowels with the acoustic qualities of the vowels which their predecessors, a few generations back, had spoken in the same linguistic forms. When they heard a dialect which had not made the change, they may have noticed a difference, but they could have had no assurance as to how this difference had arisen. Phonetic change acquires significance only if it results in a change of the phonemic pattern. For instance, in the early modern period, the Middle English vowel [ɛː], as in *sed* [sɛːd] 'seed,' was raised until it coincided with the [eː] in *ges* [geːs] 'geese,' and this coincidence for all time changed the distribution of phonemes in the forms of the language. Again, the Middle English short [e] in a so-called "open" syllable — that is, before a single consonant followed by another vowel, as in *ete* ['ete] 'eat' — was lengthened and ultimately coincided with the long vowels just mentioned. Accordingly, the phonemic structure of modern English is different from that of medieval English. Our phoneme [ij] continues, among others, these three older phonemes; we may note, especially, that this coincidence has given rise to a number of homonyms.

Old and Middle English [eː] has changed to modern [ij] in *heel, steel, geese, queen, green, meet* (verb), *need, keep*.

Old and Middle English [ɛː] has changed to modern [ij] in *heal, meal* ('taking of food'), *cheese, leave, clean, lean* (adjective), *street, mead* ('meadow'), *meet* (adjective).

Old and Middle English [e] has changed to modern [ij] in *steal, meal* ('flour'), *weave, lean* (verb), *quean, speak, meat, mete, eat, mead* ('fermented drink')

On the other hand, the restriction of this last change to a limited phonetic position, has produced different phonemes in forms that used to have the same phoneme: the old [e] was lengthened in Middle English *weve* > *weave*, but not in Middle English *weft* > *weft*. In the same way, a phonetic change which consisted of shortening long vowels before certain consonant-clusters has produced the difference of vowel between *meadow* (< Old English ['mɛːdwe]) and *mead*, or between *kept* (< Old English ['keːpte]) and *keep*.

A few hundred years ago, initial [k] was lost before [n]: the result was a change in the phonemic system, which included such features as the homonymy of *knot* and *not*, or of *knight* and *night*, and the alternation of [n-] and [-kn-] in *know, knowledge : acknowledge*.

21. 2. The general direction of a great deal of sound-change is toward a simplification of the movements which make up the utterance of any given linguistic form. Thus, consonant-groups are often simplified. The Old English initial clusters [hr, hl, hn, kn, gn, wr] have lost their initial consonants, as in Old English *hring* > *ring, hlēapan* > *leap, hnecca* > *neck, cnēow* > *knee, gnagan* > *gnaw, wringan* > *wring*. The loss of the [h] in these groups occurred in the later Middle Ages, that of the other consonants in early modern time; we do not know what new factor intervened at these times to destroy the clusters which for many centuries had been spoken without change. The [h]-clusters are still spoken in Icelandic; initial [kn] remains not only in the other Germanic languages (as, Dutch *knie* [kniː], German *Knie* [kniː], Danish [knɛːʔ], Swedish [kneː]), but also in the English dialects of the Shetland and Orkney Islands and northeastern Scotland. The [gn] persists almost as widely — in English, more widely; [wr-], in the shape of [vr-], remains in Scandinavian, the northern part of the Dutch-German area, including standard Dutch, and in several scattered dialects of English. As long as we do not know what factors led to these changes at one time and place but not at another, we cannot claim to know the causes of the change —

TYPES OF PHONETIC CHANGE

that is, to predict its occurrence. The greater simplicity of the favored variants is a permanent factor; it can offer no possibilities of correlation.

Simplification of final consonant-clusters is even more common. A Primitive Indo-European *[peːts] 'foot' (nominative singular) appears in Sanskrit as [paːt] and in Latin as *pes* [peːs]; a Primitive Indo-European *['bheronts] 'bearing' (nominative singular masculine) appears in Sanskrit as ['bharan], and in Latin as *ferens* ['ferens], later ['fereːs]. It is this type of change which leads to habits of permitted final (§ 8.4) and to morphologic alternations of the type described in § 13.9. Thus, a Primitive Central Algonquian *[axkehkwa] 'kettle,' plural *[axkehkwaki], reflected in Fox [ahkoːhkwa, ahkoːhkoːki], loses its final vowel and part of the consonant-cluster in Cree [askihk, askihkwak] and in Menomini [ahkɛːh, ahkɛːhkuk], so that the plural-form in these languages contains a consonant-cluster that cannot be determined by inspection of the singular form. In English, final [ŋg] and [mb] have lost their stop; hence the contrast of *long : longer* [lɔŋ — 'lɔŋgə], *climb : clamber* [klajm — 'klɛmbə].

Sometimes even single final consonants are weakened or disappear. In pre-Greek, final [t, d] were lost, as in Primitive Indo-European *[tod] 'that,' Sanskrit [tat]: Greek [to]; final [m] became [n], as in Primitive Indo-European *[ju'gom] 'yoke,' Sanskrit [ju'gam]: Greek [zu'gon]. The same changes seem to have occurred in pre-Germanic. Sometimes all final consonants are lost and there results a phonetic pattern in which every word ends in a vowel. This happened in pre-Slavic, witness forms like Old Bulgarian [to] 'that,' [igo] 'yoke.' It is a change of this sort that accounts for morphologic situations like that of Samoan (§ 13.9); a Samoan form like [inu] 'drink' is the descendant of an older *[inum], whose final consonant has been kept in Tagalog [i'num].

When changes of this sort appear at the beginning or, more often, at the end of words, we have to suppose that the languages in which they took place had, at the time, some phonetic marking of the word-unit. If there were any forms in which the beginning or the end of a word had not the characteristic initial or final pronunciation, these forms would not suffer the change, and would survive as sandhi-forms. Thus, in Middle English, final [n] was lost, as in *eten > ete* 'eat,' but the article *an* before vowels must have been pronounced as if it were part of the following word — that is, without the phonetic peculiarities of final position — so that the [n] in this case was not lost (liké a final [n]), but preserved (like a medial [n]): *a house* but *an arm*. Latin *vōs* 'ye' gives French *vous* [vu], but Latin phrase-types like *vōs amātis* 'ye love' are reflected in the French sandhi-habit of saying *vous aimez* [vuz eme]. Latin *est* 'he is' gave French *est* [ɛ] 'is,' but the phrase-type of Latin *est ille?* 'is that one?' appears in the French sandhi-form in *est-il?* [ɛt i?] 'is he?' In the same way, a Primitive Indo-European *['bheronts] is reflected not only in Sanskrit ['bharan], above cited, but also in the Sanskrit habit of adding a sandhi [s] when the next word began with [t], as in ['bharās 'tatra] 'carrying there.'

21. 3. Simplification of consonant-clusters is a frequent result of sound-change. Thus, a pre-Latin *['fulgmen] 'flash (of lightning)' gives a Latin *fulmen*. Here the group [lgm] was simplified by the change to [lm], but the group [lg], as in *fulgur* 'flash,' was not changed, and neither was the group [gm], as in *agmen* 'army.' In describing such changes, we speak of the conditions as *conditioning factors* (or *causing factors*) and say, for instance, that one of these was absent in cases like *fulgur* and *agmen*, where the [g], accordingly, was preserved. This form of speech is inaccurate, since the change was really one of [lgm] to [lm], and cases like *fulgur*, *agmen* are irrelevant, but it is often convenient to use these terms. The result of a conditioned change is often a morphologic alternation. Thus, in Latin, we have the suffix *-men* in *agere* 'to lead': *agmen* 'army' but *fulgere* 'to flash': *fulmen* 'flash (of lightning).' Similarly, pre-Latin [rkn] became [rn]; beside *pater* 'father': *paternus* 'paternal,' we have *quercus* 'oak' : *quernus* 'oaken.'

Quite commonly, clusters change by way of *assimilation:* the position of the vocal organs for the production of one phoneme is altered to a position more like that of the other phoneme. The commoner case is *regressive* assimilation, change of the prior phoneme.

Thus, the voicing or unvoicing of a consonant is often altered into agreement with that of a following consonant; the [s] of *goose* and *house* has been voiced to [z] in the combinations *gosling, husband*. This, again, may give rise to morphologic alternations. In the history of Russian the loss of two short vowels (I shall transcribe them as [ɪ] and [ʊ]) produced consonant-clusters; in these clusters a stop or spirant was then assimilated, as to voicing, to a following stop or spirant. The old forms can be seen in Old

TYPES OF PHONETIC CHANGE

Bulgarian, which did not make the changes in question. Thus *['svatɪba] 'marriage' gives Russian ['svadba]; compare Russian [svat] 'arranger of a marriage.' Old Bulgarian [otube:ʒati] 'to run away' appears in Russian as [odbe'ʒat]; compare the simple Old Bulgarian [otʊ] 'from, away from' : Russian [ot]. On the other hand, Old Bulgarian [podʊkopati] 'to ɪ ɪdermine' appears in Russian as [potko'pat]; contrast Old Bulgarian [podʊ igo] 'under the yoke' : Russian ['pod igo].

The assimilation may affect the action of the velum, tongue, or lips. If some difference between the consonants is kept, the assimilation is *partial;* thus in pre-Latin [pn] was assimilated to [mn], as in Primitive Indo-European *['swepnos] 'sleep,' Sanskrit ['svapnah] : Latin *somnus.* If the difference entirely disappears, the assimilation is *total,* and the result is a long consonant, as in Italian *sonno* ['sɔnno]. Similarly, Latin *octō* 'eight' > Italian *otto* ['ɔtto]; Latin *ruptum* 'broken' > Italian *rotto* ['rotto].

In *progressive* assimilation the latter consonant is altered. Thus, pre-Latin *[kolnis] 'hill' gives Latin *collis;* compare Lithuanian ['ka:lnas] 'mountain.' Our word *hill* underwent the same change [ln] > [ll] in pre-Germanic; witness Primitive Indo-European *[pl̩:'nos] 'full,' Sanskrit [pu:r'ɴah], Lithuanian ['pilnas] : Primitive Germanic *['follaz], Gothic *fulls,* Old English *full,* or Primitive Indo-European *['wl̩:na:] 'wool,' Sanskrit ['u:rɴa:], Lithuanian ['vilna] : Primitive Germanic *['wollo:], Gothic *wulla,* Old English *wull.*

21. 4. A great many other changes of consonants can be viewed as assimilative in character. Thus, the unvoicing of final consonants, which has occurred in the history of various languages, can be viewed as a sort of regressive assimilation: the open position of the vocal chords which follows upon the end of speech, is anticipated during the utterance of the final consonant. Thus, many dialects of the Dutch-German area, including the standard languages, have unvoiced all final stops and spirants; the result is an alternation of unvoiced finals with voiced medials (§ 13.9):

Old High German *tag* 'day' > New High German *Tag* [ta:k], but, plural, *taga* 'days' > *Tage* ['ta:ge], with unchanged [g];

Old High German *bad* 'bath' > New High German *Bad* [ba:t], but, genitive case, *bades* > *Bades* ['ba:des];

Old High German *gab* '(he) gave' > New High German *gab* [ga:p], but, plural, *gābun* '(they) gave' > *gaben* ['ga:ben].

The voiced consonant may be preserved in sandhi — that is, in traditional phrase-types where it did not come at the end of speech. This does not happen in standard German; here the final-form has been carried out for every word-unit. In Russian, however, we have not only the final-form, by which an old [podʊ], after loss of the vowel, became [pot], but also phrasal types like ['pod igo] 'under the yoke.' There is a type of Dutch pronunciation where an old *hebbe* '(I) have' appears, after loss of the final vowel, not only in the final-form with [-p], as in *ik heb* [ek 'hep], but also in the phrasal sandhi-type, *heb ek?* ['heb ek?] 'have I?' This is the origin of reminiscent sandhi (§ 12.5).

A very common type of change is the weakening of consonants between vowels or other open sounds. This, too, is akin to assimilation, since, when the preceding and following sounds are open and voiced, the less marked closure or the voicing of a stop or spirant represents an economy of movement. The change which gave rise to the American English voiced tongue-flip variety of [t], as in *water, butter, at all* (§ 6.7), was surely of this sort. Latin [p, t, k] between vowels are largely weakened in the Romance languages: Latin *rīpam* 'bank, shore,' *sētam* 'silk,' *focum* 'hearth' appear in Spanish as *riba, seda, fuego* 'fire,' where the [b, d, g] are largely spirant in character, and in French as *rive, soie, feu* [riːv, swa, fø]. Some languages, such as pre-Greek, lose sounds like [s, j, w] between vowels. The Polynesian languages and, to some extent, the medieval Indo-Aryan languages, show a loss of the old structure of medial consonants, much like that in the French forms just cited. In the history of English, loss of [v] is notable, as in Old English ['hɛvde, 'havok, 'hlaːvord, 'hlaːvdije, 'heːavod, 'navogaːr] > modern *had, hawk, lord, lady, head, auger;* this change seems to have occurred in the thirteenth century.

If the conditioning factors are removed by subsequent change, the result is an irregular alternation. In this way, arose, for example, the sandhi-alternation of initial consonants in Irish (§ 12.4). In the history of this language, stops between vowels were weakened to spirants, as in Primitive Indo-European *['piboːmi] 'I drink,' Sanskrit ['pibaːmi]: Old Irish *ebaim* ['evimʹ]. Apparently the language at this stage gave little phonetic recognition to the word-unit, and carried out this change in close-knit phrases, changing, for instance, an *[eso bowes] 'his cows' (compare Sanskrit [a'sja 'gaːvah]) to what is now [a vaː], in contrast with

TYPES OF PHONETIC CHANGE

the absolute form [baː] 'cows.' This type of sandhi is preserved in a limited number of cases, as, in our instance, after the pronoun [a] 'his.' In the same way, [s] between vowels was weakened to [h] and then lost: a Primitive Indo-European *['swesoːr] 'sister,' Sanskrit ['svasaː], giving first, presumably, *['swehoːr], and then Old Irish *siur*. Final [s] similarly was lost: a Gallic *tarbos* 'bull' appears in Old Irish as *tarb*. We have to suppose, now, that the change [s > h] between vowels took place also in close-knit phrases, so that an *[esaːs oːwjo] 'her egg' (compare Sanskrit [a'sjaːh] 'her,' with [-h] from [-s]) resulted in a modern [a huv] 'her egg,' in contrast with the independent [uv] 'egg' — again, a habit preserved only in certain combinations, as after the word for 'her.' Similarly, [m] was first changed to [n] and then lost at the end of words, but between vowels was preserved; both treatments appear in *[nemeːtom] 'holy place,' Old Gallic [nemeːton], Old Irish *nemed*. At the stage where [-m] had become [-n], an old *[sen-toːm oːwjoːm] 'of these eggs' (compare the Greek genitive plural [ˈtoːn]) gave what is now [na nuv], in contrast with the absolute [uv] 'egg.' To a similar, but more complicated development we owe the sandhi-alternant with initial [t], as in [an tuv] 'the egg'; ultimately this is due to the fact that the Primitive Indo-European nominative-accusative singular neuter pronoun-forms ended in [d], as Sanskrit [tat] 'that,' Latin *id* 'it.'

We may interpret the pre-Germanic change discovered by Verner (§§ 18.7; 20.8) as a weakening of unvoiced spirants [f, θ, h, s] between musical sounds to voiced [v, ð, ɣ, z]; then the restriction of the change to cases where the preceding vowel or diphthong was unstressed is subject to a further interpretation of the same sort: after a loudly stressed vowel there is a great amount of breath stored up behind the vocal chords, so that their opening for an unvoiced spirant is easier than their closure for a voiced. We cannot view these interpretations as correlating ("causal") explanations, however, for enough languages keep unvoiced spirants intact between vowels, while others change them to voiced regardless of high stress on a preceding vowel. Here, too, the conditioning factor was afterwards removed by other changes: in an early pre-Germanic *['werθonon] 'to become' versus *[wurðuˈme] 'we became,' the alternation [θːð] depended on the place of the stress; later, when the stress had changed to the first syllable of all words, the alternation in Primitive Germanic *['werθanan — 'wurdume], Old English ['weorðan — 'wurdon], was an arbitrary irregularity, just as is the parallel *was : were*, from Primitive Germanic *['wase — 'we:zume], in modern English. A similar change occurred much later in the history of English; it accounts for such differences as *luxury : luxurious* ['lʌkʃ- əri — lʌg'ʒuəriəs] in a common type of pronunciation, and for the two treatments of French [s] in forms like *possessor* [pə'zesə]. This change involved the voicing of old [s] after an unstressed vowel in suffixes, as in *glasses, misses, Bess's;* a few forms like *dice* (plural of *die*) and *pence* show the preservation of [s] after a stressed vowel. Immediately after this change the stressed forms must have been *off* [of], *with* [wiθ], *is* [is], *his* [his], and the atonic forms *of* [ov] and [wið, iz, hiz,] but this alternation has been destroyed: *off* and *of* have been redistributed by analogic change, [wiθ] survives as a variant of [wið], and the [s]-forms of *is* and *his* have fallen into disuse.

21. 5 Consonants are often assimilated to the tongue-position of preceding or following vowels. The commonest case is the assimilation especially of dentals and velars to a following front vowel; this is known as *palatalization*. A change of this kind which did not cause phonemic alterations, must have occurred not too long ago in English, for phoneticians assure us that we make the tongue-contact of [k, g] farther forward before a front vowel, as in *kin, keep, kept, give, geese, get*, than before a back vowel, as in *cook, good*. In pre-English there occurred a change of the same sort which led to alteration of the phonemic structure. To begin with, the palatalized form of [g] — presumably this phoneme had a spirant character — coincided with another phoneme, [j]. The change in phonemic distribution appears plainly when we compare the cognate forms from North German (Old Saxon), where the old phonemic distribution remained intact:

North German	Pre-English	>	Old English	>	Modern English
gold	*[gold]		*gold*	[gold]	*gold*
gōd	*[go:d]		*god*	[go:d]	*good*
geldan	*['ɡeldan]		*gieldan*	['jeldan]	*yield*
garn	*[gɛrn]		*gearn*	[jarn]	*yarn*
jok	*[jok]		*geoc*	[jok]	*yoke*
jār	*[je:r]		*gear*	[je:ar]	*year*

TYPES OF PHONETIC CHANGE

Another way in which the pre-English palatalization in time affected the structure of the language, was by the obscuration of the conditioning factor. The back vowels [o, u], which did not affect a preceding velar, were changed, under certain conditions, to front vowels [ø, y] and later to [e, i], which coincided with old front vowels that had effected palatalization. Hence, in the later stages of English, both palatalized and unpalatalized velars occurred before front vowels.

Palatalized velars, before old front vowels:

Pre-English	>	Old English	>	Modern English
*['kɛːsi]		ciese ['kiːese]		cheese
*[kinn]		cinn [kin]		chin
*['geldan]		gieldan ['jeldan]		yield
*[gern]		gearn [jarn]		yarn

Unpalatalized velars, before new front vowels:

Pre-English	>	Old English	>	Modern English
*['koːni > 'køːni]		cene ['keːne]		keen
*['kunni > 'kynni]		cynn [kyn]		kin
*['goːsi > 'gøːsi]		ges [geːs]		geese
*['guldjan > 'gyldjan]		gyldan ['gyldan]		gild

A third factor of the same kind was the loss, by later sound-change, of the conditioning feature, — that is, of the front vowel [e, i, j] which had caused the palatalization:

Palatalized velars, followed, at the critical time, by a front vowel:

Pre-English	>	Old English	>	Modern English
*['drenkjan]		drencean ['drenkan]		drench
*['stiki]		stice ['stike]		stitch
*['sengjan]		sengan ['sengan]		singe
*['bryggju]		brycg [brygg]		bridge

Unpalatalized velars, not followed by front vowel:

Pre-English	>	Old English	>	Modern English
*['drinkan]		drincan ['drinkan]		drink
*['stikka]		sticca ['stikka]		stick
*['singan]		singan ['singan]		sing
*['frogga]		frogga ['frogga]		frog

The sound-change which we call palatalization changes consonants at first to varieties which the phonetician calls palatalized; the modern English forms in our preceding examples, with their [tʃ, dʒ, j], show us that these palatalized types may undergo further changes. These, in fact, are extremely common, although their direction varies. In the case of both velars and dentals, affricate types [tʃ, dʒ] and sibilant types, both abnormal [ʃ, ʒ] and normal [s, z], are fairly frequent. In modern English we have a development of [tj > tʃ, dj > dʒ, sj > ʃ, zj > ʒ], as in *virtue*, *Indian*, *session*, *vision* [ˈvəːtʃuw, ˈindʒn, ˈseʃn, ˈviʒn]; more formal variants, such as [ˈvəːtjuw, ˈindjn̩], have arisen by later changes. The Romance languages exhibit a great variety of development of palatalized velars:

	LATIN	>	ITALIAN	FRENCH	SPANISH
'hundred'	*centum*		*cento*	*cent*	*ciento*
	[ˈkentum]		[ˈtʃɛnto]	[sã]	[ˈθjento]
'nation'	*gentem*		*gente*	*gens*	*gente*
	[ˈgentem]		[ˈdʒɛnte]	[ʒã]	[xente]

Part of the French area has a palatalization of [k] before [a]; in the Middle Ages, when English borrowed many French words, this had reached the stage of [tʃ], so that a Latin type like *cantare* [kanˈtaːre] 'to sing' > Old French *chanter* [tʃanˈteːr] appears in English as *chant*; similarly, Latin *cathedram* [ˈkatedram] appears as *chair*; Latin *catenam* [kaˈteːnam] as *chain*; Latin *cameram* [ˈkameram] as *chamber*. In modern standard French, further change of this [tʃ] has led to [ʃ]: *chanter*, *chaire*, *chaîne*, *chambre* [ʃãte, ʃɛːr, ʃɛːn, ʃãbr].

Palatalization has played a great part in the history of the Slavic languages: it has occurred at different times with different results, and has affected every type of consonant, including even labials.

A case of palatalization whose causing factor was obscured by later change, played an important part in the development of Indo-European studies. In the Indo-Iranian languages a single vowel-type [a] corresponds to the three types [a, e, o] of the other Indo-European languages. Thus, Latin *ager* 'field,' *equos* 'horse,' *octō* 'eight' are cognate with Sanskrit [ˈaɟrah, ˈaçvah, aʃˈtaːw]. For a long time students believed that the Indo-Iranian languages had here preserved the Primitive Indo-European state of affairs,

TYPES OF PHONETIC CHANGE

and that the diverse vowels of the European languages were due to later change, made during a common pre-European period. Before the [a] of the Indo-Iranian languages, Primitive Indo-European, velars [k, g] appeared sometimes unchanged and sometimes as [c, ɟ]. In the 1870's several students independently saw that these latter reflexes are probably due to palatalization, and, in fact, correlate fairly well with the cases where the European languages have [e]. Thus we find, with back vowels in the languages of Europe and velar stops in Indo-Iranian, correspondences like

Primitive Indo-European *[kʷod], Latin *quod* [kwod] 'what': Sanskrit kat- (as first member in compounds);

Primitive Indo-European *[gʷo:ws], Old English *cu* [ku:] 'cow': Sanskrit [ga:wh].

On the other hand, with the front vowel [e] in the languages of Europe and affricates instead of velar stops in Indo-Iranian, we find correspondences like

Primitive Indo-European *[kʷe], Latin *que* [kwe] 'and' : Sanskrit [ca];

Primitive Indo-European *[gʷe:nis], Gothic *qens* [kwe:ns] 'wife': Sanskrit [-ɟa:nih] (final member in compounds).

From cases like these we conclude that the uniform [a] of Indo-Iranian is due to a later development: in pre-Indo-Iranian there must have been an [e] distinct from the other vowels, and this [e] must have caused palatalization of preceding velar stops. Since this [e], moreover, agrees with the [e] of the European languages, the distinction must have existed in Primitive Indo-European, and cannot be due to a joint innovation by the languages of Europe. This discovery put an end to the notion of a common parent speech intermediate between Primitive Indo-European and the European (as opposed to the Indo-Iranian) languages.

21. 6 The weakening or loss of consonants is sometimes accompanied by *compensatory lengthening* of a preceding vowel. The Old English combination [ht], preserved to this day in northern dialects, has lost the [h] and lengthened the preceding vowel in most of the area. Thus, Old English *niht* [niht, nixt] 'night,' modern Scotch [nixt, next], became [ni:t], whence modern *night* [najt]. Loss of a sibilant before voiced non-syllabics with compensatory lengthening of a vowel is quite common, as in pre-Latin *['dis-lego:] 'I pick out, I like' > Latin *dīligō* (compare *dis-* in *dispendō* 'I weigh out,' and *legō* 'I pick, gather'); early Latin *cosmis* 'kind' > Latin *cōmis;* pre-Latin *['kaznos] 'gray-haired' > Latin *cānus* (compare, in Paelignian, a neighboring Italic dialect, *casnar* 'old man'); Primitive Indo-European *[nisdos] 'nest' (compare English *nest*) > Latin *nīdus*.

If the lost consonant is a nasal, the preceding vowel is often nasalized, with or without compensatory lengthening and other changes. This is the origin of the nasalized vowels of many languages, as of French: Latin *cantāre* > French *chanter* [ʃɑ̃te], Latin *centum* > French *cent* [sɑ], and so on. The morphology of Old Germanic shows parallel forms with and without nasal, such as Gothic ['bringan — 'bra:hta] 'bring, brought,' ['θankjan — 'θa:hta] 'think, thought.' The forms without [n] all have an [h] immediately following a long vowel. The suspicion that in these forms an [n] has been lost with compensatory lengthening, is confirmed by a few comparisons with other Indo-European languages, such as Latin *vincere* 'to conquer' : Gothic ['wi:han] 'to fight.' Further, we have a twelfth-century Icelandic grammarian's statement that in his language forms like [θe:l] 'file' (from *['θinhlo:]) had a nasalized vowel. In Old English, the [a:] of the other Germanic languages, in forms like these, is represented by [ɔ:], as in ['bro:hte] 'brought,' ['θo:hte] 'thought.' We have reason to believe that this divergent vowel quality is a reflex of older nasalization, because in other cases also, Old English shows us an [o:] as a reflex of an earlier nasalized [a]. The loss of [n] before [h] occurred in pre-Germanic; before the other unvoiced spirants [f, s, θ] an [n] remained in most Germanic dialects, but was lost, with compensatory lengthening, in English, Frisian, and some of the adjacent dialects. In these cases, too, we find an [o:] in Old English as the reflex of a lengthened and nasalized [a]. Thus, the words *five, us, mouth, soft, goose, other* appear in the oldest German documents as [finf, uns, mund, sanfto, gans, 'ander] (with [d] as reflex of an old [θ]), but in Old English as [fi:f, u:s, mu:θ, 'so:fte, go:s, 'o:ðer].

When a consonant has been lost between vowels, the resulting succession of vowels often suffers *contraction* into a single vowel or diphthongal combination. Our earliest English records still show us an [h] between vowels, but very soon afterward this *h* disappears from the texts, and single vowels are written. Thus, the word *toe* appears first as *tahæ*, presumably ['ta:hɛ], but soon as *ta* [ta:];

TYPES OF PHONETIC CHANGE 381

a pre-English type *['θanho:n] 'clay' appears first as *thohæ* ['θo:hɛ], then as [θo:]; Gothic ['ahwa] 'river' (cognate with Latin *aqua* 'water') is paralleled by Old English *ea* [e:a], from pre-English *['ahwu]; Gothic ['sehwan] 'to see' is matched by Old English *seon* [se:on].

21. 7. Vowels are often assimilated to vowels that precede or follow in the next syllable. During the early Middle Ages, changes of this kind occurred in several Germanic dialects. These changes in the Germanic languages are known by the name of *umlaut;* somewhat confusingly, this term is applied also to the resultant grammatical alternations. The commonest type of umlaut is the partial assimilation of a stressed back vowel to a following [i, j]. The resulting alternations, after the loss of the conditioning [i, j], became purely grammatical:

Pre-English	>	Old English		>	Modern English
*[gold]		*gold*			*gold*
*['guldjan]¹		*gyldan*			*gild*
*[mu:s]		*mus*	[mu:s]		*mouse*
*['mu:si]		*mys*	[my:s]		*mice*
*[fo:t]		*fot*	[fo:t]		*foot*
*['fo:ti]		*fet*	[fe:t]		*feet*
*[gans]		*gos*	[go:s]		*goose*
*['gansi]		*ges*	[ge:s]		*geese*
*[drank]		*dranc*	[drank]		*drank*
*['drankjan]		*drencean*	['drenkan]		*drench*

Old Norse had also other types of umlaut, such as assimilation of [a] toward the back-vowel quality of a following [u], as in *['saku] 'accusation' (compare Old English *sacu* 'dispute') > Old Norse [sɔk]. Similar changes, supplemented, no doubt by regularizing new-formations, must have led to the vowel-harmony that prevails in Turco-Tartar and some other languages (§ 11.7).

The effect of simplification appears most plainly in shortening and loss of vowels. In the final syllables of words, and especially in final position, this occurs in all manner of languages. Among the Central Algonquian languages, Fox alone has kept the final vowels: Primitive Central Algonquian *[eleniwa] 'man' > Fox [neniwa], Ojibwa [inini], Menomini [enɛːniw], Plains Cree [ijiniw]. Certain

---
[1] The [u] in this form is due to an earlier assimilation of [o] to the high-vowel position of the following [j].

types of two-syllable words are exempt from this shortening: *[chkwa] 'louse' > Fox [ehkwa], Ojibwa [ihkwa], Menomini [ehkuah], Cree [ihkwa].

Languages with strong word-stress often weaken or lose their unstressed vowels. The loss of final vowels, as in Old English (*ic*) *singe* > (*I*) *sing*, is known as *apocope;* that of medial vowels, as in Old English *stānas* > *stones* [stownz], as *syncope*. The contrast between the long forms of Primitive Germanic, the shorter forms of Old English, and the greatly reduced words of modern English, is due to a succession of such changes. Thus, a Primitive Indo-European *['bheronom] 'act of bearing,' Sanskrit ['bharaɴam], Primitive Germanic *['beranan], gives Old English *beran*, Middle English *bere*, and then modern (*to*) *bear*. The habit of treating certain words in the phrase as if they were part of the preceding or following word, was inherited from Primitive Indo-European; when, in pre-Germanic time, a single high stress was placed on each word, these atonic forms received none; later, the weakening of unstressed vowels led to sandhi-variants, stressed and unstressed, of such words. Weakenings of this kind have occurred over and over again in the history of English, but the resultant alternations have been largely removed by re-formations which consisted either of using the full forms in unstressed positions, or of using the weakened forms in stressed positions. Our *on*, for instance, was in the medieval period the unweakened form; the weakened form of this word was *a*, as in *away*, from Old English *on weg* [on 'wej]; this weakened form survives only in a limited number of combinations, such as *away, ashore, aground, aloft,* and the unweakened *on* is now used in atonic position, as in *on the table,* but has here been subjected to a new weakening, which has resulted in unstressed [ən] beside stressed [ɔn], as in *go on* [gow 'ɔn]. In contrast with this, our pronoun *I*, which we use in both stressed and unstressed positions, reflects an old unstressed form, in which the final consonant of Old English *ic* has been lost; the old stressed form survives in the [itʃ] 'I' of a few local dialects. These changes have left their mark in the unstressed sandhi-variants of many words, such as *is*, but [z] in *he's here; will*, but [l] in *I'll go; not*, but [nt] in *isn't;* and in the weakened forms of some unstressed compound members: *man*, but [-mən] in *gentleman; swain* but [-sn] in *boatswain*. The same factor accounts for the shortness of French words compared to Latin; as in *centum* > *cent*

TYPES OF PHONETIC CHANGE

[să]; since the time of these shortenings, however, French has lost the strong word-stress and ceased shortening its forms.

If a language goes through this kind of change at a time when morphologically related forms stress different syllables, the result may be an extremely irregular morphology. We can see the beginnings of this in our foreign-learned vocabulary, which stresses different syllables in different derivatives: *angel* ['ejnʤl], but *angelic* [ɛn'ʤelik]. In Primitive Germanic the prefixes were unstressed in verb-forms but stressed in most other words; the weakenings that ensued broke up some morphologic sets, such as

pre-English *[bi-'ha:tan] 'to threaten' > Old English *behatan* [be'ha:tan], but

pre-English *['bi-ha:t] 'a threat' > Old English *beot* [be:ot].

A similar process rendered the morphology and, as to sandhi, the syntax of Old Irish extremely irregular:

pre-Irish *['bereti] 'he bears' > Old Irish *berid* ['berið];

pre-Irish *[eks 'beret] 'he bears out, brings forth' > Old Irish *asbeir* [as'ber] 'he says';

pre-Irish *[ne esti 'eks beret] 'not it-is that-he-forth-brings' (that is, 'he does not bring forth') > Old Irish *nī epir* [ni: 'epir] 'he does not say.'

21. 8. Some changes which superficially do not seem like weakenings or abbreviations of movement, may yet involve a simplification. In a good many languages we find an intermediate consonant arising in a cluster. A Primitive Indo-European [sr] appears as [str] in Germanic and in Slavic; thus, Primitive Indo-European *[srow-] (compare Sanskrit ['sravati] 'it flows') is reflected in Primitive Germanic *['strawmaz] 'stream,' Old Norse [strawmr], Old English [stre:am], and in Old Bulgarian [struja] 'stream.' English, at more than one time, has inserted a [d] in the groups [nr, nl] and a [b] in the groups [mr, ml]: Old English ['θunrian] > (*to*) *thunder;* Old English ['alre] (accusative case) > *alder;* Gothic has ['timrjan] 'to construct' as well as ['timbrjan], but Old English has only ['timbrian] and [je'timbre] 'carpentry-work,' whence modern *timber;* Old English ['θymle] > *thimble.* These changes involve no additional movement, but merely replace simultaneous movements by successive. To pass from [n] to [r], for instance, the speaker must simultaneously raise his velum and move his tongue from the closure position to the trill position:

384 TYPES OF PHONETIC CHANGE

```
        [n]                              [r]
  velum lowered   ⟫⟶       velum raised
  dental closure  ⟫⟶       trill position
```

If, with a less delicate co-ordination, the velum is raised before the change of tongue-position, there results a moment of unnasalized closure, equivalent to the phoneme [d]:

```
        [n]                  [d]                       [r]
  velum lowered   ⟫⟶  velum raised
  dental closure                         ⟫⟶   trill position
```

The second of these performances is evidently easier than the first.

In other cases, too, an apparent lengthening of a form may be viewed as lessening the difficulty of utterance. When a relatively sonorous phoneme is non-syllabic, it often acquires syllabic function; this change is known by the Sanskrit name of *samprasarana*. Thus, in sub-standard English, *elm* [elm] has changed to [ˈelm̩]. This is often followed by another change, known as *anaptyxis*, the rise of a vowel beside the sonant, which becomes non-syllabic. Primitive Indo-European *[aɡros] 'field' gives pre-Latin *[aɡr̩]; in this the [r] must have become syllabic, and then an anaptyctic vowel must have arisen, for in the historical Latin form *ager* [ˈager] the *e* represents a fully formed vowel. Similarly, Primitive Germanic forms like *[ˈakraz] 'field,' *[ˈfoglaz] 'bird,' *[ˈtajknan] 'sign,' *[ˈmajθmaz] 'precious object' lost their unstressed vowels in all the old Germanic dialects. The Gothic forms [akrs, fugls, tajkn, majθms] may have been monosyllabic or may have had syllabic sonants; anaptyxis has taken place in the Old English forms [ˈeker, ˈfugol, ˈtaːken, ˈmaːðom], though even here spellings like *fugl* are not uncommon.

Another change which may be regarded as a simplification occurs in the history of some stress-using languages: the quantities of stressed vowels are regulated according to the character of the following phonemes. Generally, long vowels remain long and short vowels are lengthened in "open" syllables, that is, before a single consonant that is followed by another vowel; in other positions, long vowels are shortened and short ones kept short. Thus, Middle English long vowels remained long in forms like *clene* [ˈkleːne] > *clean*, *kepe* [ˈkeːpe] > *keep*, *mone* [ˈmoːne] > *moon*, but were shortened in forms like *clense* > *cleanse*, *kepte* > *kept*, *mon(en)dai* > *Monday:* and short vowels were lengthened in forms like *weve* ['weve] > *weave*, *stele* ['stele] > *steal*, *nose* ['nose] > *nose*, but stayed short in forms like *weft*, *stelth* > *stealth*, *nos(e)thirl* > *nostril*. In some languages, such as Menomini, we find a very complicated regulation of long and short vowels according to the preceding and following consonants and according to the number of syllables intervening after the last preceding long vowel.

The complete loss of quantitative differences, which occurred, for instance, in medieval Greek and in some of the modern Slavic languages, makes articulation more uniform. The same can be said of the abandonment of distinctions of syllable-pitch, which has occurred in these same languages; similarly, the removal of word-accent uniformly to some one position such as the first syllable, in pre-Germanic and in Bohemian, or the next-to-last, in Polish, probably involves a facilitation.

In the same sense, the loss of a phonemic unit may be viewed as a simplification. Except for English and Icelandic, the Germanic languages have lost the phoneme [θ] and its voiced development [ð]; the reflexes coincide in Frisian and in Scandinavian largely with [t], as in Swedish *torn* [to:rn] : *thorn*, with the same initial as *tio* ['ti:e] : *ten*, and in the northern part of the Dutch-German area with [d], as in Dutch *doorn* [do:rn] : *thorn*, with the same initial as *doen* [du:n] : *do*. Old English [h] before a consonant, as in *niht* 'night,' or in final position, as in *seah* '(I) saw,' was acoustically doubtless an unvoiced velar or palatal spirant; in most of the English area this sound has been lost or has coincided with other phonemes.

21. 9. Although many sound-changes shorten linguistic forms, simplify the phonetic system, or in some other way lessen the labor of utterance, yet no student has succeeded in establishing a correlation between sound-change and any antecedent phenomenon: the causes of sound-change are unknown. When we find a large-scale shortening and loss of vowels, we feel safe in assuming that the language had a strong word-stress, but many languages with strong word-stress do not weaken the unstressed vowels; examples are Italian, Spanish, Bohemian, Polish. The English change of [kn-, gn-] to [n-] seems natural, after it has occurred, but why did it not occur before the eighteenth century, and why has it not occurred in the other Germanic languages?

Every conceivable cause has been alleged: "race," climate, topographic conditions, diet, occupation and general mode of life, and so on. Wundt attributed sound-change to increase in the rapidity of speech, and this, in turn to the community's advance in culture and general intelligence. It is safe to say that we speak as rapidly and with as little effort as possible, approaching always the limit where our interlocutors ask us to repeat our utterance, and that a great deal of sound-change is in some way connected with this factor. No permanent factor, however, can account for specific changes which occur at one time and place and not at another. The same consideration holds good against the theory that sound-change arises from imperfections in children's learning of language. On the other hand, temporary operation of factors like the above, such as change of habitat, occupation, or diet, is ruled out by the fact that sound-changes occur too often and exhibit too great a variety.

The *substratum theory* attributes sound-change to transference of language: a community which adopts a new language will speak it imperfectly and with the phonetics of its mother-tongue. The transference of language will concern us later; in the present connection it is important to see that the substratum theory can account for changes only during the time when the language is spoken by persons who have acquired it as a second language. There is no sense in the mystical version of the substratum theory, which attributes changes, say, in modern Germanic languages, to a "Celtic substratum" — that is, to the fact that many centuries ago, some adult Celtic-speakers acquired Germanic speech. Moreover, the Celtic speech which preceded Germanic in southern Germany, the Netherlands, and England, was itself an invading language: the theory directs us back into time, from "race" to "race," to account for vague "tendencies" that manifest themselves in the actual historical occurrence of sound-change.

Aside from their failure to establish correlations, theories of this kind are confuted by the fact that when sound-change has removed some phonetic feature, later sound-change may result in the renewal of just this feature. If we attribute some particular character to the Primitive Indo-European unvoiced stops [p, t, k] — supposing, for the sake of illustration, that they were unaspirated fortes — then the pre-Germanic speakers who had begun to change these sounds in the direction of spirants [f, θ, h], were

TYPES OF PHONETIC CHANGE

doubtless incapable of pronouncing the original sounds, just as the English-speaker of today is incapable of pronouncing the French unaspirated [p, t, k]. At a later time, however, Primitive Indo-European [b, d, g] were changed in pre-Germanic to unvoiced stops [p, t, k]. These sounds did not coincide with those of the first group: the sounds of the first group had no longer the [p, t, k] character, having changed to aspirates or affricates or perhaps already to spirants; the sounds of the second group, on the other hand, were not subjected to the same change as those of the first group, because, as we say, the sound-change of [p, t, k] to [f, θ, h] was *past*. More accurately, we should say that the sound-change of [p, t, k] was *already under way:* the new [p, t, k] constituted a different habit, which did not take part in the displacement of the old habit. In time, the new [p, t, k] became aspirated, as they are in present-day English; so that, once more, we are incapable of pronouncing unaspirated unvoiced stops.

The English sound-changes that are known under the name of "the great vowel-shift," are of a type that has little effect beyond altering the acoustic shape of each phoneme; the long vowels were progressively shifted upward and into diphthongal types:

Middle English	>	Early Modern	>	Present-Day	
['naːme]		[neːm]		[nejm]	*name*
[deːd]		[diːd]		[dijd]	*deed*
[geːs]		[giːs]		[gijs]	*geese*
[wiːn]		[wejn]		[wajn]	*wine*
[stɔːn]		[stoːn]		[stown]	*stone*
[goːs]		[guːs]		[guws]	*goose*
[huːs]		[hows]		[haws]	*house*

Another theory seeks the cause of some sound-changes in formal conditions of a language, supposing that forms of weak meaning are slurred in pronunciation and thereby permanently weakened or lost. We have met this doctrine as one of those which deny the occurrence of purely phonemic changes (§ 20.10). We have no gauge by which we could mark some formal features of a language as semantically weak or superfluous. If we condemn all features of meaning except business-like denotations of the kind that could figure in scientific discourse, we should have to expect, on this theory, the disappearance of a great many forms in almost every language. For instance, the inflectional endings of adjectives in modern German are logically superfluous; the use of adjectives is quite like the English, and a text in which these endings are covered up is intelligible.

In fact, sound-changes often obliterate features whose meaning is highly important. No grammatical difference could be more essential than is that of actor and verbal goal in an Indo-European language. Yet the difference between the Primitive Indo-European nominative in *[-os], as in Sanskrit ['vr̥kah], Greek ['lukos], Latin *lupus*, Primitive Germanic *['wolfaz], Gothic *wulfs*, and the accusative in *[-om], as in Sanskrit ['vr̥kam], Greek ['lukon], Latin *lupum*, Primitive Germanic *['wolfan], Gothic *wulf*, had been obliterated by the weakening of the word-final in pre-English, so that the two cases were merged, even in our earliest records, in the form *wulf* 'wolf'. In Old English a few noun-types, such as nominative *caru* : accusative *care* 'care,' still had the distinction; by the year 1000 these were probably merged in the form ['kare], thanks to the weakening of unstressed vowels. In the same way, sound-change leads to all manner of homonymies, such as *meet* : *meat*; *meed* : *mead* ('meadow'): *mead* ('drink'), *knight* : *night*. The classical instance of this is Chinese, for it can be shown that the vast homonymy of the present-day languages, especially of North Chinese, is due to phonetic changes. Homonymy and *syncretism*, the merging of inflectional categories, are normal results of sound-change.

The theory of semantic weakness does seem to apply, however, to fixed formulas with excess slurring (§ 9.7). Historically, these formulas can be explained only as weakenings far in excess of normal sound-change. Thus, *good-bye* represents an older *God be with ye*, *ma'm* an older *madam*, Spanish *usted* [u'sted] an older *vuestra merced* ['vwestra mer'θed], and Russian [s], as in [da s] 'yes, sir,' an older ['sudar] 'lord.' In these cases, however, the normal speech-form exists by the side of the slurred form. The excess weakening in these forms has not been explained and doubtless is connected in some way with what we may call the sub-linguistic status of these conventional formulae. In any event, their excess weakening differs very much from ordinary phonetic change.

Since a sound-change is a historical happening, with a beginning and an end, limited to a definite time and to a definite body of speakers, its cause cannot be found in universal considerations or by observing speakers at other times and places. A phonetician tried to establish the cause of a change of the type [azna > asna], which occurred in the pre-history of the Avesta language, by observing in the laboratory a number of persons who were directed to pronounce the sequence [azna] many times in succession. Most of the persons — they were Frenchmen — yielded no result, but at last came one who ended by saying [asna]. The phonetician's joy was not clouded by the fact that this last person was a German, in whose native language [z] occurs only before syllabics.

It has been suggested that if a phoneme occurs in a language with more than a certain relative frequency (§ 8.7), this phoneme will be slurred in articulation and subjected to change. The upper limit of tolerable frequency, it is supposed, varies for different types of phonemes; thus, [t] represents in English more than 7 per cent of the total of uttered phonemes, and in several other languages (Russian, Hungarian, Swedish, Italian) the unvoiced dental stop runs to a similar percentage, while the type [d], on the other hand, with a lower relative frequency (in English it is less than 5 per cent) would in any language suffer sound-change, according to this theory, before it reached a relative frequency like that of English [t] The relative frequency of a phoneme is governed by the frequency of the significant forms that contain it; thus, [ð] in English is evidently favored by the high frequency of the word *the*. The frequency of significant forms is subject, as we shall see, to unceasing fluctuation, in accordance with changes in practical life. This theory, therefore, has the merit of correlating sound-change with an ever present and yet highly variable factor. It could be tested if we could determine the absolute upper limit for types of phonemes, and the actual frequency of a phoneme at a stage of a language just before this phoneme was changed — as, say, of [v] in English just before the change *havok* > *hawk*. We should then still have to account for the specific nature of the change, since phonemes of any one general type have changed in different ways in the history of various languages. Against the theory we must weigh the great phonetic difference between languages and the high frequency, in some languages, of what we may call unusual phonetic types; [ð], which plays such a great part in English, was at one time eliminated (by a pre-West-Germanic change to [d]) and has remained so in Dutch-German; later it was re-introduced into English by a change from [θ] to [ð]:

TYPES OF PHONETIC CHANGE

21. 10. Certain linguistic changes which are usually described as sound-change, do not come under the definition of phonetic change as a gradual alteration of phonemic units. In various parts of Europe, for instance, the old tongue-tip trill [r] has been replaced, in modern times, by a uvular trill. This has happened in Northumbrian English, in Danish and southern Norwegian and Swedish, and in the more citified types of French (especially in Paris) and Dutch-German. Aside from its spread by borrowing, the new habit, in whatever times and places it may first have arisen, could have originated only as a sudden replacement of one trill by another. A replacement of this sort is surely different from the gradual and imperceptible alterations of phonetic change.

Some changes consist in a redistribution of phonemes. The commonest of these seems to be *dissimilation:* when a phoneme or type of phoneme recurs within a form, one of the occurrences is sometimes replaced by a different sound. Thus, Latin *peregrīnus* 'foreigner, stranger' is replaced in the Romance languages by a type **pelegrīnus*, as in Italian *pellegrino*, and in English *pilgrim*, borrowed from Romance; the first of the two [r]'s has been replaced by [l]. In the languages of Europe, the sounds [r, l, n] are especially subject to this replacement; the replacing sound is usually one of the same group. Where the replacement occurs, it follows quite definite rules, but we cannot predict its occurrence. The change, if carried out, would produce a state of affairs where recurrence of certain sounds, such as [r] and [l], was not allowed within a word — the state of affairs which actually prevails in the modern English derivation of symbolic words, where we have *clatter, blubber,* but *rattle, crackle* (§ 14.9). Probably this type of change is entirely different from ordinary phonetic change.

There is also a type of dissimilation in which one of the like phonemes is dropped, as when Latin *quinque* ['kwi:nkwe] 'five' is replaced, in Romance, by a type *['ki:nkwe], Italian *cinque* ['ʧinkwe], French *cinq* [sɛ̃k].

There are several other kinds of phonetic replacement which cannot properly be put on a level with ordinary sound-change. In *distant assimilation* a phoneme is replaced by another of related acoustic type which occurs elsewhere in the same word. Thus, Primitive Indo-European *['penkʷe] 'five,' Sanskrit ['panca], Greek ['pente] appears in Latin not as *[pinkwe], but as *quinque*. In pre-Germanic this word seems to have suffered the reverse as-

TYPES OF PHONETIC CHANGE

similation, to *['pempe], for we have Primitive Germanic *['fimfe] in Gothic and Old High German *fimf*, Old English *fīf*, and so on. Sanskrit has [ç — ç] in words where we expect [s — ç].

Metathesis is the interchange of two phonemes within a word. Beside the expected *āscian* 'ask,' Old English has also *ācsian*. In Tagalog some morphologic alternations seem to be due to changes of this kind; thus, the suffix [-an], as in [a'sin] 'salt' : [as'nan] 'what is to be salted,' is sometimes accompanied by interchange of two consonants that come together: [a'tip] 'roofing' : [ap'tan] 'what is to be roofed'; [ta'nim] 'that planted' : [tam'nan] 'what is to have plants put into it.' In the languages of Europe distant metathesis of [r-l] is fairly common. To Old English *alor* 'alder' there corresponds in Old High German not only *elira* but also *erila* (> modern *Erle*). For Gothic ['werilo:s] 'lips,' Old English has *weleras*. Latin *parabola* 'word' (a borrowing from Greek) appears in Spanish as *palabra*.

When a phoneme or group of phonemes recurs within a word, one occurrence together with the intervening sounds, may be dropped: this change is known as *haplology*. Thus, from Latin *nūtriō* 'I nourish' the regular feminine agent-noun would be **nūtrī-trīx* 'nurse,' but the form is actually *nūtrīx*. Similarly, the compound which would normally have the form **stipi-pendium* 'wage-payment' appears actually as *stipendium*. Ancient Greek [amphi-pho'rews] 'both-side-carrier' appears also as [ampho'rews] 'amphora.' Changes like these are very different from those which are covered by the assumption of sound-change; it is possible that they are akin rather to the types of linguistic change which we have still to consider — analogic change and borrowing.

CHAPTER 22

FLUCTUATION IN THE FREQUENCY OF FORMS

22. 1. The assumption of phonetic change divides linguistic changes into two principal types. Phonetic change affects only the phonemes, and alters linguistic forms only by altering their phonetic shape. The English form *wolf* is the modern pronunciation of Primitive Germanic nominative *['wolfaz], accusative *['wolfan], and several other case-forms, and the merging of these (syncretism) is merely the result of the phonetic change. English [mijd] *meed, mead* is the modern pronunciation of Old English [mɛːd] 'meadow,' [meːd] 'reward,' and ['medu] 'honey-drink'; the homonymy results simply from the change in habits of articulation. When we have listed the phonetic correlations, there remain a great many discrepancies. Thus, having found that Old English [aː] appears in modern standard English as [ow], as in [baːt] > *boat*, and so on, we see a discrepancy in the parallelism of Old English [baːt] 'bait' with the modern *bait*. Seeing Old English initial [f] preserved in *father, five, foot*, and so on, we find a discrepancy in the sets Old English [fet] : modern *vat* and Old English ['fyksen] : modern *vixen*. While the modern form *cow* stands in a normal phonetic correlation with Old English [kuː], just as *house, mouse, out* correspond to Old English [huːs, muːs, uːt], the plural *cows* cannot be the modern form of the Old English plural [kyː] 'cows,' in view of cases like Old English [hwyː] > *why*, [fyːr] > *fire*, [myːs] > *mice*. If we adhere to the assumption of regular phonetic change, we cannot class forms like *bait, vat, vixen, cows* as modern pronunciations of Old English forms, but must view them as the products of factors other than simple tradition. Our problem, therefore, is to find among these residual forms some uniformity or correlation; to the extent that we succeed in this, we shall have confirmed the value of the assumption of phonetic change and of the particular phonetic correspondences we have set up. The neo-grammarians claim that the assumption of phonetic change leaves residues which show striking correlations and allow us to understand the factors of

FLUCTUATION IN FORMS

linguistic change other than sound-change. The opponents of the neo-grammarian hypothesis imply that a different assumption concerning sound-change will leave a more intelligible residue, but they have never tested this by re-classifying the data.

If the residual forms are not continuants of ancient forms with only the alterations of sound-change, then they must have come into the language as innovations. We shall see that two kinds of innovation account for the residual forms — namely, the adoption of forms from other languages (*bait* from Old Norse) or other dialects (*vat*, *vixen* from southern-English local dialects) and the combining of new complex forms (*cow-s* on the pattern "singular noun plus plural-suffix gives plural noun"). These two kinds of innovation, *borrowing* and *analogic change*, will occupy us in the following chapters; now we are concerned merely with the claim that the forms which are not accounted for by phonetic correlation, got into the language at various points in time.

22. 2. If a form which has been introduced into a language prevails in general usage — as, for instance, *cows* prevails as the ordinary plural of *cow* — we have to suppose that it has gained in popularity since its first introduction. Conversely, if an old form — such as the Old English plural [ky:], which, by phonetic development, would today be pronounced *[kaj] — has disappeared, we must suppose that it went through a period of decline, during which it was used less and less as the years went by. *Fluctuation in the frequency of speech-forms* is a factor in all non-phonetic changes. This fluctuation can be observed, to some extent, both at first hand and in our written records. For instance, since the introduction of the automobile, the word *garage*, borrowed from French, has become very common. We can actually name the speakers who first used the words *chortle*, *kodak*, and *blurb*; since the moment of that first use, each of these words has become common. The disappearance of a form cannot be observed at first hand, since we can have no assurance that it will not be used again, but in older written records we find many speech-forms that are no longer in use. In Old English, ['weorθan] 'to become' was one of the commonest words: [he: 'wearθ 'torn] 'he got angry,' [he: je'wearθ 'mɛːre] 'he became famous,' [he: 'wearθ of'slɛjen] 'he got killed,' [heo 'wearθ 'widuwe] 'she became a widow.' In the Dutch-German area this verb, Dutch *worden* ['wurde], German *werden* ['verden], is still so used. The ordinary Old English word for 'large,' *mycel*, survives in Scotch *mickle*, but has disappeared from standard English. In our fragments of the Gothic Bible-translation, the word *mother* is entirely replaced by a term ['ajθi:], and the word *father* occurs only once (*Galatians* 4, 6) and is in all other passages replaced by ['atta], a word familiar to us from the Gothic nickname of the king of the Huns, *Attila* 'little father.' This, apparently in its original connotation a nursery-word, is perhaps somehow connected with the Slavic term for 'father,' Primitive Slavic *[otɪ'tsɪ], Russian [o'tets], which in pre-Slavic must have crowded out the reflex of Primitive Indo-European *[pə'te:r].

Most frequently we observe the complementary fluctuation of two forms; thus, *it's I* and *it's me* or *rather* with [ɛ] and with [a], are evidently *rival forms* in present-day American English. The plural-form *kine* beside *cows* is still very rarely used as a poetic archaism. In Elizabethan writings we still find the spelling *fat* for *vat*, evidencing a survival of Old English [fɛt], which has since been crowded out by *vat*. Where a speaker knows two rival forms, they differ in connotation, since he has heard them from different persons and under different circumstances.

Fluctuations in the frequency of forms could be accurately observed if we had a record of every utterance that was made in a speech-community during whatever period of time we wanted to study. We could then keep a tally-sheet for every form (including grammatical forms, such as the type *he ran away; he fell down* in contrast with *away he ran; down he fell*); whenever an utterance was made, we could score a point on the tally-sheet of every form in this utterance. In this way we should obtain tables or graphs which showed the ups and downs in frequency of every form during the time covered by our records. Such a system of scoring will doubtless remain beyond our powers, but this imaginary system gives us a picture of what is actually going on at all times in every speech-community. We can observe the fluctuation with the naked eye when it is especially rapid, as in the sudden rise and equally sudden disuse of popular slangy witticisms. On a smaller scale, but contributing to the total fluctuations in the community, small groups and individuals indulge in similar whims; everyone can recall old favorite words and phrases which he and perhaps his associates once used at every turn. Most fluctuation is less rapid and escapes direct observation, but reveals itself in its results — in

FLUCTUATION IN FORMS

the differences of vocabulary and grammar which appear when we compare different historical stages of a language, or dialects of an area, or related languages.

Leaving aside the origination of new forms, which will concern us in the following chapters, we must now consider the factors which lead to the rise or to the decline in frequency of speech-forms. Until recently this topic was neglected, and our knowledge is still far from satisfactory.

22. 3. We naturally ask at once whether any linguistically definable characteristics of a form may favor or disfavor its use. The stylist and the rhetorician tell us that some speech-forms sound better than others. The only criterion of a phonetic sort seems to be this, that repetition of phonemes or sequences is often avoided: a phrase like *the observation of the systematization of education* is disfavored. In ordinary speech, however, euphony seems to play no part; the stock examples of troublesome phonetics are far-fetched combinations like *Peter Piper picked a peck of pickled peppers* or *she sells sea-shells*. On the other hand, various patternings of recurrent phonemes, such as alliteration (*hearth and home, cabbages and kings*), assonance (*a stitch in time saves nine*), and rime, and rhythmic repetitions (*first come, first served*), seem to favor many a speech-form.

In all ordinary cases, semantic rather than formal factors contribute to the favor or disfavor of a form. It is natural to suppose, however, that a form which differs strikingly from the other forms of comparable meaning, will be disfavored. Several students have conjectured that certain speech-forms fell into disuse because they were shorter than ordinary speech-forms of similar meaning. Gillieron believed that Latin *apis* 'bee' has died out in nearly all dialects of the French area because its modern pronunciation would consist of only a single phoneme [e]. It would be no counter-argument to say that French has grammatical and relational words of this pattern, such as *et* [e] 'and,' but a case like *eau* [o] 'water' (< *aquam*) does militate against the theory. It seems that some verb-forms in the older stages of the Indo-European languages fell into disuse because they were shorter than ordinary forms of the same kind. The Menomini language, like French and English, seems to tolerate words of all sizes. Menomini [o:s] 'canoe' is shorter than ordinary nouns, and [uah] 'he uses it' shorter than ordinary verb-forms. These forms, which are ancient inheritances, have been largely replaced in the sister languages: Primitive Central Algonquian *[oːʃi] 'canoe' by longer derivative nouns, such as Fox [anakɛːweni], Cree and Ojibwa [tʃiːmaːn], — though Cree has also [oːsi] — and Primitive Central Algonquian *[oːwa] 'he uses it' by a reduplicated form, Fox [ajoː-wa] or by other words, such as Cree [aːpatʃihtaːw]. All this, however, is doubtful.

The semantic factor is more apparent in the disfavoring of speech-forms that are homonymous with tabu-forms. The reader will have no difficulty in finding speech-forms that he avoids for this reason. In America, *knocked up* is a tabu-form for 'rendered pregnant'; for this reason, the phrase is not used in the British sense 'tired, exhausted.' In older French and English there was a word, French *connil, connin*, English *coney*, for 'rabbit'; in both languages this word died out because it resembled a word that was under a tabu of indecency. For the same reason, *rooster* and *donkey* are replacing *cock* and *ass* in American English. In such cases there is little real ambiguity, but some hearers react nevertheless to the powerful stimulus of the tabu-word; having called forth ridicule or embarrassment, the speaker avoids the innocent homonym. It is a remarkable fact that the tabu-word itself has a much tougher life than the harmless homonym.

22. 4. These cases suggest that homonymy in general may injure the frequency of a form. Many homonyms are distinguished by differences of grammatical function, as are *leader* (noun) and *lead'er* (infinitive phrase) or *bear* (noun), *bear* (verb), and *bare* (adjective); in French, [sã] is *sang* 'blood,' *cent* 'hundred,' *sans* 'without,' *sent* 'feels, smells,' and *s'en* 'oneself of it,' as in *s'en aller* 'to go away.' Even with largely similar grammatical functions, homonymies like *pear, pair* or *piece, peace* or *mead, meed* do not seem to lessen the frequency of forms.

Nevertheless, there is some evidence that homonymy may lead to troubles of communication which result in disuse of a form. The classical instance is Gilliéron's explanation of the disappearance of Latin *gallus* 'cock' in southwestern France (Figure 14). In southern France generally this word is still in use in its modern forms, such as [gal] or [ʒal]. A fair-sized area in the extreme south, however, uses for 'cock' another Latin word, *pullus*, modern [pul], which originally meant 'chick.' Now, the southwestern corner of the French area has made a sound-change by which

Latin [ll] at the end of a word has become [t]; thus, Latin *bellus* 'pretty,' modern [bɛl],[1] appears in the southwestern corner as [bɛt]. The isogloss of this sound-change cuts the *pullus*-district into an eastern part, where one says [pul] and a western part where one says [put]. Outside the *pullus*-district we should accordingly expect to find a form *[gat] 'cock,' corresponding to the

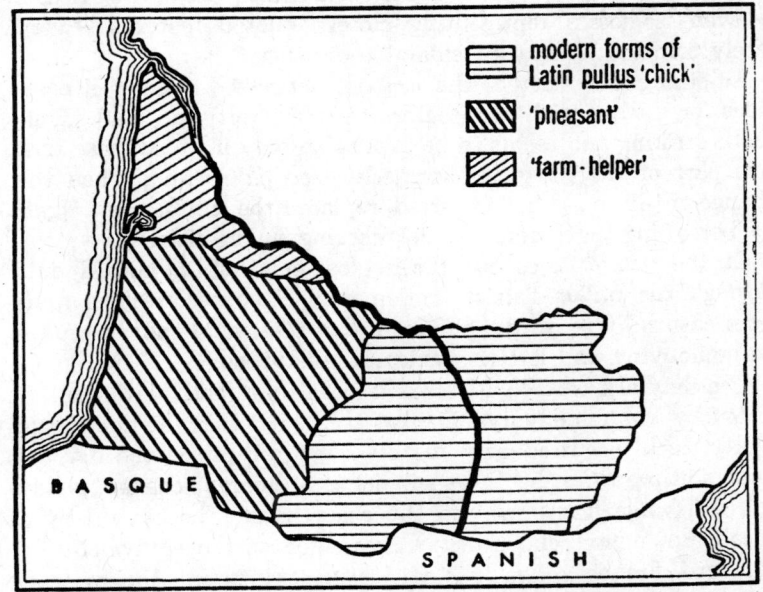

FIGURE 14. The southwestern part of the French dialect-area. — Southwest of the heavy line ——— Latin [ll] appears in final position as [t]. The unshaded part of the area uses modern forms of Latin *gallus* "cock." The shaded areas use other words for "cock." — After Dauzat.

[gal] of ordinary southern French, but actually this form nowhere appears: the entire [-t]-area, in so far as it does not say [put], calls the cock by queer and apparently slangy names, either by local forms of the word *pheasant*, such as [azã], from Latin *phāsiānus*, or by a word [begej] which means 'farm-helper, handyman' and is thought to represent Latin *vicārius* 'deputy, proxy, vicar.'

Now, Gilliéron points out, the form *[gat] 'cock' in this district would be homonymous with the word 'cat,' namely [gat],

[1] Standard French *bel* [bɛl] before vowels, *beau* [bo] before consonants.

from Latin *gattus*. This homonymy must have caused trouble in practical life; therefore *[gat] 'cock' was avoided and replaced by makeshift words.

What lends weight to this theory is the remarkable fact that the isogloss which separates the queer words [azã] and [begej] from the ordinary [gal], coincides exactly with the isogloss between [-t] and [-l]; this is highly significant, because isoglosses — even isoglosses representing closely related features — very rarely coincide for any considerable distance.

Adjoining this stretch, the isogloss between [-t] and [-l] coincides for a ways with the isogloss between [put] and [gal]. This too is striking and seems to be explicable only if we suppose that this part of the [-t]-region formerly used *gallus* and, when the change of [-ll] to [-t] had occurred, replaced the troublesome *[gat] by borrowing [put] from the neighboring *pullus*-district.

On the rest of its course, the isogloss between [-t] and [-l] cuts through the *pullus*-district, and merely separates western [put] from eastern [pul]; in the *pullus*-district the sound-change caused no homonymy and left the lexicon undisturbed.

One may ask why *[gat] 'cock' rather than [gat] 'cat' was affected by the homonymy. Dauzat points out that the morpheme *[gat] 'cock' occurred only in this one word, since the derived form, Latin *gallīna* 'hen' was subject to a different change, giving [garina], while [gat] 'cat,' on the other hand, was backed by a number of unambiguous derivatives, such as the equivalents of standard French *chatte* 'she-cat,' *chaton* 'kitten,' *chatière* 'cat-hole.'

While few instances are as cogent as this, it is likely that homonymy plays more than an occasional part in the obsolescence of forms. A few centuries ago, English had not only our present-day verb *let* (which represents the paradigm of Old English ['lɛːtan]), but also a homonymous verb which meant 'to hinder' (representing Old English ['lettan]); we still have the phrases *without let or hindrance* and *a let ball*, at tennis. When Shakspere has Hamlet say *I'll make a ghost of him that lets me*, he means 'of him that hinders me.' After it had become homonymous with *let* 'permit,' this word must have been singularly ineffective. A speaker who wanted his hearers to stop someone — say, a child that was running into danger, or a thief — and cried *Let him!* might find his hearers standing aside to make way. Then he would have to add

FLUCTUATION IN FORMS

Stop him! or *Hold him!* After a few such experiences he would use one of the effective forms at the first trial.

22. 5. We frequently find regular, or at least more regular, combinations by the side of irregular complex forms, as, *roofs, hoofs, dwarfs* by the side of *rooves, hooves, dwarves,* or *dreamed, learned* by the side of *dreamt, learnt,* or *you ought to* by the side of *you had better.* In some cases the irregular form is decidedly infrequent, as in *cows, eyes, shoes, brothers* versus *kine, eyne, shoon, brethren.* Other examples are, regular *forehead* [ˈfɔə-ˌhed], *gooseberry* [ˈguws-ˌberi], *seamstress* [ˈsijmstris] against irregular [ˈfɔrid, ˈguzbri, ˈsemstris]. History shows us that in such cases the irregular form frequently dies out, or survives only in special senses, as when *sodden,* the old participle of *seethe,* survives only in a transferred meaning. The plurals of *goat, book, cow,* if we continued using the Old English forms [gɛːt, beːk, kyː] would be today *[gijt, bijtʃ, kaj]. Whenever we know the history of a language through any considerable period, we find many cases of this kind, but the operation of this factor is obscure, because in many cases the regular form makes no headway at all. The utterance of a regular *foots* instead of *feet,* or *bringed* instead of *brought* is so rare as to be classed as a childish "mistake" or, in older people, as a "slip of the tongue." Languages seem to differ in toleration of irregular forms, but in general it would seem that a regular rival, given a good start, has much the better chance. Very common forms, such as in English the paradigm of the verb *be* and the pronouns *I, we, he, she, they,* with their over-differentiation, persist in spite of great irregularity.

22. 6. For the most part, fluctuation does not depend upon formal features, but upon meaning, and accordingly escapes a purely linguistic investigation. The changes which are always going on in the practical life of a community, are bound to affect the relative frequencies of speech-forms. The introduction of railways, street-cars, and motor-cars has lessened the frequency of many terms relating to horses, wagons, and harness, and increased that of terms relating to machinery. Even in the most remote and conservative community there is a constant displacement of things talked about; if nothing else should alter, there is at least the change of birth and death.

A new object or practice which gains in vogue, carries a speech-form, old or new, into increased frequency; examples are many in modern life, such as the terms of motoring, flying, and wireless. If the practical situation ceases to exist, the forms which are used in this situation are bound to become less common and may die out. The terms of falconry, for instance, have suffered this fate. Though we still hear beauty in Othello's words, we do not understand them:

> *If I do prove her haggard,*
> *Though that her jesses were my dear heart-strings,*
> *I'd whistle her off, and let her down the wind,*
> *To prey at fortune.*

The word *haggard* was used of a wild-caught, unreclaimed mature hawk; *jesses* were leather straps fastened to the legs of a hawk, and were not removed when the hawk was unleashed; if a hawk flew with the wind behind her, she seldom returned.

In the early centuries of our era, some of the Germanic tribes contained a class of people called [laːt], South-German [laːts], who were intermediate in rank between freemen and serfs. The English form of this word, [lɛːt], occurs only once in our records, in the oldest English law-code, and even here the word is explained — incorrectly, at that — by the word [θeːow] 'serf' written above the line. The new social organization of the English-speaking tribes in Britain contained no such class of people, and the word went out of use along with the institution.

22. 7. Words that are under a ritual or ill-omened tabu, are likely to disappear. The Indo-European languages use the most varied words for 'moon'; it is notable that Russian has borrowed Latin ['luːna] as [luˈna], though otherwise it makes scarcely any but highly learned borrowings from Latin. It may be due to a ritual or hunters' tabu that the Primitive Indo-European word for 'bear,' surviving in Sanskrit ['r̥kʃah], Greek ['arktos], Latin *ursus*, has disappeared in Germanic and in Balto-Slavic. In Slavic it has been replaced by the type of Russian [medˈvetʲ], originally a transparent compound meaning 'honey-eater.' The like of this seems to have happened in Menomini, where the old word for 'bear,' preserved in Fox [mahkwa], Cree [maskwa], has been replaced by [aweːhsɛh], a diminutive formation that seems to have meant originally 'little what-you-may-call-him.' Cree ['maːtʃiːw] 'he goes hunting' originally meant simply 'he goes away' — presumably there was danger of being overheard by the game or by its spiritual representatives. The term for the 'left' side appears to have been replaced in various languages; the Indo-European languages use many words, among which Ancient Greek [ew-'o:-numos], literally 'of good name,' is evidently euphemistic. One can often observe people avoiding unpleasant words, such as *die*, *death* — these words in pre-Germanic replaced the Primitive Indo-European term represented by Latin *morī* 'to die' — or names of serious diseases. The term *undertaker* was, to begin with, vaguely evasive, but the undertakers are now trying to replace it by *mortician*. In cases like these, where the unpleasantness inheres in the practical situation, the speech-form becomes undesirable as soon as it is too specifically tied up with the painful meaning.

Tabus of indecency do not seem to lead to obsolescence; the tabu-forms are excluded in many or most social situations, but by no means avoided in others. The substitutes may in time become too closely associated with the meaning and in turn become tabu. Our word *whore*, cognate with Latin *cārus* 'dear,' must have been at one time a polite substitute for some word now lost to us. On the whole, however, words of this type do not seem especially given to obsolescence.

The practical situation works in favor of words that call forth a good response. In commerce, the seller finds advantage in labeling his goods attractively. This is probably why terms for the young of animals sometimes replace the more general name of the species, as when we say *chicken* for 'hen.' French *poule* [pul] 'hen' and dialectal [pul] 'cock' continue a Latin word for 'chick.' The word *home* for 'house' has doubtless been favored by speculative builders. In Germany, an *express* train has come to mean a slow train, as has *Schnellzug* ['ʃnel-ˌtsu:k], literally 'fast-train'; a really fast train is *Blitzzug* ['blits-ˌtsu:k], literally 'lightning-train' — just as in the United States *first class* on a railroad means the ordinary day-coach accommodation.

There is an advantage, often, in applying well-favored terms to one's hearer. The habit of using the plural pronoun 'ye' instead of the singular 'thou,' spread over Europe during the Middle Ages. In English, *you* (the old dative-accusative case-form of *ye*) has crowded *thou* into archaic use; in Dutch, *jij* [jej] has led to the entire obsolescence of *thou*, and has in turn become the intimate form, under the encroachment of an originally still more honorific *u* [y:], representing *Uwe Edelheid* ['y:we 'e:delhejt] 'Your

Nobility.' Honorifics of this sort often replace the ordinary second-person substitutes (§ 15.7). Similarly, one speaks in honorific terms of what pertains to the hearer. In Italian, 'my wife' is *mia moglie* [mia 'moʎe], but for 'your wife' one says rather *la sua signora* [la sua si'ɲora] 'your lady.' In French and in German one prefixes 'Mr., Mrs., Miss' to the mention of the hearer's relatives, as, *madame votre mère* [madam vɔtr mɛːr] 'your mother' in German, moreover, one likes to use for the hearer's husband or wife archaic terms of distinguished flavor: *meine Frau* [majne 'fraw] 'my wife,' but *Ihre Frau Gemahlin* ['iːre fraw ge'maːlin] 'your Mrs. consort,' and *mein Mann* [majn 'man] 'my husband', but *Ihr Herr Gemahl* [iːr her ge'maːl] 'your Mr. consort.' In the Central Algonquian languages the literal terms for both 'my wife' and 'thy wife' are tabu — ogres use them in fairy-tales — and one says rather 'the old woman' or 'the one I live with' or even 'my cook.'

In general, honorific terms for persons spread at the cost of plain ones; *gentleman* and *lady* are more genteel than *man* and *woman*.

22. 8. General effectiveness, in the shape of violence or wit, is a powerful factor in fluctuation, which unfortunately quite escapes the linguist's control. It leads, for instance, to the sudden rise and fall of slang expressions. Round 1896 or so, a transferred use of the word *rubber* in the sense of 'stare, pry' played a great part in slang; ten years later it was obsolescent, and only *rubberneck-wagon* 'sight-seeing omnibus' has now any great frequency. Then, round 1905, an interjection *skidoo* 'be off' and, in the same meaning, an interjectional use of *twenty-three*, came into fashion and as suddenly died out. The rise of such forms is due, apparently, to their effectiveness in producing a response from the hearer. At first they owe this to their novelty and apt yet violent transference of meaning; later, the hearer responds well because he has heard them in favorable situations and from attractive people. All these favorable factors disappear from sheer repetition; the novelty wears off, the violent metaphor lapses when the transferred meaning becomes more familiar than the central meaning; the average of situations and speakers associated with the form becomes indifferent. Thereupon the slang form dies out. In some cases, however, the older form has meanwhile gone out of use or become archaic or specialized; the witticism, having lost its point, remains in use as a normal form. Thus, Latin *caput* 'head' survives in Italian and French in specialized and transferred senses, but in the central meaning has been displaced by reflexes of Latin *testa* 'potsherd, pot,' Italian *testa* ['tɛsta], French *tête* [tɛ:t]. Similarly, in German, the cognate of our *head*, namely *Haupt* [hawpt], survives in transferred uses and as a poetic archaism, but has been replaced, in the sense of 'head' by *Kopf*, cognate with English *cup*. The forceful or witty term, weakened through frequency, may suffer encroachment by new rivals, as in the countless slang words for 'head' or 'man' or 'girl' or 'kill,' or in a set like *awfully, terribly, frightfully (glad to see you)*.

This factor is easily recognized in extreme cases, but figures doubtless in many more which elude our grasp, especially when the fluctuation is observable only from far-off time.

22. 9. The most powerful force of all in fluctuation works quite outside the linguist's reach: the speaker favors the forms which he has heard from certain other speakers who, for some reason of prestige, influence his habits of speech. This is what decides, in countless instances, whether one says *it's me* or *it's I*, *rather* with [ɛ] or with [a], *either* and *neither* with [ij] or with [aj], *roofs* or *rooves*, *you ought to* or *you'd better*, and so on, through an endless list of variants and nearly synonymous forms. Dialect geography and the history of standard languages show us how the speech of important communities is constantly imitated, now in one feature and now in another, by groups and persons of less prestige. The more striking phases of this leveling process will concern us in connection with linguistic borrowing. We may suppose that many features of lexicon and grammar, and some features of phonetics, have a social connotation, different for different groups and even for individual speakers. In the ideal diagram of density of communication (§ 3.4) we should have to distinguish the arrows that lead from each speaker to his hearers by gradations representing the prestige of the speaker with reference to each hearer. If we had a diagram with the arrows thus weighted, we could doubtless predict, to a large extent, the future frequencies of linguistic forms. It is in childhood, of course, that the speaker is most affected by the authority of older speakers, but all through life he goes on adapting his speech to the speech of the persons whom he strives to resemble or to please.

CHAPTER 23

ANALOGIC CHANGE

23. 1. Many speech-forms are not continuants of forms that existed in an older stage of the same language. This is obvious in the case of borrowings: a word like *toboggan*, taken over from an American Indian language, cannot have been used in English before the colonization of America, and, of course, we do not find it in documents of the English language which date from before that time. In very many instances, however, the new form is not borrowed from a foreign language. Thus, the plural-form *cows* does not appear in Old and Middle English. The Old English plural of *cu* [ku:] (whence modern *cow*) is *cy* [ky:], which survives, as [kaj], in a number of modern English dialects. Round the year 1300 there appears in our records a form *kyn*, which survives in the modern archaic-poetic form *kine*. Only some centuries later do we meet the form *cows;* the *New English Dictionary's* first reference, from the year 1607, has it as an alternative of the older form: *Kine or Cows.* Evidently *cows* is not the continuant, with only phonetic change, of *kine*, any more than *kine* bears this relation to *kye:* in both cases a new speech-form has come into the language.

The fact that the form *cows* is not the continuant, with only alterations of sound-change, of the older forms, is self-evident. Strictly speaking, however, this is only an inference which we make from the primary fact of phonetic discrepancy. We know that Old English [y:] appears in modern standard English as [aj], e.g. in *why, mice, bride* from Old English [hwy:, my:s, bry:d], and that modern [aw], as in *cows*, represents an Old English [u:], as in *cow, how, mouse, out* from Old English [ku:, hu:, mu:s, u:t]. Further, we know that modern [z], as in *cows*, is not added by any sound-change, but represents Old English [s], as in *stones* from Old English ['sta:nas]. In many cases, however, the novelty of a speech-form is not so apparent and is revealed only by a systematic comparison of sounds. The form *days* superficially resembles the Old English plural-form *dagas*, which we interpret as ['dagas], presumably with a spirant [g], but the phonetic development of the

ANALOGIC CHANGE

Old English sound-group [ag] appears rather in forms like ['sage] > *saw* (implement), ['sagu] > *saw* 'saying,' ['hagu-'θorn] > *hawthorn*, ['dragan] > *draw*. This is confirmed by the fact that in earlier Middle English we find spellings like *daues, dawes* for the plural of *dei* 'day,' and that spellings which agree with the modern form *days* appear only round the year 1200. If our statements of phonetic correspondence are correct, the residues will contain the new forms. One of the strongest reasons for adopting the assumption of regular phonetic change is the fact that the constitution of the residues (aside from linguistic borrowings, which we shall consider in later chapters) throws a great deal of light upon the origin of new forms. Most of the word-forms which arise in the course of time and reveal themselves by their deviation from normal phonetic correspondence, belong to a single well-defined type. This cannot be due to accident: it confirms the assumption of phonetic change, and, on the other hand allows us to study the process of new-formation.

The great mass of word-forms that arise in the course of history consists in new combinations of complex forms. The form *cows*, arising by the side of *kye, kine*, consists of the singular *cow* (< Old English [ku:]) plus the plural-suffix [-z] (< Old English [-as]); similarly, *days*, arising by the side of older *daws*, consists of the singular *day* (< Old English [dej]) plus the same suffix. A vast number of such instances, from the history of the most diverse languages, leads us to believe that the analogic habits (§ 16.6) are subject to displacement — that at a time when the plural of *cow* was the irregular form *kine*, the speakers might create a regular form *cows*, which then entered into rivalry with the old form. Accordingly, this type of innovation is called *analogic change*. Ordinarily, linguists use this term to include both the original creation of the new form and its subsequent rivalry with the old form. Strictly speaking, we should distinguish between these two events. After a speaker has heard or uttered the new form (say, *cows*), his subsequent utterance of this form or of the older form (*kine*) is a matter of fluctuation, such as we considered in the last chapter; what we did not there consider and what concerns us now, is the utterance, by someone who has never heard it, of a new combination, such as *cow-s* instead of *kine*.

23. 2. In most cases — and these are the ones we come nearest to understanding — the process of uttering a new form is quite like that of ordinary grammatical analogy. The speaker who, without having heard it, produced the form *cows*, uttered this form just as he uttered any other regular plural noun, on the scheme

$$sow : sows = cow : x.$$

The model set (*sow : sows*) in this diagram represents a series of models (e.g. *bough : boughs, heifer : heifers, stone : stones*, etc., etc.), which, in our instance, includes all the regular noun-paradigms in the language. Moreover, the sets at either side of the sign of equality are not limited to two members. The independent utterance of a form like *dreamed* instead of *dreamt* [dremt], could be depicted by the diagram:

$$\begin{aligned}&scream : screams : screaming : screamer : screamed \\ =\ &dream\ \ : dreams\ \ : dreaming\ \ : dreamer\ \ : x\end{aligned}$$

Psychologists sometimes object to this formula, on the ground that the speaker is not capable of the reasoning which the proportional pattern implies. If this objection held good, linguists would be debarred from making almost any grammatical statement, since the normal speaker, who is not a linguist, does not describe his speech-habits, and, if we are foolish enough to ask him, fails utterly to make a correct formulation. Educated persons, who have had training in school grammar, overestimate their own ability in the way of formulating speech-habits, and, what is worse, forget that they owe this ability to a sophisticated philosophical tradition. They view it, instead, as a natural gift which they expect to find in all people, and feel free to deny the truth of any linguistic statement which the normal speaker is incapable of making. We have to remember at all times that the speaker, short of a highly specialized training, is incapable of describing his speech-habits. Our proportional formula of analogy and analogic change, like all other statements in linguistics, describes the action of the speaker and does not imply that the speaker himself could give a similar description.

In studying the records of past speech or in comparing related languages and dialects, the linguist will recognize many differences of word-form, such as the emergence of *cows* beside older *kine*. The habits of morphology are fairly rigid; word-lists and tables of inflection are relatively easy to prepare and help us to detect innovations. It is otherwise with phrasal forms. Aside from the imperfection of our descriptive technique in syntax, retarded, as it has been, by philosophic habits of approach, the syntactic positions of a language can be filled by so many different forms that a survey is hard to make. The linguist who suspects that a certain phrase departs from the older syntactic habits of its language, may yet find it difficult or impossible to make sure that this older usage really excluded the phrase, or to determine the exact boundary between the older and the newer usage. Nevertheless, we can sometimes recognize syntactic innovations on the proportional pattern. From the sixteenth century on, we find English subordinate clauses introduced by the word *like*. We can picture the innovation in this way:

to do better than Judith : *to do better than Judith did*
= *to do like Judith* : x,

where the outcome is the construction *to do like Judith did*.

A phrasal innovation which does not disturb the syntactic habit may involve a new lexical use. In this case, our lack of control over meanings, especially, of course, where the speech of past times is concerned, acts as an almost insuperable hindrance. The practical situations which make up the meaning of a speech-form are not strictly definable: one could say that every utterance of a speech-form involves a minute semantic innovation. In older English, as in some modern dialects, the word *meat* had a meaning close to that of *food*, and the word *flesh* was used freely in connection with eating, as in this passage (from the year 1693): *who flesh of animals refused to eat, nor held all sorts of pulse for lawful meat*. A compound *flesh-meat* served, for a while, as a compromise. The prevalence of *food* and *fodder* where at an earlier time the word *meat* was common, and the prevalence of *flesh-meat* and *meat* where at an earlier time *flesh* would have been the normal term, must be attributed to a gradual shifting of usage. The difficulty of tracing this has led linguists to view the process as a kind of whimsical misapplication of speech-forms. If we remember that the meaning of a speech-form for any speaker is a product of the situations and contexts in which he has heard this form, we can see that here too a displacement must be merely an extension of some pattern:

leave the bones and bring the flesh : *leave the bones and bring the meat*
= *give us bread and flesh* : x,

resulting in *give us bread and meat*. Doubtless we have to do, in both grammatical and lexical displacements, with one general type of innovation; we may call it *analogic-semantic change*. We shall leave the lexical phase of this, *semantic change*, for the next chapter, and consider first the more manageable phase which involves grammatical habits.

23. 3. We can distinguish only in theory between the actual innovation, in which a speaker uses a form he has not heard, and the subsequent rivalry between this new form and some older form. An observer who, a few years ago, heard the form *radios*, might suspect that the speaker had never heard it and was creating it on the analogy of ordinary noun-plurals; the observer could have no assurance of this, however, since the form could be equally well uttered by speakers who had and by those who had not heard it before. Both kinds of speakers, knowing the singular *radio*, would be capable of uttering the plural in the appropriate situation.

It may be worth noticing that in a case like this, which involves clear-cut grammatical categories, our inability to define meanings need give us no pause. A formula like

$$\begin{array}{c} \text{Singular} \quad \text{Plural} \\ piano \; : \; pianos \\ = radio \; : \; x \end{array}$$

will hold good even if our definitions of the meanings of these categories (e.g. 'one' and 'more than one') should turn out to be inexact.

The form *radios* did not conflict with any older form. The difficulty about most cases of analogic change is the existence of an older form. An observer round the year 1600 who heard, let us suppose, the earliest utterances of the form *cows*, could probably have made the same observations as we, a few years ago, could make about the form *radios:* doubtless many speakers uttered it independently, and could not be distinguished from speakers who had already heard it. However, the utterances of the form *cows* must have been more thinly sown, since there was also the traditional form *kine*. In the ensuing rivalry, the new form had the advantage of regular formation. It is safe to say that the factors which lead to the origination of a form are the same as those which favor the frequency of an existing form.

ANALOGIC CHANGE

We do not know why speakers sometimes utter new combinations instead of traditional forms, and why the new combinations sometimes rise in frequency. A form like *foots*, instead of *feet*, is occasionally uttered by children; we call it a "childish error" and expect the child soon to acquire the traditional habit. A grown person may say *foots* when he is tired or flustered, but he does not repeat the form and no one adopts it; we call it a "slip of the tongue."

It seems that at any one stage of a language, certain features are relatively stable and others relatively unstable. We must suppose that in the sixteenth century, owing to antecedent developments, there were enough alternative plural-forms (say, *eyen : eyes, shoon : shoes, brethren : brothers*) to make an innovation like *cows* relatively inconspicuous and acceptable. At present, an innovation like *foots* seems to have no chance of survival when it is produced from time to time; we may suppose that innovation and fluctuation are at work rather in the sphere of plurals with spirant-voicing: *hooves : hoofs, laths* [$lɑːðz : lɑːθs$], and so on.

The creation of a form like *cow-s* is only an episode in the rise in frequency of the regular plural-suffix [-iz, -z, -s]. Analogic-semantic change is merely fluctuation in frequency, in so far as it displaces grammatical and lexical types. The extension of a form into a new combination with a new accompanying form is probably favored by its earlier occurrence with phonetically or semantically related forms. Thus, the use of [-z] with *cow* was probably favored by the existence of other plurals in [-aw-z], such as *sows, brows*. Similarity of meaning plays a part: *sows, heifers, ewes* will attract *cows*. Frequent occurrence in context probably increases the attraction of a model. The Latin noun *senatus* [se'naːtus] 'senate' had an irregular inflection, including a genitive *senatus* [se'naːtuːs]; by the side of this there arose a new genitive on the regular model, *senati* [se'naːtiː]. It has been suggested that the chief model for this innovation was the regular noun *populus* ['populus] 'people,' genitive *populi* ['populiː], for the two words were habitually used together in the phrase *senatus populusque* [se'naːtus popu'lus kwe] 'the Senate and People.' The most powerful factor is surely that of numbers and frequency. On the one hand, regular form-classes increase at the cost of smaller groups, and, on the other hand, irregular forms of very high frequency resist innovation. Irregular forms appear chiefly among the commonest words and phrases of a language.

23. 4. The regularizing trend of analogic change appears plainly in inflectional paradigms. The history of the regular plural-formation of English is a long series of extensions. The suffix [-iz, -z, -s] is the modern form of an Old English suffix [-as], as in *stan* [sta:n] 'stone,' plural *stanas* ['sta:nas] 'stones.' This suffix in Old English belonged only to the nominative and accusative cases of the plural; the genitive plural *stana* ['sta:na] and the dative plural *stanum* ['sta:num] would both be represented today by the form *stone*. The replacement of this form by the nominative-accusative form *stones*, which is now used for the whole plural, regardless of syntactic position, is part of a larger process, the loss of case-inflection in the noun, which involved both phonetic and analogic changes.

The Old English nominative-accusative plural in *-as* occurred with only one type (the largest, to be sure) of masculine nouns. There were some classes of masculine nouns which formed the plural differently, as, ['sunu] 'son,' plural ['suna]; among these was a large class of *n*-plurals, such as ['steorra] 'star,' plural ['steorran]. Some nouns fluctuated: [feld] 'field,' plural ['felda] or ['feldas]. We do not know the origin of this fluctuation, but, once granted its existence, we can see in it a favoring condition for the spread of the [-as]-plural. A neologism like ['sunas] instead of older ['suna] 'sons' would perhaps have had no better chance of success than a modern *foots*, had it not been for the familiar fluctuation in cases like the word 'field.'

Neuter and feminine nouns in Old English had not the *s*-plural. Examples of neuter types are [word] 'word,' with homonymous plural, ['spere] 'spear,' plural ['speru], ['e:aje] 'eye,' plural ['e:agan]; feminine types, ['karu] 'care,' plural ['kara], ['tunge] 'tongue,' plural ['tungan], [bo:k] 'book,' plural [be:k].

Even where the *s*-plural was traditional, sound-change led to divergent forms. Thus an early voicing of spirants between vowels led to the type *knife : knives*. Other irregularities of this sort have been overlaid by new-formations. In pre-English, [a] became [ɛ] in monosyllables and before [e] of a following syllable; after this change, [g] became [j] before a front vowel and in final position after a front vowel. The result was a set of alternations, as in the paradigm of 'day':

ANALOGIC CHANGE

	Singular	Plural
nom.-acc.	[dɛj]	['dagas]
dat.	['dɛje]	['dagum]
gen.	['dɛjes]	['daga]

Later, there came a change of [g] to [w], whence the Middle English irregularity of *dei*, plural *dawes;* the latter form, as we have seen, was superseded by the regular new combination of *day* plus [-z].

The early Old English loss of [h] between vowels with contraction (§ 21.6), led to paradigms like that of 'shoe,' which were regular in Old English, but by subsequent phonetic change, would have led to highly irregular modern sets:

	Old English	Modern Phonetic Result
singular		
nom.-acc.	[skoːh]	*[ʃʌf]
dat.	[skoː]	[ʃuw]
gen.	[skoːs]	*[ʃʌs]
plural		
nom.-acc.	[skoːs]	*[ʃʌs]
dat.	[skoːm]	*[ʃuwm, ʃum]
gen.	[skoː]	[ʃuw]

Among the Old English paradigms of other types, that of 'foot' shows us an interesting redistribution of forms:

	Singular	Plural
nom.-acc.	[foːt]	[feːt]
dat.	[feːt]	['foːtum]
gen.	['foːtes]	['foːta]

Here the form with [oː], modern *foot*, has been generalized in the singular, crowding out the old dative, and the form with [eː], modern *feet*, in the plural, crowding out the old dative and genitive forms.

In a few cases, two forms have survived with a lexical difference. Our words *shade* and *shadow* are reflexes of different forms of a single Old English paradigm:

ANALOGIC CHANGE

	OLD ENGLISH	MODERN PHONETIC EQUIVALENT	
singular			
nominative	['sk̆adu]	[ʃejd]	*shade*
other cases	['sk̆adwe]	['ʃɛdow]	*shadow*
plural			
dative	['sk̆adwum]	['ʃɛdow]	*shadow*
other cases	['sk̆adwa]	['ʃɛdow]	*shadow*

Both forms, *shade* and *shadow*, have been generalized for the whole singular, and have served as underlying forms for new regular plurals, *shades, shadows;* the rivalry of the two resulting paradigms has ended in a lexical differentiation. The words *mead* and *meadow* arose in the same way, but in this case the fluctuation seems to be ending in the obsolescence of the form *mead*.

The word 'gate' had in Old English the nominative-accusative singular *geat* [jat], plural *gatu* ['gatu]. The old singular, which would give a modern **yat*, has died out; the modern form *gate* represents the old plural, and the new plural *gates* has been formed on the regular model.

Analogic creation is not limited to complex forms. A simple form may be created on the analogy of cases where a complex form and a simple form exist side by side. The Middle English noun *redels* 'riddle,' with homonymous plural, was subjected to analogic change of the pattern

PLURAL		SINGULAR
stones	:	*stone*
= *redels*	:	x,

whence the modern singular form *riddle*. This creation of shorter or underlying forms is called *back-formation*. Another example is Old English ['pise] 'pea,' plural ['pisan]; all the forms of the paradigm lead to modern *pease, peas* [pijz], and the singular *pea* is a back-formation. Similarly, Old French *cherise* 'cherry' was borrowed in Middle English as *cheris*, whence modern *cherries;* the singular *cherry* is an analogic creation.

23. 5. In word-formation, the most favorable ground for analogic forms is a derivative type which bears some clear-cut meaning. Thus, we form all manner of new agent-nouns in *-er*, on what is at present a normal grammatical analogy. This suffix was borrowed in pre-English time from Latin, and has replaced a number

ANALOGIC CHANGE

of native types. In Old English, the agent of ['huntian] 'to hunt' was ['hunta], which has been replaced by *hunter*. At a later time, *webster* was replaced by *weaver*, and survives only as a family-name. In *boot-black, chimney-sweep* old forms survive as compound-members. We not only form new agent-nouns, such as *camou-flager, debunker, charlestoner*, but also make back-formations, such as the verb *chauffe* [ʃowf] 'drive (someone) about in a motor-car' from *chauffeur* ['ʃowfə]. An analogy that permits of new formations is said to be "living."

The old suffix *-ster* in *webster* is an example of a type which perhaps never could have been described as "regular" or "living" and yet had its period of expansion. It seems to have denoted (as is still the case in Dutch) a female agent. The female meaning survives in *spinster*, originally 'spinneress.' Apparently, the female meaning was not obvious in all the words: the suffix became indifferent as to sex and appears in *tapster, huckster, teamster, maltster, webster* 'weaver,' *dunster* 'dunner, bailiff.' The action was not necessarily useful, witness *songster, rimester, trickster, gamester, punster*. A non-human agent appears in *lobster*, which probably represents Old English *loppestre*, originally 'jumper.' An inanimate object is *roadster*. An adjective, instead of verb or noun, underlies *youngster*. After the restriction to females was lost, words in *-ster* combined with *-ess: huckstress, songstress, seamstress*. This last, by the shortening of vowels before clusters, became ['semstris]; the more regular rival form ['sijmstris] is analogic, with the vowel of the underlying *seam*. In cases like *-ster* we see a formation spreading from form to form without ever attaining to the free expansion of "living" types.

Some formations become widely usable without pre-empting a domain of meaning. In English, the suffixes *-y, -ish, -ly*, which derive adjectives, have all remained quite "alive" through the historical period, spreading from word to word, and settling in various semantic patches. Thus, with the suffix *-y* (from Old English *-ig*), some words appear in our Old English records (e.g. *mighty, misty, moody, bloody, speedy*), while others appear only later (e.g. *earthy, wealthy, hasty, hearty, fiery*). When the suffix is added to words of foreign origin, the date of the borrowing gives us a limit of age ("terminus post quem") for the new combination: *sugary, flowery, creamy*. At present, this suffix is expanding in certain zones of meaning, such as 'arch, affected': *summery* (e.g.

of clothes), *sporty, swanky, arty* ('pretendedly artistic'), *booky* ('pretendedly bookish'). In the same way, *-ish*, in some combinations a mere adjective-former (*boyish, girlish*), has staked a claim in the zone of 'undesirably, inappropriately resembling,' as in *mannish, womanish* (contrast *manly, womanly*), *childish* (contrast *childlike*). The starting-point of semantic specialization is to be sought in forms where the underlying word has the special value; thus, the unpleasant flavor of *-ish* comes from words like *loutish, boorish, swinish, hoggish*.

The shape of morphologic constituents is subject to analogic change, especially in the way of enlargement. In Latin, the set *argentum* [ar'gentum] 'silver' : *argentarius* [argen'ta:rius] 'silversmith' represents a regular type of derivation. In the history of French there was repeated losses of final phonemes; the modern forms are *argent* [arʒã] : *argentier* [arʒãtje]. The formula of derivation has become: add the suffix [-tje]. This suffix, accordingly, appears in words which (as the historian, quite irrelevantly, remarks) never contained a [t] in the critical position: French *ferblanc* [fɛr-blã] 'tin' (Latin type *ferrum blankum* 'white iron,' with the Germanic adjective *blank*) underlies *ferblantier* [fɛrblãtje] 'tinsmith'; *bijou* [biʒu] 'jewel' (from Breton *bizun*) underlies *bijoutier* [biʒutje] 'jeweler,' and so on.

In time, an affix may consist entirely of accretive elements, with no trace of its original shape. In Old English, verb-paradigms were derived from nouns on the pattern [wund] 'a wound': ['wundian] 'to wound,' and this is still the living type, as in *wound : to wound, radio : to radio*. In a few instances, however, the underlying noun was itself derived, by means of a suffix [-en-], from an adjective, as in the set [fɛst] 'firm, strong' : ['fɛsten] 'strong place, fortress' : ['fɛstenian] 'to make firm, to fortify,' Thanks to some fluctuation in frequency or meaning — such, perhaps, as a decline or specialization of the noun ['fɛsten] — the pair [fɛst] 'firm' : ['fɛstenian] 'to make firm' served as a model for new-formations on the scheme

$$fast : fasten = hard : x,$$

with the result of forms like *harden, sharpen, sweeten, fatten, gladden*, in which a suffix *-en* derives verbs from adjectives.

Less often, a relatively independent form is reduced to affixal status. Compound-members are occasionally reduced, by sound-change, to suffixes; thus, the suffix *-ly* (*manly*) is a weakened form of *like*, and the suffix -*dom* (*kingdom*) of the word *doom*. This happens especially when the independent word goes out of use, as in the case of -*hood* (*childhood*), which is a relic of an Old English word [ha:d] 'person, rank.' German *Messer* ['meser] 'knife' is the modern form, with analogic as well as phonetic shortening, of Old High German ['messi-rahs] originally 'food-knife,' in which the second member, [sahs] 'knife,' had been disfigured by Verner's change (§ 20.8) and the subsequent change of [z] to [r]. In German *Schuster* [ʃuːster] 'shoemaker' the unique suffix [-ster] reflects an old compound-member [suˈteːre] 'cobbler.' Merging of two words into one is excessively rare; the best-known instance is the origin of the future tense-forms in the Romance languages from phrases of infinitive plus 'have': Latin *amare habeo* [aˈmaːre ˈhabeoː] 'I have to, am to love' > French *aimerai* [emre] '(I) shall love'; Latin *amare habet* [aˈmaːre ˈhabet] 'he has to, is to love' > French *aimera* [emra] '(he) will love,' and so on. This development must have taken place under very unusual conditions; above all, we must remember that Latin and Romance have a complicated set of verb-inflections which se. ed as a model for one-word tense-forms.

Back-formations in word-structure are by no means uncommon, though often hard to recognize. Many verbs in the foreign-learned vocabulary of English resemble Latin past participles; this is all the more striking since English has borrowed these words from French, and in French the Latin past participles have been obscured by sound-change or replaced by new-formations: Latin *agere* [ˈagere] 'to lead, carry on, do,' past participle *actus* [ˈaktus] 'led, done' : French *agir* [aʒiːr] 'to act,' participle (new-formation) *agi* [aʒi] 'acted' : English *to act;* Latin *affligere* [afˈliːgere] 'to strike down, afflict,' participle *afflictus* [afˈfliktus] 'stricken, afflicted' : French *affliger* [afliʒe], participle *affligé* [afliʒe] : English *to afflict;* Latin *separare* [seːpaˈraːre] 'to separate,' participle *separatus* [seːpaˈraːtus] : French *séparer* [separe], participle *séparé* [separe] : English *to separate*. The starting-point for this habit of English seems to have been back-formation from nouns in -*tion:* Eng'sh verbs like *act, afflict, separate* are based on nouns like *action, affliction, separation*, from Latin *actionem, afflictionem, separationem* [aktiˈoːnem, afflikti'oːnem, seːparaːtiˈoːnem] via French *action, affliction, séparation* in modern pronunciation [aksjɔ̃, afliksjɔ̃, separasjɔ̃]. The immediate models must have been cases like *communion: to commune* (Old French *communion : comuner*); the general background was the English homonymy of adjective and verb in cases like *warm : to warm = separate : to separate*. This supposition is confirmed by the fact that the nouns in *-tion* appear in our records at an earlier time, on the whole, than the verbs in *-t*. Of the 108 pairs with initial A in the *New English Dictionary*, the noun appears earlier than the verb in 74 cases, as, *action* in 1330, but *to act* in 1384; *affliction*, in 1303, but *to afflict* in 1393. Moreover, we sometimes see the late rise of the verb with *-t:* in the case of *aspiration : to aspire* we have stuck to the Latin-French scheme, but round 1700 there appears the new-formation *to aspirate*. Modern formations of this sort are *evolute*, based on *evolution*, as a rival of the older *evolve*, and *elocute* based on *elocution*.

23. 6. The task of tracing analogy in word-composition has scarcely been undertaken. The present-day habits of word-composition in English produce the illusion that compounds arise by a simple juxtaposition of words. The reader need scarcely be told that the modern English pattern, in which the compound word equals the independent forms of the members, with modification only of word-stress, is the product of a long series of regularizing analogic changes. Thus, [ˈfɔə-ˌhed] *forehead*, as a rival of [ˈfɔrid], which has been irregularized by sound-change, is due to analogic re-formation:

fore, arm : fore-arm [ˈfɔər-ˌɑːm]
= *fore, head : x*.

The relation of the compound to independent words often suffers displacement. Primitive Indo-European did not use verb-stems as compound-members; to this day, English lacks a verbal type, *to meat-eat, which would match the noun and adjective types *meat-eater* and *meat-eating* (§ 14.3). Several Indo-European languages, however, have developed compounds with verbal members. In English we have a few irregular forms like *housekeep, dressmake, backbite*. From a compound noun like *whitewash* we derive, with a zero-element, a verb *to whitewash*, and from this an agent-noun *whitewasher*. The irregular type *to housekeep* is probably a back-formation on this model:

whitewasher : to whitewash
= *housekeeper : x*.

ANALOGIC CHANGE

In a now classical investigation, Hermann Osthoff showed how forms of this kind arose in several of the Indo-European languages. In Old High German, abstract nouns like ['beta] 'prayer' were used, in the normal inherited fashion, as prior members of compounds: ['beta-ˌhuːs] 'prayer-house, house for prayer.' The morphologically connected verb ['betoːn] 'to pray' had a different suffixal vowel and did not interfere with the compound. During the Middle Ages, however, unstressed vowels were weakened to a uniform [e] and in part lost; hence in Middle High German (round the year 1200), in a set like ['beten] 'to pray' : ['bete] 'prayer' : ['bete-ˌhuːs] 'house for prayer,' the compound-member resembled the verb as much as it resembled the noun. If the noun lost in frequency or was specialized in meaning, the compound-member became equivalent to the verb-stem. Thus ['bete] 'prayer' lost in frequency — the modern language uses a different derivative, *Gebet* [geˈbeːt] 'prayer' — and, for the rest, was specialized in a meaning of 'contribution, tax.' As a result of this, compounds like *Bethaus* ['beːt-ˌhaws] 'house for praying,' *Bettag* ['beːt-ˌtaːk] 'day of prayer,' *Betschwester*, ['beːt-ˌʃvester] 'praying-sister,' that is 'nun' or 'over-pious woman,' can be described only as containing the verb-stem [beːt-] of *beten* [beːten] 'to pray.' Accordingly, ever since the Middle Ages, new compounds of this sort have been formed with verbal prior members, as *Schreibtisch* [ˈʃrajp-ˌtiʃ] 'writing-table,' from *schreiben* 'to write,' or *Lesebuch* [ˈleːze-ˌbuːx] 'reading-book' from *lesen* 'to read.'

The fluctuation between irregular compounds, such as [ˈfɔrid] *forehead*, and analogically formed regular variants, such as [ˈfɔə-ˌhed], serves as a model for new-formations which replace an obscure form by a compound-member. Thus, *inmost, northmost, utmost* (and, with regularization of the first member, *outmost*), with the word *most* as second member, are analogic formations which replace the Old English type [ˈinnemest, ˈnorθmest, ˈuːtemest]; the [-mest] in these words was a special form (with accretion) of the superlative suffix [-est]. Regularizing new-formations like this, which (as the historian finds) disagree with the earlier structure of the form, are sometimes called *popular etymologies*.

23. 7. Analogic innovation in the phrase is most easily seen when it affects the shape of single words. Conditioned sound-changes may produce different forms of a word according to its phonetic positions in the phrase. In the types of English which lost [r] in final position and before consonants, but kept it before vowels, there resulted sandhi-alternants of words like *water:* in final position and before consonants this became ['wɔːtə], but before a vowel in a close-knit phrase it kept its [r]: *the water is* ['wɔːtər iz], *the water of* ['wɔːtər əv]. The final vowel of *water* was now like that of a word like *idea* [aj'diə], which had never had final [r]. This led to a new-formation:

water ['wɔːtə] : *the water is* ['wɔːtər iz]
= *idea* [aj'diə] : *x*,

which resulted in the sandhi-form *the idea-r is* [aj'diər iz].

In a language like modern English, which gives special phonetic treatment to the beginning and end of a word, the phonemes in these positions rarely fulfil the terms of an ordinary conditioned sound-change, but are subject rather to conditioned changes of their own. Only phrases with atonic words parallel the conditions which exist within a word. Hence English sandhi-alternation is limited largely to cases like the above (. . . *of*, . . . *is*) or to such as *don't, at you* ['ɛtʃuw], *did you* ['diʤuw].Moreover, the plain phonetic marking of most words, and in some positions even of ordinarily atonic words, favors the survival or new-formation of variants that agree with the absolute form: *do not, at you* ['ɛt juw], *did you* ['did juw].

In languages which give a less specialized treatment to word-boundaries, sandhi-alternants arise in great numbers and give rise to irregularities which are in turn leveled out by new-formations. We saw in § 21.4 the origin of the initial-sandhi of Irish. In French, the noun is on the whole free from sandhi-alternation: words like *pot* [po] 'pot' or *pied* [pje] 'foot' are invariable in the phrase. However, we need only look to phrase-like compounds (§ 14.2), such as *pot-au-feu* [pɔt o fø] 'pot-on-the-fire,' that is 'broth,' or *pied-à-terre* [pjɛt a tɛːr] 'foot-on-ground,' that is 'lodgings,' to see that the apparent stability is due to analogic regularization. Third-person singular verbs which were monosyllabic in the early Middle Ages, have, by regular phonetic development, a final [t] in sandhi before a vowel: Latin *est* > French *est* [ɛ] 'is,' but Latin *est ille* > French *est-il* [ɛt i] 'is he?' On the other hand, verb-forms of more than one syllable had not this [t]; Latin *amat* 'he loves' gives French *aime* [ɛm] 'loves' even before a vowel. However, the pattern

[ɛ] : [ɛt i] = [ɛm] : *x*

ANALOGIC CHANGE

resulted in a modern sandhi-form *aime-t-il* [ɛmt i] 'does he love?'

In the later Old English period, final [n] after an unstressed vowel was lost, except in sandhi before a vowel. Thus, *eten* 'to eat' became *ete*, *an hand* became *a hand*, but *an arm* remained. In the case of the article *a : an* the resulting alternation has survived; in early modern English one still said *my friend : mine enemy*. One must suppose that at the time of the loss of *-n*, the language did not distinguish word-boundaries in the manner of present-day English. The sandhi [n] was generalized in a few cases as a word-initial. Old English *efeta* ['eveta] 'lizard' appears in Middle English as *ewte* and *newte*, whence modern *newt*. A phrase like *an ewte* must have been pronounced [a'newte] and (doubtless under some special conditions of frequency or meaning) subjected to the new-formation

[a'na:me] 'a name' : ['na:me] 'name'
= [a'newte] 'a lizard' : *x*,

with the result that one said *newte*. Similarly, *eke-name* 'supplementary name' gave rise to a by-form with *n-*, modern *nickname*; *for then anes* is now *for the nonce*. On the other hand, an initial [n] was in some forms treated as a sandhi [n]. Thus, Old English *nafogar* ['navo-₁ga:r], literally 'nave-lance,' Middle English *navegar*, has been replaced by *auger*; Old English ['nɛ:dre] gives Middle English *naddere* and *addere*, whence modern *adder*; Old French *naperon*, borrowed as *napron*, has been replaced by *apron*.

After this loss of final [n], another sound-change led to the loss of certain final vowels, through which many hitherto medial [n]'s got into final position, as in *oxena > oxen*. These new final [n]'s came into final position too late to suffer the dropping; hence the language had now, beside the sandhi [n], which appeared only before vowels, also a stable final [n]. This led to some complicated relations:

	OLD ENGLISH >	EARLY MIDDLE ENGLISH	
		before vowel	otherwise
singular			
nominative	*oxa*	*ox*	*oxe*
other cases	*oxan*	*oxen*	*oxe*
plural			
nom.-acc.	*oxan*	*oxen*	*oxe*
dat.	*oxum*	*oxen*	*oxe*
gen.	*oxena*	*oxen*	*oxen*

This complicated habit was re-shaped into our present distribution of singular *ox*, plural *oxen*.

In most cases, a phrasal innovation results not in a new word-form, but in a new syntactic or lexical usage, such as the use of *like* as a conjunction (§ 23.2). In German we find such appositional groups as *ein Trunk Wasser* [ajn 'truŋk 'vaser] 'a drink of water,' where the related languages would lead us to expect the second noun in genitive case-form, *Wassers* 'of water.' The genitive case-ending in feminine and plural nouns has been reduced to zero by phonetic change: the genitive of *Milch* [milx] 'milk' (feminine noun) is homonymous with the nominative and accusative. The old locution *ein Trunk Wassers* has been replaced by the present one, which arose on the scheme

Milch trinken 'to drink milk' : *ein Trunk Milch* 'a drink of milk'
= *Wasser trinken* 'to drink water' : x.

This was favored, no doubt, by the existence of nouns whose genitive wavered between zero and *-es*, and by the circumstance that the genitive case was declining in frequency. It seems likely, in spite of the obvious difficulties, that further research will find many examples of analogic innovation in the phrase, both syntactic and lexical. Our philosophic prepossessions have led us too often to seek the motives of change in the individual word and in the meaning of the individual word.

23. 8. For many new-formations we are not able to give a proportional model. We believe that this is not always due to our inability to find the model sets, and that there is really a type of linguistic change which resembles analogic change, but goes on without model sets. These *adaptive* new-formations resemble an old form with some change in the direction of semantically related forms. For instance, of the two slang forms *actorine* 'actress' and *chorine* 'chorus-girl,' only the former can be described as the result of a proportional analogy (*Paul* : *Pauline* = *actor* : x). Now, *chorine* seems to be based in some way on *actorine*, but the set *chorus* : *chorine* is not parallel with *actor* : *actorine* either in form or in meaning. The set *Josephus* : *Josephine* [jow'sijfəs, 'jowzi-fijn] is uncommon, remote in meaning, and phonetically irregular. We can say only that many nouns have a suffix [-ijn], e.g. *chlorine, colleen;* that this suffix derives some women's names and

ANALOGIC CHANGE

especially the noun *actorine;* and that the *-us* of *chorus* is plainly suffixal, in view of the adjective *choral.* This general background must have sufficed to make someone utter the form *chorine,* even though there was no exact analogy for this form.

A new form (such as *chorine*), which is based on a traditional form (*chorus, chorus-girl*), but departs from it in the direction of a series of semantically related forms (*chlorine, colleen, Pauline,* etc., including especially *actorine*), is said to originate by *adaptation.* Adaptation seems to be favored by more than one factor, but all the factors taken together would not allow us to predict the new form. Often, as in our example, the new form has a facetious connotation; this connotation is probably connected with the unpredictable, far-fetched shape of the new word. This is true of mock-learned words, like *scrumptious, rambunctious, absquatulate.* It seems unlikely that more than one speaker hit upon these forms: we suspect them of being individual creations, determined by the linguistic and practical peculiarities of some one speaker. They must have agreed to some extent, however, with the general habits of the community, since they were taken up by other speakers.

Some adaptations are less far-fetched and merely produce a new form which agrees better with semantically related forms. English has borrowed many French words with a suffix *-ure,* such as *measure, censure, fracture.* The Old French words *plaisir, loisir, tresor,* which contain other suffixes, have in English been adapted to the *-ure* type, for the [-ɜə] of *pleasure, leisure, treasure* reflects an old [-zju:r]. Among our foreign-learned words, *egoism* follows the French model, but *egotism* is an adaptive formation in the direction of *despotism, nepotism.*

In the Romance languages, Latin *reddere* [ˈreddere] 'to give back' has been largely replaced by a type **rendere*, as in Italian *rendere* [ˈrɛndere], French *rendre* [rãdr], whence English *render.* This **rendere* is an adaptation of *reddere* in the direction of the series Latin *prehendere* [preˈhendere, ˈprendere] 'to take' > Italian *prendere* [ˈprendere], French *prendre* [prãdr]; Latin *attendere* [atˈtendere] 'to pay attention' > Italian *attendere* [atˈtɛndere] 'to wait,' French *attendre* [atãdr] (and other compounds of Latin *tendere*); Latin *vendere* [ˈweːndere] 'to sell' > Italian *vendere* [ˈvendere], French *vendre* [vãdr]; here the word for 'take,' with its close kinship of meaning, was doubtless the main factor.

Sometimes it is a single form which exercises the attraction. Beside the old word *gravis* 'heavy,' later Latin has also a form *grevis*, whose vowel seems to be due to the influence of *levis* 'light (in weight).' Formations of this sort are known as *blendings* or *contaminations*. We cannot always be sure that the attraction was exercised by only a single form; in our example, the word *brevis* 'short' may have helped toward the ormation of *grevis*.

The paradigm of the word for 'foot,' Primitive Indo-European *[poːds], genitive *[poˈdos], Sanskrit [paːt], genitive [paˈdah], appears in one ancient Greek dialect in the expected shape, [ˈpoːs], genitive [poˈdos], but in the Attic dialect has the unexpected nominative form [ˈpows]; this has been explained as a contamination with the word for 'tooth,' [oˈdows], genitive [oˈdontos], which is a phonetically normal reflex of a Primitive Indo-European type *[oˈdonts].

In the earlier stages of the Germanic languages, the personal pronouns must have been in a state of instability. The old form for 'ye' seems to have been a Primitive Germanic type *[juːz, juz], which appears in Gothic as *jus* [juːs] or [jus]. The other Germanic dialects reflect a Primitive Germanic type *[jiz]: Old Norse [eːr], Old English [jeː], Old High German [ir]. This form has been explained as a contamination of *[juz] 'ye' with the word for 'we,' Primitive Germanic *[wiːz, wiz], reflected in Gothic [wiːs], Old Norse [veːr], Old English [weː], Old High German [wir].

Similarly, in Gothic the accusative case of 'thou' is [θuk] and the dative case [θus]. These forms disagree with the other dialects, which reflect the Primitive Germanic types accusative *[ˈθiki], Old Norse [θik], Old English [θek], Old High German [dih], and dative *[θiz], Old Norse [θeːr], Old English [θeː], Old High German [dir]. The Gothic forms have been explained as contaminations with the nominative *[θuː], Gothic, Old Norse, Old English [θuː], Old High German [duː]. For this, the word 'I,' which had the same vowel in all three forms, Gothic [ik, mik, mis], may have served as a kind of model, but there is no exact analogy covering the two paradigms, and we might equally well expect [mik, mis] to work in favor of *[θik, θis].

Numerals seem to have been contaminated in the history of various languages. In Primitive Indo-European. 'four' was *[kʷeˈtwoːres], and 'five' *[ˈpenkʷe]; witness Sanskrit [caˈtvaːrah, ˈpanca] or Lithuanian [ketuˈri, penˈki]. In the Germanic languages

ANALOGIC CHANGE

both words begin with [f], which reflects a Primitive Indo-European [p], as in English *four, five;* and *five,* moreover, has an [f] for the [kʷ] of the second syllable, as in Gothic [fimf]. In Latin, on the other hand, both words begin with [kw]: *quattuor, quinque* ['kwattuor, 'kwi:nkwe]. All of these deviant forms could be explained as due to "distant assimilation"; it seems more probable, however, that the changes described under this and similar terms (§ 21.10) are in reality contaminative or adaptive. Ancient Greek [hep'ta] 'seven' and [ok'to:] 'eight' led in one dialect to a contaminative [op'to:] 'eight,' and in others to [hok'to:]. The words 'nine' and 'ten,' Primitive Indo-European *['newn, 'dek m̥], as in Sanskrit ['nava, 'daça], Latin *novem, decem,* both have initial [d] in Slavic and Baltic, as in Old Bulgarian [devĕtɪ, desĕtɪ].

Psychologists have ascertained that under laboratory conditions, the stimulus of hearing a word like 'four' often leads to the utterance of a word like 'five' — but this, after all, does not account for contamination. There is perhaps more relevance in the fact that contaminative "slips of the tongue" are not infrequent, e.g. "I'll just *grun* (*go* plus *run*) over and get it."

Innovations in syntax sometimes have a contaminative aspect. The type *I am friends with him* has been explained as due to contamination of *I am friendly with him* and *we are friends.* Irregularities such as the "attraction" of relative pronouns (§ 15.11) seem to be of this nature.

So-called popular etymologies (§ 23.6) are largely adaptive and contaminative. An irregular or semantically obscure form is replaced by a new form of more normal structure and some semantic content — though the latter is often far-fetched. Thus, an old *sham-fast* 'shame-fast,' that is, 'modest,' has given way to the regular, but semantically queer compound *shame-faced.* Old English *sam-blind,* containing an otherwise obsolete first member which meant 'half,' was replaced by the Elizabethan *sand-blind.* Old English *bryd-guma* ['bry:d-ˌguma] 'bride-man' was replaced by *bride-groom,* thanks to the obsolescence of *guma* 'man.' Foreign words are especially subject to this kind of adaptation. Old French *crevisse,* Middle English *crevise* has been replaced by *cray-fish, craw-fish: mandragora* by *man-drake; asparagus* in older substandard speech by *sparrow-grass.* Our *gooseberry* seems to be a replacement of an older *groze-berry,* to judge by dialect forms such as *grozet, groser;* these forms reflect a borrowed French form akin to modern French *groseille* [grɔzɛːj] 'currant; gooseberry.'

Probably forms like our symbolic words, nursery words, and short-names are created on general formal patterns, rather than on exact analogic models. It seems, however, that forms like *Bob, Dick* existed as common nouns, perhaps with symbolic connotation, before they were specialized as hypochoristic forms of *Robert, Richard*. It is a great mistake to think that one can account for the origin of forms like these by merely stating their connotation.

In some instances we know that a certain person invented a form. The most famous instance is *gas*, invented in the seventeenth century by the Dutch chemist van Helmont. In the passage where he introduces the word, van Helmont points out its resemblance to the word *chaos*, which, in Dutch pronunciation, is not far removed (though phonemically quite distinct) from *gas*. Moreover, van Helmont used also a technical term *blas*, a regular derivative, in Dutch, of the verb *blazen* 'to blow.'

It is evident that in such cases we cannot reconstruct the inventor's private and personal world of connotations; we can only guess at the general linguistic background. Charles Dodgson ("Lewis Carroll") in his famous poem, "The Jabberwocky" (in *Through the Looking-Glass*), uses a number of new-formations of this sort and, later in the book, explains the connotative significance they had for him. At least one of them, *chortle*, has come into wide use. More recent examples are the mercantile term *kodak*, invented by George Eastman, and *blurb*, a creation of Gelett Burgess.

CHAPTER 24

SEMANTIC CHANGE

24. 1. Innovations which change the lexical meaning rather than the grammatical function of a form, are classed as *change of meaning* or *semantic change*.

The contexts and phrasal combinations of a form in our older written records often show that it once had a different meaning. The King James translation of the Bible (1611) says, of the herbs and trees (*Genesis* 1, 29) *to you they shall be for meat*. Similarly, the Old English translation in this passage used the word *mete*. We infer that the word *meat* used to mean 'food,' and we may assure ourselves of this by looking into the foreign texts from which these English translations were made. Sometimes the ancients tell us meanings outright, chiefly in the form of glosses; thus, an Old English glossary uses the word *mete* to translate the Latin *cibus*, which we know to mean 'food.'

In other instances the comparison of related languages shows different meanings in forms that we feel justified in viewing as cognate. Thus, *chin* agrees in meaning with German *Kinn* and Dutch *kin*, but Gothic *kinnus* and the Scandinavian forms, from Old Norse *kinn* to the present, mean 'cheek.' In other Indo-European languages we find Greek ['genus] 'chin' agreeing with West Germanic, but Latin *gena* 'cheek' agreeing with Gothic and Scandinavian, while Sanskrit ['hanuh] 'jaw' shows us a third meaning. We conclude that the old meaning, whatever it was, has changed in some or all of these languages.

A third, but much less certain indication of semantic change, appears in the structural analysis of forms. Thus, *understand* had in Old English time the same meaning as now, but since the word is a compound of *stand* and *under*, we infer that at the time the compound was first formed (as an analogic new-formation) it must have meant 'stand under'; this gains in probability from the fact that *under* once meant also 'among,' for the cognates, German *unter* and Latin *inter*, have this meaning. Thus, *I understand these things* may have meant, at first, 'I stand among these things.' In other cases, a form whose structure in the present state of the language does not imply anything as to meaning, may have been semantically analyzable in an earlier stage. The word *ready* has the adjective-forming suffix *-y* added to a unique root, but the Old English form [je'rɛːde], which, but for an analogic re-formation of the suffix, can be viewed as the ancestor of *ready*, meant 'swift, suited, skilled' and was a derivative of the verb ['riːdan] 'to ride,' past tense [raːd] 'rode,' derived noun [raːd] 'a riding, a road.' We infer that when [je'rɛːde] was first formed, it meant 'suitable or prepared for riding.'

Inferences like these are sometimes wrong, because the make-up of a form may be of later date than its meaning. Thus, *crawfish* and *gooseberry*, adaptations of *crevise* and **groze-berry* (§ 23.8), can tell us nothing about any older meanings.

24. 2. We can easily see today that a change in the meaning of a speech-form is merely the result of a change in the use of it and other, semantically related speech-forms. Earlier students, however, went at this problem as if the speech-form were a relatively permanent object to which the meaning was attached as a kind of changeable satellite. They hoped by studying the successive meanings of a single form, such as *meat* 'food' > 'flesh-food,' to find the reason for this change. This led them to classify semantic changes according to the logical relations that connect the successive meanings. They set up such classes as the following:

Narrowing:

Old English *mete* 'food' > *meat* 'edible flesh'

Old English *dēor* 'beast' > *deer* 'wild ruminant of a particular species'

Old English *hund* 'dog' > *hound* 'hunting-dog of a particular breed'

Widening:

Middle English *bridde* 'young birdling' > *bird*

Middle English *dogge* 'dog of a particular (ancient) breed' > *dog*

Latin *virtūs* 'quality of a man (*vir*), manliness' > French *vertu* (> English *virtue*) 'good quality'

Metaphor:

Primitive Germanic *['bitraz] 'biting' (derivative of *['biːtoː] 'I bite' > *bitter* 'harsh of taste'

Metonymy — the meanings are near each other in space or time:
Old English *cēace* 'jaw' > *cheek*
Old French *joue* 'cheek' > *jaw*
Synecdoche — the meanings are related as whole and part:
Primitive Germanic *['tu:naz] 'fence' (so still German *Zaun*) > *town*
pre-English *['stobo:] 'heated room' (compare German *Stube*, formerly 'heated room,' now 'living-room') > *stove*
Hyperbole — from stronger to weaker meaning:
pre-French *ex-tonāre* 'to strike with thunder' > French *étonner* 'to astonish' (from Old French, English borrowed *astound, astonish*)
Litotes — from weaker to stronger meaning:
pre-English *['kwalljan] 'to torment' (so still German *quälen*) > Old English *cwellan* 'to kill'
Degeneration:
Old English *cnafa* 'boy, servant' > *knave*
Elevation:
Old English *cniht* 'boy, servant' (compare German *Knecht* 'servant') > *knight*.

Collections of examples arranged in classes like these are useful in showing us what changes are likely to occur. The meanings 'jaw,' 'cheek,' and 'chin,' which we found in the cognates of our word *chin*, are found to fluctuate in other cases, such as that of *cheek* from 'jaw' (Old English meaning) to the present meaning; *jaw*, from French *joue* 'cheek,' has changed in the opposite direction. Latin *maxilla* 'jaw' has shifted to 'cheek' in most modern dialects, as in Italian *mascella* [ma'ʃella] 'cheek.' We suspect that the word *chin* may have meant 'jaw' before it meant 'cheek' and 'chin.' In this case we have the confirmation of a few Old High German glosses which translate Latin *molae* and *maxillae* (plural forms in the sense 'jaw' or 'jaws') by the plural *kinne*. Old English ['weorθan] 'to become' and its cognates in the other Germanic languages (such as German *werden*, § 22.2) agree in form with Sanskrit ['vartate:] 'he turns,' Latin *vertō* 'I turn,' Old Bulgarian [vr̥te:ti] 'to turn,' Lithuanian [ver'tʃu] 'I turn'; we accept this etymology because the Sanskrit word has a marginal meaning 'to become,' and because English *turn* shows a parallel development, as in *turn sour, turn traitor.*

24. 3. Viewed on this plane, a change of meaning may imply a connection between practical things and thereby throw light on the life of older times. English *fee* is the modern form of the paradigm of Old English *feoh*, which meant 'live-stock, cattle, property, money.' Among the Germanic cognates, only Gothic *faihu* ['fehu] means 'property'; all the others, such as German *Vieh* [fi:] or Swedish *fä* [fe:], have meanings like '(head of) cattle, (head of) live-stock.' The same is true of the cognates in the other Indo-European languages, such as Sanskrit ['paçu] or Latin *pecu;* but Latin has the derived words *pecūnia* 'money' and *pecūlium* 'savings, property.' This confirms our belief that live-stock served in ancient times as a medium of exchange.

English *hose* corresponds formally to Dutch *hoos* [ho:s], German *Hose* ['ho:ze], but these words, usually in plural form, mean not 'stockings' but 'trousers.' The Scandinavian forms, such as Old Norse *hosa*, mean 'stocking' or 'legging.' An ancient form, presumably West Germanic, came into Latin in the early centuries of our era, doubtless through the mediation of Roman soldiers, for the Romance languages have a type **hosa* (as, Italian *uosa* ['wɔsa]) in the sense 'legging.' We conclude that in old Germanic our word meant a covering for the leg, either including the foot or ending at the ankle. Round his waist a man wore another garment, the *breeches* (Old English *brōc*). The English and Scandinavian terminology indicates no change, but the German development seems to indicate that on the Continent the *hose* were later joined at the top into a trouser-like garment.

In this way, a semantically peculiar etymology and cultural traces may confirm each other. The German word *Wand* [vant] denotes the wall of a room, but not a thick masonry wall; the latter is *Mauer* ['mawer], a loan from Latin. The German word sounds like a derivative of the verb *to wind*, German *winden* (past tense *wand*), but etymologists were at loss as to the connection of these meanings, until Meringer showed that the derivative noun must have applied at first to wattled walls, which were made of twisted withes covered with mud. In the same way, Primitive Germanic *['wajjuz] 'wall,' in Gothic *waddjus*, Old Norse *veggr*, Old English *wāg*, is now taken to have originated as a derivative of a verb that meant 'wind, twist.' We have seen that scholars try, by a combination of semantic and archaeologic data, to throw light on prehistoric conditions, such as those of the Primitive Indo-

SEMANTIC CHANGE

European parent community (§ 18.14). The maxim "Words and Things" has been used as the title of a journal devoted to this aspect of etymology.

Just as formal features may arise from highly specific and variable factors (§ 23.8), so the meaning of a form may be due to situations that we cannot reconstruct and can know only if historical tradition is kind to us. The German *Kaiser* ['kajzer] 'emperor' and the Russian [tsar] are offshoots, by borrowing, of the Latin *caesar* ['kajsar], which was generalized from the name of a particular Roman, *Gaius Julius Caesar*. This name is said to be a derivative of the verb *caedō* 'I cut'; the man to whom it was first given was born by the aid of the surgical operation which, on account of this same tradition, is called the *caesarian* operation. Aside from this tradition, if we had not the historical knowledge about Caesar and the Roman Empire, we could not guess that the word for 'emperor' had begun as a family-name. The now obsolescent verb *burke* 'suppress' (as, *to burke opposition*) was derived from the name of one *Burke*, a murderer in Edinburgh who smothered his victims. The word *pander* comes from the name of *Pandarus;* in Chaucer's version of the ancient story of Troilus and Cressida, Pandarus acts as a go-between. *Buncombe* comes from the name of a county in North Carolina, thanks to the antics of a congressman. *Tawdry* comes from *St. Audrey;* at St. Audrey's fair one bought *tawdry lace.* Terms like *landau* and *wiener* come from the original place of manufacture. The word *dollar* is borrowed ultimately from German *Taler*, short for *Joachimstaler*, derived from *Joachimstal* ('Joachim's Dale'), a place in Bohemia where silver was minted in the sixteenth century. The Roman mint was in the temple of *Jūnō Monēta* 'Juno the Warner'; hence the Romans used the word *monēta* both for 'mint' and for 'coin, money.' English *mint* is a pre-English borrowing from this Latin word, and English *money* is a medieval borrowing from the Old French continuation of the Latin word.

The surface study of semantic change indicates that refined and abstract meanings largely grow out of more concrete meanings. Meanings of the type 'respond accurately to (things or speech)' develop again and again from meanings like 'be near to' or 'get hold of.' Thus, *understand,* as we saw, seems to have meant 'stand close to' or 'stand among.' German *verstehen* [ferˈʃteːn] 'understand' seems to have meant 'stand round' or 'stand before'; the

Old English equivalent *forstandan* appears both for 'understand' and for 'protect, defend.' Ancient Greek [eˈpistamaj] 'I understand' is literally 'I stand upon,' and Sanskrit [avaˈgacchati] is both 'he goes down into' and 'he understands.' Italian *capire* [kaˈpire] 'to understand' is an analogic new-formation based on Latin *capere* 'to seize, grasp.' Latin *comprehendere* 'to understand' means also 'to take hold of.' The Slavic word for 'understand, as in Russian [poˈnat], is a compound of an old verb that meant 'seize, take.' A marginal meaning of 'understand' appears in our words *grasp, catch on, get* (as in *I don't get that*). Most of our abstract vocabulary consists of borrowings from Latin, through French or in gallicized form; the Latin originals can largely be traced to concrete meanings. Thus Latin *dēfinīre* 'to define' is literally 'to set bounds to' (*finis* 'end, boundary'). Our *eliminate* has in Latin only the concrete meaning 'put out of the house,' in accordance with its derivative character, since Latin *ēlimināre* is structurally a synthetic compound of *ex* 'out of, out from' and *līmen* 'threshold.'

24. 4. All this, aside from its extra-linguistic interest, gives us some measure of probability by which we can judge of etymologic comparisons, but it does not tell us how the meaning of a linguistic form can change in the course of time. When we find a form used at one time in a meaning A and at a later time in a meaning B, what we see is evidently the result of at least two shifts, namely, an expansion of the form from use in situations of type A to use in situations of a wider type A-B, and then a partial obsolescence by which the form ceases to be used in situations which approximate the old type A, so that finally the form is used only in situations of type B. In ordinary cases, the first process involves the obsolescence or restriction of some rival form that gets crowded out of use in the B-situations, and the second process involves the encroachment of some rival form into the A-situations. We can symbolize this diagrammatically as follows:

meaning:	'nourishment'	'edible thing'	'edible part of animal body'	'muscular part of animal body'
first stage:	*food*	*meat*	*flesh*	*flesh*
second stage:	*food*	*meat* ➡	*meat*	*flesh*
third stage:	*food* ➡	*food*	*meat*	*flesh*

SEMANTIC CHANGE

In the normal case, therefore, we have to deal here with fluctuations of frequency like those of analogic change; the difference is only that the fluctuations result in lexical instead of grammatical displacements, and therefore largely elude the grasp of the linguist. The first student, probably, to see that semantic change consists of expansion and obsolescence, was Hermann Paul. Paul saw that the meaning of a form in the habit of any speaker, is merely the result of the utterances in which he has heard it. Sometimes, to be sure, we use a form in situations that fairly well cover its range of meaning, as in a definition ("a *town* is a large settlement of people") or in a very general statement ("vertebrate animals have a *head*"). In such cases a form appears in its *general* meaning. Ordinarily, however, a form in any one utterance represents a far more specific practical feature. When we say that *John Smith bumped his head*, the word *head* is used of one particular man's head. When a speaker in the neighborhood of a city says *I'm going to town*, the word *town* means this particular city. In such cases the form appears in an *occasional* meaning. In *eat an apple a day* the word *apple* has its general meaning; in some one utterance of the phrase *eat this apple*, the word *apple* has an occasional meaning: the apple, let us say, is a large baked apple. All marginal meanings are occasional, for — as Paul showed — marginal meanings differ from central meanings precisely by the fact that we respond to a marginal meaning only when some special circumstance makes the central meaning impossible (§ 9.8). Central meanings are occasional whenever the situation differs from the ideal situation that matches the whole extent of a form's meaning.

Accordingly, if a speaker has heard a form only in an occasional meaning or in a series of occasional meanings, he will utter the form only in similar situations: his habit may differ from that of other speakers. The word *meat* was used of all manner of dishes; there must have come a time when, owing to the encroachment of some other word (say, *food* or *dish*), many speakers had heard the word *meat* only (or very predominantly) in situations where the actual dish in question consisted of flesh; in their own utterances these speakers, accordingly, used the word *meat* only when flesh-food was involved. If a speaker has heard a form only in some marginal meaning, he will use this form with this same meaning as a central meaning — that is, he will use the form for a meaning in which other speakers use it only under very special conditions — like the city child who concluded that pigs were very properly called *pigs*, on account of their unclean habits. In the later Middle Ages, the German word *Kopf*, cognate with English *cup*, had the central meaning 'cup, bowl, pot' and the marginal meaning 'head'; there must have come a time when many speakers had heard this word only in its marginal meaning, for in modern German *Kopf* means only 'head.'

24. 5. Paul's explanation of semantic change takes for granted the occurrence of marginal meanings and of obsolescence, and views these processes as adventures of individual speech-forms, without reference to the rival forms which, in the one case, yield ground to the form under consideration, and, in the other case, encroach upon its domain. This view, nevertheless, represents a great advance over the mere classification of differences of meaning. In particular, it enabled Paul to show in detail some of the ways in which obsolescence breaks up a unitary domain of meaning — a process which he called *isolation*.

Thus, beside the present central meaning of the word *meat* 'flesh-food,' we have today the strange marginal (apparently, widened) uses in *meat and drink* and in *sweetmeats;* for dishes other than flesh, the word *meat* went out of use, except in these two expressions, which are detached from what is now the central meaning of the word: we may say that these two expressions have been *isolated* by the invasion of the intermediate semantic domain, which is now covered by *food, dish*. In the same way, *knave* has been shifted from 'boy, young man, servant' to 'scoundrel,' but the card-player's use of *knave* as a name for the lowest of the three picture-cards ('jack') is an isolated remnant of the older meaning. The word *charge* is a loan from Old French *charger* which meant originally 'to load a wagon.' Its present multiplicity of meanings is evidently due to expansion into marginal spheres followed by obsolescence of intermediate meanings. Thus, the agent-noun *charger* is no longer used for 'load-bearer, beast of burden,' but only in the special sense 'war-horse'; the meaning *charge* 'make a swift attack (on)' is a back-formation from *charger* 'war-horse.' The word *board* had in Old English apparently the same central meaning as today, 'flat piece of wood,' and, in addition to this, several specialized meanings. One of these, 'shield,' has died out entirely. Another, 'side of a ship,' has led to some isolated forms, such as *on board, aboard, to board* (a ship), and these have been extended to use in connection with other vehicles, such as railway cars. A third marginal meaning, 'table,' survives, again, in elevated turns of speech, such as *festive board*. Before its general obsolescence, however, *board* 'table' underwent a further transference to 'regular meals,' which is still current, as in *bed and board, board and lodging, to board (at a boarding-house)*, and so on. This use of *board* is so widely isolated today from *board* 'plank' that we should perhaps speak of the two as homonymous words.

In Old Germanic the adjective *['hajlaz] meant 'unharmed, well, prosperous,' as *heil* still does in German; this meaning remains in our verb *to heal*. In modern English we have only a transferred meaning in *whole*. Derived from *[hajlaz] there was another adjective *['hajlagaz] which meant 'conducive to welfare, health, or prosperity.' This word seems to have been used in a religious or superstitious sense. It occurs in a Gothic inscription in runes, but as Bishop Ulfila did not use it in his Bible, we may suspect that it had heathen associations. In the other Germanic languages it appears, from the beginning of our records, only as an equivalent of Latin *sanctus* 'holy.' Thus, the semantic connection between *whole* and *holy* has been completely wiped out in English; even in German *heil* 'unharmed, prosperous' and *heilig* 'holy' lie on the border-line between distant semantic connection and mere homonymy of roots.

The Old English adjective *heard* 'hard' underlay two adverbs, *hearde* and *heardlice;* the former survives in its old relation, as *hard*, but the latter, *hardly*, has been isolated in the remotely transferred meaning of 'barely, scarcely,' through loss of intermediate meanings such as 'only with difficulty.'

Isolation may be furthered by the obsolescence of some construction. We find it hard to connect the meaning of *understand* with the meanings of *under* and *stand*, not only because the meaning 'stand close to' or 'stand among,' which must have been central at the time the compound was formed, has been obsolete since prehistoric time, but also because the construction of the compound, preposition plus verb, with stress on the latter, has died out except for traditional forms, which survive as irregularities, such as *undertake, undergo, underlie, overthrow, overcome, overtake, forgive, forget, forbid*. The words *straw* (Old English *strēaw*) and *to strew* (Old English *strewian*) were in prehistoric time morphologically connected; the Primitive Germanic types are *['strawwan] 'a strewing, that strewn,' and *['strawjo:] 'I strew.' At that time *strawberry* (Old English *strēaw-berige*) 'strewn-berry' must have described the strawberry-plant as it lies along the ground; as *straw* became specialized to 'dried stalk, dried stalks,' and the morphologic connection with *strew* disappeared, the prior member of *strawberry* was isolated, with a deviant meaning, as a homonym of *straw*.

Phonetic change may prompt or aid isolation. A clear case of this is *ready*, which has diverged too far from *ride* and *road;* other examples are *holiday* and *holy, sorry* and *sore, dear* and *dearth*, and especially, with old umlaut (§ 21.7) *whole* and *heal, dole* and *deal*. The word *lord* (Old English *hlāford*) was at the time of its formation 'loaf-ward,' doubtless in a sense like 'bread-giver'; *lady* (Old English *hlāfdige*) seems to have been 'bread-shaper.' The word *disease* was formerly 'lack of ease, un-ease'; in the present specialized meaning 'sickness' it is all the better isolated from *dis-* and *ease* through the deviant form of the prefix, with [z] for [s] after unstressed vowel (§ 21.4).

Another contributory factor is the intrusion of analogic new-formations. Usually these overrun the central meaning and leave only some marginal meanings to the old form. Thus, *sloth* 'laziness' was originally the quality-noun of *slow*, just as *truth* is still that of *true*, but the decline of the *-th* derivation of quality-nouns and the rise of *slowness*, formed by the now regular *-ness* derivation, has isolated *sloth*. An Old English compound *$h\bar{u}s$-$w\bar{\imath}f$* 'housewife' through various phonetic changes reached a form which survives today only in a transferred meaning as *hussy* ['hʌzi] 'rude, pert woman.' In the central meaning it was replaced by an analogic new composition of *hūs* and *wīf*. This, in its turn, through phonetic change reached a form *nussif* ['hʌzif] which survives, though now obsolescent, in the transferred meaning 'sewing-bag,' but has been crowded out, in the central meaning, by a still newer compounding, *housewife* ['haws-₁wajf]. In medieval German, some adjectives with an umlaut vowel had derivative adverbs without umlaut: *schoene* ['ʃøːne] 'beautiful,' but *schone* ['ʃoːne] 'beautifully'; *feste* 'firm' but *faste* 'firmly.' In the modern period, these adverbs have been crowded out by regularly formed adverbs, homonymous with the adjective: today *schön* [ʃøːn] is both 'beautiful' and, as an adverb, 'beautifully,' and *fest* both 'firm, vigorous' and 'firmly, vigorously,' but the old adverbs have survived in remotely marginal uses, *schon* 'already' and 'never fear,' and *fast* 'almost.'

Finally, we may be able to recognize a change in the practical world as a factor in isolation. Thus, the isolation of German *Wand* 'wall' from *winden* 'to wind' is due to the disuse of wattled walls. Latin *penna* 'feather' (> Old French *penne*) was borrowed in Dutch and in English as a designation of the *pen* for writing. In French *plume* [plym] and German *Feder* ['fe:der], the vernacular word for 'feather' is used also for 'pen.' The disuse of the goose-quill pen has isolated these meanings.

24. 6. Paul's explanation of semantic change does not account for the rise of marginal meanings and for the obsolescence of forms in a part of their semantic domain. The same is true of so-called psychological explanations, such as Wundt's, which merely paraphrase the outcome of the change. Wundt defines the central meaning as the *dominant element* of meaning, and shows how the dominant element may shift when a form occurs in new typical contexts. Thus, when *meat* had been heard predominantly in situations where flesh-food was concerned, the dominant element became for more and more speakers, not 'food' but 'flesh-food.' This statement leaves the matter exactly where it was.

The obsolescence which plays a part in many semantic changes, need not present any characteristics other than those of ordinary loss of frequency; what little we know of fluctuations in this direction (Chapter 22) will apply here. The expansion of a form into new meanings, however, is a special case of rise in frequency, and a very difficult one, since, strictly speaking, almost any utterance of a form is prompted by a novel situation, and the degree of novelty is not subject to precise measurement. Older students accepted the rise of marginal meanings without seeking specific factors. Probably they took for granted the particular transferences which had occurred in languages familiar to them (*foot* of a mountain, *neck* of a bottle, and the like, § 9.8). Actually, languages differ in this respect, and it is precisely the spread of a form into a new meaning that concerns us in the study of semantic change.

The shift into a new meaning is intelligible when it merely reproduces a shift in the practical world. A form like *ship* or *hat* or *hose* designates a shifting series of objects because of changes in the practical world. If cattle were used as a medium of exchange, the word *fee* 'cattle' would naturally be used in the meaning 'money,' and if one wrote with a goose-feather, the word for 'feather' would naturally be used of this writing-implement. At this point, however, there has been no shift in the lexical structure of the language. This comes only when a learned loan-word *pen* is distinct from *feather*, or when *fee* on the one hand is no longer used of cattle and, on the other hand, loses ground in the domain of 'money' until it retains only the specialized value of 'sum of money paid for a service or privilege.'

The only type of semantic expansion that is relatively well understood, is what we may call the accidental type: some formal change — sound-change, analogic re-shaping, or borrowing — results in a locution which coincides with some old form of not too remote meaning. Thus, Primitive Germanic *['awzo:] denoted the 'ear' of a person or animal; it appears as Gothic ['awso:], Old Norse *eyra*, Old German *ōra* (> modern Dutch *oor* [o:r]), Old English ['e:are], and is cognate with Latin *auris*, Old Bulgarian [uxo], in the same meaning. Primitive Germanic *['ahuz] denoted the grain of a plant with the husk on it; it appears in Gothic *ahs*, Old Norse *ax*, Old German *ah* and, with an analogic nominative form due to oblique case-forms, Old German *ahir* (> modern Dutch *aar* [a:r]), Old English ['ɛhher] and ['e:ar], and is cognate with Latin *acus* 'husk of grain, chaff.' The loss of [h] and of unstressed vowels in English has made the two forms phonetically alike, and, since the meanings have some resemblance, *ear* of grain has become a marginal (transferred) meaning of *ear* of an animal. Since Old English [we:od] 'weed' and [we:d] 'garment' have coincided through sound-change, the surviving use of the latter, in *widow's weeds*, is now a marginal meaning of the former. Of course, the degree of nearness of the meanings is not subject to precise measurement; the lexicographer or historian who knows the origins will insist on describing such forms as pairs of homonyms. Nevertheless, for many speakers, doubtless, a *corn* on the foot represents merely a marginal meaning of *corn* 'grain.' The latter is a continuation of an old native word; the former a borrowing from Old French *corn* (< Latin *cornū* 'horn,' cognate with English *horn*). In French, *allure* is an abstract noun derived from *aller* 'to walk, to go,' and means 'manner of walking, carriage,' and in a specialized meaning 'good manner of walking, good carriage.' In English we have borrowed this *al-*

SEMANTIC CHANGE 437

lure; since it coincides formally with the verb *to allure* (a loan from Old French *aleurer*), we use it in the meaning 'charm.' It may be that *let* in *let or hindrance* and *a let ball* is for some speakers a queer marginal use of *let* 'permit,' and that even the Elizabethan *let* 'hinder' (§ 22.4) had this value; we have no standard for answering such questions.

Phonetic discrepancies in such cases may be removed by new-formation. Thus, the Scandinavian loan-word *būenn* 'equipped, ready' would give a modern English *[bawn]. This form was phonetically and in meaning so close to the reflex of Old English *bunden*, past participle of *bindan* 'to bind,' (> modern *bound* [bawnd], past participle of *bind*), that a new-formation *bound* [bawnd] replaced it; the addition of [-d] was probably favored by a habit of sandhi. The result is that *bound* in such phrases as *bound for England, bound to see it* figures as a marginal meaning of the past participle *bound*. Both the word *law* and its compound *by-law* are loan-words from Scandinavian. The first member of the latter was Old Norse [by:r] 'manor, town' — witness the older English forms *bir-law, bur-law* — but the re-shaping *by-law* turned it into a marginal use of the preposition and adverb *by*.

Beside the central meaning *please* 'to give pleasure or satisfaction,' we have the marginal meaning 'be willing' in *if you please.* This phrase meant in Middle English 'if it pleases you.' The obsolescence of the use of finite verbs without actors, and of the postponement of the finite verb in clauses, the near-obsolescence of the subjunctive (*if it please you*), and the analogic loss of case-distinction (nominative *ye* : dative-accusative *you*), have left *if you please* as an actor-action clause with *you* as the actor and an anomalous marginal use of *please*. The same factors, acting in phrases of the type *if you like*, seem to have led to a complete turn-about in the meaning of the verb *like*, which used to mean 'suit, please,' e.g. Old English [he: me: 'wel 'li:kaθ] 'he pleases me well, I like him.'

Partial obsolescence of a form may leave a queer marginal meaning. To the examples already given (e.g. *meat, board*) we may add a few where this feature has led to further shifts. The Latin-French loan-word *favor* had formerly in English two well-separated meanings. The more original one, 'kindly attitude, inclination,' with its offshoot, 'kindly action,' is still central; the other, 'cast of countenance,' is in general obsolete, but survives as a marginal meaning in *ill-favored* 'ugly.' In the aphoristic sentence *Kissing goes by favor*, our word had formerly this marginal value (that is, 'one prefers to kiss good-looking people'), but now has the central value ('is a matter of inclination'). Similarly, *prove, proof* had a central meaning 'test' which survives in the aphorism *The proof of the pudding is in the eating;* this was the meaning also in *The exception proves the rule*, but now that *prove, proof* have been shifted to the meaning '(give) conclusive evidence (for),' the latter phrase has become a paradox.

The old Indo-European and Germanic negative adverb *[ne] 'not' has left a trace in words like *no, not, never*, which reflect old phrasal combinations, but has been supplanted in independent use. Its loss in the various Germanic languages was due partly to sound-change and led to some peculiar semantic situations. In Norse it left a trace in a form which, owing to its original phrasal make-up, was not negative: *[ne 'wajt ek hwerr] 'not know I who,' that is, 'I don't know who,' resulted, by phonetic change, in Old Norse ['nøkurr, 'nekkwer] 'someone, anyone.' In other phonetic surroundings, in pre-Norse, *[ne] was entirely lost. Some forms which were habitually used with the negation must have got in this way two opposite meanings: thus, an *['ajnan] 'once' and a *[ne 'ajnan] 'not once, not' must have led to the same phonetic result. Actually, in Old Norse, various such expressions have survived in the negative value: *[ne 'ajnan] gives Old Norse *a* 'not'; *[ne 'ajnato:n] 'not one thing' gives Old Norse *at* 'not'; *[ne 'ajnaz ge] 'not even one' gives Old Norse *einge* 'no one'; *[ne 'ajnato:n ge] 'not even one thing' gives *etke, ekke* 'nothing'; *[ne 'ajwan ge] 'not at any time' gives *eige* 'not'; *[ne 'mannz ge] 'not even a man' gives *mannge* 'nobody.' In German, where *ne* has been replaced by *nicht* [nixt], originally 'not a whit,' the double meanings due to its loss in some phonetic surroundings, still appear in our records. At the end of the Middle Ages we find clauses of exception ('unless . . . ') with a subjunctive verb formed both with and without the adverb *ne, en, n* in apparently the same meaning:

with *ne: ez en mac mih nieman troesten, si en tuo z* 'there may no one console me, unless she do it'

without *ne: nieman kan hie fröude finden, si zergē* 'no one can find joy here, that does not vanish.'

The first example here is reasonable; the second contains a

SEMANTIC CHANGE

whimsical use of the subjunctive that owes its existence only to the phonetic disappearance of *ne* in similar contexts. We observe in our examples also a plus-or-minus of *ne*. *en* in the main clause along with *nieman* 'nobody.' This, too, left an ambiguous type: both an old *dehein* 'any' and an old *ne dehein* 'not any' must have led, in certain phonetic contexts, to *dehein* 'any; not any.' Both these meanings of *dehein* appear in our older texts, as well as a *ne dehein* 'not any'; of the three possibilities, only *dehein* 'not any' (> *kein*) survives in modern standard German.

In French, certain words that are widely used with a verb and the negative adverb, have also a negative meaning when used without a verb. Thus, *pas* [pa] 'step' (< Latin *passum*) has the two uses in *je ne vais pas* [ʒə n ve pa] 'I don't go' (originally 'I go not a step') and in *pas mal* [pa mal] 'not badly, not so bad'; *personne* [pɛrsɔn] 'person' (< Latin *persōnam*) appears also in *je ne vois personne* [ʒə n vwa pɛrsɔn] 'I don't see anyone,' and in *personne* 'nobody'; *rien* [rjɛ̃] (< Latin *rem* 'a thing') has lost ordinary noun values, and occurs in *je ne vois rien* [ʒə n vwa rjɛ̃] 'I don't see anything' and in *rien* 'nothing.' This development has been described as *contagion* or *condensation*. It can be better understood if we suppose that, during the medieval period of high stress and vowel-weakening, French *ne* (< Latin *nōn*) was phonetically lost in certain contexts.

The reverse of this process is a loss of content. Latin forms like *cantō* 'I-sing,' *cantās* 'thou-singest,' *cantat* 'he-she-it-sings' (to which more specific mention of an actor was added by cross-reference, § 12.9), appear in French as *chante(s)* [ʃɑ̃t] 'sing(s),' used only with an actor, or, rarely, in completive speech, just like an English verb-form. This loss of the pronominal actor-meaning is evidently the result of an analogic change which replaced the type *cantat* 'he-sings' by a type *ille cantat* 'that-one sings' (> French *il chante* [i ʃɑ̃t] 'he sings'). This latter change has been explained, in the case of French, as a result of the homonymy, due to sound-change, of the various Latin inflections; however, in English and in German, forms like *sing, singest, singeth* have come to demand an actor, although there is no homonymy.

24. 7. Special factors like these will account for only a small proportion of the wealth of marginal meanings that faces us in every language. It remained for a modern scholar, H. Sperber, to point out that extensions of meaning are by no means to be taken for granted, and that the first step toward understanding them must be to find, if we can, the context in which the new meaning first appears. This will always be difficult, because it demands that the student observe very closely the meanings of the form in all older occurrences; it is especially hard to make sure of negative features, such as the absence, up to a certain date, of a certain shade of meaning. In most cases, moreover, the attempt is bound to fail because the records do not contain the critical locutions. Nevertheless, Sperber succeeded in finding the critical context for the extension of older German *kopf* 'cup, bowl, pot' to the meaning 'head': the new value first appears in our texts at the end of the Middle Ages, in battle-scenes, where the matter is one of smashing someone's head. An English example of the same sort is the extension of *bede* 'prayer' to the present meaning of *bead:* the extension is known to have occurred in connection with the use of the rosary, where one *counted one's bedes* (originally 'prayers,' then 'little spheres on a string').

In the ordinary case of semantic extension we must look for a context in which our form can be applied to both the old and the new meanings. The obsolescence of other contexts — in our examples, of German *kopf* applied to earthen vessels and of *bead* 'prayer' — will then leave the new value as an unambiguous central meaning. The reason for the extension, however, is another matter. We still ask why the medieval German poet should speak of a warrior smashing his enemy's 'bowl' or 'pot,' or the pious Englishman of counting 'prayers' rather than 'pearls.' Sperber supposes that intense emotion (that is, a powerful stimulus) leads to such transferences. Strong stimuli lead to the favoring of novel speech-forms at the cost of forms that have been heard in indifferent contexts (§ 22.8), but this general tendency cannot account for the rise of specific marginal meanings.

The methodical error which has held back this phase of our work, is our habit of putting the question in non-linguistic terms — in terms of meaning and not of form. When we say that the word *meat* has changed from the meaning 'food' to the meaning 'edible flesh,' we are merely stating the practical result of a linguistic process. In situations where both words were applicable, the word *meat* was favored at the cost of the word *flesh*, and, on the model of such cases, it came to be used also in situations where formerly the word *flesh* alone would have been applicable. In the same way, words like *food* and *dish* encroached upon the word *meat*. This second displacement may have resulted from the first because the ambiguity of *meat* 'food' and *meat* 'flesh-food' was troublesome in practical kitchen life. We may some day find out why *flesh* was disfavored in culinary situations.

Once we put the question into these terms, we see that a normal extension of meaning is the same process as an extension of grammatical function. When *meat*, for whatever reason, was being favored, and *flesh*, for whatever reason, was on the decline, there must have occurred proportional extensions of the pattern (§ 23.2):

leave the bones and bring the flesh : *leave the bones and bring the meat*
= *give us bread and flesh* : *x*,

resulting in a new phrase, *give us bread and meat*. The forms at the left, containing the word *flesh*, must have borne an unfavorable connotation which was absent from the forms at the right, with the word *meat*.

A semantic change, then, is a complex process. It involves favorings and disfavorings, and, as its crucial point, the extension of a favored form into practical applications which hitherto belonged to the disfavored form. This crucial extension can be observed only if we succeed in finding the locutions in which it was made, and in finding or reconstructing the model locutions in which both forms were used alternatively. Our records give us only an infinitesimal fraction of what was spoken, and this fraction consists nearly always of elevated speech, which avoids new locutions. In Sperber's example of German *kopf* 'pot' > 'head,' we know the context (head-smashing in battle) where the innovation was made; there remains the problem of finding the model. One might surmise, for instance, that the innovation was made by Germans who, from warfare and chivalry, were familiar with the Romance speaker's use of the type of Latin *testam, testum* 'potsherd, pot' > 'head,' which in French and Italian has crowded the type of Latin *caput* 'head' out of all but transferred meanings. We confront this complex problem in all semantic changes except the fortuitous ones like English *let, bound, ear*, which are due to some phonetic accident.

We can best understand the shift in modern cases, where the connotative values and the practical background are known. During the last generations the growth of cities has led to a lively trade in city lots and houses, "development" of outlying land into residence districts, and speculative building. At the same time, the prestige of the persons who live by these things has risen to the point where styles pass from them to the working man, who in language is imitative but has the force of numbers, and to the "educated" person, who enjoys a fictitious leadership. Now, the speculative builder has learned to appeal to every weakness, including the sentimentality, of the prospective buyer; he uses the speech-forms whose content will turn the hearer in the right direction. In many locutions *house* is the colorless, and *home* the sentimental word:

COLORLESS	SENTIMENTAL, PLEASANT CONNOTATION
Smith has a lovely house = *a lovely new eight-room house*	: *Smith has a lovely home* : *x*.

Thus, the salesman comes to use the word *home* of an empty shell that has never been inhabited, and the rest of us copy his style. It may be too, that, the word *house*, especially in the substandard sphere of the salesman, suffers from some ambiguity, on account of meanings such as 'commercial establishment' (*a reliable house*), 'hotel,' 'brothel,' 'audience' (*a half-empty house*).

The learned word *transpire* in its Latin-French use, meant 'to breathe or ooze (Latin *spīrāre*) through (Latin *trans*),' and thus, as in French *transpirer* [trãspire], 'to exhale, exude, perspire, ooze out,' and with a transfer of meaning, 'to become public (of news).' The old usage would be to say *of what really happened, very little transpired*. The ambiguous case is *it transpired that the president was out of town*. On the pattern

COLORLESS	ELEGANT-LEARNED
it happened that the president was out of town	: *it transpired that the president . . .*
= *what happened, remains a secret*	: *x*,

we now get the formerly impossible type *what transpired, remains a secret*, where *transpire* figures as an elegant synonym of *happen, occur*.

This parallelism of transference accounts for successive encroachments in a semantic sphere. As soon as some form like *terribly*, which means 'in a way that arouses fear,' has been extended into use as a stronger synonym of *very*, the road is clear for a similar transference of words like *awfully, frightfully, horribly*.

Even when the birth of the marginal meaning is recent, we shall not always be able to trace its origin. It may have arisen under some very special practical circumstances that are unknown to us, or, what comes to the same thing, it may be the successful coinage of some one speaker and owe its shape to his individual circumstances. One suspects that the queer slang use, a quarter of a century ago, of *twenty-three* for 'get out' arose in a chance situation of sportsmanship, gambling, crime, or some other rakish environment; within this sphere, it may have started as some one person's witticism. Since every practical situation is in reality unprecedented, the apt response of a good speaker may always border on semantic innovation. Both the wit and the poet often cross this border, and their innovations may become popular. To a large extent, however, these personal innovations are modeled on current forms. Poetic metaphor is largely an outgrowth of the transferred uses of ordinary speech. To quote a very well chosen example, when Wordsworth wrote

The gods approve
The depth and not the tumult of the soul,

he was only continuing the metaphoric use current in such expressions as *deep, ruffled,* or *stormy* feelings. By making a new transference on the model of these old ones, he revived the "picture." The picturesque saying that "language is a book of faded metaphors" is the reverse of the truth, for poetry is rather a blazoned book of language.

CHAPTER 25

CULTURAL BORROWING

25. 1. The child who is learning to speak may get most of his habits from some one person — say, his mother — but he will also hear other speakers and take some of his habits from them. Even the basic vocabulary and the grammatical features which he acquires at this time do not reproduce exactly the habits of any one older person. Throughout his life, the speaker continues to adopt features from his fellows, and these adoptions, though less fundamental, are very copious and come from all manner of sources. Some of them are incidents in large-scale levelings that affect the whole community.

Accordingly, the comparatist or historian, if he could discount all analogic-semantic changes, should still expect to find the phonetic correlations disturbed by the transfer of speech-forms from person to person or from group to group. The actual tradition, could we trace it, of the various features in the language of any one speaker, runs back through entirely diverse persons and communities. The historian can recognize this in cases of formal discrepancy. He sees, for instance, that forms which in older English contained a short [a] in certain phonetic surroundings, appear in Central-Western American English as [ɛ] in *man, hat, bath, gather, lather,* etc. This represents the basic tradition, even though the individual forms may have had very different adventures. Accordingly, when the speaker uses an [a] for the same old phoneme in the word *father* and in the more elegant variant of the word *rather*, the historian infers that somewhere along the line of transmission these forms must have come in from speakers of a different habit. The adoption of features which differ from those of the main tradition, is *linguistic borrowing*.

Within the sphere of borrowing, we distinguish between *dialect borrowing*, where the borrowed features come from within the same speech-area (as, *father, rather* with [a] in an [ɛ]-dialect), and *cultural borrowing*, where the borrowed features come from a different language. This distinction cannot always be carried out,

CULTURAL BORROWING

since there is no absolute distinction to be made between dialect boundaries and language boundaries (§ 3.8). In this chapter and the next we shall speak of borrowing from foreign languages, and in Chapter 27 of borrowing between the dialects of an area.

25. 2. Every speech-community learns from its neighbors. Objects, both natural and manufactured, pass from one community to the other, and so do patterns of action, such as technical procedures, warlike practices, religious rites, or fashions of individual conduct. This spread of things and habits is studied by ethnologists, who call it *cultural diffusion*. One can plot on a map the diffusion of a cultural feature, such as, say, the growing of maize in pre-Columbian North America. In general, the areas of diffusion of different cultural features do not coincide. Along with objects or practices, the speech-forms by which these are named often pass from people to people. For instance, an English-speaker, either bilingual or with some foreign knowledge of French, introducing a French article to his countrymen, will designate it by its French name, as: *rouge* [ru:ʒ], *jabot* [ʒabo], *chauffeur* [ʃofœ:r], *garage* [gara:ʒ], *camouflage* [kamufla:ʒ]. In most instances we cannot ascertain the moment of actual innovation: the speaker himself probably could not be sure whether he had ever before heard or used the foreign form in his native language. Several speakers may independently, none having heard the others, make the same introduction. In theory, of course, we must distinguish between this actual introduction and the ensuing repetitions by the same and other speakers; the new form embarks upon a career of fluctuation in frequency. The historian finds, however, that some of the later adventures of the borrowed form are due to its foreign character.

If the original introducer or a later user has good command of the foreign language, he may speak the foreign form in foreign phonetics, even in its native context. More often, however, he will save himself a twofold muscular adjustment, replacing some of the foreign speech-movements by speech-movements of the native language; for example, in an English sentence he will speak his French *rouge* with an English [r] in place of the French uvular trill, and an English [uw] in place of the French tense, non-diphthongal [u:]. This *phonetic substitution* will vary in degree for different speakers and on different occasions; speakers who have not learned to produce French phonemes are certain to make it.

The historian will class it as a type of adaptation (§ 23.8), in which the foreign form is altered to meet the fundamental phonetic habits of the language.

In phonetic substitution the speakers replace the foreign sounds by the phonemes of their language. In so far as the phonetic systems are parallel, this involves only the ignoring of minor differences. Thus, we replace the various [r] and [l] types of European languages by our [r] and [l], the French unaspirated stops by our aspirated, the French postdentals by our gingivals (as, say, in *tête-à-tête*), and long vowels by our diphthongal types [ij, uw, ej, ow]. When the phonetic systems are less alike, the substitutions may seem surprising to members of the lending community. Thus, the older Menomini speakers, who knew no English, reproduced *automobile* as [atamo:pen]: Menomini has only one, unvoiced series of stops, and no lateral or trill. Tagalog, having no [f]-type, replaced Spanish [f] by [p], as in [pi'jesta] from Spanish *fiesta* ['fjesta] 'celebration.'

In the case of ancient speech, phonetic substitutions may inform us as to the acoustic relation between the phonemes of two languages. The Latin name of the Greek nation, *Graeci* ['grajki:], later ['gre:ki:], was borrowed, early in the Christian Era, into the Germanic languages, and appears here with an initial [k], as in Gothic *krēkōs*, Old English *crēcas*, Old High German *kriahha* 'Greeks.' Evidently the Latin voiced stop [g] was acoustically closer to the Germanic unvoiced stop [k] than to the Germanic phoneme which we transcribe as [g], say, in Old English *grēne* 'green'; presumably, at the time the old word for 'Greek' was borrowed, this Germanic [g] was a spirant. Latin [w] at this early time was reproduced by Germanic [w], as in Latin *vinum* ['wi:num] 'wine' > Old English *win* [wi:n], and similarly in Gothic and in German. In the early Middle Ages, the Latin [w] changed to a voiced spirant of the type [v]; accordingly, this Latin phoneme in loan-words of the missionary period, from the seventh century on, was no longer reproduced by Germanic [w], but by Germanic [f]. Thus, Latin *versus* ['vɛrsus] 'verse,' from older ['wersus], appears in Old English and in Old High German as *fers*. A third stage appears in modern time: German, having changed its old [w] to a spirant type, and English, having in another way acquired a phoneme of the [v]-type, now give a fairly accurate reproduction of Latin [v], as in French *vision* [vizjõ] (from Latin *visionem* [wi:-

si'o:nem]: > German [vi'zjo:n], English ['viʒn].¹ In Bohemian, where every word is stressed on the first syllable, this accentuation is given to foreign words, such as ['ạkvarijum] 'aquarium,' ['konstelatse] 'constellation,' ['ʃofe:r] 'chauffeur.'

25. 3. If the borrowing people is relatively familiar with the lending language, or if the borrowed words are fairly numerous, then foreign sounds which are acoustically remote from any native phoneme, may be preserved in a more or less accurate rendering that violates the native phonetic system. In this respect, there are many local and social differences. Thus, the French nasalized vowels are very widely kept in English, even by people who do not speak French, as in French *salon* [salõ] > English [sə'lõ, 'sɛlõ], French *rendez-vous* [rãde-vu] > English ['rã:divuw], French *restaurant* [rɛstɔrã] > English ['restərõ]. Some speakers, however, substitute vowel plus [ŋ], as in ['rɔŋdivuw], and others vowel plus [n], as in ['rɔndivuw]. The Germans do the like; the Swedes always replace French nasalized vowels by vowel plus [ŋ]. In some forms English does not reproduce the nasalized vowel, as in French *chiffon* [ʃifõ] > English ['ʃifɔn], and in the more urbane variant ['envilowp] *envelope*.

This adoption of foreign sounds may become quite fixed. In English the cluster [sk] is due to Scandinavian loan-words; the [sk] of Old English had changed in later Old English time to [ʃ], as in Old English [sko:h] > modern *shoe*. The Scandinavian cluster occurs not only in borrowed words, such as *sky, skin, skirt* (beside native *shirt*), but also in new-formations, such as *scatter, scrawl, scream;* it has become an integral part of the phonetic system. The initials [v-, z-, dʒ-] came into English in French words, such as *very, zest, just;* all three are quite at home now, and the last two occur in new-formations, such as *zip, zoom, jab, jounce.* Thus, the phonetic system has been permanently altered by borrowing.

Where phonetic substitution has occurred, increased familiarity with the foreign language may lead to a newer, more correct version of a foreign form. Thus, the Menomini who knows a little English no longer says [atamo:pen] 'automobile,' but [atamo:pil], and the modern Tagalog speaker says [fi'jesta] 'celebration.' The old form of the borrowing may survive, however, in

---

¹ The discrepancies in this and similar examples are due to changes which the various languages have made since the time of borrowing.

special uses, such as derivatives: thus, even the modern Tagalog speaker says [kapijes'taːhan] 'day of a festival,' where the prefix, suffix, and accentuation are native, and in English the derived verb is always *envelop* [in'velɔp], with vowel plus [n] in the first syllable.

A similar adjustment may take place, at a longer interval of time, if the borrowing language has developed a new phoneme that does better justice to the foreign form. Thus, English *Greek*, German *Grieche* ['griːxe] embody corrections made after these languages had developed a voiced stop [g]. Similarly, English *verse* is a revision of the old *fers;* German has stuck to the old form *Vers* [fɛːrs]. In revisions of this sort, especially where literary terms are concerned, learned persons may exert some influence: thus, the replacement of the older form with [kr-] by the later form *Greek* was surely due to educated people.

For the most part, however, the influence of literate persons works also against a faithful rendering. In the first place, the literate person who knows nothing of the foreign language but has seen the written notation of the foreign form, interprets the latter in terms of native orthography. Thus, French forms like *puce, ruche, menu, Victor Hugo* [pys, ryʃ, məny, viktɔr ygo] would doubtless be reproduced in English with [ij] for French [y], were it not for the spelling with the letter *u*, which leads the literate English-speaker to pronounce [(j)uw], as in [pjuws, ruwʃ, ˈmenjuw, ˈviktə ˈhjuwgow]. Spanish *Mexico*, older [ˈmeʃiko], modern [ˈmexiko], has [ks] in English because of literate people's interpretation of the symbol *x;* similarly, the older English rendering of *Don Quixote* (Spanish [don kiˈxote]) is [dɔn ˈkwiksɔt]. The latter has been revised, certainly under learned influence, to [dɔn kiˈhowti], but the older version has been retained in the English derivative *quixotic* [kwikˈsɔtik]. We reproduce initial [ts] in *tsar* or *tse-tsc-fly*, but not in German forms like *Zeitgeist* [ˈtsajt-ˌgajst] > English [ˈzajtgajst], or *Zwieback* [ˈtsvibːak] > English [ˈzwijbɛk], where the letter *z* suggests only [z]. Even where there is no phonetic difficulty, as in German *Dachshund* [ˈdaks-ˌhunt], *Wagner* [ˈvaːgner], *Wiener* [ˈviːner], the spelling leads to such reproductions as [ˈdɛʃ-ˌhawnd, ˈwɛgnə, ˈwijnə, ˈwijni].

This relation is further complicated by literate persons who know something of the foreign pronunciation and orthography. A speaker who knows the spelling *jabot* and the English form

CULTURAL BORROWING 449

[ˈʒɛbow] (for French [ʒabo]), may revise *tête-à-tête* [ˈtejtəˌtejt] (from French [tɛːt a tɛːt]) to a *hyper-foreign* [ˈtejtətej], without the final [t]. The literate person who known *parlez-vous français?* [ˈparlej ˈvuw ˈfrɑ̃ːsej?] (for French [parle vu frɑ̃sɛ?]), may decide to join the *Alliance Française* [aliˈjɑ̃ːs ˈfrɑ̃ːsej], although the Frenchman here has a final [z]: [aljɑ̃s frɑ̃sɛːz].

25. 4. The borrowed word, aside from foreign sounds, often violates the phonetic pattern. Thus, a German initial [ts], even aside from the orthography, may be troublesome to many English-speakers. Generally, adaptation of the phonetic pattern takes place together with adaptation of morphologic structure. Thus, the final [ʒ] of *garage*, which violates the English pattern, is replaced by [dʒ] and the accent shifted in the form [ˈgɛridʒ], which conforms to the suffixal type of *cabbage, baggage, carriage*. Likewise, beside *chauffeur* [ʃowˈfəː] with normal phonetic substitution, we have a more fully adapted [ˈʃowfə].

The description of a language will thus recognize a layer of *foreign forms*, such as *salon* [səˈlõ], *rouge* [ruwʒ], *garage* [gəˈrɑːʒ], which deviate from the normal phonetics. In some languages a descriptive analysis will recognize, further, a layer of *semi-foreign* forms, which have been adapted up to a conventional point, but retain certain conventionally determined foreign characteristics. The foreign-learned vocabulary of English is of this type. Thus, a French *préciosité* [presiɔsite] was anglicized only to the point where it became *preciosity* [presiˈɔsiti, preʃiˈɔsiti]; the unstressed prefix, the suffix *-ity* (with presuffixal stress), and the formally and semantically peculiar relation to *precious* [ˈpreʃəs], do not lead to further adaptation. The English-speakers (a minority) who use the word at all, include it in a set of habits that deviates from the structure of our commonest words. This secondary layer of speech-habit owes its existence, historically, to old waves of borrowing, which will concern us in the sequel.

When the adaptation is completed, as in *chair* (anciently borrowed from Old French) or in [ˈʃowfə] *chauffeur*, the foreign origin of the form has disappeared, and neither the speaker nor, consequently, a relevant description can distinguish it from native forms. The historian, however, who is concerned with origins, will class it as a *loan-form*. Thus, *chair* and [ˈʃowfə] *chauffeur*, in the present state of the language, are ordinary English words, but the historian, taking the past into view, classes them as *loan-words*.

At all stages, the assimilation of foreign words presents many problems. The phenomena of the type of phonetic dissimilation (§ 21.10), as in French *marbre* > English *marble*, are fairly frequent. We probably have to reckon here with highly variable factors, including adaptations based on the habits of individual speakers. Both during the progress toward the status of a loan-form, and after this status has been reached, the structure is likely to be unintelligible. The languages and, within a language, the groups of speakers that are familiar with foreign and semi-foreign forms, will tolerate this state of affairs; in other cases, a further adaptation, in the sense of popular etymology, may render the form structurally or lexically more intelligible, as in *groze > *groze-berry > *gooseberry; asparagus* > *sparrow-grass; crevise* > *crayfish* > *crawfish* (§ 23.8). The classical instance is the replacement, in medieval German, of Old French *arbaleste* 'crossbow' by an adaptive new-formation *Armbrust* ['arm-ˌbrust], literally 'arm-breast.'

The borrowed form is subject to the phonetic changes that occur after its adoption. This factor is distinct from phonetic substitution and other adaptive changes. Thus, we must suppose that an Old French form like *vision* [vi'zjoːn] (reflecting a Latin [wiːsi'oːnem]) was taken into medieval English with some slight amount of no longer traceable phonetic substitution, and that it gave rise to a successful adaptive variant, with stress on the first syllable. The further changes, however, which led to the modern English ['viʒn] are merely the phonetic changes which have occurred in English since the time when this word was borrowed. These two factors, however, cannot always be distinguished. After a number of borrowings, there arose a fairly regular relation of adapted English forms to French originals; a new borrowing from French could be adapted on the model of the older loans. Thus, the discrepancy between French *préciosité* [presiɔsite] and English *preciosity* [preˑsi'ɔsiti, preʃiɔsiti] is not due to sound-changes that occurred in English after the time of borrowing, but merely reflects a usual relation between French and English types — a relation which has set up in the English-speakers who know French a habit of adapting forms along certain lines.

25. 5. Where we can allow for this adaptive factor, the phonetic development of borrowed forms often shows us the phonetic form

CULTURAL BORROWING

at the time of borrowing and accordingly the approximate date of various sound-changes. The name of *Caesar* appears in Greek in a spelling (with the letters *k, a, i*) which for earlier time we can interpret as ['kajsar] and for later as ['kɛːsar], and it appears in a similar spelling in Gothic, where the value of the digraph *ai* is uncertain and the form may have been, accordingly, either ['kajsar] or ['kɛːsar]. These forms assure us that at the time of these borrowings, Latin still spoke an initial [k] and had not yet gone far in the direction of modern forms like Italian *cesare* ['tʃezare] (§ 21.5). In West Germanic, the foreign word appears as Old High German *keisur*, Old Saxon *kēsur*, Old English *casere*, this last representing presumably something like ['kaːseːre]. These forms confirm the Latin [k]-pronunciation; moreover, they guarantee a Latin diphthong of the type [aj] for the first syllable, since the correspondence of southern German *ei*, northern [eː], and English [aː] is the ordinary reflex of a Primitive Germanic diphthong, as in *['stajnaz] 'stone' > Old High German *stein*, Old Saxon [steːn], Old English [staːn]. Thus, for the time of the early contact of Rome with Germanic peoples, we are assured of [kaj-] as the value of the first syllable of Latin *caesar*. On the other hand, the West Germanic forms show us that the various changes of the diphthong [aj], in Old Saxon to [eː] and in Old English to [aː] occurred after the early contact with the Romans. The vowel of the second syllable, and the addition of a third syllable in Old English, are surely due to some kind of an adaptation; the English form, especially, suggests that the Roman word was taken up as though it were *[kaj'soːrius] > pre-English *['kajsoːrjaz]. The word was borrowed from a Germanic language, doubtless from Gothic, by the Slavs; it appears in Old Bulgarian as [tseˈsarĭ]. Now, in pre-Slavic time, as we know from the correspondences of native words, [aj] was monophthongized to [eː], and then a [k] before such an [eː] changed to [ts]. Thus, Primitive Indo-European *[kʷojˈnaː] 'penalty,' Avestan [kaenaː], Greek [pojˈneː] appears in Old Bulgarian as [tseˈnaː] 'price.' The Slavic borrowing, accordingly, in spite of its actual deviation, confirms our reconstruction of the old Germanic form, and, in addition to this, enables us to date the pre-Slavic changes of [kaj] to [tseː] after the time of early borrowing from Germanic, which, history tells us, occurred from round 250 to round 450 A.D. Moreover, the second and third syllables of the Slavic form show the same adaptation as the Old

English, to a Germanic type *['kajso:rjaz]; we may conclude that this adapted form existed also among the Goths, although our Gothic Bible, representing a more learned stratum of speech, has the correctly Latin *kaisar*.

Latin *strāta (via)* 'paved road' appears in Old Saxon as ['stra:ta], in Old High German as ['stra:ssa], and in Old English as [strɛ:t]. We infer that this term, like *caesar*, was borrowed before the emigration of the English. The correspondence of German [a:] English [ɛ]: reflects, in native words, a Primitive Germanic [e:], as in *['de:diz] 'deed,' Gothic [ga-'de:θs], Old Saxon [da:d], Old High German [ta:t], Old English [dɛ:d]; accordingly we conclude that at the time when Latin *strāta* was borrowed, West Germanic speakers had already made the change from [e:] to [a:], since they used this vowel-phoneme to reproduce the Latin [a:]. On the other hand, the Anglo-Frisian change of this [a:] toward a front vowel, Old English [ɛ:], must be later than the borrowing of the word *street;* this is confirmed by the Old Frisian form (of much later documentation, to be sure), namely *strete*. The medial [t] of the Germanic words shows us that, at the time of borrowing, Latin still said ['stra:ta] and not yet ['strada] (Italian *strada*). This contrasts with later borrowings, such as Old High German ['si:da] 'silk,' ['kri:da] 'chalk,' which have [d] in accordance with later Latin pronunciation ['se:da, 'kre:da] from earlier Latin ['se:ta, 'kre:ta] (§ 21.4). Finally, the [ss] of the High German form shows us that the South-German shift of Germanic medial [t] to affricate and sibilant types (§ 19.8) occurred after the adoption of the Latin *strāta*. In the same way, Latin ['te:gula] 'tile' appears in Old English as ['ti:gol] (whence the modern *tile*), but in Old High German as ['tsiagal] (whence modern German *Ziegel* ['tsi:gel]): the borrowing occurred before the South-German consonant-shift, and this is the case with a whole series of borrowings in the sphere of useful objects and techniques. In contrast with this, Latin words in the literary and scientific domains, which were borrowed presumably in the missionary period, from the seventh century onward, came too late for the South-German consonant-shift: Latin *templum* 'temple' appears in Old High German as ['tempal], Latin *tincta* 'colored stuff, ink' as ['tinkta], and Latin *tēgula* was borrowed over again as Old High German ['tegal] 'pot, retort' (> modern German *Tiegel* ['ti:gel]). The same re-borrowing of this last word appears in Old English ['tijele]; but here we have no striking sound-change to distinguish the two chronological layers of borrowing.

The South-German change of [t] to affricate and sibilant types shows us, in fact, a remarkable instance of dating by means of borrowed forms. A Primitive Germanic type *['mo:to:] is represented by the Gothic word ['mo:ta] which translates the Greek words for 'tax' and for 'toll-station' (e.g. in *Romans* 13, 7 and *Matthew* 9, 9-10); there is also a derivative ['mo:ta:ri:s] 'tax-gatherer, publican.' The Old English cognate [mo:t] occurs once, in the meaning 'tribute money' (*Matthew* 22, 19); the Middle High German ['muosse] 'miller's fee' shows us the regular High German shift of [t] to a sibilant and an equally regular shift of [o:] to [uo]. Now, in the southeastern part of the German area we find also an Old High German ['mu:ta] 'toll' (> modern *Maut*) and the place-name ['mu:ta:run] (literally, 'at the toll-takers") of a town on the Danube (> modern *Mautern*). These forms not only lack the shift of [t] but also have an altogether unparalleled [u:] in place of Germanic [o:]. We have reason to believe that Gothic [o:] was close to [u:] and in later time perhaps coincided with it. History tells us that in the first half of the sixth century, Theodoric the Great, the Gothic emperor of Italy, extended his rule to the Danube. We conclude that the German word is a borrowing from Gothic, and, accordingly, that at the time of borrowing, Primitive Germanic [t] in Bavarian German had already changed toward a sibilant: the [t] of the Gothic word was reproduced by the German reflex of Primitive Germanic [d], as in Old High German [hlu:t] 'loud' (> modern *laut*) from Primitive Germanic *['hlu:-daz]; compare Old English [hlu:d]. The spread of the Gothic ['mo:ta] or rather *['mu:ta] is confirmed by the borrowing into Primitive Slavic *['myto, 'mytarɪ], e.g. Old Bulgarian [myto] 'pay, gift,' [mytarɪ] 'publican.'

25. 6. Grammatically, the borrowed form is subjected to the system of the borrowing language, both as to syntax (*some rouge, this rouge*) and as to the indispensable inflections (*garages*) and the fully current, "living" constructions of composition (*rouge-pot*) and word-formation (*to rouge; she is rouging her face*). Less often, a simultaneous borrowing of several foreign forms saves this adaptation; thus, from Russian we get not only *bolshevik* but also the Russian plural *bolsheviki*, which we use alongside the English plural-derivation *bolsheviks*. On the other hand, native grammatical constructions which occur, at the time of borrowing, only in a few traditional forms, will scarcely be extended to cover the foreign word. After complete adaptation, the loan-word is subject to the same analogies as any similar native word. Thus, from the completely nativized ['ʃowfə] *chauffeur,* we have the back-formation *to chauffe* [ʃowf], as in *I had to chauffe my mother around all day.*

When many forms are borrowed from one language, the foreign forms may exhibit their own grammatical relations. Thus, the Latin-French semi-learned vocabulary of English has its own morphologic system (§ 9.9). The analogies of this system may lead to new-formations. Thus, *mutinous, mutiny, mutineer* are derived, in English, according to Latin-French morphology, from an old *mutine,* a loan from French *mutin;* French has not these derivatives. Similarly, *due* is a loan from French, but *duty, duteous, dutiable* (and, with a native English suffix, *dutiful*) probably had no French source, but were formed, with French-borrowed suffixes, in English. The back-formation of pseudo-French verbs in *-ate* (§ 23.5) is a case in point.

When an affix occurs in enough foreign words, it may be extended to new-formations with native material. Thus, the Latin-French suffix *-ible, -able,* as in *agreeable, excusable, variable,* has been extended to forms like *bearable, eatable, drinkable,* where the underlying verb is native. Other examples of French suffixes with native English underlying forms are *breakage, hindrance, murderous, bakery.* In Latin, nouns for 'a man occupied with such-and-such things' were derived from other nouns by means of a suffix *-āriu-,* as *monētārius* 'coiner; money-changer' from *monēta* 'mint; coin'; *gemmārius* 'jeweler' from *gemma* 'jewel'; *telōnārius* 'tax-gatherer, publican' from *telōnium* 'toll-house.' Many of these were borrowed into the old Germanic languages; thus, in Old English we have *myntere, tolnere,* and in Old High German *gimmāri.* Already in our earliest records, however, we find this Latin suffix extended to native Germanic underlying nouns. Latin *lāna* 'wool' : *lānārius* 'wool-carder' is matched in Gothic by *wulla* 'wool' : *wullāreis* ['wulla:ri:s] 'wool-carder'; similarly, *bōka* 'book' : *bōkāreis* 'scribe,' *mōta* 'toll' : *mōtāreis* 'toll-gatherer,' or, in Old English, [wɛjn] 'wagon' : ['wɛjnere] 'wagoner.' Cases like Old English [re:af] 'spoils, booty' : ['re:avere] 'robber,' where there was a morphologically related verb, ['re:avian] 'to despoil, rob,' led to new-formations on the model ['reːavian: 'reːavere] even in cases where there was no underlying noun, such as ['reːdan] 'to read' : ['reːdere] 'reader' or ['wriːtan] 'to write' : ['wriːtere] 'writer.' Thus arose our suffix *-er* 'agent,' which appears in all the Germanic languages. Quite similarly, at a much later time, the same suffix in Spanish pairs like *banco* ['banko] 'bank' : *banquero* [ban'keroj 'banker,' was added to native words in Tagalog, as ['siːpaʔ] 'football' : [si'peːro] 'football-player,' beside the native derivation [maːniˈniːpaʔ] 'football-player.'

If many loans have been made from some one language, the foreign structure may even attract native words in the way of adaptation. In some German dialects, including the standard language, we find native words assimilated to Latin-French accentuation: Old High German ['forhana] 'brook-trout,' ['holuntar] 'elder, lilac,' ['wexxolter] 'juniper' are represented in modern standard German by *Forelle* [fo'rele], *Holunder* [hoˈlunder], *Wacholder* [vaˈxolder].

25. 7. The speakers who introduce foreign things may call them by the native name of some related object. In adopting Christianity, the Germanic peoples kept some of the heathen religious terms: *god, heaven, hell* were merely transferred to the new religion. Needless to say, the leveling to which these terms owe their uniform selection in various Germanic languages, is only another instance of borrowing. The pagan term *Easter* is used in English and German; Dutch and Scandinavian adopted the Hebrew-Greek-Latin term *pascha* (Danish *paaske*, etc.).

If there is no closely equivalent native term, one may yet describe the foreign object in native words. Thus the Greek-Latin technical term *baptize* was not borrowed but paraphrased in older Germanic: Gothic said *daupjan* and (perhaps under Gothic influence) German *taufen* 'to dip, to duck'; Old English said [ˈfulljan], apparently from *[ˈfull-wiːhjan] 'to make fully sacred'; Old Norse said ['skiːrja] 'to make bright or pure.' This involves a semantic extension of the native term. American Indian languages resort to descriptive forms more often than to borrowing. Thus, they render *whiskey* as 'fire-water,' or *railroad* as 'fire-wagon.' Menomini uses [riːtewew] 'he reads,' from English *read*, less often than the native description [waːpahtam], literally 'he looks at it.' For *electricity* the Menomini says 'his glance' (meaning the Thunderer's) and *telephoning* is rendered as 'little-wire speech' rather than by [tɛlɛfoːnewɛw] 'he telephones'; a compound 'rubber-wagon' is commoner than the borrowed [atamoːpen]. Tools and kitchen-utensils are designated by native descriptive terms.

If the foreign term itself is descriptive, the borrower may reproduce the description; this occurs especially in the abstract domain. Many of our abstract technical terms are merely translations of Latin and Greek descriptive terms. Thus, Greek [sun-'ejdeːsis] 'joint knowledge, consciousness, conscience' is a derivative of the verb [ej'denaj] 'to know' with the preposition [sun] 'with.' The Romans translated this philosophical term by *conscientia*, a compound of *scientia* 'knowledge' and *con-* 'with.' The Germanic languages, in turn, reproduced this. In Gothic ['miθ-wissiː] 'conscience' the first member means 'with' and the second is an abstract noun derived from the verb 'to know,' on the Greek model. In Old English [je-'wit] and Old High German [gi-'wissida] the prefix had the old meaning 'with'; in North-German and Scandinavian forms, such as Old Norse ['sam-vit], the prefix is the regular replacer of an old [ga-]. Finally, the Slavic languages translate the term by 'with' and 'knowledge,' as in Russian ['so-*vest*] 'conscience.' This process, called *loan-translation*, involves a semantic change: the native terms or the components which are united to create native terms, evidently undergo an extension of meaning. The more literate and elevated style in all the languages of Europe is full of semantic extensions of this sort, chiefly on ancient Greek models, with Latin, and often also French or German, as intermediaries. The Stoic philosophers viewed all deeper emotion as morbid and applied to it the term ['pathos] 'suffering, disease,' abstract noun of the verb ['paskhoː] 'I suffer' (aorist tense ['epathon] 'I suffered'). The Romans translated this by *passiō* 'suffering,' abstract of *patior* 'I suffer,' and it is in this meaning that we ordinarily use the borrowed *passion*. German writers, in the seventeenth century, imitated the Latin use, or that of French *passion*, in *Leidenschaft* 'passion,' abstract of *leiden* 'to suffer,' and the Slavic languages followed the same model, as, for instance, in Russian [stra*st*] 'passion,' abstract of [stra'da*t*] 'to suffer.' Ancient Greek [pro-'balloː] 'I throw (something) before (someone)' had also a transferred use of the middle-voice forms, [pro-'ballomaj] 'I accuse (someone) of (something).' The Latin usage of a similar compound may be a loan-translation: one said not only *canibus cibum ob-jicere* 'to throw food to the dogs,' but also *alicuī probra objicere* 'to reproach someone for his bad actions.' This was imitated in German: *er wirft den Hunden Futter vor* 'he throws food before the dogs,' and *er wirft mir meine Missetaten vor* 'he reproaches me for my misdeeds.' The use of terms like *call, calling* for 'professional occupation,' derives from a familiar notion of Christian theology. Our terms imitate the late Latin use in this sense of *vocātiō*, abstract noun of *vocāre* 'to call'; similarly, German *Beruf* 'calling, vocation, profession' is derived from *rufen* 'to call,' and Russian ['zvanije] 'calling, vocation' is the abstract of [zva*t*] 'to call.' A great deal of our grammatical terminology has gone through this process. With a very peculiar extension, the ancient Greek grammarians used the term ['pto:sis] 'a fall' at first for 'inflectional form' and then especially for 'case-form.' This was imitated in Latin where, *cāsus*, literally 'a fall,' was used in the same way (whence our borrowed *case*); this, in turn, is reproduced in the German *Fall* 'fall; case,' and in Slavic, where Russian [pa'deʃ] 'case' is the learned-foreign (Old Bulgarian) variant of [pa'doʃ] 'a fall.' In English the loan-translations have been largely replaced, as in these examples, by Latin-French semi-learned borrowings; thus, the complex semantic sphere of Latin *commūnis*, now covered by the borrowed *common*, was in Old English imitated by extensions of the native word [je-'mɛːne], of parallel formation, just as it still is in German by the native forms *gemein* and *gemeinsam*. In Russian, the loan-translations are often in Old Bulgarian form, because this language served as the medium of theological writing.

In a less elevated sphere, we have Gallicisms, such as *a marriage of convenience* or *it goes without saying*, or *I've told him I don't know how many times*, word-for-word imitations of French phrases. The term *superman* is a translation of the German term coined by Nietzsche. For 'conventionalized,' French and German use a derivative of the noun *style*, as, French *stylisé* [stilize]; one occasionally hears this imitated in English in the form *stylized*.

These transferences are sometimes so clumsily made that we may say they involve a misunderstanding of the imitated form. The ancient Greek grammarians called the case of the verbal goal (the "direct object") by the term [ajtia:ti'ke: 'pto:sis] 'the case pertaining to what is effected,' employing an adjective derived from [ajtia:'tos] 'effected,' with an ultimately underlying noun [aj'tia:] 'cause.' This term was chosen, evidently, on account of constructions like 'he built a house,' where 'house' in Indo-

European syntax has the position of a verbal goal. The word [aj'tia:], however, had also the transferred meaning 'fault, blame, and the derived verb [ajti'aomaj] had come to mean 'I charge accuse.' Accordingly, the Roman grammarians mistranslated the Greek grammatical term by *accūsātīvus*, derived from *accūsō* 'I accuse.' This unintelligible term, *accusative*, was in turn translated into Russian, where the name of the direct-object case is [vi'nitelnoj], derived from [vi'nit] 'to accuse.' The Menomini, having only one (unvoiced) series of stops, interpreted the English term *Swede* as *sweet*, and, by mistaken loan-translation, designate the Swedish lumber-workers by the term [saje:wenet] literally 'he who is sweet.' Having neither the types [l, r] nor a voiced [z], they interpreted the name of the town *Phlox* (Wisconsin) as *frogs* and translated it as [uma:hkahkow-mɛni:ka:n] 'frog-town.'

25. 8. Cultural loans show us what one nation has taught another. The recent borrowings of English from French are largely in the sphere of women's clothes, cosmetics, and luxuries. From German we get coarser articles of food (*frankfurter, wiener, hamburger, sauerkraut, pretzel, lager-beer*) and some philosophical and scientific terms (*zeitgeist, wanderlust, umlaut*); from Italian, musical terms (*piano, sonata, scherzo, virtuoso*). From India we have *pundit, thug, curry, calico*; from American Indian languages, *tomahawk, wampum, toboggan, moccasin*. English has given *roast beef* and *beefsteak* to other languages, (as, French *bifteck* [biftɛk], Russian [bif'ʃteks]); also some terms of elegant life, such as *club, high life, five-o'clock* (*tea*), *smoking* (for 'dinner-jacket'), *fashionable*, and, above all, terms of sport, such as *match, golf, football, baseball, rugby*. Cultural loans of this sort may spread over a vast territory, from language to language, along with articles of commerce. Words like *sugar, pepper, camphor, coffee, tea, tobacco* have spread all over the world. The ultimate source of *sugar* is probably Sanskrit ['çarkara:] 'gritty substance; brown sugar'; the various shapes of such words, such as French *sucre* [sykr], Italian *zucchero* ['tsukkero] (whence German *Zucker* ['tsuker]), Greek ['sakkharon] (whence Russian ['saxar]), are due to substitutions and adaptations which took place under the most varied conditions in the borrowing and lending languages; Spanish *azucar* [a'θukar], for instance, is a borrowing from an Arabic form with the definite article, [as sokkar] 'the sugar' — just as *algebra, alcohol, alchemy* contain the Arabic article [al] 'the.' It is this same

CULTURAL BORROWING

factor of widespread cultural borrowing which interferes with our reconstruction of the Primitive Indo-European vocabulary, in cases like that of the word *hemp* (§ 18.14). Words like *axe*, *sack*, *silver* occur in various Indo-European languages, but with phonetic discrepancies that mark them as ancient loans, presumably from the Orient. The word *saddle* occurs in all the Germanic languages in a uniform type, Primitive Germanic *['sadulaz], but, as it contains the root of *sit* with Primitive Indo-European [d] (as in Latin *sedeō* 'I sit') unshifted, we must suppose *saddle* to have been borrowed into pre-Germanic, too late for the shift [d > t], from some other Indo-European language — presumably from some equestrian nation of the Southeast. The Slavic word for 'hundred,' Old Bulgarian [suto], phonetically marked as a loan-word from a similar source, perhaps Iranian, belongs to the same geographic sphere. The early contact of the Germanic-speaking peoples with the Romans appears in a layer of cultural loan-words that antedates the emigration of the English: Latin *vīnum* > Old English [wi:n] > *wine;* Latin *strāta* (*via*) > Old English [stre:t] > *street;* Latin *caupō* 'wine-dealer' is reflected in Old English ['ke:apian] 'to buy' (German *kaufen*) and in modern *cheap*, *chapman;* Latin *mangō* 'slave-dealer, peddler' > Old English ['mangere] 'trader' (still in *fishmonger*); Latin *monēta* 'mint, coin' > Old English *mynet* 'coin.' Other words of this layer are *pound*, *inch*, *mile;* Old English [kirs] 'cherry,' ['persok] 'peach,' ['pise] 'pea.' On the other hand, the Roman soldiers and merchants learned no less from the Germanic peoples. This is attested not only by Roman writers' occasional use of Germanic words, but, far more cogently, by the presence of very old Germanic loan-words in the Romance languages. Thus, an old Germanic *['werro:] 'confusion, turmoil' (Old High German ['werra]) appears, with a usual substitution of [gw-] for Germanic [w-], as Latin *['gwerra] 'war' in Italian *guerra* ['gwɛrra], French *guerre* [gɛ:r] (in English *war*, we have, as often, a borrowing back from French into English); Old Germanic *['wi:so:] 'wise, manner' (Old English [wi:s]) appears as Latin *['gwi:sa] in Italian and Spanish *guisa*, French *guise* [gi:z]; English *guise* is a loan from French, alongside the native *wise*. Germanic *['wantuz] 'mitten' (Dutch *want*, Swedish *vante*) appears as Latin *['gwantus] in Italian *guanto* 'glove,' French *gant* [gã]; English *gauntlet* is a loan from French. Other Germanic words which passed into Latin in the early centuries of our era are *hose* (> Italian *uosa* 'legging'; cf. above, § 24.3), *soap* (> Latin *sāpō*), *['θwahljo:] 'towel' (> French *touaille*, whence, in turn, English *towel*), *roast* (>French *rôtir*, whence, in turn, English *roast*), *helmet* (> French *heaume*), *crib* (> French *crèche*), *flask* (> Italian *fiasca*), *harp* (> French *harpe*). An example of a loan-translation is Latin *compāniō* 'companion,' a synthetic compound of *con-* 'with, along' and *pānis* 'bread,' on the model of Germanic *[ga-'hlajbo:], Gothic [ga'hlajba] 'companion,' a characteristically Germanic formation containing the prefix *[ga-] 'along, with' and *['hlajbaz] 'bread' (> English *loaf*).

CHAPTER 26

INTIMATE BORROWING

26. 1. Cultural borrowing of speech-forms is ordinarily mutual; it is one-sided only to the extent that one nation has more to give than the other. Thus, in the missionary period, from the seventh century onward, Old English borrowed Latin terms relating to Christianity, such as *church, minister, angel, devil, apostle, bishop, priest, monk, nun, shrine, cowl, mass,* and imitated Latin semantics in the way of loan-translation, but Old English gave nothing, at this time, in return. The Scandinavian languages contain a range of commercial and nautical terms from Low German, which date from the trading supremacy of the Hanseatic cities in the late Middle Ages; similarly, Russian contains many nautical terms from Low German and Dutch.

In spite of cases like these, we can usually distinguish between ordinary cultural borrowing and the *intimate borrowing* which occurs when two languages are spoken in what is topographically and politically a single community. This situation arises for the most part by conquest, less often in the way of peaceful migration. Intimate borrowing is one-sided: we distinguish between the *upper* or *dominant* language, spoken by the conquering or otherwise more privileged group, and the *lower* language, spoken by the subject people, or, as in the United States, by humble immigrants. The borrowing goes predominantly from the upper language to the lower, and it very often extends to speech-forms that are not connected with cultural novelties.

We see an extreme type of intimate borrowing in the contact of immigrants' languages with English in the United States. English, the upper language, makes only the most obvious cultural loans from the languages of immigrants, as *spaghetti* from Italian, *delicatessen, hamburger,* and so on (or, by way of loan-translation, *liver-sausage*) from German. The immigrant, to begin with, makes far more cultural loans. In speaking his native language, he has occasion to designate by their English names any number of things which he has learned to know since coming to America: *baseball, alderman, boss, ticket,* and so on. At the very least, he makes loan-translations, such as German *erste Papiere* 'first papers' (for naturalization). The cultural reason is less evident in cases like *policeman, conductor, street-car, depot, road, fence, saloon,* but we can say at least that the American varieties of these things are somewhat different from the European. In very many cases, however, not even this explanation will hold. Soon after the German gets here, we find him using in his German speech, a host of English forms, such as *coat, bottle, kick, change.* He will say, for instance, *ich hoffe, Sie werden's enjoyen* [ix 'hofe, zi: 'verden s en'tʃojen] 'I hope you'll enjoy it,' or *ich hab' einen kalt gecatched* [ix ha:p ajnen 'kalt ge'ketʃt] 'I've caught a cold.' He makes loan-translations, such as *ich gleich' das nicht* [ix 'glajx das 'nixt] 'I don't like that,' where, on the model of English *like,* a verb with the meaning 'be fond of' is derived from the adjective *gleich* 'equal, resemblant.' Some of these locutions, like this last, have become conventionally established in American immigrant German. The phonetic, grammatical, and lexical phases of these borrowings deserve far more study than they have received. The assignment of genders to English words in German or Scandinavian has proved a fruitful topic of observation.

The practical background of this process is evident. The upper language is spoken by the dominant and privileged group; many kinds of pressure drive the speaker of the lower language to use the upper language. Ridicule and serious disadvantages punish his imperfections. In speaking the lower language to his fellows, he may go so far as to take pride in garnishing it with borrowings from the dominant speech.

In most instances of intimate contact, the lower language is indigenous and the upper language is introduced by a body of conquerors. The latter are often in a minority; the borrowing rarely goes on at such headlong speed as in our American instance. Its speed seems to depend upon a number of factors. If the speakers of the lower language stay in touch with speech-fellows in an unconquered region, their language will change less rapidly. The fewer the invaders, the slower the pace of borrowing. Another retarding factor is cultural superiority, real or conventionally asserted, of the dominated people. Even among our immigrants, educated families may keep their language for generations with little admixture of English.

INTIMATE BORROWING

The same factors, apparently, but with some difference of weight, may finally lead to the *disuse* (extinction) of one or the other language. Numbers count for more here than in the matter of borrowing. Among immigrants in America, extinction, like borrowing, goes on at great speed. If the immigrant is linguistically isolated, if his cultural level is low, and, above all, if he marries a person of different speech, he may cease entirely to use his native language and even lose the power of speaking it intelligibly. English becomes his only language, though he may speak it very imperfectly; it becomes the native language of his children. They may speak it at first with foreign features, but outside contacts soon bring about a complete or nearly complete correction. In other cases the immigrant continues to speak his native language in the home; it is the native language of his children, but at school age, or even earlier, they cease using it, and English becomes their only adult language. Even if their English keeps some foreign coloring, they have little or no command of the parental language; bilingualism is not frequent. In the situation of conquest the process of extinction may be long delayed. One or more generations of bilingual speakers may intervene; then, at some point, there may come a generation which does not use the lower language in adult life and transmits only the upper language to its children.

The lower language may survive and the upper language die out. If the conquerors are not numerous, or, especially, if they do not bring their own women, this outcome is likely. In less extreme cases the conquerors continue, for generations, to speak their own language, but find it more and more necessary to use also that of the conquered. Once they form merely a bilingual upper class, the loss of the less useful upper language can easily take place; this was the end of Norman-French in England.

26. 2. The conflict of languages, then, may take many different turns. The whole territory may end by speaking the upper language: Latin, brought into Gaul round the beginning of the Christian Era by the Roman conquerers, in a few centuries crowded out the Celtic speech of the Gauls. The whole territory may end by speaking the lower language: Norman-French, brought into England by the Conquest (1066), was crowded out by English in three hundred years. There may be a territorial distribution: when English was brought into Britain in the fifth century of our era, it crowded the native Celtic speech into the remoter parts of the island. In such cases there follows a geographic struggle along the border. In England, Cornish died out round the year 1800, and Welsh, until quite recently, was losing ground.

In all cases, however, *it is the lower language which borrows predominantly from the upper.* Accordingly, if the upper language survives, it remains as it was, except for a few cultural loans, such as it might take from any neighbor. The Romance languages contain only a few cultural loan-words from the languages that were spoken in their territory before the Roman conquest; English has only a few cultural loan-words from the Celtic languages of Britain, and American English only a few from American Indian languages or from the languages of nineteenth-century immigrants. In the case of conquest, the cultural loans which remain in the surviving upper language are chiefly place-names; witness, for example, American Indian place-names such as *Massachusetts, Wisconsin, Michigan, Illinois, Chicago, Milwaukee, Oshkosh, Sheboygan, Waukegan, Muskegon.* It is interesting to see that where English in North America has superseded Dutch, French, or Spanish as a colonial language, the latter has left much the same traces as any other lower language. Thus, from Dutch we have cultural loan-words like *cold-slaw, cookie, cruller, spree, scow, boss,* and, especially, place-names, such as *Schuylkill, Catskill, Harlem, the Bowery.* Place-names give valuable testimony of extinct languages. Thus, a broad band of Celtic place-names stretches across Europe from Bohemia to England; *Vienna, Paris, London* are Celtic names. Slavic place-names cover eastern Germany: *Berlin, Leipzig, Dresden, Breslau.*

On the other hand, if the lower language survives, it bears the marks of the struggle in the shape of copious borrowings. English, with its loan-words from Norman-French and its enormous layer of semi-learned (Latin-French) vocabulary, is the classical instance of this. The Battle of Hastings, in 1066, marks the beginning. The first appearances of French words in written records of English fall predominantly into the period from 1250 to 1400; this means probably that the actual borrowing in each case occurred some decades earlier. Round 1300 the upper-class Englishman, whatever his descent, was either bilingual or had at least a good foreign-speaker's command of French. The mass of the people spoke only English. In 1362 the use of English was prescribed for law-courts;

INTIMATE BORROWING

in the same year Parliament was opened in English. The conflict between the two languages, lasting, say, from 1100 to 1350, seems not to have affected the phonetic or grammatical structure of English, except in the sense that a few phonemic features, such as the initials [v-, z-, dʒ-], and many features of the morphologic system of French were kept in the borrowed forms. The lexical effect, however, was tremendous. English borrowed terms of government (*state, crown, reign, power, country, people, prince, duke, duchess, peer, court*), of law (*judge, jury, just, sue, plea, cause, accuse, crime, marry, prove, false, heir*), of warfare (*war, battle, arms, soldier, officer, navy, siege, danger, enemy, march, force, guard*), of religion and morals (*religion, virgin, angel, saint, preach, pray, rule, save, tempt, blame, order, nature, virtue, vice, science, grace, cruel, pity, mercy*), of hunting and sport (*leash, falcon, quarry, scent, track, sport, cards, dice, ace, suit, trump, partner*), many terms of general cultural import (*honor, glory, fine, noble, art, beauty, color, figure, paint, arch, tower, column, palace, castle*), and terms relating to the household, such as servants might learn from master and mistress (*chair, table, furniture, serve, soup, fruit, jelly, boil, fry, roast, toast*); in this last sphere we find the oft-cited contrast between the native English names of animals on the hoof (*ox, calf, swine, sheep*), and the French loan-word names for their flesh (*beef, veal, pork, mutton*). It is worth noting that our personal names are largely French, as *John, James, Frances, Helen,* including even those which ultimately are of Germanic origin, such as *Richard, Roger, Henry.*

26. 3. The presence of loan words in a wider semantic sphere than that of cultural novelties enables us to recognize a surviving lower language, and this recognition throws light not only upon historical situations, but also, thanks to the evidence of the loan-words themselves, upon the linguistic features of an ancient time. Much of our information about older stages of Germanic speech comes from loan-words in languages that once were under the domination of Germanic-speaking tribes.

Finnish, Lappish, and Esthonian contain hundreds of words that are plainly Germanic in origin, such as, Finnish *kuningas* 'king,' *lammas* 'sheep,' *rengas* 'ring,' *niekla* 'needle,' *napakaira* 'auger,' *pelto* 'field' (§ 18.6). These loan-words occur not only in such semantic spheres as political institutions, weapons, tools, and garments, but also in such as animals, plants, parts of the body, minerals, abstract relations, and adjective qualities. Since the sound-changes which have occurred in Finnish differ from those which have occurred in the Germanic languages, these loan-words supplement the results of the comparative method, especially as the oldest of these borrowings must have been made round the beginning of the Christian Era, centuries before our earliest written records of Germanic speech.

In all the Slavic languages we find a set of Germanic loan-words that must have been taken, accordingly, into pre-Slavic. There is an older layer which resembles the Germanic loan-words in Finnish, as, Old Bulgarian [kʊnĕdzɪ] 'prince' < *['kuninga-], Old Bulgarian [xleːbʊ] 'grain, bread' < *['hlajba-] (Gothic *hlaifs* 'bread,' English *loaf*), Old Bohemian [nebozeːz] 'auger' < *['nabagajza-]. A later stratum, which includes cultural terms of Greco-Roman origin, shows some specifically Gothic traits; to this layer belong terms like Old Bulgarian [kotɪlʊ] 'kettle' < *['katila-], Old Bulgarian [myto] 'toll' < *['moːta], Old Bulgarian [tseːsarɪ] 'emperor' < *['kajsoːrja-] (§ 25.5), Old Bulgarian [userĕdzɪ] 'earring' < *['awsa-hringa-]. We infer that the earlier stratum is pre-Gothic and dates from the beginning of the Christian Era, and that the later stratum comes from the stage of Gothic that is represented in our written documents of the fourth century.

In what is known as the Great Migrations, Germanic tribes conquered various parts of the Roman Empire. At this time Latin already contained a number of old cultural loan-words from Germanic (§ 25.8); the new loans of the Migration Period can be distinguished, in part, either by their geographic distribution, or by formal characteristics that point to the dialect of the conquerors. Thus, the vowel of Italian *elmo* ['elmo] 'helmet' reflects an old [i], and the Germanic [e] of a word like *['helmaz] (Old English *helm*) appears as [i] only in Gothic; the Goths ruled Italy in the sixth century. On the other hand, a layer of Germanic words with a consonant-shift like that of South German, represents the Lombard invasion and rule. Thus, Italian *tattera* ['tattera] 'trash' is presumably a loan from Gothic, but *zazzera* ['tsattsera] 'long hair' represents the Lombard form of the same Germanic word. Italian *ricco* 'rich,' *elso* 'hilt,' *tuffare* 'to plunge' are similarly marked as loans from Lombard.

The most extensive borrowing in Romance from Germanic appears in French. The French borrowings from the Frankish rulers, beginning with the name of the country *France*, pervade the vocabulary. Examples are Frankish *[helm] 'helmet' > Old French *helme* (modern *heaume* [o:m]); Frankish *['falda-₁sto:li] 'folding-stool' > Old French *faldestoel* (modern *fauteuil* [fotœ:j]); Frankish *[bru:n] 'brown' > French *brun;* Frankish *[bla:w] 'blue' > French *bleu;* Frankish *['hatjan] 'to hate' > French *haïr;* Frankish *['wajdano:n] 'to gain' > Old French *gaagnier* (modern *gagner;* English *gain* from French). This last example illustrates the fact that many of the French loan-words in English are ultimately of Germanic origin. Thus, English *ward* is a native form and represents Old English ['weardjan]; the cognate Frankish *['wardo:n] appears in French as *garder* [garde], whence English has borrowed *guard*.

It is not surprising that personal names in the Romance languages are largely of Germanic origin, as French *Louis, Charles, Henri, Robert, Roger, Richard,* or Spanish *Alfonso* (presumably < Gothic *['haθu-funs] 'eager for fray'), *Adolfo* (presumably < Gothic *['aθal-ulfs] 'wolf of the land'). The upper-class style of name-giving survives even when the upper language is otherwise extinct.

Repeated domination may swamp a language with loan-words. Albanese is said to contain a ground-stock of only a few hundred native words; all the rest are dominance-loans from Latin, Romance, Greek, Slavic, and Turkish. The European Gipsies speak an Indo-Aryan language: it seems that in their various abodes they have been sufficiently segregated to keep their language, but that this language figured always as a lower language and taker of loan-words. All the Gipsy dialects, in particular, contain loan-words from Greek. F. N. Finck defines German Gipsy simply as that dialect of the Gipsy language in which "any expression lacking in the vocabulary" is replaced by a German word, as ['flikerwa:wa] 'I patch' from German *flicken* 'to patch,' or ['ʃtu:lo] 'chair' from German *Stuhl*. The inflectional system, however, is intact, and the phonetics apparently differ from those of German.

The model of the upper language may affect even the grammatical forms of the lower. The anglicisms, say, in the American German of immigrants, find many a parallel in the languages of dominated peoples; thus, Ladin is said to have largely the syntax of the neighboring German, though the morphemes are Latin. In English we have not only Latin-French affixes, as in *eatable, murderous,* (§ 25.6), but also a few foreign features of phonetic pattern, as in *zoom, jounce*. Non-distinctive traits of phonemes do not seem to be borrowed. When we observe the American of German parentage (whose English, at the same time, may show some German traits) using an American-English [l] or [r] in his German, we may account for this by saying that German is for him a foreign language.

With a change of political or cultural conditions, the speakers of the lower language may make an effort to cease and even to undo the borrowing. Thus, the Germans have waged a long and largely successful campaign against Latin-French loan-words, and the Slavic nations against German. In Bohemian one avoids even loan-translations; thus, [zanaːʃka] 'entry (as, in a ledger),' abstract of a verb meaning 'to carry in,' a loan-translation of German *Eintragung* 'a carrying in, an entry,' is being replaced by a genuinely native [zaːpis] 'writing in, notation.'

26. 4. Beside the normal conflict, with the upper language, if it survives, remaining intact, and the lower language, if it survives, bearing off a mass of loan-words and loan-translations, or even syntactic habits, we find a number of cases where something else must have occurred. Theoretically, there would seem to be many possibilities of an eccentric outcome. Aside from the mystic version of the substratum theory (§ 21.9), it seems possible that a large population, having imperfectly acquired an upper language, might perpetuate its version and even crowd out the more original type spoken by the upper class. On the other hand, we do not know the limit to which a lower language may be altered and yet survive. Finally, it is conceivable that a conflict might end in the survival of a mixture so evenly balanced that the historian could not decide which phase to regard as the main stock of habit and which as the borrowed admixture. However, we do not know which of these or of other imaginable complications have actually occurred, and no one, apparently, has succeeded in explaining the concrete cases of aberrant mixture.

From the end of the eighth century on, Danish and Norwegian Vikings raided and settled in England; from 1013 to 1042 England was ruled by Danish kings. The Scandinavian elements in English, however, do not conform to the type which an upper language leaves behind. They are restricted to the intimate part of the vocabulary: *egg, sky, oar, skin, gate, bull, bait, skirt, fellow, husband, sister, law, wrong, loose, low, meek, weak, give, take, call cast, hit.* The adverb and conjunction *though* is Scandinavian, and so are the pronoun forms *they, their, them;* the native form [m̩], as in *I saw 'em* (< Old English *him,* dative plural), is now treated as an unstressed variant of the loan-form *them.* Scandinavian place-names abound in northern England. We do not know what circumstances led to this peculiar result. The languages at the time of contact were in all likelihood mutually intelligible. Perhaps their relation as to number of speakers and as to dominance differed in different localities and shifted variously in the course of time.

Most instances of aberrant borrowing look as though an upper language had been affected by a lower. The clearest case is that of Chilean Spanish. In Chile, the prowess of the natives led to an unusually great influx of Spanish soldiers, who settled in the country and married native women. In contrast with the rest of Latin America, Chile has lost its Indian languages and speaks only Spanish, and this Spanish differs phonetically from the Spanish that is spoken (by the dominant upper class) in the rest of Spanish America. The differences run in the direction of the indigenous languages that were replaced by Spanish; it has been surmised that the children of the first mixed marriages acquired the phonetic imperfections of their mothers.

Some features of the normal type of the Romance languages have been explained as reflections of the languages that were superseded by Latin. It would have to be shown that the features in question actually date from the time when speakers of the earlier languages, having imperfectly acquired Latin, transmitted it in this shape to their children. If this were granted, we should have to suppose that the official and colonizing class of native Latin-speakers was not large enough to provide an ever-present model, such as would have led to the leveling out of these imperfections. Actually, the peculiar traits of the Romance languages appear at so late a date that this explanation seems improbable, unless one resorts to the mystical (atavistic) version of the substratum theory (§ 21.9).

Indo-Aryan speech must have been brought into India by a relatively small group of invaders and imposed, in a long progression of dominance, by a ruling caste. Some, at least, of the languages which were superseded must have been kin to the present-day non-Aryan linguistic stocks of India. The principal one of these stocks, Dravidian, uses a domal series of stops [т, d, n] alongside the dental [t, d, n]; among the Indo-European languages, only the Indo-Aryan have the two series, and in their history the domals have become more numerous in the course of time. The Indo-Aryan languages exhibit also an ancient confusion of [l] and [r] which has been explained as due to substrata that possessed only one or neither of these sounds. The noun-declension of later Indo-Aryan shows a re-formation, by which the same case-endings are added to distinct stems for the singular and plural, as in Dravidian; this replaced the characteristic Indo-European habit of different sets of case-endings, as the sole distinction between singular and plural, added to one and the same stem.

In Slavic, especially in Russian and Polish, the impersonal and partitive constructions closely parallel the Finnish habit. The languages of the Balkan peninsula show various resemblances, although they represent four branches of Indo-European: Greek, Albanese, Slavic (Bulgarian, Serbian), and Latin (Roumanian). Thus, Albanese, Bulgarian, and Roumanian, all use a definite article that is placed after the noun; the Balkan languages generally lack an infinitive. In other parts of the world, too, we find phonetic or grammatical features prevailing in unrelated languages. This is the case with some phonetic features in the Caucasus, which are common both to the several non-Indo-European stocks and to Armenian and to the Iranian Ossete. On the Northwest Coast of North America, phonetic and morphologic peculiarities appear in similar extensions. Thus, Quilleute, Kwakiutl, and Tsimshian all have different articles for common nouns and for names, and distinguish between visibility and invisibility in demonstrative pronouns; the latter peculiarity appears also in the neighboring Chinook and Salish dialects, but not in those of the interior. The suggestion has been made that different tribes captured women from one another, who transmitted their speech, with traces of their native idiom, to the next generation.

Where we can observe the historical process, we occasionally find phonetic and grammatical habits passing from language to language without actual dominance. In the modern period the uvular-trill [r] has spread over large parts of western Europe as a replacement of the tongue-tip [r]; today, in France and in the Dutch-German area the former is citified and the latter rustic or old-fashioned. At the end of the Middle Ages, large parts of the

English, Dutch, and German areas, including the socially favored dialects, diphthongized the long high vowels. The rise of the articles and of phrasal verb-forms consisting-of 'have,' 'be,' or 'become' plus past participle, in perfectic and passive values, took place in both the Latin and the Germanic areas during the early Middle Ages.

26. 5. There remains a type of aberrant borrowing in which we have at least the assurance that an upper language has been modified, though the details of the process are no less obscure.

The English (now largely American) Gipsies have lost their language and speak a phonetically and grammatically normal variety of sub-standard English; among themselves, however, they use anywhere from a few dozen to several hundred words of the old Gipsy language. These words are spoken with English phonemes and English inflection and syntax. They are terms for the very commonest things, and include grammatical words, such as pronouns. They are used interchangeably with the English equivalents. Older recordings show great numbers of these words: apparently a long speech could be made almost entirely in Gipsy words with English phonetics and grammar. Modern examples are: [ˈmɛndi] 'I,' [ˈlɛdi] 'you,' [sɔː] 'all,' [kejk] 'not,' [pʌn] 'say,' [ˈgrajə] 'horse,' [aj ˈdownt ˈkaːm tu ˈdik ə ˈmuʃ ə-ˈtʃumərən ə ˈgrʊvn] 'I don't like to see a man a-kissin' a cow.' Occasionally one hears a Gipsy inflection, such as [ˈrukjə], plural of [ruk] 'tree.' The phonetics and grammar of the Gipsy words mark them unmistakably as borrowings by native speakers of English from a foreign language. Presumably they passed from native speakers of the Gipsy language, or from bilinguals, into the English of their children or other persons for whom Gipsy was no longer a native language. It is remarkable, however, that speakers of the latter sort should have interlarded their English with borrowings from the senescent lower language. Under the general circumstances of segregation, these borrowings had perhaps a facetious value; certainly they had the merit of making one's speech unintelligible to outsiders. Americans of non-English parentage who do not speak their parents' language, sometimes, by way of jest, use words of this language, speaking them with English sounds and inflections. Thus, German-Americans will occasionally use forms like [ʃwits] 'to sweat' (from German *schwitzen*), or [klatʃ] 'to gossip' (from German *klatschen*). This trick seems to be commonest among Jews, who live under a measure of segregation, and the borrowings, moreover, are to a large extent the very words which in German also are peculiarly Jewish, namely, semi-learned words of literary Hebrew origin, such as ['ganef] 'thief,' [gɔj] 'gentile,' [me'ʃuga] 'crazy,' [me'zuma] 'money,' or dialect-forms of Judeo-German, such as ['nebix] 'poor fellow' (< Middle High German ['n eb ix] 'may I not have the like'). It seems likely that the Gipsy forms in English represent merely an extension of this habit under conditions that made it especially useful.

Speakers of a lower language may make so little progress in learning the dominant speech, that the masters, in communicating with them resort to "baby-talk." This "baby-talk" is the masters' imitation of the subjects' incorrect speech. There is reason to believe that it is by no means an exact imitation, and that some of its features are based not upon the subjects' mistakes but upon grammatical relations that exist within the upper language itself. The subjects, in turn, deprived of the correct model, can do no better now than to acquire the simplified "baby-talk" version of the upper language. The result may be a conventionalized *jargon*. During the colonization of the last few centuries, Europeans have repeatedly given jargonized versions of their language to slaves and tributary peoples. Portuguese jargons are found at various places in Africa, India, and the Far East; French jargons exist in Mauritius and in Annam; a Spanish jargon was formerly spoken in the Philippines; English jargons are spoken in the western islands of the South Seas (here known as *Beach-la-Mar*), in Chinese ports (*Pidgin English*), and in Sierra Leone and Liberia. Unfortunately, these jargons have not been well recorded. Examples from Beach-la-Mar are:

What for you put diss belonga master in fire? Him cost plenty money and that fellow kai-kai him. 'Why did you put the master's dishes into the fire? They cost a lot of money and it has destroyed them' — spoken to a cook who had put silverware into the oven.

What for you wipe hands belonga you on clothes belonga esseppoon? 'Why did you wipe your hands on the napkin?'

Kai-kai he finish? 'Is dinner ready?'

You not like soup? He plenty good kai-kai. 'Don't you like the soup? It's very good.'

What man you give him stick? 'To whom did you give the stick?'

Me savey go. 'I can go there.'

In spite of the poor recording, we may perhaps reconstruct the creation of speech-forms like these. The basis is the foreigner's desperate attempt at English. Then comes the English-speaker's contemptuous imitation of this, which he tries in the hope of making himself understood. This stage is represented, for instance, by the lingo which the American, in slumming or when traveling abroad, substitutes for English, to make the foreigner understand. In our examples we notice, especially, that the English-speaker introduces such foreign words as he has managed to learn (*kai-kai* 'eat' from some Polynesian language), and that he does not discriminate between foreign languages (*savey* 'know,' from Spanish, figures in all English jargons). The third layer of alteration is due to the foreigner's imperfect reproduction of the English-speaker's simplified talk, and will differ according to the phonetic and grammatical habit of the foreigner's language. Even the poor orthography of our examples shows us substitution of [s] for [ʃ] in *dish* and failure to use final [ŋ], in *belonga*, and initial [sp], in *esseppoon* for *spoon*.

A jargon may pass into general commercial use between persons of various nationality; we then call it a *lingua franca*, using a term which seems to have been applied to an Italian jargon in the eastern Mediterranean region in the early modern period. Pidgin English, for instance, is used quite generally in commerce between Chinese and Europeans of other than English speech. In Washington and Oregon, Indians of various tribes, as well as French and English-speaking traders, formerly used a lingua franca known as "Chinook Jargon," which was based, strangely enough, on a jargonized form of the Chinook language, with admixtures from other Indian languages and from English.

It is important to keep in view the fact, often neglected, that a jargon or a lingua franca is nobody's native language but only a compromise between a foreign speaker's version of a language and a native speaker's version of the foreign speaker's version, and so on, in which each party imperfectly reproduces the other's reproduction. In many cases the jargon or lingua franca dies out, like Chinook Jargon, without ever becoming native to any group of speakers.

In some cases, however, a subject group gives up its native language in favor of a jargon. This happens especially when the subject group is made up of persons from different speech-communities, who can communicate among themselves only by means of the jargon. This was the case, presumably, among Negro slaves in many parts of America. When the jargon has become the only language of the subject group, it is a *creolized language*. The creolized language has the status of an inferior dialect of the masters' speech. It is subject to constant leveling-out and improvement in the direction of the latter. The various types of "Negro dialect" which we observe in the United States show us some of the last stages of this leveling. With an improvement of social conditions, this leveling is accelerated; the result is a caste-dialect whose speakers, so far as linguistic factors are concerned, have no more difficulty than other sub-standard speakers in acquiring the standard language.

It is a question whether during this process the dialect that is being de-creolized may not influence the speech of the community — whether the creolized English of the southern slaves, for instance, may not have influenced local types of sub-standard or even of standard English. The Dutch of South Africa, known as *Afrikaans*, shows some features that remind one of creolized languages — such, for instance, as extreme inflectional simplification. Since it is spoken by the whole community, one would have to suppose that the Dutch settlers developed a jargonized form of Dutch in communication with native Africans, and that this jargon, through the medium of native servants (especially, of nurses) then influenced the language of the masters.

In the very unusual case where the subject group, after losing its native language or languages and speaking only a creolized language, is removed from the dominance of the model language, the creolized language escapes assimilation and embarks upon an independent career. A few such cases have been observed. Thus, the descendants of runaway slaves who settled on the island of San Thomé off the coast of West Africa, spoke a creolized Portuguese. A creolized Dutch was long spoken on the Virgin Islands. Two creolized forms of English are spoken in Suriname (Dutch Guiana). One of these, known as *Ningre Tongo* or *taki-taki*, is spoken by the descendants of slaves along the coast. The other, more divergent from ordinary types of English, is known as *Jew-Tongo;* it is spoken by the Bush Negroes on the Saramakka River, descendants of slaves who won their liberty in the eighteenth century by rebellion and flight. It owes its name to the fact that some of the slaves were owned by Portuguese Jews. The remarkable feature of Bush-Negro English is its extreme adaptation to the phonetics and structure of West African languages, and the retention of much West African vocabulary: if the slaves still spoke an African language, it is a puzzle why they should have abandoned it in favor of English jargon.

The following examples of Ningre-Tongo are taken from texts recorded by M. J. Herskovits:

['kom na 'ini:-sej. mi: sɛ 'gi: ju wan 'sani: fo: ju: de 'njam.] 'Come inside. I shall give you something to eat.'

[a 'taki: , 'gran 'taŋgi: fo: 'ju:] 'He said, "Thank you very much."'

[mi: 'njam mi: 'bɛre 'furu.] 'I have eaten my belly full.'

In the first of the following Bush-Negro English proverbs, kindly supplied by Professor Herskovits, the tones are indicated by numbers: [1]rising, [2]level, [3]falling, and by combinations of numbers, such as [13]rising then falling, [23]level then falling, and so on.

[fu[13] kri[21] ki[23] a[n1] taŋ[13] hɔn[2] wi[21]] 'full creek not stand uproot weeds,' that is, 'A full creek doesn't uproot any weeds' — said when a person boasts of what he is going to accomplish.

[ɛfi: ju: sɛi: ju: hɛdɛ, tɛ ju: baj hati:, pɛ ju: pɔti: ɛŋ] 'If you sell your head, then you buy hat, where you put him?' that is, 'If you sell your head to buy a hat, where will you put it?'

[pi:ki: matʃaw faa gã paw] 'Small axe fell great stick,' that is, 'A small axe can cut down a large tree.'

CHAPTER 27

DIALECT BORROWING

27. 1. The infant begins by acquiring the speech-habits of the people who take care of him. He gets most of his habits from some one person, usually from his mother, but he does not reproduce this person's speech exactly, because he takes some forms from other persons. It is a matter of dispute whether any permanent habits, in the normal case, arise as mere inaccuracies of imitation. Later on, the child acquires speech-forms from more people; children are especially imitative in their first contacts outside the immediate family circle. As time goes on, the range of imitated persons becomes wider; throughout his life, the speaker continues to adopt speech-habits from his fellows. At any moment, his language is a unique composite of habits acquired from various people.

Very often whole groups of speakers agree in adopting or favoring or disfavoring a speech-form. Within an age-group, an occupational group, or a neighborhood group, a turn of speech will pass from person to person. The borrowing of speech-habits within a community is largely one-sided; the speaker adopts new forms and favoritisms from some people more than from others. In any group, some persons receive more imitation than others; they are the leaders in power and prestige. Vaguely defined as they are, the different groups make similarly one-sided adoptions. Every person belongs to more than one minor speech-group; a group is influenced by the persons who, along some other line of division, belong to a dominant class. Among his occupational companions, for example, a speaker will imitate those whom he believes to have the highest "social" standing. To take the extreme case, when a speaker comes in contact with persons who enjoy much greater prestige, he eagerly imitates not only their general conduct, but also their speech. Here the direction of leveling is most plainly apparent. The humble person is not imitated; the lord or leader is a model to most of those who hear him. In conversation with him, the common man avoids giving offense or cause for ridicule; he suppresses such of his habits as might seem peculiar, and tries to ingratiate himself by talking as he hears. Having conversed with the great, he himself may become a model in his own group for those who have not had that privilege. Every speaker is a mediator between various groups.

The adjustments are largely minute and consist in the favoring of speech-forms more often than in the adoption of wholly new ones. A great deal of adjustment probably concerns non-distinctive variants of sound. On the other hand, when rival forms enjoy something like equality, the choice may be actually discussed: a speaker deliberates whether he will say *it's I* or *it's me*, or speak *either, neither* with [ij] or with [aj]. In our community, with its tradition about the "correctness" of speech-forms, the speaker asks "Which form is better?" instead of asking "With which persons shall I agree in speech?" In the main, however, the process does not rise to the level of discussion.

Every speaker, and, on a larger scale, every local or social group, acts as an imitator and as a model — as an agent in the leveling process. No person and no group acts always in one or the other capacity, but the privileged castes and the central and dominating communities act more often as models, and the humblest classes and most remote localities more often as imitators.

27. 2. The important historical process in this leveling is the growth of central speech-forms that spread over wider and wider areas. Suppose, for instance, that in a locally differentiated area, some one town, thanks to personalities that live in it or thanks to a favorable topographic situation, becomes the seat of a recurrent religious rite or political gathering or market. The inhabitants of the villages round about now resort at intervals to this central town. On these visits they learn to avoid the strikingly divergent forms of their domestic speech, replacing them by forms that do not call forth misunderstanding or mockery. These favored speech-forms will be such as are current in all or most of the local groups; if no one form is predominant, the choice will fall usually upon the form that is used in the central town. When the villager goes home, he continues to use one or another of these new locutions, and his neighbors will imitate it, both because they know its source and because the speaker who has visited the central town has gained in prestige at home. At second, third, and later hand, these locutions may pass to still more remote persons and places. The central town becomes a *speech-center*, whose forms of speech, when there is not too much weight against them, become the "better" forms for a whole area of the surrounding country.

As commerce and social organization improve, this process repeats itself on a larger and larger scale. Each center is imitated over a certain area. A new concentration of political power elevates some of these centers to a higher rank; the lesser centers themselves now imitate this main center, and continue to spread both its forms and their own over their petty spheres. This development took place in the Middle Ages in Europe. At the end of the medieval period, countries like England, France, and Germany contained a number of provincial speech-centers, though even by that time, in England and in France, the capital city was taking the rank of a supreme speech-center for the whole area. These levelings, where they occurred on a large scale, are reflected in the great isogloss-bundles that mark the conflict of cultural systems, such as the bundles which separate Low German and High German or Northern and Southern French. The lesser provincial and parochial levelings appear as minor isoglosses; thus, we saw that the boundaries of the petty states along the lower Rhine that were swamped by the French invasion of 1789 are reflected in lesser isogloss-bundles of today. All this would be plainer, were it not for the frequent shifting both of political boundaries and of the relative influence of centers. The most variable factor, however, is the difference between the speech-forms themselves, since some will spread more vigorously than others, either for semantic reasons or, less often, for reasons of formal structure.

A similarity of speech in a district of any size may date from the time when the speech-community first spread over this district. The word *house*, for example, spread over England with the entrance of the English language, at the time of the Saxon conquest. It then had the form [huːs], and in the northern dialects which still speak so, the modern form may be a direct continuation of the old form.

In very many instances, however, we know that a uniformity does not date from the time of settlement. Thus, we know that the diphthong [aw] in *house, mouse*, etc., arose from older [uː] long after the settlement of England. In these cases, older students took for granted a uniform linguistic change over a large area, supposing, for instance, that a large part of the English area made a phonetic change of [uː] to [aw]. At present, we believe rather that the actual change occurred among a relatively small group of speakers, and that after this, the new form spread by linguistic borrowing over the large area. We are led to this opinion by the fact that isoglosses for parallel forms do not coincide. A divergence like that of the isoglosses of the vowels in *mouse* and *house* in the Netherlands (§ 19.4) fits into our classification of linguistic borrowing, but not into our classification of phonetic change. Some students see in this a reason for giving up our classifications, and insist that a "phonetic change" spreads in this irregular fashion. This statement, however, is inconsistent with the original application of the term "phonetic change" to phonemic parallelism in cognate speech-forms (§ 20.4). Accordingly, we should have to devise a new classification or else to find some way of reconciling the two kinds of phenomena that are included in the new use of the term "phonetic change" — and no one has even attempted to do either of these things. The method which distinguishes between a uniform *phonetic change* and the spread by *borrowing* of resultant variants, is the only formula that has so far been devised to fit the facts.

Even when a uniform feature could represent the type that was imported in the original settlement, we may find upon closer investigation that this feature has merely overlaid an older diversity. This may be disclosed by isolated relic forms (§ 19.5), or by the characteristic phenomenon of *hyper-forms*. Of these, Gamillscheg gives a beautiful example. In the Ladin of the Dolomite Mountains, Latin [wi-] has become [u-]: a Latin [wiˈkiːnum] 'neighbour,' for instance, appears as [uʒiṇ]. In one corner of this district, however, the Rau Valley, this change apparently did not take place: Latin [wi-] is represented by [vi-], as in [viʒin] 'neighbour.' However, there is a queer discrepancy. The Latin type [awˈkɛllum] 'bird,' which appears in Italian as [utˈtʃello] and in the Ladin of the Dolomites as [utʃel], and did not have initial [wi-], has in the Rau valley the form [vitʃel] 'bird.' If the Rau valley had really preserved Latin [wi-] as [vi-], the form [vitʃel] 'bird' would be inexplicable. It can be understood only if we suppose that the Rau dialect, like the other Dolomite dialects, changed [wi-] to [u-], and afterwards took to borrowing the more urbane Italian [vi-] as a replacement for the native [u-]. In doing this, the Rau speakers went too far, and substituted [vi-] for [u-] even in the word *[utʃel] 'bird,' where Italian has [u-] and not [vi-].

An isogloss tells us only that there has occurred somewhere and at some time a sound-change, an analogic-semantic change, or a cultural loan, but the isogloss does not tell us where or when this change occurred. The form which resulted from the change was spread abroad and perhaps pushed back, we know not with what vicissitudes, in a process of dialect borrowing whose outcome is represented by the isogloss. The present area of a form may even fail to include the point at which this form originated. It is a very naïve error to mistake isoglosses for the limits of simple linguistic changes. The results of dialect geography tell us of linguistic borrowing.

27. 3. If the geographic domain of a linguistic form is due to borrowing, we face the problem of determining who made the original change. A cultural loan or an analogic-semantic innovation may be due to a single speaker; more often, doubtless, it is made independently by more than one. Perhaps the same is true of the non-distinctive deviations which ultimately lead to a sound-change, but this matter is more obscure, since the actual, linguistically observable change is here the result of a cumulation of minute variants. The speaker who favors or exaggerates some acoustic variant, as well as the speaker who adopts such a variant, has merely altered a non-distinctive feature. By the time a succession of such favorings has resulted in a change of phonemic structure, the borrowing process has doubtless long been at work. There must have been a time, for instance, when some parts of the American English speech-community favored the lower and less rounded variants of the vowel in words like *hot, cod, bother*. It is useless to ask what person or set of persons first favored these variants; we must suppose only that he or they enjoyed prestige within some group of speakers, and that this group, in turn, influenced other groups, and so on, in the manner of widening circles: the new variants were fortunate enough through some time and in repeated situations, to belong to the more dominant speakers and groups. This favoring went on until, over a large part of the area, and doubtless not everywhere at the same time, the vowel of *hot, cod, bother* coincided with that of *far, palm, father*. Only at this moment could an observer say that a sound-change had occurred; by this time, however, the distribution of the variants among speakers, groups, and localities, was a result of borrowing. The moment of the coincidence of the two former phonemes into one could not be determined; doubtless even one speaker might at one time make a difference and at another time speak the two alike. By the time a sound-change becomes observable, its effect has been distributed by the leveling process that goes on within each community.

The linguist's classification of changes into the three great types of phonetic change, analogic-semantic change, and borrowing, is a classification of facts which result from minute and complicated processes. The processes themselves largely escape our observation; we have only the assurance that a simple statement of their results will bear some relation to the factors that created these results.

Since every speaker acts as an intermediary between the groups to which he belongs, differences of speech within a dialect area are due merely to a lack of mediatory speakers. The influence of a speech-center will cause a speech-form to spread in any direction until, at some line of weakness in the density of communication, it ceases to find adopters. Different speech-forms, with different semantic values, different formal qualifications, and different rival forms to conquer, will spread at different speeds and over different distances. The advance of the new form may be stopped, moreover, by the advance of a rival form from a neighboring speech-center, or, perhaps, merely by the fact that a neighboring speech-center uses an unchanged form.

One other possible source of differentiation must be reckoned with: absorption of a foreign area, whose inhabitants speak their new language with peculiar traits. We have seen (§ 26.4) that this is entirely problematic, since no certain example has been found. For the most part, then, differentiation within a dialect area is merely a result of imperfect leveling.

27. 4. Increases in the area and intensity of unification are due to a number of factors which we sum up by saying that the economic and political units grow larger and that the means of communication improve. We know little about the details of this process of centralization, because our evidence consists almost entirely of written documents, and written documents are in this matter especially misleading; to begin with, they are in Europe mostly couched in Latin and not in the language of the country.

In the non-Latin (*vernacular*) records of the English and Dutch-German areas, we find at the outset, — that is, from the eighth century on, — provincial dialects. Internal evidence shows that even these have arisen through some degree of unification, but we do not know how much of this unification existed in actual speech. In the later Middle Ages we find beginnings of greater centralization. In the Dutch-German area, especially, we find three fairly uniform types of language: a Flemish ("Middle Dutch") type, a decidedly uniform North German ("Middle Low German") type in the Hanseatic area, and a South German ("Middle High German") type in the aristocratic literature of the southern states. The language of these documents is fairly uniform over wide geographic areas. In some respects, we can see how local peculiarities are excluded. The North German type is based predominantly on the speech of the city of Lübeck. The southern type strikes a kind of average between provincial dialects, excluding some of the localisms that appear in present-day dialect. In old Germanic the personal pronouns had separate forms for the dual and plural numbers; in general, the distinction was removed by an extension of the plural forms to the case where only two persons were involved, but in some regions the old dual forms were extended to plural use. In most of the German area the old plural forms, Middle High German *ir* 'ye' (dative *iu;* accusative *iuch*), survived, but certain districts, notably Bavaria and Austria, took the second alternative: the modern local dialects use the old dual form *ess* 'ye' (dative and accusative *enk*). Now, our Middle High German documents from the latter region scarcely ever show us these provincial forms, but write only the generally German *ir* 'ye.' On the other hand, careful study of a text will usually show in what part of southern Germany it originated, because many details had not been standardized. Poets' rimes, especially, conform, on the one hand, to certain conventions, but, on the other hand, betray each poet's provincial phonetics. It is remarkable that at the beginning of the modern period, in the fifteenth and early sixteenth centuries, this South German convention had broken down and our documents are again decidedly provincial, until the coming of the modern national standard language.

The modern standard languages, which prevail within the bounds of an entire nation, supersede the provincial types. These standard languages become more and more uniform as time goes on. In most instances they have grown out of the provincial type that prevailed in the upper class of the urban center that became the capital of the unified nation; modern standard English is based on the London type, and modern standard French on that of Paris. In other instances even the center of origin is obscure. Modern standard German is not based on any one provincial dialect, but seems to have crystallized out of an official and commercial type of speech that developed in the eastern frontier region. It was not created, but only helped toward supremacy, by Luther's use in his Bible-translation. This origin is reflected in the fact that the documents of standard German until well into the eighteenth century are far less uniform and show many more provincial traits than do those of English or French; the same can be said of the standard language as it is spoken today.

The modern state, then, possesses a standard language, which is used in all official discourse, in churches and schools, and in all written notation. As soon as a speech-group attains or seeks political independence, or even asserts its cultural peculiarity, it works at setting up a standard language. Thus, the Serbo-Croatians, emerging from Turkish rule, possessed no standard language; a scholar, Vuk Stefanovich Karadjich (1787–1864) made one on the basis of his local dialect, writing a grammar and lexicon. Bohemia, governed from German-speaking centers, had nevertheless developed something like a standard language at the time of the Reformation. The great reformer, Jan Hus (1369–1415), in particular, had devised an excellent system of spelling. In the seventeenth and eighteenth centuries this movement died down, but, with the national revival at the end of this period, a new standard language, based on the old, was created largely by the efforts of a philologian, Josef Dobrowsky (1753–1829). Within the memory of persons now living, the Lithuanian standard language, today official and fully current in the confines of its nation, arose from out of a welter of local dialects. Groups that have not gained political independence, such as the Slovaks, the Catalans, and the Frisians, have developed standard languages. The case of Norway is especially interesting. For some centuries Norway belonged politically to Denmark and used standard Danish as its national language. The latter was similar enough to Norwegian speech-forms to make this possible for persons who got school training.

484   DIALECT BORROWING

The Norwegians modified their standard Danish in the direction of Norwegian speech-forms. This Dano-Norwegian *Riksmaal* ('national language') became the native speech of the educated upper class; for the uneducated majority, who spoke local dialects, it was almost a foreign language, even though after the political separation from Denmark in 1813, it was more and more assimilated to the general type of the native dialects. In the 1840's a language-student, Ivar Aasen (1813-1896) constructed a standard language on the basis of Norwegian local dialects and proposed its adoption in place of Dano-Norwegian. With many changes and variations, this new standard language, known as *Landsmaal* ('native language'), has been widely adopted, so that Norway has today two officially recognized standard languages. The advocates of the two are often in earnest conflict; the two standard languages, by concessions on either side, are growing more and more alike.

27. 5. The details of the rise of the great standard languages, such as standard English, are not known, because written sources do not give us a close enough picture. In its early stages, as a local dialect and later as a provincial type, the speech which later became a standard language, may have borrowed widely. Even after that, before its supremacy has been decided, it is subject to infiltration of outside forms. The native London development of Old English [y] is probably [i], as in *fill, kiss, sin, hill, bridge;* the [o] which appears in *bundle, thrush*, seems to represent a West-of-England type, and the [e] in *knell, merry* an eastern type. In *bury* ['beri] the spelling implies the western development, but the actual pronunciation has the eastern [e]; in *busy* ['bizi] the spelling is western, but the actual spoken form indigenous. The foreign [o] and [e] must have come at a very early time into the official London speech. The change of old [er] into [ɑ:], as in *heart, parson, far, dark, 'varsity,* or *clerk* in British pronunciation (contrasting with the development in *earth, learn, person, university,* or *clerk* in American pronunciation) seems to have been provincial; the [ɑ:]- forms filtered into upper-class London speech from the fourteenth century on. Chaucer uses *-th* as the third-person singular present-tense ending of verbs (*hath, giveth,* etc.); our [-iz, -z, -s] ending was provincial (northern) until well into the sixteenth century. Especially the East Midlands influenced London English during the early centuries of the latter's pre-eminence. In later times, the standard language borrows from other dialects only technical terms, such as *vat, vixen* (§ 19.1), or *laird, cairn* (from Scotch), or else facetiously, as in *hoss, cuss* as jesting-forms for *horse, curse;* here *bass* ('species of fish') for **berse*, (Old English *bears*) represents a more serious borrowing of earlier date.

The standard language influences the surrounding dialects at wider range and more pervasively as it gains in prestige. It affects especially provincial centers and, through them, their satellite dialects. This action is relatively slow. We have seen that a feature of the standard language may reach outlying dialects long after it has been superseded at home (§ 19.4). In the immediate surroundings of the capital, the standard language acts very strongly; the neighboring dialects may be so permeated with standard forms as to lose all their individuality. We are told that within thirty miles of London there is no speech-form that could be described as local dialect.

The standard language takes speakers from the provincial and local dialects. The humblest people make no pretense at acquiring it, but with the spread of prosperity and education, it becomes familiar to a larger and larger stratum. In western European countries today most people possess at least a good smattering of the standard language. The person who rises in the world speaks it as his adult language and transmits only it to his children: it comes to be the native dialect of a growing upper layer of the population.

Both in the gradual assimilation of lesser dialects and in the conversion of individuals and families to standard speech, the result is usually imperfect and is to be described as sub-standard or, in the favorable case, as provincially colored standard (§ 3.5). The evaluation of these types varies in different countries: in England they are counted inferior and their speakers are driven toward a more rigid standardization, but in the United States or in Germany, where the standard language belongs to no one local group, the standard is less rigid and a vaguely-defined range of varieties enjoys equal prestige. The English which the first settlers brought to America consisted, apparently, of provincialized types of the standard language and of sub-standard, rather than of local dialects. The characteristic features of sub-standard American English seem to be general features of dialectal and sub-standard British English, rather than importations from any special British local dialects.

27. 6. The study of written records tells us little about the centralization of speech and the rise of standard languages, not only because the conventions of writing develop to a large extent independently of actual speech, but also because they are more rapidly standardized and then actually influence the standardizing of speech. We have seen that even the early written notations of a language tend to use uniform graphs which soon become traditional (§ 17.7). The spellings of medieval manuscripts seem very diverse to the modern student, yet closer inspection shows that they are largely conventional. At the end of the Middle Ages, as the use of writing increases, the provincial types of orthography become more and more fixed. After the invention of printing and with the spread of literacy, the convention grows both more unified and more rigid; at last come grammars and dictionaries whose teachings supplement the example that everyone has before him in the shape of printed books. Schooling becomes more common, and insists upon conventional style.

This development conceals from us the actual centralization of the spoken language. The historian has to deal constantly with two opposite possibilities. The written convention, at bottom, reflects the forms that have prestige in actual speech; on the other hand, it conventionalizes much more rapidly and affects the prestige of rival spoken forms. The decisive events occur in the spoken language, yet the written style, once it has seized upon a form, retains it more exclusively, and may then weight the scales in its favor. We get a glimpse of the state of affairs in the spoken language from occasional aberrant spellings or from rimes. Thus, occasional spellings and rimes show us a rivalry in standard English between pronunciations with [aj] and with [ɔj] in words like *oil, boil, join;* the decisive victory, in the last two centuries, of the latter type is doubtless due to its agreement with the spelling; we may contrast the still unsettled fluctuation in similar matters where the spelling does not exert pressure, such as [a] versus [ɛ] in American *rather,* [ɑː] versus [ɛ] in British *lather*.

In syntax and vocabulary the message of the written record is unmistakable, and it exerts a tremendous effect upon the standard language. In Old English and to this day in sub-standard English, certain negative forms require a negative adverb with a finite verb: *I don't want none;* the habit of the standard language seems to have arisen first in writing, as an imitation of

Latin syntax. Everyone has had the experience of starting to speak a word and then realizing that he does not know how to say it, because he has seen it only in writing. Some words have become obsolete in actual speech and have then been restored, from written sources: thus, *sooth, guise, prowess, paramour, behest, caitiff, meed, affray* were revived by eighteenth-century poets.

We get a clearer notion of the influence of written notation in cases where it leads to actual changes in the language. Now and then a reviver of ancient forms misunderstands his text and produces a *ghost-word*. Thus, *anigh* 'near' and *idlesse* 'idleness' are pseudo-antique formations made by nineteenth-century poets. In Hamlet's famous speech, *bourne* means 'limit,' but moderns, misunderstanding this passage, use *bourne* in the sense of 'realm.' Chaucer's phrase *in derring do that longeth to a knight* 'in daring to do what is proper for a knight,' was misunderstood by Spenser, who took *derring-do* to be a compound meaning 'brave actions' and succeeded in introducing this ghost-form into our elevated language. Misinterpretation of an old letter has led to the ghost-form *ye* for *the* (§ 17.7).

It is not only archaic writings, however, that lead to change in actual speech. If there is any rivalry between speech-forms, the chances are weighted in favor of the form that is represented by the written convention; consequently, if the written convention deviates from the spoken form, people are likely to infer that there exists a preferable variant that matches the written form. Especially, it would seem, in the last centuries, with the spread of literacy and the great influx of dialect-speakers and sub-standard speakers into the ranks of standard-speakers, the influence of the written form has grown — for these speakers, unsure of themselves in what is, after all, a foreign dialect, look to the written convention for guidance. The school-teacher, coming usually from a humble class and unfamiliar with the actual upper-class style, is forced to the pretense of knowing it, and exerts authority over a rising generation of new standard-speakers. A great deal of *spelling-pronunciation* that has become prevalent in English and in French, is due to this source. In a standard language like the German, which belongs originally to no one class or district, this factor is even more deep-seated: the spoken standard is there largely derived from the written.

In standard English an old [sjuː] developed to [ʃuw], as we see in the words *sure* [ʃuə] and *sugar* [ˈʃugə]. This change is reflected in occasional spellings since about 1600, such as *shuite* 'suit,' *shewtid* 'suited.' John Jones' *Practical Phonography* in 1701 prescribes the pronunciation with [ʃ] for *assume, assure, censure, consume, ensue, insure, sue, suet, sugar*. The modern [s] or [sj] in some of these words is doubtless a result of spelling-pronunciation. The same is probably true of [t, d] or [tj, dj] in words like *tune, due*, which replaces an authentic [tʃ, ʤ]; witness forms like *virtue* [ˈvəːtʃuw], *soldier* [ˈsowlʤə]. The British standard pronunciation [ˈinʤə] *India* is probably older than the now usual [ˈindjə]. Since old final [mb, ŋg], as in *lamb, long* have lost the stop, it may be that the preservation of the stop in [nd], as in *hand*, is due to spelling-pronunciation; in the fifteenth, sixteenth, and seventeenth centuries we find occasional spellings like *blyne* 'blind,' *thousan, poun*. The old [t] in forms like *often, soften, fasten* is being constantly re-introduced by the lower reaches of standard-speakers.

The most cogent evidence appears where purely graphic devices lead to novel speech-forms. Written abbreviations like *prof., lab., ec.* lead to spoken forms [prɔf, lɛb, ek] in students' slang for *professor, laboratory, economics*. These serve as models for further innovations, such as [kwɔd] for *quadrangle*, [dɔəm] for *dormitory*. The forms [ej em, pij em] come from the A.M. and P.M. of railroad time-tables. Other examples are [juw es ej] for *United States of America*, [aj sij] for *Illinois Central (Railroad)*, and [ej bij, ej em, em dij, pij ejtʃ dij] for academic degrees whose full designations, *Bachelor of Arts, Master of Arts, Doctor of Medicine, Doctor of Philosophy*, are actually less current; the abbreviations, moreover, have the word-order of the original Latin terms. French has forms like [te ɛs ɛf] for *télégraphe sans fil* 'wireless telegraphy, radio'; in Russia many new republican institutions are known by names read off from graphic abbreviations, such as [komsoˈmol] for [kommuniˈstitʃeskoj soˈjus moloˈdoʒi] 'communistic union of young people,' or [ftsik] for [fserosˈsijskoj tsenˈtralnoj ispolˈnitelnoj komiˈtet] 'all-Russian central executive committee.'

The influence of written notation works through the standard language, but features that are thus introduced may in time seep down into other levels of speech. Needless to say, this influence can be described only in a superficial sense as conservative or regularizing: the loans from written notation deviate from the results of ordinary development.

27. 7. The full effect of borrowing from written documents can be seen in the cases where written notation is carried on in some speech-form that deviates widely from the actual language.

Among the Romans, the upper-class dialect of the first century B.C. — the Latin that we find in the writings of Caesar and Cicero — became established as the proper style for written notation and for formal discourse. As the centuries passed, the real language came to differ more and more from this convention, but, as literate people were few, the convention was not hard to maintain: whoever learned to write, learned, as part of the discipline, to use the forms of classical Latin. By the fifth century A.D., an ordinary speaker must have needed serious schooling before he could produce writings in the conventional form. In reading aloud and in formal speech, the custom apparently was to follow the written form, giving each letter the phonetic value that was suggested by the current forms of the language. Thus, a graph like *centum* 'hundred,' which in the classical period represented the form ['kentum], was now pronounced successively as ['kentum, 'tʃentum, 'tsentum] and the like, in accordance with the phonetic development of the actual language, which spoke, in the respective cases, say ['kentu, 'tʃentu, 'tsentu]. To this day, in reading Latin, the different nationalities follow this practice: the Italian reads Latin *centum* as ['tʃentum] because in his own language he writes *cento* and speaks ['tʃento]; the Frenchman reads it as [sentɔm] because in his own language he writes *cent* and speaks [sã]; the German got his tradition of Latin-reading from a Romance tradition that used [ts] for *c* and accordingly reads Latin *centum* as ['tsentum]; in England one can still hear an "English" pronunciation of Latin, which says *centum* ['sentʌm], because it derives from a French tradition. These traditional pronunciations of Latin are now being superseded by a system which attempts to reconstruct the pronunciation of classical times.

This custom of carrying on written and formal or learned discourse in classical Latin passed, with Christianity, to non-Latin countries. Records in the actual Romance languages, or in Celtic or Germanic, begin round the year 700; they are scarce at first and become copious only in the twelfth and thirteenth centuries; until some time after the invention of printing, Latin books remain in the majority. Since Latin is still the official language of the Roman Catholic church, we may say that its use as a written and formal language persists to the present day.

As soon as classical Latin had begun to antiquate, persons who had not been sufficiently schooled, were sure to make mistakes in writing it. In the non-Latin countries this was true, of course, from the moment when Latin-writing was introduced. As to the thoroughness of the training, there were differences of time and place. The Latin written in Merovingian France, from the sixth to the eighth centuries, is decidedly unclassical, and reveals many characteristics of the authors' spoken language — the language whose later form we call French. In the ninth century, under Charles the Great, there came a revival of schooling: our texts return to a far more conventional Latin. Needless to say that in the Romance countries, and to some extent, perhaps, even in the others, errors in Latin-writing give us information about the actual language spoken by the authors. We have already seen that earlier scholars misconstrued this situation, mistaking changes in Latin-writing for linguistic change and drawing the moral that linguistic changes were due to ignorance and carelessness and represented a kind of decay (§ 1.4). Another error has proved more tenacious — namely, that of viewing the "medieval Latin" of our documents as an ordinary language. When we find a new form in these documents, there is only a remote possibility that this form represents an actual tradition of a classical Latin form; in by far the most instances, it is either a new-formation on the basis of classical Latin, or a latinization of some spoken form. Thus, the form *quiditas* 'whatness, characteristic quality' which appears in medieval Latin-writing, is roughly constructed on the analogies of classical Latin, and does not reflect any spoken form either of classical or of medieval times. The form *mansionaticum* 'place for a feudal lord to stop over night; domestic establishment' does not evidence the use of this form in classical Latin: it is merely a latinization of an actually spoken Old French *masnage* (or of its pre-French antecedent), which appears in later French as *mesnage*, modern *ménage* [menaːʒ] 'household'; English *manage* is borrowed from a derived verb, French *ménager*. The latinization is correct, to be sure, in the sense that *masnage* is a morphologic combination whose elements, if we put them back into classical Latin form, would have combined as *$mansi\bar{o}n\bar{a}ticum$:

the medieval scribe hit upon the historically correct Latin equivalents, although, actually, classical Latin formed no such combination. When we read a perfect tense form *presit* 'he took' in Merovingian documents, we should do wrong to call this the ancestor of forms like Italian *prese* ['prese] 'he took,' or French *prit* [pri]; it is merely an error in Latin-writing, on the part of a scribe who was not familiar enough with the classical Latin form *prehendit* 'he took,' and wrote instead a pseudo-Latin form based on his spoken usage. This error tells us that the scribe's language already employed the new-formation of the type Latin *prensit, which underlies the Romance forms and probably dates from a very early time, but it would be a grave methodic confusion to say that the Romance forms are derived from the "medieval Latin form." Again, when we find in Latin documents of German provenience a word *muta* 'toll,' it would be a naïve error to see in this "medieval Latin" word the source of Old High German *muta* 'toll' (§ 25.5); the writer merely used the German technical term in Latin-writing, because he knew no exact equivalent; one writer even speaks of *nullum teloneum neque quod lingua theodisca muta vocatur* 'no toll or what is in German called *muta*.' Moreover, we find the derivatives *mutarius, mutnarius* 'toll-taker' the latter with an analogic *-n-* that is peculiar to German morphology (modern *Mautner*). In sum, then, the medieval Latin-writer's deviations from classical Latin usage may throw light upon his actual speech, but dare not be confused with the antecedents of the latter, even in cases where the scribe succeeded in making a correct latinization.

27. 8. We find, now, that at all times, and especially with the modern spread of education, the Romance peoples introduced into their formal speech and then into ordinary levels, expressions from book-Latin in the phonetic form of the traditional reading-pronunciation. These borrowings from the written language are known as *learned words*, or, by the French term, as *mots savants* [mo savã]. After a book-Latin word came into current spoken use, it was subject, of course, to the normal changes which thereafter occurred in the language; however, these were sometimes followed by re-shaping in the direction of the bookish form. Many a Latin word appears in a Romance language both in its normally developed modern form, as a so-called *popular word*, and in a half-modernized Latin (or pseudo-Latin) form, as a learned word.

Latin *redemptionem* [redempti'o:nem] 'redemption' appears, by normal development, as modern French *rançon* [rãsõ] 'ransom' (English *ransom* is a loan from Old French), but, as a borrowing from the written form, in modern French *rédemption* [redãpsjõ] 'redemption.' At the time of bookish borrowings, the Frenchman, when reading Latin, used a pronunciation (based, as we have seen, upon the actual linguistic correspondences) which rendered a graph like *redemptionem* by a pronunciation, say, of [redɛmp'(t)sjo:nɛm]: the differences between this and the present-day French [redãpsjõ] are due to subsequent changes in the French language. Only some — perhaps only a minority — of the learned words actually went through this development, but on the model of those that did, one re-shapes any new ones that may be taken from the books; thus, if an educated Frenchman wanted to take up the Latin *procrastinationem* 'procrastination,' he would render it, in accordance with these models, as *procrastination* [prɔkrastinasjõ].

Other examples of twofold development are: Latin *fabricam* ['fabrikam] 'factory' > French *forge* [fɔrʒ] 'forge,' learned *fabrique* [fabrik] 'factory'; Latin *fragile* ['fragile] 'fragile' > French *frêle* [frɛ:l] 'frail,' learned *fragile* [fraʒil] 'fragile'; Latin *securum* [se:'ku:rum] 'secure' > French *sûr* [sy:r] 'sure,' Latin *securitatem* [se:ku:ri'ta:tɛm] > French *sûreté* [syrte] 'sureness, guarantee,' learned *sécurité* [sekyrite] 'security.'

Sometimes the book-word got into the language early enough to undergo some sound-change which gives it a superficially normal look. Thus Latin *capitulum* [ka'pitulum] 'heading' was taken into French speech early enough to share in the development [ka > tʃa > ʃa], and appears in modern French as *chapitre* [ʃapitr] 'chapter.' The [r] for Latin [l] is due apparently to an adaptation of the type usually classed as aberrant sound-change (§ 21.10); doubtless quite a few such changes are really due to re-shapings of bookish words that presented an unusual aspect. In other cases, a bookish word borrowed after a sound-change, is still, by way of adaptation, put into a form that partly or wholly imitates the effects of this change. Thus, a Latin *discipulum* [dis'kipulum] 'disciple, pupil' would give by normal development a modern Italian *[de'ʃeppjo]; this does not exist, but the learned loan in Italian partly apes these vowel-changes; it is not *[di'ʃipulo], but *discepolo* [di'ʃepolo]. The number of learned and semi-learned forms in the western Romance languages is very large, especially as the standard languages have extended the analogy to the point where almost any Latin or Greco-Latin word can be modernized.

Among the French forms that were borrowed by English during the period after the Norman Conquest, there were many of these learned French borrowings from the Latin of books. The literate Englishman, familiar with both French and Latin, got into the habit of using Latin words in the form they had as French *mots savants*. We have seen how the Englishman made his own adaptations (§ 25.4). In later time, the English writer continued to use Latin words. In making these loans, we alter the Latin graph and pronounce it in accordance with a fairly well-fixed set of habits; these habits are composed of (1) the adaptations and phonetic renderings that were conventional in the French use of book-Latin words round the year 1200, (2) adaptations that have become conventional in the English usage of Latin-French forms, and (3) phonetic renderings due to English sound-changes that have occurred since the Norman time. Thus, the Latin *procrastinationem*, which is not current in French, is borrowed from Latin books into English as *procrastination* [prə‚krɛsti'nejʃn], in accordance with the above set of analogies. Under (1) we have the fact that French borrows its Latin words not in nominative singular form (Latin *procrastinatio*), but in accusative or ablative form, with loss of ending: had the word been used, as a bookish loan, in the Old French of 1200 to 1300, it would have appeared as *procrastination *[prokrastina'sjoːn], with phonetic changes which, like the selection of the case-form, are due ultimately, to the model of non-learned French words. The remaining deviations of the actual English form, namely [ɛ] for *a* in the second syllable, [ej] for *a* in the third, [ʃ] for *ti* before vowel, and the weakening of the end of the word to [-ņ], are modeled on the phonetic changes which have been undergone by words of similar structure that really were borrowed during the Norman period, such as Latin *nationem* > Old French [na'sjoːn] > English *nation* ['nejʃn]. Finally, the shift of accent to pre-suffixal position copies an adaptation which English made in its actual loans from French. In the same way, when we borrow from Latin books the verb *procrastinare*, we render it as *procrastinate*, adding the suffix *-ate* in accordance with an adaptation that has become habitual in English (§ 23.5).

Both the Romance languages and English can borrow, in this way, not only actual Latin words, but even medieval scribal coinages, such as English *quiddity* from scholastic *quiditas*. We even invent new words on the general model of Latin morphology: *eventual, immoral, fragmentary* are examples of learned words whose models do not occur in Latin. Since the Romans borrowed words from Greek, we can do the same, altering the Greek word in accordance with the Roman's habit of latinization, plus the Frenchman's habit of gallicizing Latin book-words, plus the English habit of anglicizing French learned words. Ancient Greek [philoso'phia:] thus gives an English [fi'lɔsəfi] *philosophy*. As in the case of Latin, we are free to coin Greek words: *telegraphy* represents, with the same modifications, a non-existent ancient Greek *[te:legra'phia:] 'distance-writing.'

Needless to say, we sometimes confuse the analogies. We render ancient Greek [th] in English, against the custom of the Romance languages, by [θ], as in [mu:tholo'gia:] > *mythology*. It is true that ancient Greek [th] has changed to [θ] in modern Greek, but the English habit is probably independent of this and due merely to the spelling. Moreover, medieval scribes, knowing *th* as an abstruse Greek graph and pronouncing it simply as *t* [t], occasionally put it into words that were not Greek at all. Thus, the name of the Goths, old Germanic *['goto:z], appears in medieval Latin-writing not only as *goti* but also as *gothi*, and it is from the latter graph that we get our pronunciation of *Goth, Gothic* with [θ]; the use of [θ] in *Lithuanian* is a modern instance of the same pseudo-learned pedantry. The same thing has happened in English to an ordinary Latin word, *auctorem* > French *autor* (modern *auteur* [otœ:r]) > Middle English *autor;* in English it was spelled *author* and finally got the spelling-pronunciation with [θ].

The habit of learned borrowing from the classical languages has spread to the other languages of Europe; in each one, the learned borrowing is accompanied by adaptations which reflect the circumstances of the contact, immediate or mediate, with the Romance-speaker's use of book-Latin. Thus, the German, who says *Nation* [na'tsjo:n], *Station* [ʃta'tsjo:n], could conceivably borrow a *Prokrastination *[prokrıstina'tsjo:n], — and similar habits exist in the other languages of Europe.

This whole history finds its parallel, including even the graphic archaization of spoken forms (like the medieval scribe's *mansionaticum, presit*), in the use of Sanskrit in India. In the languages of India, graphic loans from Sanskrit are known as *tatsama* ('like-to-it'). Like the *mots savants* of Europe, these formations show us written notation exercising an influence upon language.

CHAPTER 28

APPLICATIONS AND OUTLOOK

28. 1. The normal speaker faces a linguistic problem whenever he knows variant forms which differ only in connotation — for instance, *it's I* and *it's me*. He states this problem in the question, "How shall I talk?" In most cases he has no difficulty, because the social connotations are obvious, and the speaker knows that some of the variants, (e.g. *I done it*) have an undesirable connotation and lead people to deal unkindly with the user. We express this traditionally by saying that the undesirable variant is "incorrect" or "bad English" or even "not English" at all. These statements, of course, are untrue: the undesirable variants are not foreigners' errors, but perfectly good English; only, they are not used in the speech of socially more privileged groups, and accordingly have failed to get into the repertory of standard speech-forms. Even in smaller and less stratified speech-communities, which have segregated no standard speech-forms, the speaker usually knows which variants will do him better service.

When there is no obvious difference between the variant forms, there should be no problem at all, since it evidently will make no difference which variant the speaker uses. A speaker who is in doubt whether to say *it's I* or *it's me*, has heard these two variants from approximately the same kinds of fellow-speakers, since otherwise they would bear clear-cut connotations of desirability and undesirability. Since his associates, then, use both forms, his standing will not be affected by his use of one or the other. Nevertheless, people devote time and energy to such problems, and suffer anxiety on account of them.

The background of our popular ideas about language is the fanciful doctrine of the eighteenth-century "grammarians." This doctrine, still prevalent in our schools, brands all manner of forms as "incorrect," regardless of fact. Having heard the term "incorrect" applied to variants which bear no undesirable connotation, the speaker grows diffident and is ready to suspect almost any speech-form of "incorrectness."

APPLICATIONS AND OUTLOOK 497

It would not have been possible for "grammarians" to bluff a large part of our speech-community, and they would not have undertaken to do so, if the public had not been ready for the deception. Almost all people, including even most native speakers of a standard language, know that someone else's type of language has a higher prestige. At the top, of course, there should be a most privileged group, whose members are sure of themselves in speech as in all other issues of mannerism; in the English-speaking community, this should be the British upper class, which speaks the "public school" variety of southern English. One may suspect, however, that even within this group, the model of printed books and the minor variations of modish cliques, make many speakers unsure. Snobbery, the performance of acts which belong to a more privileged group, often takes the shape, therefore, of unnatural speech: the speaker utters forms which are not current among his associates, because he believes (very often, mistakenly) that these forms are favored by some "better" class of speakers. He, of course, falls an easy prey to the authoritarian.

It is no accident that the "grammarians" arose when they did. During the eighteenth and nineteenth centuries our society went through great changes: many persons and families rose into relatively privileged positions and had to change from non-standard to standard speech. The problem that faces the speaker who makes this change, will concern us later; we see now that the authoritarian doctrine battened on the diffidence of speakers whose background was non-standard — speakers who were afraid to trust the speech-forms they had heard from their parents and grandparents. In the United States this is complicated by the fact that even many native speakers of standard English have a foreign background and are easily frightened into thinking that a speech-form which is natural to them is actually "not English."

Indeed, diffidence as to one's speech is an almost universal trait. The observer who sets out to study a strange language or a local dialect, often gets data from his informants only to find them using entirely different forms when they speak among themselves. They count these latter forms inferior and are ashamed to give them to the observer. An observer may thus record a language entirely unrelated to the one he is looking for.

The tendency to revise one's speech is universal, but the revision consists normally in adopting forms which one hears from one's fellows. The doctrine of our grammarians has had very little effect in the way of banishing or establishing specific speech-forms, but it has set up among literate people the notion that forms which one has not heard may be "better" than those which one actually hears and speaks. The only danger that threatens the native speaker of a standard language is artificiality: if he is snobbish, priggish, or timid, he may fill his speech (at least, when he is on his good behavior) with spelling-pronunciations and grotesque "correct" forms. The speaker to whom the standard language is native, will hardly ever find good reason for replacing a form that is natural to him. Variants such as *it's I: it's me* have been used for centuries in the upper levels of English speech; there is no reason why anyone should make himself uncomfortable about them.

It is not often that a speaker has to choose between genuine and relatively well-defined variants within the standard language. In the United States, the speaker of Central-Western standard English, who uses the vowel [ɛ] indifferently in *man, mad, mat* and in *laugh, bath, can't,* is confronted by a higher-toned type of the standard language, which uses a different vowel [a] in words of the latter set. Whether he tries to acquire this more elegant feature, will depend upon how highly he values conformity with the speakers who use it. If he is placed entirely among them, say, by residence in New England or in Great Britain, he may naturally fall into the new habit. One does well to remember that the change is not easy to make, and that a novice is likely to put the new feature into places where it does not belong, producing outlandish hyperforms, such as [maːn] for [mɛn] *man*. Unless the speaker constantly hears the preferred type from his associates, he had better not meddle with it. Unnatural speech is not pleasing. In England, where provincially tinged types of the standard language are inferior to the "public-school" type, this question may wear a different aspect.

As to non-distinctive features of speech, the situation is different. Although they are habitual, they do not form part of the signaling-system, and are subject to divergence and improvement. Just as one may be considerate and agreeable in other mannerisms, one may speak in a pleasant "tone of voice" — that is, with a pleasant regulation of non-distinctive acoustic features. The same may be said of the combination of non-distinctive and semantic features

APPLICATIONS AND OUTLOOK

which we call *style;* here too, one may, without affectation, use apt and agreeable forms. Unfortunately our handbooks of rhetoric confuse this with the silly issue of "correctness."

For the native speaker of sub-standard or dialectal English, the acquisition of standard English is a real problem, akin to that of speaking a foreign language. To be told that one's habits are due to "ignorance" or "carelessness" and are "not English," is by no means helpful. Our schools sin greatly in this regard. The non-standard speaker has the task of replacing some of his forms (e.g. *I seen it*) by others (*I saw it*) which are current among people who enjoy greater privilege. An unrealistic attitude — say, of humility — is bound to impede his progress. The unequal distribution of privilege which injured him in childhood, is a fault of the society in which he lives. Without embarrassment, he should try to substitute standard forms which he knows from actual hearing, for those which he knows to be non-standard. In the beginning he runs a risk of using hyper-urbanisms; such as *I have saw it* (arising from the proportion *I seen it : I saw it = I have seen it : x*). At a later stage, he is likely to climb into a region of stilted verbiage and over-involved syntax, in his effort to escape from plain dialect; he should rather take pride in simplicity of speech and view it as an advantage that he gains from his non-standard background.

28. 2. Society deals with linguistic matters through the school system. Whoever is accustomed to distinguish between linguistic and non-linguistic behavior, will agree with the criticism that our schools deal too much with the former, drilling the child in speech-response phases of arithmetic, geography, or history, and neglecting to train him in behavior toward his actual environment. In the simpler community of a few generations ago, matters of art and science were remote, and mechanical and social processes worked on a scale which placed them (or seemed to place them) within direct everyday observation: the child learned practical matters without the help of the school, which needed to train him only in the three R's. The schools have clung to this pattern, in spite of the complexities of modern life. Attempts at improvement have not been encouraging: practical (that is, non-linguistic) matters have been introduced in the shape of ill-considered fads. In view of our schools' concentration on verbal discipline, it is surprising to see that they are utterly benighted in linguistic matters. How training is best imparted must be for the pedagogue to determine.

but it is evident that no pedagogic skill will help a teacher who does not know the subject which is to be taught.

Our unfortunate attitude toward matters of standard and non-standard speech ("correct English") is largely kept up by our schools. Their attitude is authoritarian; fanciful dogmas as to what is "good English" are handed down by educational authorities and individual teachers who are utterly ignorant of what is involved — dogmas such as the *shall*-and-*will* rules or the alleged "incorrectness" of well-established locutions (*I've got it*) or constructions (*the house he lived in*). Meanwhile the differences between standard and prevalent non-standard forms (such as *I saw it : I seen it*) are made the subject not so much of rational drill as of preachment about "ignorance," "carelessness," and "bad associations." All of this, moreover, is set in a background of pseudo-grammatical doctrine, which defines the categories of the English language as philosophical truths and in philosophical terms ("a noun is the name of a person, place, or thing," "the subject is that talked about," and so on).

The chief aim, of course, is literacy. Although our writing is alphabetic, it contains so many deviations from the alphabetic principle as to present a real problem, whose solution has been indefinitely postponed by our educators' ignorance of the relation of writing to speech. Nothing could be more discouraging than to read our "educationalists' " treatises on methods of teaching children to read. The size of this book does not permit a discussion of their varieties of confusion on this subject. The primers and first reading books which embody these doctrines, present the graphic forms in a mere hodge-podge, with no rational progression. At one extreme, there is the metaphysical doctrine which sets out to connect the graphic symbols directly with "thoughts" or "ideas" — as though these symbols were correlated with objects and situations and not with speech-sounds. At the other extreme are the so-called "phonic" methods, which confuse learning to read and write with learning to speak, and set out to train the child in the production of sounds — an undertaking complicated by the crassest ignorance of elementary phonetics.

Pedagogues must determine how reading and writing are to be taught. Their study of eye-movements is an instance of progress in this direction. On the other hand, they cannot hope for success until they inform themselves as to the nature of writing. The person who learns to read, acquires the habit of responding to the sight of letters by the utterance of phonemes. This does not mean that he is learning to utter phonemes; he can be taught to read only after his phonemic habits are thoroughly established. Of course, he cannot utter phonemes in isolation; to make him respond, say, to the letter *b* by uttering the phoneme [b], which in the English phonetic pattern cannot be spoken alone, is to create a difficulty. The co-ordination between letters and phonemes, accordingly, has to be established as an analogic process by practice on graphs in which the symbols have a uniform value, such as *bat, cat, fat, hat, mat, pat, rat, sat — can, Dan, fan, man, pan, ran, tan, van — bib, fib, rib* — and so on. The real factor of difficulty is the host of irregular spellings which will remain, no matter what values are assigned as regular. Two devices obviously demand to be tried. One is to teach children to read a phonetic transcription, and to turn to traditional writing only after the essential reading habit has been set up. The other is to begin with graphs that contain only one phonemic value for each letter — sets such as were illustrated above — and either to postpone other graphs until the elementary habit has been fixed, or else to introduce them, in some rationally planned way, at earlier points. The irregular graphs should be presented systematically (e.g. silent *gh: fight, light, might, night, right, sight, tight; a* for [ɔ:] before *l: all, ball, call, fall, gall, hall, tall, wall, halt, malt, salt, bald, false*). It may prove advantageous to use some distinguishing mark (such as different colors) for silent letters and for letters in irregular phonemic values. The methods of procedure, the order of presentation, and the various minor devices can be determined only by experiment; from the outset, however, one must know what one is trying to do.

28. 3. The difficulty of our spelling greatly delays elementary education, and wastes even much time of adults. When one sees the admirably consistent orthographies of Spanish, Bohemian, or Finnish, one naturally wishes that a similar system might be adopted for English. It is not true that to change our orthography would be to "change our language": our language is the same, regardless of how we write it. In the long run, to be sure, the orthography does cause some linguistic alterations (§ 27.6); esthetically — and this is here the only consideration — we should gain by eliminating the factor of ugly spelling-pronunciations.

It is an error, also, to suppose that English is somehow an "unphonetic language," which cannot be consistently symbolized by alphabetic writing; like all languages, English moves within a precisely definable range of phonemic units. It would be necessary only to reach some compromise between the regional types of standard English pronunciation; thus, the [r] of types like Central-Western American would have to be kept, because it gives the simplest phonemic analysis for forms like British *red* [red], *far* [fɑː], *bird* [bəːd], *bitter* ['bitə]. On the other hand, the Southern British distinction of [ɛ] as in *bad* and [ɑ] as in *bath* would evidently have to be maintained. It is wrong to suppose that writing would be unintelligible if homonyms (e.g. *pear, pair, pare* or *piece, peace*) were spelled alike; writing which reproduces the phonemes of speech is as intelligible as speech. Moreover, our present irregular writing sins exactly in this respect by using identical graphs for phonemically different forms, such as *read* [rijd, red], *lead* [lijd, led], or *tear* [tiɔ, tɛə]. Literary people entertain the notion that graphic eccentricities, such as the spellings of *ghost* or *rhyme*, somehow contribute to the connotation of words; for a small minority of over-literate persons they undoubtedly produce the sort of bookish connotation which good writers try to avoid. There would be no serious difficulty about devising a simple, effective orthography for all types of standard English; the use of it would save an enormous amount of time and labor, and, far from injuring our language, would raise the general level of standard speech, both by reassuring native speakers of non-standard and by removing the tendency to spelling-pronunciations.

The real difficulty is economic and political. A new orthography would within fifty years or so turn our whole present stock of printed texts into something difficult and antiquated; for our grandchildren the printed forms of today would bear the same quaint connotation that Chaucerian spellings bear for us. The confusion and expense of reproducing all the more useful texts would be enormous. Moreover, the change itself, extending to every printer and every school-teacher (not to speak of the public at large), would demand a uniformity of co-operation in changing deep-seated habits that far transcends our present political and administrative powers. Some years ago there was a movement to "reform" our spelling by a series of lesser changes. Small

APPLICATIONS AND OUTLOOK

changes have worked well for orthographies like the Spanish, German, Dutch, Swedish, or Russian, where the irregularities were few and could be removed or noticeably lessened by a few simple adjustments. In our case, however, fragmentary changes can only increase the trouble; for instance, the spelling of no English word in the present orthography ends with the letter *v;* to omit a final silent *e* after *v* in some words (writing, for instance, *hav* for *have*), but not in others, is a doubtful expedient. As long as our main habits are kept up, minor alterations only make things harder. We may expect that at some time in the future our social organism will reach a degree of co-ordination and flexibility where a concerted change becomes possible, or else that mechanical devices for reproducing speech will supersede our present habits of writing and printing.

28. 4. At a later stage in schooling we encounter the many-sided problem of foreign-language teaching. For the sake of what is called cultural tradition or continuity, some part of the population ought to be familiar with ancient languages, especially with Latin and Greek. For the sake of contact with other nations, and, especially, to keep up with technologic and scientific progress, a fairly large body of persons must understand modern foreign languages. The large part of the work of high schools and colleges that has been devoted to foreign-language study, includes an appalling waste of effort: not one pupil in a hundred learns to speak and understand, or even to read a foreign language. The mere disciplinary or "transfer" value of learning the arbitrary glossemes of a foreign language can be safely estimated at almost nil. The realization of all this has led to much dispute, particularly as to the methods of foreign-language teaching. The various "methods" which have been elaborated differ greatly in the mere exposition, but far less in actual classroom practice. The result depends very little upon the theoretical basis of presentation, and very much upon the conditions of teaching and on the competence of the teacher; it is only necessary to avoid certain errors to which our tradition inclines.

A minority of the population stays in school long enough to reach the stage where foreign-language instruction begins. In the old days, this minority was condemned *en bloc* to study Latin and Greek. The bitter struggle against the abandonment of this custom seems unwarranted, in view of the fact that the pupils learned to read neither of these languages. There remains the fairly widespread four years' Latin course of our high schools; apart from other factors, its ineffectiveness is explained by the fact that scarcely any of the teachers have a reading knowledge of Latin. The modern foreign languages are better taught, because some of the teachers know the subject; here too, however, the results are scarcely good enough to counter a movement for abolishing the instruction. Even as it is, very few persons, even of our middle-class population, have a useful command of any foreign language. Whether the number of such persons should be increased, and, if so, how the selection is to be made, is a large-scale educational problem. We are far from the point where this is determined by the pupil's aptitude rather than by his parents' economic means, combined with chance or whim. In particular, we could gain by having children of foreign background study the language they had heard at home.

Another question of general bearing is that of the student's age. Our eight years' grammar-school course represents a downright waste of something like four years of every child's time. The European, after four or five years of elementary schooling, enters upon an eight or nine years' course in a secondary school, in which he obtains his general education; at the end of this, he is ready to take up professional studies. At about the same age, the American has had only four years of high-school study, and, to get a general education, must still go through a four years' college course. In all respects except formal education, he is too mature to find satisfaction in general and elementary studies; accordingly, he turns, instead, to the snobberies and imbecilities which make a by-word of the American college. The four years' delay which appears plainly in the history of the students who go on into professional study, is as serious, if less apparent, for the great majority who do not, and works most adversely upon the effectiveness of foreign-language study. The eight years' grammar-school course has become something of a vested interest of administrators and educational experts; there seems to be little hope of beginning secondary-school studies, and foreign languages in particular, in the fifth or sixth year of schooling. Yet it is probably to this earlier beginning that we must attribute the vastly greater success of foreign-language instruction in Europe. The formal and repetitious nature of this study, the necessarily simple content of the reading-matter, and the need of make-believe, all work in favor of young children. The pupil who takes up his first foreign language at high-school age or later, is likely to substitute analysis for mere repetition, and thus to meet halfway the incompetent teacher, who talks about the foreign language instead of using it. Between the two, they have kept alive the eighteenth-century scheme of pseudo-grammatical doctrine and puzzle-solving translation.

The goal to be sought in an ancient language, and, for many students, in a modern, is the ability to read. This circumstance serves too often as an excuse for slovenly teaching. A student who does not know the sound of a language, finds great difficulty in learning to read it. He cannot remember the foreign forms so long as they figure for him as a mere jumble of letters. Aside from the esthetic factor, a clear-cut set of phonetic habits, whether perfectly correct or not, is essential to fluent and accurate reading. For the students who are to speak the foreign language — and they should be more numerous than they are — this question requires no argument.

The matter that is to be presented, the thousands of morphemes and tagmemes of the foreign language, can be mastered only by constant repetition. The lexical phase, being the more extensive, presents the greater difficulty. Every form that is introduced should be repeated many times. Many of our text-books are profligate in their introduction of new words, and fail to let them recur in later lessons. Recent experience has shown the tremendous gain that results from control of the lexical matter: text-book-writer and teacher should know exactly when a new lexical unit (in most instances, a new word) is introduced, and keep exact track of its recurrences, which must be frequent. Word-formation, the stepchild of traditional school grammar, must play an important part in the presentation of some languages, such as Latin or German. The meaning of the foreign forms is hard to convey. Translation into the native language is bound to mislead the learner, because the semantic units of different languages do not match, and because the student, under the practised stimulus of the native form, is almost certain to forget the foreign one. The nucleus of the foreign language should be presented in connection with practical objects and situations — say, of the classroom or of pictures. Much can be gathered from the contexts of reading, provided the native speech-forms are kept as remotely as possible in the background.

Grammatical doctrine should be accepted only where it passes a test of usefulness, and even there it should be re-shaped to suit the actual need. In Latin or German the case-forms, and in Latin or French the verb-forms, are essential to understanding, but the traditional presentation is uneconomic and confusing. The memorizing of paradigms, especially, produces collocations of forms that bear so little relation to actual speech as to be nearly worthless.

It is essential, in all linguistic phases of education, that the practical bearing be kept in view. The content of what is read in a foreign language should show the life and history of the foreign nation. Above all, what is read or spoken should be well within the competence of the learner; solving puzzles is not language-learning.

28. 5. The application of linguistics to the recording and transmission of speech, as in stenography or codes, depends largely upon the phonemic principle and requires no special discussion. There is one undertaking, however, which would seem to demand all the resources of our knowledge, and more to boot, and that is the setting up of a universal language. The advantages of an international medium of communication are self-evident. An international language would not involve anyone's giving up his native speech; it would mean only that in every nation there would be many foreign speakers of the international language. We should need to agree only upon some one language which would be studied in every country. It has been argued that actually existing languages are difficult and that the adoption of any one would give rise to jealousy; accordingly, various artificial languages have been devised. The only type that has met with any success is that of simplified Latin or Romance, especially in the shape of Esperanto. Languages of this sort are semi-artificial. They retain the chief grammatical categories of the languages of western Europe. They are morphologically simpler than actual languages; the syntax and the semantic pattern are taken quite naïvely from the western European type, with not enough analysis to insure uniformity. In the semantic sphere, especially, we can scarcely hope to set up a rational or stable scheme; there are no natives to whom we could go for decisions. The political difficulty of getting any considerable number of people all over the world to study, say, Esperanto, will probably prove so great that some natural language will outstrip it.

English is the most likely choice; it is handicapped chiefly by its irregular written notation.

28. 6. The movement for a universal language is an attempt to make language more useful extensively. One might expect the linguist to try also to increase the usefulness of language intensively, by working out speech-forms that will lead to valuable responses in practical life. However, it seems that all languages are flexible enough to provide such speech-forms without artificial aid. We can coin, and define scientific terms at will; mathematical reasoning can be translated into any language. The problem is not one of linguistic structure, but of practical application. The logic and dialectics of ancient and medieval times represent a mistaken effort to arrive at pregnantly useful formulae of discourse. Meanwhile, a genuine system of this kind has grown up, in the shape of mathematics. If we can state a situation in mathematical terms, mathematics enables us to re-state it in various simplified shapes, and these, in the end, lead to a useful practical response. These procedures, however, depend upon our understanding of the practical world. The tasks of stating a situation in mathematical (usually, in numerical) terms, and of deciding what types of re-statement are consistent (that is, lead to a correct response), are independent of linguistic features. When we have defined *two* as 'one plus one,' *three* as 'two plus one,' and *four* as 'three plus one,' it is not the linguist who can tell us that we shall get into trouble if we now act on the statement that *two plus two equals three*. All that linguistics can do is to reveal the verbal character of mathematics and save us from mystical aberrations on this score.

If this is true of the relatively simple speech-forms that are involved in mathematical discourse, it holds good all the more of vaguer and more complicated forms of speech. Lexical and grammatical analysis cannot reveal the truth or falsity of a doctrine; linguistics can merely make us critical of verbal response habits. Linguistics cannot tell us whether it is helpful to subject one tenth of the children born into the community to desperate handicaps, because their parents failed to go through a ceremony of marriage. The linguist will merely note that this matter is hardly ever discussed and that until quite recently its mention was under a tabu. Assuming that certain practices are injurious, the linguist will observe that failure to react to them by speech (*evasion*) is a characteristic symptom. At a higher level, when such practices come into discussion, we often observe a speech-response that invokes some obviously valuable but irrelevant sanction, as when the Cree Indian says that he does not speak his sister's name because he *respects* her too much. This *appeal to a higher sanction* merges, at a later stage, into *rationalization,* a habit of discussing the practice in apparently reasonable ("common-sense" or "logical") terms.

Something more like a practical application of linguistics can be made in the analysis of popular (and philosophic-scholastic) beliefs that account for phenomena which in reality are due to language. It is remarkable that popular belief, the world over, exaggerates the effect of language in superstitious ways (magic formulae, charms, curses, name-tabu, and the like), but at the same time takes no account of its obvious and normal effects. When one person stimulates another by speech, popular belief deems the speech alone insufficient, and supposes that there is also a transference of some non-physical entity, an *idea* or *thought.* When a person describes an act by speech before performing it, popular belief is not satisfied with the obvious connection, but views the speech as the more immediate manifestation of a metaphysical *will* or *purpose,* which determines the subsequent act. The analogy is then transferred to the conduct of inanimate objects in the guise of *teleologic* explanations: trees strive toward the light; water seeks its own level; nature abhors a vacuum.

28. 7. Although the linguist cannot go far toward the explanation of practical things, he has the task of classifying linguistic forms wherever their meaning has been determined by some other science. Thus, we can vouch for the existence, in every language that has been studied, of a set of cardinal numbers, and we can investigate the grammatical structure of these forms, finding, for instance, that arrangements in groups of ten, *decimal* systems, are decidedly widespread. The anthropologist tells us at once that this is due to the habit of counting on one's fingers. Both the restriction of our extra-linguistic knowledge and, what concerns us more, our lack of accurate and complete information about the languages of the world, have so far frustrated attempts at general grammar and lexicology. Until we can carry on this investigation and use its results, we cannot pretend to any sound knowledge of communal forms of human behavior.

Adequate descriptive information about languages is a prerequisite for historical understanding. It is apparent even now that we can see historical change in human affairs most intimately in the change of language, but it is evident also, that we shall have to know far more both of practical (that is, extra-linguistic) events and of linguistic changes that have actually occurred, before we can reach the level of scientific classification and prediction. Even now it is clear that change in language tends toward shorter and more regularly constructed words: sound-change shortens the word, and analogic change replaces irregular derivatives by regular. The speed and the consistent direction of this process differ in different times and places. Starting from a common parent language, we find modern English with greatly shortened words and simple morphology, but Lithuanian with fairly long words and a complex morphology. The result of this simplification seems to be a greater number of words in response to like practical situations; modifying and relational features and substitute forms that were once expressed by affixes or other morphologic features, appear later in the shape of separate words. The ultimate outcome may be the state of affairs which we see in Chinese, where each word is a morpheme and every practical feature that receives expression receives it in the shape of a word or phrase.

The methods and results of linguistics, in spite of their modest scope, resemble those of natural science, the domain in which science has been most successful. It is only a prospect, but not hopelessly remote, that the study of language may help us toward the understanding and control of human events.

NOTES

Full titles of books and journals will be found in the Bibliography at the end of these Notes.

CHAPTER 1

History of linguistic studies: Pedersen, *Linguistic science.* Older period: Benfey. Indo-European studies: Delbrück, *Einleitung;* Streitberg, *Geschichte.* Germanic studies: Raumer; Paul, *Grundriss* 1.9; W. Streitberg and V. Michels in Streitberg, *Geschichte* 2.2. The history of a single scholastic tradition: Jellinek, *Geschichte der deutschen Grammatik.* Some interesting details in the first chapter of Oertel.

1..2. The ancients' philosophical views about language: Steinthal, *Geschichte.* The anecdote about the children in the park: Herodotus 2.2.

The etymology of *lithos* in *Eymologicon magnum* (ed. T. Gaisford, Oxford, 1848) 565.50; that of *lucus* from Quintilian 1.6.34, and in Lactantius Placidus' gloss on Statius, *Achilleis* 593 (ed. R. Jahnke, Leipzig, 1898, p. 502).

Greek grammarians: G. Uhlig, *Grammatici Graeci,* Leipzig, 1883 ff.; Herodian edited by A. Lentz, Leipzig, 1867 ff.

1. 3. Theories about the origin of language: Steinthal, *Ursprung;* Wundt, *Sprache* 2.628.

The epigram about etymology is attributed to Voltaire by Max Müller, *Lectures on the science of language; Second series* (London, 1864), p. 238; I have sought it in vain in Voltaire's writings.

Latin grammarians: H. Keil, *Grammatici Latini,* Leipzig, 1857 ff.; H. Funaioli, *Grammaticae Romanae fragmenta,* Leipzig, 1907.

Medieval work in Latin grammar: Wackernagel, *Vorlesungen* 1.22; Thurot.

The Port-Royal grammar was written by A. Arnauld and C. Lancelot; it appeared in Paris in 1660, a second edition in 1664, another in Brussels in 1676; I have seen only this last (at the Newberry Library, Chicago); modern reprints with additions appeared at Paris in 1803 and 1810.

Eighteenth-century normative grammar: Fries; Leonard (very full account). The *shall* and *will* doctrine: C. C. Fries in *PMLA* 40.963 (1925).

Pallas, Peter Simon, *Linguarum totius orbis vocabularia comparativa,* St. Petersburg, 1786-89, two volumes (Newberry Library, Chicago). I have not seen the second edition. An alphabetical index, anonymous (according to the Newberry Library catalog, by Theodor Jankovic von Mirijevo) under the title *Sravnitel'nyj slovar' vsex jazykov i narečij,* in four volumes, appeared in St. Petersburg, 1790-91. Vuk Stefanovich (Karadjich) published a supplement (*Dodatak*) at Beč in 1822, correcting the Serbian and adding Bulgarian forms (copy in Newberry Library).

Adelung-Vater's *Mithridates* was named after the first book of its kind, an alphabetical list of languages, with a very few specimens, by Konrad Gessner

(1516–65), which appeared in Zurich in 1555; a new edition of this, with a commentary by Kaspar Waser, Zurich, 1660 (both editions in Newberry Library).

Junius, F., *Quatuor D. N. Jesu Christi Euangeliorum versiones perantiquae duae*, Dordrecht, 1665.

Hickes, G., *Institutiones grammaticae Anglo-Saxonicae et Moesogothicae*, Oxford, 1689; *Antiquae literaturae septentrionalis libri duo (Linguarum vett. thesaurus)*, Oxford, 1705.

1. 5. On the philological-linguistic work of the Chinese, Karlgren, *Philology*. On Hindu grammar, Belvalkar; bibliography in *Lg* 5.267 (1929).

1. 6. Jones' address appeared in *Asiatick researches* (Calcutta, 1788) 1.422; this volume has been reprinted, repeatedly, as volume 1 of the *Transactions of the Royal Asiatic society of Bengal*.

1. 7. Etymology: Thurneysen; Thomas 1.

On Brugmann: W. Streitberg in *IJ* 7.143 (1921). On Delbrück: Hermann.

1. 8. The second edition (1886) of Paul's *Prinzipien* served as the basis for the excellent English adaptation by Strong-Logeman-Wheeler. On Paul's life and work: W. Streitberg in *IJ* 9.280 (1924).

1. 9. On Leskien: W. Streitberg in *IJ* 7.138 (1921); K. Brugmann in *Berichte Leipzig* 68.16 (1916). On Böhtlingk: B. Delbrück in *IF Anzeiger* 17.131 (1905). On de Saussure: A. Meillet in *BSL* 18.clxv (1913).

CHAPTER 2

Psychologists generally treat language as a side-issue. General discussion: Marett 130; Boas 1.5; Wundt, *Sprache;* Sapir; Allport; de Laguna; and, especially, Weiss.

2. 1. The term *philology*, in British and in older American usage, is applied not only to the study of culture (especially through literary documents), but also to linguistics. It is important to distinguish between *philology* (German *Philologie*, French *philologie*) and *linguistics* (German *Sprachwissenschaft*, French *linguistique*), since the two studies have little in common. On the confusion in English usage: H. Pedersen in *Litteris* 5.150 (1928); G. M. Bolling in *Lg* 5.148 (1929).

2. 4. The popular belief seems to be that in thinking we finally suppress the speech-movements altogether, like the horse in the story, that finally learned to go without fodder.

The use of numbers is characteristic of speech-activity at its best. Who would want to live in a world of pure mathematics? Mathematics is merely the best that *language* can do.

2. 5. The child's learning of language: Allport 132; Weiss 310. Almost nothing is known because observers report what the child says, but not what it has heard; so Stern; Preyer; Bühler. Learning to speak is the greatest feat in one's life: Jespersen, *Language* 103.

2. 8. Disturbances of speech: Kussmaul; Gutzmann, *Sprachheilkunde;* Wilson; Head; Travis.

2. 9. Gesture: Wundt, *Sprache* 1.143.

The universe symbolically reduced to library dimensions: A. P. Weiss in *Lg* 1.52 (1925).

NOTES

Chapter 3

3. 2. The largest speech-communities: Jespersen, *Growth* 252; L. Tesnière in Meillet, *Langues*. For the languages of India, Tesnière's figures deviate slightly from those of Grierson (volume 1); both estimates are based on the census of 1921.

3. 3. Sex-differences: Jespersen, *Language* 237; E. Sapir in *Donum Schrijnen* 79.

3. 9. Saer discusses children's shift of language in Wales. Saer uses the term *bilingual* of children who have shifted from Welsh to English — an unfortunate extension; thus, in spite of Saer's careful distinction (32 ff.), West, *Bilingualism* confuses the situation of these children with genuine bilingualism, and both of these things with the position of a child who hears an entirely foreign language in school.

On real bilingualism: Ronjat; a realistic fictional account, based on the author's childhood, will be found in George Du Maurier's *Peter Ibbetson*, published in *Harper's new monthly magazine*, volume 83 (1891) and in book form.

Chapter 4

F. Müller surveys the languages of the world, giving grammatical sketches and bits of text. Finck, *Sprachstämme* gives a bare list. Meillet-Cohen is a collection of surveys by specialists; it contains maps and some bibliography. W. Schmidt has excellent bibliographies and, in a separate atlas, several maps. Useful charts also in Kroeber; for America in Wissler. India: Grierson. Africa: Meinhof, *Moderne Sprachforschung*.

4. 3. Relation of Hittite to Indo-European: E. H. Sturtevant in *Lg* 2.25 (1926); *TAPA* 40.25 (1929); *AJP* 50.360 (1929); a different view: W. Petersen in *AJP* 53.193 (1932).

4. 4. Languages now extinct: Pedersen, *Linguistic science*. A few legible but unintelligible inscriptions represent the language of the Picts in Scotland; it is uncertain whether Pictish was Indo-European (Celtic) or not; see Hubert 247.

4. 8. Deny in Meillet-Cohen. Chinese dialects: Arendt, *Handbuch* 258; 340; map.

4. 9. Papuan: S. H. Ray in *Festschrift Meinhof* 377.

4. 10. On the grouping of the Algonquian languages (in the text listed geographically) see T. Michelson in *BAE Annual report* 28.221 (1912).

Chapter 5

5. 1. *Semantics*, from *semantic* 'pertaining to meaning.' These words are less clumsy than *semasiology, semasiological*. Literally, then, semantics is the study of meaning. If one disregards the speech-forms and tries to study meaning or meanings in the abstract, one is really trying to study the universe in general; the term *semantics* is sometimes attached to such attempts. If one studies speech-forms and their meanings, semantics is equivalent to the study of grammar and lexicon; in this sense I have defined it in the text.

5. 2. Laboratory phonetics: Rousselot, *Principes*; Scripture; Panconcelli-Calzia, *Einführung* (excellent introductory survey); *Experimentelle Phonetik* (theoretical outline); Gutzmann, *Physiologie;* Russell; Fletcher (especially for analysis of sound-waves and on the ear); Paget (except Chapters 7, 8, 9 and Appendix 8, which deal inadequately with unrelated topics).

5. 3. The phoneme: Baudouin de Courtenay 9; de Saussure 55; 63; E. Sapir in *Lg* 1.37 (1925); see also *Lg* 2.153 (1926); *Modern philology* 25.211 (1927); H. Pedersen in *Litteris* 5.153 (1928).

5. 8. The chief systems of phonetic transcription are assembled by Heepe. Visible Speech: Sweet, *Primer.* Analphabetic Notation: Jespersen, *Lehrbuch.* Other systems: Lepsius; Lundell; Bremer; *Phonetic transcription.*

International Phonetic Association Alphabet: Sweet, *Handbook; Collected papers* 285; Passy-Jones; Jespersen-Pedersen. Discussion and texts in *Maître phonétique.*

5. 10. On transliteration and the like: G. M. Bolling and L. Bloomfield in *Lg* 3.123 (1927); Palmer, *Romanization.*

Chapter 6

6. 1. Practical phonetics: Passy, *Phonétique* (the best introduction); Sweet, *Primer;* Rippmann; Soames; Noël-Armfield. Larger works: Sievers, *Grundzüge* (the classical text); Jespersen, *Lehrbuch;* Viëtor, *Elemente.*

American English: Krapp; Kenyon; H. Kurath in *SPE* 30.279 (1928); L. Strong in *RP* 5.70 (1928); *Maître phonétique* 3.5.40 (1927); bibliography: H. Kurath in *Lg* 5.155 (1929).

British English: Sweet, *Sounds;* Jones, *Outline;* Palmer, *First course;* Lloyd. Phonetic dictionaries: Michaelis-Jones; Jones, *English pronouncing dictionary;* Palmer-Martin-Blandford (the American part is inadequate).

German: Hempl; Viëtor, *German pronunciation; Aussprache; Ausspracheworterbuch;* Bremer; Siebs.

French: Passy, *Sons; Sounds;* Passy-Rambeau; G. G. Nicholson; Michaelis-Passy; Passy-Hempl.

Dutch: Kruisinga, *Grammar;* Scharpé. Danish: Jespersen, *Fonetik;* Forchhammer. Swedish: Noreen *VS.* Spanish: Navarro Tomás. Russian: Trofimov-Jones. North Chinese: Guernier.

6. 2. African languages: Meinhof, *Moderne Sprachforschung* 57.

6. 3. Voiced *h:* Broch 67; E. A. Meyer in *NS* 8.261 (1900). Resonance: Paget.

6. 6. Domals: E. Srámek in *RP* 5.206 (1928); Noël-Armfield 99. Palatal stops: Noël-Armfield 91. Glottal stop: Jespersen, *Fonetik* 297. Glottalized stops: Boas 1.429; 565; 2.33. South-German stops: Winteler 20.

6. 7. Trills: Jespersen, *Fonetik* 417; *Lehrbuch* 137; Bohemian: Chlumsky in *RP* 1.33 (1911). Tongue-flips: Lundell 48; Noreen *VS* 1.451.

6. 8. German spirants: *Maître phonétique* 3.8.27 (1930). Arabic glottal spirants: Gairdner 27; W. H. Worrell in *Vox* 24.82 (1914); G. Panconcelli-Calzia in *Vox* 26.45 (1916).

6. 10. Laterals: Sweet, *Collected papers* 508; Boas 1.429; 565; Broch 45.

6. 12. Vowels: Russell, *Vowel;* Paget; C. E. Parmenter and S. N. Treviño in *Quarterly journal* 18.351 (1932). Vowel systems: N. Troubetzkoy in *Travaux* 1.39 (1929). For the English-speaker, study of the French vowels is especially enlightening: H. Pernot in *RP* 5.108; 289; 337 (1928).

NOTES

CHAPTER 7

7. 2. Mora: E. Sapir in *Lg* 7.33 (1931).

7. 4. For the contrast between American and British treatment of unstressed vowels, see the introductory remarks of Palmer-Martin-Blandford; their general outlook, however, will scarcely find acceptance.

7. 5. *A name: an aim:* many examples are assembled by D. Jones in *Maître phonétique* 3.9.60 (1931).

7. 6. Pitch in (British) English: Jones, *Curves;* Palmer, *Intonation;* Armstrong-Ward. German: Barker; Klinghardt. French: Klinghardt-de Fourmestraux.

Eduard Sievers (1850–1932) gave many years to the study of non-distinctive speech-patterns; summary and bibliography: Sievers, *Ziele;* Ipsen-Karg.

7. 7. Word-pitch in Swedish and Norwegian: Noreen *VS* 2.201; E. Selmer in *Vox* 32.124 (1922). In Japanese: K. Jimbo in *BSOS* 3.659 (1925). North Chinese: Guernier; Karlgren, *Reader.* Cantonese: Jones-Woo. Lithuanian: R. Gauthiot in *Parole* 1900.143; Leskien, *Lesebuch* 128; in Serbian: R. Gauthiot in *MSL* 11.336 (1900); Leskien, *Grammatik* 123; in African languages: E. Sapir in *Lg* 7.30 (1931); in Athabascan: E. Sapir in *Journal de la Société* 17.185 (1925).

7. 8. Palatalization: Broch 203; velarization: 224.

CHAPTER 8

8. 1. An example of two languages with similar sounds in entirely different phonemic distribution: E. Sapir in *Lg* 1.37 (1925).

8. 7. Relative frequency of phonemes: Dewey; Travis 223; Zipf. The conclusions of Zipf do not seem warranted by his data; see also his essay in *Harvard studies* 40.1 (1929).

CHAPTER 9

Many of the examples in the text are taken from the excellent popular treatise of Greenough-Kittredge. See also Bréal; Paul, *Prinzipien* 74; McKnight; Nyrop *Liv;* Darmesteter, *Vie;* Hatzfeld. For individual English words, see *NED.* Position of the study of meaning: L. Weisgerber in *GRM* 15.161 (1927). The mentalistic view of meaning: Ogden-Richards. Bibliography: Collin; G. Stern.

9. 1. Kinship terms: L. Spier in *University of Washington publications* 1.69 (1925). Demonstration: Weiss 21. The definition of *apple* is taken from *Webster's new international dictionary,* Springfield, 1931.

9. 7. Facetious malformation: M. Reed in *American speech* 7.192 (1932). Over-slurred formulas: Horn, *Sprachkörper* 18.

9. 8. See especially Collin 35.

9. 9. Examples of speech-levels: Noreen *VS* 1.21, with table on p. 30. Slang: Farmer-Henley; Mencken, *The American Language.*

9. 10. Tabu: Meillet, *Linguistique* 281; G. S. Keller in *Streitberg Festgabe* 182.

9. 11. Jespersen, *Language* 396; Hilmer; Wheatley. Hypochoristic forms: Sundén; Rotzoll; L. Müller in *Giessener Beiträge* 1.33 (1923).

NOTES

Chapter 10

On the structure of languages: Sweet, *Practical study;* de Saussure; Sapir; Hjelmslev; see also *Lg* 2.153 (1926). The best example of descriptive analysis is the Hindus' work on Sanskrit; see note on § 1.6. English: Jespersen, *Grammar; Philosophy;* Kruisinga, *Handbook;* Poutsma, *Grammar;* German: Curme; French: Beyer-Passy. Various languages are analyzed in Boas and by Finck, *Haupttypen.*

10. 1. The asterisk before a form (as, *cran) indicates that the writer has not heard the form or found it attested by other observers or in written documents. It appears, accordingly, before forms whose existence the writer is denying (as, *ran John), and before theoretically constructed forms (such as *cran, the theoretically posited independent word corresponding to the compound-member *cran-* in *cranberry*). Among the latter the most important are ancient speech-forms not attested in our written records, but reconstructed by the linguist.

Chapter 11

In this and the following chapters, examples from less familiar languages have been taken from the following sources: Arabic, Finck, *Haupttypen;* Bantu (Subiya), same; Chinese, same, and Arendt, *Einführung;* Cree in *Atti* 2.427; Eskimo, Finck, *Haupttypen* and Thalbitzer in Boas 1.967; Finnish, Rosenqvist; Fox, T. Michelson in various publications listed in *IJAL* 3.219 (1925); Georgian, Finck, *Haupttypen;* Gothic, Streitberg, *Elementarbuch;* Irish, Borthwick; Menomini, *Proceedings 21st* 1.336; Polish, Soerensen; Russian, Berneker, *Grammatik;* Samoan, Finck, *Haupttypen;* Sanskrit, Whitney, *Grammar;* Tagalog, Bloomfield; Turkish, Finck, *Haupttypen.*

11. 1. Traditionally and in school grammar, the term *sentence* is used in a much narrower value, to designate the subject-and-predicate sentence-type of the Indo-European languages. If we adhered to this use, we should have to coin a new term to designate the largest form in an utterance. The older definitions are philosophical rather than linguistic; they are assembled by Ries, *Satz*. The definition in the text is due to Meillet, *Introduction* 339; compare *Lg* 7.204 (1931).

11. 2. Impersonal sentence-types are usually confused with pseudo-impersonal types, which contain a pronominal actor (as, *it's raining*, § 15.6).

11. 5. Difficulty of making word-divisions: Passy, *Phonétique* 21.

11. 7. The French-speaker occasionally uses stress to mark word-divisions (Passy, *Sons* 61), but this use is not distinctive; it is comparable to our or the Frenchman's occasional pause between words. The word-unit in South German: Winteler 185; 187.

Chapter 12

On syntax: Morris; Wackernagel, *Vorlesungen;* Blümel; Jespersen, *Philosophy*. For English, beside the books cited for Chapter 10, see Curme-Kurath; for German, Paul, *Grammatik.*

12. 1. Definition of syntax: Ries, *Syntax.*

12. 4. Pitch and stress in Chinese sandhi: Karlgren, *Reader* 23; examples from Arendt, *Einführung* 14.

NOTES

12. 10. Ranks: Jespersen, *Philosophy* 96.
12. 12. Bibliography of writings on word-order: E. Schwendtner in *Wörter und Sachen* 8.179 (1923); 9.194 (1926).

CHAPTER 13

Description of a complex morphologic system (ancient Greek): Debrunner.
13. 1. Classification of languages according to their morphology: Steinthal, *Charakteristik;* Finck, *Klassifikation;* Haupttypen; Sapir.

CHAPTER 14

14. 1. Compounds: Künzel; Darmesteter, *Traité.*
14. 4. Inclusion of words between members of compounds: T. Michelson in *IJAL* 1.50 (1917).
14. 6. Exocentric compounds: Uhrström; Last; Fabian.
14. 7. Denominative verbs: Bladin. On *drunken: drunk* and the like, M. Deutschbein in *Streitberg Festgabe* 36. Male and female in English: Knutson.
14. 8. Concrete suffixes of Algonquian in *Festschrift Meinhof* 393. Incorporation: Steinthal, *Charakteristik* 113. English *flip: flap: flop,* etc.: Warnke.

CHAPTER 15

15. 6. Impersonal and pseudo-impersonal types, bibliography: Ljunggren.
15. 7. Annatom Island: F. Müller 2.2.73.

CHAPTER 16

Some dictionaries:
English: *NED*; Bosworth-Toller; Stratmann; German: Grimm, *Wörterbuch;* Benecke-Müller-Zarncke; Lexer; Graff; Dutch: Verwijs-Verdam; de Vries-te Winkel; Danish: Dahlerup; Swedish: *Ordbok;* Old Norse: Cleasby-Vigfusson; Fritzner; Russian: Blattner; Latin: *Thesaurus;* French: Hatzfeld-Darmesteter-Thomas; Sanskrit: Böhtlingk-Roth; Chinese: Giles.
16. 5. English aspects: Poutsma, *Characters;* Jespersen, *Grammar* 4.164; Kruisinga, *Handbook* 2.1.340.
16. 7. Number of words used: Jespersen, *Language* 126; *Growth* 215.
Relative frequency of words: Zipf; Thorndike.
16. 8. Kham Bushman numerals: F. Müller, *Grundriss* 4.12; numerals, bibliography: A. R. Nykl in *Lg* 2.165 (1926).

CHAPTER 17

Linguistic change: Paul, *Prinzipien;* Sweet, *History of language;* Oertel; Sturtevant; de Saussure.
History of various languages:
The Indo-European family: the best introduction is Meillet, *Introduction;* standard reference-book, with bibliography, Brugmann-Delbrück; summary, Brugmann, *Kurze vergleichende Grammatik;* recent, more speculative, Hirt, *Indogermanische Grammatik;* etymological dictionary, Walde-Pokorny.
The Germanic branch: Grimm, *Grammatik* (still indispensable); Streitberg,

Grammatik; Hirt, *Handbuch des Urgermanischen;* Kluge, *Urgermanisch;* etymological dictionary, Torp, *Wortschatz.*

English: readable introduction, Jespersen, *Growth;* Sweet, *Grammar; History of sounds;* Horn, *Grammatik;* Kaluza; Luick; Wyld, *Historical study; History; Short history;* Wright, *Elementary;* Jespersen, *Progress;* etymological dictionaries: *NED;* Skeat, *Dictionary;* Weekley, *Dictionary.* Old English: Sievers, *Grammatik;* Sweet, *Primer; Reader.*

German: readable summaries, Kluge, *Sprachgeschichte;* Behaghel, *Sprache;* larger works: Wilmanns; Paul, *Grammatik;* Sütterlin; Behaghel, *Geschichte; Syntax;* etymological dictionary, Kluge, *Wörterbuch.* Old High German, Braune; Old Low German (Old Saxon), Holthausen; Middle High German: Michels.

Dutch: Schönfeld; van der Meer; etymological dictionary, Franck-van Wijk.

Old Norse: Heusler; Noreen, *Grammatik.* Danish, Dahlerup, *Historie.* Dano-Norwegian: Seip; Torp-Falk, *Lydhistorie;* Falk-Torp, *Syntax;* etymological dictionaries: Falk-Torp, *Wörterbuch;* Torp, *Ordbok.* Swedish: Noreen *VS;* etymological dictionary, Tamm; see also Hellquist.

Gothic: Streitberg, *Elementarbuch;* Jellinek, *Geschichte der gotischen Sprache;* etymological dictionary, Feist.

Latin: Lindsay; Sommer; Stolz-Schmalz; Kent; etymological dictionary, Walde.

Romance: introductions, Zauner; Bourciez; Meyer-Lübke, *Einführung;* larger works: Gröber; Meyer-Lübke, *Grammatik;* etymological dictionary, Meyer-Lübke, *Wörterbuch.* French: Nyrop, *Grammaire;* Dauzat, *Histoire;* Meyer-Lübke, *Historische Grammatik.* Italian: d'Ovidio; Grandgent. Spanish: Hanssen; Menéndez Pidal.

Oscan and Umbrian: Buck; Conway.

Celtic: Pedersen, *Grammatik.* Old Irish: Thurneysen, *Handbuch.*

Slavic: Miklosich, *Grammatik;* Vondrák; Meillet, *Slave;* etymological dictionaries: Miklosich, *Wörterbuch;* Berneker, *Wörterbuch.* Russian: Meyer. Old Bulgarian: Leskien.

Greek: Meillet *Aperçu;* Brugmann-Thumb; Hirt, *Handbuch;* etymological dictionary, Boisacq; ancient dialects: Buck; modern Greek: Thumb.

Sanskrit: Wackernagel, *Grammatik;* etymological dictionary, Uhlenbeck. Marathi: Bloch.

Finno-Ugrian: Szinnyei. Semitic: Brockelmann. Bantu: Meinhof, *Grundzüge; Grundriss.*

On writing: Sturtevant; Jensen; Pedersen, *Linguistic science;* Sprengling.

17. 1. Picture messages: Wundt, *Sprache* 1.241; in America: G. Mallery in *BAE Annual reports* 4 (1886); 10 (1893); Ojibwa song record in W. Jones, *Ojibwa texts, Part 2,* New York, 1919 (*Publications of the American ethnological society,* 7.2), 591.

17. 2. Egyptian writing: Erman. Chinese: Karlgren, *Sound.* Cuneiform: Meissner. Runes: Wimmer; O. v. Friesen in Hoops, *Reallexikon* 4.5.

17. 9. Conventional spellings in Old English: S. Moore in *Lg* 4.239 (1928); K. Malone in *Curme volume* 110. Occasional spellings as indications of sound: Wyld, *History.* Inscriptions: Kent. Re-spelling of Homeric poems: J. Wackernagel in *Beiträge zur Kunde* 4.259 (1878); R. Herzog; of Avesta: F. C. Andreas and J. Wackernagel in *Nachrichten Göttingen* 1909.42; 1911.1 (especially this); 1913.363.

17. 10. Rimes: Wyld, *Studies;* theoretical discussion: Schauerhammer. Alliteration as evidence: Heusler 11. Inaccuracy of older English phoneticians: Wyld, *History* 115.

CHAPTER 18

Comparative method: Meillet, *Linguistique* 19; *Méthode;* K. Brugmann in *IZ* 1.226 (1884).

18. 4. Latin *cauda, coda: Thesaurus* under *cauda;* Schuchardt, *Vokalismus* 2.302; Meyer-Lübke, *Einführung* 121. Latin *secale:* same 136. Suetonius: *Vespasian* 22.

18. 6. Gallehus horn: Noreen, *Altisländische Grammatik* 379. Germanic loan-words in Finnish: see note on § 26.3.

18. 7. On K. Verner: H. Pedersen in *IF Anzeiger* 8.107 (1898). Verner's discovery in *ZvS* 23.97; 131 (1877).

The acoustic value of the Primitive Indo-European vowel phoneme which in our formulae is represented by the inverted letter *e*, is unknown; linguists sometimes speak of this phoneme by the name *shwa*, a term taken from Hebrew grammar.

Primitive Indo-European form of Latin *cauda:* Walde under *cauda;* K. Ettmayer in *ZrP* 30.528 (1906).

Hittite: see note on § 4.3.

18. 8. The Indonesian example from O. Dempwolff in *Zeitschrift für Eingeborenensprachen* 15.19 (1925), supplemented by data which Professor Dempwolff has kindly communicated.

18. 11. Dialect differences in Primitive Indo-European: J. Schmidt; Meillet, *Dialectes;* Pedersen, *Groupement*. Figures 1 and 3 are modeled on those given by Schrader, *Sprachvergleichung* 1.59; 65.

18. 13. Hemp: Schrader, *Sprachvergleichung* 2.192. Herodotus 4.74.

18. 14. Schrader, *Sprachvergleichung;* Meillet, *Introduction* 364, Hirt, *Indogermanen;* Feist, *Kultur;* Hoops, *Waldbäume;* Hehn; Schrader, *Reallexikon*. Germanic pre-history: Hoops, *Reallexikon*. General: Ebert.

Terms of relationship: B. Delbrück in *Abhandlungen Leipzig* 11.381 (1889).

CHAPTER 19

Dialect geography: Jaberg; Dauzat, *Géographie; Patois;* Brøndum-Nielsen; Gamillscheg; Millardet; Schuchardt, *Klassifikation;* E. C. Roedder in *Germanic review* 1.281 (1926). Questions of principle in special studies: L. Gauchat in *Archiv* 111.365 (1903); Terracher; Haag; Kloeke; A. Horning in *ZrP* 17.160 (1893), reprinted in *Meisterwerke* 2.264.

Discussion of a single dialect: Winteler; of an area: Schmeller, *Mundarten;* Bertoni; Jutz. Dictionaries: Schmeller, *Wörterbuch;* Feilberg.

English dialects: Ellis, volume 5; Wright, *Dictionary; Grammar;* Skeat, *Dialects; Publications of the English dialect society; Dialect notes*. On the American atlas: H. Kurath in *Dialect notes* 6.65 (1930); M. L. Hanley in *Dialect notes* 6.91 (1931).

19. 2. With the fifth issue (1931), the German atlas takes up some of the hitherto omitted parts of the area. Studies based on the German atlas: *Deutsche Dialektgeographie; Teuthonista.*
19. 3. Kaldenhausen: J. Ramisch in *Deutsche Dialektgeographie* 1.17; 62 (1908).
19. 4. Every word has its own history: Jaberg 6.
19. 5. Latin *multum* in France: Gamillscheg 51; *fallit:* Jaberg 8.
19. 6. Latin *sk-* in French: Jaberg 5; my figures, taken directly from Gilliéron-Edmont's maps, differ slightly from Jaberg's.
19. 8. French and Provençal: Tourtoulon-Bringuier. Low and High German: W. Braune in *Beiträge zur Geschichte* 1.1 (1874); T. Frings in *Beiträge zur Geschichte* 39.362 (1914); Behaghel, *Geschichte* 156 and map; see also map 3 of Wrede and the map given by K. Wagner in *Deutsche Dialektgeographie* 23 (1927).
19. 9. Rhenish fan: J. Ramisch in *Deutsche Dialektgeographie* 1 (1908); plates 1 and 2 of Wagner's study, cited in the preceding note; Frings.

Chapter 20

20. 2. Germanic consonant-shift: Russer.
20. 3. H. Grassmann in *ZvS* 12.81 (1863).
20. 6. The neo-grammarian hypothesis: E. Wechssler in *Festgabe Suchier* 349; E. Herzog; Delbrück, *Einleitung* 171; Leskien, *Declination* xxviii; 2; Osthoff-Brugmann, preface of volume 1; Brugmann, *Stand;* Ziemer. Against the hypothesis: Curtius; Schuchardt, *Lautgesetze;* Jespersen, *Language;* Horn, *Sprachkörper:* Hermann, *Lautgesetz.*
20. 7. Tabulations of Old English and modern English correspondences in Sweet, *History of sounds.*
20. 8. Algonquian forms: *Lg* 1.30 (1925); 4.99 (1928); E. Sapir in S. A. Rice 292.
20. 9. English *bait,* etc.: Luick 387; Björkman 36.
20. 10. Greek forms: Brugmann-Thumb 143; 362.
20. 11. Observation of sub-phonemic variants: Passy *Étude:* Rousselot, *Modifications;* L. Gauchat in *Festschrift Morf* 175; E. Hermann in *Nachrichten Göttingen* 1929.195. Relative chronology: O. Bremer in *IF* 4.8 (1893).

Chapter 21

21. 1. The symbol > means 'changed into' and the symbol < means 'resulting from.'
21. 2. Simplification of final consonants: Gauthiot.
21. 3. Latin clusters: Sommer 215. Russian assimilations: Meyer 71.
21. 4. Origin of Irish sandhi: Thurneysen, *Handbuch* 138; Brugmann-Delbrück 1.922. English voicing of spirants: Jespersen, *Grammar* 1.199; Russer 97.
21. 5. Palatalization in Indo-Iranian: Delbrück, *Einleitung* 128; Bechtel 62; Wackernagel, *Grammatik* 1.137.
21. 6. Nasalization in Old Norse; Noreen, *Altisländische Grammatik* 39.
21. 7. English *away,* etc.: Palmgren. Irish verb-forms: Thurneysen, *Handbuch* 62.

21. 8. Insertion of stops: Jespersen, *Lehrbuch* 62. Anaptyxis, etc.: Brugmann-Delbrück 1.819.

21. 9. Causes of sound-change: Wundt, *Sprache* 1.376; 522. Relative frequency: Zipf (see note on § 8.7). Experiment misapplied: J. Rousselot in *Parole* 1901.641. Substratum theory: Jespersen, *Language* 191. Homonymy in Chinese: Karlgren, *Études*.

21. 10. Types of *r* in Europe: Jespersen, *Fonetik* 417. Dissimilation: K. Brugmann in *Abhandlungen Leipzig* 27.139 (1909); Grammont; A. Meillet in *MSL* 12.14 (1903). Assimilation: J. Vendryes in *MSL* 16.53 (1910); M. Grammont in *BSL* 24.1 (1923). Metathesis: Brugmann-Delbrück 1.863; M. Grammont in *MSL* 13.73 (1905); in *Streitberg Festgabe* 111; in *Festschrift Wackernagel* 72. Haplology: Brugmann-Delbrück 1.857.

CHAPTER 22

22. 2. The Old English word for "become": F. Klaeber in *JEGP* 18.250 (1919). Obsolescence: Teichert.

22. 3. Latin *apis* in France: Gilliéron, *Généalogie*; Meyer-Lübke, *Einführung* 103. Short verb-forms: A. Meillet in *MSL* 11.16 (1900); 13.359 (1905); J. Wackernagel in *Nachrichten Göttingen* 1906.147. English *coney NED* under *coney*; Jaberg 11.

22. 4. Homonymy: E. Richter in *Festschrift Kretschmer* 167. Latin *gallus* in southern France: Gilliéron-Roques 121; Dauzat, *Géographie* 65; Gamillscheg 40.

22. 6. Othello's speech (Act 3, Scene 3) explained in H. H. Furness' *New variorum edition*, volume 6 (Philadelphia, 1886).

22. 7. Tabu: see note on § 9.10.

CHAPTER 23

Analogic change: Wheeler; Paul, *Prinzipien* 106; 242; Strong-Logeman-Wheeler 73; 217; de Saussure 221; Darmesteter, *Création*; Goeders.

23. 1. Regular versus irregular combinations: Jespersen, *Philosophy* 18.

23. 2. Objections to proportional diagram of analogy: Herman, *Lautgesetz* 86.

23. 3. English *s*-plural: Roedler. Latin *senati*: Hermann, *Lautgesetz* 76.

23. 5. Back-formation: Nichtenhauser; O. Jespersen in *Festskrift Thomsen* 1. English verbs in *-en*: Raith. English verbs in *-ate*: Strong-Logeman-Wheeler 220.

23. 6. Verbal compound-members: Osthoff; de Saussure 195; 311.

Popular etymology: A. S. Palmer; Andresen; Hasse; W. v. Wartburg in *Homenaje Menéndez Pidal* 1.17; Klein 55; H. Palander in *Neuphilologische Mitteilungen* 7.125 (1905); J. Hoops in *Englische Studien* 36.157 (1906).

23. 7. Analogic change in syntax: Ziemer; Middleton.

23. 8. Adaptation and contamination: M. Bloomfield in *AJP* 12.1 (1891); 16.409 (1895); *IF* 4.66 (1894); Paul, *Prinzipien* 160; Strong-Logeman-Wheeler 140; L. Pound in *Modern language review* 8.324 (1913); Pound, *Blends*; Bergström; G. H. McKnight in *JEGP* 12.110 (1913); bibliography: K. F. Johansson in *ZdP* 31.300 (1899). In pronouns: Brugmann-Delbrück 3.386. Psychological study: Thumb-Marbe; Esper; Oertel 183. Slips of the tongue: Meringer-Meyer. *Bob, Dick*, etc.: Sundén.

NOTES

CHAPTER 24

See the references to Chapter 9.
24. 3. The wattled wall: R. Meringer in *Festgabe Heinzel* 173; H. Collitz in *Germanic review* 1.40 (1926). Words and things: *Wörter und Sachen*.
24. 4. Paul, *Prinzipien* 74.
24. 5. On *hard : hardly*, Uhler.
24. 6. Marginal meanings in aphoristic forms: Taylor 78.
24. 7. Sperber; S. Kroesch in *Lg* 2.35 (1926); 6.322 (1930); *Modern philology* 26.433 (1929); *Studies Collitz* 176; *Studies Klaeber* 50. Latin *testa*: A. Zauner in *Romanische Forschungen* 14.355 (1903). Passage from Wordsworth: Greenough-Kittredge 9.

CHAPTER 25

25. 2. First phonetic adaptation of borrowed words: S. Ichikawa in *Grammatical miscellany* 179.
25. 3. Scandinavian *sk-* in English: Björkman 10.
25. 5. Latin *Caesar* in Germanic: Stender-Petersen 350. German *Maut* from Gothic: F. Kluge in *Beiträge zur Geschichte* 35.156 (1909).
25. 6. English words with foreign affixes: G. A. Nicholson; Gadde; Jespersen, *Growth* 106. Suffix *-er*: Sütterlin 77.
25. 7. Loan-translation: K. Sandfeld Jensen in *Festschrift Thomsen* 166. Grammatical terms: Wackernagel, *Vorlesungen*.
25. 8. Early Germanic loans from Latin: Kluge, *Urgermanisch* 9; Jespersen, *Growth* 31. Latin loans from early Germanic: Brüch; Meyer-Lübke, *Einführung* 43.

CHAPTER 26

26. 1. Latin missionary words in English: Jespersen, *Growth* 41. Low German words in Scandinavian: Hellquist 561. Low German and Dutch in Russian: van der Meulen; O. Schrader in *Wissenschaftliche Beihefte* 4.99 (1903). Gender of English words in American German: A. W. Aron in *Curme volume* 11; in American Norwegian: G. T. Flom in *Dialect notes* 2.257 (1902).

West's erroneous statement (*Bilingualism* 46) about the fate of immigrant languages in America is based on an educationist's article (which contains a few figures with diametrically false interpretation) and on some haphazard remarks in a literary essay.

26. 2. Conflict of languages, bibliography: Paul, *Prinzipien* 390; see especially E. Windisch in *Berichte Leipzig* 1897.101; G. Hempl in *TAPA* 1898.31; J. Wackernagel in *Nachrichten Göttingen, Geschäftliche Mitteilungen* 1904.90. Welsh: Parry-Williams.

Place-names: Mawer-Stenton; Meier 145; 322; Dauzat, *Noms de lieux;* Meyer-Lübke, *Einführung* 254; Olsen.

Dutch words in American English: van der Meer xliv; these are not to be confused with the much older stratum discussed by Toll.

French words in English: Jespersen, *Growth* 84; 115.

Personal names: Barber; Ewen; Weekley, *Romance; Surnames;* Bähnisch; Dauzat, *Noms de personnes;* Meyer-Lübke, *Einführung* 244.

26. 3. Germanic words in Finnish: Thomsen; E. N. Setälä in *Finnisch-*

ugrische Forschungen 13.345 (1913); later references will be found in W. Wiget in *Streitberg Festgabe* 399; K. B. Wiklund in same, 418; Collinder.

Germanic words in Slavic: Stender-Petersen. In Romance: Meyer-Lübke, *Einführung* 43 with references.

Gipsy: Miklosich, *Mundarten;* bibliography: Black; German Gipsy: Finck, *Lehrbuch.*

Ladin: Meyer-Lübke, *Einführung* 55.

26. 4. Scandinavian elements in English: Björkman; Xandry: Flom; Lindkvist; A. Mawer in *Acta philologica Scandinavica* 7.1 (1932); E. Ekwall in *Grammatical miscellany* 17.

Chilean Spanish: R. Lenz in *ZrP* 17.188 (1893); M. L. Wagner in *ZrP* 40.286; 385 (1921), reprinted in *Meisterwerke* 2.208. Substrata in Romance languages: Meyer-Lübke, *Einführung* 225.

Dravidian traits in Indo-Aryan: S. Konow in Grierson 4.278.

Balkan languages: Sandfeld. Northwest Coast languages: F. Boas in *Lg* 1.18 (1925); 5.1 (1929); *American anthropologist* 22.367 (1920).

26. 5. English and American Gipsies: J. D. Prince in *JAOS* 28.271 (1907); A. T. Sinclair in *Bulletin* 19.727 (1915); archaic form: Sampson.

Jargons, trade languages, creolized languages: Jespersen, *Language* 216. English: Kennedy 416; American Negro: J. A. Harrison in *Anglia* 7.322 (1884); J. P. Fruit in *Dialect notes* 1.196 (1892); Smith; Johnson. West African: P. Grade in *Archiv* 83.261 (1889); *Anglia* 14.362 (1892); E. Henrici in *Anglia* 20.397 (1898). Suriname: Schuchardt, *Sprache;* M. J. Herskovits in *Proceedings 23d* 713; *West-Indische gids* 12.35. Pidgin: F. P. H. Prick van Wely in *Englische Studien* 44.298 (1912). Beach-la-mar: H. Schuchardt in *Sitzungsberichte Wien.* 105.151 (1884); *Englische Studien* 13.158 (1889); Churchill. India: H. Schuchardt in *Englische Studien* 15.286 (1890).

Du ch: H. Schuchardt in *Tijdschrift* 33.123 (1914); Hesseling; de Josselin de Jong; Afrikaans: van der Meer xxxiv; cxxvi.

For various Romance jargons, see the studies of H. Schuchardt, listed in *Schuchardt-Brevier* 22 ff.

Chinook jargon: M. Jacobs in *Lg* 8.27 (1932). Slavic German and Italian: Schuchardt, *Slawo-Deutsches.* Russian-Norwegian trade language: O. Broch in *Archiv für slavische Philologie* 41.209 (1927).

CHAPTER 27

27. 1. The child: Jespersen, *Language* 103; J. M. Manly in *Grammatical miscellany* 287.

27. 2. Gamillscheg 14.

27. 4. Rise of standard languages: Morsbach; Flasdieck; Wyld, *History;* L. Morsbach in *Grammatical miscellany* 123. German: Behaghel, *Geschichte* 182; Kluge, *Luther.* Dutch: van der Meer. French: Brunot. Serbian: Leskien, *Grammatik* xxxviii. Bohemian: Smetánka 8. Lithuanian: E. Hermann in *Nachrichten Göttingen* 1929.25. Norwegian: Burgun; Seip.

27. 5. English *busy,* etc.: H. C. Wyld in *Englische Studien* 47.1; 145 (1913). English *er; ar,* etc.: Wyld, *History.*

Obsolete words revived: Jespersen, *Growth* 232; *derring-do:* Greenough-Kittredge 118.

Half-learned words in Romance: Zauner 1.24; Meyer-Lübke, *Einführung* 30.

27. 7. Medieval Latin: Strecker; Bonnet; C. C. Rice; forms in Du Cange.

CHAPTER 28

28. 1. Rise of new speakers to the standard language: Wyld, *Historical study* 212.

28. 2. Reading: Passy, *Enseignement;* Erdmann-Dodge; Fechner.

28. 4. Foreign-language teaching: Sweet, *Practical study;* Jespersen, *How to teach;* Viëtor, *Methodik;* Palmer, *Language study;* Coleman; McMurry. Bibliography: Buchanan-McPhee. Vocabulary: West, *Learning.*

28. 5. Artificial languages: R. M. Meyer in *IF* 12.33; 242 (1901); Guérard; R. Jones in *JEGP* 31.315 (1932); bibliography in *Bulletin* 12.644 (1908).

26. 6. General tendency of linguistic development: Jespersen, *Progress.*

BIBLIOGRAPHY

General bibliographic aids, including the periodic national bibliographies, are described in H. B. Van Hoesen and F. K. Walter, *Bibliography; practical, enumerative, historical; an introductory manual* (New York, 1928) and in Georg Schneider, *Handbuch der Bibliographie* (fourth edition, Leipzig, 1930). Bibliography of various language families: W. Schmidt; Meillet-Cohen. Oriental languages, annually: *Orientalische Bibliographie*. Indo-European: Brugmann-Delbrück; annually in *IF Anzeiger*, since 1913 in *IJ;* these annuals list also some general linguistic publications. Greek: Brugmann-Thumb; Latin: Stolz-Schmalz; both of these languages annually in Bursian. Romance: Gröber; annually in Vollmöller, then in *ZrP Supplement*. Germanic, including English, in Paul, *Grundriss;* annually in *Jahresbericht;* the latter, up to 1900, is summarized in Bethge. English: Kennedy; current in *Anglia Beiblatt*. Serials dealing with Germanic languages are listed in Diesch. Germanic and Romance, bi-monthly in *Literaturblatt*.

Items I have not seen are bracketed.

Abhandlungen Leipzig: Sächsische Akademie der Wissenschaften, Leipzig; Philologisch-historische Klasse; Abhandlungen. Leipzig, 1850–.
Acta philologica Scandinavica. Copenhagen, 1926–.
AJP: American journal of philology. Baltimore, 1880–.
Allport, F. H., *Social psychology.* Boston, 1924.
American speech. Baltimore, 1925–.
Andresen, K. G., *Über deutsche Volksetymologie.* Sixth edition, Leipzig, 1899.
Anglia. Halle, 1878–; bibliographic supplement: *Beiblatt; Mitteilungen,* since 1890.
Archiv: Archiv für das Studium der neueren Sprachen. Elberfeld (now Braunschweig) 1846–. Often referred to as *HA* ("Herrigs Archiv").
Archiv für slavische Philologie. Berlin, 1876–.
Arendt, C., *Einführung in die nordchinesische Umgangssprache.* Stuttgart and Berlin, 1894 (= *Lehrbücher des Seminars für orientalische Sprachen zu Berlin,* 12).
Arendt, C., *Handbuch der nordchinesischen Umgangssprache. Erster Theil.* Stuttgart, 1891 (= same series as preceding, 7).
Armstrong, L. E., and Ward, I. C., *Handbook of English intonation.* Cambridge, 1926.
Atti del XXII congresso internazionale degli Americanisti. Rome, 1928.
BAE: Bureau of American ethnology; Annual reports. Washington, 1881–.
Bahlsen, L., *The teaching of modern languages.* Boston, 1905.
Bähnisch, A., *Die deutschen Personennamen.* Third edition, Leipzig, 1920 (= *Aus Natur und Geisteswelt,* 296).
Barber, H., *British family names.* Second edition, London, 1903.

Barker, M. L., *A handbook of German intonation.* Cambridge, 1925.
Baudouin de Courtenay, J., *Versuch einer Theorie der phonetischen Alternationen.* Strassburg, 1895.
Bechtel, F., *Die Hauptprobleme der indogermanischen Lautlehre seit Schleicher.* Göttingen, 1892.
Behaghel, O., *Die deutsche Sprache.* Seventh edition, Vienna, 1923 (= *Das Wissen der Gegenwart,* 54).
Behaghel, O., *Deutsche Syntax.* Heidelberg, 1923–32 (= *Germanische Bibliothek,* 1.10).
Behaghel, O., *Geschichte der deutschen Sprache.* Fifth edition, Berlin and Leipzig, 1928 (= *Grundriss der germanischen Philologie,* 3).
Beiträge zur Geschichte der deutschen Sprache und Literatur. Halle, 1874–. Often referred to as *PBB* ("Paul und Braunes Beiträge").
Beiträge zur Kunde der indogermanischen Sprachen. Göttingen, 1877–1906. Often referred to as *BB* ("Bezzenbergers Beiträge").
Belvalkar, S. K., *An account of the different existing systems of Sanskrit grammar.* Poona, 1915.
Benecke, G. F., Müller, W., Zarncke, F., *Mittelhochdeutsches Worterbuch.* Leipzig, 1854–61. Supplemented by Lexer, below.
Benfey, T., *Geschichte der Sprachwissenschaft und Philologie in Deutschland.* Munich, 1869 (= *Geschichte der Wissenschaften in Deutschland; Neuere Zeit,* 8).
Bennicke, V., and Kristensen, M., *Kort over de danske folkemaal.* Copenhagen, 1898–1912.
Bergström, G. A., *On blendings of synonymous or cognate expressions in English.* Dissertation, Lund, 1906.
Berichte über die Verhandlungen der sächsischen Akademie der Wissenschaften zu Leipzig; Philologisch-historische Klasse. Leipzig, 1849–.
Berneker, E., *Russische Grammatik.* Second edition, Leipzig, 1911 (= *Sammlung Göschen,* 68).
Berneker, E., *Slavisches etymologisches Wörterbuch.* Heidelberg, 1908– (= *Indogermanische Bibliothek,* 1.2.2).
Bertoni, G., *Italia dialettale.* Milan, 1916 (*Manuali Hoepli*).
Bethge, R., *Ergebnisse und Fortschritte der germanistischen Wissenschaft im letzten Vierteljahrhundert.* Leipzig, 1902.
Beyer, F., and Passy, P., *Elementarbuch des gesprochenen Französisch.* Cöthen, 1893.
Björkman, E., *Scandinavian loan-words in Middle English.* Halle, 1900–02 (= *Studien zur englischen Philologie,* 7; 11).
Black, G. F., *A Gypsy bibliography.* London, 1914 (= *Gypsy lore society monographs,* 1).
Bladin, V., *Studies on denominative verbs in English.* Dissertation, Uppsala, 1911.
Blattner, K., *Taschenwörterbuch der russischen und deutschen Sprache.* Berlin, 1906.
Bloch, J., *La formation de la langue marathe.* Paris, 1920 (= *Bibliothèque de l'École des hautes études; Sciences historiques et philologiques,* 215).
Bloomfield, L., *Tagalog texts.* Urbana, Illinois, 1917 (= *University of Illinois studies in language and literature,* 3.2–4).

BIBLIOGRAPHY

Blümel, R., *Einführung in die Syntax*. Heidelberg, 1914 (= *Indogermanische Bibliothek*, 2.6).

Boas, F., *Handbook of American Indian languages*. Washington, 1911– (= *Smithsonian institution; Bureau of American ethnology; Bulletin* 40).

Böhtlingk, O., *Panini's Grammatik*. Second edition, Leipzig, 1887.

Böhtlingk, O., *Die Sprache der Jakuten*. St. Petersburg, 1851 (= volume 3 of A. T. von Middendorf, *Reise im äuszersten Norden und Osten Sibiriens*).

Böhtlingk, O., and Roth, R., *Sanskrit-Wörterbuch*, St. Petersburg, 1855–75; additional matter in O. Böhtlingk, *Sanskrit-Wörterbuch in kürzerer Fassung*, St. Petersburg, 1879–89 and in R. Schmidt, *Nachträge zum Sanskrit-Wörterbuch*, Hannover, 1924.

Boisacq, E., *Dictionnaire étymologique de la langue grecque*. Heidelberg and Paris, 1916.

Bonnet, M., *Le latin de Grégoire de Tours*. Paris, 1890.

Bopp, F., *Über das Konjugationssystem der Sanskritsprache*. Frankfurt am Main, 1816.

Bopp, F., *Vergleichende Grammatik des Sanskrit, Zend, Griechischen, Lateinischen, Litthauischen, Gothischen und Deutschen*. Berlin, 1833. Third edition, 1868–71.

Borthwick, N., *Ceachda beoga gāluingi*. *Irish reading lessons*, edited in simplified spelling by O. Bergin. Dublin, 1911.

Bosworth, J., and Toller, T. N., *An Anglo-Saxon dictionary*. Oxford, 1898. *Supplement*, by T. N. Toller, 1921.

Bourciez, E., *Éléments de linguistique romane*. Second edition, Paris, 1923.

Braune, W., *Althochdeutsche Grammatik*. Third-fourth edition, Halle, 1911 (= *Sammlung kurzer Grammatiken germanischer Dialekte*, 5).

Bréal, M., *Essai de sémantique*. Fourth edition, Paris, 1908. An English translation of the third (1897) edition, by Mrs. H. Cust, appeared under the title *Semantics* in London, 1900.

Bremer, O., *Deutsche Phonetik*. Leipzig, 1893 (= *Sammlung kurzer grammatiken deutscher Mundarten*, 1).

Broch, O., *Slavische Phonetik*. Heidelberg, 1911 (= *Sammlung slavischer Elementar- und Handbücher*, 1.2).

Brockelmann, C., *Semitische Sprachwissenschaft*. Leipzig, 1906 (= *Sammlung Göschen*, 291).

Brøndum-Nielsen, J., *Dialekter og dialektforskning*. Copenhagen, 1927.

Brüch, J., *Der Einfluss der germanischen Sprachen auf das Vulgärlatein*. Heidelberg, 1913 (= *Sammlung romanischer Elementar- und Handbücher*, 5.1).

Brugmann, K., *Kurze vergleichende Grammatik der indogermanischen Sprachen*. Strassburg, 1902–04.

Brugmann, K., *Zum heutigen Stand der Sprachwissenschaft*. Strassburg, 1885.

Brugmann, K., and Delbrück, B., *Grundriss der vergleichenden Grammatik der indogermanischen Sprachen*. Strassburg, 1886–1900. Second edition, 1897–1911.

Brugmann, K., and Thumb, A., *Griechische Grammatik*. Fourth edition, Munich, 1913 (= *Handbuch der klassischen Altertumswissenschaft*, 2.1).

Brunot, F., *Histoire de la langue française des origines à 1900.* Paris, 1905 –.
BSL: *Bulletin de la Société de linguistique de Paris.* Paris, 1869 –.
BSOS: *Bulletin of the School of Oriental studies, London institution.* London, 1917–.
Buchanan, M. A., and McPhee, E. D., *An annotated bibliography of modern language methodology.* Toronto, 1928 (= *Publications of the American and Canadian committees on modern languages,* 8); also in volume 1 of *Modern language instruction in Canada* (= same series, 6).
Buck, C. D., *A grammar of Oscan and Umbrian.* Boston, 1904.
Buck, C. D., *Introduction to the study of the Greek dialects.* Second edition, Boston, 1928.
Bühler, K., *Die geistige Entwicklung des Kindes.* Fifth edition, Jena, 1929.
Bulletin of the New York Public Library, New York, 1897–.
Burgun, A., *Le développement linguistique en Norvège depuis 1814.* Christiania, 1919–21 (= *Videnskapsselskapets skrifter; Historisk-filologisk klasse,* 1917.1; 1921.5).
Bursian, K., *Jahresbericht über die Fortschritte der klassischen Altertumswissenschaft.* Berlin (now Leipzig), 1873–.
Churchill W., *Beach-la-mar.* Washington, 1911 (= *Carnegie institution of Washington; Publications,* 154).
Cleasby, R., and Vigfusson, G., *An Icelandic-English dictionary.* Oxford, 1874.
Coleman, A., *The teaching of modern foreign languages in the United States.* New York, 1929 (= *Publications of the American and Canadian committees on modern languages,* 12).
Collin, C. S. R., *Bibliographical guide to sematology.* Lund, 1914.
Collinder, B., *Die urgermanischen Lehnwörter in Finnischen.* Uppsala, 1932 (= *Skrifter utgivna av K. humanistiska vetenskaps-samfundet i Uppsala,* 28.1).
Conway, R. S., *The Italic dialects.* Cambridge, 1897.
Curme, G. O., *A grammar of the German language.* Second edition, New York, 1922.
Curme, G. O., and Kurath, H., *A grammar of the English language;* volume 3, *Syntax,* by G. O. Curme. New York, 1931.
Curme volume of linguistic studies. Baltimore, 1930. (= *Language monographs published by the Linguistic society of America,* 7).
Curtius, G., *Zur Kritik der neuesten Sprachforschung.* Leipzig, 1885.
Dahlerup, V., *Det danske sprogs historie.* Second edition, Copenhagen, 1921.
Dahlerup, V., *Ordbog over det danske sprog.* Copenhagen, 1919–.
Darmesteter, A., *De la création actuelle de mots nouveaux dans la langue française.* Paris, 1877.
Darmesteter, A., *Traité de la formation des mots composés dans la langue française.* Second edition, Paris, 1894.
Darmesteter, A., *La vie des mots.* Twelfth edition, Paris, 1918.
Dauzat, A., *La géographie linguistique.* Paris, 1922.
Dauzat, A., *Histoire de la langue française.* Paris, 1930.
Dauzat, A., *Les noms de lieux.* Paris, 1926.
Dauzat, A., *Les noms de personnes.* Paris, 1925.

BIBLIOGRAPHY

Dauzat, A., *Les patois*. Paris, 1927.
Debrunner, A., *Griechische Wortbildungslehre*. Heidelberg, 1927 (= *Indogermanische Bibliothek*, 2.8).
de Josselin de Jong, J. P. B., *Het huidige Negerhollandsch*. Amsterdam, 1926 (= *Verhandelingen der K. akademie van wetenschappen; Afdeeling letterkunde; Nieuwe reeks*, 14.6).
de Laguna, G. A., *Speech; its function and development*. New Haven, 1927.
Delbrück, B., *Einleitung in das Studium der indogermanischen Sprachen*. Sixth edition, Leipzig, 1919 (= *Bibliothek indogermanischer Grammatiken*, 4).
Delbrück B., *Grundfragen der Sprachforschung*. Strassburg, 1901.
de Saussure, F., *Cours de linguistique générale*. Second edition, Paris, 1922.
Deutsche Dialektgeographie. Marburg, 1908–.
de Vries, M., and te Winkel, L. A., *Woordenboek der Nederlandsche taal*. The Hague, 1882–.
Dialect notes. New Haven, 1890–.
Diesch, C., *Bibliographie der germanistischen Zeitschriften*. Leipzig, 1927 (= *Bibliographic publications, Germanistic section, Modern language association of America*, 1).
Diez, F., *Grammatik der romanischen Sprachen*. Bonn, 1836–44. Fifth edition, 1882.
Donum natalicum Schrijnen. Nijmegen and Utrecht, 1929.
d'Ovidio, F., *Grammatica storica della lingua e dei dialetti italiani*. Milan, 1906 (*Manuali Hoepli*).
Du Cange, C. du Fresne, *Glossarium mediae et infimae Latinitatis*. Second edition, Niort, 1883–87.
Ebert, M., *Reallexikon der Vorgeschichte*. Berlin, 1924–.
Ellis, A. J., *On early English pronunciation*. London, 1869–89 (= *Early English text society; Extra series*, 2; 7; 14; 23; 56).
Englische Studien. Heilbronn (now Leipzig), 1877–.
Erdmann, B., and Dodge, R., *Psychologische Untersuchungen über das Lesen*. Halle, 1898.
Erman, A., *Die Hieroglyphen*. Leipzig, 1912 (= *Sammlung Göschen*, 608).
Esper, E. A., *A technique for the experimental investigation of associative interference in artificial linguistic material*. Philadelphia, 1925 (= *Language monographs published by the Linguistic society of America*, 1).
Ewen, C. L'Estrange, *A history of surnames of the British Isles*. London, 1931.
Fabian, E., *Das exozentrische Kompositum im Deutschen*. Leipzig, 1931 (= *Form und Geist*, 20).
Falk, H., and Torp, A., *Dansk-Norskens syntax*. Christiania, 1900.
Falk, H., and Torp, A., *Norwegisch-dänisches etymologisches Wörterbuch*. Heidelberg, 1910 (= *Germanische Bibliothek*, 1.4.1).
Farmer, J. S., and Henley, W. E., *Slang and its analogues*. London, 1890–1904. Second edition 1903–. Abridged version: *A dictionary of slang and colloquial English*. New York, 1921.
Fechner, H., *Grundriss der Geschichte der wichtigsten Leselehrarten*. Berlin, 1884.

Feilberg, H. F., *Bidrag til en ordbog over jyske almuesmaal.* Copenhagen, 1886–1910.
Feist, S., *Etymologisches Wörterbuch der gotischen Sprache.* Second edition, Halle, 1923.
Feist, S., *Kultur, Ausbreitung und Herkunft der Indogermanen.* Berlin, 1913.
Festgabe Heinzel: Abhandlungen zur germanischen Philolgoie; Festgabe für R. Heinzel. Halle, 1898.
Festgabe Suchier: Forschungen zur romanischen Philologie; Festoabe für H. Suchier. Halle, 1900.
Festschrift für . . . P. Kretschmer. Berlin, 1926.
Festschrift Meinhof. Hamburg, 1927.
Festschrift Morf: Aus romanischen Sprachen und Literaturen; Festschrift H. Morf. Halle, 1905.
Festschrift V. Thomsen. Leipzig, 1912.
Festschrift Wackernagel: Antidoron; Festschrift J. Wackernagel. Göttingen, 1924.
Festskrift til V. Thomsen. Copenhagen, 1894.
Finck, F. N., *Die Aufgabe und Gliederung der Sprachwissenschaft.* Halle, 1905.
Finck, F. N., *Die Haupttypen des Sprachbaus.* Leipzig, 1910 (= *Aus Natur und Geisteswelt*, 268).
Finck, F. N., *Die Klassifikation der Sprachen.* Marburg, 1901.
Finck, F. N., *Lehrbuch des Dialekts der deutschen Zigeuner.* Marburg, 1903.
Finck, F. N., *Die Sprachstämme des Erdkreises.* Leipzig, 1909 (= *Aus Natur und Geisteswelt*, 267).
Finnisch-ugrische Forschungen. Helsingfors, 1901–.
Fischer, H., *Geographie der schwäbischen Mundart.* Tübingen, 1895.
Flasdieck, H. M., *Forschungen zur Frühzeit der neuenglischen Schriftsprache.* Halle, 1922 (= *Studien zur englischen Philologie*, 65; 66).
Fletcher, H., *Speech and hearing.* New York, 1929.
Flom, G. T., *Scandinavian influence on southern Lowland Scotch.* New York, 1901 (= *Columbia University Germanic studies*, 1).
Forchhammer, H., *How to learn Danish.* Heidelberg, 1906. I have seen only the French version, *Le danois parlé*, Heidelberg, 1911.
Franck, J., and van Wijk, N., *Etymologisch woordenboek der Nederlandsche taal.* The Hague, 1912.
Fries, C. C., *The teaching of the English language.* New York, 1927.
Frings, T., *Rheinische Sprachgeschichte.* Essen, 1924. Also as contribution to *Geschichte des Rheinlandes*, Essen, 1922.
Fritzner, J., *Ordbog over det gamle norske sprog.* Christiania, 1886-96.
Gabelentz, G. von der, *Die Sprachwissenschaft.* Second edition, Leipzig, 1901.
Gadde, F., *On the history and use of the suffixes -ery (-ry), -age and -ment in English.* Lund, 1910 (*Svea English treatises*).
Gairdner, W. H. T., *The phonetics of Arabic.* London, 1925 (*The American University at Cairo; Oriental studies*).

Gamillscheg, E., *Die Sprachgeographie*. Bielefeld and Leipzig, 1928 (= *Neuphilologische Handbibliothek*, 2).
Gauthiot, R., *La fin de mot en indo-européen*. Paris, 1913.
The Germanic review. New York, 1926–.
Giessener Beiträge zur Erforschung der Sprache und Kultur Englands und Nordamerikas. Giessen, 1923–.
Giles, H. A., *A Chinese-English dictionary*. London, 1892.
Gilliéron, J., *L'aire clavellus*. Neuveville, 1912.
Gilliéron, J., *Généalogie des mots qui désignent l'abeille*. Paris, 1918 (= *Bibliothèque de l'École des hautes études; Sciences historiques et philologiques*, 225).
Gilliéron, J., *Pathologie et thérapeutique verbales*. Paris, 1921 (= *Collection linguistique publiée par la Société de linguistique de Paris*, 11).
Gilliéron, J., and Edmont, E., *Atlas linguistique de la France*. Paris, 1902–10. Supplement, 1920; maps for Corsica, 1914–15.
Gilliéron, J., and Mongin, J., *Scier dans la Gaule romane du sud et de l'est*. Paris, 1905.
Gilliéron, J., and Roques, M., *Études de géographie linguistique*. Paris, 1912.
Goeders, C., *Zur Analogiebildung im Mittel- und Neuenglischen*. Dissertation, Kiel, 1884.
Graff, E. G., *Althochdeutscher Sprachschatz*. Berlin, 1834–42. Index by H. F. Massmann, 1846. A supplement, *Die althochdeutschen Präpositionen*, Königsberg, 1824, appeared before the main work.
A grammatical miscellany offered to O. Jespersen. Copenhagen, 1930.
Grammont, M., *La dissimilation consonantique dans les langues indo-européennes et dans les langues romanes*. Dijon, 1895.
Grandgent, C. H., *From Latin to Italian*. Cambridge, Mass., 1927.
Greenough, J. B., and Kittredge, G. L., *Words and their ways in English speech*. New York, 1901.
[Griera, A., *Atlas lingüistic de Catalunya*. Barcelona, 1923–.]
Grierson, G. A., *Linguistic survey of India*. Calcutta, 1903–22.
Grimm, J., *Deutsche Grammatik*. Göttingen, 1819–37. Second edition of first volume, 1822. Index by K. G. Andresen, 1865. Reprint with additions from Grimm's notes, Berlin, then Gütersloh, 1870–98.
Grimm, J. and W., *Deutsches Wörterbuch*. Leipzig, 1854–.
GRM: Germanisch-romanische Monatsschrift. Heidelberg, 1909–.
Gröber, G., *Grundriss der romanischen Philologie*. Second edition, Strassburg, 1904–06.
Guérard, A. L., *A short history of the international language movement*. London, 1922.
Guernier, R. C., *Notes sur la prononciation de la langue mandarine de Pékin*. London, 1912 (Supplement to *Maître phonétique*).
Gutzmann, H., *Physiologie der Stimme und Sprache*. Second edition, Braunschweig, 1928 (= *Die Wissenschaft*, 29).
Gutzmann, H., *Sprachheilkunde*. Third edition, Berlin, 1924.
Haag, C., *Die Mundarten des oberen Neckar- und Donaulandes*. School program, Reutlingen, 1898.

Hanssen, F., *Spanische Grammatik auf historischer Grundlage.* Halle, 1910 (= *Sammlung kurzer Lehrbücher der romanischen Sprachen,* 6).
Harvard studies in classical philology. Boston, 1890–.
Hasse, A., *Studien über englische Volksetymologie.* Dissertation, Strassburg, 1904.
Hatzfeld, A., Darmesteter, A., Thomas, A., *Dictionnaire général de la langue française.* Sixth edition, Paris, 1920.
Hatzfeld, H., *Leitfaden der vergleichenden Bedeutungslehre.* Second edition, Munich, 1928.
Head, H., *Aphasia and kindred disorders of speech.* New York, 1926.
Heepe, M., *Lautzeichen.* Berlin, 1928.
Hehn, V., *Kulturpflanzen und Haustiere.* Seventh edition, Berlin, 1902.
Hellquist, E., *Det svenska ordförrådets ålder och ursprung.* Lund, 1929–30.
Hempl, G., *German orthography and phonology.* Boston, 1897.
Hermann, E., *Berthold Delbrück.* Jena, 1923.
Hermann, E., *Lautgesetz und Analogie.* Berlin, 1931 (= *Abhandlungen der Gesellschaft der Wissenschaften zu Göttingen; Philologisch-historische Klasse; Neue Folge,* 23.3).
Herzog, E., *Streitfragen der romanischen Philologie.* Halle, 1904.
Herzog, R., *Die Umschrift der älteren griechischen Literatur in das ionische Alphabet.* University program, Basel, 1912.
Hesseling, D. C., *Het Negerhollands der Deense Antillen.* Leiden, 1905.
Heusler, A., *Altisländisches Elementarbuch.* Second edition, Heidelberg, 1921 (= *Germanische Bibliothek,* 1.1.3).
Hilmer, H., *Schallnachahmung.* Halle, 1914.
Hirt, H., *Handbuch der griechischen Laut- und Formenlehre.* Second edition, Heidelberg, 1912 (= *Indogermanische Bibliothek,* 1.1.2).
Hirt, H., *Handbuch des Urgermanischen.* Heidelberg, 1931– (= *Indogermanische Bibliothek,* 1.1.21).
Hirt, H., *Die Indogermanen.* Strassburg, 1905.
Hirt, H., *Indogermanische Grammatik.* Heidelberg, 1921– (= *Indogermanische Bibliothek,* 1.13).
Hjelmslev, L., *Principes de grammaire générale.* Copenhagen, 1928 (= *Det k. danske videnskabernes selskab; Historisk-filologiske meddelelser,* 16.1).
Holthausen, F., *Altsächsisches Elementarbuch.* Second edition, Heidelberg, 1921 (= *Germanische Bibliothek,* 1.5).
Homenaje ofrecido a Menéndez Pidal. Madrid, 1925.
Hoops, J., *Reallexikon der germanischen Altertumskunde.* Strassburg, 1911–19.
Hoops, J., *Waldbäume und Kulturpflanzen im germanischen Altertum.* Strassburg, 1905.
Horn, W., *Historische neuenglische Grammatik; Erster Teil, Lautlehre.* Strassburg, 1908.
Horn, W., *Sprachkörper und Sprachfunktion.* Second edition, Leipzig, 1923 (= *Palaestra,* 135).
Hubert, H., *Les Celtes et l'expansion celtique.* Paris, 1932 (= *L'évolution de l'humanité,* 1.21).
Humboldt, W. von, *Über die Kawisprache.* Berlin, 1836–39 (in *Abhandlungen der Akademie der Wissenschaften zu Berlin,* as of 1832). Part 1 was

republished with an elaborate commentary, in two volumes and a supplement, by A. F. Pott, Berlin, 1876–80.

IF: Indogermanische Forschungen. Strassburg (now Berlin), 1892–. Supplement: *Anzeiger.*

IJ: Indogermanisches Jahrbuch. Strassburg (now Berlin), 1914–.

IJAL: International journal of American linguistics. New York, 1917–.

Ipsen, G., and Karg, F., *Schallanalytische Versuche.* Heidelberg, 1928 (= *Germanische Bibliothek,* 2.24).

IZ: Internationale Zeitschrift für allgemeine Sprachwissenschaft. Leipzig, 1884–90.

Jaberg, K., *Sprachgeographie.* Aarau, 1908.

Jaberg, K., and Jud, J., *Sprach- und Sachatlas Italiens und der Südschweiz.* Zofingen, 1928–.

Jahresbericht über die Erscheinungen auf dem Gebiete der germanischen Philologie. Berlin, 1880–.

JAOS: Journal of the American Oriental society. New York (now New Haven), 1850–.

JEGP: Journal of English and Germanic Philology. Bloomington, Indiana (now Urbana, Illinois), 1897–.

Jellinek, M. H., *Geschichte der deutschen Grammatik.* Heidelberg, 1913–14 (= *Germanische Bibliothek,* 2.7).

Jellinek, M. H., *Geschichte der gotischen Sprache.* Berlin and Leipzig, 1926 (= *Grundriss der germanischen Philologie,* 1.1).

Jensen, H., *Geschichte der Schrift.* Hannover, 1925.

Jespersen, O., *Fonetik.* Copenhagen, 1897–99.

Jespersen, O., *Growth and structure of the English language.* Fourth edition, New York, 1929.

Jespersen, O., *How to teach a foreign language.* London, 1904.

Jespersen, O., *Language; its nature, development, and origin.* London and New York, 1923.

Jespersen, O., *Lehrbuch der Phonetik.* Second edition, Leipzig, 1913.

Jespersen, O., *A modern English grammar on historical principles.* Heidelberg, 1909– (= *Germanische Bibliothek,* 1.9).

Jespersen, O., *The philosophy of grammar.* London and New York, 1924.

Jespersen, O., *Progress in language.* London, 1894.

(Jespersen, O., and Pedersen, H.,) *Phonetic transcription and transliteration.* Oxford, 1926 (Supplement to *Maître phonétique*).

Johnson, G. B., *Folk culture on St. Helena Island.* Chapel Hill, 1930 (in *University of North Carolina social study series*).

Jones, D., *An English pronouncing dictionary.* London, 1917.

Jones, D., *Intonation curves.* Leipzig, 1909.

Jones, D., *Outline of English phonetics.* Second edition, Leipzig and Berlin, 1922.

Jones, D., and Woo, K. T., *A Cantonese phonetic reader.* London, 1912.

Journal de la Société des américanistes de Paris, 1895–.

Jutz, L., *Die alemannischen Mundarten.* Halle, 1931.

Kaluza, M., *Historische Grammatik der englischen Sprache.* Second edition, Berlin, 1906–07.

Karlgren, B., *Études sur la phonologie chinoise*. Leiden and Stockholm, 1915 (= *Archives d'études orientales*, 15).
Karlgren, B., *A Mandarin phonetic reader*. Uppsala, 1917 (= *Archives d'études orientales*, 13).
Karlgren, B., *Philology and ancient China*. Oslo, 1926 (= *Instituttet for sammenlignende kulturforskning; Serie A: Forelesninger*, 8).
Karlgren, B., *Sound and symbol in Chinese*. London, 1923 (*Language and literature series*).
Kennedy, A. G., *A bibliography of writings on the English language*. Cambridge and New Haven, 1927.
Kent, R. G., *The sounds of Latin*. Baltimore, 1932 (= *Language monographs published by the Linguistic society of America*, 12).
Kent, R. G., *The textual criticism of inscriptions*. Philadelphia, 1926 (= *Language monographs published by the Linguistic society of America*, 2).
Kenyon, J. S., *American pronunciation*. Ann Arbor, 1924.
Klein, E., *Die verdunkelten Wortzusammensetzungen im Neuenglischen*. Dissertation, Königsberg, 1911.
Klinghardt, H., *Übungen im deutschen Tonfall*. Leipzig, 1927.
Klinghardt, H., and de Fourmestraux, M., *Französische Intonationsübungen*. Cöthen, 1911. English translation by M. L. Barker: *French intonation exercises*, Cambridge, 1923.
Kloeke, G. G., *De Hollandsche expansie*. The Hague, 1927 (= *Noorden Zuid-Nederlandsche dialectbibliotheek*, 2).
Kluge, F., *Deutsche Sprachgeschichte*. Second edition, Leipzig, 1925.
Kluge, F., *Etymologisches Wörterbuch der deutschen Sprache*. Tenth edition, Berlin and Leipzig, 1924; eleventh edition, 1930–
Kluge, F., *Urgermanisch*. Third edition, Strassburg, 1913 (= *Grundriss der germanischen Philologie*, 2).
Kluge, F., *Von Luther bis Lessing*. Fifth edition, Leipzig, 1918.
Knutson, A., *The gender of words denoting living beings in English*. Dissertation, Lund, 1905.
Krapp, G. P., *The English language in America*. New York, 1925.
Krapp, G. P., *The pronunciation of standard English in America*. New York, 1919.
Kroeber, A. L., *Anthropology*. New York, 1923.
Kruisinga, E., *A grammar of modern Dutch*. London, 1924.
Kruisinga, E., *A handbook of present-day English*. Fourth edition, Utrecht, 1925; Part 2 in fifth edition, Groningen, 1931–32.
Künzel, G., *Das zusammengesetzte Substantiv und Adjektiv der englischen Sprache*. Dissertation, Leipzig, 1910.
Kussmaul, A., *Die Störungen der Sprache*. Fourth edition, Leipzig, 1910.
Last, W., *Das Bahuvrihi-Compositum im Altenglischen, Mittelenglischen und Neuenglischen*. Dissertation, Greifswald, 1925.
Leonard, S. A., *The doctrine of correctness in English usage 1700–1800*. Madison, 1929 (= *University of Wisconsin studies in language and literature*, 25).
Lepsius, C. R., *Standard alphabet*. Second edition, London, 1863.

Le Roux, P., *Atlas linguistique de la Basse Bretagne.* Rennes and Paris, 1924–.

Leskien, A., *Die Declination im Slavisch-Litauischen und Germanischen.* Leipzig, 1876 (= *Preisschriften der Jablonowski'schen Gesellschaft,* 19).

Leskien, A., *Grammatik der altbulgarischen Sprache.* Second edition, Heidelberg, 1919 (= *Sammlung slavischer Lehr- und Handbücher,* 1.1).

Leskien, A., *Grammatik der serbokroatischen Sprache. 1. Teil.* Heidelberg, 1914 (= *Sammlung slavischer Lehr- und Handbücher,* 1.4).

Leskien, A., *Handbuch der altbulgarischen (altkirchenslavischen) Sprache.* [Fifth edition, Weimar, 1910.]

Leskien, A., *Litauisches Lesebuch.* Heidelberg, 1919 (= *Indogermanische Bibliothek,* 1.2).

Lexer, M., *Mittelhochdeutsches Handwörterbuch.* Leipzig, 1872–78.

Lg: Language; Journal of the Linguistic society of America. Baltimore, 1925–.

Lindkvist, H., *Middle English place-names of Scandinavian origin. Part 1.* Dissertation, Uppsala, 1912 (also in *Uppsala universitets årsskrift,* 1911.1).

Lindsay, W. M., *The Latin language.* Oxford, 1894.

Literaturblatt für germanische und romanische Philologie. Heilbronn (now Leipzig), 1880–.

Ljunggren, R., *Om den opersonliga konstruktionen.* Uppsala, 1926.

Lloyd, R. J., *Northern English.* Second edition, Leipzig, 1908 (= *Skizzen lebender Sprachen,* 1).

Luick, K., *Historische Grammatik der englischen Sprache.* Leipzig, 1914–.

Lundell, J. A., *Det svenska landsmålsalfabetet.* Stockholm, 1879 (= *Nyare bidrag till kännedom om de svenska landsmålen,* 1.2).

Le maître phonétique. Bourg-la-Reine (now London), 1889–.

Marett, R. R., *Anthropology,* New York, 1911 (= *Home university library,* 37).

Mawer, A., and Stenton, F. M., *Introduction to the survey of English place-names.* Cambridge, 1924 (= *English place-name society,* 1.1).

McKnight, G. H., *English words and their background.* New York, 1923.

McMurry, R. E., Mueller, M., Alexander, T., *Modern foreign languages in France and Germany.* New York, 1930 (= *Studies of the International institute of Teachers college,* 9).

Meier, J., *Deutsche Volkskunde.* Berlin and Leipzig, 1926.

Meillet, A., *Aperçu d'une histoire de la langue grecque.* Third edition, Paris, 1930.

Meillet, A., *Les dialectes indo-européens.* Second edition, Paris, 1922 (= *Collection linguistique publiée par la Société de linguistique de Paris,* 2).

Meillet, A., *Introduction a l'étude comparative des langues indo-européennes.* Third edition, Paris, 1912.

Meillet, A., *Les langues dans l'Europe nouvelle.* Second edition, Paris, 1928.

Meillet, A., *Linguistique historique et linguistique générale.* Paris, 1921 (= *Collection linguistique publiée par la Société de linguistique de Paris,* 8).

Meillet, A., *La méthode comparative en linguistique historique.* Oslo, 1925 (= *Instituttet for sammenlignende kulturforskning; Serie A: Forelesninger,* 2).

Meillet, A., *Le slave commun.* Paris, 1924 (= *Collection de manuels publiée par l'Institut d'études slaves,* 2).

Meillet, A., and Cohen, M., *Les langues du monde*, Paris, 1924 (= *Collection linguistique publiée par la Société de linguistique de Paris*, 16).
Meinhof, C., *Grundriss der Lautlehre der Bantusprachen*. Second edition, Berlin, 1910.
Meinhof, C., *Grundzüge einer vergleichenden Grammatik der Bantu-Sprachen*. Berlin, 1906.
Meinhof, C., *Die moderne Sprachforschung in Afrika*. Berlin, 1910.
Meissner, B., *Die Keilschrift*. Leipzig, 1913 (= *Sammlung Göschen*, 708).
Meisterwerke der romanischen Sprachwissenschaft. Munich, 1929–30.
Menéndez Pidal, R., *El idioma español en sus primieros tiempos*. Madrid, 1927 (= *Collección de manuales Hispania*, B2).
Menéndez Pidal, R., *Manual de gramática historica española*. Fourth edition, Madrid, 1918.
Menéndez Pidal, R., *Orígenes del español*. Madrid, 1926 (= *Revista de filología española; Anejo* 1).
Meringer, R., and Meyer, K., *Versprechen und Verlesen*. Stuttgart, 1895.
Meyer, K. H., *Historische Grammatik der russischen Sprache*. Bonn, 1923.
Meyer-Lübke, W., *Einführung in das Studium der romanischen Sprachen*. Third edition, Heidelberg, 1920 (= *Sammlung romanischer Elementar- und Handbücher*, 1.1).
Meyer-Lübke, W., *Grammatik der romanischen Sprachen*. Leipzig, 1890–1902. French translation, *Grammaire des langues romanes*. Paris, 1890–1906.
Meyer-Lübke, W., *Historische Grammatik der französischen Sprache; 1. Teil*. Second edition, Heidelberg, 1913; *2. Teil*, 1921 (= *Sammlung romanischer Elementar- und Handbücher*, 1.2).
Meyer-Lübke, W., *Romanisches etymologisches Wörterbuch*. Heidelberg, 1911–19; third edition, 1930– (= *Sammlung romanischer Elementar- und Handbücher*, 3.3).
Michaelis, H., and Jones, D., *A phonetic dictionary of the English language*. Hannover, 1913.
Michaelis, H., and Passy, P., *Dictionnaire phonétique de la langue française*. Second edition, Hannover, 1914.
Michels, V., *Mittelhochdeutsches Elementarbuch*. Third edition, Heidelberg, 1921 (= *Germanische Bibliothek*, 1.1.7).
Middleton, G., *An essay on analogy in syntax*. London, 1892.
Miklosich, F., *Etymologisches Wörterbuch der slavischen Sprachen*. Vienna, 1886.
Miklosich, F., *Über die Mundarten und die Wanderungen der Zigeuner Europa's*. Vienna, 1872–81 (also in volumes 21–23, 25–27, 30, 31 of *Denkschriften der Akademie der Wissenschaften; philosophisch-historische Klasse*).
Miklosich, F., *Vergleichende Grammatik der slavischen Sprachen*. Weimar, 1852–74; second edition of volume 1, 1879; of volume 3, 1876.
Millardet, G., *Linguistique et dialectologie romanes*. Montpellier and Paris, 1923 (= *Publications spéciales de la Société des langues romanes*, 28).
The modern language review. Cambridge, 1906–.
Modern philology. Chicago, 1903–.
Morris, E. P., *On principles and methods in Latin syntax*. New York, 1901.

Morsbach, L., *Über den Ursprung der neuenglischen Schriftsprache.* Heilbronn, 1888.
MSL: Mémoires de la Société de linguistique de Paris. Paris, 1868–.
Müller, F., *Grundriss der Sprachwissenschaft.* Vienna, 1876–88.
Müller, M., *Die Reim- und Ablautkomposita des Englischen.* Dissertation, Strassburg, 1909.
Nachrichten von der Gesellschaft der Wissenschaften zu Göttingen; Philologisch-historische Klasse. Göttingen.
Navarro Tomás, T., *Manual de pronunciación española.* Madrid, 1918. [English adaptation by A. M. Espinosa, *Primer of Spanish pronunciation.* New York, 1926.]
NED: A new English dictionary on historical principles, edited by J. A. H. Murray. Oxford, 1888–1928.
Neuphilologische Mitteilungen. Helsingfors, 1899–.
Nicholson, G. A., *English words with native roots and with Greek, Latin, or Romance suffixes.* Dissertation, Chicago, 1916 (= *Linguistic studies in Germanic,* 3).
Nicholson, G. G., *A practical introduction to French phonetics.* London, 1909.
Nichtenhauser, D., *Rückbildungen im Neuhochdeutschen.* Dissertation, Freiburg, 1920.
Noël-Armfield, G., *General phonetics.* Third edition, Cambridge, 1924.
Noreen, A., *Altnordische Grammatik: 1. Altisländische und altnorwegische Grammatik.* Fourth edition, Halle, 1923. *2. Altschwedische Grammatik,* Halle, 1904 (= *Sammlung kurzer Grammatiken germanischer Dialekte,* 4; 8).
Noreen VS: Noreen, A., *Vårt språk.* Lund, 1903–18. Selections translated into German by H. W. Pollak, *Einführung in die wissenschaftliche Betrachtung der Sprache.* Halle, 1923.
NS: Die neueren Sprachen. Marburg, 1894–.
Nyrop, K., *Grammaire historique de la langue française.* Copenhagen, 1899–1930.
Nyrop, K., *Ordenes liv.* Second edition, Copenhagen, 1925–26. A German translation by L. Vogt, *Das Leben der Wörter,* Leipzig, 1903. [Second edition, 1923.]
Oertel, H., *Lectures on the study of language.* New York, 1901.
Ogden, C. K., and Richards, I. A., *The meaning of meaning.* London, 1923.
Olsen, M., *Farms and fanes of ancient Norway.* Oslo, 1926 (= *Institutet for sammenlignende kulturforskning; Serie A: Forelesninger,* 9).
Ordbok över svenska språket, utgiven av Svenska akademien. Lund, 1898–.
Orientalische Bibliographie. Berlin, 1888–.
Osthoff, H., *Das Verbum in der Nominalcomposition.* Jena, 1878.
Ostoff, H., and Brugmann, K., *Morphologische Untersuchungen.* Leipzig, 1878–1910.
Paget, R., *Human speech.* London, 1930.
Palmer, A. S., *Folk-etymology.* London, 1882.
Palmer, H. E., *English intonation.* Cambridge, 1922.
Palmer, H. E., *A first course in English phonetics.* Cambridge, 1922.
Palmer, H. E., *A grammar of spoken English.* Cambridge, 1924.
Palmer, H. E., *The principles of language-study.* London, 1921.

Palmer, H. E., *The principles of romanization.* Tokyo, 1931.
Palmer, H. E., Martin, J. V., Blandford, M. A., *A dictionary of English pronunciation with American variants.* Cambridge, 1926.
Palmgren, C., *A chronological list of English forms of the types alive, aloud, aglow.* School program, Norrköping, 1923.
Panconcelli-Calzia, G., *Einführung in die angewandte Phonetik.* Berlin, 1914.
Panconcelli-Calzia, G., *Experimentelle Phonetik.* Berlin and Leipzig, 1921 (= *Sammlung Göschen*, 844).
La parole. Paris, 1891–1904.
Parry-Williams, T. H., *The English element in Welsh.* London, 1923.
Passy, J., and Rambeau, A., *Chrestomathie française.* Fourth edition, Leipzig, 1918.
Passy, P., *L'enseignement de la lecture.* London, 1916 (Supplement to *Maître phonétique*).
Passy, P., *Étude sur les changements phonétiques.* Paris, 1890.
Passy, P., *Petite phonétique comparée.* Second edition, Leipzig, 1912.
Passy, P., *Les sons du français.* Eighth edition, Paris, 1917 [English translation, *The sounds of the French language.* Second edition, Oxford, 1913.]
Passy, P., and Hempl, G., *International French-English and English-French dictionary.* New York, 1904.
(Passy, P., and Jones, D.,) *Principles of the International phonetic association.* London, 1912 (Supplement to *Maître phonétique*).
Paul, H., *Deutsche Grammatik.* Halle, 1916–20.
Paul, H., *Grundriss der germanischen Philologie.* Second edition, Strassburg, 1900–09. Some of the contributions have appeared in later editions, as separate volumes; see Behaghel, *Geschichte;* Kluge, *Urgermanisch.*
Paul, H., *Prinzipien der Sprachgeschichte.* Halle, 1880; fifth edition, 1920. The second (1886) edition was translated into English by H. A. Strong, *Principles of the history of language,* London, 1889; an adaptation of the same edition is Strong-Logeman-Wheeler.
Pedersen, H., *Le groupement des dialectes indo-européens.* Copenhagen, 1925 (= *Det k. danske videnskabernes selskab; Historisk-filologiske meddelelser,* 11.3).
Pedersen, H., *Linguistic science in the nineteenth century;* English translation by J. Spargo. Cambridge, Mass., 1931.
Pedersen, H., *Vergleichende Grammatik der keltischen Sprachen.* Göttingen, 1909–13.
The phonetic transcription of Indian languages. Washington, 1916 (= *Smithsonian miscellaneous collections,* 66.6).
PMLA: Publications of the Modern language association of America. Baltimore (now Menasha, Wis.), 1886–.
Pott, A. F., *Etymologische Forschungen auf dem Gebiete der indo-germanischen Sprachen.* Lemgo, 1833. Second (entirely different) edition, 1859–76.
Pound, L., *Blends; their relation to English word formation.* Heidelberg, 1914 (= *Anglistische Forschungen,* 42).
Poutsma, H., *The characters of the English verb.* Groningen, 1921.
Poutsma, H., *A grammar of late modern English.* Groningen, 1904–26.
Preyer, W., *Die Seele des Kindes.* Seventh edition, Leipzig, 1908.

BIBLIOGRAPHY

Proceedings of the 21st international congress of Americanists. Part 1. The Hague, 1924.
Proceedings of the 23d international congress of Americanists. New York, 1930.
Publications of the English dialect society. London, 1873–.
The quarterly journal of speech. Chicago, 1915–.
Raith, J., *Die englischen Nasalverben.* Leipzig, 1931 (= *Beiträge zur englischen Philologie*, 17).
Rask, R. K., *Undersøgelse om det nordiske eller islandske sprogs oprindelse.* Copenhagen, 1818.
Raumer, R. von, *Geschichte der germanischen Philologie.* Munich, 1870 (= *Geschichte der Wissenschaften in Deutschland; Neuere Zeit*, 9).
Revue des patois gallo-romans. Paris, 1887–93.
Rice, C. C., *The Phonology of Gallic clerical Latin after the sixth century.* Dissertation, Cambridge, Mass., 1902.
Rice, S. A., *Methods in social science.* Chicago, 1931.
Ries, J., *Was ist ein Satz?* Prague, 1931 (= his *Beiträge zur Grundlegung der Syntax*, 3).
Ries, J., *Was ist Syntax?* Second edition, Prague, 1927 (= his *Beiträge zur Grundlegung der Syntax*, 1).
Rippmann, W., *Elements of phonetics.* Second edition, New York, 1903.
Roedler, E., *Die Ausbreitung des s-Plurals im Englischen.* Dissertation, Kiel, 1911.
Romania. Paris, 1872–.
Romanische Forschungen. Erlangen, 1883–.
Ronjat, J., *Le développement du langage observé chez un enfant bilingue.* Paris, 1913.
Rosenqvist, A., *Lehr- und Lesebuch der finnischen Sprache.* Leipzig, 1925 (*Sammlung Jügel*).
Rotzoll, E., *Die Deminutivbildungen im Neuenglischen.* Heidelberg, 1910 (= *Anglistische Forschungen*, 31).
Rousselot, J., *Les modifications phonétiques du langage.* Paris, 1893 (also in *Revue des patois*, volumes 4, 5, and 5 supplement).
Rousselot, J., *Principes de phonétique expérimentale.* Paris, 1897–1908.
RP: Revue de phonétique. Paris, 1911–.
Russell, G. O., *Speech and voice.* New York, 1931.
Russell, G. O., *The vowel.* Columbus, 1928.
Russer, W. S., *De Germaansche klankverschuiving.* Haarlem, 1931 (= *Nederlandsche bijdragen op het gebied van Germaansche philologie en linguistiek*, 1).
Saer, D. J., Smith, F., Hughes, J., *The bilingual problem.* Aberystwyth, 1924.
Sampson, J., *The dialect of the Gypsies of Wales.* Oxford, 1926.
Sandfeld, K., *Linguistique balkanique.* Paris, 1930 (= *Collection linguistique publiée par la Société de linguistique de Paris*, 31).
Sapir, E., *Language.* New York, 1921.
Scharpé, L., *Nederlandsche uitspraakleer.* Lier, 1912.
Schauerhammer, A., *Mundart und Heimat Kaspar Scheits.* Halle, 1908 (= *Hermaea*, 6).

Schleicher, A., *Compendium der vergleichenden Grammatik der indogermanischen Sprachen.* Weimar, 1861; fourth edition, 1876.
Schmeller, J. A., *Bayerisches Wörterbuch.* Second edition, Munich, 1872–77.
Schmeller, J. A., *Die Mundarten Bayerns.* Munich, 1821. A partial reprint, with an index as a separate volume (*Registerband*), by O. Mausser, appeared in 1929.
Schmidt, J., *Die Verwandtschaftsverhältnisse der indogermanischen Sprachen.* Weimar, 1872.
Schmidt, W., *Die Sprachfamilien und Sprachenkreise der Erde.* Heidelberg, 1926 (= *Kulturgeschichtliche Bibliothek,* 1.5).
Schönfeld, M., *Historiese grammatika van het Nederlands.* Second edition, Zutphen, 1924.
Schrader, O., *Reallexikon der indogermanischen Altertumskunde.* Second edition, Berlin and Leipzig, 1917–29.
Schrader, O., *Sprachvergleichung und Urgeschichte.* Third edition, Jena, 1906–07. English translation of the second (1890) edition, *Prehistoric antiquities of the Aryan peoples.* London, 1890.
Schuchardt, H., *Slawo-Deutsches und Slawo-Italienisches.* Graz, 1884.
Schuchardt, H., *Die Sprache der Saramakkaneger in Surinam.* Amsterdam, 1914 (= *Verhandelingen der k. Akademie van wetenschappen; Afdeeling letterkunde; Nieuwe reeks,* 14.6).
Schuchardt, H., *Über die Klassifikation der romanischen Mundarten.* [Graz, 1900.] Reprinted in *Schuchardt-Brevier,* 166.
Schuchardt, H., *Über die Lautgesetze.* Berlin, 1885. Reprinted in *Schuchardt-Brevier,* 51.
Schuchardt, H., *Der Vokalismus des Vulgärlateins.* Leipzig, 1866–67.
Schuchardt-Brevier: Hugo Schuchardt-Brevier. Second edition, Halle, 1928.
Scripture, E. W., *The elements of experimental phonetics.* New York, 1902.
Seip, D. A., *Norsk sproghistorie.* Christiania, 1920.
Siebs, T., *Deutsche Bühnenaussprache.* Fifteenth edition, Cologne, 1930.
Sievers, E., *Angelsächsische Grammatik.* Third edition, Halle, 1898 (= *Sammlung kurzer Grammatiken germanischer Dialekte,* 3). English translation by A. S. Cook, under the title *An Old English grammar,* Boston, 1903.
Sievers, E., *Grundzüge der Phonetik.* Fifth edition, Leipzig, 1901 (= *Bibliothek indogermanischer Grammatiken,* 1).
Sievers, E., *Ziele und Wege der Schallanalyse.* Heidelberg, 1924 (= *Germanische Bibliothek,* 2.14; also in *Stand und Aufgaben,* 65).
Sitzungsberichte der philosophisch-historischen Klasse der Akademie der Wissenschaften. Vienna, 1848–.
Skeat, W. W., *An etymological dictionary of the English language.* Third edition, Oxford, 1898.
Skeat, W. W., *English dialects.* Cambridge, 1911 (*Cambridge manuals of science and literature*).
Smetánka, E., *Tschechische Grammatik.* Berlin and Leipzig, 1914 (= *Sammlung Göschen,* 721).
Smith, R., *Gullah.* Columbia, S. C., 1926 (= *Bulletin of the University of South Carolina,* 190).

BIBLIOGRAPHY

Soames, L., *Introduction to English, French, and German phonetics.* Third edition, London, 1913.

Soerensen, A., *Polnische Grammatik.* Berlin, 1900.

Sommer, F., *Handbuch der lateinischen Laut- und Formenlehre.* Second edition, Heidelberg, 1914 (= *Indogermanische Bibliothek*, 1.1.3).

SPE: Society for pure English; Tracts. Oxford, 1919–.

Sperber, H., *Einführung in die Bedeutungslehre.* Bonn and Leipzig, 1923.

Sprengling, M., *The alphabet.* Chicago, 1931 (= *Oriental institute communications*, 12).

Stand und Aufgaben der Sprachwissenschaft; Festschrift für W. Streitberg. Heidelberg, 1924.

Steinthal, H., *Charakteristik der hauptsächlichsten Typen des Sprachbaues.* Second edition, revised by F. Misteli. Berlin, 1893 (= his *Abriss der Sprachwissenschaft*, 2).

Steinthal, H., *Geschichte der Sprachwissenschaft bei den Griechen und Römern.* Berlin, 1863.

Steinthal, H., *Der Ursprung der Sprache.* Fourth edition, Berlin, 1888.

Stender-Petersen, A., *Slavisch-germanische Lehnwortkunde.* Gothenburg, 1927 (= *Göteborgs k. vetenskaps- och vitterhets-samhälles handlingar*, 4.31.4).

Stern, C. and W., *Die Kindersprache.* Leipzig, 1907.

Stern, G., *Meaning and change of meaning.* Gothenburg, 1932 (= *Göteborg högskolas årsskrift*, 38.1).

Stolz, F., and Schmalz, J. H., *Lateinische Grammatik.* Fifth edition, Munich, 1928 (= *Handbuch der klassischen Altertumswissenschaft*, 2.2).

Stratmann, F. H., *A Middle English dictionary.* Oxford, 1891.

Strecker, K., *Einführung in das Mittellatein.* Berlin, 1928.

Streiff, C., *Die Laute der Glarner Mundarten.* Frauenfeld, 1915 (= *Beiträge zur schweizerdeutschen Grammatik*, 8).

Streitberg, W., *Gotisches Elementarbuch.* Fifth edition, Heidelberg, 1920 (= *Germanische Bibliothek*, 1.2).

Streitberg, W., *Urgermanische Grammatik.* Heidelberg, 1896 (= *Sammlung von Elementarbüchern der altgermanischen Dialekte*, 1).

Streitberg, W., and others, *Geschichte der indogermanischen Sprachwissenschaft.* Strassburg (now Berlin), 1916– (part of *Grundriss der indogermanischen Altertumskunde*, begründet von K. Brugmann und A. Thumb).

Streitberg Festgabe. Leipzig, 1924.

Strong, H. A., Logeman, W. S., Wheeler, B. I., *Introduction to the study of the history of language.* London, 1891 (see Paul, *Prinzipien*).

Studies in English philology; A miscellany in honor of F. Klaeber. Minneapolis, 1929.

Studies in honor of Hermann Collitz. Baltimore, 1930.

Sturtevant, E. H., *Linguistic change.* Chicago, 1917.

Sundén, K., *Contributions to the study of elliptical words in modern English.* Uppsala, 1904.

Sütterlin, L., *Geschichte der Nomina Agentis im Germanischen.* Strassburg, 1887.

Sütterlin, L., *Neuhochdeutsche Grammatik.* Munich, 1924–.

Sweet, H., *An Anglo-Saxon primer.* Eighth edition, Oxford, 1905.

Sweet, H., *An Anglo-Saxon reader*. Eighth edition, Oxford, 1908.
Sweet, H., *Collected papers*. Oxford, 1913.
Sweet, H., *Handbook of phonetics*. Oxford, 1877.
Sweet, H., *A history of English sounds*. Oxford, 1888.
Sweet, H., *The history of language*. London, 1900.
Sweet, H., *A new English grammar*. Oxford, 1892–98.
Sweet, H., *The practical study of languages*. New York, 1900.
Sweet, H., *A primer of phonetics*. Third edition, Oxford, 1906.
Sweet, H., *The sounds of English*. Second edition, Oxford, 1910.
Szinnyei, J., *Finnisch-ugrische Sprachwissenschaft*. Leipzig, 1910 (= *Sammlung Göschen*, 463).
Tamm, F., *Etymologisk svensk ordbok*. Uppsala, 1890–.
TAPA: Transactions of the American philological association. Hartford, Conn. (now Middletown, Conn.), 1871–.
Taylor, A., *The proverb*. Cambridge, Mass., 1931.
Teichert, F., *Über das Aussterben alter Wörter im Verlaufe der englischen Sprachgeschichte*. Dissertation, Erlangen, 1912.
Terracher, A. L., *Les aires morphologiques*. Paris, 1914.
Teuthonista; Zeitschrift für deutsche Dialektforschung und Sprachgeschichte. Bonn und Leipzig, 1924–.
Thesaurus linguae Latinae editus auctoritate et consilio academiarum quinque Germanicarum. Leipzig, 1904–.
Thomas, A., *Nouveaux essais de philologie française*. Paris, 1904.
Thomsen, W., *Über den Einfluss der germanischen Sprachen auf die finnischlappischen*. Halle, 1870.
Thorndike, E. L., *A teacher's word book*. New York, 1931.
Thumb, A., *Grammatik der neugriechischen Volkssprache*. Berlin and Leipzig, 1915 (= *Sammlung Göschen*, 756).
Thumb, A., *Handbuch der neugriechischen Volkssprache*. Strassburg, 1910.
Thumb, A., and Marbe, K., *Experimentelle Untersuchungen über psychologische Grundlagen der sprachlichen Analogiebildung*. Leipzig, 1901.
Thurneysen, R., *Die Etymologie*. Freiburg i. B., 1905.
Thurneysen, R., *Handbuch des Altirischen*. Heidelberg, 1909 (= *Indogermanische Bibliothek*, 1.1.6).
Thurot, C., *Notices et extraits de divers manuscrits latins pour servir à l'histoire des doctrines grammaticales au moyen âge*. Paris, 1868 (= *Notices et extraits des manuscrits de la bibliothèque impériale et autres bibliothèques*, 22.2).
Tijdschrift voor Nederlandsche taal- en letterkunde. Leiden, 1881–.
Toll, J. M., *Niederländisches Lehngut im Mittelenglischen*. Halle, 1926 (= *Studien zur englischen Philologie*, 69).
Torp, A., *Nynorsk etymologisk ordbok*. Christiania, 1919.
Torp, A., *Wortschatz der germanischen Spracheinheit*. Göttingen, 1909 (= A. Fick, *Vergleichendes Wörterbuch der indogermanischen Sprachen*, volume 3, fourth edition).
Torp, A., and Falk, H., *Dansk-Norskens lydhistorie*. Christiania, 1898.
Tourtoulon, C. J. M., and Bringuier, M. O., *Étude sur la limite géographique de la langue d'oc et de la langue d'oïl*. Paris, 1876.
Travaux du Cercle linguistique de Prague. Prague, 1929–.

Travis, L. E., *Speech pathology*. New York, 1931.
Trofimov, M. V., and Jones, D., *The pronunciation of Russian*. Cambridge, 1923.
Uhlenbeck, C. C., *Kurzgefasstes etymologisches Wörterbuch der altindischen Sprache*. Amsterdam, 1898–99.
Uhler, K., *Die Bedeutungsgleichheit der altenglischen Adjektiva und Adverbia mit und ohne -lic (-lice)*. Heidelberg, 1926 (= *Anglistische Forschungen*, 62).
Uhrström, W., *Pickpocket, turnkey, wrap-rascal and similar formations in English*. Stockholm, 1918.
University of Washington publications in anthropology. Seattle, 1920–.
van der Meer, M. J., *Historische Grammatik der niederländischen Sprache*. Heidelberg, 1927 (= *Germanische Bibliothek*, 1.1.16).
van der Meulen, R., *De Hollandsche zee- en scheepstermen in het Russisch*. Amsterdam, 1909 (= *Verhandelingen der K. akademie van wetenschappen; Afdeeling letterkunde; Nieuwe reeks*, 10.2).
Verwijs, E., and Verdam. J., *Middelnederlandsch woordenboek*. The Hague, 1885–1930.
Viëtor, W., *Die Aussprache des Schriftdeutschen*. Tenth edition, Leipzig, 1921.
Viëtor, W., *Deutsches Aussprachewörterbuch*. Third edition, Leipzig, 1921.
Viëtor, W., *Elemente der Phonetik*. Sixth edition, Leipzig, 1915.
Viëtor, W., *German pronunciation*. Third edition, Leipzig, 1903.
Viëtor, W., *Die Methodik des neusprachlichen Unterrichts*. Leipzig, 1902.
Vollmöller, K. G., *Kritischer Jahresbericht über die Fortschritte der romanischen Philologie*. Munich and Leipzig (then Erlangen), 1890–1915.
Vondrák, V., *Vergleichende slavische Grammatik*. Second edition, Göttingen, 1924–28.
Vox: Internationales Zentralblatt für experimentelle Phonetik; Vox. Berlin, 1891–1922.
Wackernagel, J., *Altindische Grammatik*. Göttingen, 1896–.
Wackernagel, J., *Vorlesungen über Syntax; Erste Reihe*. Second edition, Basel, 1926. *Zweite Reihe*, Basel, 1924.
Walde, A., *Lateinisches etymologisches Wörterbuch*. Second edition, Heidelberg, 1910; third edition, 1930– (= *Indogermanische Bibliothek*, 1.2.1).
Walde, A., and Pokorny, J., *Vergleichendes Wörterbuch der indogermanischen Sprachen*. Berlin and Leipzig, 1930.
Warnke, C., *On the formation of English words by means of ablaut*. Dissertation, Halle, 1878.
Weekley, E., *A concise etymological dictionary of modern English*. New York, 1924.
Weekley, E., *The romance of names*. Third edition, London, 1922.
Weekley, E., *Surnames*. New York, 1916.
Weigand, G., *Linguistischer Atlas des dacorumänischen Sprachgebeites*. Leipzig, 1909.
Weiss, A. P., *A theoretical basis of human behavior*. Second edition, Columbus, 1929.
West, M., *Bilingualism*. Calcutta, 1926 (= *Bureau of education, India; Occasional reports*, 13).

West, M., *Leaning to read a foreign language*. London, 1926.
De West-Indische gids. The Hague, 1919–.
Wheatley, H. B., *A dictionary of reduplicated words in the English language*. London, 1866 (Appendix to the *Transactions of the Philological society* for 1865).
Wheeler, B. I., *Analogy and the scope of its application to language*. Ithaca, 1887 (= *Cornell university studies in classical philology*, 2).
Whitney, W. D., *Language and the study of language*. New York, 1867.
Whitney, W. D., *The life and growth of language*. New York, 1874.
Whitney, W. D., *A Sanskrit grammar*. Third edition. Boston, 1896.
Wilmanns, W., *Deutsche Grammatik*; volume 1, third edition, Strassburg, 1911; volume 2, second edition, 1899; volume 3, 1906.
Wilson, S. A. Kinnier, *Aphasia*. London, 1926.
Wimmer, L., *Die Runenschrift*. Berlin, 1887.
Winteler, J., *Die Kerenzer Mundart*. Leipzig, 1876.
Wissenschaftlich Beihefte zur Zeitschrift des Allgemeinen deutschen Sprachvereins. Leipzig, 1891–.
Wissler, C., *The American Indian*. Second edition, New York, 1922.
Wörter und Sachen. Heidelberg, 1909–.
Wrede, F., *Deutscher Sprachatlas*. Marburg, 1926–.
Wright, J., *The English dialect dictionary*. London, 1898–1905.
Wright, J., *The English dialect grammar*. Oxford, 1905 (also as part of his *English dialect dictionary*).
Wright, J., and E. M., *An elementary historical New English grammar*. London, 1924.
Wright, J. and E. M., *An elementary Middle English grammar*. Second edition, London, 1928.
Wundt, W., *Sprachgeschichte und Sprachpsychologie*. Leipzig, 1901.
Wundt, W., *Völkerpsychologie; Erster Band: Die Sprache*. Third edition, Leipzig, 1911.
Wyld, H. C., *Historical study of the mother tongue*. London and New York, 1906.
Wyld, H. C., *A history of modern colloquial English*. London, 1920.
Wyld, H. C., *A short history of English*. Third edition, London and New York, 1927.
Wyld, H. C., *Studies in English rhymes from Surrey to Pope*. London, 1923.
Xandry, G., *Das skandinavische Element in den neuenglischen Dialekten*. Dissertation (Münster University), Neu Isenburg, 1914.
Zauner, A., *Romanische Sprachwissenschaft; 1. Teil*. Fourth edition, Berlin and Leipzig, 1921. *2. Teil*. Third edition, 1914. (= *Sammlung Göschen*, 128; 250).
ZdP: Zeitschrift für deutsche Philologie. Halle, 1869–. Often referred to as ZZ ("Zachers Zeitschrift").
Zeitschrift für Eingeborenensprachen. Berlin, 1910–.
Zeuss, J. K., *Grammatica Celtica*. Berlin, 1853; second edition, by H. Ebel, 1871.
Ziemer, H., *Junggrammatische Streifzüge im Gebiete der Syntax*. Second edition, Colberg, 1883.

Zipf, G. K., *Selected studies of the principle of relative frequency in language.* Cambridge, Mass., 1932.

ZrP: Zeitschrift für romanische Philologie. Halle, 1887–; Supplement: *Bibliographie.*

ZvS: Zeitschrift für vergleichende Sprachforschung. Berlin, 1852–. Often referred to as *KZ* ("Kuhns Zeitschrift").

TABLE OF PHONETIC SYMBOLS

The phonetic alphabet used in this book is a slightly modified form of the alphabet of the International Phonetic Association. The main principle of this alphabet is the use of a single letter for each phoneme (distinctive sound, see Chapter 5) of a language. The symbols are used very flexibly, and represent rather different sounds in the transcription of different languages, but the use is consistent within each language. Thus, [t] represents an English sound in *tin* [tin] and a somewhat different French sound in *tout* [tu] 'all.' Additional symbols are used only when a language distinguishes additional phonemes; symbols such as italic [*t*] or capital [T] are used in addition to [t] only for languages like Russian or Sanskrit which distinguish more than one phoneme of the general type of [t].

The following indications are to be read: "The symbol . . . represents the general type of the sound in . . ."

[a] American English *palm* [pam], French *patte* [pat]
[ɑ] British English *palm* [pɑ:m], American English *top* [tɑp]
[ʌ] English *cut* [kʌt]
[b] *bib* [bib]
[c] unvoiced palatal stop
[ç] unvoiced palatal spirant
[d] *did* [did]
[ð] *then* [ðen]
[dʒ] *jam* [dʒɛm]
[e] *pet* [pet], French *été* [ete]
[ɛ] *add* [ɛd], French *dette* [dɛt]
[ə] *bird* [bə:d], *bitter* [ˈbitə], *fair* [fɛə]
[f] *fat* [fɛt]
[g] *gag* [gɛg]
[ɣ] voiced velar spirant
[h] *hid* [hid]
[i] *bit* [bit], French *fini* [fini]
[ï] high unrounded back vowel
[j] *yes* [jes], *gay* [gej]
[k] *cook* [kuk]

TABLE OF PHONETIC SYMBOLS

[l] *lull* [lʌl]
[ʎ] Italian *figlio* [ˈfiʎo]
[m] *mad* [mɛd]
[n] *none* [nʌn]
[ŋ] *sing* [siŋ]
[ɲ] French *signe* [siɲ]
[o] American English *cut* [kot], French *eau* [o]
[ɔ] *top* [tɔp], *saw* [sɔː]
[ø] French *peu* [pø]
[œ] French *peuple* [pœpl]
[p] *pin* [pin]
[r] *red* [red], French *riz* [ri]
[s] *see* [sij]
[ʃ] *show* [ʃow]
[t] *ten* [ten]
[tʃ] *chin* [tʃin]
[θ] *thin* [θin]
[u] *put* [put], French *tout* [tu]
[v] *veil* [vejl]
[w] *woo* [wuw]
[x] German *ach* [ax]
[y] French *vu* [vy]
[ɥ] French *lui* [lɥi]
[z] *zoo* [zuw]
[ʒ] *rouge* [ruwʒ]
[ʔ] glottal stop

Additional signs:

When a language distinguishes more than one phoneme within any one of the above types, variant symbols are introduced; thus, capitals denote the domal sounds of Sanskrit [T, D, N], which are distinct from dental [t, d, n], and capital [I, U] denote opener varieties, distinct from [i, u], as in Old Bulgarian; italic letters are used for palatalized consonants, as in Russian [*bit*] 'to beat,' distinct from [bit] 'way of being.'

A small vertical stroke under a letter means that the sound forms a syllable, as in *brittler* [ˈbritl̩ə].

A tilde over a letter means that the sound is nasalized, as in French *bon* [bõ]. A small raised [ʷ] means that the preceding sound is labialized.

The mark [ˈ] means that the next syllable is accented, as *be-*

TABLE OF PHONETIC SYMBOLS 549

nighted [beˈnajted]. The signs [ʺ ˊ ˌ] are used in the same way, wherever several varieties of accent are distinguished. Numbers [¹ ² ³ ⁴] indicate distinctions of pitch.

The colon means that the preceding sound is long, as in German *Kahn* [kaːn], contrasting with *kann* [kan].

Other marks of punctuation [. , ?] denote modulations in the sentence; [¿] is used for the modulation in *Who's there?* [ˈhuw z ˈðɛə¿], contrasting with *Are you there?* [ɑː ju ˈðɛə?].

ADDITIONS AND CORRECTIONS

Page 13. *Albanese*, the form used throughout the book, should perhaps be replaced by the more current *Albanian*.

Page 14. On Rask, see the Introduction by H. Pedersen to Rask, R. K., *Ausgewählte Abhandlungen*, Copenhagen, 1932-33.

Page 53. In expressions like "our Southwest," the angle of vision is that of the United States of North America.

Page 59. For *Faroese* read *Faroe*.

Page 61. Ladin is spoken also in the southern Tyrol and in north-eastern Italy.

Page 65. The term *Accadian* is now preferred to *Babylonian-Assyrian*.

Page 70. On the basis of an entirely new definition and theory of the relationship of languages, the Russian scholars N. I. Marr and F. Braun view the Caucasian languages as survivals of a once widespread *Japhetic* family, some features of which appear also in Basque, in Semitic, and even in Indo-European languages, notably Armenian. However, the statements of these relations and the evidence for them do not seem precise enough to warrant acceptance. See *Materialy po jafetičeskomu jazykoznaniju*, Leningrad, 1910-; Marr, N. I., *Der japhetitische Kaukasus*, Berlin, 1923 (= *Japhetitische Studien*, 2); Marr, N. I., *Etapy razvitija jafetičeskoj teorii*, Leningrad, 1933 (= *Izbrannyje raboty*, 1).

Page 143. Instead of "(2) are so distantly correlated," etc., it would be better to say: "(2) are so variably correlated with speech-forms that these cannot guide us in determining the speaker's situation."

Page 164. The example *Backwater!* seems to be an unusual speech-form; *Dismount!* would be better.

Page 284. The cuneiform characters were not "scratched," but pressed with a stylus into tough clay.

Page 323. On Joseph Wright (1866-1930), see Wright, S. M., *The Life of Joseph Wright*, London, 1932.

Page 328. On the map, the dotted patch which represents the Frisian area extends too far southward; the dots should reach only to the boundary line which can be seen on the map.

Page 332. On the map, for *Kerensen* read *Kerenzen*.

Page 358. The Old English word for 'become' was doubtless pronounced not with [θ], but with [ð] representing an older [θ].

Page 363. Greek [ˈelejpsa] 'I left' is probably a late formation; a relevant example would be Primitive Indo-European *[ˈeteːrpsm̩] 'I satisfied' (Sanskrit [ˈataːrpsam] 'I was pleased'), Greek [ˈeterpsa].

Page 372. Latin *agmen* is a new formation and does not preserve old *-g-m-*; in this combination the *g* was lost, witness *exāmen* 'swarm.' With *fulmen* we should contrast, rather, *mūnımĕn* 'rampart' derived from *mūnīre* 'to fortify.'

Page 413. Jespersen, *Linguistica*, Copenhagen, 1933, page 420, does not believe that the suffix *-ster* was ever restricted to females.

Page 414. We should add the following example, because it gives the historical explanation of a phenomenon described earlier in the book.

The Latin adjective *grandis* (accusative *grandem*, etc.) leads phonetically to a French *grand* [grã], masculine and feminine; actually a new feminine form *grande* [grãd] has been created analogically, according to the type of adjective that loses a final consonant in the masculine inflection (§ 13.7); the old feminine form survives as a prior member in certain compound words (§ 14.3).

Page 423. To *crayfish*, etc., add: French *mousseron* re-shaped in English as *mushroom*.

Page 512. Note on Chapter II: see also the lively and readable survey of linguistics by J. R. Firth, *Speech*, London, 1930.

Page 514. See also Armstrong, L. E., *The Phonetics of French*, London, 1932.

Page 515. On pitch in Japanese, see also O. Pletner in *BSOS* 3.447 (1924).

Page 519. On Verner, see also Jespersen, *Linguistica*, 12. On Primitive Indo-European formulæ, see C. D. Buck in *Lg* 2.99 (1926).

Page 520. On English voicing of spirants, see also Jespersen, *Linguistica*, 346.

Page 524. On foreign-language teaching, see also Palmer, H. E., *The Scientific Study and Teaching of Languages*, London, 1917.

Page 533. A third edition of D. Jones' *Outline of English Phonetics*, London, 1932.

INDEX

Aasen, I., 484
abbreviation 288, 488
ablative 263, 315
abnormal 100, 378
absolute 170, 186–189
abstract 205, 271, 429f., 456f.
accent 80, 82, 182, 308f., 358f., 385, 450, *see* pitch, stress
accretion 414, 417
accusative 165, 272, 388, 392, 457f.
Açoka 63
acoustic 77–79, 93, 128
action 172–175, 267, 271
action-goal 192, 197, 267
action noun 236
active, *see* actor-action
actor 172–175, 267, 297
actor-action 165–167, 172–175, 184f., 190f., 194, 196f.
adam's-apple 27
adaptation 420–424, 426, 446, 449f., 458, 492f.
address 148, 152, 255f., 401f.
Adelung, J. C., 7
adjective 6, 165, 173, 188, 192, 198, 202–206, 231, 261, 271, 387f
adult language 55, 463, 485
adverb 175, 177, 197f., 237, 258, 260, 262f., 271, 433–435
affix 218, 414, 454, 509
affricate 120, 133, 214, 342, 378
Afghan 62
Africa 7, 56, 67, 87, 94, 99, 117, 472
Afrikaans 474
agent 221, 366, 412f., 454f.
agglutination 207f.
agreement 165f., 190–194
Ainu 70
Albanese 13, 15, 62, 312, 315f., 467, 470
Alfred, King, 17, 47, 281, 295
Algonquian 72, 193, 198, 241, 256f., 271f., 359f., 371, 381f., 396, 402
alliteration 296, 395
alphabet 79, 85f., 128, 290–294, 500–503
Alsatian, *see* German
Altaic 68f.
alternation 164, 210–219, 370–376, 381f., 410f., 418f.
alveolar 98
American English 44, 47–52, 81, 98, 100, 102–106, 109f., 112, 114, 117, 121f., 124f., 127, 129, 152, 187, 325, 361, 366f., 374, 394, 396, 401, 444, 464, 471, 480, 484f., 488, 498, 502
American Indian 7, 19, 42f., 71–73, 87, 97, 102, 127, 283, 404, 455f., 458, 464, 469, 473
Amharic 66
amredita 235
anacolouthon 186
analogic change 362–366, 376, 391, 393, 404–424, 426, 436, 439, 509
analogy 275–277, 454, 501
analphabetic notation 86
analytic 207
anaphora 249–266
anaptyxis 384
Anglo-Frisian 58, 304, 311f., 452
Anglo-Saxon, *see* Old English
animal 27, 155
animate 193, 232, 262, 272
animated 156, 197
Annamite 44, 71
Annatom 257
answer 91, 115, 159, 163, 176f., 179, 250
antecedent 249–263
antepenult 182
anticipatory 254, 258
aorist 362–364, 456
Apache 72
aphasia 35f.
aphoristic 152, 177, 438
apical 98, 100, 102
apocope 382
Apollonius Dyscolus 5
aposiopesis 186
apposition 6, 186, 420
apraxia 36
Arabic 7, 10, 21, 44, 66f., 89, 99, 101, 154, 243f., 289, 458
Aramaic 66, 289, 294
Arapaho 72
Araucanian 73
Arawak 73
archaic 152f., 292, 331, 401–404, 487
Aristarchus 5
Armenian 13, 15, 62, 307, 312, 315f., 319f., 470
arrangement 163–168
article 147, 192, 204, 259, 261, 371f., 419, 458, 470f.

INDEX

artificial language 506
arytenoids 94f., 102
aspect 270, 272f., 280
aspiration 80–82, 84, 89, 99f., 129, 348–351, 446
assimilation 273–381, 390, 423
Assiniboine 72
assonance 395
Assyrian 65f., 288, 293, 320
asterisk 516
asyntactic 233–235
Athabascan 72
atonic 187, 204, 244, 247, 250, 256, 261, 266, 364, 376, 382, 418
attraction 263, 423
attribute 188, 191, 194–206, 230–235, 251–263, 266–269
Australia 71
Austric 71
Austronesian 71
authority 3, 7f., 496–500
auxiliary, *see* secondary phoneme
Avesta 15, 62, 295, 315, 389, 451
avyayibhava 237
axis 192, 194, 199, 263, 265, 267
ayin 101
Azerbaijan 68
Aztec 72f., 241, 287

Babylonian 65, 288, 293
baby-talk 148, 472
back formation 412–416, 432, 454
back vowel 103–107, 117–119, 181, 376–381
bahuvrihi 235
Bali 71
Baltic 13, 18, 60f., 312–319, 400, 423
Baluchi 62
Bantu 19, 67, 192, 272
basic alternant 164, 209, 211f., 217–219, 222, 231, 242–244
basis 127
Basque 64
Batak 310
Bavarian, *see* German
Beach la Mar 472f.
Beaver 72
Bell, A. M., 86
Bengali 44, 63
Bennicke, V., 325
Benrath Line 343
Berber 65, 67
Bihari 44, 63
bilabial 98, 101
bilingual 56, 290, 293f., 445, 463f., 471, 513
Bisaya 71
Blackfoot 72
blend 422–424
Bodo 70

Bohemian 9f., 44, 54, 61, 86f., 89, 95, 100f., 113, 182, 291, 385, 447, 466, 468, 483, 501
Böhtlingk, O., 18f.
Bopp, F., 14f.
borrowing 298, 306f., 320–345, 361–367, 398, 412–416, 429, 444–495
bounded noun 205, 265
bound form 160, 177–184, 207–246, 257
Brahmana 63
Brahui 70
brain 36f.
Brant 295f.
breath 27, 31, 80, 93–102, 110, 120, 375
Bremer, O., 87
Breton 13, 60, 325, 414
British English 44, 47, 49–52, 81, 98, 100, 102–104, 112, 114, 118, 152, 367, 396, 484f., 488, 497f., 502
Broca, P., 36
Brugmann, K., 15
Bulgarian 15, 61, 154, 290f., 306–308, 314f., 363, 371, 373, 383, 423, 427, 437, 451, 453, 457, 459, 466, 470
Burgess, G., 424
Burgundian 59
Burmese 70
Bushman 67, 279f.

call 115, 164, 169, 177
Cambogian 71
Canarese 44, 70
Cantonese 44, 69, 116
Carelian 68
Carian 65
Carib 46, 73
Caroline 71
Carroll, L., 424
Carthage 66
case 5, 165, 192, 256, 272, 297, 388, 392, 457, 506
Caspian 62
Catalan 61, 483
category 204, 270–273, 388, 408
Catharine, Empress, 7
Caucasian 70
Cayuga 72
Celtic 12f., 16, 60f., 188, 307f., 312, 315f., 319, 386, 463f., 489
center 174, 195f., 202, 265
central meaning 149, 151, 402f., 431–437
centum languages 316
Champollion, J. F., 293
change 5, 13–20, 38, 158, 208, 277, 281–495, 509
character 284–286, 294
character-substance 194, 202–206

INDEX 555

Chaucer 281, 295, 429, 484, 487
Cheremiss 68
Cherokee 72, 288
Cheyenne 72
Chickasaw 72
child 28–31, 43, 46, 56f., 84, 140f., 148, 157, 386, 399, 403, 409, 432, 444, 476, 485, 512
Chinese 10, 44, 57, 69, 76f., 80, 83f., 91, 100, 109, 111, 116, 176, 182f., 188, 199–201, 207f., 243f., 252, 269, 271, 278f., 296, 388, 509
Chinese writing 21, 69, 90, 284–288
Chinook 470, 473
Chinook jargon 473
Chipewyan 72
Choctaw 72
chronology 309, 340, 346, 368, 413, 416, 451–453
Chukchee 70
circumlocution 140
citation 89f.
class-cleavage 204–206, 241, 251, 258–270
classification 207f.
classifier 286–288
class-meaning 146, 166, 202–205, 247–251, 266–268, 271
clause 192–194, 197, 204, 251f., 263, 273, 407, 437f.
click 93f.
close transition 119f.
closed construction 196f., 223, 268
closed vowel 103
closure, see stop
cluster 131–136, 183, 219, 228, 243, 335, 367, 370–373, 383
collective 221
colloquial 52, 153
color 140, 280
Comanche 72
command 164, 172, 174, 176
common noun 205, 273, 470
comparative 215, 238f.
comparative method 11–20, 38, 64, 297–321, 346–364, 466
compensatory 379f.
complement 230, 254, 260, 263
completion 224, 270, 273
completive 176f., 262, 266, 439
complex 160–170, 240, 244–246, 268f., 276, 405, 412
compounding form 225
compound phoneme 90f., 120, 124f., 130–132, 135f., 167, 182
compound word 17, 38, 180–184, 209f., 224–237, 275, 382, 413–418
condensation 439
conditioned sound-change 353, 372–385, 417–420

conflict 463–475
congruence 6, 191f., 204, 224, 253, 256, 263, 270, 273
conjunct 179f., 197f., 256, 260
conjunction 195, 198, 244, 269, 420, 469
connotation 151–157, 163, 197, 214, 402f., 421, 424, 441f., 496–498, 502
conquest 42f., 57, 60f., 64, 66, 68–70, 313f., 361, 386, 461–470, 472
consonant 102, 117–121, 217, 219, 243–246, 370–381
constituent 160f.
construction 169, 183–246, 407, 433, 437f., 453f.
contamination 422–426
context 409, 440f.
contraction 380f., 411
co-ordination 195, 198, 232, 235, 269
Coptic 67
copulative 235
Cornish 13, 60, 307, 464
coronal 98
correctness 3, 21f., 48, 477, 496
Cossean 65
Cottian 70
counting 28f.
Cree 72, 136, 145, 147, 155, 176, 182, 193f., 257–259, 288, 359f., 371, 381f., 396, 400, 508
Creek 72
creolized 474f.
Cretan 65, 293
Croatian 61
cross-reference 193f., 197, 257, 439
Crow 72
cuneiform 21, 64f., 284, 287f., 293f., 309
Curtius, G., 354
Cushite 65, 67
Cyprian 288
Czech 61

Dakota 72
Dalmatian 61
Danish 8–10, 53f., 59, 99–101, 106, 127, 279, 287, 299f., 314, 325, 370, 390, 455, 468, 483f.
Dano-Norwegian 59, 483f.
Darius 62
dative 272, 437
Dauzat, A., 398
deaf-mute 39, 144
decay 8f., 490
decipherment 64f., 72, 293f.
de-compound 210, 227
defective 223
definite 203–206, 251–261, 266, 270
definition 139–146, 152, 266–268, 280, 408

INDEX

Delaware 72
Delbrück, B., 15, 18
demonstration 140
demonstrative 147, 248, 250, 258–260, 470
Dempwolff, O., 519
denotation 146
density of communication 46f., 282, 326, 328, 340, 345, 403, 481
dental 98, 100, 102, 214, 376, 378, 384, 470
dependent, *see* anaphora, subordinate
derived 209–227, 237–246, 412–416, 453–458, 491
deriving form 225
de Saussure, F., 19
descriptive adjective 202f.
descriptive order 213
descriptive study 11f., 16–20, 158, 274, 311
determinative 240–245
determinative compound 235
determiner 203–206, 262, 265–269
diacritical 86–88, 289–291
dialect 5, 47–52, 152, 314–318, 321–345, 476–485, 499
dialect area 51, 477–481
dialect atlas 51, 322–325
dialect geography 51, 321–345, 361f., 480
dictionary 3, 87, 140, 142, 152, 178, 293, 320–323, 486
dictionary meaning 142, 148
Diez, F., 16
digraph 79, 85f., 89, 291, 451
diminutive 150, 157, 226, 400
Dinka 67
Dionysius Thrax 5
diphthong 90, 124f., 131f.
displaced speech 28, 30, 141–143, 149f.
dissimilation 349–351, 390, 450
distinctive 77–80, 141, 366
disturbance of speech 34–37
Dobrowsky, J., 483
Dodgson, C., 424
Dogrib 72
domain 247–251
domal 98, 102, 470
dominant 435
Donatus 6
dorsal 98, 101
double consonant 110, 119, 132–134, 181, 228, 363, 368, 373
Dravidian 44, 70, 470
dual 255, 257, 482
Du Maurier, G., 513
duration, *see* quantity
durative 272f.
Dutch 44, 59, 328–331, *passim*.

dvandva 235
dvigu 237

ear-drum 25, 31, 74f., 128, 514
East Germanic 59
Easter Island 71
Eastern Hindi 44, 63
Eastman, G., 424
Edda 296
Edmont, E., 324
Egyptian 21, 65, 67, 90, 283–289, 293
Elamitic 65
elegant, elevated 48, 152f., 156, 330, 402
Ellis, A. J., 87, 323
emphatic 111, 171, 174, 186, 197f., 204, 261
enclitic 187, 212
endocentric 194–196, 199, 202, 235f., 268
English 43–45, 57f., *passim*.
episememe 166–168, 172
equational 173–176, 201, 260
Eskimo 72, 207f., 259
Esperanto 506
Esthonian 68, 306, 465
Ethiopian 66f., 289
Etruscan 64, 290, 294
etymology 4, 6, 15, 346, 351–355, 427–430
euphemism 401
euphony 395
Ewe 67
exclamation 6, 92, 115, 147, 156, 164, 166–172, 176f.
exclusive 232, 255–257
exocentric 194–196, 199, 235–237, 240, 268
experiment 4, 34, 75f., 389, 423
explicit 174
explosive 97
expression 196
extinct languages 13, 57, 59–61, 63–66, 68, 70, 72, 463f., 513

facetious 147f., 151, 153f., 394, 402f., 421, 443, 471
false palate 75
family-tree 311f., 316, 318
Faroese 59
favorite sentence-form 171–177, 199, 254, 262
female 146, 238, 248, 253, 270
feminine 192, 211, 217, 253, 410, 420
field of selection 204, 260
Fiji 71
final 131–136, 181–183, 218f., 245, 371–374, 381f., 418f.
final-pitch 114f., 163–171, 185

INDEX 557

Finck, F. N., 19, 467
finite 165–167, 172, 185, 190–197, 251f., 256f., 267, 270
Finnish 19, 68, 86, 89, 106, 109f., 175, 177, 255, 272, 291, 298f., 306f., 465f., 470, 501·
Finno-Ugrian 19, 65, 67f., 298, 306, 319
first person 247f., 255–258
Fischer, H., 325
Flemish, see Dutch
foreign form 131, 153f., 423f., 449, 454
foreign language 45, 54–56, 80–84, 93, 142, 148, 248, 365–367, 386, 445–475, 481, 497, 499, 503–506
foreign-learned 153f., 220, 239, 241–243, 292, 383, 415f., 421, 449, 454–458, 464f.
form-class 146, 164–167, 185, 190, 194–196, 199–204, 210f., 247–251, 265–276, 409
Formosa 71
fortis 99f., 386
Fox 72, 136, 177, 181, 218, 232, 241, 288, 359f., 371, 396, 400
Frankish 466f., see German
free form 160, 178, 181–206, 209, 219, 243
French 43f., 61, *passim*.
frequency of forms 277, 354, 389, 392–403, 405, 408f., 414, 420, 431, 435, 445
frequency of phonemes 136f., 389
friction, see spirant
Frisian 8, 14f., 17, 58, 303–305, 311, 330, 380, 385, 452, 483
front vowel 103–107, 117–119, 125, 181, 376–381, 410, 452
Ful 67
full sentence 171–177, 252, 259, 262f.
full word 199f.
function 185, 194–196, 265–274
fundamental assumption 78, 144f., 158f., 162
futhark 291
future 224, 272f., 415

von der Gabelentz, G., 18
Galla 67
Gallic 13, 60, 375, 463
Gamillscheg, E., 479
gender 5, 192, 211, 217, 236, 253f., 271–273, 278, 280, 462
general grammar 6, 20, 233, 270f., 297, 508f.
general meaning 431
genitive 231, 375, 409, 420
Georgian 70, 174
German 43f., 58f., *passim*.

Germanic 57–59, 298–301, *passim*.
gerund 269
Gessner, K., 511f.
gesture 39f., 111, 114f., 144, 147, 176, 250
ghost-form 293, 487
Gilbert Islands 71
Gilliéron, J., 325, 395–397
Gilyak 70
gingival 98, 100, 102, 446
Gipsy 63, 313, 467, 471
Gipsy English 50, 471f.
Glarus 331
glide 96f., 118–120, 147
glosseme 264, 277f., 503
glottal 80, 82, 99, 101, 113, 118f., 147, 289, 299
glottalized 99, 101f.
glottis 94f., 97, 101, 118
goal 165, 173, 192, 197f., 229, 233, 241, 257f., 265, 269, 272, 297, 457f.
goal-action 173, 201, 316, 471
Goropius 9
Gothic 8, 14, 17, 59, 453, 466, *passim*.
government 6, 192f., 197, 273
grammar 3, 7, 135, 138, 183, 266, 274, 322f., 365, 408, 506
grammatical feature 35, 166–169, 209, 214, 216, 239, 264f., 268, 275, 277, 394, 467f.
grammatical terms 457
Grassmann, H., 349–355
Grebo 67
Greek 43, 62, *passim*.
Greek alphabet 64f., 86f., 288–296
Greek grammar 4–7, 12, 208, 457
greeting 148
Griera, A., 325
Grimm, J., 347–351, 355, 360
Grotefend, G. F., 293
Gujerati 44, 63
gums 96, 98, 100, 119
guttural 98, 127

Haag, K., 325
Hakka 69
Hamitic 65, 67
haplology 391
Haussa 67
Hawaiian 71
head 195f., 199–202, 235–237
Head, H., 35f.
Hebrew 9f., 66, 89, 289, 455, 472, 519
Herero 67
Hermann, G., 6
Herodian 5
Herodotus 4, 318
Herskovits, M. J., 475
hesitation 186

hiatus 134
Hickes, G., 8
hieroglyphs, see picture writing
high vowel 103–107, 120
Hincks, E., 293
hiss 100
historical present 156, 272
Hittite 64f., 293, 309
hoarse h 101
home language 56, 60
Homeric poems 5, 62, 295, 319
homonym 145, 150, 161, 179, 183, 205, 209, 214, 223–225, 232, 286, 354, 367, 369f., 388, 392, 396–399, 410, 412, 416, 420, 433f., 436, 439, 502
Hopi 72
Hottentot 67
Humboldt, W. v., 18f.
Hungarian 19, 44, 61, 68, 99, 313f., 389
hunting 155, 400
Hupa 72
Huron 72
Hus, J., 483
hyperbole 426
Hyperborean 70
hyper-forms 302, 309, 330, 449, 479, 499
hypochoristic 157, 424
hypostasis 148, 180

Iberian 64
Icelandic 59, 182, 296, 314, 370, 380, 385, see Norse
idea 142, 508
identification 146f., 203f., 249–263
ideogram 285
Illinois 72
Illyrian 64
imitation 6, 30, 127, 148, 156f., 365f., 403, 472, 476–478, 496–500
immediate constituents 161, 167, 209f., 221f.
immigrant 43, 55f., 461–463, 467
imperative 331
imperfect 224, 273
impersonal 174, 254f., 470, 516
implosion 97, 119
inanimate 241, 262, 272
included 170, 183, 186, 219, 262
inclusive 255–257
incorporation 241
indefinite 203–206, 260–262, 270
independent 249, 255–266
India 42, 55, 98, 102, 154, 289, 458, 469, 472, 495
Indic 62f., 296, 312, 319, 374, 467–469
indicative 190, 208, 273, 358

individual 22, 30, 45–47, 75f., 142f., 152, 155, 157, 393, 403, 421, 424, 431, 443, 450
indivisibility 180f., 232, 240, 252
Indo-Aryan, see Indic
Indo-Chinese 69f.
Indo-European 12–19, 57–65, 306–321, passim.
Indo-Iranian 62, 307f., 315–318, 351, 378f.
Indonesian 71, 243f., 271, 309f.
infinitive 164–166, 172–175, 197, 210, 215f., 252, 254, 265, 268f., 273, 470
infix 218, 222
inflecting languages 207f.
inflection 5, 11, 222–232, 237f., 256, 263, 270, 294, 387f., 406, 410–412, 453, 470f.
Ingrian 68
Ingweonic 58
initial 99, 131, 134–136, 147, 181–183, 188, 243–246, 296, 367, 370, 374f., 418, 447–449, 465, 473
inscription 60–66, 68f., 71f., 289–294, 302, 305f., 433
instrument 173f.
instrumental 315, 318
intense 156f., 198, 245
interdental 98
interjection 121, 156, 176f., 181, 198, 250, 265, 402
intermarriage 43, 343, 463, 469f.
International Phonetic Alphabet 87–92, 96, 101, 103f.
interpretation 64f., 293–296
interrogative 171, 204, 244, 248, 252, 260, 262, 265, 269, 315f.
intimate 255f., 401
intransitive 150, 241
invasion, see conquest
inverse spelling 294
inverted 98, 102f.
inverted order 174f.
inverted speech 156
Iowa 72
Iranian 13, 15, 62f., 70, 312, 320, 459, 470
Irish 13, 15, 60, 188, 291f., 307, 315, 319, 374f., 383, 418
Iroquoian 72
irregular 177, 188, 203, 207f., 213–217, 223, 228, 231f., 238f., 247, 256, 269–275, 279, 309, 318f., 331, 358, 374, 376, 383, 399, 405, 409–411, 416–420, 423, 433, 509
isogloss 51, 58, 317f., 321–345, 398, 478–480
isolating 207f.
isolation 432–435
Italian 43f., 61, passim.

INDEX

Italic 61, 308, 312, 319, 350, 380
iterative 221, 272f.

Jaberg, K., 325
Japanese 10, 21, 44, 70, 101, 116, 256, 288
jargon 472-474
Javanese 44, 71, 310, 330
jaw 25, 97, 127
Jespersen, O., 43, 86
Jones, D., 87
Jones, W., 12f.
Jud, J., 325
Junius, F., 8

Kabyle 67
Kachin 70
Kaffir 67
Kamchadal 70
Kansa 72
Karadjich, V. S., 483, 511
karmadharaya 235
Kechua 73
kernel 225
Kickapoo 72
King James Bible 281, 425
Kirgiz 68
Kloeke, G. G., 325, 329
Koiné 62
Korean 44, 70
Koryak 70
Kristensen, M., 325
Kurath, H., 325
Kurdish 62
Kwakiutl 259, 470
kymograph 76

labial 98, 339, 378
labialized 118, 315
labiodental 100
labiovelar 118, 315f.
laboratory 75-77, 85, 128, 137, 389, 423
Ladin 61, 300f., 341, 467, 479f.
Landsmaal 59, 484
language boundary 53f., 56, 314, 317f., 464
Lappish 19, 68, 306, 465
laryngal 99, 289
laryngoscope 75
larynx 25, 27, 36, 43, 94f., 108
lateral 97, 101f., 120, 446
Latin 43, 47, 61f., *passim*.
Latin alphabet 21, 86-90, 237, 288, 290-292, 296, 300, 302
Latin grammar 4-8, 237f., 296, 458
law 354
learned 153, 277, 400, 436, 442, 448, 452, 472, 491-495
Lemnian 65

length, *see* quantity
lenis 99f.
Lepsius, C. R., 87
Le Roux, P., 325
Leskien, A., 18, 353
letter 79, 284, 290-294, 300, 304, 487, 489, 501
Lettish 13, 60
levels 47-50, 52
lexical form 35, 166-168, 264-269, 277
lexical meaning 169, 174, 271, 425
lexicon 21, 39f., 138, 162, 269, 274-280, 297, 316, 319f., 365, 407f., 431, 459, 465, 486
liaison, *see* sandhi
Libyan 67
Ligurian 64
limiting 202-206, 250, 252, 258-262
lingua franca 473
linguistic form 138, 141, 145, 158-162, 166, 168f., 208f., 265, 283-287, 353f., 389
linguistic meaning 141, 145, 158, 280
lips 31, 43, 80, 86, 97-107, 117f., 123, 373
lisp, *see* stammering
list 38, 203, 213, 219, 238, 269, 280
literacy 21
literary 52, 291f.
literature 21f., 286
Lithuanian 13, 15, 60, 117, 125, 307, 309, 315, 319, 373, 422, 427, 483, 509
litotes 426
living analogy 413f., 453
Livonian 68
loan-translation 456-458, 460-462, 468
loan-word 449
local difference 47-52, 112, 114
logogram 285-288, 293, 296
Lo-lo 70
Lombard 59, 466
loose vowel 103, 107, 109, 112
low vowel 103-107, 109, 120, 367
lower language 461-475
lucus a non lucendo 4
Ludian 68
Luganda 67
Lundell, J. A., 87
Lusatian 60
Luther 483
Lycian 65
Lydian 65, 294

macaronic 153
Macedonian 64
Maduran 71
Malagasy 71

malapropism 154
Malay 45, 55, 71, 256, 297
Malayalam 70
Malayan 71
Malayo-Polynesian 19, 71, 297
male 146, 238, 248, 251, 253, 270
Manchu 69
Mandan 72, 283f.
Mandarin 69
Manx 60
Maori 71
Marathi 44, 63
marginal 149-151, 254, 427, 430-437
Marianne Islands 71
marker 199f., 258, 265, 268-271, 280
Marshall Islands 71
Masai 67
masculine 192, 211, 217, 253, 280, 410
Massachusetts 72
mass noun 205, 214, 252, 265
mass observation 37f.
mathematics 29, 146f., 249, 507, 512
Matole 72
Maya 72f., 293
meaning 27, 74-78, 84f., 93, 128, 138-159, 247-251, 264, 407f., 425-443
mechanical record 76, 85, 87, 93, 128, 365
mechanistic 33, 38, 142-144
medial 131f., 134, 136, 181f., 189, 373f., 382, 452
medieval use of Latin 6, 8, 13, 61, 301f., 316, 346, 481, 489-494
Melanesian 71, 257
member 195, 209, 227-237
Mencken, H. L., 515
Menomini 72, 80, 82-84, 111, 150, 171, 175-177, 219, 244, 256, 260, 262, 279, 359f., 371, 381f., 385, 395, 400, 446f., 455f., 458
mentalism 17, 32f., 38, 142-144
Meringer, R., 428
Mesha 66
Mesopotamia 21, 65, 284, 287
Messapian 64
metals 320
metaphor 149, 426, 443
metathesis 391
metonymy 426
Miami 72
Micmac 72
Micronesian 71
mid vowel 103-109, 112
Middle English 365, 368-371, 382, 384f., 387, 404f., 411f., 419, 423, 426, 437
middle voice 258, 456
migration 12f., 58, 60, 64, 69, 312f., 461-475

Miklosich, F. v., 16
Milton 277
minor sentence 171f., 176f.
minus feature 217f., 231
Missouri 72
Mitanni 65
Mithridates 7, 511
mixed vowel 104
Moabite 66
mock foreign 153
mock learned 154, 421
mode 5, 193, 200, 224, 270, 273
modified phoneme 117f.
modifier, *see* attribute
modulation 163, 166-171, 183-186, 207-210, 220f., 239, 263, 290
Mohawk 72
Mohican 72
Mongol 69
Mon-Khmer 70f.
Montagnais 72
mora 110
Mordvine 68
morpheme 161-168, 209, 244-246, 264, 274-278, 412, 509
morpheme word 209, 218, 240, 412
morphology 183f., 189, 207-246, 308, 349, 352, 371, 380, 383, 391, 406, 449, 454, 465, 506, 509
mots savants 491-495
mouth 97
muffled 102
Müller, F., 19
Munda 70f.
murmur 95, 99, 101f., 112
musical 97, 120-126, 375
Muskogean 72
mute 130, 218f.

Naga 70
Nahuatl 72, 241
name 57, 64, 131, 155, 157, 201, 205, 288, 294, 413, 420, 429, 451, 465, 467, 470
Narraganset 72
narrative 173 175f., 200f.
narrow vowel 107
narrowed meaning 151, 426
nasal 96f., 101f., 120, 130, 136, 339, 380
nasalized 96f., 102, 106, 110, 117, 217, 380, 384, 447
Natick 72
native 43
natural syllable 122f., 126
Navajo 72
negative 174-177, 197, 204, 248f., 262, 438f., 486
neo-grammarian 354-364, 392f.
nervous system 26, 33f., 36, 141, 158

INDEX   561

neuter 192, 211, 253, 375, 410
new formation 214, 276, 363f., 368, 381f., 393, 405–425, 430, 434, 437, 447, 454f., 490f.
Nietzsche, F., 457
noeme 264
nominative 165–167, 185, 190–196, 237f., 267, 269, 388, 392, 422
non-distinctive 77–85, 96–105, 110–129, 141, 144, 147, 365–367, 468, 477, 480, 498f., 516
non-personal 146, 236, 248, 253, 260f., 263, 273
nonsense form 153, 157
non-standard 48–52
non-syllabic 120–125, 131f., 134, 182, 238, 243, 287, 379, 384
Norman Conquest 291, 463–465, 493
Norse 15, 303–308, *passim*.
Northumbrian burr 100, 390
Norwegian 54, 59, 100, 110, 116, 390, 468, 483f., *see* Norse
nose 80, 95f.
noun 166, 190, 192, 194, 198, 202–206, 210–216, 224f., 228–231, 236f., 249, 251–254, 266, 269, 272, 297, 388, 392, 406, 408–412, 418, 470
Nuba 67
number 5, 192, 204–206, 224, 234, 236, 254–257, 271f., 297, 320
number of speakers 43–45, 57–73
numeral 29, 147, 152, 206, 237, 249, 279f., 294, 320, 422f., 508
numeral symbol 86, 287
numerative 200, 203, 205f., 249, 262, 266
nursery form 157, 394, 424

object 146, 165, 167, 173, 198, 202, 205, 216, 221, 232, 236, 250f., 257f., 260, 267f., 271f., 278
object expression 199–201, 244, 249
object of verb, *see* goal, of preposition, *see* axis
obscene 155, 396, 401
obsolescence 154, 241, 321, 331–340, 365–368, 376, 393–403, 412, 415, 423, 430–435, 437, 440, 487
Ob-Ugrian 68
obviative 193f., 257
occasional meaning 431
occupation 50
Oglala 72
Ojibwa 72, 283f., 359f., 381f., 396
Old English 8f., 15, 17, 89, 303–308, *passim*.
Olonetsian 68
Omaha 72
ominous form 155, 400f.
Oneida 72

onomatopoeia 156f.
Onondaga 72
onset of stress 113f., 126, 182
open syllable 369, 384
open transition 119
open vowel 103
Oppert, J., 293
oral 96f.
order 163, 167f., 184f., 197, 201, 207, 210, 213, 222, 227, 229f., 234, 236f., 247, 263, 285
origin of language 6, 40
Oriya 44, 63
Orkhon inscriptions 293
Osage 72
Oscan 61
Ossete 62, 70, 470
Osthoff, H., 417
Ostyak 68
outcry 6, 147
over-differentiation 223f., 269, 399

Paelignian 380
Paiçachi 63
Paiute 72
palatal 99, 101f., 385
palatalized 117–120, 315, 376–379
palate 86, 95–103, 118
paleography 295
Pali 63
Pallas, P. S., 7
Pamir 62
Panini 11, 19, 63
Panjabi 44, 63
Papuan 71
papyrus 295
paradigm 223–226, 229–231, 237–239, 257, 270, 349, 358f., 399, 406, 410–412, 422, 506
parataxis 171, 176f., 185f., 254, 259, 263
parent language 12, 14, 298–321, 350, 352, 360, 379, 509
parenthesis 186
Parthian 63
participle 197, 225, 230, 233, 237, 252, 358, 399, 415, 437, 471
particle 171, 173, 176, 199–201, 232, 241, 244, 252, 269
parts of speech 5, 17, 20, 190, 196, 198–202, 240, 249, 268–271, 274
passive, *see* goal-action
Passy, P., 87
past 164, 174, 210, 212, 214–216, 224, 272f., 316, 358
Paul, H., 16f., 19, 431f., 435
pause 92, 114f., 171, 181, 185f.
Pehlevi 62
Penobscot 72
penult 182

Peoria 72
perfect 224, 273, 316, 471, 491
Permian 68
permitted, *see* phonetic pattern
Persian 13f., 62, 65, 154, 288, 293
person 5, 224, 297
personal 146, 164, 167, 236, 248, 251, 253, 258, 260f., 263, 265, 270, 273
personal substitute 255-258, 422, 482
pet-name 157
phememe 264
Philippine 7, 42, 71
philology 21, 512
philosophy 6, 17, 172, 201, 270, 456, 508
Phoenician 66, 289
phoneme 79-138 158, 162, 166f., 179, 264, 289-292, 300, 302-305, 308-310, 350-360, 389, 395, 465, 501f.
phonemic, *see* alphabet, distinctive
phonetic alphabet 85-92
phonetic alternant 154, 211
phonetic change 309, 329f., 335, 339, 342, 346-393, 404, 410f., 415, 418-420, 434, 436, 438f., 450f., 479-481, 492, 509
phonetic form 138, 145, 148, 159f., 162, 164, 166, 168, 209, 223, 285, 287
phonetic modification 156, 163-168, 179f., 183f., 207-218, 222, 226, 228f. 235, 238f., 242-244
phonetic pattern 103, 124f., 128-138, 147f., 153, 181f., 187, 214, 217-219, 221, 228, 250, 290, 295, 324, 350, 369-371, 376f., 385, 395f., 449, 467f.
phonetic substitution 81-84, 365, 445-449, 458f., 472
phonetic symbol 286f.
phonetics 74-138, 294, 328, 365
phonic method 500
phonogram 287, 293
phonograph 41, 76
phonology 78, 137f., 323
phrase 178-209, 372, 374f., 417-419, *passim*.
phrase derivative 178f., 183, 227, 239
phrase word 180, 184, 207, 239f.
Phrygian 4, 64
physiology 25, 32, 75f., 78, 127, 130-133, 137, 296
Pictish 513
picture writing 65, 73, 283-288, 293
Pidgin English 472f.
Piman 72
pitch 76f., 80, 84, 91f., 94, 109, 114-117, 147, 163, 167, 169-172, 174, 182, 185, 188, 221, 243, 299, 385

place 173f., 201, 221
place-name 60, 64, 339f., 453, 464, 469
place of stress 111
Plato 4
plural 190f., 195, 205f., 209-216, 219, 224, 226, 236, 255-261, 265f., 270f., 358, 376, 392-394, 399, 401, 404-406, 408-412, 453, 470, 482
Polabian 60
Polish 9f., 42, 44, 54, 61, 86, 96, 102, 113, 119, 126, 177, 182, 187, 256, 291, 385, 470
Polynesian 71, 374, 473
polysynthetic 207f.
popular etymology 417, 423f., 450
Port Royal 6
Portuguese 13, 44, 61, 96, 341, 472, 474
position 185, 192, 265, 267, 271, 273, 297
possession 178, 193f., 203, 212, 216, 223f., 226, 230, 236, 256f., 267, 297
postdental 98, 102, 446
Potawatomi 72
Pott, A. F., 15
practical event 23-27
practical phonetics 78, 84f., 93-127, 129, 137
Prakrit 63
pre- 309, 311f.
predicate 5, 173f., 199-201, 206, 244, 252, 260, 262
predisposition 23-34, 75, 141
prefix 154, 180f., 218, 220, 230, 232, 241, 383, 434
pre-history 12, 16, 319f., 428
preposition 194f., 198, 216, 228, 234, 244, 252, 265, 268, 271
present 156, 174, 212, 214, 224, 272f. 278, 358, 364
pre-suffixal 220f., 449, 493
primary derivative 209, 227, 240-246, 366
primary phoneme 85, 90f., 109, 111, 114, 116, 126, 135f., 163, 182, 290f., 308
primitive 13, 299, 302, 311f.
printing 21, 41, 286, 486, 502f.
Priscian 6
proclitic 187, 259
pronoun 146f., 152, 188, 193f., 244, 249-263, 266, 269f., 375, 382, 399, 401, 422f., 439, 469f., 482
proper noun 194, 205, 265
proportion 276, 406-420, 441f.
propriety 155
prothetic 335-338
protrusion 101, 103, 105f.

INDEX

proverb 152
provincial 49, 52, 62, 296, 340, 478, 482–485
Prussian 13, 60
Psammetichus 4
pseudo-impersonal 254f.
psychology 17f., 32–38, 78, 142, 199, 248, 297, 406, 423, 435
punctual 272f., 362
Pushto 62

quality 198, 202, 205, 236, 239, 271, 434, 465
quantity 89, 104, 107, 109f., 129, 177, 217, 221, 290, 294, 296, 302, 366, 369, 379–381, 384f.
question 91f., 114f., 147, 169, 171, 174–177, 186, 193, 204, 250, 260
Quilleute 470
quotation 148

race 43, 386
Ragusan 61
Rajasthani 44, 63
rank 195, 222, 224, 226
Rask, R. K., 14, 347, 355, 360
Rawlinson, H. C., 293
reading 37, 282, 285f., 500
real, *see* indicative
reciprocal 221
reconstruction 15, 300–310, 351, 451, 459, 516
reduplication 218, 221f., 349, 396
reflexive 193, 197
register 94f.
regular 189, 211, 213, 216f., 224f., 238f., 273–276, 399, 405f., 409–413, 434, 509
relation-axis 192, 194, 199, 263, 267, 271
relationship 140, 177, 278f., 320
relationship of languages 9–13, 57, 59, 64, 68f., 71f., 293f., 297–318, 346, 425
relative substitute 204, 262f., 423
relayed speech 28, 141
relic form 331–340, 479
religion 42, 50, 155, 343, 455, 461
reminiscent sandhi 189, 219, 374
Renaissance 7f., 10
repetition 156f., 235
resonance 94–97, 102
re-spelling 62, 295
response 23–34, 74f., 128, 139, 142–144, 147, 158, 250, 285f., 365
resultant 194–196, 207, 221, 223, 274
retraction 103, 105f., 117f.
Rhaetian 64
Rhaeto-Romanic 61
Rhenish Fan 343, 478

rhythm 395
Rig-Veda 10, 63
rime 78, 295f., 330, 395, 482, 486
ritual 400
rival, *see* variant
Romance 6, 9f., 61, 300–302, 489–494, *passim*.
root 10, 240–246, 289, 362f., 426, 433, 459
root forming 245f., 275f.
root word 239f., 243
Rosetta Stone 293
Roumanian 13, 44, 61, 300f., 314, 325, 470
rounding 105–107, 117f., 125
runes 290f., 293, 305f., 433
Russian 43f., 47, 61, 457, *passim*.
rustic 152, 331–340

Sakian 63
Salish 470
Samoan 71, 181, 219, 255, 257, 371
Samoyede 68
samprasarana 384
sandhi 110, 113f., 135f., 163f., 173, 178f., 181, 183, 186–189, 201, 204, 219, 222, 228, 275, 371f., 374f., 378, 382f., 418f., 437
Sanskrit 11–15, 63, 495, *passim*.
Sanskrit grammar 10–12, 18, 208f., 235, 237, 296, 384
Sarsi 72
satem-languages 316
Sauk 72
Saxon 303–305, 358, 376, 451f.
Scandinavian 58f., *passim*.
Schleicher, A., 15
Schmeller, J. A., 323
Schmidt, J., 317
scholastic 6
school grammar 6, 102, 178, 237f., 266, 268, 400, 496, 500, 505, 516
Schuchardt, H., 354
Scotch English 152, 300, 329, 370, 394, 485
Scotch Gaelic 60
second person 152, 188, 197, 224, 247, 250, 255–258, 400f.
secondary derivative 209f., 217f., 220, 224, 237–242, 244, 297, 366
secondary phoneme 90–92, 109, 111, 114–116, 122, 134, 136, 156, 163, 169–171, 220f.
secret dialect 50, 471
selection 164–169, 171, 174, 177, 179f., 184f., 190–199, 201f., 207, 229–237, 247, 265f.
semantic change 335, 407f., 414, 425–443, 456
semantics 74, 138, 141, 160, 513

sememe 162, 166, 168, 174, 216, 238, 264, 276
semi-absolute 185f., 193
Seminole 72
semi-predicative 206
Semitic 19, 65–67, 198, 243f., 288f
semivowel 102, 123f., 130, 132, 134, 136
Seneca 72
sensation 174
sentence 90–92, 114f., 138, 167, 170–177, 179, 185, 197, 200, 262, 297, 516
sentence-type 152, 169–177, 184, 197, 247, 260, 265, 275f.
sentence-word 172, 175
Serbian 9f., 61f., 87, 117, 290f., 314, 470, 483
serial, see co-ordination
sex 46
Shakspere 22, 277, 281, 398, 400, 487
shift of language 55, 463
Shoshone 72
shwa 519
Siamese 69
sibilant 100, 120, 133, 211f., 214, 315f., 378f., 452f.
Sicilian 64
Sievers, E., 515
signal 80, 128, 136, 139, 144, 157f., 162, 166, 168, 281
significant, see distinctive
Sikwaya 288
Silver Codex 8, 59
simple, see morpheme, taxeme
Sinai inscriptions 289
singular 146, 165, 190f., 205f., 208–213, 219, 223f., 236, 270f., 358, 371, 401, 405, 408–412, 470
Sino-Tibetan 69
Siouan 72
situation, see stimulus
slang 49, 133f., 147, 154, 254, 394, 397, 402f., 420, 443
Slavic 9f., 60f., 466, passim.
slip of the tongue 399, 409, 423
Slovak 61, 483
Slovene 61, 314
slurred form 148, 388
social levels 47–52, 112, 476f.
society 24–34, 42
Sogdian 63
Solomon Islands 71
Somali 67
sonant 102, 121–124, 384
sonority 100, 120–126, 147, 384
Sorbian 60
sound-waves 25–28, 31, 75–80, 87, 95, 111, 128, 142
Spanish 42–44, 61, 467, passim.

specialized meaning 150, 214f., 227–229, 265, 276, 402f., 414, 417, 432, 434, 436
species 146f., 202, 204f., 236, 249–253, 258, 260, 263
speech 22–27, 74, 248
speech community 29, 42–56, 140, 155, 281, 298, 311, 313f., 317, 319, 394, 445
speech-island 53, 56, 58, 61
spelling pronunciation 487f., 494, 498, 501f.
spelling reform 501–503
Spenser 487
Sperber, H., 439f.
spirant 95–97, 100–102, 119f., passim.
sporadic sound-change 353–364
stage 49
stammering 34, 101, 148
standard language 48–52, 57, 59–63, 68, 296, 321–323, 329, 334, 339, 474, 482–487, 496–500
statement 92, 114, 156, 169, 171
static 200
Steinthal, H., 18
stem 221, 225f., 229–232, 237, 241, 315, 331, 349, 362f., 416f., 470
stimulus 23–34, 74, 114, 128, 139–144, 151, 156, 158, 166f., 177, 285, 365, 435, 440
stop 80, 86, 97–102, 214, passim.
Streiff, C., 331, 333
stress 90–92, 110–114, 120–126, 130, 154, 163, 168, 174, 180, 182f., 186f., 220f., 228, 233, 259, 303, 375f., 382f., 385, 447, 450
stridulation 27
structural order 210, 213, 222, 227, 247
structure 135, 264, 268
stuttering 34
style 45, 153, 499
Subiya 67
subject 5, 173f., 199–201, 252
subjunctive 152, 190, 224, 273, 358, 437–439
subordinate 192–195, 197f., 204, 235, 237, 251f., 269, 407
sub-standard 50–52
substantive 146, 164f., 177, 185, 196, 198, 249, 267–271
substitute 146f., 169, 184, 247–263, 509
substitution feature 112, 216–218, 222, 228, 243, 274
substratum 386, 468–470, 481
sub-vocal 143
Suetonius 302
suffix 154, 218–221, 230–232, 240f., 244f., 314f., 318, 366, 410–417, 454f

INDEX

Sumerian 65, 288, 293
Sundanese 71
superlative 417
suppletion 215f., 218, 223, 238f., 270
Swaheli 67
Swedish 9f., 54, 59, 87, 100f., 106, 110, 116, 151, 193, 221, 256, 299f., 370, 385, 389f., 428, 447, 459, 503
Sweet, H., 86f.
syllabic 120–125, 130–137, 181, 384
syllabic stress 122f., 136
syllabic writing 287f.
syllable 120–126, 243f., 287–290, 349–351
symbol 283–290
symbolic 6, 156, 243–246, 390, 424
syncope 382
syncretism 388, 392
synecdoche 426
synonym 145, 442
syntactic compound 233–235
syntax 5, 11, 183–206, 212, 216, 224, 232–235, 247–264, 268, 270–273, 407, 417–420, 423, 453, 467f., 486f.
synthetic compound 231–234, 236, 430, 460
synthetic languages 207
syrinx 27

tabu 155, 396, 400–402, 507f.
tactic form 166
Tagalog 71, 105, 171, 173f., 176, 200f. 218, 221f., 243f., 252, 255, 260, 269, 278, 310, 371, 391, 446–448, 455
tagmeme 166–168, 264, 276f., 505
Tahiti 71
Tai 69
Tamil 44, 70
Tartar 68
tatpurusha 235
tatsama 495
taxeme 166–171, 174, 184f., 190–192, 197–199, 210, 220, 264–266
Tebele 67
technical 49f., 152f., 277
teeth 98, 100, 118f.
telephone 41, 45
Telugu 44, 70
tense 5, 200, 224, 270, 272, 297
tense vowel 103, 107, 109, 124, 136, 445
Tesnière, L., 44f.
Teton 72
textual criticism 5, 295
theoretical form 218–220, 223, 237, 242, 516
thinking 28f., 142f., 508
third person 152, 188, 193, 198, 212, 214f., 224, 253f., 256–258, 418f.

Thomsen, V., 293
Thracian 64
Tibetan 69
Tigre 66
Tocharian 64, 316
tone of voice 39, 114f., 144, 147, 498
tones 116, 475
tongue 25, 31, 36, 75, 94–97, 99, 101–105, 108, 112f., 117–119, 123, 127, 365, 373, 376, 383f., 390, 470
tongue-flip 81, 100, 187, 374
transcription 85–92, 96, 98–104, 109, 112–114, 117, 120–123, 128, 135, 168, 296, 366, 501
transferred meaning 39, 149f., 198, 402f., 425–443, 456, 458
transient 173f., 200f.
transition 118–120
transitive 150, 165
translation 140
transliteration 90, 101
transmission 294f.
trial 255, 257
trill 98, 100–102, 104, 120, 127, 383f., 390, 445, 470
triphthong 124, 131, 135, 137
Tsimshian 470
Tuareg 67
Tunguse 69
Tupi-Guarani 73
Turco-Tartar 44, 68f., 381
Turkish 21, 68f., 107, 154, 181, 208, 293, 467
Tuscarora 72

Ukrainian 44
ultimate constituent 161, 182, 195, 242
Umbrian 61
umlaut 381, 434
unbounded 205
undergoer, *see* goal
underlying form 209–226, *passim*.
understanding 31, 55, 80–82, 84, 93, 127, 149, 179, 250, 277, 281, 295, 386, 457f., 487
unique 160f., 210, 213f., 234f., 275, 415, 426
unreal 224, 273
unrounded 107
upper language 461–475
Ural-Altaic 69
Ürdingen Line 343
Ute 72
uvula 95–97, 99–101, 127, 390, 445, 470
Uzbeg 68

Vai 288
Van 65, 293

INDEX

Vandal 59
van Helmont 424
variant 81, 83, 98–103, 105, 110–114, 117f., *passim*.
Vater, J. S., 8
Vedic 63
velar 98f., 101f., 127, 315f., 339, 376–379, 385
velarized 118f.
Veliote 61
velum 95f., 98, 103, 117, 119, 373, 383f.
Venetic 64
Vepsian 68
verb 20, 165–167, 172–175, 190–194, 197f., 210, 212, 214–216, 223–225, 229–233, 238f., 251, 254, 256, 258, 260, 297, 358f., 362–364, 383, 395, 414–417, 439, 471, 506
vernacular 482
Verner, K., 308, 357–359, 374, 415
verse 78, 295f., 302
Visible Speech 86f.
vocabulary, *see* lexicon
vocal chords 25, 27, 31, 75, 94f., 99, 102, 111, 373, 375, 505
vocative 177, 225
Vogule 68
voice 27, 94–97, 101f., 112, 114, 117f., 120, 224, 258, 364
voice of verb 173, 201, 224
voicing 94–97, 99–102, 118, 120, 135, 137, 189, 218f., 357f., 372–376, 389, 458
Voltaire 6
Votian 68
Votyak 68
vowel 81f., 102–126, 134f., 216, 243, 288–290, 292, 295, 300–302, 306f., 329, 356–358, 376–387
vowel harmony 181, 381
vowel-shift 387
vulgar 147, 152, 156, 302
Vulgar Latin 302

war 156
wave-theory 317f., 340
Weigand, G., 325
Welsh 13, 55, 60, 97, 307, 464
Wendish 60
Wenker, G., 322
West Germanic 59, 304, 311–389, 425, 428, 451
Western Hindi 44, 63
whisper 95, 102
Whitney, W. D., 16
wide vowel 107
widened meaning 151, 426, 432
Winnebago 72
Winteler, J., 331
Wolof 67
word 90, 99, 102, 110–114, 116, 138, 171f., 176, 178–189, 195f., 200, 207–247, 254, 265, 268, 277f., 284–287, 291, 297, 303, 309, 328, 371, 374f., 381f., 395f., 414f., 417–420, 447, 509
word-class 190, 196, 202
word-formation 222f., 226, 231, 237–240, 412–416, 453, 505
word order 156, 171–175, 197–201, 229, 234, 254, 260, 263, 286, 437, 470
Wordsworth 443
Wrede, F., 322, 325
Wright, J., 323
writing 3, 8, 13, 21f., 37, 40, 66, 73, 79, 85f., 129, 144, 152f., 178, 282–296, 448f., 486–495, 500–503, 506
written records 5–7, 10, 13, 21f., 38, 57–73, 152, 277, 281–296, 298–305, 309–311, 319, 330, 346, 359, 380f., 393, 400, 404f., 416, 425, 438, 440f., 455, 459, 464, 481f., 484
Wundt, W., 18, 386, 435
Wyandot 72

x-ray 75

Yakut 19, 69
Yana 46
Yap 71
Yenisei-Ostyak 70
Yoruba 67

zero-feature 209, 215–219, 223, 231, 236, 238f., 252, 256, 263, 416, 420
Zeuss, J. K., 16
Zulu 67
Zyrian 68